BARRON'S
THE TRUSTED NAME IN TEST PREP

2026

AP® U.S. History
PREMIUM

Eugene V. Resnick, M.A.

AP® is a registered trademark of the College Board, which is not affiliated with Barron's and was not involved in the production of, and does not endorse, this product.

AP® is a registered trademark of the College Board, which is not affiliated with Barron's and was not involved in the production of, and does not endorse, this product.

Copyright © 2025, 2024, 2023, 2022, 2020, 2018, 2016, 2014, 2012 by Kaplan North America, LLC, d/b/a Barron's Educational Series

All rights reserved.
No part of this publication may be reproduced or distributed in any form or by any means without the written permission of the copyright owner.

Published by Kaplan North America, LLC d/b/a Barron's Educational Series
1515 West Cypress Creek Road
Fort Lauderdale, Florida 33309
www.barronseduc.com

ISBN: 978-1-5062-9770-5

10 9 8 7 6 5 4 3 2 1

Kaplan North America, LLC d/b/a Barron's Educational Series print books are available at special quantity discounts to use for sales promotions, employee premiums, or educational purposes. For more information or to purchase books, please call the Simon & Schuster special sales department at 866-506-1949.

About the Author

Eugene V. Resnick has taught in the Social Studies Department at Midwood High School in Brooklyn, New York, for thirty-three years; he has taught AP United States History for twenty-four of those years. He received a master's degree in United States history from Brooklyn College.

Acknowledgments

I would like to extend my gratitude to Sharone David for her invaluable editorial assistance and guidance, to Mark Willner, Joe Peters, and Danielle Shapiro for their assistance with this project, and to my colleagues, past and present, at Midwood High School, who have provided me with advice, feedback, and inspiration. In addition, I would like to thank the many students who have taken my Advanced Placement United States History class; I have learned much from them. Finally, many thanks to the staff at Barron's Educational Series. I am indebted to Stuart Murray, John Evans, and Aarthi Padmanaban for their excellent copyediting work, and to the outstanding editorial work of Peter Mavrikis, Kristen Girardi, Christine Ricketts, and Lauren Manoy. I would like to also thank the anonymous reviewers who have commented insightfully on this manuscript over the years. This book is dedicated to Aviv David-Paris—a bright young scholar who never ceases to amaze me.

How to Use This Book

Review and Practice

This book's review chapters are aligned with the curriculum for the AP U.S. History course, as outlined in the College Board's *Course and Exam Description*. You may find it helpful to read the text along with your classroom assignments when you are first learning the material and studying for classroom tests, or you may choose to read the chapters together as a review after you have completed most of your AP U.S. History course. By answering the practice questions that follow each chapter, you will be able test your learning as you progress through the book.

Practice Tests

The final section of the book offers the opportunity to take two full-length practice tests that include all question types found on the actual exam. It is suggested that you time yourself as you take these exams. In this way, you will get used to the pacing required for the actual exam. The exams are followed by explanations for the multiple-choice questions and descriptions of high-scoring responses for the written sections of the exam. Please consult these explanations and descriptions if the material in the questions is not clear to you.

Online Practice

In addition to the two practice tests within this book, there are also three full-length online practice exams. You can take these exams in practice (untimed) mode or in timed mode. All questions include answer explanations.

Table of Contents

About the Author iii
How to Use This Book... iv
Barron's Essential 5.. x

PART 1: INTRODUCTION

Preparing for the Advanced Placement United States History Exam 3
    Using This Book to Help You Prepare for the Exam 3

1 Historical Thinking Skills, Reasoning Processes, and Themes 5
    Historical Thinking Skills and Reasoning Processes 5
    Historical Thinking Skills 5
    History Reasoning Processes 11
    Themes in U.S. History 13

2 Navigating the Advanced Placement United States History Exam 17
    Multiple-Choice Questions 19
    Short-Answer Questions 21
    Document-Based Question 23
    Long Essay Question 29
    Answers and Explanations 32

PART 2: REVIEW SECTION—TIME PERIODS

3 Period 1: 1491–1607 The Meeting of Three Peoples 43
    Topic 1.1 Contextualizing Period 1 44
    Topic 1.2 Native American Societies Before European Contact 44
    Topic 1.3 European Exploration in the Americas 46
    Topic 1.4 Columbian Exchange, Spanish Exploration, and Conquest 47
    Topic 1.5 Labor, Slavery, and Caste in the Spanish Colonial System 49
    Topic 1.6 Cultural Interactions Between Europeans, Native Americans, and Africans 51
    Topic 1.7 Subject to Debate 53
    Practice Multiple-Choice Questions 54
    Answers and Explanations 55

4 Period 2: 1607–1754 Patterns of Empire and Resistance 57
    Topic 2.1 Contextualizing Period 2 58
    Topic 2.2 European Colonization 58
    Topic 2.3 The Regions of British Colonies 62
    Topic 2.4 Transatlantic Trade 71
    Topic 2.5 Interactions Between American Indians and Europeans 76
    Topic 2.6 Slavery in the British Colonies 79
    Topic 2.7 Colonial Society and Culture 81

Topic 2.8 Subject to Debate...86
Practice Multiple-Choice Questions 87
Answers and Explanations 89

5 Period 3: 1754–1800 The Crisis of Empire, Revolution, and Nation Building..........................91

Topic 3.1 Contextualizing Period 3 93
Topic 3.2 The Seven Years' War (The French and Indian War)...93
Topic 3.3 Taxation Without Representation..97
Topic 3.4 Philosophical Foundations of the American Revolution......................................100
Topic 3.5 The American Revolution 104
Topic 3.6 The Influence of Revolutionary Ideas 106
Topic 3.7 The Articles of Confederation..108
Topic 3.8 The Constitutional Convention and Debates over Ratification...........................111
Topic 3.9 The Constitution...114
Topic 3.10 Shaping the New Republic...116
Topic 3.11 Developing an American Identity 122
Topic 3.12 Movement in the Early Republic...123
Topic 3.13 Subject to Debate 125
Practice Multiple-Choice Questions 127
Answers and Explanations 131

6 Period 4: 1800–1848 The Meaning of Democracy in an Era of Economic and Territorial Expansion...133

Topic 4.1 Contextualizing Period 4 135
Topic 4.2 The Rise of Political Parties and the Era of Jefferson..135
Topic 4.3 Politics and Regional Interests...138
Topic 4.4 America on the World Stage...140
Topic 4.5 The Market Revolution: Economic Transformations...144
Topic 4.6 Market Revolution: Society and Culture..148
Topic 4.7 Expanding Democracy..151
Topic 4.8 Jackson and Federal Power 153
Topic 4.9 The Development of an American Culture..156
Topic 4.10 The Second Great Awakening 158
Topic 4.11 An Age of Reform...160
Topic 4.12 African Americans in the Early Republic..163
Topic 4.13 The Society of the South in the Early Republic...166
Topic 4.14 Subject to Debate 168
Practice Multiple-Choice Questions 170
Answers and Explanations 174

7 Period 5: 1844–1877 The Civil War and Reconstruction 177

- Topic 5.1 Contextualizing Period 5 178
- Topic 5.2 Manifest Destiny 179
- Topic 5.3 The Mexican-American War 181
- Topic 5.4 The Compromise of 1850 184
- Topic 5.5 Sectional Conflict: Regional Differences 186
- Topic 5.6 Failure to Compromise 189
- Topic 5.7 Election of 1860 and Secession 191
- Topic 5.8 Military Conflict in the Civil War 192
- Topic 5.9 Government Policies During the Civil War 195
- Topic 5.10 Reconstruction 197
- Topic 5.11 Failure of Reconstruction 202
- Topic 5.12 Subject to Debate 204
- Practice Multiple-Choice Questions 206
- Answers and Explanations 211

8 Period 6: 1865–1898 The Challenges of the Era of Industrialization 213

- Topic 6.1 Contextualizing Period 6 214
- Topic 6.2 Westward Expansion: Economic Development 215
- Topic 6.3 Westward Expansion: Social and Cultural Development 218
- Topic 6.4 The "New South" 222
- Topic 6.5 Technological Innovation 223
- Topic 6.6 The Rise of Industrial Capitalism 224
- Topic 6.7 Labor in the Gilded Age 226
- Topic 6.8 Immigration and Migration in the Gilded Age 230
- Topic 6.9 Responses to Immigration in the Gilded Age 231
- Topic 6.10 Development of the Middle Class 233
- Topic 6.11 Reform in the Gilded Age 235
- Topic 6.12 Controversies over the Role of Government in the Gilded Age 237
- Topic 6.13 Politics in the Gilded Age 238
- Topic 6.14 Subject to Debate 242
- Practice Multiple-Choice Questions 244
- Answers and Explanations 248

9 Period 7: 1890–1945 Economic Dislocation and Reform in the Age of Empire and World War 251

- Topic 7.1 Contextualizing Period 7 254
- Topic 7.2 Imperialism: Debates 255
- Topic 7.3 The Spanish-American War and Its Aftermath 257
- Topic 7.4 The Progressives 262
- Topic 7.5 World War I: Military and Diplomacy 271
- Topic 7.6 World War I: Home Front 276
- Topic 7.7 1920s: Innovation in Communications and Technology 279
- Topic 7.8 1920s: Cultural and Political Controversies 282
- Topic 7.9 The Great Depression 286
- Topic 7.10 The New Deal 288
- Topic 7.11 Interwar Foreign Policy 295

Topic 7.12 World War II: Mobilization ... 298
Topic 7.13 World War II: Military ... 300
Topic 7.14 Postwar Diplomacy ... 304
Topic 7.15 Subject to Debate ... 305
Practice Multiple-Choice Questions ... 308
Answers and Explanations ... 312

10 Period 8: 1945–1980 Redefining Democracy in the Era of Cold War and Liberal Ascendancy ... 315

Topic 8.1 Contextualizing Period 8 ... 317
Topic 8.2 The Cold War from 1945 to 1980 ... 318
Topic 8.3 The Red Scare ... 322
Topic 8.4 The Economy After 1945 ... 325
Topic 8.5 Culture After 1945 ... 327
Topic 8.6 Early Steps in the Civil Rights Movement (1940s and 1950s) ... 328
Topic 8.7 America as a World Power ... 331
Topic 8.8 The Vietnam War ... 333
Topic 8.9 The Great Society ... 335
Topic 8.10 The African-American Civil Rights Movement (1960s) ... 338
Topic 8.11 The Civil Rights Movement Expands ... 343
Topic 8.12 Youth Culture of the 1960s ... 345
Topic 8.13 The Environment and Natural Resources from 1968 to 1980 ... 349
Topic 8.14 Society in Transition ... 352
Topic 8.15 Subject to Debate ... 355
Practice Multiple-Choice Questions ... 357
Answers and Explanations ... 360

11 Period 9: 1980–Present Political and Foreign Policy Adjustments in a Globalized World ... 363

Topic 9.1 Contextualizing Period 9 ... 365
Topic 9.2 Reagan, Conservatism, and Partisan Divisions ... 365
Topic 9.3 The End of the Cold War ... 380
Topic 9.4 A Changing Economy ... 383
Topic 9.5 Migration and Immigration, 1980 to the Present ... 386
Topic 9.6 Defining America's Role in the World in the 21st Century ... 388
Topic 9.7 Subject to Debate ... 395
Practice Multiple-Choice Questions ... 397
Answers and Explanations ... 399

PART 3: PRACTICE TESTS

Practice Test 1 .... **405**
   Answers and Explanations 436
   Scoring the Test 455

Practice Test 2 .... **459**
   Answers and Explanations 486
   Scoring the Test 504

Index **505**

BARRON'S ESSENTIAL 5

As you review the content in this book and work toward earning that **5** on your AP U.S. HISTORY exam, here are five things that you **MUST** know above everything else.

1 **How to think like a historian.** The questions on the AP U.S. History exam are all built around historical thinking skills and reasoning processes. The College Board has identified six historical thinking skills and three reasoning processes that are central to the exam and to the broader field of history. The six skills—developments and processes, sourcing and situation, claims and evidence in sources, contextualization, making connections, and argumentation—encourage you to develop the habits of mind required for a critical examination of the past. The three reasoning processes—comparison, causation, and continuity and change—focus on constructing and evaluating historical arguments about the past. These skills and processes encourage students to go beyond memorization and to engage with the past in complex and sophisticated ways.

2 **How to read documents.** Documents are the building blocks of history and are central to the AP exam. All of the multiple-choice questions and the first two short-answer questions are built around primary or secondary documents. In addition, the document-based essay question asks you to analyze a series of documents as you construct a response to the question. Focus on how documents relate to the question and on how documents often relate to one another. Remember that historical documents contain a point of view. You should be able to read a diary entry, a newspaper article, a speech, or an argument by a historian and ascertain the point of view and intent of the author.

3 **Themes of growth and conflict in American history.** The rapid growth of the United States—territorially, economically, and demographically—is unprecedented in world history. On the one hand, this growth decimated Native American cultures; on the other, the nation has provided a haven for immigrants. The territorial growth of the country—inspired by the spirit of "manifest destiny"—intensified the debate over slavery in the antebellum period. The series of compromises over expansion eventually unraveled and helped bring about the Civil War. The economic and territorial growth of the United States continued in the period following the Spanish-American War, as the United States joined the other imperialist powers of the world. Be familiar with the causes of American expansion as well as the profound impacts.

4 **The changing nature of the American experiment in democracy.** The United States had made major contributions to the literature and the practice of modern representative government. However, be aware that democracy did not emerge fully formed with the birth of the nation. Americans have struggled over the meaning of democracy throughout American history. Abigail Adams encouraged her husband, John, to "remember the ladies" at the time of the creation of the United States. Slavery and the "Jim Crow" system excluded African Americans from the American experiment in democracy. The civil rights movement struggled to fully include African Americans in the democratic system. These conflicts over the meaning of democracy are crucial to understanding the evolution of the United States.

5 **The dynamic nature of history.** Traditional historians saw history as unidirectional—emanating from the minds and priorities of the elites in society. More recently, historians have seen events as part of a more dynamic process. Social and cultural historians have explored "history from below." As you study, look for such connections and interactions in history. For instance, while it is important to remember that President Lyndon Johnson endorsed and pushed for passage of the 1964 Civil Rights Act, you should be able to connect that with the growth of the grassroots civil rights movement, with the violent backlash against the movement, with shifts within the major political parties, and with the dynamics of the Cold War. Historical events do not occur in isolation of one another. Therefore, memorizing discrete events in American history is not sufficient for success on the AP exam.

PART 1
Introduction

Preparing for the Advanced Placement United States History Exam

Congratulations on taking the Advanced Placement course in United States History. If taken seriously, the class and the exam will develop your critical thinking skills and your ability to understand the world in nuanced ways. The class and the exam ask more of you than merely memorizing facts. You are asked to think through problems, to engage in debates, to organize your thinking, to develop your communication skills, and to take thoughtful stands on important issues.

The College Board's course framework, included in its AP U.S. History Course and Exam Description, identifies nine periods in United States history. Within each period, there are seven to fifteen topics. This sequence of topics is designed to mirror the sequence of units often found in college courses and textbooks. The College Board has also identified specific historical thinking skills and reasoning processes, as well as themes, that students must show proficiency in to earn high scores on the AP exam.

The skills, processes, and themes in the framework reflect the College Board's desire to align the AP curriculum and exam with history courses at the university level. The College Board has put more of an emphasis on developing the skills and processes that will deepen your understanding and appreciation of history, and less of an emphasis on memorizing hundreds of seemingly unrelated facts. Yes, you still must be familiar with a wide variety of developments in United States history. However, the exam focuses on your ability to use this historical content in analyzing and developing arguments, in making connections across time, in understanding the broader context of particular developments, in assessing causation, and in evaluating interpretations and developing new ones. The course and exam will push you toward greater intellectual growth and will help you think in new and more sophisticated ways about the world we live in.

Using This Book to Help You Prepare for the Exam

This book has been written and revised with the explicit aim of helping you succeed on the AP United States History exam. In the following chapter you will find descriptions of the historical thinking skills and reasoning processes, as well as themes, that are central to the exam. The book provides examples of how these skills and themes apply to the content of American history. These descriptions are followed by a detailed description of the exam. Each of the four sections of the exam is explored, along with tips, strategies, and approaches for achieving high scores on the exam.

Next, the book contains nine chapters of historical content corresponding to the breakdown of United States history in the College Board's course framework. Each content chapter is broken down into seven to fifteen topics, mirroring the sequence of topics in the College Board's course framework. The content chapters in this book provide you with a wealth of illustrative examples that are most relevant to the topics in the course framework and will be most useful to you as you prepare for the AP exam.

Each of the nine content chapters concludes with a "Subject to Debate" section. These sections will help you recognize the contentious nature of historical interpretation, which is the focus of the first short-answer question on the AP exam. This short-answer question will provide you with two historians' interpretations of a historical development or process and will assess your ability to describe and compare these interpretations. As you become more familiar with historians' interpretations of the past, you will begin to develop your own interpretations of historical developments. It will become clear that you are becoming a participant in ongoing debates about the past. By gaining a deeper understanding of the nature of these debates, you will become better prepared to develop your own interpretive ideas.

Finally, the book contains two practice exams. It is suggested that you time yourself as you take these exams. In this way, you will get used to the pacing required for the actual Advanced Placement exam. The exams are followed by explanations for the multiple-choice questions and descriptions of high-scoring responses for the written sections of the exam. Please consult these explanations and descriptions if the material in the questions is not clear to you.

Good luck as you prepare for the AP exam.

1

Historical Thinking Skills, Reasoning Processes, and Themes

> **Learning Objectives**
> In this chapter, you will learn about:
> → Historical thinking skills and reasoning processes
> → Historical thinking skills
> → Historical reasoning processes
> → Themes in U.S. history

The College Board has identified a set of historical thinking skills and reasoning processes as well as thematic learning objectives that it expects AP U.S. History students to develop. These skills, processes, and themes, used in all the AP history courses, are central to all the questions on the exam. The skills and processes outlined by the College Board reflect the skills used by professional historians in their day-to-day work. The themes are windows to help students see continuities and enduring debates and challenges in U.S. history.

Below, these skills, processes, and themes are described and discussed; it is crucial to be familiar with them during the AP course and, of course, as you prepare for the AP exam.

Historical Thinking Skills and Reasoning Processes

The College Board has identified five historical thinking skills and four reasoning processes that are commonly used by those who participate in the field of historical study. These nine skills and processes outlined by the College Board for the AP U.S. History exam are the same as those used on the AP World History exam and on the AP European History exam. Therefore, familiarity with these skills and processes can aid you in other AP history courses you may take. These skills and processes, discussed in this chapter and illustrated in boxes throughout the content chapters of this book, are at the heart of the practice of history—in college, in graduate school, and in the field. At least one of these skills or processes is built into every question on the AP exam. Therefore, an understanding of these skills and processes is essential to success on the AP exam.

Historical Thinking Skills

Skill 1: Developments and Processes

This skill calls on you to identify and explain historical developments and processes. Developing a broad base of empirical historical knowledge represents the beginning point of historical inquiry.

Identifying and Explaining Historical Developments and Processes
- *Identify a historical concept, development, or process.*
- *Explain a historical concept, development, or process.*

You attain knowledge of historical concepts, developments, and processes from a variety of sources—participating in classroom activities, engaging in public history (monuments, museums, documentaries), reading textbooks, and analyzing primary and secondary sources. Before you can carry out the more sophisticated skills discussed below, you need to establish a solid foundation of historical events, processes, and people and their actions.

Skill 2: Sourcing and Situation

This skill calls on you to analyze sourcing and situation of primary and secondary sources. "Sourcing" refers to analyzing the origins of a document; "situation" refers to the context it was created in. You must be able to carefully describe and evaluate evidence about the past from a variety of primary and secondary sources.

Identifying and Explaining Sourcing and Situation
- *Identify a source's point of view, purpose, historical situation, and/or audience.*
- *Explain a source's point of view, purpose, historical situation, and/or audience.*

Primary and secondary sources are essential building blocks of the historian. Primary sources can include written documents, artifacts, oral traditions, works of music and art, and other sources. Secondary sources include a variety of historical accounts created after the event in question—history books, textbooks, journal articles, documentaries, museum exhibits, public monuments, and other sources. You should be proficient in "reading" a variety of sources, including documents from the point of view of traditionally underrepresented groups and cultures. For example, in understanding the impact of Protestant missionary work in nineteenth-century Irish-Catholic immigrant neighborhoods, you might be asked to look at different types of evidence—from the point of view of the Protestant missionaries as well as from the point of view of the Irish immigrants. The exam might also invite you to analyze historical evidence beyond the written word; you might have to evaluate archaeological evidence or geographical analyses. In addition, you should be prepared to examine popular culture in gaining an understanding of a period, such as the 1950s or 1960s. Finally, not all relevant evidence will be from an American point of view; in examining the role of the United States in the world, it is important to be able to understand evidence offered by non-American actors.

This practice calls on you to understand the content of sources, but also to interrogate sources by looking beyond the explicit content and by thinking critically about how to use documents in a meaningful and effective way. Specifically, you are expected to identify and explain the following elements of sources:

POINT OF VIEW: The point of view of the author—his or her ideology, background, way of understanding the world—can shape the content of a document. An author's point of view, in turn, can be shaped by a number of factors, including his or her gender, race, ethnicity, class, sexual orientation, and age.

PURPOSE: The purpose of the author also helps us better understand a document's meaning. Is the document aimed at convincing others or is it merely a recording of one's private thoughts? Does the author have a score to settle or is he or she attempting to remain above the fray? Related to purpose is audience.

AUDIENCE: Individuals often shape the content of a speech or a letter to appeal to an intended audience—allies or antagonists, a close friend or a powerful figure, a select group or the general public. One might emphasize or leave out certain points based on the purpose and audience.

HISTORICAL SITUATION: The historical situation of a document helps us better understand the author's purpose. Thomas Paine's tract, *Common Sense* (published in January 1776), for instance, can be better understood when seen in its particular historical situation—namely, the deteriorating relationship between Great Britain and the Thirteen Colonies and the bitter debates among Americans about what course of action to pursue. A better understanding of a document's historical situation will also help us better understand how it was received by contemporaries.

Significance of Sourcing and Usefulness of Sources
- *Explain the significance of a source's point of view, purpose, historical situation, and/or audience, including how these might limit the uses(s) of a source.*

You are expected not to simply identify and explain the above elements of sourcing and situation but also to determine the relative significance of these elements. This part of the skill calls on you to evaluate which elements of sourcing (discussed on pages 6–7) are most important in understanding a document. In addition, this part of the skill asks you to determine the degree to which the sourcing of a document might limit the usefulness of that document. Here, you must employ the four elements of sourcing and situation (point of view, purpose, audience, and historical situation) to better assess a document's credibility and limitations. Perhaps an author's background or social position might limit his or her ability to comprehend a situation. A document describing an event years earlier might contain inaccuracies as memories become less vivid over time. A closing argument from a judicial proceeding may leave out certain elements or emphasize other elements that advance a lawyer's contention of "guilty" or "not guilty." Noting a document's credibility and limitations also begs the question of what additional documents would be helpful to fill in gaps.

Skill 3: Claims and Evidence in Sources

This skill calls on you to analyze arguments in primary and secondary sources. It requires you to first identify a source's argument and then to cite the specific evidence that an author uses to support his or her argument. In addition, you should be able to compare the main idea of two sources, and finally to explain how additional evidence can support, modify, or refute a source's argument.

Identifying Claims and Arguments
- *Identify and describe a claim and/or argument in a text-based or non-text-based source.*

Claims can be found in primary or secondary sources. In regard to primary sources, be prepared to identify the main argument of a manifesto, letter, speech, or other pronouncement. What specifically, for example, is Nathaniel Bacon attempting to prove in his 1676 manifesto? What is Frederick Douglass asserting in his speech, "What to the Slave Is the Fourth of July?" What is the main claim that Woodrow Wilson is making in his argument for entering World War I in his 1917 "Joint Address to Congress"? Be prepared to also identify claims in secondary sources—notably the writings of historians. How, for example, does Eric Foner interpret the Reconstruction period in his (1988) book, *Reconstruction: America's Unfinished Revolution, 1863–1877*? What is the main argument of Gar Alperovitz in *The Decision to Use the Atomic Bomb* (1995)? Excerpts from historical writing can appear on the AP exam in the document-based question as well as in multiple-choice questions. In addition, the focus of the first short-answer question on each AP exam will include two excerpts of historical writing that you must compare (see page 21).

Identifying Evidence in Claims
- *Identify the evidence used in a source to support an argument.*

A compelling argument includes evidence to support that argument. Be prepared to identify specific pieces of evidence that authors provide to bolster their points, both in primary sources and secondary sources. What evidence, for example, does President Lyndon B. Johnson provide in his 1965 State of the Union Address to support his claim that the nation needs to invest in his Great Society agenda? Does historian Richard Hofstadter provide sufficient evidence in *The Age of Reform* (1955) to support his claim that the Populists were driven more by provincial prejudices and irrational fears than by legitimate political and economic injustices? What evidence does the historian Carl Degler (*Out of Our Past*, 1959) provide in support of his thesis that the New Deal represented a dramatic break with American traditions, a "revolutionary response" to the economic crisis of the 1930s?

Comparing Arguments
- *Compare the main ideas of two sources.*

This skill requires you to note different arguments among historical actors (in primary sources) as well as among historians (in secondary sources). Often historians come to very different interpretations about historical developments and processes. Many factors shape a historian's interpretation of the past—the era the historian was writing in, the availability of sources, the background of the historian (in regard to gender, race, class, age, ethnicity), and the allegiances and political inclinations of the historian, as well as the methods and approach of the historian. Historians realize that their interpretations are contingent and will likely be modified or even refuted by future historians as new evidence emerges and new approaches to understanding the past develop. Historical inquiry is an ongoing conversation about the past. Historians, therefore, can come up with widely divergent interpretations of events in the past. You should be prepared to evaluate and engage with a variety of historical arguments and to compare competing interpretations of the past. It is important, then, to be familiar with historiographical debates of historical topics. Debates have occurred between historians over the reasons for the American Revolution, the nature of slavery, the causes of the Civil War, the impact of progressivism, American conduct in the Cold War, and many others. The "Subject to Debate" section of each of the content chapters of this book introduces you to the historiographical debates of that time period.

This part of the skill can be assessed on multiple-choice questions and on the document-based essay question on the AP exam. In addition, it will be the focus of the first short-answer question. The question, which addresses historical developments or processes between the years 1754 and 1980 (Period 3 to Period 8), will require you to grapple with two historical sources and to compare how they differ on a particular topic (see more on the short-answer question section, page 21).

Modify and Refuting a Source's Argument
- *Explain how claims or evidence support, modify, or refute a source's argument.*

In addition to explaining a source's claim and explaining how the author uses evidence to support his or her claim, you should be able to explain how additional evidence can support or contradict a particular claim. In terms of claims in primary sources, this skill can involve first identifying an argument in a source and then evaluating the impact of additional evidence. You could be asked, for example, to identify the arguments of the Declaration of Independence, and then to evaluate whether additional evidence from the time supports or refutes the arguments of the document. A document by an American Indian critiquing colonial encroachments on Indian lands might refute the Declaration's claim that the King "excited domestic insurrections." Does the additional evidence support or refute the claim the King established an "absolute Tyranny"? A similar approach can be applied to secondary sources. After familiarizing yourself with a historian's argument, you should be able to test its validity by examining additional evidence.

Skill 4: Contextualization

This skill requires you to look at historical events and processes and to be able to evaluate how they connect with a broader historical setting. The context of a particular event can be regional, national, or global.

Identifying and Explaining Historical Context
- *Identify and describe an accurate historical context for a specific historical development or process.*
- *Explain how a specific historical development or process is situated with a broader historical context.*

Contextualization deepens our understanding of how and why particular events and developments occur. The skill of contextualization requires you to situate a particular development or process within broader developments. The skill will be assessed on all essay questions. Although the essay questions can focus on one of the three reasoning processes—comparison, causation, or continuity and change—*all* essay questions (the document-based question as well as the long essay question) will require you to contextualize the subject of the prompt.

Contextualizing the civil rights movement of the 1950s and 1960s, for example, requires going beyond the stories of the individuals and organizations involved. Contextualization involves examining relevant developments during and before the period in question—in the South, in the United States, and even in the world. You could look at the context of economic changes in the South in the post–World War II period or the experiences of African-American veterans. More broadly, an understanding of the origins of the movement might lead one to examine changes in the Democratic Party as it distanced itself from the ideology of its base in the white South. You could also look at the context of the Cold War to understand why calls for African-American civil rights found a receptive audience; many political leaders found it difficult to accuse the Soviet Union of denying democracy to its people while a certain section of the United States practiced Jim Crow segregation. These layers of context help students of history to more fully understand a particular event or phenomenon.

Skill 5: Making Connections

This skill requires you to use the historical reasoning processes—comparison, causation, and continuity and change—in order to identify and explain patterns and connections between and among historical developments and processes.

Identifying and Explaining Patterns and Relationships in History
- *Identify patterns among or connections between historical developments or processes.*
- *Explain how a historical development or process relates to another historical development or process.*

The skill of Making Connections encourages you to pull together the previously discussed skills and find patterns among historical developments, processes, claims, and evidence. However, it is not enough to simply note connections. You must be able explain *how* developments are connected. One can readily see that there is a connection between antebellum reform movements and Progressive-era reform movements: reform activity existed during both periods. However, this skill requires that you use the historical reasoning processes—comparison, causation, and continuity and change—to explain and evaluate how a phenomenon, event, or process connects to similar developments across space and time.

Analyzing patterns and making connections is the bridge between all of the previous historical thinking skills. This skill pulls everything together and allows you to connect all concepts. Whether you are using sources or your own historical knowledge, you will use the historical reasoning processes (discussed in the next section of this chapter) to identify and explain patterns and connections between historical events and developments.

Skill 6: Argumentation

Argumentation is a basic skill in the field of history. This skill calls on you to develop an evaluative thesis and to use evidence in making an argument. Argumentation draws together many of the other skills discussed in this chapter—identifying developments and processes, analyzing sources, analyzing arguments, putting events into a broader context, making connections between developments and processes—and invites you to develop meaningful and compelling new understandings of the past. In addition, you should understand that historians have been addressing major interpretative questions for generations. Therefore, in constructing an argument, you are entering, and interacting with, a community of scholars.

Developing a Claim/Argument
- *Make a historically defensible claim.*

You should be able to develop an argument about the past. A convincing argument contains a compelling and comprehensive thesis and draws on relevant evidence.

Using Evidence to Support an Argument
- *Support an argument using specific and relevant evidence.*

This element of the skill requires you to both describe and explain how specific pieces of historically relevant evidence support an argument. The skill is used in both the document-based essay and the long essay. In the long essay, you will have to supply appropriate and relevant evidence to support a thesis. It might be useful to brainstorm a wide variety of pieces of evidence that are relevant to the topic of the prompt and then to narrow the list to items that support your argument. In regard to the document-based question, you will need to evaluate the evidence provided, and determine whether the evidence supports, refutes, or modifies a possible argument.

Explaining Relationships Among Pieces of Evidence
- *Use historical reasoning to explain relationships among pieces of historical evidence.*

This element of Argumentation is especially relevant in tackling the document-based essay question. The question provides you with a variety of pieces of evidence, but it is up to you to determine how they are related to one another. The prompt will involve one of the three reasoning processes (discussed in the next section). The question might call for comparison. In that case, establish meaningful categories in which to compare the pieces of evidence. If the question is built around the reasoning process of causation, note how the varied evidence shows a pattern of causes or a pattern of effects. Finally, if the question calls for noting patterns of continuity and/or change, look for patterns among the documents and draw conclusions to support an argument.

Developing Complexity in Historical Argumentation
- *Corroborate, qualify, or modify an argument using diverse and alternative evidence in order to develop a complex argument.*

This element of Argumentation invites you to move beyond simplistic understandings of the past and to use a diversity of approaches to add shades of gray to arguments and claims. You should be able to consider ways in which diverse or alternative evidence could be used to qualify or modify an argument. The College Board has identified the following methods of adding complexity to arguments and claims:

MULTIPLE VARIABLES: *Explain the nuance of an issue by analyzing multiple variables.* An argument could add nuance by analyzing multiple variables. Such variables can include different categories of analysis, such as economic, political, social, and cultural factors, or the impact of a historic development on different groups of people. The lack of multiple voices was evident in traditional accounts of the Reconstruction period. The African-American historian W. E. B. Du Bois criticized the historical profession in his 1935 book, *Black Reconstruction*, for failing to include the views of African Americans and working people in analyzing Reconstruction, and for refusing to look at alternative evidence. In the decades since, historians have taken up his call in studying the Reconstruction period. Additionally, the use of multiple themes can add nuance to an essay. For example, an essay prompt dealing with antebellum westward expansion might primarily focus on the theme of migration and settlement. A complex response could include multiple perspectives from a variety of themes: politics and power; work, exchange, and technology; and/or social structure. These multiple perspectives can be used to confirm or challenge the validity of an argument. A compelling essay can demonstrate complexity by doing the same. As you attempt to create new arguments, you should be prepared to challenge traditional narratives and ask what voices, perspectives, and categories of analysis might be missing.

CONNECTIONS ACROSS TIME: *Explain relevant and insightful connections within and across periods.* A response could explain connections across and within time periods—applying understandings and insights about the past to other contexts and circumstances, including the present. For example, in an essay about the Progressive movement of the early twentieth century, you may wish to draw connections between the Progressive movement and other reform movements that followed it. To what degree is it similar to or different from the New Deal of the 1930s or the Great Society of the 1960s? Such connections across time allow you to add depth and nuance to your argument.

THE CREDIBILITY AND LIMITATIONS OF SOURCES: *Explain the historical significance of a source's credibility and limitations.* This element is especially relevant to the document-based essay question on the AP exam, but it can be applied to any historical writing that draws on sources. It calls on you to use the elements of Sourcing and Situation—point of view, purpose, historical situation, and/or audience (see Skill 2: Sourcing and Situation)—in developing an argument. For example, if there was a document-based essay question about conditions of Irish-Americans living in the Five Points neighborhood of New York City in the 1850s, a document written by a Protestant member of the Know-Nothing Party should be handled cautiously. By assessing the point of view of the author (vehemently anti-Catholic and anti-Irish), you can question its reliability as an accurate description of the Five Points neighborhood.

THE EFFECTIVENESS OF CLAIMS: *Explain how or why a historical claim or argument is or is not effective.* Students in AP U.S. History are entering an ongoing conversation about the past. Sophisticated students will be able to see that not all claims are created equal. Some are more sound and are supported by stronger evidence than others. Be prepared to judge whether evidence supports a particular claim. Is there additional evidence that goes against the claim? Can a counterclaim be put forward? Is the counterclaim more or less effective than the initial claim?

History Reasoning Processes

Reasoning Process 1: Comparison

You should be able to look at two or more different historical developments or processes and note similarities and differences. You should also be able to compare different perspectives on a particular process or development. This process is often presented in history class as the directive to "compare and contrast." Specifically, in order to show proficiency with this process, you should be able to:

- Describe similarities and/or differences between different historical developments or processes.
- Explain relevant similarities and/or differences between specific historical developments and processes.
- Explain the relative historical significance of similarities and/or differences between different historical developments or processes.

Questions on the AP exam might ask you to compare developments or processes across time and place. The developments might be from different societies or from within the same society. A sophisticated analysis might compare different developments and processes across more than one variable—such as across time and across place. In any case, a successful comparison will demonstrate the ability to describe, compare, and evaluate different historical developments or processes.

There is a wide variety of comparison-based questions that you might encounter on the AP exam: How similar and how different were the antebellum reform movements and the Progressive-era reform movements? How does the anti-imperialism movement of the early twentieth century compare to the antiwar movement of the 1960s and 1970s? You might be asked to compare thematic developments in different time periods, such as how ideas and debates around gender norms and roles in the 1920s compare to those in the 1950s.

Reasoning Process 2: Causation

This practice involves thinking about the causes and effects of historical events. You must see that events in history do not happen in a vacuum—that they are connected to and influenced by previous events in history. Specifically, in order to show proficiency with this process, you should be able to:

- Describe the causes or effects of a specific historical development or process.
- Explain the relationship between causes and effects of a specific historical development or process.
- Explain the differences between primary and secondary causes and between short-term and long-term effects.
- Explain the relative historical significance of different causes and/or effects.

This process also requires you to assess historical contingency. Historical contingency presumes that each event in history depends on a whole array of events and circumstances—that each event is contingent on this universe of previous conditions. If one or more of the antecedent conditions were absent, then perhaps a historical event would have occurred differently or not at all. This process requires you to interrogate and dissect the myths of inevitability that have shaped many people's thinking about the past. The events that led the United States to expand its borders, for example, were contingent on earlier events—expansion was not simply the "manifest destiny" of the American nation.

Thinking about historical contingency requires you to distinguish among coincidence, causation, and correlation in looking at different events. Perhaps two events happening around the same time are not related to each other in any significant way—they are merely coincidental. Perhaps one can be seen as the cause of the other. Or, perhaps, the two events are related, but one cannot clearly be seen as the cause of the other. Teasing out the relationship of events in history is key to historical interpretation and to critiquing existing interpretations of causality.

Reasoning Process 3: Continuity and Change

Recognizing patterns of continuity and change requires you to see patterns and trends in history and at the same time to see that not all events can fit neatly into existing patterns. Students of history can readily see change over time—that our predecessors functioned with different technologies, lived under different laws, participated in different cultural pursuits. This process requires you to identify and evaluate these changes over time, but also to note continuities as well. Specifically, in order to show proficiency with this process you should be able to:

- Understand and describe patterns of continuity and/or change over time.
- Explain patterns of continuity and change over time.
- Explain the relative significance of specific historical developments in relation to a larger pattern of continuity and/or change.

An essay prompt might invite you to explore continuity and change in regard to attitudes around immigrants by examining the pre–Civil War responses to large-scale Irish and German immigration, and the responses to the large influx of "new immigrants" in the late nineteenth and early twentieth centuries. A response could explore thematic continuities—in terms of fears, rhetoric, actions—between the anti-immigrant sentiment that led to the Emergency Quota Act of 1921 and the earlier Know-Nothing Party of the 1840s and 1850s. The context of the "red scare" and pseudo-scientific ideas about race in the later period might show discontinuities with the antebellum nativist movement. A continuity and change essay prompt could have you examine any one of a host of historical issues as they were manifested in different time frames—living conditions for certain groups, popular culture, American foreign policy, race relations.

Themes in U.S. History

The AP curriculum highlights eight themes that are woven into the entire AP course. These themes are broader ideas that are revisited at different points in the curriculum. They help develop a deeper understanding of the topics covered in the curriculum. All the questions on the exam are designed to assess your proficiency in one or more of these themes.

Below is a list of the eight themes in the Advanced Placement curriculum, followed by a description of each theme. Familiarity with the themes is crucial for success on the AP exam. The different themes run through the entire curriculum and allow you to develop meaningful connections across time periods.

> The eight themes are:
> 1. American and National Identity
> 2. Work, Exchange, and Technology
> 3. Geography and the Environment
> 4. Migration and Settlement
> 5. Politics and Power
> 6. America and the World
> 7. American and Regional Culture
> 8. Social Structures

American and National Identity

The development of and debates about democracy, freedom, citizenship, diversity, and individualism shape American national identity, cultural values, and beliefs about American exceptionalism, and in turn, these ideas shape political institutions and society. Throughout American history, notions of national identity and culture have coexisted with varying degrees of regional and group identities.

This theme encourages you to analyze both the identity of the American people as a national entity as well as to explore the ways that various groups of individuals have sought to define their identities within the broader American culture. This theme requires you to understand that identity changes over time and that participants in these various groups themselves play an important role in reshaping and redefining identity. Groups have sought to define themselves along lines of gender, class, race, and ethnicity.

The concept of national identity involves topics such as citizenship, foreign policy, constitutionalism, and assimilation. In addition, this theme invites us to grapple with the idea of American exceptionalism. This idea posits the uniqueness of the United States, based on democratic ideals and individual liberty. It sees the United States as unique in that it was formed around a creed, rather than around a shared history or common ethnicity. Others view these "American" qualities as manifestations of broader developments in global history.

The following are sub-themes of the theme of American and National Identity:

- **DEMOCRACY, FREEDOM, AND INDIVIDUALISM:** Ideas about democracy, freedom, and individualism have found expression in the development of cultural values, political institutions, and American society.
- **THE CONSTITUTION AND CITIZENSHIP:** Interpretations of the Constitution and debates over rights, liberties, and definitions of citizenship have affected American values, politics, and society.
- **AMERICAN IDENTITY IN A GLOBAL CONTEXT:** Ideas about national identity have changed in response to U.S. involvement in international conflicts and the growth of the United States.
- **REGIONAL AND NATIONAL IDENTITY:** Different regional, social, ethnic, and racial groups have developed different identities and these groups' experiences have contributed to national identity in the United States.

Work, Exchange, and Technology

The interplay between markets, private enterprise, labor, technology, and government policy shape the American economy. In turn, economic activity shapes society and government policy and drives technological innovation.

This theme expands on the traditional theme in the American history curricula of "economic history." The theme looks broadly at the development of the American economy from the colonial period through the present. The College Board identifies agriculture, commerce, and manufacturing as the basis of the American economy.

The following are sub-themes of the theme of Work, Exchange, and Technology:

- **LABOR SYSTEMS:** Different labor systems have developed in North America and the United States, affecting workers' lives and American society.
- **MARKETS AND GOVERNMENT POLICY:** Different patterns of exchange, markets, and private enterprise have developed over time, and governments have responded to changing economic patterns in diverse ways.
- **TECHNOLOGY AND DEVELOPMENT:** Technological innovation has affected economic development and society is diverse ways.

Geography and the Environment

Geographic and environmental factors, including competition over and debates about natural resources, shape the development of America and foster regional diversity. The development of America impacts the environment and reshapes geography, which leads to debates about environmental and geographic issues.

The inclusion of this theme represents a coming together of two traditionally discrete disciplines—history and geography. In the last decade, geographers have become increasingly interested in the historical patterns of the human imprint on the physical world, and historians have become increasingly interested in the degree to which the physical environment has shaped human patterns of behavior over time. The theme focuses on interactions. Specifically, how have interactions between the physical environment and various North American groups shaped their institutions and values? In addition, the theme invites you to examine decisions and policies related to the environment. Geography and the Environment is the only theme of the eight that has no sub-themes.

Migration and Settlement

Push and pull factors shape immigration into and migration within America, and the demographic change as a result of these moves shapes the migrants, society, and the environment.

The theme of Migration and Settlement covers migration into the United States, out of the United States, and within the United States. Further, this theme recognizes the impact that the adjustments of borders have had on the people who did not migrate. Migrants bring with them ideas, beliefs, technologies, gender roles, and traditions. This theme explores the ways in which people adapt to new settings, and how these adaptations have shaped American society.

The following are sub-themes of the theme of Migration and Settlement:

- **IMMIGRATION FROM ABROAD:** There have been a variety of causes and effects of the migration of different groups of people to colonial North America and, later, to the United States.
- **INTERNAL MIGRATIONS:** There have been a variety of causes and effects of internal migrations and patterns of settlement in what would become the United States.

Politics and Power

Debates fostered by social and political groups about the role of government in American social, political, and economic life shape government policy, institutions, political parties, and the rights of citizens.

This theme expands on the traditional theme of political history, which has been at the center of standard American history curricula for decades. The theme of politics and power goes well beyond the traditional focus of elections, presidents, parties, and policies. This theme invites you to explore the interactions between power on the one hand, and popular participation on the other. Attempts have been made to limit participation by certain groups throughout American history; likewise, reform movements have attempted to expand avenues for participation in the political process. The theme of politics and power also examines the debates about the proper role of government in society. You should be familiar with changes in the relationship among the three branches of government and between the national government and the state governments. Finally, this theme invites you to explore the ongoing tensions between liberty and authority in American history.

The following are sub-themes of the theme of Politics and Power:

- **IDEAS, INSTITUTIONS, AND PARTIES:** Political ideas, beliefs, institutions, party systems, and alignments have developed and changed over time.
- **MOVEMENTS FOR CHANGE:** Various popular movements, reform efforts, and activist groups have sought to change American society and institutions.
- **THE ROLE OF THE FEDERAL GOVERNMENT:** Different beliefs about the federal government's role in American social and economic life have affected political debates and policies.

America in the World

Diplomatic, economic, cultural, and military interactions between empires, nations, and peoples shape the development of America and America's increasingly important role in the world.

Traditional U.S. history curricula have certainly focused on the diplomatic and military history of the United States. Such traditional history courses have focused almost exclusively on the decisions made by leaders and on the impact of those decisions. The College Board, however, goes beyond this traditional approach by looking at the United States in a global context and looking at a wide range of factors that have shaped the role of the United States in the world. The primary focus is no longer on the diplomatic and military decisions of American political leaders. Rather, you are asked to put the United States in a global context. You should be able to look at the broad array of factors and motives that have shaped specific decisions in relation to American military, economics, and diplomatic interventions abroad. This theme places foreign policy in the broader context of American social, economic, and political history.

The following are sub-themes of the theme of America in the World:

- **EMPIRE AND THE SHAPING OF COLONIAL NORTH AMERICA:** Cultural interactions, cooperation, competition, and conflict between empires, nations, and peoples have influenced political, economic, and social developments in North America.
- **AMERICAN DIPLOMATIC, ECONOMIC, AND MILITARY INITIATIVES:** There have been a variety of reasons for and results of U.S. diplomatic, economic, and military initiatives in North America and overseas.

American and Regional Culture

Creative expression, demographic change, philosophy, religious beliefs, scientific ideas, social mores, and technology shape national, regional, and group cultures in America, and these varying cultures often play a role in shaping government policy and developing economic systems.

In traditional history courses, cultural history often occupies a marginal place, relegated to the random song or poem introduced as a precursor to the more "serious" history. Over the last generation, historians have worked to integrate cultural, religious, moral, and intellectual history into the mainstream of historical study. The College Board's curriculum framework recognizes this shift in the American and Regional Culture theme. The theme explores the roles that ideas, beliefs, social mores, and creative expression have played in the ongoing development of the United States. Part of understanding the identity of the United States is understanding the development of aesthetic, religious, scientific, and philosophical principles. In addition, you should be prepared to examine how these principles have affected individual and group actions. Beliefs and value systems do not exist in isolation—they intersect with ideas about community and economics, and with movements for social change.

The following are sub-themes of the theme of American and Regional Culture:

- **RELIGION AND AMERICAN LIFE:** Various religious groups and ideas have affected American society and political life.
- **CULTURE AND SOCIETY:** Artistic, philosophical, and scientific ideas have developed and shaped American society and institutions.

Social Structures

Social categories, roles, and practices are created, maintained, challenged, and transformed throughout American history, shaping government policy, economic systems, culture, and the lives of citizens.

This theme looks at the variety of ways that social groups have been organized and maintained in U.S. history. These groups can be organized around religious institutions, schools, type of work, political affiliations, kinship and friendship networks, as well as around different forms of identity—race, class, ethnicity, sexual orientation, gender, and others. These social structures are formed and altered by the needs, desires, and actions of individual members of society, and they also work to determine social behavior of individuals.

The following are sub-themes of the theme of Social Structures:

- **GENDER AND SOCIETY:** Evolving ideas about women's rights and gender roles have affected society and politics.
- **THE EVOLUTION OF SOCIAL GROUPS:** Different groups identities, including those based on race, ethnicity, class, and region, have emerged and changed over time.

2

Navigating the Advanced Placement United States History Exam

Learning Objectives

In this chapter, you will learn about:
- → Multiple-choice questions
- → Short-answer questions
- → Document-based questions
- → Long essay questions

AP Exams Are Going Digital

Starting in May 2025, the AP U.S. History Exam will be fully digital. You will take the exam using the Bluebook digital testing application, which will include multiple-choice, short-answer, and essay sections.

How You'll Take the Exam

You'll complete the exam on the Bluebook application, using a personal or school-issued device. This setup gives you flexibility and ensures a smooth testing experience.

Exam Structure Stays the Same

The format and content of the AP U.S. History Exam will remain unchanged. You'll still analyze historical documents, answer questions about key themes, and demonstrate your understanding of U.S. history from 1491 to the present.

Tools to Support You

Bluebook provides tools like highlighting, annotating, and answer elimination to help you stay organized during the exam. You'll also type your written responses directly in the app, which simplifies the submission process.

Practice Opportunities

Practice tests and resources will be available in AP Classroom and the Bluebook app. These tools are designed to help you get comfortable with the digital format and the app's features ahead of the exam.

Take time to explore these resources and familiarize yourself with Bluebook so you're fully prepared to succeed on the AP U.S. History Exam in 2025!

The AP U.S. History exam is focused explicitly on assessing your achievement with the historical thinking skills, reasoning processes, and themes. Familiarity with the skills, processes, and themes discussed in the previous chapter is essential to success on the exam.

The AP exam has two sections; each section has two parts. Section I consists of the multiple-choice and short-answer questions, and Section II consists of the document-based question and long essay question.

Section I, Part A: Multiple-Choice Questions

Part A of Section I consists of 55 multiple-choice questions. You have 55 minutes to complete this part; it accounts for 40 percent of your total exam grade.

Section I, Part B: Short-Answer Questions

Part B of Section I consists of three short-answer questions—Questions 1 and 2 are required; you can choose between Questions 3 and 4. Question 1 will require you to analyze secondary source material. Question 2 will be based on primary source material and will require you to employ one of the following two skills—comparison or causation. Both questions will be drawn from material within Periods 3 to 8.

Questions 3 and 4 will have no stimulus material. They will both employ the same skill—comparison or causation (the skill not used in Question 2). Question 3 will draw from material within Periods 1 to 5; Question 4 will draw from material within Periods 6 to 9. Again, for Questions 3 and 4, you can choose the one you feel most confident answering. You will have 40 minutes for this part; it accounts for 20 percent of your total exam grade.

Section II, Part A: Document-Based Question

Part A of Section II consists of a document-based question. You will have 60 minutes for this part; it accounts for 25 percent of your total exam grade. The document-based question will draw from material within Periods 3 to 8.

> **KEEP IN MIND**
>
> **Pace Yourself**
>
> All told, the exam is lengthy—3 hours and 15 minutes long. You will have 95 minutes for the multiple-choice and short-answer section and 100 minutes for the essay section. You should pace yourself so you have sufficient time for all the sections.

Section II, Part B: Long Essay Questions

Part B of Section II requires you to complete one of three long essay questions. The three questions will all address the same theme and will all be based on the same historical reasoning process (causation, comparison, or continuity and change). However, each of the three choices will deal with material from different time periods—Periods 1 to 3, Periods 4 to 6, and Periods 7 to 9. You will have 40 minutes to complete the long essay; it accounts for 15 percent of your total exam grade.

Breakdown of Questions on the AP Exam

In terms of content, the questions on the AP exam focus on the points in each topic of the course framework in the College Board's AP U.S. Course and Exam Description. These topics, and the points outlined in the course framework, are described and elaborated upon in this book within each of the nine chronological periods. Multiple-choice questions on the AP exam are based on the points in the course framework. However, the written portions of the exam invite you to introduce illustrative examples from history to add depth and insight to your responses. As you respond to the short-answer and essay questions, you have the flexibility to introduce illustrative examples that are appropriate and compelling.

Questions on the AP exam can address topics in any of the nine time periods. The written portions of the exam emphasize the core periods of the curriculum—Periods 3 through 8, covering material from the beginning of the French and Indian War through the election of President Ronald Reagan. These core periods represent approximately 80 percent of the material on the AP exam, with Periods 6 through 8 weighted more heavily (45 percent of the total) than Periods 3 through 5 (35 percent). Two of the three short-answer questions and the document-based question will be based on material from within these core periods. Periods 1, 2, and 9 are not ignored, but they are given less weight in the written sections. These three periods could be explored in the third short-answer question and in the long essay question, but in both of these questions you will have options in terms of which time period(s) to address. The approximate overall breakdown of time periods for exam questions and the curriculum is outlined in the following chart:

Period	Approximate percentage of instructional time	Approximate percentage of the AP exam
1. 1491–1607	5%	5%
2. 1607–1754	10%	45%
3. 1754–1800	12%	
4. 1800–1848	10%	
5. 1844–1877	13%	
6. 1865–1898	13%	45%
7. 1890–1945	17%	
8. 1945–1980	15%	
9. 1980–Present	5%	5%

Multiple-Choice Questions

Section I, Part A of the exam consists of 55 multiple-choice questions. You will have 55 minutes to complete this part of the exam; 40 percent of your grade on the exam is based on this section.

The multiple-choice questions focus on your ability to reason about different types of historical evidence. Questions are organized in sets of two to five, with each set referring to specific stimulus material. All of the multiple-choice questions require you to show proficiency in one or more of the themes and require you to apply one or more of the historical thinking skills or reasoning processes. Each multiple-choice question has four choices.

> **KEEP IN MIND**
>
> **Tips for Completing the Exam**
>
> Bring a watch with you and try to work at a steady pace. You have about a minute for each question. This means that you cannot get hung up on difficult questions. If the answer does not immediately come to you, make a notation in the test book and come back to it if you have time. Make sure you leave yourself time to get to all the questions.

The multiple-choice questions require you to reason about the specific stimulus material provided with each set of questions. The stimulus material could be drawn from graphs, charts, maps, paintings, photographs, political cartoons, historical interpretations, letters, diary entries, speeches, books, manifestos, proclamations, political platforms, laws, legal proceedings and decisions, newspaper articles—virtually any primary or secondary source. The multiple-choice questions ask you to draw on the stimulus material as well as on your knowledge of the concepts and historical developments in the College Board's course framework. These concepts and historical developments are all described in this book.

The following is a sample set of multiple-choice questions. In this case, you are presented with a political cartoon and then four questions related to the cartoon. (Answers and explanations to the following multiple-choice questions can be found on pages 32–33.)

Questions 1–4 refer to the following image:

—Thomas Nast, "This Is a White Man's Government," *Harper's Weekly*, September 5, 1868

1. The political cartoon shown above makes the point that

    (A) northern capitalists benefit as much from the institution of slavery as southern plantation owners do.
    (B) Reconstruction was brought to an unfortunate end by a coalition of forces in the North and South.
    (C) African Americans were incapable of effectively participating in the political process.
    (D) nativist politicians were unfairly presenting Irish Americans as ignorant and brutish.

2. Which of the following would most likely support the perspective of the cartoon?

    (A) Radical Republicans
    (B) Southern Democrats
    (C) Working-class Irish immigrants
    (D) Northern opponents of the Civil War

3. The sentiments expressed in the cartoon most directly contributed to which of the following?

    (A) The compromise ending Reconstruction
    (B) The rise of the Ku Klux Klan in the South
    (C) The enactment of segregation laws in Southern states
    (D) The passage of the Fifteenth Amendment

4. The ideas expressed in the cartoon most directly reflect which of the following continuities in United States history?

   (A) Debates about immigration policy
   (B) Debates about the regulation of big business
   (C) Debates about access to voting rights
   (D) Debates about nullification and secession

Short-Answer Questions

Section I, Part B of the exam consists of four short-answer questions, of which you will answer three. The first two questions are required; you will have a choice of whether to respond to the third or fourth question. You will have 40 minutes to complete this part of the exam; 20 percent of your grade on the exam is based on this section. Each short-answer question has three parts, with each part given a grade of 0 or 1. Therefore, the maximum grade for each of the short-answer questions is 3.

The first question will assess the skill of analyzing secondary sources. You will be presented with one or two secondary sources—generally excerpts from the work of one or more historians. The question will ask you to describe a historical interpretation or to describe differences in historical interpretation. Then it will ask you to explain how evidence from the period under discussion could be used to support the interpretation(s). This question will draw on material from Periods 3 through 8.

The second question will include some sort of primary source material, such as letters, diary entries, political cartoons, newspaper articles, posters, photographs, legal documents, speeches, manifestos, and other material. This question will use one of two historical reasoning processes—causation or comparison. You will be asked to describe the significance of the source document or documents and to use historical evidence to explain a historical development related to the image. This question will draw on material from Periods 3 through 8.

The third question will provide you with a choice of two questions. These questions will not have any stimulus material. They will both use the same historical reasoning process—either causation or comparison (whichever of the two skills that was not used in the second question). A causation question will ask you to describe a historical development and explain its causes and/or effects. A comparison question will present you with two historical developments and ask you to describe how they are similar and how they are different. In addition, it may ask you to explain reasons for differences or the impact of one or the other historical development. Again, you will be asked to provide historical evidence relevant to the task at hand. The first of these two questions (Question 3) will draw from material in Periods 1 through 5; the second of the two questions (Question 4) will draw from material in Periods 6 through 9.

The following are examples of the types of short-answer questions you will encounter on the AP exam (see pages 33–35 for explanations of good answers):

Question 1

"Out of this frontier democratic society where the freedom and abundance of land in the great Valley opened a refuge to the oppressed in all regions, came the Jacksonian democracy. . . . It was because Andrew Jackson personified these essential Western traits that in his presidency he became the idol and mouthpiece of the popular will. . . . [H]e went directly to his object with the ruthless energy of a frontiersman. . . . The triumph of Andrew Jackson marked the end of the old era of trained statesmen for the Presidency. With him began the era of the popular hero."

Frederick Jackson Turner, historian, *The Frontier in American History*, 1920

"Not only was [Andrew] Jackson not a consistent politician, he was not even a real leader of democracy. He had no part whatever in the promotion of the liberal movement which was progressing in his own state. . . . [H]e always believed in making the public serve the ends of the politician. Democracy was good talk with which to win the favor of the people and thereby accomplish ulterior objectives. Jackson never championed the cause of the people; he only invited them to champion his."

Thomas P. Abernathy, historian, *From Frontier to Plantation in Tennessee*, 1932

1. Using the excerpts above, answer (a), (b), and (c).

    (a) Briefly describe ONE major difference between Turner's and Abernathy's historical interpretations of President Andrew Jackson.

    (b) Briefly explain how ONE specific historical event or development during the period 1820 to 1850 that is not explicitly mentioned in the excerpts could be used to support Turner's interpretation.

    (c) Briefly explain how ONE specific historical event or development during the period 1820 to 1850 that is not explicitly mentioned in the excerpts could be used to support Abernathy's interpretation.

Question 2

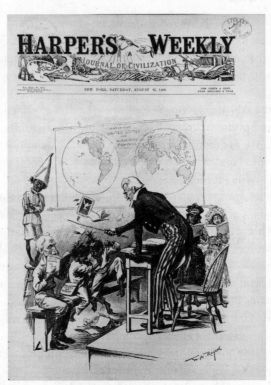

—W. A. Rogers, "Uncle Sam's New Class in the Art of Self-Government," 1898

2. Using the image above, answer (a), (b), and (c).

    (a) Briefly describe ONE perspective about American foreign policy in the period 1890 to 1910 expressed in the image.

    (b) Briefly explain ONE specific event or development that led to the perspective expressed in the image.

    (c) Briefly explain ONE specific effect of the foreign policy actions referenced in the image.

Question 3 or Question 4

3. Answer (a), (b), and (c).

    (a) Briefly describe ONE specific historical similarity between the First Great Awakening of the 1730s through the 1740s and the Second Great Awakening of the 1810s through the 1840s.

    (b) Briefly describe ONE specific historical difference between the First Great Awakening of the 1730s through the 1740s and the Second Great Awakening of the 1810s through the 1840s.

    (c) Briefly explain ONE specific historical reason for a difference between the First Great Awakening of the 1730s through the 1740s and the Second Great Awakening of the 1810s through the 1840s.

4. Answer (a), (b), and (c).

    (a) Briefly describe ONE specific historical similarity between the government reforms enacted in the 1900s to the 1920s and the government reforms enacted in the 1930s.
    (b) Briefly describe ONE specific historical difference between the government reforms enacted in the 1900s to the 1920s and the government reforms enacted in the 1930s.
    (c) Briefly explain ONE specific historical reason for a difference between the government reforms enacted in the 1900s to the 1920s and the government reforms enacted in the 1930s.

Document-Based Question

Section II, Part A of the AP exam consists of one document-based question. You will have 60 minutes to complete this part of the exam; 25 percent of your grade on the exam comes from the document-based question. The DBQ evaluates your ability to assess, analyze, and synthesize a wide variety of types of historical evidence and to construct a coherent essay. Your response to the document-based question is judged on your ability to formulate a thesis and support it with relevant evidence.

> **KEEP IN MIND**
>
> **Historical Neutrality**
>
> Try to avoid using the words "us," "our," and "we" when discussing the United States. Refer to the United States in a neutral manner. Strong essays should be intellectually engaged, but not emotionally invested in a particular outcome or position. Such personal investment tends to undermine one's argument.

The documents can include written materials, charts, graphs, cartoons, and pictures. The documents are carefully chosen to allow you to explore the interactions and complexities of the topic at hand.

Each document-based question will focus on one of the following historical reasoning processes: comparison, causation, or continuity and change (see pages 11–12 for a description of these reasoning processes). In addition, the document-based question assesses all six historical thinking skills—developments and processes, sourcing and situation, claims and evidence in sources, contextualization, making connections, and argumentation (see pages 5–11 for a description of these skills).

Elements and Scoring Rubric for the Document-Based Question

The maximum score you can receive for the document-based question is 7. Below is a description of the specific scoring criteria for each element of the document-based essay, along with a description of each element.

Thesis: 0–1 points

1 point: Responds to the prompt with a historically defensible thesis/claim that establishes a line of reasoning.

Your thesis must make a claim that directly addresses all parts of the question. The thesis must consist of one or more sentences located in one place. It can be in the introduction or the conclusion; however, it is a stronger strategy to state your claim in the introduction so that the reader is readily aware of what you are attempting to demonstrate.

You must do more than restate the question. The last element of the document-based essay requires you to demonstrate a complex understanding of the topic (see pages 25–26). A strong thesis will reflect this complex understanding. Such a thesis could break down the topic into different categories of analysis, such as social, political, and economic factors. It could make connections over time, could include multiple perspectives across themes, or could consider alternative viewpoints. A strong thesis should avoid overly simplistic assertions and should acknowledge gray areas—similarities as well as differences, multiple causes, changes as well as continuities, causes as well as effects.

Contextualization: 0–1 points

1 point: Describes a broader historical context relevant to the prompt.

This element of the rubric assesses your ability to place your essay in a broader context. To earn this point, you must accurately and explicitly relate the topic of the prompt to broader historical events, developments, and processes that occurred before or during the time frame of the question, or continued afterward. The element requires an explanation, consisting of multiple sentences or a full paragraph—not simply a word or a phrase. The College Board does not specify where in the essay contextualization should appear, but it is often advantageous to put it in the introductory paragraph before the thesis statement. This sets the stage for the argument that the essay will make and shows the reader the larger world that shaped the particular development you will be discussing. Another strategy is to devote the paragraph immediately following the introduction to contextualization—to establish a line of reasoning first and then strengthen it by connecting the particular to the general. Either strategy can be effective, as long as the contextual points you raise shed light on the topic and strengthen your argument.

Evidence: 0–3 points

Evidence from the Documents

1 point: Uses the content of at least three documents to address the topic of the prompt. Or 2 points: Supports an argument in response to the prompt using at least four documents.

The use of evidence—one of the basic building blocks of the historical profession—is at the heart of the document-based question. You may earn the basic one point by simply using three of the seven documents to address the topic. However, you should aim to use at least four of the documents in ways that support your overall argument.

As you develop your skill in constructing responses to the document-based question, it is important to work on integrating documents into your overall response so that the documents support your argument. You are on the wrong track when the paragraphs of your essay begin as follows: "According to Document 1 . . ." or "As Document 3 indicates . . . ." In such an essay, you may be using the documents to *address* the topic of the prompt, but to support an argument you must incorporate the documents into that argument.

Try to begin the paragraphs of your essay with ideas rather than with mentioning a document. Then, within the paragraph, discuss the appropriate document or documents that illustrate that paragraph's idea. For example, in an essay comparing the temperance movement with the abolitionist movement in the pre–Civil War period, you might have a paragraph that leads with the following sentence: "Both the temperance movement and the abolitionist movement drew on middle-class Protestant fears of licentiousness; both stressed the importance of individuals possessing self-control." Within the paragraph, you might discuss an image of an out-of-control slave owner violently whipping a defenseless slave, as well as a newspaper article describing an out-of-control drunkard. A strong paragraph will explain how both documents relate to the idea of the paragraph and ultimately support the overall argument of the essay.

Evidence Beyond the Documents

1 point: Uses at least one additional piece of specific historical evidence (beyond that found in the documents) relevant to an argument about the prompt.

To earn this point, you must provide evidence beyond what is in the documents to support or qualify your argument. This must consist of more than a word or phrase; you must explain *how* the outside evidence you have chosen supports or qualifies your argument. For example, a document-based question looking at changes in the civil rights movement from the 1950s to the 1960s might provide you with a reading from a Black Panther platform in 1967, illustrating a more militant direction for the movement in the 1960s. Outside evidence could include a discussion of the ideas or actions of Malcolm X or Stokely Carmichael. A discussion of each figure could be used to support the idea that the movement was moving in a more militant direction. Or to qualify your argument you could bring in evidence from the anti-Vietnam War movement, such as an account of college students preventing a representative of Lyndon Johnson's administration from speaking—the growing militancy of the civil rights movement in the 1960s, you might argue, was part of a more general increase in militancy and frustration among 1960s protest movements.

Analysis and Reasoning: 0–2 points

Sourcing and Situation

1 point: For at least two documents, explain how or why the document's point of view, purpose, historical situation, and/or audience is relevant to an argument.

Sourcing and situation, as discussed in Chapter 1 (see pages 6–7), refers to examining the origins and/or author of a primary document to make better sense of it. To earn this point, however, it is not enough to simply identify one or more of the elements of sourcing—point of view, purpose, historical situation, and/or audience. You must explain how one or more of these elements is relevant to the larger argument that the essay is making.

Complex Understanding

1 point: Demonstrates a complex understanding of the historical development that is the focus of the prompt through sophisticated argumentation and/or effective use of evidence.

A response may demonstrate a complex understanding through sophisticated argumentation that is relevant to the prompt. There are a variety of ways to do this, such as:

- Explaining multiple themes or perspectives to explore complexity or nuance, *or*
- Explaining multiple causes or effects, multiple similarities or differences, or multiple continuities or changes, *or*
- Explaining both cause and effect, both similarity and difference, or both continuity and change, *or*
- Explaining relevant and insightful connections within and across periods or geographical areas. These connections should clearly relate to an argument that responds to the prompt.

A response may demonstrate a complex understanding through effective use of evidence relevant to an argument that addresses the prompt. There are a variety of ways to do this, such as:

- Effectively using all seven documents to support an argument that responds to the prompt, *or*
- Explaining how the point of view, purpose, historical situation, and/or audience of at least four documents supports an argument that responds to the prompt, *or*
- Using documents and evidence beyond the documents effectively to demonstrate a sophisticated understanding of different perspectives relevant to the prompt.

This complex understanding must be developed as part of the argument. There are various ways to demonstrate this complexity. For example, if an essay prompt asks you to evaluate causes of America's expanding role in the world after 1945, you can add complexity by looking at the effects of this growing engagement, such as the "witch hunt" of suspected Communists in the early Cold War period, or the shifting of money away from Great Society programs during the Vietnam War (*explaining both cause and effect*). If an essay prompt asks you to evaluate the extent of change in ideas about American independence from 1763 to 1783, you can add complexity by incorporating evidence beyond the documents that gives voice to groups often left out of the debates around independence, such as the voices of slaves and American Indians (*using documents and evidence beyond the documents effectively to demonstrate a sophisticated understanding of different perspectives relevant to the prompt*).

The College Board's rubric for the document-based question states that the complex understanding can be demonstrated in any part of the essay. It is not essential that this complex understanding be woven throughout the response. Certain approaches to demonstrating a complex understanding—such as using all seven documents or sourcing four or more of the documents—will be evident throughout your essay. Other approaches—such as drawing connections across time periods or geographical areas—could be demonstrated in a particular paragraph. However, attempting to weave your complex understanding throughout your essay is generally considered a powerful approach. In any case, this point cannot be earned by merely including a phrase or reference. In many cases, it would be wise to incorporate your approach to argument complexity into your thesis statement. Adding complexity will strengthen the thesis statement and will let the reader know what to look for as he or she reads your essay.

Sample Document-Based Question

The following is an example of a document-based question. The document-based question is Part A of Section II of the AP exam. You will have a total of 1 hour and 40 minutes to complete Section II of the exam (which includes the document-based question and the long essay question). (A guide to answering the following sample document-based question can be found on pages 35–37.)

Document-Based Question

Time: Suggested reading and writing time: 1 hour
(It is suggested that you spend 15 minutes reading the documents and 45 minutes writing your response. Note: You may begin writing your response before the reading period is over.)

> **DIRECTIONS:** Question 1 is based on the accompanying documents. The documents have been edited for the purpose of this exercise.

1. In your response, you should do the following:
   - Respond to the prompt with a historically defensible thesis or claim that establishes a line of reasoning.
   - Describe a broader historical context relevant to the prompt.
   - Support an argument in response to the prompt using at least four documents.
   - Use at least one additional piece of specific historical evidence (beyond that found in the documents) relevant to an argument about the prompt.
   - For at least two documents, explain how or why the document's point of view, purpose, historical situation, and/or audience is relevant to an argument.
   - Demonstrate a complex understanding of a historical development related to the prompt through sophisticated argumentation and/or effective use of evidence.

   Evaluate the extent to which participation in World War I fostered political, economic, and social change in the United States in the period from 1915 to 1935.

DOCUMENT 1

Source: Amendment to Section 3 of the Espionage Act (excerpt), June 15, 1917.

SECTION 3. Whoever, when the United States is at war, shall willfully make or convey false reports or false statements with intent to interfere with the operation or success of the military or naval forces of the United States, or to promote the success of its enemies, or shall willfully make or convey false reports, or false statements, . . . or incite insubordination, disloyalty, mutiny, or refusal of duty, in the military or naval forces of the United States, or shall willfully obstruct . . . the recruiting or enlistment service of the United States, or . . . shall willfully utter, print, write, or publish any disloyal, profane, scurrilous, or abusive language about the form of government of the United States, or the Constitution of the United States, or the military or naval forces of the United States . . . or shall willfully display the flag of any foreign enemy, or shall willfully . . . urge, incite, or advocate any curtailment of production . . . or advocate, teach, defend, or suggest the doing of any of the acts or things in this section enumerated and whoever shall by word or act support or favor the cause of any country with which the United States is at war or by word or act oppose the cause of the United States therein, shall be punished by a fine of not more than $10,000 or imprisonment for not more than twenty years, or both.

DOCUMENT 2

Source: William Charles Morris, "Mr. President, Why Not Make America Safe for Democracy?" *The Kansas City Sun*, July 14, 1917

DOCUMENT 3

Source: "Another Tar and Feather Party Is Staged," *Ashland* [Wisconsin] *Daily Press*, April 11, 1918.

Adolph Anton, residing at 1100 Sixth Avenue West, was taken from his home at about nine o'clock last night by a party of five or six who came to the house in an auto, carried to a spot on the Beaser Avenue road known as the Chequamego Ice Company's farm, and given a coat of tar and feathers for alleged pro-German sentiments. He was then released and told to beat it for home. Stark naked and covered with a profuse coat of tar and feathers, he walked the distance to his home, about a mile.

DOCUMENT 4

Source: War Industries Board, announcement, June 6, 1918, reprinted in *The New York Times*, June 7, 1918.

Be it Resolved, by the War Industries Board, That the following agreement reached as a result of several conferences between a committee of the board and the American Iron and Steel Institute, be and the same is hereby ratified, confirmed, and approved, to become effective at once:

Whereas, A careful study of the sources of supply in connection with the present and rapidly increasing direct and indirect war requirements for iron and steel products has convinced the War Industries Board of the necessity for (1) a strict conservation of the available supply of iron and steel products, on the one hand, and (2) the expansion of existing sources and the development of new sources of supply of iron and steel products, on the other hand; and

Whereas, the producers iron and of iron and steel products in the main concur in this conclusion reached by the said board, and have expressed their willingness to cooperate wholeheartedly with the said board. . . .

DOCUMENT 5

Source: President Woodrow Wilson, Address to the Senate, September 30, 1918.

Are we alone to ask and take the utmost that our women can give—service and sacrifice of every kind—and still say we do not see what title that gives them to stand by our sides in the guidance of the affairs of their nation and ours? We have made partners of the women in this war; shall we admit them only to a partnership of suffering and sacrifice and toil and not to a partnership of privilege and right? This war could not have been fought, either by the other nations engaged or by America, if it had not been for the services of the women—services rendered in every sphere—not merely in the fields of effort in which we have been accustomed to see them work, but wherever men have worked and upon the very skirts and edges of the battle itself. . . .

DOCUMENT 6

Source: Billy Ireland, "We Can't Digest the Scum," *Columbus Dispatch*, March 4, 1919.

Credit: Granger, NYC

> **DOCUMENT 7**
>
> **Source:** Senator Warren G. Harding, address to the Home Market Club, Boston, May 14, 1920.
>
> America's present need is not heroics, but healing; not nostrums, but normalcy; not revolution, but restoration; not agitation, but adjustment; not surgery, but serenity; not the dramatic, but the dispassionate; not experiment, but equipoise; not submergence in internationality, but sustainment in triumphant nationality. It is one thing to battle successfully against world domination by military autocracy, because the infinite God never intended such a program, but it is quite another thing to revise human nature and suspend the fundamental laws of life and all of life's acquirements . . .
>
> If we can prove a representative popular government under which a citizenship seeks what it may do for the government rather than what the government may do for individuals, we shall do more to make democracy safe for the world than all armed conflict ever recorded . . .
>
> The world needs to be reminded that all human ills are not curable by legislation, and that quantity of statutory enactment and excess of government offer no substitute for quality of citizenship. The problems of maintained civilization are not to be solved by a transfer of responsibility from citizenship to government . . .

Long Essay Question

Section II, Part B of the exam gives you a choice between three comparable long essay questions. You will have 40 minutes to complete this part of the exam; 15 percent of your grade on the exam is based on the long essay. Each of the three questions will focus on the same historical reasoning process—comparison, causation, or continuity and change (see pages 11–12 for a description of these reasoning processes). In addition, the long essay question assesses four of the historical thinking skills—developments and processes, contextualization, making connections, and argumentation (see pages 5–6 and 8–11 for a description of these thinking skills). The three questions will cover material from different time periods. The first question will draw on material from Periods 1 through 3, the second from Periods 4 through 6, and the third from Periods 7 through 9. You should pick the essay question that you are best prepared to write about. The long essay requires you to develop a thoughtful historical thesis or argument and to support your thesis with an analysis of specific and relevant historical evidence.

Elements and Scoring Rubric for the Long Essay Question

The maximum score you can receive for the long essay question is 6. Below is a description of the specific scoring criteria for each element of the long essay, along with a description of each element.

Thesis: 0–1 points

1 point: Responds to the prompt with a historically defensible thesis/claim that establishes a line of reasoning.

Your thesis must make a claim that directly addresses all parts of the question. The thesis must consist of one or more sentences located in one place. It can be in the introduction or the conclusion, but, it is a stronger strategy to state your claim in the introduction so that the reader is readily aware of what you are attempting to demonstrate.

You must do more than restate the question. A strong thesis demonstrates a complex understanding of the topic. The last element of the long essay requires you to demonstrate a complex understanding (see "Analysis and Reasoning," below). A strong thesis will reflect this complex understanding.

Contextualization: 0–1 points

1 point: Describes a broader historical context relevant to the prompt.

This element of the rubric assesses your ability to place your essay in a broader context. To earn this point, you must accurately and explicitly relate the topic of the prompt to broader historical events, developments, and processes that occurred before or during the time frame of the question, or continued afterward. The element requires an explanation, consisting of multiple sentences or a full paragraph—not simply a word or a phrase. As discussed earlier in the section on the document-based question, it is advisable to include contextualization toward the beginning of the essay. One strategy would be to place contextualization in the opening paragraph before the thesis statement. This allows you to establish a setting for the historical development under discussion. An alternative strategy would be to include contextualization in the first paragraph *after* the thesis statement. In either case, be sure to connect the broader context to the argument of the essay. How does the context help us to better understand the topic at hand? (See more on contextualization, pages 8–9.)

Evidence: 0–2 points

1 point: Provides specific examples of at least two pieces of evidence relevant to the topic of the prompt. Or 2 points: Supports an argument in response to the prompt using at least two pieces of specific and relevant evidence.

The use of evidence—one of the basic building blocks of the historical profession—is at the heart of the long-essay question. This basic skill of historical work is central to successful responses to the long essay question. You will earn one point for identifying evidence that is relevant to the topic of the essay. For the second point, you will have to use that evidence to support your argument. Evidence can include references to primary source material, such as speeches, legal decisions, or specific detailed examples of relevant historical information. The College Board does not specify a limit to the number of pieces of evidence necessary for a successful response, but for one point, it notes that the essay must contain at least two pieces of evidence. A strong essay should include multiple pieces of evidence for each paragraph or point of the essay.

Analysis and Reasoning: 0–2 points

1 point: Uses historical reasoning (comparison, causation, or continuity and change over time) to frame and structure an argument that addresses the prompt. Or 2 points: Demonstrates a complex understanding of the historical development that is the focus of the prompt through sophisticated argumentation and/or effective use of evidence.

To earn the first point, you must use one of the historical reasoning processes to frame or structure an argument. The College Board will still grant this first point if the reasoning is "uneven or unbalanced," or if the evidence is "general or lacking specificity." The structure of the essay must logically support the thesis statement. To earn the second point for Analysis and Reasoning, your essay must go beyond a basic argument and demonstrate a complex understanding of the topic through sophisticated argumentation that is relevant to the prompt. This may be done in a variety of ways, such as:

- Explaining multiple themes or perspectives to explore complexity or nuance, *or*
- Explaining multiple causes or effects, multiple similarities or differences, or multiple continuities or changes, *or*
- Explaining both cause and effect, both similarity and difference, or both continuity and change, *or*
- Explaining relevant and insightful connections within and across periods or geographical areas. These connections should clearly relate to an argument that responds to the prompt.

A response may demonstrate a complex or nuanced understanding through effective use of evidence relevant to an argument that addresses the prompt. There are a variety of ways to do this, such as:

- Explaining how multiple pieces of specific and relevant evidence (at least four) support a nuanced or complex argument that responds to the prompt, or
- Using evidence effectively to demonstrate a sophisticated understanding of different perspectives relevant to the prompt.

This complex understanding must be developed as part of the argument. As discussed earlier, in the description of the elements of the document-based question, there are various ways to demonstrate this complexity. For example, if the essay prompt asks you to evaluate the extent of change for African Americans during the period from 1890 to 1930, your essay might focus on changes connected with the Great Migration of African Americans between 1910 and 1930. You might add complexity by noting connections between the Great Migration and the wave of "new immigrants" arriving in the United States at the same time, noting how these groups adapted differently to a changing society (*explaining relevant connections within or across time periods*). Or, you could add complexity by discussing the large number of African Americans who did not participate in the Great Migration and continued to labor in the South under the burdens of Jim Crow laws and lynching (*explaining both continuity and change*).

It is not essential that this complex understanding be woven throughout the response. You may wish to devote a paragraph to one of the options listed above. However, attempting to weave your complex understanding throughout your essay is generally considered a powerful approach. In any case, this point cannot be earned by merely including a phrase or reference. In many cases, it would be wise to incorporate your approach to argument complexity into your thesis statement. Adding complexity will strengthen the thesis statement and will let the reader know what to look for as he or she reads your essay.

Sample Long Essay Questions

Below are three sample long essay questions. The three questions are all built around the same theme and the same historical reasoning process. The theme for each question is "Culture and Society." These questions ask you to analyze patterns of continuity and change in regard to roles and conditions for women during three different periods in American history. The first long essay question will always draw on material from Periods 1 through 3; the second from Periods 4 through 6; and the third from Periods 7 through 9. They will be labeled Questions 2, 3, and 4. (A guide to answering the following sample long essay questions can be found on pages 37–40.)

Long Essay Questions

Time: Suggested writing time: 40 minutes

> **DIRECTIONS:** Answer Question 2 *or* Question 3 *or* Question 4.

In your response, you should do the following:
- Respond to the prompt with a historically defensible thesis or claim that establishes a line of reasoning.
- Describe a broader historical context relevant to the prompt.
- Support an argument in response to the prompt using at least two pieces of specific and relevant evidence.
- Use historical reasoning (e.g., comparison, causation, continuity or change) to frame or structure an argument that addresses the prompt.
- Demonstrate a complex understanding of a historical development related to the prompt through sophisticated argumentation and/or effective use of evidence.

2. Evaluate the extent to which roles and conditions for women changed in the United States in the period 1750 to 1800.
3. Evaluate the extent to which roles and conditions for women changed in the United States in the period 1800 to 1850.
4. Evaluate the extent to which roles and conditions for women changed in the United States in the period 1940 to 1980.

Answers and Explanations

Multiple-Choice Questions

1. **(B)** This evocative political cartoon requires you to read a whole host of clues before you can understand its meaning. The man on the left is an Irish immigrant; the "5 Points" on his hat refers to the Irish neighborhood in New York City. Note his almost ape-like face. This was typical of representations of Irish immigrants as drawn by nativist cartoonists. The man in the middle has "C.S.A." on his belt buckle: Confederate States of America. His knife says "Lost Cause," an allusion to the southern nostalgia for the noble fight the South put up in the Civil War. The man on the right has "Capital" written on the object he is holding; he is a northern capitalist, ready to use money to purchase votes. These three sinister forces are working together in the Democratic Party to deny African Americans the right to vote. Note the ballot box contents strewn on the ground in the lower right-hand corner of the cartoon. Thomas Nast intended the cartoon as a warning about the dangers of a Democratic victory in the upcoming presidential election. The cartoon does not allude to the slave system or cotton production (A). The cartoon is drawn sympathetically toward African Americans; there is no allusion that the man on the ground is ignorant or debased (C). It is true that Irish immigrants were presented as ignorant, but the cartoonist is not critiquing that. In fact, he himself is presenting an Irish immigrant in an unflattering manner (D).

2. **(A)** The sentiment in the cartoon is that of the Radical Republicans. In the years after the Civil War, they grew alarmed at the assertiveness of the old plantation-owning class and the supporters of secession. This cartoon, published in the weeks before the 1868 presidential election, was intended to warn voters of the dangers of a victory by the Democratic Party. The cartoon is meant as a critique of the Democratic Party's agenda in the South (B); they would certainly not support the sentiment of the cartoon. The cartoon depicts working-class Irish immigrants (C) in a stereotypically brutish manner; they would be unlikely to support the overall point of the cartoon. Northern opponents of the Civil War (D), a war that undid the system of slavery, were unlikely to embrace the cause of suffrage for African Americans.

3. **(D)** The sentiments expressed in the cartoon most directly contributed to the passage of the Fifteenth Amendment. The Fifteenth Amendment states that the vote may not be denied to someone based on "race, color, or previous condition of servitude." Voting rights for African Americans was a key element of the Reconstruction program of the radical Republicans. The cartoon shows empathy for African Americans, depicted being pushed to the ground and having the vote denied them. The other choices all reflect the point of view of white southern opponents of Reconstruction. The compromise in 1877 that allowed Republican Rutherford B. Hayes to assume the White House also led to the end of Reconstruction, allowing Democrats in the South to reestablish power (A). One factor in pushing African Americans from meaningful participation in the political process was the rise of the Ku Klux Klan in the South (B). After Reconstruction southern states enacted segregation laws (C), further solidifying the second-class status of African Americans.

4. **(C)** The ideas expressed in the cartoon most directly reflect debates about access to voting. The Constitution left voting procedures up to each state. This lack of a federal mandate on voting opened the door to an ongoing debate about equal access to the ballot box. Initially, many states had property qualifications for voting. By the 1820s and 1830s, however, most states had eliminated these qualifications. Even by the turn of the twentieth century, most states had not extended the right to vote to women. After debates on the state level, the U.S. Constitution was amended in 1919 to extend the right to vote to women. Access to voting for African Americans has been an ongoing source of debate and struggle. Though the Fifteenth Amendment barred racial discrimination in voting, southern states devised strategies to suppress the African-American vote. The debates about access to voting

rights led to passage of the Voting Rights Act in 1965, removing many impediments to African Americans voting. More recently, the federal oversight provisions of the Voting Rights Act were greatly reduced by the Supreme Court decision in *Shelby County v. Holder* (2013).

Short-Answer Questions

Good Responses to Question 1

(a) A good response would explain differences between Turner's and Abernathy's historical interpretations of President Andrew Jackson, such as:

Both Turner and Abernathy address the issue of whether President Andrew Jackson was a "man of the people," an upholder and proponent of democratic values. Turner argues that Jackson does live up to his reputation as a true democrat. He traces Jackson's democratic spirit back to his upbringing in the frontier region, along the border of the colonies of North and South Carolina. Turner asserts that the region fostered an independent and egalitarian spirit that was reflected in Jackson's actions. Abernathy, however, argues that Jackson's talk of democracy was hollow. He asserts that Jackson was typical of most politicians in that he was self-serving. He talked about the interests of the common man, but his policies did not advance a democratic agenda.

(b) Good responses would cite evidence that would support Turner's interpretation of Jackson, such as:

Jackson supported the rotation of office in government, also known as the "spoils system." Jackson brought new individuals into government positions rather than allowing the old established officeholders to continue to exercise power.

Jackson attacked the corrupt Second Bank of the United States, vetoing its recharter. He saw the "monster" bank as a tool used by the eastern elite to suppress common men of the West. By attacking the Bank of the United States and promoting state banks, he was promoting the interests of ordinary Americans.

(c) Good responses would cite evidence that would support Abernathy's interpretation of Jackson, such as:

Jackson did not attempt to promote the right to vote for people other than white males. As a slaveholder, he did not want to extend democratic rights to African Americans or to challenge the institution of slavery. Nor did he support extending democratic rights to women.

Jackson's veto of the Second Bank of the United States was undemocratic in that it went against an institution that was supported by the majority of Congress and that established a degree of stability in the United States.

Jackson's promotion of the Indian Removal Act and his determination to carry out the removal of American Indians from Georgia to the West showed a disregard for the rights and lives of American Indians. In promoting Indian removal, he was denying the Cherokee and other tribes the democratic right to remain on their own property.

Good Responses to Question 2

(a) A good response would describe one perspective about American foreign policy in the period 1890 to 1910 expressed in the image, such as:

The cartoonist is expressing support for America's imperialist foreign policy in the late 1890s. In the cartoon, Uncle Sam is depicted using a switch to separate a classroom of unruly children labeled "Cuban Ex-patriot" and "Guerilla." The cartoon is acknowledging the difficulties the United States had in "disciplining" the people of recently acquired territories, but it is asserting that it is a worthwhile venture. Reflecting the racial attitudes of the time, the cartoonist is claiming that many of people in these territories were not capable of self-government and would require the steady hand and stern disposition of the U.S. government.

(b) Good responses would explain a specific event or development that led to the perspective expressed in the image, such as:

*The United States gained control of the Philippines, Puerto Rico, and Cuba as part of the terms that ended the Spanish-American War in

1898. Many Americans debated what to do with the people in these newly acquired territories, especially in light of resistance in the Philippines to United States control. The cartoon is taking a position in that debate.

*The United States annexed Hawaii in 1898, the same year of the cartoon. Earlier, the United States had intervened in Hawaii (1893) to protect American businessmen who had toppled the regime of the local ruler, Queen Lili'uokalani. The cartoon is implying that the Hawaiian people had peacefully accepted U.S. control.

(c) Good responses would explain a specific effect of the foreign policy actions referenced in the image, such as:

*One effect of the United States playing a more active role in the world was a long and bitter war in the Philippines. The 1898 cartoon shows the Filipino rebel Emilio Aguinaldo standing in the corner wearing a dunce cap. In the subsequent years (1899–1902), he would lead a resistance movement in the Philippines that would challenge United States control. It resulted in approximately 200,000–250,000 Filipino deaths.

*One effect of the United States asserting its might in newly acquired countries was the development of strong anti-imperialist movements. A sizable number of Americans came to see the actions depicted in the cartoon in a negative light. These critics wondered how the United States, a country born in an anticolonial war, could acquire an empire of its own. The most prominent anti-imperialist was the author Mark Twain, who chaired the American Anti-Imperialist League.

Good Responses to Question 3

(a) A good response would explain a specific historical similarity between the First Great Awakening of the 1730s through the 1740s and the Second Great Awakening of the 1810s through the 1840s, such as:

*Both the First and Second Great Awakenings responded to declining church membership and enthusiasm, and both were marked by enthusiastic revivals with an emphasis on salvation.

*Both the First and Second Great Awakenings led to a greater role for women in the church and also to the spread of new Protestant denominations.

(b) A good response would explain a specific historical difference between the First Great Awakening of the 1730s through the 1740s and the Second Great Awakening of the 1810s through the 1840s, such as:

*The First Great Awakening did not result in an increase in moral reform movements, though the Second Great Awakening did. The Second Great Awakening inspired a host of reform movements, such as the temperance movement, the abolitionist movement, and the movement to improve treatment for the mentally ill.

*The First Great Awakening put more of an emphasis on introspection, sin, guilt, and personal morality. The Second Great Awakening put forth a more optimistic view of religion and God, and also put more emphasis on the redemption of society, not just of the individual.

(c) A good response would explain a specific historical reason for a difference between the First Great Awakening of the 1730s through the 1740s and the Second Great Awakening of the 1810s through the 1840s, such as:

*An important reason for the differences between the First and the Second Great Awakenings was their respective contexts. The First Great Awakening grew out of the trials and tribulations of Calvinist Puritanism in New England. As the Puritan experiment was declining in enthusiasm, ministers such as Jonathan Edwards attempted to rekindle the fire that had animated earlier Puritans. As such, he maintained the Calvinist belief that salvation could occur only through God's grace, not through the works of man. Later, the Second Great Awakening, which began after the old Puritan faith had gone by the wayside, allowed that humans could perfect themselves and could achieve salvation through their actions. The departure from Calvinist ideas about salvation helps explain the emphasis on reform and social perfection in the Second Great Awakening.

Good Responses to Question 4

(a) Good responses would explain a specific historical similarity between the government reforms enacted in the 1900s to the 1920s and the government reforms enacted in the 1930s, such as:

*Both the reforms of the Progressive era in the 1900s to the 1920s and of the New Deal of the 1930s expanded the role of the government in the economic life of the United States. Out of the Progressive era came federal programs such as the Food and Drug Administration and the Federal Trade Commission. The New Deal brought about government agencies such as the Securities and Exchange Commission and the National Labor Relations Board.

*Both the reforms of the Progressive era in the 1900s to the 1920s and of the New Deal of the 1930s attempted to address the needs of working-class people. During the Progressive era, Congress passed the Keating-Owen Act to challenge the practice of child labor (the act was declared unconstitutional by the Supreme Court). Also, many states passed laws to promote worker safety during the Progressive era, especially in the aftermath of the Triangle Shirtwaist Factory fire in 1911. During the New Deal, the National Industrial Recovery Act included provisions to set standards for hours and safety for workers. Later, the Wagner Act protected the rights of workers to organize unions.

(b) Good responses would explain a specific historical difference between the government reforms enacted in the 1900s to the 1920s, and the government reforms enacted in the 1930s, such as:

*The reforms of the Progressive era in the 1900s to the 1920s were different from the reforms of the New Deal of the 1930s in that there was a greater emphasis on moral reform during the earlier period. Although progressives were concerned about economic issues, they spent a great deal of effort on moral reform, such as moving toward the prohibition of the sale, production, importation, and transportation of alcoholic beverages. The social purity movement campaigned to clean up a variety of forms of vice, including prostitution. The New Deal did not attempt to reform people's personal morality; it stuck to the broad goals of economic recovery, reform, and relief.

*The reforms of the Progressive era in the 1900s to the 1920s were different from the reforms of the New Deal of the 1930s in that progressive reform occurred on the local, state, and national levels, while the New Deal was primarily a set of federal initiatives. In many ways, progressive reform grew out of a multifaceted set of grassroots organizations. It addressed issues from prohibition to women's suffrage, from greater democratic participation to food hygiene. The New Deal, more of a top-down set of initiatives, focused on the economic catastrophe of the 1930s.

(c) A good response would explain a specific historical reason for a difference between the government reforms enacted in the 1900s to the 1920s and the government reforms enacted in the 1930s, such as:

*The main reason for differences between the government reforms enacted in the 1900s to the 1920s and the government reforms enacted in the 1930s is that the first reforms occurred in the context of a growing economy, while the second set occurred during the most profound economic collapse in American history. The Progressive era occurred as industrialization and immigration were contributing to an expanding economy. Despite economic downturns following the Panics of 1893 and 1907, the standard of living for most Americans rose during the Progressive era. The New Deal was a response to the Great Depression. As such, it was more focused on economic recovery, relief, and reform, and less focused on the broad agenda of change that characterized the Progressive era.

Document-Based Question

QUESTION 1

This document-based question asks you to evaluate the extent to which participation in World War I fostered political, economic, and social change in the United States in the period from 1915 to 1935. As you look at the documents, several themes should emerge.

One development that is suggested by the documents is growth in the role of the federal government. In Document 4, the War Industries Board is exercising control over major industries (steel and iron) by directing conservation efforts and the expansion of production. The War Industries Board is one of several federal agencies that organized the nation's war effort and expanded federal power. In some ways, this represents a continuity with Progressive-era agencies from the pre-war period, such as the Federal Trade Commission. By the end of the war, we can see that political leaders sought to move away from large-scale government planning. In Document 7, Warren Harding argues for a retreat from the experimentation and activist governance of the Progressive era and of World War I. His election represents a change toward more limited government in the 1920s. However, to some degree, the growth of the government during World War I inspired the array of agencies of the New Deal of the 1930s.

A second change that could be made involves the erosion of civil liberties. Document 1, an excerpt from the Espionage Act, highlights the whittling away of First Amendment rights, such as freedom of speech and freedom of the press. After the war, these abridgments of civil liberties continued with the Red Scare of the 1920s. The Red Scare also represented a continuation of the anti-immigrant sentiment that can be seen in both Document 3 and Document 6. Document 3 shows the growth of anti-German sentiment evident during World War I, specifically the assault of a man who allegedly held pro-German views. In Document 6, Uncle Sam, stirring "the world's melting pot," laments that "the scum" cannot be incorporated. The words in the pot, "Bolshevism," "Un-American Ideals," and "The Mad Notion of Europe," reflect a desire for United States to disengage from European conflicts and ideas. The isolationism and anti-immigrant sentiment that developed during the war and continued into the 1920s mark a change from idealism that drew the United States into World War I.

Social aspects of World War I are also evident in the documents. Document 2 depicts an African-American woman pleading with President Woodrow Wilson to push for democratic reform not just abroad, but at home as well. The war opened up many opportunities for African Americans, both in the military and in war industries. The war was a catalyst for the Great Migration of African Americans from the rural South to the urban North. However, we can see in the document that violence against African-American communities continued from the pre-war period. The cartoon alludes to a massacre in East St. Louis, Illinois, that resulted in hundreds of African Americans killed. It could be noted in the essay that the race riots and the growth of the Ku Klux Klan that characterized post-war society represent a continuity from before the war.

Finally, shifting ideas around gender are alluded to in Document 5. The document is an excerpt from a speech by President Wilson recognizing the contributions that women made to the war effort. When Wilson is calls for admitting women into a "partnership of privilege and right," he is urging Congress to pass the Nineteenth Amendment, extending voting rights to women. The document makes clear the role that the war played in pushing the issue of suffrage onto center stage. The essay could note that after gaining the right to vote, in 1920, a variety of other changes could be seen in regard to ideas around gender. The "New Woman," emancipated from the constraints of Victorianism and engaged in public issues and debates, represents a change from pre-war society.

A successful essay would earn a point for developing a strong **thesis** that addresses the prompt—one that makes a claim in regard to the extent of social, political, and economic change fostered by World War I. The thesis should reflect a complex understanding of the topic, an understanding that would then be developed in the body of the essay (see below for a discussion of historical complexity). A possible thesis would be: *"In some ways, certain social patterns persisted from the period before World War I to the period after the war. This is evident in the persistence of racism and violence against African Americans. However, changes brought about by the war are more significant, as the Progressive politics of the* *pre-war era gave way to the conservative politics of the post-war era. This is evident in the erosion of civil liberties, the growth of anti-immigrant sentiment, and the rejection of business reform in the period after the war."*

The second possible point in the essay would be for **contextualization**. You must put the developments around the war into a wider context. For instance, this essay could focus on ongoing social and economic changes—urbanization and industrialization—that provide context to the changes wrought specifically by the war. Also, America's involvement in World War I can be seen in the context of America's growing stature on the world stage, starting with the Spanish-American War of 1898.

The next three points would be for using **evidence**—both within and outside of the documents. For the first of these points, the essay must successfully use the content of at least three of the documents to address the topic of the prompt. The next point can be earned for using the content of at least four of the documents in a way that supports an argument in response to the prompt. The third evidence point would be for using evidence outside the documents. Examples of such outside information could include the *Schenck v. United States* case, the Tulsa race riots, the Palmer raids, the Committee on Public Information, the Ludlow Massacre, the movement around Marcus Garvey, and the Emergency Quota Act. To earn this point, the essay must explain how the outside evidence is relevant to the argument. It is not enough to simply mention or describe this information.

The last two points are for **analysis and reasoning**. The first of these two points is for **sourcing**—for at least three of the documents, explaining how or why the document's point of view, purpose, historical situation, and/or audience is relevant to the argument. For example, the essay could discuss the purpose of the Espionage Act (Document 4) during World War I. This point could note that the act was designed to blunt objections to a war that was widely criticized by Americans. This could be connected with a broader point about the role of government in organizing and producing enthusiasm for American participation in military ventures.

The last point is for demonstrating a **complex understanding** of the historical development that is the focus of the essay. This point could be earned by extending the argument to another time period—such as the Civil War or the Vietnam War—and drawing conclusions about how wartime upheavals often result in social or political change. In addition, the complex understanding point can be earned by effectively using **seven** of the documents to support your argument, or by sourcing (see explanation of sourcing above) at least **four** of the documents. Finally, the point can be earned by demonstrating a sophisticated understanding of different perspectives relevant to the prompt. For instance, the essay could discuss how working class people or immigrants reacted to the reorganization of labor during World War I or to the Red Scare of the post-war world.

Long Essay Questions

QUESTION 2

Question 2, on **change's and continuities** in regard to women's roles and conditions, covers the time period of the crisis of empire, from the end of the French and Indian War through the ratification of the Declaration of Independence, the American Revolutionary War (1765–1783), and the development of an independent United States, up to 1800. In addition, Enlightenment thinking— much of which explicitly challenged traditional gender roles—became important in the Revolution and in the early republic. These political and intellectual developments could be used in this essay to establish the **context** of the essay.

A key change to note in terms of roles and conditions for women in this period is the increasingly public role women played in these major events. This was the era of the Daughters of Liberty, boycotts, spinning bees, and homespun cloth. In North Carolina in 1774, fifty-one women signed a declaration vowing to give up tea and other British products, in what is known as the Edenton Tea Party. Abigail Adams reflected Enlightenment ideals when she encouraged her husband, John, to "remember the ladies" as the structure of a new nation was being debated in 1776. Some women participated in the fighting of the American Revolution, including Deborah Sampson of Massachusetts, who dressed as a man and served in several theaters of war. Many women participated in supplying the soldiers and working as nurses. In the early republic, the ideas of republican motherhood developed. These are all pieces of **evidence** that could be used to support an argument in this essay.

As you develop an argument to respond to this prompt, think about the final point for demonstrating a **complex understanding** of the topic. For instance, if an essay focuses on changes for women in this period, it might acknowledge continuities as well (*explaining both continuity and change*). By 1800 women still did not have the right to run for office or vote. Many of the legal strictures on married women, under the doctrine of *feme covert*, were in place. And though republican motherhood asserted that women had an important role to play in the new republic, it was still as mothers. Further, some of the changes that impacted white women had no impact on enslaved African-American women (*explaining multiple themes or perspectives to explore complexity or nuance*).

A strong **thesis** to this question could attempt to acknowledge change, while stressing its limited nature. *"During the period of 1750 to the 1800s, conflicts between the colonists and the British opened new avenues for women to participate in public life. By 1800, however, the laws and constitutions that were created in the new republic relegated women to second-class status just as they had been under British rule."* A different tack in developing a thesis might acknowledge different perspectives: *"For many white women, the crisis of empire and the birth of a new country offered new opportunities and possibilities to participate in the public realm. However, for enslaved African-American women, the rhetoric of the American Revolution changed little."*

A successful essay would bring all the elements of the essay together—relevant contextualization, a strong thesis, evidence in support of the argument of the essay, and a complex understanding of the topic.

QUESTION 3

Question 3, on **changes and continuities** in women's roles and conditions, covers the first half of the nineteenth century. This period witnessed the Second Great Awakening and the proliferation of reform movements; the advent of the market revolution and the beginnings of industrial production; the growth of the middle class and the spread of new ideas about the public realm and the private realm. This essay could elaborate on any of these developments to establish the **context** for the essay.

A major development in this period in regard to gender was the growing popularity of the idea of separate spheres for men and women—of a public sphere of business and politics for men, and of a private sphere of home, hearth, and family for women. The idea that women were to maintain a proper Christian home became known as the "cult of domesticity." However, despite the strictures of the "cult of domesticity," women became increasingly involved in the public realm. Women were active in the churches that were part of the Second Great Awakening, and they played important roles in the reform movements inspired by religious revival, including the temperance movement and the abolitionist movement. Toward the end of this period, a group of women challenged their unequal treatment in society by organizing the Seneca Falls Convention in 1848. Many of these trends were more pronounced among middle-class women. Different trends can be seen for women at the lower end of the socioeconomic spectrum. Many young women left family farms in the period of the 1820s to the 1840s to work in textile mills in New England. Also, many women performed piecework at home, including shoe binding. These and other developments in the period could be used as **evidence** in this essay.

A **complex understanding** of the period might look at different categories of historical developments, such as social, political, and economic, or might explore change and continuity as it affected women of different classes (*explaining multiple themes or perspectives to explore complexity or nuance*).

A strong **thesis** might read as follows: *"In terms of economics, women experienced changes in their roles as the market revolution opened up new opportunities for them. In regard to social life, women played a growing role in the Second Great Awakening and in reform movements. However, in the political realm, women continued to be excluded from formal participation."* In addition to looking at multiple variables, this thesis also acknowledges continuity as well as change. Another thesis could focus on economic class: *"Changes for women were often determined by economic class. For middle-class women, the antebellum period provided new opportunities to participate in churches and reform movements, despite the cultural pressure on women to assume domestic roles. For many farm women and working-class women, economic necessity required them to enter occupations in the expanding economy."* Such a thesis, combined with appropriate contextualization, relevant evidence, and complex argumentation, would make a strong essay.

QUESTION 4

Question 4, on **changes and continuities** in women's roles and conditions, focuses on the middle of the twentieth century, specifically the period 1940–1980. This period witnessed World War II, the Cold War, and the Vietnam War; the rise of suburbia in the 1950s; the protest movements of the 1950s and 1960s; and major economic fluctuations, from the sustained economic expansion of the 1950s and 1960s to the "stagflation" of the 1970s. Any of these historical developments could be developed into the **context** for this essay.

There are several historical developments related to women and work during this forty-year span that could be explored in this essay. During World War II, women took on jobs in heavy industry that had previously been closed to them. The government used the image of "Rosie the Riveter" in a publicity campaign to assure women (and men) that such jobs were appropriate for women. After the war, women were encouraged to give up their factory jobs for returning male veterans. Advertising and television in the 1950s depicted women as suburban homemakers. Despite this, women continued to work outside the home in large numbers as many new office jobs opened up. This trend continued steadily in the 1960s and then began to grow more dramatically as a "quiet revolution" began in the 1970s, when large numbers of women assumed positions in the workforce. In addition, by the 1960s and 1970s women were getting married later and having children later, allowing for greater participation in the workforce. Accompanying changes in the workforce were changes in gender expectations. Participation in the war effort during the 1940s led many women to question traditional roles. The writer Betty Friedan captured this sense of longing for something more than a domestic existence in her book, *The Feminine Mystique* (1963). This questioning led to the development of the women's liberation movement in the 1960s, challenging unequal treatment, marginalization, objectification, and discrimination in the workplace. Changes in women's private lives—including the development of the birth-control pill, starting in 1960, and the widespread legalization of abortion with the Supreme Court decision in *Roe v. Wade* (1973)—opened up new opportunities in the public realm. The counterculture of the 1960s also encouraged a broad rethinking of societal norms, including around gender. These trends can be used to shape a thesis about changing roles and conditions for women and could be mined for **evidence** to support such a thesis.

A **complex understanding** of the period might incorporate evidence of different developments in this period—such as the growth in the percentage of women in the job market and changing cultural norms in regard to gender (*explaining how multiple pieces of specific and relevant evidence—at least four—support a nuanced or complex argument*). An essay could also demonstrate complexity by looking at changes for other marginalized groups, such as African Americans during the same period, or at changes for women during earlier periods, such as the Gilded Age (*explaining relevant and insightful connections within and across periods or geographical areas*). If the essay focused on the material conditions of women during this period, a complex understanding of the period might examine portrayals of women in popular culture (*explaining multiple themes or perspectives to explore complexity or nuance*).

A strong **thesis** for this question might acknowledge continuities but focus more on change: *"While sexism persisted in the period of 1940 to 1980, the role of women in regard to job discrimination and everyday life changed dramatically as a result of the requirements of a wartime economy, broad changes in cultural values, and the militancy of the women's liberation movement."* Another thesis might focus less on economics and more on social history: *"During the period of 1940 through 1980, women became liberated from the rigid role of the suburban housewife as they married later in life, had fewer children because of the availability of new forms of birth control, and had greater control over their bodies and their time. Although inequalities continued to exist, women were liberated to pursue a fuller, more well-rounded life."* Again, a successful essay would contextualize the argument, include appropriate evidence to support the thesis statement, and demonstrate a degree of historical complexity.

PART 2
Review Section—Time Periods

3

Period 1: 1491–1607 The Meeting of Three Peoples

TIMELINE

1492	Christopher Columbus (Italian, in the service of the Spanish monarchy) sails to the New World, beginning era of European colonization of the Americas
1498	Vasco da Gama (Portugal) sails to India
1517	Martin Luther challenges Roman Catholic beliefs and practices; initiates Protestant Reformation
1521	Spanish forces, led by Hernán Cortés, defeat the Mexica people, led by Montezuma
1530	John Calvin breaks with the Catholic Church
1532	Spanish forces, led by Francisco Pizarro, defeat the Inca people
1542	Bartolomé de Las Casas writes *A Short Account of the Destruction of the Indies*
1549	The *repartimiento* reforms begin to replace the *encomienda* system
1587	Founding of the "lost" English colony of Roanoke
1588	English defeat of the Spanish Armada
1597	Juanillo's Revolt in Florida
1598	Acoma Pueblo Massacre in New Mexico

Topics in Period 1

In this chapter, you will learn about:
→ Topic 1.1 Contextualizing Period 1
→ Topic 1.2 Native American societies before European contact
→ Topic 1.3 European exploration in the Americas
→ Topic 1.4 Columbian Exchange, Spanish exploration, and conquest
→ Topic 1.5 Labor, slavery, and caste in the Spanish colonial system
→ Topic 1.6 Cultural interactions between Europeans, Native Americans, and Africans
→ Topic 1.7 Subject to debate

Topic 1.1 Contextualizing Period 1

> The meeting of three peoples—American Indians, Europeans, and West Africans—on land held by American Indians on the North American continent created a "new world." From the late 1400s to the early 1600s, a remarkable series of events led to a broad transformation of much of the world.

The age of exploration and colonization brought peoples together from far-flung corners of the globe. The local and regional systems of an earlier era gave way to a global system. The encounters of peoples from the Americas, Europe, and Africa led to a reordering of the world and created great wealth for some and utter destruction for others. Out of these encounters, new settlements and colonies emerged in the New World. People from all three regions had to adapt to one another as they developed new cultural patterns.

Topic 1.2 Native American Societies Before European Contact

A wide variety of social, political, and economic structures had developed among the native peoples in North America in the period before the arrival of Europeans. These structures grew, in part, out of the interactions among native peoples and between native peoples and the environment. As native peoples migrated across North America, over time they developed a great diversity of complex social structures. These peoples both adapted to the environment and transformed it.

A. Societies of the Southwest

The peoples of the Southwest came to depend on the cultivation of maize (corn). Maize cultivation spread from present-day Mexico through the Southwest and across much of North America. The cultivation of maize fostered economic development and social diversification among Native Americans.

The Pueblo People of the Southwest

The **Pueblo** people lived in areas that are part of the current southwestern United States. The Pueblo were named by the Spanish because many lived in small towns, or *pueblos*. Ancestral Pueblo culture developed around the year 900 in the area that is today known as the **Four Corners** region of the Southwest—where Utah, Colorado, Arizona, and New Mexico meet. These early Pueblos, sometimes called the **Anasazi** people, became increasingly dependent on the cultivation of maize. Their settled communities developed complex, technologically advanced societies. Many lived in architecturally sophisticated structures, including those found in the Chaco Canyon of New Mexico, some of which contained hundreds of rooms.

Because of climatic change, including volcanic eruptions and severe drought in the thirteenth and fourteenth centuries, the Pueblo people began to disperse from the complex settlements around the Four Corners region. This dispersal led to conflict with neighboring peoples. Some Pueblos united with **Zunis** and **Hopis** in western New Mexico, while others joined with settled communities in the Rio Grande valley. This movement led the Pueblo to abandon the sophisticated towns they had developed over hundreds of years of civilization and to join other groups in the Southwest. This development weakened Pueblo communities on the eve of European contact.

B. Societies of the Great Basin and Great Plains

The peoples of the Great Basin and the western Great Plains tended to develop mobile lifestyles in response to the lack of natural resources.

The Shoshone, Paiute, and Ute Peoples of the Great Basin

The **Great Basin** refers to the 400,000-square-mile area between the Rocky Mountains and the Sierra Nevada Mountains. The area has a great deal of environmental diversity but is characterized by a pronounced lack of natural resources. This dearth of resources was especially severe, historians believe, after a rise in temperatures, approximately 5,000 years ago, created hot, arid conditions. Historians and archeologists refer to a **"desert culture"** that was common among most of the pre-contact American Indian tribes of the Great Basin. "Desert culture" was characterized by seasonable mobility, as hunters and foragers searched for food throughout the year. "Desert culture" peoples often developed basketmaking, whereas more sedentary groups often developed pottery. Three large groupings of native peoples of the Great Basin were the **Shoshone**, the **Paiute**, and the **Ute**.

American Indians of the Great Plains

The **Great Plains** refers to the vast stretch of land in the United States and Canada that stretches from the Mississippi River to the Rocky Mountains. The **Plains Indians** are the native groups most commonly stereotyped in images of Indians in American popular culture. The stereotype often involves Plains Indians riding horses, wearing feathered headdresses, and hunting buffalo. In the minds of many Americans who know this stereotype from movies and television shows, this image represents not just Plains Indians, but all American Indians. The stereotype has little validity even when it comes to Plains Indians. Although many Plains Indian groups, especially those of the western Great Plains, did depend on hunting buffalo for survival, it was not until European contact that horses were introduced into Plains Indian cultures. Before that, many American Indian cultures of the Great Plains, such as the **Sioux**, the **Blackfoot**, the **Arapaho**, and the **Cheyenne**, hunted for buffalo on foot, maintaining a mobile lifestyle. Some American Indian groups of the Great Plains, especially the eastern Great Plains closer to the Mississippi River (such as the **Osage**, the **Wichita**, and the **Omaha**), developed more sedentary, agrarian lifestyles.

C. Societies of the East

Along the Atlantic seaboard, many native societies developed a mix of agricultural and hunter-gatherer economies. These economic developments fostered the development of permanent settlements.

The Algonquian Peoples

The Algonquian language group included hundreds of American Indian tribes along the east coast of the present-day United States and in the interior of the continent, around the St. Lawrence River and the Great Lakes. The Atlantic coast **Algonquians** hunted, fished, and grew corn. In northern New England and the upper Great Lakes region, the colder climate tended to make agriculture impractical, forcing Algonquians in these areas to rely on hunting and fishing.

The Iroquois Great League of Peace

In present-day New York state, groups of Iroquoian-speaking peoples formed the **Iroquois League**, a confederation made up of the **Mohawks**, **Oneidas**, **Onondagas**, **Cayugas**, and **Senecas**. (Later, in 1720, a sixth group, the **Tuscaroras**, joined the league.) The founding of the Iroquois League dates back to perhaps the fifteenth century (although some oral traditions assert an earlier founding date). The league formed in order to end infighting among the groups. Over time, the cohesion of the five nations grew, and the Iroquois League became one of the most powerful forces in the pre-contact Northeast.

The Iroquois lived in settled, permanent villages. They relied on farming, gathering, hunting, and fishing for their sustenance, but the majority of their food came from farming. Their three most important crops were corn, beans, and squash—the **"three sisters"** of crops common to many agrarian American Indian societies. The Iroquois are, traditionally, a **matrilineal society**—inheritance and descent pass through the mother's line.

D. Societies of the Pacific Northwest

Societies in the Northwest and in areas of present-day California experienced economic development and social diversification in the period before European contact, developing a mix of foraging and hunting. In some areas, the peoples of the Northwest supported themselves with the vast resources of the Pacific Ocean and the rivers.

Chinook People of the Pacific Northwest

In the Pacific Northwest, the **Chinook** people lived along the Columbia River in present-day Washington and Oregon. The Chinook consisted of several groups, all speaking related languages. These groups practiced foraging, hunting, and fishing and tended to live in settled communities. Chinook communities had a high degree of economic development and social stratification. A higher caste of Chinook people—shamans, warriors, and successful merchants—lived in relative isolation from Chinook commoners. Many Chinook people lived in longhouses, which contained up to fifty people.

Topic 1.3 European Exploration in the Americas

In the late 1400s and 1500s, European overseas exploration, conquest, and settlement resulted in a series of interactions and adaptations among Europeans, American Indians, and Africans. Eventually, the impact of conquest and settlement in the New World was felt in the Old World. Expansion in the Americas resulted in increased competition among the nations of Europe as well as in the promotion of empire building.

A. Factors Contributing to European Exploration

The efforts by European nations to explore and conquer the New World starting in the late fifteenth century stemmed from a variety of factors. These factors include a desire for new sources of wealth, competition for power and status, and a push among Christian sects for new converts. Several important changes in Europe set the groundwork for exploration and conquest.

The Crusades and the Revival of Trade

The series of religious wars known as the **Crusades** shook the stability of European feudal society and whet the appetites of Europeans for foreign trade goods. Starting in 1095, with a proclamation from Pope Urban II, the goal of the wars was to establish Christian control of the Muslim-ruled "Holy Land" (Jerusalem and its surrounding area). Although, by the end of the thirteenth century, the wars ended in defeat for the Crusaders, the experience of the Crusades sparked change in Europe. The relatively self-sufficient manorial world of feudal Europe began its long demise during this period, as trade routes and regional and international economic activity shifted power and priorities. Europeans became interested in circumventing the Italian city-states and finding new trade routes with the East.

The Black Death and the Decline of Feudalism

The **Black Death**, probably caused by a pandemic outbreak of bubonic plague in the fourteenth century, reduced the European population by 30 to 60 percent. Although the effects of the Black Death were devastating for Europe, the plague also opened up opportunities for the survivors. Food and land were more plentiful in the aftermath of the Black Death. Individuals became more willing to take risks and seek opportunities. The Black Death also played an important role in undermining the stability of the **feudal system**.

The Impact of the Renaissance

The **Renaissance** spirit of curiosity about the world inspired people to explore and map new areas. Universities and scholarly books—also infused with the spirit of Renaissance humanism—spread knowledge of these new discoveries. **Johannes Gutenberg's printing press** (developed in the 1440s) helped disseminate information and stimulated interest in new discoveries.

The Protestant Reformation and the Catholic Counter-Reformation

Religious movements in the sixteenth century renewed many people's religious zeal and their desire to spread their gospels. The most important religious movement was the Protestant Reformation. Theologians Martin Luther and John Calvin both led breaks with the Roman Catholic Church over church practices and beliefs. Both believed that the church had drifted from its spiritual mission. The Catholic Church's practice of selling indulgences—or remissions of sin—was especially galling to Luther.

Although his reasons were more political than theological, **King Henry VIII** of England led a break with Rome when the Pope refused to grant Henry a divorce. Some English Protestants, the **Puritans**, believed that the English Protestant Reformation did not go far enough. Motivated by Calvinist thinking, the Puritans argued for a complete reformation in the Church of England (see pages 64–68 for more on the Puritans).

The Catholic Church itself underwent a reform in the sixteenth century. This **Counter-Reformation** focused on a renewed sense of spirituality within the Catholic Church. Out of this movement came the **Jesuits**, a Catholic order devoted to spreading their gospel throughout the world.

Topic 1.4 Columbian Exchange, Spanish Exploration, and Conquest

Historians refer to the introduction of new products and organisms on each side of the Atlantic as the "Columbian Exchange." The Columbian Exchange and the expansion of the Spanish Empire in the fifteenth and sixteenth centuries ushered in momentous demographic, economic, and social changes.

A. The Impact of Exploration and Conquest on Europe

The introduction of new sources of wealth in the form of precious metals transformed the European economy and helped facilitate the ongoing transition from feudalism to capitalism. In addition, new crops and livestock contributed to population growth in Europe.

The Impact of the "Columbian Exchange" on Europe

The **"Columbian Exchange"** led to the introduction to Europe of crops and livestock that were native to the Americas in the 1500s. The list of organisms brought by Europeans back to the Old World included turkeys, corn, potatoes, sweet potatoes, cacao (cocoa), and tomatoes. These foods revolutionized agricultural and culinary traditions in Europe and supplemented the meager diets of the European peasantry. In addition, Spanish sailors brought syphilis back to Europe—the result of sexual encounters in the New World. Tobacco, too, was introduced and started a craze among Europeans.

The Economic Impact of Conquest

It is assumed that since conquest brought so much hardship to **American Indians** as well as to **Africans**, it must surely have brought improvements to the status of **Europeans**. However, this was for the most part not the case. The position of ordinary Spaniards declined during the age of exploration and conquest. First, the influx of silver and gold into Spain set off a wave of inflation in the 1500s that made many ordinary items considerably more expensive. Second, in Spain taxes went up more than fivefold in the 1500s, so that the monarchy could pay for the military expenditures necessary to secure its New World empire. Third, Spain went into debt, as it borrowed more and more from European banks to maintain its empire. The interest on this debt also depressed the Spanish economy; in many ways, ordinary Spaniards did not recover from this period until the nineteenth century.

B. Technological Advances and New Economic Structures

New forms of technology and new business models facilitated extensive changes in the economies of both Europe and the Americas.

Technological Advances and a Revolution in Navigation

A series of developments in maritime technology encouraged exploration and transformed the global economy. The **compass**, the **astrolabe**, the **quadrant**, and the **hourglass** all aided navigation, helping sailors plot direction, determine speed, and assess latitude. *Portulanos*, detailed maps, also helped navigators find their way around the world, many sailing on Portugal's maneuverable and sturdy ships called **caravels**.

The Joint-stock Company

The **joint-stock company** model was developed in Europe in the 1500s and became an important engine for exploration and colonization in the New World. In a joint-stock company, shareholders control part of the company in proportion to the number of shares they own. The joint-stock company model was embraced by many of the European nations embarking on risky expeditions of exploration, colonization, and trade. The risks involved would then be spread out among multiple investors. Another advantage of the joint-stock company is the concept of limited liability; the shareholders can be held liable for company debts, but their liability is limited to the face value of their shareholding.

C. The Spanish and Portuguese Models

The first explorers and settlers in the New World were sponsored by Spain and Portugal. Their presence in the New World led to deadly epidemics that decimated native populations. Over time, a racially mixed population developed in the Americas, characterized by caste distinctions that grew out of the intermixture of Spanish settlers, African slaves, and American Indians.

Portugal and Spain Lead the Way

Portugal, with the encouragement and guidance of **Prince Henry the Navigator**, embarked on a search for new trade routes to Asia that would bypass the Italian city-states that controlled Mediterranean trade. Portuguese explorers moved down the coast of Africa with the goal of rounding the Cape of Good Hope and crossing the Indian Ocean to arrive at India and China. **Bartolomeu Dias** sailed around the Cape of Good Hope in 1488 and **Vasco da Gama** reached India by 1498.

Spain also sought new trade routes. The Italian navigator **Christopher Columbus** convinced the Spanish monarchs, **Isabella** and **Ferdinand**, to fund a venture west, across the Atlantic, to reach the East. Columbus argued that the circumference of the Earth was smaller than cartographers believed and that a venture in a westerly direction was both possible and feasible. (Despite the common myth, most educated Europeans, including Columbus, believed the Earth was round.) Columbus's three ships, the *Niña*, the *Pinta*, and the *Santa María*, set sail in 1492 and, six weeks later, reached a Caribbean island that he named **San Salvador**. Columbus assumed that he had reached the East Indies, and he named the **Taíno** people he encountered "Indians." The misnomer stuck. Columbus made two more voyages but never fully realized that he had voyaged to an entirely new continent. Others who followed in his footsteps made that realization, paving the way for a century of exploration, conquest, and riches.

Spanish and Portuguese Ambitions

Spain was able to secure a dominant role in the New World following the **Treaty of Tordesillas** (1494) between Spain and Portugal. The treaty settled the competing claims of the two countries to the newly explored lands outside of Europe by drawing a longitudinal line through the Atlantic Ocean and South America. Portugal was granted lands to the east of the line, including Brazil in the Western Hemisphere and Africa. Spain was granted the rest of the lands of the Americas. Spain made those claims real by establishing settlements throughout Central and South America. Spanish explorers even made it as far north as California and New Mexico, the area around the Mississippi River, and Florida. **Ponce de León** reached Florida in 1513. Spaniards later established the first permanent European settlement in what would become the United States, at **St. Augustine, Florida** (1585).

The Conquistadores and the Defeat of Native Peoples

Within a generation of Columbus's first journey to the New World, Spanish forces wrested control of much of **Central and South America** from the native inhabitants, transforming the economic and social structures of the region and devastating the native population.

The sixteenth century saw brutal fighting in the Americas as Spain extended its dominance over much of the New World. One of the more brutal episodes of violence between the Spanish **conquistadores** and native peoples was the defeat of the **Mexica** (also known as the **Aztecs**, and led by **Montezuma**) by Spanish forces led by **Hernán Cortés** (1518–1521). The **Incas** of South America were defeated by a Spanish expedition led by **Francisco Pizarro** (1532).

Disease and Death

The peoples of the **New World**, having evolved and adapted separately from the peoples of the **Old World**, had no immunities to many of the germs and infectious diseases that foreign explorers and settlers inadvertently brought with them. These diseases included bubonic plague, influenza, cholera, scarlet fever, and, most important, **smallpox**. It is estimated that between 50 and 90 percent of the native peoples of the Americas died between 1500 and 1650. For instance, on the island of **Hispaniola** (the island that today is comprised of Haiti and the Dominican Republic) the population rapidly declined from over a million to a mere 500 in the decades following contact with Christopher Columbus and Spaniards in the 1490s.

The rapid decline of the various peoples in the areas of Spanish conquest should not be attributed solely to disease. Spanish policies focused on subjugating the native peoples of the New World. Warfare, brutal conquest, and harsh working conditions, fueled by the desire for riches and an ideology of racial superiority, contributed to the decline of native populations. Many were killed outright; many were physically weakened under Spanish occupation and became more susceptible to disease.

The Columbian Exchange Transforms the Americas

By far, the most important organisms brought from Europe to the New World were germs, which caused widespread disease and death. The **Columbian Exchange**, however, also brought useful products to the inhabitants of the New World. Europeans introduced important crops, including sugar, wheat, and bananas, as well as domestic livestock, including goats, cows, and chickens. The exchange also brought the horse to the New World, which proliferated and transformed many native cultures.

> **KEEP IN MIND**
>
> **The Impact of Disease**
>
> Remember that the main cause of the massive die-off of American Indians in the 1600s was disease, not warfare. Warfare was brutal, but it could not have affected the large number of people the way disease could.

Topic 1.5 Labor, Slavery, and Caste in the Spanish Colonial System

Spaniards first turned to the forced labor of native Indians in a system known as the *encomienda*. This exploitative system was used in plantation agriculture and in the extraction of precious metals. Over time, native labor was replaced by enslaved Africans.

A. Spanish Exploitation of New World Resources

Upon gaining control of much of the Americas, Spain created a system to extract precious metals, such as gold and silver, and to ship them to Spain, which soon became the wealthiest country in Europe with the influx of New World resources.

Silver and the *Encomienda* System

In Spain's ***encomienda*** system, the initial Spanish settlers were granted tracts of land and the right to extract labor from local inhabitants. In many ways, this system of New World colonization resembled Old World feudalism. Acting as feudal lords, the ***encomenderos*** had a free hand to manage their holdings, as long as a percentage of gold and silver was sent back to the monarchy. The *encomienda* system led to brutal exploitation. Spurred by Spanish critics such as **Bartolomé de Las Casas** (see page 53), the Crown issued a series of reforms in regard to the governance of Spain's New World colonies known as the ***repartimiento*** (1549). Treatment of native peoples did not improve appreciably, but control of Spanish America came to be exercised more directly by the Crown (see page 59).

B. Spain and the African Slave Trade

Soon after European settlement in the Americas, a system of slave labor developed. Spain participated in the international slave trade to import enslaved Africans to the New World in order to labor in plantation agriculture and mining.

The Impact of the Slave Trade

Even before the settlement of the New World, Africans had been taken from their villages and forced into slavery. Africans and Europeans had been enslaving and trading Africans for centuries. Slavery has existed since ancient times, but the concept of slavery changed in the age of New World colonization. Starting in the 1500s, captured Africans were thought of as slaves for life; it was not a temporary condition. Also, the children of slaves would now be considered slaves as well. This, too, was a break from tradition. African slaves came to be considered property, with no rights, as opposed to people who were enslaved for a period of time.

There were two main impacts of the slave trade on Africa from the 1500s onward. First, entire generations of strong, young people were kidnapped and taken out of the continent. These individuals would otherwise have comprised the next generation of leaders of their tribes or villages. Second, the introduction of European manufactured items undermined the traditional African economy.

> **USING REASONING PROCESSES: COMPARISON**
>
> **Parallels Between Colonial Systems**
>
> There are many parallels between the Spanish and English colonial systems. In both cases, the Crown initially gave local governors a free hand in the New World. Subsequently, in both cases, the Crown exercised direct control over its colonial holdings. In Spain's New World colonies, we can look at the *repartimiento*; in English America, we can look at the creation of the Dominion of New England.

Resistance to Slavery and the Development of Maroon Communities

As Africans were brought into the slavery system, they developed forms of cultural resistance that attempted, against great odds, to preserve traditional cultural patterns and to maintain a sense of autonomy. In New Spain, one notable form of resistance was the establishment of **"Maroon"** communities.

> **KEEP IN MIND**
>
> **Slavery in History**
>
> It is true that slavery has existed since ancient times. However, be prepared to discuss the aspects of modern slavery that differentiate it from ancient slavery.

Maroons were Africans who had escaped from slavery in the New World and established independent communities. These communities existed throughout the New World, with many in the Caribbean and Brazil. Often, these communities were formed by slaves who were the first generation brought out of Africa. The Maroons, with memories of Africa, were in the best position to preserve African traditions in the New World. These traditions included the use of medicinal herbs, often combined with special drumming and dancing as part of healing rituals. Other African healing traditions and rites have survived over the centuries through the descendants of these original Maroons. One of the most significant Maroon communities was **Palmares**, established in Brazil in the early 1600s. It had more than 30,000 residents and remained an independent community until it was conquered by the Portuguese in 1694. When the English took over Jamaica from the Spanish in 1655, many enslaved Africans fled into the interior and joined communities of **Arawak** Indians. Over time, the Maroons came to control large areas of the Jamaican interior.

C. The Social Structure of Spanish America

Spanish colonizers developed an elaborate caste system in the New World. The Spanish caste system was a key element in the establishment of rigidly hierarchical society defined by social origin and race.

The *Casta* System

Despite traditional notions of the superiority of "pure blood" among Spaniards (see page 53), a good deal of intermixing occurred in the Spanish colonies. In Spain's New World colonies, Spaniards were always greatly outnumbered by native peoples. Further, Spanish men greatly outnumbered Spanish women. In these circumstances, intermarriage was common. The Spanish used the term ***casta*** to describe the variety of mixed race people in the new world. The *casta* system included **peninsulares** (born in Spain) and **creoles** (those born in the New World of Spanish parents) at the top of the social structure. These groups usually consisted of only one or two percent of the population. Just below them in social status were **mestizos**, the children of Spanish men and Indian women. *Mestizos* comprised four to five percent of the population of Spain's New World empire. Below them were **mulattos** (children of Spanish men and African women), followed by American Indians and Africans at the bottom of the social pyramid. The *casta* system recognized even finer gradations, based on the specific percentage of each lineage an individual possessed.

Topic 1.6 Cultural Interactions Between Europeans, Native Americans, and Africans

In the sixteenth century, the divergent worldviews of Europeans and American Indians became increasingly evident. Both groups attempted to assert worldviews about religion, gender roles, family, land use, and power.

A. Interactions, Trade, and Cultural Adaptations in the New World

The divergent worldviews of Europeans and American Indians were evident in the first century of Spanish conquest of the Americas. Each side often misunderstood the cultural assumptions of the other. In the process of conquest and domination by the Spanish, each side adopted some useful aspects of the other's culture.

Cultural Misunderstandings

Early encounters between American Indians and Europeans were marked by profound misunderstandings, as both groups attempted to make sense of the other. Many American Indian societies were **matrilineal**—members of the community were identified by their mothers' lineage; European societies were patrilineal. In addition, the two groups had very different ideas about wealth and material possessions. In regard to land ownership, American Indians did not understand the concept of individual ownership of land. Land was seen as a resource controlled by the entire community. Europeans, on the other hand, put a high premium on individual land ownership. These cultural differences often led to conflicting understandings of arrangements made between the two groups over the status of land.

Religious Adaptation in the New World

In many cases, American Indians made accommodations with the Spanish, adopting Christianity and adapting it to fit their needs and circumstances. Some native peoples adopted Catholicism completely, while others incorporated certain Spanish spiritual beliefs into traditional religious practices.

B. Resistance by American Indians and Africans

As Europeans encroached upon Native Americans' land and attempted to impose their ideas about culture, propriety, gender roles, family structure, religion, and the natural world, native peoples developed strategies for resistance and contestation. In the face of enslavement, subjugation, and defeat, Africans and American Indians attempted to maintain a sense of political and cultural autonomy.

Native American Resistance in Spain's New World Colonies

The responses of American Indians to the catastrophe of conquest were varied. Some fled from the invading Spaniards, abandoning their ancestral homelands. These migrations led to population pressures and conflicts elsewhere in the Americas. Native people engaged in violent resistance as well as more passive cultural resistance. The **Guale** people lived near the Spanish mission in St. Augustine—one of four missions in Spanish Florida in the sixteenth century. As missionaries tried to bring Guale Indians into the mission system, a revolt, known as **Juanillo's Revolt**, occurred in 1597, resulting in the deaths of several missionaries.

Juan de Oñate and the Acoma Pueblo People

In the western reaches of Spain's New World empire, a violent confrontation occurred with the Pueblo people in what is now New Mexico. The Spanish conquistador **Juan de Oñate** and his soldiers had, in the 1590s, occupied land held by the **Acoma Pueblo** people. In 1598, the Acoma resisted an order by the Spaniards to hand over certain supplies that the Acoma needed to survive the upcoming winter. They attacked the Spanish occupiers, killing 15, including the nephew of Oñate. Oñate responded by firing cannons from a mesa above the Acoma people, killing over 800 native people. The survivors were put on trial by the Spanish, whose punishments included cutting off one foot for males over the age of 25. As many as 80 men had a foot cut off. The remaining 500 Acoma people were enslaved by the Spaniards.

C. Debates Around Perceptions of American Indians

Before the age of exploration, most Europeans had little or no knowledge of people who were different from themselves. Initially, Spanish and Portuguese explorers did not know what to make of the people they encountered in the Americas. Over time, debates occurred among Europeans around how "civilized" these peoples were by European standards.

The Development of the Belief in White Superiority

As Europeans solidified their control over the New World and brought more American Indians and Africans under their control, a set of racist ideas developed to justify the continued subjugation of nonwhite people. These racist ideas often grew out of earlier notions of race that had existed in Europe. For the Spaniards, for instance, these included traditional notions about **"pure blood"** (*limpieza de sangre*). In Spain, this description was used for those without Jewish or Muslim ancestry. The idea that "pure blood" was superior shaped Spanish understandings of race in the New World. As **miscegenation**—the mixing of races—occurred in the New World, Spaniards erected an elaborate hierarchy of racial classes. The degree of "pure blood" determined one's place in this hierarchy. Indians and Africans were at the bottom (see page 51). This model drew on traditional Spanish beliefs and adapted them to a New World setting. The model was useful to the Spanish because it justified their position at the top of the hierarchy and the continued subjugation of those at the bottom.

Debates over Spain's Actions in the New World

As reports of the actions of the Spanish conquistadores and officials in the *encomienda* system reached Spain, a heated debate ensued about Spanish behavior in the New World. The priest **Bartolomé de Las Casas** roundly criticized Spanish actions as being among "the most unpardonable offenses committed against God and mankind." His book, *A Short Account of the Destruction of the Indies* (written in 1542; published in 1552), chronicled atrocities against native peoples in the New World. He has been criticized as paving the way for the enslavement of Africans in order to replace American Indian laborers. He did advocate such a transition, but later came to believe that all forms of slavery were morally wrong.

Las Casas was challenged by another Spanish theologian, **Juan Ginés de Sepúlveda**. Sepúlveda defended the treatment that the Spaniards meted out to the native peoples of the Americas. He asserted that American Indians were beings of an inferior order. Because they could not be expected to perform duties beyond manual labor, he argued that they were "natural slaves." He insisted that the battles of conquest in the New World were "just wars." His justifications for taking native peoples' lands and for destroying their culture—including the idea that it was in native people's best interests—would resonate with Spanish policymakers in their assertion of power in the New World in the coming centuries.

Topic 1.7 Subject to Debate

The Nature of Spanish Conquest and Colonization

Most American history textbooks provide vivid accounts of the brutality of the Spanish conquistadores toward American Indians. That the Spaniards were often cruel to the native peoples of the Americas is not in question, but recently historians have begun to question the extent of Spanish brutality. The term **"Black Legend"** was used by a Spanish historian in 1914 to describe the anti-Spanish propaganda written by English, Italian, Dutch, and other European writers. Although English sources from the 1500s onward should not be discounted, it would be prudent for the student to take into account the authorship of these sources and their motives. English writers might have been trying to demonize Spanish behavior in order to portray English behavior in the New World in a more favorable light. The English portrayed themselves as altruistic, bringing God and civilization to the inhabitants of the New World, while the Spanish were portrayed as greedy and cruel. Of course, the historical record demonstrates that the English committed their share of atrocities in the New World, probably comparable to those committed by the Spanish. The controversy provides us with a cautionary lesson: Look carefully at the source of documents as you use them to write about the past, taking into account their point of view, purpose, historical situation, and audience.

Practice Multiple-Choice Questions

> **DIRECTIONS:** Pick the letter that best answers the following questions.

Questions 1–3 refer to the following passage:

"The gold and silver mined with forced labor in Mexico and what is now Bolivia constituted a windfall that could have been used to develop Spanish agriculture, industry, and commerce. It could have helped the country catch up with northwestern Europe's more developed economies. . . .

"But Spain [in the 1500s] was in the grip of a tiny ruling class of royalty, Catholic Church hierarchy, and landed aristocracy. Two to three per cent of the population owned 97 per cent of the land in Castile, Spain's heartland. The great landowners had no incentive to modernize Spain. They just wanted to raise more sheep and sell more wool. The environmental degradation that overgrazing vast numbers of sheep entailed seems to have bothered the ruling class no more than the cutting of forests for timber to build ships and provide charcoal to smelt domestic Spanish silver ore. And so, what if the wool went to Holland to be manufactured into cloth rather than being processed in Spain itself.

"Meanwhile, successes in the New World swelled the Spanish monarchy's ambitions in the Old. The bonanza of bullion from the Americas encouraged Spain's rulers to build up the army into Europe's largest military force, setting off an arms race that forced rivals to multiply their armed forces as well. . . . Hegemonic wars against the French, Dutch, and English followed. . . .

"The most lasting and far-reaching effect of the increase of money in circulation was to set off a long wave of inflation that spread throughout Western Europe. To be sure, deficit spending on unproductive armies, navies, and wars as well as debasement of coinage by monarchs in search of additional royal revenue contributed to the run-up in prices."

—A. Kent MacDougall, University of California, Berkeley, March 1992.

1. Which of the following best describes a central point of MacDougall's argument above?

    (A) During the age of exploration and conquest, a growing divide developed in Spain between the Catholic Church and the monarchy over the treatment of American Indians.
    (B) The large-scale migration of Spanish peasants to the New World left Spain with a scarcity of workers and a depressed economy.
    (C) Spanish conquest of the New World led Spain to focus its military and diplomatic efforts toward subduing resistance in the New World and removing itself from the conflicts of Europe.
    (D) The successes of Spanish conquest in the New World did not result in a general economic improvement in Spain itself.

2. MacDougall's description of Spanish actions contributes to an understanding of which of the following developments beyond the 1500s?

    (A) The industrial growth of Spain in the seventeenth century
    (B) The growing gap between the wealthy and the poor in the seventeenth century
    (C) Spanish military domination over its European rivals in the seventeenth century
    (D) The success of independence movements in Spanish America in the seventeenth century

3. Concerns raised in Spain in the 1540s about "forced labor in Mexico and what is now Bolivia," mentioned in the first paragraph of MacDougall's article, led to which of the following changes?

   (A) Limits being placed on the *encomienda* system and a shift toward African slavery
   (B) The growth of the Spanish abolitionist movement and a royal decree ending slavery in the New World
   (C) A shift in Spanish economic activities in the New World from export-oriented activities toward production for local consumption
   (D) The establishment of a line of demarcation in Spanish-held territories in the New World between areas for American Indians and areas for Spanish colonists

Answers and Explanations

1. **(D)** The successes of Spanish conquest in the New World did not result in a general economic improvement in Spain itself. The article focuses on the shortsightedness of the wealthy class and the impact of ongoing warfare. The elite class in Spain did not try to improve infrastructure or develop new forms of processing and manufacturing.

2. **(B)** The article is attempting to account for a curious outcome. With all the gold and silver coming into Spain in the 1500s, why did the standard of living for most Spaniards decline from the 1500s until, according to the article, the late 1800s? MacDougall argues that the wealth was squandered rather than reinvested. Further, taxes and inflation both increased, putting the peasantry in a deeper hole. The author states, in another part of the article, "Super-exploitation of labor on the periphery of the world capitalist economy leads to increased exploitation of workers at the core."

3. **(A)** The article focuses on the impact of Spanish colonization on Spain itself, rather than on the Americas. However, it does allude to "forced labor in Mexico and what is now Bolivia." The super-exploitation of indigenous peoples by the Spaniards was raised in the 1640s by the Dominican Friar Bartolomé de Las Casas. He described the brutality of slavery under the *encomienda* system. He asserted that Indians were free people in the natural order and deserved the same treatment as others. He also initially suggested replacing Indian labor with African labor (although he later recanted that suggestion). In the coming decades, Spain shifted toward a reliance on African slavery for labor in its New World empire.

4

Period 2: 1607–1754 Patterns of Empire and Resistance

TIMELINE

1588	England defeats the Spanish Armada
1607	Jamestown colony founded
1609	Henry Hudson explores area that will become New York
1609–1610	"Starving time" in Virginia
1619	House of Burgesses established
1620	Founding of Plymouth Colony
	Mayflower Compact signed
1622	Attack on Jamestown by local Algonquin Indians
1624	New Amsterdam founded by the Dutch
1630	Founding of Massachusetts Bay Colony
1630–1640	"Great Migration" of Puritans from England to Massachusetts
1632	Founding of Maryland Colony
1636	Founding of Rhode Island Colony
1638	Anne Hutchinson banned from Massachusetts
1639	The Fundamental Orders of Connecticut adopted
1649	Act of Religious Toleration passed in Maryland
1662	The Halfway Covenant
1663	Founding of Carolina Colony
1675	King Philip's War
1676	Bacon's Rebellion
1679	New Hampshire Colony separated from Massachusetts
1680	Pueblo Revolt (Popé's Rebellion)
1681	Founding of the Pennsylvania Colony
1686	Creation of the Dominion of New England
1688	The Glorious Revolution
1689	Colonists bring down the Dominion of New England
1692	Salem witch trials
1711	Founding of North Carolina Colony
1733	Molasses Act
1735	Zenger trial
1739	Stono Rebellion
1741	Arrests and executions in the supposed "Negro Plot" in New York City
	Jonathan Edwards's sermon, "Sinners in the Hands of an Angry God"

Topics in Period 2

In this chapter, you will learn about:
- Topic 2.1 Contextualizing Period 2
- Topic 2.2 European colonization
- Topic 2.3 The regions of British colonies
- Topic 2.4 Transatlantic trade
- Topic 2.5 Interactions between American Indians and Europeans
- Topic 2.6 Slavery in the British colonies
- Topic 2.7 Colonial society and culture
- Topic 2.8 Subject to debate

Topic 2.1 Contextualizing Period 2

> Throughout the seventeenth century and the first half of the eighteenth century, the major European imperial powers and various groups of American Indians maneuvered and fought for control of the North American continent. Out of these conflicts, native societies experienced dramatic changes and distinctive colonial societies emerged.

England was eager to duplicate the stunning success of the Spanish in the New World. Emerging as the most powerful nation on the high seas after defeating the Spanish Armada in 1588, England then set its sights on North America. England, Spain, the Netherlands, and France all made attempts to establish control over extensive areas of North America. These efforts led to different patterns of colonization and different types of interactions with American Indian groups.

Once established, the thirteen British colonies developed along diverse, but parallel, paths. We see distinct patterns of development in the four regions of colonial America. The colonies of the Chesapeake and the upper South—Virginia, Maryland, and North Carolina—all developed economies based on the cultivation of tobacco, grown by indentured servants, and later, by enslaved Africans. The New England colonies of Massachusetts, Rhode Island, Connecticut, and New Hampshire all experienced economic transformations that undermined the community cohesion and intense piety of the founding generation of Puritan settlers. The middle colonies of New York, New Jersey, Pennsylvania, and Delaware saw the development of economic and ethnic diversity as immigrants from Europe began to fill up the region. The colonies of the lower South and the British West Indies—South Carolina and Georgia, as well as Barbados—used their long growing season to develop staple-crop export economies, relying on the extensive use of enslaved people (who often outnumbered white colonists). However, the thirteen North American colonies were united by shared experiences as much as they were separated by different patterns of development. All lived under the British Crown and practiced some form of Protestantism (along with Catholicism in Maryland); all maneuvered within mercantilist trade rules; all pushed back and fought with American Indians; and all were exposed to new philosophical and religious ideas. We begin to see, in the eighteenth century, a pattern of development in North America distinct from Britain (by then England, Wales, and Scotland had formed a union known as Great Britain). These distinctions begin to lay the groundwork for the political break that followed the intellectual break from the British.

Topic 2.2 European Colonization

In the seventeenth century, several European empires competed for control of North America. These colonial powers had various priorities and goals. As they sought to exert control over different parts of North America, the

Spanish, French, Dutch, and British developed various patterns for colonizing the New World. These patterns reflected the different economic and social goals, cultural assumptions, and traditions of these major powers. The different patterns were also shaped by environmental factors in North America and by competition for resources among the European powers and between them and the diverse American Indian groups.

A. Spain's New World Colonies

Spain maintained tight control over its colonial empire in the New World. Spanish colonizers focused on converting American Indians to Christianity and on exploiting the labor of the native population.

The Evolution of Spanish America

The basis of Spain's New World empire was the exploitation of the labor of native peoples. By 1550, Spain abandoned the **encomienda system**. Under this system, the initial Spanish settlers in the Americas were granted the right to extract labor from local inhabitants. This system led to harsh treatment of Indians. The worst excesses of Spanish behavior were chronicled by the Spanish Dominican friar, **Bartolomé de Las Casas** (see page 53). The Spanish government replaced the *encomienda* system with the ***repartimiento* system**—banning outright Indian slavery and mandating that Indian laborers be paid wages. However, Spain's empire remained highly exploitative of native labor. Colonial authorities could still require that local people work for Spanish landlords. In many colonies the work of Indians was supplemented by African slave labor.

By 1650, approximately 350,000 Spaniards had migrated to the New World. This population was supplemented by more than a quarter million Africans. Indians were still the majority in Spanish America, but their population, by 1570, had been reduced by approximately 90 percent from what it was in 1492. Intermarriage was common in Spain's New World colonies. A complex social hierarchy resulted from the mixing of peoples of different backgrounds (see page 51).

Spain's New World empire was tightly controlled by the Crown, especially after the *repartimiento* system was established. In the sixteenth and seventeenth centuries, administration of the empire was divided between two administrative units. The northern portion of the empire, called the **Viceroyalty of New Spain**, was headquartered in Mexico City. The southern portion of the empire was called the **Viceroyalty of Peru**, consisting of Spanish holdings in South America and headquartered in Lima. New Spain attempted to extend its reach into modern-day Florida and New Mexico, but failed to establish a strong presence in the northern reaches of its imperial holdings (see page 49).

Most Indians lived removed from Spanish colonists—remaining in their own communities under the authority of native leaders and speaking their own languages. Spanish priests were, however, aggressive in leaving the imprint of Catholicism on native communities. Priests converted communities en masse; Spanish efforts at conversion seemed successful. However, the Catholicism that was practiced in native communities was different from what Catholic priests had originally intended. Indians often accepted Jesus as one among many gods and interwove Catholic practices with traditional Indian spiritual practices. At the same time, local ideas and expectations frequently reshaped Catholic practices. Catholic priests realized they had to accept certain adaptations in order to better reach native peoples.

B. French and Dutch Colonies

Both France and the Netherlands established colonies in North America, but they differed markedly from the Spanish and British models. Few French or Dutch people actually settled in the New World. Rather, the French and Dutch colonies served as trading outposts. Their colonials often intermarried with the native peoples, thereby combining new family connections to promote trade, acquiring furs and other valuable goods for export to Europe.

France's New World Empire

France's North American colonies were vast on paper but thinly populated when it came to French colonials. New France stretched from the mouth of the St. Lawrence River in Quebec to the port of New Orleans, encompassing the Great Lakes region, the Ohio River Valley, the Mississippi River Valley, and much of the Great Plains in what would later become the United States. The first permanent French settlements were **Port Royal** (1605), in what would later become Nova Scotia, and **Quebec** (1608), founded by **Samuel de Champlain**. In 1642, French traders established a small settlement at what would later become **Montreal**. It was not until the latter part of the seventeenth century that the French established settlements at **New Orleans** and in the southern Great Lakes region.

French-American Indian Diplomacy

Because the French had relatively few actual colonists in the New World, they had to rely on diplomacy with American Indian groups. French military officers in the New World learned native languages and became well versed in American Indian diplomatic protocol, including smoking the long-stemmed **calumet** ("peace pipe") and giving and receiving gifts, including **wampum belts**. French officers and agents often married Indian wives, which promoted their efforts at maintaining good relations with native peoples. Despite these efforts, American Indians maintained actual control of the heart of the North American continent. In these areas, French agents had to adjust to Indian ways to maintain France's colonial presence. The **Osages**, for example, south of the Missouri River, accepted some French agents into their kinship networks. This French accommodation of and adaptation to American Indian ways was in marked contrast to the actions of British and Spanish colonists.

The Métis of the French Colonies

In many French settlements in the interior of the North American continent, French women were few and far between. In these frontier communities, a certain intermingling of French and American Indian peoples and lifeways occurred. The fort and trading post at **Detroit**, for instance, combined French as well as American Indian elements. The layout of the village resembled a French village, but many of the buildings were covered by bark, in the style of local American Indians. Clothing among French colonists also included European and native elements: European shirts and Indian shoes, for example. In addition, intermarriage with American Indians was common in these far-flung French colonies. The children of these marriages were known as **Métis**—an old French word for "mixed" or "mixed-blood." In Métis communities, American Indian women often played important roles, in contrast to traditional French family structures. These women served as cultural mediators and were an important part of the fur trade as brokers. Métis communities, combining Catholic and indigenous religious practices, continued to exist after France officially surrendered its North American colonies in 1763.

The Dutch Presence in the Americas

The Dutch presence in the New World dates from the 1590s. Like the French, the first Dutch colonies in the New World functioned more as trading outposts rather than as populated settlements. The Dutch established forts and small settlements in Guyana in 1590, followed by a string of island settlements in the Caribbean in the early 1600s. Dutch efforts at colonization were often stymied by rival European powers. In Tobago, for example, the Dutch attempted four different times to build settlements in the seventeenth century, with each settlement destroyed by either the French, the Spanish, or the British. Later in the seventeenth century, the Dutch obtained control of the colony of **Surinam**, in South America. Earlier, in the 1650s, the British had established a colony there. It was captured by a Dutch expedition in 1667 and was formally transferred to the Dutch as part of the **Treaty of Breda**, following the **Second Anglo-Dutch War**, 1665–1667. By this treaty, the Dutch formally relinquished control of New Amsterdam (see page 61). The Dutch focused on sugar production in Surinam, relying on African slave labor to work the fields.

Dutch New Amsterdam

In the early 1600s, the Dutch set their sights on North America. The **Dutch Republic** commissioned an expedition to North America led by English explorer **Henry Hudson (1609)**. The project was funded by the **Dutch East India Company**, which instructed Hudson to search for a Northwest Passage to Asia. Hudson sailed into the river that would later bear his name, and past Manhattan Island, part of present-day New York City. Continuing northward, he sailed almost as far as present-day Albany before turning back. Hudson never found a Northwest Passage, but his reports of abundant fur, timber, and fertile lands generated further interest among Dutch merchants. After several more journeys of exploration and repeated attempts to find a Northwest Passage, the Dutch Republic chartered the **Dutch West India Company** to develop colonies in North America. The Dutch claimed a vast stretch of land from the Delaware River in the south to Cape Cod in the north. The Dutch later acquiesced to claims by the growing population of Puritan Connecticut (a 1650 treaty with the Connecticut colony formalized a new border, close to the present border between New York and Connecticut).

The administrative seat, and most important settlement of New Netherland, was **New Amsterdam**. A settlement was established in 1624 on what is now Governor's Island, in New York Harbor. Fort Amsterdam was soon built at the southern tip of Manhattan and a settlement was begun near the fort the following year. Legend has it that in 1626, **Peter Minuit**, the company director general of New Amsterdam, purchased the island of Manhattan from the local people for goods estimated to be worth $24. Almost all aspects of this transaction are in doubt—the value of the goods, the intentions of the American Indians, and even the legitimacy of the unnamed native people to "sell" the island. However, the myth of the **"$24 Deal"** has persisted.

The Economy of New Amsterdam

The Dutch West India Company did not see immediate profits, as the colony of **New Amsterdam** floundered during its first twenty years. Initially, few Dutch settlers came to the New World. The company tried to induce immigrants with generous land grants along the Hudson River. Slowly, settlers began to arrive—an amalgam of Europeans of diverse national and religious backgrounds, including a group of Sephardic Jewish colonists who had fled Brazil to escape Portuguese persecution. The Dutch also brought African slaves to New Amsterdam to address the colony's chronic labor shortage.

The colony began to thrive under the leadership of the heavy-handed **Peter Stuyvesant**, who was hired by the company in 1647. New Amsterdam became a center for the thriving trade in beaver furs and a growing commercial seaport town. However, **King Charles II of England** soon set his sights on the "Dutch wedge," which divided England's holdings in North America. The king sent a fleet of warships to New Amsterdam. The outnumbered and outgunned Stuyvesant surrendered in 1664 without a fight. Charles II granted the colony to his brother **James, the Duke of York**, who renamed it **New York**. Formal transfer to the English occurred in 1667, as part of the settlement following the Second Anglo-Dutch War (see page 60).

C. English Colonial Patterns

Of the European empires that established colonies in the New World, the English pattern differed markedly from the Spanish, Dutch, and French. Whereas their European competitors sent relatively few colonists to the New World, the English migrated in substantial numbers to the new colonies.

The English Merchant Class and the Expansion of Trade

As England was facing the crisis of a population surplus (see box, "Population Pressures and English Colonization," page 62), a class of merchants and landowners was accumulating a great deal of capital. Landowners, for much of the 1500s, profited from the expanding market for wool. Entrepreneurs established a domestic wool-processing industry, while merchants began to establish **joint-stock companies** (see page 48), laying claim to exclusive trading rights in different regions. The Crown, guided by **mercantilist principles** (see page 74), granted charters to these companies, such as the **East India Company** (1600). As joint-stock companies made profits on trade, investors set their sights on New World colonization, especially after the international wool market weakened in the second half of the 1500s. Oxford clergyman **Richard Hakluyt** wrote an influential tract in which he argued that overseas expansion could benefit England in two ways—drawing off England's surplus population and providing new markets for manufactured goods.

The Colonization of Ireland

The English pattern of colonizing new lands with large numbers of settlers had been established in **Ireland**, well before the English founded colonies in the **New World**. In the 1560s and 1570s, English and Scottish colonists flooded across the Irish Sea to Ireland, establishing settlements and driving out the native population. The brutal subjugation of the Irish in the sixteenth and seventeenth centuries foreshadowed the English conquest of North America in several ways. The English saw themselves as both superior to and separate from the native population of Ireland, just as they did in regard to American Indians in the seventeenth and eighteenth centuries. This attitude of supremacy, subjugation, and separation set the English apart from other powers settling in the New World; Spain and France sought to control native populations, but both also accepted a degree of social interaction between colonists and natives. The English, on the other hand, sought to transplant purely "English" societies in the New World.

> **USING HISTORICAL THINKING SKILLS: CONTEXTUALIZATION**
>
> **Population Pressures and English Colonization**
>
> English colonization in the New World can be seen in the context of economic transformations in England in the 1400s and 1500s. For centuries, much of the land in the English countryside had been considered common land—tracts in which landless peasants and rural laborers traditionally had a right to gather hay or graze their animals. However, in the 1500s, the demand for wool grew throughout Europe, pressuring landowners to convert their "common lands" to sheep pastures. Much of the common and rented lands of England were enclosed in order to create pastures. Despite protests, the enclosure movement led to the eviction of thousands of farmers, creating a class of landless and poor people, some roaming the countryside, some making their way to England's growing cities. The enclosures also took land out of cultivation, creating a food crisis in England, just as the population was rising. These factors created a population surplus at the same time as English explorers were making claims in the New World.

Topic 2.3 The Regions of British Colonies

Although the thirteen colonies in British North America had much in common, each of the four regions was distinct from the others. The characteristics of each of the four regions—the New England colonies, the middle colonies, the Chesapeake colonies, and the lower South and West Indian colonies—were shaped by each region's particular geographic and environmental features.

A. The Chesapeake and the Upper South

The upper South was the most populous part of the South, containing 90 percent of the white population and 80 percent of the Black population of the South. The colonists of the Chesapeake region and North Carolina came to rely on labor-intensive tobacco, using white indentured servants and slaves as their workforce.

The Founding of Jamestown and the "Starving Time"

The first settlers to **Jamestown, Virginia,** arrived in 1607. Investors in England formed a **joint-stock company**, the **Virginia Company**, to fund the expedition. **King James I** chartered the company and granted territory in the New World. The Jamestown colony nearly collapsed during its first few years of existence. The colonists were not prepared to establish a community, grow crops, and sustain themselves. They were mostly male gentlemen as well as their personal servants, unaccustomed to working with their hands. These early settlers hoped to find gold and silver and to quickly duplicate the Spanish successes in Central and South America. They did not find precious metals, nor did they initially plant crops. Their store of food diminished quickly and, by 1608, only 38 of the original 144 colonists were still alive. By 1610, things had not improved. An additional 500 settlers had come, including many indentured servants. By 1610, only 60 were still alive, with many having perished during the **"starving time"** (winter of 1609–1610).

Jamestown and its American Indian Neighbors

Relations with local American Indians deteriorated rapidly during the early years of the Jamestown colony. The local **Algonquian-speaking** people, led by their chief, **Powhatan**, father of **Pocahontas**, traded corn with the settlers at first. However, when the American Indians could not supply a sufficient amount of corn for their English neighbors, the English initiated raids on the Powhatan Confederacy. These skirmishes occurred for years, until the Indians organized an assault on Jamestown in 1622. The series of attacks ended up killing a quarter of the colony (347 people), but it did not dislodge it. In the coming years relations between the Virginia colony and the Powhatan Confederacy worsened. The following year, Virginia leaders brought poisoned wine to a meeting with the Powhatan people, resulting in 200 deaths. After another war in 1644, the Powhatan presence in the area precipitously declined. In many ways, the incidents in Jamestown foretold the history of relations between the American Indians of North America and the white settlers from Europe. Whites consistently encroached on American Indian lands and consistently defeated them in the violent encounters that resulted.

A Tobacco Economy

Following a difficult beginning, marked by disease, starvation, and resistance by native peoples, the colonists of Virginia began the successful cultivation of **tobacco**. Tobacco was unknown in Europe before Columbus's journeys to the New World. The Spanish had first introduced tobacco to Europe in the 1500s, but it remained a scarce luxury there. In 1612, the Jamestown planter **John Rolfe** began experimenting with growing tobacco. The first shipments were sent to England in 1617. With its addictive properties, tobacco soon became extremely popular in Europe and hugely profitable for the **Chesapeake Bay** region. By 1700, the American colonies were exporting more than thirty-five million pounds of tobacco a year. Tobacco became the most important crop for the Chesapeake region, accounting for nearly three-fourths of its exports by 1750, and nearly one-third of all exports from British North America.

The shift to a tobacco economy profoundly affected the direction of Virginia's development and, subsequently, the rest of the Chesapeake and the northern part of the colony of **Carolina** (the area that would become North Carolina in the eighteenth century). First, the cultivation of tobacco required large tracts of land. Tobacco cultivation quickly exhausted the nutrients in the

---

> **USING REASONING PROCESSES: COMPARISON**
>
> **The Colonies of Virginia and Massachusetts**
>
> The struggles of the Jamestown colony, notably the "starving time" of 1609 to 1610, can be contrasted with the relative success of the early years of the Plymouth and Massachusetts Bay colonies. Be careful when selecting the focus of your comparison. For example, if you were to focus on the geography of the two regions, it would raise the question—why didn't the Puritans in bitter-cold New England die off in large numbers and the Virginians, in a mild climate, thrive? A more thorough comparison would compare the motivations, social structures, leadership, and culture of the two sets of colonists. The early years of Jamestown were characterized by an unwillingness to work, a scarcity of families, and a lack of wilderness survival skills. Many of the Puritan settlers of New England, by contrast, were driven by a cooperative spirit and an ethic of hard work. They believed that their success would demonstrate God's favor.

> **USING REASONING PROCESSES: COMPARISON**
>
> **Agriculture, North Versus South**
>
> From the start, the northern and southern colonies developed different patterns of agriculture. The southern colonies focused on a few staple crops, grown for export. The northern colonies focused on smaller scale agriculture and a variety of crops. The export-oriented agricultural practices of the southern colonies would prove to be a major factor in the development and proliferation of slavery in the region.

soil, requiring growers to seek out new tracts of land after only a few years of production. This thirst for land inevitably led to encroachments on the territory of American Indians in the interior of Virginia. Second, the success of tobacco established a pattern in the South of large-scale production of staple crops for the international market. This pattern continued with the expansion of cotton production in the nineteenth century. Finally, this reliance on the cultivation of export crops required a large number of laborers. The need for labor facilitated the development of indentured servitude and slavery.

Labor and Tobacco

The leaders of the **Chesapeake** colonies used a variety of methods to bring workers to the New World. New immigrants were enticed to come to the Chesapeake region with the offer of 50 acres, called a **head-right**, upon arrival. However, this still required a potential immigrant to scrape together the fare for passage to the New World—approximately a year's income for an agrarian worker in England. To bring lower-class English people to America, wealthy Virginians employed the system of **indentured servitude**. Under this system, a potential immigrant in England would agree to contract to work as an indentured servant for a certain number of years in America (usually four to seven) in exchange for free passage. An agent would then sell this contract to a planter in the colonies. The system accomplished its goal, allowing for tens of thousands of impoverished English men and women to migrate to the New World, but the system also created an entire underclass of mistreated workers. The first enslaved Africans were brought to Virginia in 1619. **Slavery** developed gradually; it was only later in the century that it began to grow dramatically (see more on the development of slavery, pages 80–81).

Maryland

The colony of **Maryland** bore similarities to Virginia. Both colonies focused on the cultivation of tobacco as an export crop and used indentured servants and African slaves to work the tobacco fields.

Maryland was the first **proprietary colony** established by England in North America. The Crown was moving away from the model of granting charters to joint-stock companies. It hoped that the proprietor (owner) of a colony would be more accountable to the monarch. The proprietor of Maryland was to be **George Calvert, 1st Baron Baltimore**. Calvert was Catholic and hoped to create in the New World a refuge for **Catholics**. He was granted a charter by **King Charles I**, but died just weeks before the colony was to be established. His son, **Cecelius Calvert**, became the actual proprietor of Maryland. Almost immediately, Protestants outnumbered Catholics, but Catholicism continued to be tolerated in Maryland.

North Carolina

The roots of **North Carolina** can be found in the divergent development of the Carolina colony. **Carolina** was founded in 1663 by wealthy plantation owners who had migrated from **Barbados**. These wealthy plantation owners created an agrarian system in the southern portion of Carolina that came to resemble the sugar economy of Barbados (see pages 69–70). However, from the 1670s and 1680s, when the first English settlers arrived, economy of the northern part of Carolina more closely resembled that of the Chesapeake colonies. These settlers included runaway servants as well as families of modest means. Tensions between the two regions, which were remote from one another, led to a split in 1712 and the establishment of North Carolina as a distinct colony from **South Carolina.**

B. The New England Colonies

The first settlers of the New England region were driven more by religious reasons than a quest for economic gain. These settlers were devout Puritans. Their religious motivation helps explain the unique patterns of development in New England.

Origins of Puritanism

The roots of **Puritanism** can be found in the **Protestant Reformation** of the first half of the sixteenth century. **Martin Luther** and **John Calvin** both broke with the **Catholic Church** for theological reasons. Both argued that the Catholic Church had strayed from its spiritual mission. The Protestant Reformation took hold in much of northern Europe but not, initially, in England. In the 1530s, **King Henry VIII** of England initiated his own break with the Catholic Church. His break, however, was not over theological differences with the Catholic Church, but over political control. Henry wanted control of the vast holdings of the church in England and the power to appoint members of the church hierarchy, as well as the power to annul his marriage. Because Henry's break with Rome was not theological in nature, he did not question, nor did he change, the traditional Roman Catholic religious practices. This **"halfway reformation"** upset many true Protestants in England. Those who sought a full reformation in England, who wanted the **Church of England** to be "purified" of Catholic practices, came to be known as **Puritans**. Some Puritans, who came to be known as **separatists**, went even further and argued for a complete separation from the Church of England.

> **USING HISTORICAL THINKING SKILLS: CONTEXTUALIZATION**
>
> ### The Context of the Puritan Migration
>
> The Puritan migration to the New World took place in the context of religious developments in Europe. Be familiar with the Protestant Reformation, and how the English version of the Reformation lacked the spiritual dimensions of Calvinism or Lutheranism. English Protestants who were drawn to Calvinism increasingly found themselves at odds with English religious and civil authorities. These clashes were an important factor in the decision of many Puritans to settle in North America. The religious divisions of Europe profoundly impacted colonial America and the United States.

Puritan Beliefs and Practices

The Puritans took their inspiration from **Calvinism**. Calvinist doctrine taught that individual salvation was subject to a divine plan, rather than to the actions of individuals. This belief in a divine plan in regard to salvation, known as **predestination**, left true believers in a state of anxiety, since it was impossible to know God's will. To lessen this sense of anxiety, Puritans lived lives of strict piety, framed by prayer, righteous living, and hard work. Calvinism held that everyone had a **"calling"**—work on Earth that God intended the individual to do. Being diligent at one's "calling," therefore, was central to Puritanism.

The Puritans also put a great value on community. They believed it was God's will that members of the community take care of one another and watch that members did not go astray. Individual malfeasance could result in divine punishment for the entire community.

Finally, the Puritan approach to humanity and to God was markedly dour, even dark. The Puritans put a great deal of emphasis on **"original sin"** (stemming from the biblical story in Genesis of Eve, and then Adam, violating God's injunction not to eat the forbidden fruit in the Garden of Eden) and saw humanity as tainted with this inheritance. Further, the Puritan vision of God was closer to the vengeful, jealous God found in much of the Old Testament, rather than the loving God found in much of the New Testament.

Plymouth and the Mayflower Compact

A group of **separatists**, known to history as the **"Pilgrims,"** fled England in 1608 to find a more hospitable religious climate in **the Netherlands**. The Netherlands, by this time, was tolerant of different beliefs and had a strong Calvinist presence, and it seemed like the ideal location for this group of **English Calvinists**. Although the Pilgrims did not suffer religious persecution in the Netherlands, their leaders became concerned about the country's material temptations. These leaders came to believe that the challenges of establishing a settlement in the New World would steel the congregants for the rigors of religious piety. **William Bradford** and the leadership of the separatist community got permission from the British king to settle in the land granted to the Virginia Company. They formed a joint-stock company to fund the expedition. Slightly over a hundred separatists set sail on the ***Mayflower*** in 1620, arriving on Cape Cod eleven weeks later. They quickly realized that they were well north of their targeted area, and did not have legal authority to settle. To provide a sense of legitimacy they drew up and signed the **Mayflower Compact**, an agreement calling for orderly government based on the consent of the governed. The colony of Plymouth struggled the first year. By 1630, it achieved a small degree of success, but it failed to attract large numbers of mainline Puritans from England. The **Massachusetts Bay Colony**, founded a decade later thirty-five miles up the coast, would prove to be far more successful.

Massachusetts Bay Colony—"A City Upon a Hill"

By the 1620s, many Puritans were eager to leave England. **King Charles I**, with the encouragement of his advisor, **Archbishop William Laud**, sought to suppress the religious practices of Puritans and other nonconforming sects in England. In 1629, the king, perhaps eager to rid England of Puritans, granted a charter to the **Massachusetts Bay Company** to establish a colony in the northern part of British North America. The charter did not specify the exact location of the company's headquarters, allowing the governance of the Massachusetts Bay Company to be located in the colony instead of in England. This gave the colony a high degree of autonomy. The leader of the Massachusetts Bay Colony was **John Winthrop**. Before the colonists' ship, the *Arbella*, landed in present-day **Salem** in 1630, Winthrop gave a sermon, **"A Model of Christian Charity,"** that is considered one of the more important orations in American history. He stressed the importance of the colonists' mission. They should think of their colony as being **"a city upon a hill,"** for, he insisted, "The eyes of all people are upon us."

> **USING HISTORICAL THINKING SKILLS:**
> **DEVELOPMENTS AND PROCESSES**
>
> ### The Development of the Separation of Church and State
>
> Students of American history often make a profound mistake about church and state in colonial Massachusetts. They hear in history class, "The Puritans came to America to freely practice their religion." From this they conclude that the origins of religious freedom can be found in Massachusetts. This is not accurate. The Puritans (with the exception of Roger Williams) established theocratic governments. Other developments in colonial America helped establish the separation of church and state as a foundational American value, including the establishment of Rhode Island (1636) (see page 67) and the issuing of the Flushing Remonstrance (1657) (see page 84). The separation of church and state was later codified in the "establishment clause" of the First Amendment (1791), prohibiting the establishment of an official religion in the United States (see page 114). Defenders of this separation also cite the 1797 Treaty of Tripoli, in which the federal government asserts that the United States was "not, in any sense, founded on the Christian religion."

The "Great Migration" and the Growth of New England

Like their fellow New Englanders in Plymouth, the settlers of the **Massachusetts Bay Colony**, centered in present-day **Boston**, had a difficult first year. However, unlike the Pilgrims' original settlement in Plymouth, John Winthrop's colony was soon thriving. By 1640, a **"great migration"** of more than 20,000 settlers came to Massachusetts Bay Colony. The settlers arriving in Massachusetts Bay were middling sorts—farmers, carpenters, textile workers—not the mixture of gentlemen founders and indentured servants found in Virginia. While the Jamestown settlers were primarily men, Massachusetts Bay Colony tended to attract families. The settlers in Massachusetts were eager to build permanent, cohesive communities, and they were willing to labor; they were not looking for quick riches. Massachusetts Bay Colony burgeoned with ten new towns in the first decade after 1630 and more than 130 by the end of the century.

> **USING HISTORICAL THINKING SKILLS:**
> **MAKING CONNECTIONS**
>
> ### Great Migrations
>
> Avoid confusing the seventeenth-century "Great Migration" of the Puritans to New England with the twentieth-century "Great Migration" of African Americans from the rural South to the urban North and West. Participants in both frequently used biblical imagery to describe their journeys. Both groups of participants saw their journeys as a form of deliverance to a "promised land."

New Hampshire

Some Puritans moved north to the area that would become **New Hampshire**. These settlers were predated by small fishing villages founded by the English in the 1620s. Massachusetts soon claimed the region, and a 1641 agreement gave it jurisdiction over New Hampshire. A royal decree separated the two colonies in 1679.

Roger Williams and the Founding of Rhode Island

Puritan society encouraged the intensive study of scripture. At the same time, the Puritan hierarchy enforced a rigid conformity to its own religious doctrine. This combination of a promotion of learning but insistence on conformity led to inevitable conflicts in New England. **Roger Williams** was a devout Puritan minister who became an important dissenter in Massachusetts. Williams was increasingly concerned about the mistreatment of American Indians by the Puritans (see pages 77–79). He was also critical of the involvement of the church in matters of civil governance. He was worried that the concerns of civil government would distract ministers from godly matters. He fled to the **Narragansett Bay** area in 1636 and founded the colony of **Rhode Island**. One of the distinguishing characteristics of Rhode Island was the separation of church and state in its governance.

The Banishment of Anne Hutchinson

Another important religious dispute in Puritan New England involved **Anne Hutchinson,** a deeply religious thinker who challenged contemporary gender norms by holding meetings in her house to discuss theological matters with both men and women. In many ways, she took Puritan thought to its logical conclusion, arguing that ministers were not needed to interpret and convey the teachings of the Bible; rather, God could communicate directly to true believers. Further, she accused Puritan leaders of backsliding on the idea that salvation was determined solely by God's divine plan, not by the actions of individuals. In 1638, John Winthrop and other Puritan leaders tried, excommunicated, and banished Hutchinson and her family. The Hutchinson family and several of her supporters then established a settlement in Rhode Island. Later, she and several of her children relocated to Dutch New Netherlands, where they were killed in a military conflict between the Dutch and the Lenape Indians (1643).

The Founding of Connecticut

Some Massachusetts Bay colonists sought to rid themselves of the heavy-handed rule of the colony's governor, John Winthrop. The **Reverend Thomas Hooker** disagreed with Winthrop over who should be admitted to church membership. Winthrop insisted that new members be able to demonstrate to church leaders that they had had a conversion experience. Hooker argued for a less rigorous requirement; he asserted that living a godly life was sufficient to be considered for church membership. Hooker led a group to the **Connecticut River Valley** in 1636, where they founded the town of **Hartford**, well away from the reach of Winthrop. Other towns formed along the Connecticut River, combining with Hartford to form the colony of **Connecticut**. The **Fundamental Orders of Connecticut** were adopted in 1639. In 1662, the town of **New Haven** merged into the Connecticut colony.

The Splintering of Puritanism

By the end of the seventeenth century, tensions were seen in the Puritan experiment. To some degree, the second and third generations of Puritans did not maintain the zeal and fire of the founding group. By the 1650s, Puritan leaders were noting a decline in church membership. Also, the economic vitality of the New England communities might have pulled some people away from the demands of Puritanism. The splintering of Puritanism can be seen in both the creation of the Halfway Covenant and in the Salem witch trials (see page 68).

The Halfway Covenant (1662)

Concerns about the decline of Puritan zeal led to the establishment of the **Halfway Covenant** (1662). Previously, potential new members of Puritan churches in New England—either children of original members or new arrivals—had to demonstrate to church elders that they had undergone a conversion experience. Candidates for membership in the **Congregational Church** (as the Puritan church came to be called) had to convince church elders that they had experienced the workings of God in their soul. Demonstrating a conversion experience was exceedingly difficult. In the face of declining membership, the idea of partial membership evolved. The Halfway Covenant was an initiative in the Congregational Church to allow for partial church membership for children of church members. Even if they could not demonstrate a conversion experience, they could be baptized and become partial, nonvoting members of the church.

Salem Witch Trials (1692)

The 1692 **Salem witch trials** in Massachusetts demonstrate division in the once-cohesive Puritan community. In a global sense, the Salem witch trials are a mere footnote to the centuries of **witch-hunts** in Europe that led to perhaps a hundred thousand people being executed. Events in Salem in 1692 came at the tail end of this chapter in history.

The first to be accused of **witchcraft** in Salem were teenage girls. To be accused of witchcraft meant that the defendant was thought to be working in consort with Satan. In Puritan thinking, every event had some cosmic explanation. Misfortune in one's life (a stillborn child or a bad harvest) could be divine punishment for sinful behavior. It could also, however, be the work of an enemy who was channeling the power of Satan. This second explanation of misfortune pushed blame onto someone else—a witch. The epidemic of accusations in Salem tells us much about the Puritan community three generations after John Winthrop urged his fellow Puritans to "be knit together in this work as one man." The fact that over a hundred members of the Salem community were accused of consorting with Satan speaks to the perceived lack of godly piety in New England. Also, the fact that neighbors were so ready to turn on neighbors, that men were ready to turn on women (the majority of the accused were women), and that the poorer members were ready to turn on the wealthy members all reflect a fractured community.

C. The Middle Colonies

The most diverse colonies in British North America—in regard to religion, ethnicity, and social class—were the middle colonies. The middle colonies developed a thriving export economy based on the cultivation of cereal crops. The middle colonies were "restoration colonies." That is, they were founded after the monarchy was restored in England (1660), following the period of the English Civil War (1642–1651) and the period of England being ruled as a commonwealth (1649–1660).

Pennsylvania

In 1681, **King Charles II** granted an enormous tract of land (25,000 square miles) to **William Penn** to settle a debt that the king had owed to Penn's father. William Penn and the king were on friendly terms, despite the fact that Penn had become a devout **Quaker** and was often at odds with the official Church of England. Charles was no doubt pleased to see the establishment of a colony to draw the dissenting Quakers out of England. The king named the colony **Pennsylvania** after William Penn's father, much to the embarrassment of Penn, the younger.

> **USING HISTORICAL THINKING SKILLS:**
> **CONTEXTUALIZATION**
>
> **Quaker Egalitarianism in Context**
>
> The non-hierarchical and egalitarian spirit of Quakerism is more noteworthy when looked at in the context of social practices in the European and colonial American world of the seventeenth and eighteenth centuries. This world was characterized by social titles and rules of deference. Deference describes the ritualistic display of submission by common people toward those of a "superior" class. The egalitarian spirit of Quakerism would, to a degree, come to shape social norms in the early United States.

Quakerism and the "Holy Experiment"

Quakerism provided the guiding set of beliefs in the founding of **Pennsylvania**. Quakerism developed in the religious ferment of seventeenth-century England. Its approach to religion, and indeed to life, was radically non-hierarchical. Quakers saw one another as equals in the eyes of God. They addressed one another as **"friend"** (hence, the formal name of Quakerism, the **"Religious Society of Friends"**). They avoided the practice of the "lower sorts" bowing or removing their hats to their "betters"; Quakers shook hands with one another. Quakers did not have sermons; they attended **"meetings"** in which each congregant could speak if moved. Penn wanted to establish a **"holy experiment"** in the New World to put Quakerism's egalitarian values into practice. He initiated friendly relations with local native groups. Pennsylvania's Quakers practiced religious toleration and frowned upon slavery (although it did exist in colonial Pennsylvania). Pennsylvania thrived in the seventeenth century, and its largest city, **Philadelphia**, surpassed New York as a commercial center.

New Jersey and Delaware

New Jersey and **Delaware** were both initially settled by the **Dutch**. After **Dutch New Netherlands** came into the hands of the British in 1664 (see page 61), the **Duke of York** gave the land adjacent to New York, between the Hudson and Delaware Rivers, to two friends, **Sir George Carteret** and **Lord Berkeley of Stratton**, who established the **colony of New Jersey**.

Delaware was first settled by the Dutch in 1631, but all the initial settlers were soon killed in a dispute with American Indians. In 1638, **Sweden** established a trading post and colony in Delaware at **Fort Christina** (present-day Wilmington). In 1651, the Dutch established a fort in the Swedish colony; **the Netherlands** took over the colony and incorporated it into its North American holdings, **New Netherland**, in 1655. When the Dutch were ousted by the **British** in 1664, the Duke of York granted Delaware to his friend William Penn, who incorporated it into his Pennsylvania land grant (see page 68). In 1704, **Pennsylvania's Lower Counties**, as Delaware was referred to, developed their own representative body and effectively became independent of Pennsylvania.

New York

New Amsterdam was settled by the Dutch in 1624 and came into English hands in 1664 and was renamed **New York** (see page 61). New York continued to function as a commercial port, similar to Boston or Philadelphia. One factor that distinguished New York from similar northern port cities was the central position that slavery played in the local economy. Slave labor had been used extensively by the Dutch in New Amsterdam to augment the colony's meager working population; when the colony changed hands, English officials expanded the use of slave labor. By the mid-1700s, New York had a slave population greater than North Carolina's (but less than that of other southern colonies). On the eve of the American Revolution, New York City's approximately 3,000 slaves accounted for 14 percent of the city's population.

The "Negro Plot of 1741"

Tensions in New York between whites and enslaved African Americans came to the surface in several events in 1741. A series of unexplained fires in the city led authorities to believe that a slave conspiracy was afoot. Over 150 African Americans were arrested, along with 20 whites. At least 30 people were executed, more than during the period of the Salem witch trials. Historians have debated the extent of the **"Negro Plot of 1741,"** or whether there even was a plot.

D. The Lower South and the Colonies of the West Indies

The colonies of the lower South—Carolina and Georgia—as well as British colonies in the West Indies all shared certain characteristics that set them apart from the rest of British colonial America. These colonies had longer growing seasons and came to depend on exporting staple crops and on the slave-labor system. The population of the lower South and West Indies was considerably less than that of the upper South, and the ratio of Blacks to whites was significantly different. In many cases, enslaved Africans made up the majority of a colony's population. In South Carolina by the mid-eighteenth century, there were approximately twice as many Black slaves as there were whites.

Sugar and Slavery in the West Indies

Barbados was the most profitable colony in Britain's New World empire. Although Barbados's economy was based on agriculture and slavery as were the economies of the Chesapeake region, Barbados's economic model was significantly different from those in the Chesapeake region.

Barbados was settled by English colonists in the 1630s and soon became very successful. The planters of Barbados grew wealthy by selling sugar produced from **sugarcane**, the main crop in Barbados, at high prices in England. By the end of the seventeenth century, the English colonies of the Caribbean were exporting nearly fifty million pounds of sugar per year. Sugarcane favored wealthy planters because only they could afford the high initial investment needed in a sugar growing and processing operation. Unlike Virginia, Barbados lacked a small-scale yeoman farmer class. The wealthy sugar planters of Barbados were, on average, four times as wealthy as the tobacco planters of Virginia. In addition, the slave population of Barbados was much larger than that of Virginia. By the end of the seventeenth century, slaves made up 75 percent of the population of Barbados, compared to less than 25 percent in Virginia. The average sugar grower in Barbados owned 115 slaves, far more than the average plantation in Virginia. Plantation work in Barbados was physically demanding—long hours of intense labor under the hot sun. Finally, gender and family dynamics among slaves differed considerably between Barbados and Virginia. Slaves in Barbados were much less likely to form families than were slaves in Virginia, with men outnumbering women two to one in Barbados.

Carolina

The initial settlers of the colony of **Carolina** were mostly planters who had migrated from **Barbados**. They brought with them the system of slavery that they had developed on the island, making the economy of Carolina resemble that of Barbados more than that of Virginia. Carolina was established in 1663 by **King Charles II**, who assumed the throne following the English Commonwealth period of 1649–1660. To reward eight noblemen who had helped him reinstall monarchical rule, he granted them a charter for the lands south of Virginia. These proprietors recruited additional wealthy slave-owning English settlers in Barbados to resettle in Carolina. The early Carolinians looked to replicate the export-oriented plantation economy of Barbados, but they could not find a crop nearly as profitable as sugar. By the late 1600s, they began making money growing and exporting rice.

In the 1670s and 1680s, the economy of the northern part of Carolina began to diverge from that of the southern part (see page 64). The two regions were distinct economically and relatively remote from each other. This economic division led to political division; in 1691, a deputy governor was charged with administering the northern part of the colony. The split was made official in 1712. **South Carolina**, declared a royal colony in 1719, continued to operate an economic system like that of Barbados, with thousands of slaves controlled by a relatively small number of elite planters.

Georgia

The last of the original thirteen colonies to be established was **Georgia**. Britain, becoming increasingly concerned about competition from other European powers making New World land claims, wanted to establish a buffer between South Carolina and Spanish-held Florida. Toward this end, Britain granted a charter to **James Oglethorpe** to establish the colony of Georgia in 1732. Oglethorpe was a philanthropist and hoped to establish a paternalistic colony for Britain's **"deserving poor,"** including imprisoned debtors. Oglethorpe did not grant his charges any element of representative government. He mandated military service for all males. Oglethorpe's plans did not come to fruition. Few "deserving poor" met Oglethorpe's requirements. Instead, Carolinians in search of new land moved into Georgia and brought slavery with them. In 1752, Oglethorpe gave up on his project and ceded control of the colony to the Crown.

E. The Development of Self-Government in Britain's New World Colonies

By the eighteenth century, the British colonies of North America had developed institutions of self-government that were remarkably democratic for that era. These early attempts at representative democracy can be seen as laying the groundwork for eventual independence from Great Britain.

The Evolution of Governance in Colonial North America

Institutions of **self-government** in colonial North America developed in a relative power vacuum. Great Britain did not create an extensive governing structure in its North American colonies (as it later would in India), in part because of their remoteness from the "mother country" and in part because of Great Britain's lax attention to its New World empire. In theory, all of the thirteen colonies were under the supervision of the Crown. Whether the colonies were first ruled by a **corporation** or a **proprietor**, they eventually all became **royal colonies**. The king appointed a governor to rule over each colony (sometimes one governor ruled over two colonies). However, in all cases, some sort of **colonial legislature** existed. These legislatures dealt with local matters (not trade regulations, for example), including the power to tax the inhabitants of the colony. Governors came to depend on funding from this tax revenue to run the colony. In many instances, the colonial legislatures were able to exercise a good deal of leverage over the royal governors because of this **"power of the purse,"** which instilled in many colonists a sense of their ability to govern themselves.

Town Meetings in New England

New England town meetings were face-to-face decision-making assemblies that were open to all free male residents of a town. These meetings, usually held annually, made important decisions about the town and selected a group of representatives, **"selectmen,"** who carried out governing functions until the next town meeting. This form of direct democracy allowed for a high degree of citizen participation in decision-making.

The House of Burgesses in Virginia

The **House of Burgesses** was created by the **Virginia Company** in 1619. The company had founded the colony of Virginia in 1607 as a profit-generating venture. Seeing the need for some sort of body to govern the inhabitants of the colony, the company created this representative assembly. Initially, all free adult men could vote for representatives; later, voting rights were limited to wealthy men. After the king transferred governance of Virginia from the Virginia Company to the Crown in 1624, he allowed the House of Burgesses to continue. Over time, the House of Burgesses became less powerful and more exclusive, as smaller planters were barred from voting.

Topic 2.4 Transatlantic Trade

The late 1600s and 1700s witnessed the growth of an Atlantic economy—one characterized by an increased exchange of goods. Colonial economies focused on selling commodities to Europe and in gaining new sources of labor. Ultimately, the growth of the Atlantic economy led to an expansion of colonial economies, devastation and adaptation by American Indian groups, an increase in the use of slave labor, and changes in British mercantilist policies toward its thirteen North American colonies.

A. The Atlantic Economy and the Evolution of Colonial Economies

Traditionally labeled the "triangle trade," a complex trading network, developed in the 1700s, brought manufactured items from England to both Africa and the Americas. These items included firearms, shoes, furniture, ceramics, and many other items. Kidnapped Africans were sold by human traffickers, who forced them into the international slave trade. New World colonies tended to focus on growing and obtaining foodstuffs and other natural resources that could be traded with Europeans. The colonies of the Americas produced a wide variety of raw materials.

The African Slave Trade

Slave trafficking in **sub-Saharan Africa** became a thriving business in the eighteenth century. European traders set up operations in African coastal towns and encouraged African men to venture into the interior to kidnap members of other tribal groups. In the port towns along the "Slave Coast," between the Volta River and the kingdom of Benin in West Africa, European traders exchanged manufactured items for human cargo. The **slave trade** not only resulted in kidnapping, but it also worsened ethnic and societal tensions, destabilizing the region. The victims of the slave trade were from a variety of cultural and linguistic groups. These Africans—mostly young and male, with men outnumbering women two to one—were next transported to the New World in horrid conditions. This grueling, and often deadly, part of the journey was known as the **"middle passage."** The most well-known account of the middle passage by an African is contained in the autobiographical book, *The Interesting Narrative of the Life of Olaudah Equiano*, published in 1789.

Tobacco, Indigo, Rice, Sugar, and Slavery in the South and the West Indies

By the eighteenth century, the economic status of most of the **North American colonies** improved, as the colonies focused on crops and economic activities that were suited for the local climate and geography, and that could be marketed to European nations. After several years of economic uncertainty, **Virginians** came to settle on the cultivation, processing, and export of **tobacco** (see pages 63–64). The colonies of the **lower South** specialized in **indigo** and **rice**. These two crops made up nearly two-thirds of exports from the lower South by 1750. All told, the southern colonies supplied 90 percent of the exports from British North America. However, the most profitable of all the British New World colonies were the sugar-growing islands of the **West Indies**. Throughout the South and the West Indies, agricultural work was performed primarily by slave labor (see pages 69–70).

The Fur Trade in the North American Interior

A lucrative **fur trade** drew French, Dutch, and English traders and colonists to the interior of the North American continent—specifically the broad swath of land stretching north from the Ohio River toward the St. Lawrence River and Great Lakes. This fur trade led **Europeans** to reach accommodations with **American Indian** groups, in contrast to the agricultural settlements along the Atlantic Coast, where American Indians were often exterminated or removed. The increased trade in furs often destabilized American Indian communities by pushing native peoples to extend their traditional territory in search of more furs. This territorial expansion inevitably brought conflict with neighboring Indian groups. We see an increase in the intensity of warfare in the seventeenth and eighteenth centuries, as Indian groups, allied with and armed by competing European powers, fought for territory and trading privileges (see pages 76–79).

Wheat, Indentured Servants, and Redemptioners in the Middle Colonies

By the eighteenth century, settlers in the **middle colonies** of **Pennsylvania** and **New York**, many of them German and Scots-Irish immigrants, developed the cultivation of **wheat** and other cereal crops for export to Europe. Whereas the southern colonies used the slave system to solve the problem of finding laborers in the New World, the middle colonies tended to rely on **indentured servants** (see page 64) and **"redemptioners."** Redemptioners were transported to the New World by sea captains; they promised to pay for their passage once they arrived in the New World by either borrowing money from a friend or relative already there, or by contracting for several years of servitude. Redemptioners were at a distinct disadvantage as compared to indentured servants. Indentured servants generally worked out the details of their indenture back in Europe; they could negotiate and refuse unreasonable offers. Redemptioners, on the other hand—tired, ill-fed, frequently sick, and stuck on an unsanitary ship in a New World harbor—were in no position to negotiate effectively with potential masters. Over time, however, the initial difficulties faced by the redemptioners usually paid off. Once freed from their service, they thrived, particularly in Pennsylvania. The standard of living for typical Pennsylvania farmers was higher than in any other comparable agricultural region in the eighteenth-century world.

Fish and Lumber in New England

The **New England** countryside did not lend itself to growing profitable export crops. New England farmers tended to grow a variety of crops for local consumption. Many New Englanders engaged in **fishing** in order to participate in the Atlantic trade. **Salted fish**, primarily cod, made up a third of total exports from New England to Europe. **Livestock** and **timber** accounted for another third of New England exports. New Englanders acquired **molasses** from the sugar-growing British West Indies and distilled it into **rum**, which became an increasingly important export after 1700. These distillers also purchased French molasses, in violation of mercantilist trade principles (see page 74). Great Britain responded to this by passing the **Molasses Act** of 1733. The act, which was loosely enforced and routinely violated, placed a steep duty on foreign molasses (see page 76).

New England towns grew into commercial centers engaged in an Atlantic exchange with Europe, the West Indies, and Africa. The population of New England was the most homogeneously English of any of Great Britain's New World holdings. After the waves of **Puritan migrations** in the 1600s, few immigrants ended up in New England, favoring the middle colonies instead. In fact, many New Englanders left the region in the eighteenth century. The region grew through natural reproduction in the eighteenth century, but less rapidly than the middle colonies and the South, where settlers and slaves continued to arrive in significant numbers.

B. Trade, Disease, and Demographic Changes for American Indians

The expansion of the transatlantic trade dramatically altered the traditional cultures of American Indian peoples. Patterns of trade as well as the arrival of diseases reshaped their communities. Many American Indian tribes were devastated by disease, while others managed to maintain sustainable population levels. To some degree, the choices made by American Indians themselves played an important role in the outcome of increased contact with European colonists.

Contact, Disease, Warfare, and the Collapse of the Huron

The **Huron** people, of Ontario, first made contact with the French explorer, **Samuel de Champlain**, at the beginning of the seventeenth century. Soon after, in 1609, they made an alliance with the French. By the 1630s, increased contact with **French settlers**, including **Jesuit priests**, proved to be disastrous for the Huron. It is estimated that the Huron numbered between 20,000 and 40,000 at the time of European contact. As contact increased after 1634, a major epidemic of **measles** and **smallpox** afflicted the Huron tribe, resulting in the deaths of between one-half and two-thirds of the population.

The **Beaver Wars** (see page 76) further devastated the Huron. In 1649, an **Iroquois** war party of about a thousand warriors, supplied with firearms by their Dutch allies, destroyed Huron mission villages in Ontario, killing approximately 300 people. Iroquois warriors also killed several Jesuits. The Huron ended up fleeing from the Iroquois to an island in **Georgian Bay**, Ontario, where large numbers died due to harsh conditions and lack of food. Eventually, many Huron resettled in **Quebec** and others to the upper **Lake Michigan** region. The intensity of the new form of warfare unleashed by European contact completely upended traditional methods of resolving conflicts for many American Indian groups. In the end, entire communities were often destroyed or relocated.

The Catawba—Contact, Trade, and Cultural Adaptation

In the face of conquest and encroachment by European settlers, American Indian groups were often left with stark choices—work for the settlers, move inland, resist encroachment, or join other American Indian groups. The **Catawba** people of the **American Southeast** attempted to ensure their survival by making themselves useful to the advancing settlers. They had established contact with the towns of colonial South Carolina as **traveling peddlers**, selling goods such as **pottery**, **baskets**, and **moccasins**. Sustained contact with settlers altered Catawba culture in significant ways. The nature of basket-making and pottery changed, as Catawba artisans transformed ancient practices to meet heightened demand. By the 1750s, the introduction of **alcohol** as a form of payment for goods led to drunkenness and increased brawls and instability within the Catawba community. The Catawba had generally amicable relations with colonists, but prolonged contact slowly eroded traditional cultural ways.

C. British Imperial Policies

From the late seventeenth century through the middle of the eighteenth century, the British approach to governing their North American colonies changed dramatically. In the 1680s, the British attempted to exert greater control over the colonies, enforce mercantilist rules, and integrate many of them into a single administrative unit. Because of colonial resistance, these efforts failed. By the early 1700s, the British embarked on a policy of "salutary neglect," which allowed the colonies to develop without excessive oversight.

Mercantilism

Britain's ambitions in the New World were influenced by **mercantilism**—a set of economic and political ideas that shaped colonial policy for the major powers in the early modern world. Mercantilism holds that only a limited amount of wealth exists in the world. Nations increase their power by increasing their share of the world's wealth. Nations therefore try to maximize the amount of precious metals they hold. One way of acquiring precious metals is to maintain a favorable balance of trade, with the value of exports exceeding the value of imports. Mercantilist theory encourages nations to advance these goals by maintaining colonies so as to have a steady and inexpensive source for raw materials. The theory also holds that the colonies should not develop manufacturing but should purchase manufactured goods from the **"mother country."** The British government imposed several navigation acts (see below) on the American colonies to make sure they fulfilled their role.

Navigation Acts and Mercantilism

From the 1650s until the American Revolution, Britain's Parliament passed a number of **Navigation Acts**. The goal of the acts, in conformity with mercantilist principles, was to define the colonies as suppliers of raw materials to Britain and as markets for British manufactured items. Toward this end, Parliament developed a list of **"enumerated goods"**—goods from the colonies that could be shipped only to Britain. These included goods that were essential for ship building, such as tar, pitch, and trees for masts. Also, Britain insisted that profitable staple crops from the southern slave colonies, such as rice, tobacco, sugar, and indigo, could be shipped only to Britain. These goods were sold both within England and at a considerable profit to other countries. The enumeration of these goods was a double-edged sword; the colonies could not always negotiate the highest price for their

> **USING REASONING PROCESSES:**
> **COMPARISON**
>
> **Mercantilism Versus Capitalism**
>
> Be prepared to distinguish the economic ideas that shaped mercantilism from those that shaped capitalism. Mercantilism, for example, involved extensive government regulation of trade and economic activities. During the nineteenth century, the British government moved away from a mercantilist approach and fully embraced free trade and the laissez-faire economic principles espoused by Adam Smith. These principles, central to modern capitalism, have led to a reduction of formal trade barriers among nations. However, it would be inaccurate to characterize contemporary U.S. economic policies as laissez-faire. Government subsidies and tax breaks to corporations deviate from Smith's assertion that the "invisible hand" of the market should determine economic outcomes under capitalism.

goods, but they had a consistent market for them. Several of the Navigation Acts—such as the **Wool Act** (1699), the **Hat Act** (1732), and the **Iron Act** (1750)—restricted colonial manufacturing. These policies gave an advantage to manufacturers in Britain by guaranteeing them a steady supply of reasonably priced raw materials and protecting them from colonial competition.

Greater Imperial Control

Over the course of the seventeenth century, almost all the British colonies—**charter colonies** and **proprietary colonies**—were taken over directly by the **Crown** and became **royal colonies**, as the Crown attempted to tie the colonies more closely into the imperial system. In **Virginia**, this occurred early, after **King James I** revoked the charter of the **Virginia Company** in 1624 and made Virginia a royal colony under the control of a Crown-appointed governor. James had become alarmed at the level of violence directed against American Indians, at the high mortality rate among the colonists and at the general level of mismanagement in the colony.

The Dominion of New England

The shift toward greater imperial control in New England occurred in the late seventeenth century, in the wake of **King Philip's War** (see page 78). In the aftermath of the fighting, **King Charles II** sent an agent to New England to investigate the practices of the New Englanders. Charles II became increasingly resentful of the New Englanders, especially because English Puritans had executed his father, Charles I, during the **English Civil War**. The agent found ample evidence of New Englanders not living in conformity with mercantilist laws. In 1686, royal officials revoked the charters of all the colonies north of the Delaware River and formed one massive colony called the **Dominion of New England**. This new colony was ruled directly by a royal appointee, **Sir Edmund Andros**.

England's move to incorporate several of its North American colonies into a single administrative unit was met with resistance. New England Puritans were shocked at Andros's support for the **Anglican Church** and his refusal to enforce **Sabbath laws**. Throughout the affected colonies, his rigid tactics and stern demeanor aroused ire. Colonists insisted that he was rescinding their rights as Englishmen.

The Glorious Revolution and the Restoration of Colonial Charters

The **Dominion of New England** did not last long. Events in England again had a major impact on events in English North America. In the late 1600s, a crisis developed involving religion and succession to the throne. After King Charles II died, his brother **James II** became king (1685). James had previously converted to Catholicism. Many Protestants in England were troubled by this but were calmed by the fact that James's daughter, **Mary**, the heir apparent, was Protestant, having married **William of Orange**, a Dutch prince and leader of the republic. However, in 1688, James's wife bore a male child—a new heir apparent and a Catholic. If James's son assumed the throne, England would have a Catholic king and perhaps additional Catholic monarchs in successive generations. Protestant parliamentarians would not stand for this. They rose up in the **"Glorious Revolution"** (1688), inviting William and Mary to become England's monarchs. King James was deposed in this bloodless uprising. The Glorious Revolution empowered Parliament and ended absolute monarchy in England. It also led to the establishment of the **English Bill of Rights**. The turmoil in the mother country inspired New Englanders in 1689 to arrest Sir Edmund Andros and to do away with the Dominion of New England.

Lax Enforcement of Mercantilist Policies

Following the Glorious Revolution (1688) and the Dominion of New England (1686–1689), Great Britain attempted to incorporate the thirteen colonies more closely into the empire with new charters and royal governors. However, the difficulties and costs of carrying out imperial laws in a sprawling empire, thousands of miles from the mother country, contributed to lax enforcement of mercantilist rules. In the eighteenth century, the policy of lax enforcement, or **"salutary neglect,"** came to characterize Great Britain's relationship with the thirteen colonies. The policy is often attributed to Prime Minister **Robert Walpole** (1721–1742) because he urged the Crown to not excessively interfere with the profitable trade generated by the North American colonies. In this setting, colonists routinely smuggled banned goods into and out of the thirteen colonies. For example, the Molasses Act (1733) placed a prohibitive import tax on sugar and molasses from non-British colonies into North America. Boston merchants routinely flouted this law, importing illegal sugar to supply Massachusetts rum distilleries.

Topic 2.5 Interactions Between American Indians and Europeans

In the seventeenth and eighteenth centuries, conflict intensified in North America between rival European empires and between North American colonists and American Indians. A major source of conflict in colonial North America was competition over resources—notably land and furs.

A. Imperial Conflicts and North American Political Instability

The political situation in North America grew increasingly unstable in the seventeenth and eighteenth centuries. Old rivalries in Europe among the French, Dutch, British, and Spanish spilled over to the New World, and in the process drew various American Indian groups into these conflicts. The introduction of European firearms into conflicts among American Indians altered the political and military landscape of North America.

The Beaver Wars (1640–1701)

Traditional rivalries between American Indian groups took on new dimensions in the age of European colonization. Several European powers formed alliances with American Indian groups. Further, the introduction of **European firearms**, often obtained in the **fur trade**, intensified the impact of armed conflicts. The **Beaver Wars**, an especially deadly series of events in the middle and late seventeenth century, illustrate the destabilizing influence of trade and European firepower on American Indian relations.

Competition in the fur trade, as the name of the wars implies, led to violent conflict. Both the **Dutch** and the **French** had established trading posts to obtain furs from native groups in exchange for a variety of goods, including firearms. French traders established a series of trading posts along the **St. Lawrence River** in the early 1600s, aligning themselves with **Algonquian-speaking tribes**. The Dutch had established a trading post at present-day **Albany** in 1614, at the edge of territory controlled by the **Iroquois**, and had developed an alliance and profitable trade with the **Iroquois Confederacy**. The Iroquois hoped to expand their trading network, but the **Huron**, an Algonquian-speaking tribe, stood in their way. By 1645 long-simmering tensions between the Dutch-allied Iroquois and the French-allied Algonquian-speaking tribes of the **Great Lakes** region, notably the Huron, exploded into open warfare.

Dutch rule was superseded by the **British**, who took control of **New Netherland** in 1664. The British allied themselves with the Iroquois Confederacy in its ongoing battles with the French and their American Indian allies until the Beaver Wars ended in 1701, with the **Great Peace of Montreal**. The Iroquois were able to expand their territory and influence; the Huron suffered disaster (see page 73). The Iroquois also realized that they held the balance of power between the British and the French. The wars, the pressures of the fur trade, and the introduction of European firearms all contributed to a realignment of American Indian alliances and a reorganization of their societies.

The French and Indian Wars and Control of North America (1688–1763)

There were four significant conflicts for control of much of North America between 1688 and 1763. These wars, labeled the **French and Indian Wars**, include King William's War (1688–1697), Queen Anne's War (1702–1713), and King George's War (1744–1748). The fourth war, called the French and Indian War (1754–1763), was the most decisive, eliminating the French military and governmental presence in North America (see more on the French and Indian War, pages 93–97).

These wars followed similar patterns. For one, the first three (each named after the reigning British monarch) grew out of conflicts in Europe between Great Britain and France; the fourth war originated in North America and turned into a worldwide conflict between the two empires. Second, the wars intensified ongoing rivalries between American Indian groups. Some tribes formed alliances with the British and other tribes with the French. American Indian groups were able to maintain a degree of autonomy in North America through the first half of the eighteenth century through these alliances. As long as neither the British nor the French was able to achieve a decisive victory, American Indians were able to maintain some control of their territory. This changed, as we shall see in Period 3, with the complete withdrawal of the French presence from North America following the French and Indian War (see pages 95-97). Finally, the wars tended to increase the bonds between the British colonists and the government of Great Britain. As long as enemies threatened British colonial interests along disputed and ambiguous borderlands, the colonists felt the need of British military might. After the defeat of the French in 1763, colonists began to reevaluate their role within the British Empire.

King William's War (1688-1697)

King William's War was the New World manifestation of the **Nine Years' War** in Europe between France and an alliance of countries, including Great Britain. The war in the New World had two sources. First, tensions between American Indian groups allied with the British (including the Iroquois Confederacy) and those allied with the French led to fighting in New York and Canada. Second, skirmishes occurred when British colonists encroached upon the French colony of **Acadia** (which includes present-day Nova Scotia, New Brunswick, and Maine north of the Kennebec River). Following the war, the Iroquois Confederacy skillfully negotiated the **Grand Settlement of 1701** with France and other Indian nations. For the next fifty years, the Iroquois were primarily neutral in the struggle over control of North America.

Queen Anne's War (1702-1713)

Queen Anne's War occurred on the border with Canada and in the American South. In the North, French and British forces continued the struggle for territory as they had earlier in King William's War. Fighting in the North included a bold and destructive raid by the **Wabanaki Confederacy**, with French support, on **Deerfield, Massachusetts**. In the South, European powers and allied American Indian groups fought for control of territory. British colonists had enlisted the **Chickasaw** people to procure enslaved people from their traditional enemy, the **Choctaw** people. Meanwhile, French fur traders along the Mississippi River had formed an alliance with the Choctaw. At the same time, tensions emerged between Great Britain and Spain over the boundary between Spanish Florida and British Carolina. The French and Spanish formed an alliance, also enlisting the **Apalachee**, to challenge the British presence in the South. The ensuing war did not settle boundary issues, but it weakened the Spanish presence in Florida and devastated American Indians in Spanish Florida.

King George's War (1744-1748)

The third conflict between the French and the British, **King George's War** (1744-1748), was fought in New York, Massachusetts, New Hampshire, and Nova Scotia. The war included a successful siege by New England soldiers on the newly built French **Fortress of Louisbourg** in Nova Scotia. French and Indian forces destroyed Saratoga, New York. This war did not settle ongoing territorial disputes. In the peace treaty, the British agreed to return the fort at Louisbourg to the French. This decision angered the northern colonies, which had lost a large number of men to cold and disease while occupying the fort during the harsh winter after the siege.

B. British Colonial Expansion and Conflicts with American Indians

As British colonial populations grew, colonists pushed inland, beyond their initial settlements. As they encroached upon lands held by native peoples, a series of military confrontations occurred between colonists and Indians.

Unlike the imperial struggles that occurred throughout North America (see pages 76–77), these conflicts were carried out by the colonists themselves. In many ways, these conflicts shaped the identity of the colonists in addition to transforming the lives of American Indian communities.

The Pequot War (1634–1638)

Contact between American Indians and British colonists grew increasingly violent in New England, just as it had been in Virginia (see page 63). The intensity of the clashes in New England led to major demographic changes there, as American Indians died in large numbers, with survivors moving farther into the interior of the region. The **Puritan** project of building an ideal community did not preclude them from forcing American Indian populations off land the Puritans intended to settle. The most violent episode in the first years of settlement was the **Pequot War**. The colonies of **Massachusetts Bay** and **Plymouth** worked in alliance with each other and with the **Narragansett** and the **Mohegan** peoples to defeat the **Pequots**. Later, further warfare would virtually eliminate a cohesive native presence from New England (see below).

King Philip's War (1675–1678)

Relations between New England colonists and Indians were relatively peaceful after the Pequot War of the 1630s (see above). However, violent conflict occurred again in the 1670s. The **Wampanoags**, led by **Chief Massasoit**, had forged an alliance with the Pilgrims in 1621, and afterward, the Wampanoags and the Plymouth settlers maintained peaceful relations. However, by the 1670s, relations had deteriorated. New Englanders had steadily been pushing into the interior, onto Wampanoag lands. The catalyst for combat was the 1675 execution of three Wampanoags who had been tried in a Plymouth court for killing a Christianized Wampanoag. The chief of the Wampanoag, **Metacomet**, also known to whites as **King Philip**, launched an attack on a string of Massachusetts towns. Several towns were destroyed and over a thousand colonists were killed. The counterattack by the New Englanders was fierce. They received crucial support from the Mohawks, who were longtime foes of the Wampanoags. Metacomet, the grandson of Massasoit, was killed by a group of Mohawks, and several Wampanoag villages were destroyed by the colonists. By the spring of 1676, over 40 percent of the Wampanoag were killed. The war was catastrophic for both sides— it was the deadliest of the wars of European settlement in North America in regard to the percentage of the populations of each side killed.

"Praying Indians" in Puritan New England

Some New England Indian groups mounted armed resistance to encroachments by the English; these efforts—the **Pequot War** (1634–1638) and **King Philip's War** (1675–1678)—ended tragically for the native peoples (see above). Others made efforts to coexist with the Puritan settlers of New England, including converting to Christianity. Puritan missionaries established **"praying towns"** for these **"praying Indians."** By the 1670s, there were fourteen "praying towns" in New England. "Praying Indians" were still seen by the Puritans as second-class citizens. Puritans insisted that the converted Christian Indians wear European-style clothing and that they completely abandon their spiritual traditions (in contrast with French Jesuit missionaries in Canada, who accepted that native peoples might combine elements of Catholicism with their traditional beliefs). In the end, the "praying towns" tended to impose English practices on the Indians rather than allowing native peoples to retain some elements of their traditional ways.

Racial Hierarchy and American Indians

The attitudes of English colonists toward American Indians changed over the course of the seventeenth century, as did their attitude toward enslaved Africans. Earlier in the century, the primary goal of the English settlers was to maintain peace with the native peoples. The early English settlements were precarious; maintaining peace was imperative. In this situation, English settlers made efforts to understand their neighbors and to figure out ways to coexist. As the century progressed and as the settlements became growing colonies, the colonists' primary desire was no longer to maintain the peace, but was to acquire Indian land. As the English colonists expanded their land holdings, violent conflicts with American Indians inevitably ensued. This process of expansion and conflict can be seen in King Philip's War in 1675 (see page 77). In the context of these clashes, the English colonists increasingly saw the American Indians as savages. **"Savagery"** became not just a description of American Indian behavior, but also a trait of their race. As the seventeenth century progressed, this racial hierarchy hardened and, in the minds of the English, justified the continued exploitation of American Indian lands.

C. Spain and American Indians in North America

The Spanish pattern of colonization differed from the English pattern. To a large degree, these divergent patterns reflected the cultural norms of each colonizing power as well as the power dynamics that developed between the colonizers and the colonized. Spanish colonists were more ready to make some accommodations to American Indian cultural ways, in contrast with English efforts, which more often resulted in complete destruction of American Indian communities.

Pueblo Revolt

By the second half of the seventeenth century, **Pueblo Indians** in **New Mexico** had grown increasingly resentful of Spanish rule. The Spanish *encomienda* **system** undermined the traditional economy of the Pueblos, forcing them to labor in mines and fields (see page 50). In addition, the Spanish outlawed traditional Pueblo religious practices. In 1680, these grievances came to the surface in the **Pueblo Revolt**, also known as **Popé's Rebellion**. The rebellion was centered in Santa Fe and resulted in attacks on Spanish Franciscan priests as well as ordinary Spaniards. More than 300 Spaniards were killed. Spanish colonists fled, but returned later in the decade. As a result of the uprising, Spanish authorities appointed a public defender to protect native rights and agreed to allow the Pueblo to continue their cultural practices. Also, each Pueblo family was granted land. The outcome of this rebellion was markedly different from conflicts between English settlers and native peoples, whose clashes usually resulted in Indian removal or eradication.

Topic 2.6 Slavery in the British Colonies

Slavery developed in British North America in response to the economic, demographic, and geographic characteristics of the colonies. Slavery was part of English colonial North America from the earliest years. In 1619, twenty Africans arrived in Virginia, probably as slaves. However, slavery did not become central to the southern economy until later in the seventeenth century.

A. The Development of British Slavery

A persistent problem of the wealthy planters in the British New World was attracting enough settlers to do the difficult work cultivating and processing staple crops. In the 1600s, the system of indentured servitude was used to facilitate the migration of workers to the New World. However, the system did not provide an adequate number of workers. As a result, slavery developed to meet this chronic need for additional workers. All the British colonies participated, to some degree, in the Atlantic slave trade (see more on the Atlantic slave trade, pages 71–72). Few slaves were used by the small-scale farms of New England. Most prominent port cities had significant numbers of enslaved laborers. Large slave populations existed in the colonies of the Chesapeake region as well as in the Deep South. Within the British colonial world, the great majority of enslaved Africans ended up in the West Indies.

Bacon's Rebellion and the Development of Slavery in Virginia

In the latter half of the seventeenth century, Virginia planters began to experience problems with the system of indentured servitude (see page 64). Upon the end of their indenture, these men and women were generally not integrated into Virginia society. Many moved from the fertile tidewater region of Virginia into the hilly piedmont region. This inland region was also where many American Indians had settled after being dislocated by the initial wave of English settlers. The former indentured servants grew resentful of the taxes they were required to pay the Virginia government and of their lack of representation in the House of Burgesses. Things grew worse for them as violence intensified on the frontier between these hardscrabble farmers and the nearby American Indians.

In 1676, frontier tensions erupted into a full-scale rebellion, known as **Bacon's Rebellion**. **Nathaniel Bacon**, a lower-level planter, championed the cause of the frontier farmers and became their leader. **Governor William Berkeley** refused to offer help in fighting the American Indians. Many of the wealthier Virginians engaged in a profitable trade with Indians and, therefore, did not want war waged against them. When colonial authorities refused to aid the frontier farmers, Bacon led a group of them into **Jamestown**, burning the homes of the elite planters and even the capital building. During the rebellion, Bacon himself died of disease, and the rebellion was soon put down. The rebellion proved to be an important turning point in colonial history, as the elite planters turned increasingly to enslaved Africans as their primary labor force.

> **USING HISTORICAL THINKING SKILLS:**
> **DEVELOPMENTS AND PROCESSES**
>
> **The Transition from Servitude to Slavery**
>
> Historians view Bacon's Rebellion as a key event in the shift from indentured servitude to slavery as the main form of labor in the South. African slavery allowed the planters to emphasize a commonality of interests between themselves and the frontier farmers. Although the position of these frontier farmers did not appreciably improve, they could at least take solace in the fact that they were among the free Virginians and members of the race they were told was superior.

B. Ideas about Race and the Development of Slavery in British North America

Slavery in British North America differed from earlier slave systems in other parts of the world in several fundamental ways. British notions of racial hierarchy reinforced the idea that slavery would be a permanent condition for both sub-Saharan Africans who were enslaved and their descendants.

The Origins of Racial Hierarchies

Spanish, French, and Dutch colonies, which had fewer female colonists, were relatively accepting of intermarriages with native peoples, and unions with Africans were fairly common in the Spanish colonies. In contrast, the British colonies attracted both male and female colonists and did not tolerate intermarriage. In this context, a rigid **racial hierarchy** developed in the British colonies.

The racial hierarchy that developed within the British colonial world followed a long tradition in English thought of making divisions within humanity. These divisions—between civilized and barbaric, between Christian and heathen, between English and non-English—shaped English understandings of the world. Historians continue to debate whether racism toward Africans developed as a result of the enslavement of Africans, or whether racist notions predated and allowed for the enslavement of Africans (see "Subject to Debate," page 86).

> **USING REASONING PROCESSES:**
> **COMPARISON**
>
> **Slavery in the North and South**
>
> In an essay that addresses slavery in the colonial period, do not ignore slavery in the northern colonies. Although slavery came to define southern society in the nineteenth century, slavery was legal in all thirteen colonies at one time or another in the seventeenth and eighteenth centuries. Northern slaves worked as sailors, domestic servants, longshoremen, and artisans' assistants. Colonial New York, especially, had a large slave population. In the 1740s, 20 percent of New York's inhabitants were slaves and 40 percent of households had at least one slave (see page 69). (By comparison, slaves comprised 40 percent of Virginia's population in 1740, and 70 percent of South Carolina's.) Because the northern colonies did not have an extensive export agricultural sector, slavery in the North was never as strong as it was in the South, but it did exist.

The Nature of Slavery in British North America

Historians note that slavery in the British colonies evolved considerably during the seventeenth century. Evidence suggests that the few slaves present in colonial Virginia in the early seventeenth century were treated in a manner similar to other "unfree" people, such as indentured servants. Over the course of the seventeenth century, however, rules about slavery hardened in colonial Virginia. In 1640, an indentured servant of African descent, **John Casor**, was declared by a civil court to be a slave for life. The case represents an important turning point in the shift toward permanent enslavement. Later, in 1662, the Virginia legislature passed a law stating that the child of a slave woman would inherit its mother's status—that is, would be a slave for life. This principle, called in Latin ***partus sequitur ventrum***, broke with traditional English common law; previously, the child would inherit its father's status, meaning the child of a white man and an enslaved woman would be considered a free person. This principle had a major impact on the dynamics of slavery in the British colonial system. In effect, it sanctioned the rape of slave women by their white owners.

Even the language that English settlers used to describe Africans changed by the end of the century. Early in the seventeenth century, English accounts of African slaves in Virginia usually describe them as "Negroes." By the end of the century, they are more frequently referred to as "black," a color with negative overtones for English people at the time. Colonists began to identify themselves as "white"—a color that denoted purity and beauty. After 1660, laws in Virginia made it clear that slavery was a permanent and inherited status. By the end of the century, white Virginians came to see "blacks" and "slaves" as nearly synonymous terms.

C. Resistance to Slavery

Against great odds, slaves found ways to resist the brutality, humiliations, grueling work, and dehumanizing nature of slavery and to maintain their sense of family, gender systems, culture, and religion. Resistance was both overt and covert.

The Stono Rebellion

The main fear of slave owners in the British colonies was overt resistance in the form of violent rebellion. Such rebellions were uncommon. Since slave owners and white authorities had the law behind them and a monopoly on weaponry, outright rebellion was tantamount to suicide. Yet, attempts at rebellion did occur. The most prominent slave rebellion of the colonial period was the **Stono Rebellion** in **South Carolina** (1739). The rebellion, initiated by twenty slaves who obtained weapons by attacking a country store, led to the deaths of twenty slave owners and the plundering of half a dozen plantations. But the rebellion was quickly put down and the participants beheaded with their heads placed on mileposts along the road. Lesser forms of resistance, however, occurred on a daily basis, from working slowly to breaking tools. Also, slaves resisted by retaining cultural connections to Africa, maintaining traditional names and practices (see more on resistance to slavery, pages 164–166).

Topic 2.7 Colonial Society and Culture

Great Britain and its thirteen North American colonies participated in political, cultural, and economic exchanges. These exchanges led to stronger bonds between Great Britain and the colonies and reshaped the worldviews and prerogatives of British colonists in the New World. Ultimately, the priorities and interests of the thirteen colonies diverged from those of Great Britain, leading to tensions and to resistance on the part of the colonies.

A. Religious Pluralism in Colonial America

A variety of religious and spiritual movements flourished in colonial America. Many of these movements grew out of religious debates in Great Britain, while others reflected the religious sensibilities of immigrants from the Germanic states, Ireland, and elsewhere in Europe.

The "Great Awakening"

Protestant leaders in colonial America faced several challenges in the early 1700s, notably a decline in church membership and a lessening of religious zeal (see page 67), as well as the rise of Enlightenment philosophy, which challenged religious orthodoxy (see below). By the 1730s, several charismatic ministers sought to take action and infuse a new passion into religious practice. These ministers and their followers were part of a religious resurgence known as the **"Great Awakening."** The origins of the Great Awakening can be traced to Great Britain. The most well-known Great Awakening preacher was the English minister, **George Whitefield**. Whitefield visited the North American colonies seven times, holding large revival meetings in dozens of locales in the 1740s and bringing huge audiences to a state of religious ecstasy. Other itinerant preachers brought an emotional religious message to thousands of colonists. The leaders of the movement took a more emotional, and less cerebral, approach to religion than seventeenth-century Puritans had. In Massachusetts, the Congregationalist minister **Jonathan Edwards** delivered his most famous sermon, **"Sinners in the Hands of an Angry God,"** to a mesmerized audience. The Great Awakening's core message was that anyone could be saved and that people could make choices in their lives that would affect their afterlife. This was in stark contrast with traditional Puritan ideas of **"original sin"** and **predestination**. In this regard, the Great Awakening was more egalitarian and democratic.

Immigration and Dissenting Denominations

In the seventeenth century, the great majority of churches in the British colonies were either Anglican or Congregational. These "established" churches were recognized and funded by the various colonial administrations. This was not the case in Rhode Island, New Jersey, and Pennsylvania, which separated government from religious institutions. Quakerism continued to have a strong presence in Pennsylvania (see page 69).

However, by the mid-eighteenth century, acceptance of dissenting Protestant denominations became widespread throughout the colonies. Baptist and Methodist churches grew out of the Great Awakening. In addition, immigrants from Europe brought new denominations with them. The largest group of immigrants came from the Germanic states (over 100,000 in the colonial period). Most of these Germans settled in the backcountry areas of Pennsylvania, New York, and the South. Many were Lutheran and Calvinist; smaller sects of Mennonites, Moravians, and Dunkers were also established in Germanic areas of the colonies. Urban centers such as New York, with a great diversity of immigrant populations, including Sephardic Jews, added to the religious diversity of colonial America.

Deism and the Enlightenment

In the 1700s, many educated colonists moved away from the rigid doctrines of Puritanism and other faiths and adopted a form of worship known as *deism*. In a deist cosmology, God is seen as a distant entity. Deists did not see God intervening in the day-to-day affairs of humanity. God had created the world and had also created a series of natural laws to govern it. In their beliefs, deists were aligned with the **Enlightenment** ethos, including the aspiration to understand Earth's natural laws. Deists saw God as a great clockmaker, with the Earth being analogous to a clock. Although God created the clock, it is the mechanisms of the clock, rather than God's interventions, that move the hour and the minute hands forward.

B. The Anglicization of British North America

The imprint of Great Britain on its North American colonies cannot be overstated. Many ideas and structures—from self-government to legal codes, from commerce to print culture, from religious toleration to Enlightenment thought—developed in Great Britain and found fertile soil in the New World.

Emulating the British

Many residents of the British colonies—especially the more well-to-do—consciously attempted to model their lives in the New World on British patterns of culture. In many respects, each of the American colonies had more interactions with Great Britain—through trade and communication—than they had with the other colonies. Wealthy merchants and planters frequently sent their sons to Great Britain for schooling. Colonists of even modest means became increasingly interested in acquiring British-made goods. Colonists purchased British-made bedding, clocks, silver, china, wigs, books, and more. For many colonists, the pioneering ways of the seventeenth century, characterized by homemade goods, gave way to a more **consumerist culture** in the eighteenth century. For colonists of means, connections with British culture and goods allowed them to elevate their status; they did not want to be seen as provincial bumpkins on the edge of the civilized world.

Trans-Atlantic Print Culture

Residents of the thirteen colonies had a high degree of literacy, which created a demand for printed materials. By the middle of the eighteenth century, Boston had eight printers, and New York and Philadelphia each had two. By the 1730s, newspapers existed in most colonial cities, including Charleston, South Carolina and Williamsburg, Virginia. **John Peter Zenger** created the *New York Weekly Journal* in 1733 (see more on Zenger and his trial for libel, page 85). **Benjamin Franklin** took the reins of the *Pennsylvania Gazette* in 1729. These newspapers devoted a great deal of space to European affairs—at first, reprinting items from the British press, and later writing articles covering both European and local affairs. By the time of the American Revolution, over forty weekly newspapers existed in colonial America.

Anglicanism and Enlightenment Thinking—from Great Britain to North America

In the 1600s and 1700s, the Anglican Church in Great Britain, and subsequently in colonial America, began to incorporate Enlightenment ideas. Anglicanism in the seventeenth century was beset with internal strife between High Church and Low Church factions. The more conservative and ritualistic **High Church** was embraced by the Archbishop of Canterbury, **William Laud** (1633–1640). His strict interpretation of dogma fueled the rise of oppositional Puritanism and the exodus of Puritans to the New World in the 1630s. Later, some Anglican theologians, influenced by **Enlightenment** thinking, embraced a more reform-minded, liberal approach to spirituality. This reform-minded approach to religion, referred to as the **Low Church,** tried to combine Enlightenment rationalism with broad-minded theology. Allowing for much latitude in matters of faith and practice, Low Churchmen are also known as **Latitudinarians**. These reformers, rejecting superstition and rigidity, gained a foothold in England and in the colonies. **Harvard University** (founded in 1636) moved in this more liberal, independent direction under the leadership of **John Leverett, Jr.**, who was installed as president in 1708.

Religious Toleration

The idea of **religious toleration**—allowing religious groups outside of the official, or established, religion to practice freely—had European roots and New World manifestations. In both the Old World and the New World, the concept was the object of much debate and contestation. The concept has a long history in Europe. The **Edict of Nantes** (1598) allowed Calvinist Protestants in France (known as **Huguenots**) to practice their religion in the predominantly Catholic country. Several Enlightenment thinkers advocated religious toleration. **Baruch Spinoza**, the Dutch philosopher from a Portuguese Jewish family, embraced the idea of religious toleration in the mid-1600s. In 1689, amid concerns of a Catholic ascendancy to the throne in England, **John Locke** wrote "A Letter Concerning Toleration," urging toleration of different Christian sects. Later, the French philosopher, **Voltaire**, wrote "A Treatise on Toleration" (1763), echoing Locke's sentiments but extending them to all faiths—including Islam and Judaism.

In colonial America, while religious orthodoxy shaped New England life, the idea of religious toleration emerged, haltingly, in several colonies. In 1649, Maryland passed the **Act of Religious Toleration**, guaranteeing rights to Christians of most denominations. The act did not apply to Jews or Muslims, nor to Christian sects that did not believe in the holy trinity. In Dutch New Amsterdam, several residents wrote the **Flushing Remonstrance** in 1657, requesting that **Peter Stuyvesant** lift his ban on Quaker worship in the colony. Both documents are seen as early expressions of religious tolerance—an idea that would later come to fruition in the First Amendment of the United States Constitution, guaranteeing freedom of religion.

C. Diverging Interests—British Policies and Colonial Dissatisfaction

Mercantilist principles guided British policies in the New World. However, many colonists began to chafe at imperial policies and developed a set of priorities often at odds with the powers in Britain. Colonists grew increasingly dissatisfied over a number of issues.

Tensions over Imperial Control

Tensions developed between Great Britain and its North American colonies in the late seventeenth century and the first half of the eighteenth century. Colonial resistance to British policies became evident in the years during and following the **Dominion of New England** (see page 75). The Dominion of New England had been established in 1686 when British authorities rescinded the charters of the colonies from New Jersey to Massachusetts and took direct control of these colonies. This direct control of much of colonial North America ended as the **Glorious Revolution** occurred in Great Britain in 1688. As news of the Glorious Revolution arrived in America, colonists used the opportunity to jail royal administers, including **Sir Edmund Andros**, the governor of the Dominion of New England.

In New York in 1689, rebels led by **Jacob Leisler** took power from royal authorities. The rebel movement drove Andros's lieutenant governor in New York into exile, captured Fort James in lower Manhattan, and established a new government. Also in 1689, Protestants in Maryland deposed the absentee proprietor of the colony, **Charles Calvert, 3rd Baron Baltimore** (a Catholic). They assumed (incorrectly) that Calvert had sided with the Catholic King James against William and Mary. These rebellious governments were short lived, but they reflected ongoing dissatisfaction with British policies.

The end of the Dominion of New England and the ouster of Andros did not mean the end of imperial oversight. In some ways, the opposite occurred, as the new royal charters of the affected colonies affirmed royal control and bound the colonies closer into the imperial system. As Britain attempted to exert greater control, many colonists grew critical of the erosion of the autonomy they had come to enjoy living on the edge of the British Empire. When royal governors attempted to enforce navigation acts and crack down on smuggling, many colonists protested and called for rejecting governors' requests for funding. Many residents of the thirteen colonies remained firmly loyal to British rule and thrived economically within the empire. Others, however, began to challenge imperial control.

D. The Background to Colonial Resistance to Imperial Control

Colonists who opposed and resisted British rule in the first half of the eighteenth century drew on a variety of sources—the growing

> **USING HISTORICAL THINKING SKILLS:**
> **CONTEXTUALIZATION**
>
> **Colonial Democracy in Context**
>
> It might be tempting to argue in an essay that the roots of American democracy can be found in the history of the colonial period. One can cite the Mayflower Compact, the House of Burgesses, the Flushing Remonstrance, the Zenger trial, and the remarkable degree of local democracy found in New England town meetings. However, these elements can be put into a broader context of undemocratic features—coerced labor (slavery and servitude); theocratic rules and government-established churches; edicts from the distant British monarchy; and a culture of deference and rigid class distinctions. Such contextualization can complicate assertions of the democratic nature of colonial society.

influence of Enlightenment thinkers, a long history of local self-government, new ideas about liberty, greater religious diversity, and the growing perception that the imperial system was rife with corruption.

Enlightenment Thinking and Resistance to British Rule

Many colonists who challenged imperial control drew on the political thought of the **Enlightenment**. **John Locke**, the British political theorist, was widely read in the colonies. He insisted that the primary role of government was to protect certain "natural rights"—including life, liberty, and property. Locke broke with an earlier Enlightenment thinker, **Thomas Hobbes.** Hobbes emphasized the selfish, "nasty," and "brutish" nature of humanity, and concluded that humans need ironfisted rulers to keep them in line. Locke shared with Hobbes the notion of the self-interested nature of humans, but he was much more optimistic about the ability of humans to use reason and to make sound decisions about governance. His thinking deeply influenced the colonial idea of the legitimacy of self-government (see more on John Locke, page 102).

Influence of the Country Party and "Cato's Letters"

Colonial resistance to British imperial control drew some of its inspiration from an unlikely source—British writers. In Great Britain, reformers and radicals developed a critique of the British government based on perceptions of corruption, wastefulness, and tyranny. These writers and reformers were labeled the **"Country Party"** because they were seen as representing the interest of the entire country. The opposite tendency was labeled by critics, the **"Court Party,"** because its members operated within the inner sanctum of power in London. The Country Party was critical of Prime Minister **Robert Walpole** for amassing power and wealth at the expense of the elected members of Parliament. The Country Party, also labeled **"Commonwealth men,"** accused overreaching political figures, notably Walpole, of upsetting the balanced constitution of Great Britain and endangering individual liberties. These ideas became popular among the North American colonists, providing an intellectual and political framework for grievances against the imperial system.

One of the more popular Country Party essayists in the American press was **"Cato"**—the pseudonym for the writing team of **John Trenchard** and **Thomas Gordon**. They borrowed the name "Cato" from the foe of Julius Caesar who passionately defended republican values. The essays, labeled **"Cato's Letters,"** were first published between 1720 and 1723 in British newspapers and were frequently reprinted in the colonies. "Cato's Letters," later collected in the volume *Essays on Liberty, Civil and Religious*, condemned corruption within the British political system and warned against tyrannical rule. The collection was a best-selling book in the colonies and was frequently cited by the **Patriot** cause during the American Revolution.

American Legal Procedures and Freedom of the Press

During the eighteenth century, the British colonies developed legal systems and procedures that differed in significant ways from the British system. This was partly caused by the lack of British-trained lawyers in the New World and partly the result of local circumstances. Chronic labor shortages in the colonies, for example, led to less reliance on imprisonment as a punishment (removing potential workers from the labor force), and greater reliance on whipping, branding, and public shaming. In general, procedures were streamlined and simplified in the New World.

Further, colonial legal practices redefined crimes, such as **libel**. In Great Britain, any printed criticisms of public officials could be considered libelous. In the colonies, courts ruled that critical items could not be considered libelous if they were truthful. In 1735, New York City newspaper publisher, **John Peter Zenger**, was arrested and charged with seditious libel for printing articles critical of the royal governor. His lawyer successfully argued that he had the right to print such articles because they were truthful. The jury acquitted Zenger. In the wake of the case, more newspaper publishers and editors were willing to write articles critical of royal authorities. The verdict and its effects were indicative of the value placed on a free press in the colonies.

Topic 2.8 Subject to Debate

Regional Differences in British North America

There are several important historiographical questions surrounding the English settlement of North America. One question that has engaged historians is the comparisons between the New England and the Chesapeake colonies in the seventeenth century. Historical accounts have looked for differences between the northern and southern regions—examining such differences almost from the first day of settlement. To some degree historians can be faulted for reading the more recent past (the Civil War) into the more distant past (the colonies in the 1600s) and concluding that the bloodshed of the 1860s was rooted in seventeenth-century patterns of development. It is open to interpretation whether the differences between the regions are more important than the commonalities.

Slavery and the Development of Racism

Historians continue to debate several important issues about the development of slavery. Historical work has examined the relationship between racism and slavery. Did African slavery develop because of preconceived notions of racial hierarchies, or did these notions of superior and inferior races develop over time to justify the continued enslavement of hundreds of thousands and, ultimately, millions of Black Americans?

How Oppressed Were British Colonists?

In addition, historians have debated whether the thirteen colonies' ties to Great Britain were beneficial or not to the colonies. On the one hand, mercantilist rules restricted colonial economic activity. The economic activity that was permitted was designed to benefit Great Britain more than the colonies. To support the argument that mercantilist rules hampered colonial economic development, historians have cited many colonists complaining of being "oppressed" and reduced to the status of "slaves." Other historians note that many of the mercantilist rules were simply ignored by the colonists.

Practice Multiple-Choice Questions

> **DIRECTIONS:** Pick the letter that best answers the following questions.

Questions 1–2 refer to the following passage:

"In spite of the proximity of certain Puritan values to the rising capitalistic ethic, Puritanism was more medieval than modern in its economic theory and practice. The idea of unrestrained economic individualism would have seemed a dangerous notion to any self-respecting Puritan. The statute books and court records of seventeenth-century Massachusetts abound in examples of price and wage controls instituted by the government of the colony. The Puritans, furthermore, always looked upon wealth as a gift from God given in the form of a trust; and they emphasized not only the benefits that accrued from work and wealth, but also their duties and responsibilities. In 1639, for example, one of the richest merchants in the colony was fined by the General Court (the highest legislative body) for excessive profiteering, despite the fact that there was no statute against the practice. The Puritans could never separate religion and business, and they often reiterated the medieval conception of the 'just price.'

"In the long run, however, the Puritan ethic, when divorced from its religious background, did serve to quicken and stimulate the spirit of capitalism. The limitations placed by the Puritans on the individual and the freedom of movement within society were subordinated as the time went on in favor of the enterprising and driving individual who possessed the ability and ambition to rise through his own exertions."

—Gerald N. Grob and Robert N. Beck, *American Ideas*, 1963, p. 63

1. In the second paragraph, the authors discuss the 1639 legal proceedings against "one of the richest merchants in the colony" in order to show that

    (A) impoverished New Englanders used the legal system to vent class frustrations against the wealthy.
    (B) political corruption was common in Puritan New England.
    (C) Puritan magistrates were evenhanded in that they prosecuted anyone—rich or poor—who expressed heretical religious views.
    (D) the Puritans attempted to enforce economic values that emphasized communal notions of fairness over free-market individualism.

2. Which of the following reflects the main point that authors Grob and Beck are making in the passage?

    (A) Puritan restraints on economic activity prevented the economy of New England from growing, leading it to fall behind the South and the middle colonies during the colonial period.
    (B) The economy of Puritan New England came to resemble the feudal economy of medieval Europe, dominated by large estates passed on from father to son over several generations.
    (C) The economy of New England began to thrive only when non-Puritan immigrants began to move into New England after the 1640s.
    (D) As the seventeenth century progressed, the decline of Puritan orthodoxy, combined with Puritan patterns of work, allowed for the emergence of a market-oriented economy.

Questions 3–5 are based on the following passage:

"Asked what causes or motives the said Indian rebels had for renouncing the law of God and obedience to his Majesty, and for committing so many kinds of crimes, [Josephe answered] the causes they have were alleged ill treatment and injuries received from [Spanish authorities], because they beat them, took away what they had, and made them work without pay. Thus he replies.

"Asked if he has learned if it has come to his notice during the time that he has been here the reason why the apostates burned the images, churches, and things pertaining to divine worship, making a mockery and a trophy of them, killing the priests and doing the other things they did, he said that he knows and had heard it generally stated that while they were besieging the villa the rebellious traitors burned the church and shouted in loud voices, 'Now the God of the Spaniards, who was their father, is dead, and Santa Maria, who was their mother, and the saints, who were pieces of rotten wood,' saying that only their own god lived. . . . The captains and the chiefs ordered that the names of Jesus and Mary should nowhere be uttered. . . . He has seen many houses of idolatry which they have built, dancing the dance of the cachina [part of a traditional Indian religious ceremony], which this declarant has also danced. Thus he replies to the question."

—Account of questioning of Josephe, a Spanish-speaking Pueblo Indian, by Spanish authorities following the Pueblo Revolt of 1680 (1681)

3. The events described by Josephe in the account above reflect

   (A) adaptation by American Indians to European cultural practices.
   (B) resistance by American Indians to Spanish colonial practices.
   (C) the high rate of intermarriage between American Indians and Spaniards in the New World.
   (D) conflict among American Indian groups as a result of displacement and relocation by Spanish colonial forces.

4. The testimony of Josephe indicates that the Pueblo Indians

   (A) were thoroughly Christianized by 1680.
   (B) practiced nonviolent means of protest.
   (C) targeted symbols of Spanish culture as well as the Spanish political and economic system.
   (D) traded extensively with the Spanish but resented heavy taxes imposed on trade.

5. Which of the following trends occurred in the aftermath of the events described in the account?

   (A) Spanish colonizing efforts in North America in the late 1600s and 1700s saw an accommodation with some aspects of American Indian culture.
   (B) Spanish military actions and disease wiped out the American Indian populations in Spanish North America.
   (C) Spanish forces, having been defeated by the Pueblo Indians, abandoned all land claims in North America by 1700.
   (D) Spain and Great Britain formed an alliance to establish European control over North America.

Answers and Explanations

1. **(D)** The mention of the arrest of "one of the richest merchants in the colony" by the authors of the secondary source is meant to illustrate Puritan attempts to enforce economic values that emphasized communal notions of fairness over free-market individualism. Puritan communities passed a series of laws enforcing "fair prices" and "fair wages." This notion of a moral economy precedes capitalist individualism, dating back to the Middle Ages. The existence of such laws not only helps us understand the Puritan notion of an ideal community, but these laws also demonstrate that some members of the community were moving away from the ideal. After all, why would such laws be needed if everyone observed the guidelines of a moral economy? The authors are pointing to a shift toward a more individualistic, market economy.

2. **(D)** The reading raises one of the interesting contradictions of Puritanism. The religion emphasized a rejection of worldly temptations and a rigid asceticism. Yet, its injunction to carry out one's calling—the work that God has intended one to do on Earth—with dedication and vigor often led to material success. The reading is arguing that once the white-hot zeal of Puritanism declined in New England, the road toward economic success was wide open.

3. **(B)** The events described by Josephe in the account reflect resistance by American Indians to Spanish colonial practices. The events described are part of the Pueblo Revolt of 1680. Tensions between the Pueblo people and Spanish conquerors began almost a century before the rebellion. The Spanish conquistador, Juan de Oñate, and his soldiers had, in the 1590s, occupied land held by the Acoma Pueblo people. In 1598, in response to Pueblo resistance, Oñate responded by firing cannons from a mesa above the Acoma Pueblo people, killing over 800. Resentment of Spanish rule by the Pueblo people intensified by the late 1600s. The Spanish *encomienda* system had undermined the traditional economy of the Pueblo people. In addition, Spanish officials imposed Christianity on the Pueblo people and outlawed traditional spiritual practices. This resentment led to the Pueblo Revolt, also known as Popé's Rebellion (1680). The rebellion included attacks on the Spanish clergy as well as on ordinary Spaniards. The Pueblo Revolt resulted in over 300 Spanish deaths and a temporary withdrawal of Spanish forces from the area.

4. **(C)** The testimony of Josephe indicates that the Pueblo Indians targeted symbols of Spanish culture as well as the Spanish political and economic system. Josephe notes that the Pueblo rebels burned churches and decided that the names of Jesus and Mary should never be uttered. These actions indicate that the rebellion was not only about harsh treatment; it was also an attempt to assert cultural autonomy in the face of Spanish efforts to Christianize the local people.

5. **(A)** After the Pueblo Revolt, Spanish authorities adjusted their approach to dealing with the Pueblo people. In the late 1600s and 1700s, Spanish authorities attempted to be more accommodating of some aspects of Pueblo culture. A public defender was appointed with the responsibility of protecting the rights of the Pueblo people. The Spanish reaction to the rebellion was markedly different from the response of British officials to conflicts between colonists and native peoples. The British response usually entailed removal or eradication rather than accommodation.

5

Period 3: 1754–1800 The Crisis of Empire, Revolution, and Nation Building

TIMELINE

1754	Beginning of French and Indian War
1763	Treaty of Paris ends French and Indian War
	Proclamation Act
1764	March of the Paxton Boys
1764	Sugar Act
	First Committee of Correspondence established in Boston
1765	Stamp Act
	Stamp Act Congress
1766	Declaratory Act
1767	Townshend Revenue Acts
1770	Boston Massacre
1772	*Gaspee* Affair
1773	Tea Act
	Boston Tea Party
1774	Coercive (Intolerable) Acts
	First Continental Congress
1775	Fighting at Lexington and Concord
	Second Continental Congress
1776	Publication of *Common Sense* by Thomas Paine
	Declaration of Independence
1777	Articles of Confederation written
1778	Battle of Saratoga
	France enters the war on the side of the American revolutionaries
1781	Articles of Confederation ratified by the states
1783	Treaty of Paris ends the American Revolution
1784	First Land Ordinance
	Treaty of Fort Stanwix
1785	Second Land Ordinance
1786	Shays's Rebellion
	Annapolis meeting to revise Articles of Confederation
1787	Northwest Ordinance
	Constitutional Convention in Philadelphia

1788	Publication of *The Federalist*
	Ratification of the Constitution
	First federal elections
1789	Inauguration of George Washington
	Judiciary Act
	Beginning of French Revolution
	Publication of *The Interesting Narrative of the Life of Olaudah Equiano*
1791	Ratification of the Bill of Rights
	Alexander Hamilton issues "Report on Manufacturers"
	The Bank of the United States approved
1793	War between Great Britain and France
	Washington's Neutrality Proclamation
1794	Whiskey Rebellion
	Jay's Treaty
1795	Pinckney's Treaty
1796	Washington's Farewell Address
	Election of John Adams
1798	XYZ Affair
	"Quasi-war" with France
	Alien and Sedition Acts
	Kentucky and Virginia Resolutions
1800	Election of Thomas Jefferson

Topics in Period 3

In this chapter, you will learn about:
- → Topic 3.1 Contextualizing Period 3
- → Topic 3.2 The Seven Years' War (The French and Indian War)
- → Topic 3.3 Taxation without representation
- → Topic 3.4 Philosophical foundations of the American Revolution
- → Topic 3.5 The American Revolution
- → Topic 3.6 The influence of revolutionary ideas
- → Topic 3.7 The Articles of Confederation
- → Topic 3.8 The Constitutional Convention and debates over ratification
- → Topic 3.9 The Constitution
- → Topic 3.10 Shaping the new republic
- → Topic 3.11 Developing an American identity
- → Topic 3.12 Movement in the early republic
- → Topic 3.13 Subject to debate

CHAPTER 5: PERIOD 3: 1754–1800 THE CRISIS OF EMPIRE, REVOLUTION, AND NATION BUILDING

Topic 3.1 Contextualizing Period 3

> The attempt by Great Britain to restructure its North American empire following the French and Indian War and to assert greater control over its colonies led to intense colonial resistance and finally to revolution. The American Revolution produced a new American republic. The first decades of the United States were marked by a struggle over the new nation's social, political, and economic identity.

The American Revolution was a monumental event in the history of the United States, as well as in world history. The American Revolution brought to the surface tensions that existed between the thirteen American colonies and the government of Great Britain. It also brought into existence a democratic republic. The democratic spirit that imbued the founding of the United States inspired movements for change—both within the United States and abroad. The American Revolution did not give birth to a perfect democracy. Americans have struggled with the meaning and extent of democracy for the more than 235 years since winning independence.

The decade of the 1780s was a trying one for the new American nation. The newborn United States fought and won the final stages of the American Revolution and then was faced with a series of threats from within and from abroad that threatened its very existence. By the end of the "critical period," the nation had shifted directions in regard to governance on the national level—rejecting the Articles of Confederation and adopting the Constitution.

The first dozen years after the ratification of the Constitution were key in the shaping of the United States political system. The government was restructured in conformity with the Constitution. The Bill of Rights established important civil liberties. It was in this period that many of the American political system's traditions and precedents—collectively known as the "unwritten Constitution"—were established. We see the development of political parties and of the two-party system during these years. Further, we see continuing struggles over the new nation's identity.

Topic 3.2 The Seven Years' War (The French and Indian War)

Competition among the British, French, and American Indian nations culminated in the French and Indian War (1754–1763). American Indians were forced to adjust alliances in the wake of the victory of Great Britain over France. The war proved to be a turning point in relations between Great Britain and the thirteen colonies. Before the war, the British unofficial policy of "salutary neglect" allowed both Great Britain and the colonies to benefit under loosely enforced mercantilist rules (see pages 75–76). After the war, the British government enacted a series of measures designed to assert greater control over its North American colonies.

A. Expansion and War

Both Great Britain and France had extensive land claims in North America. France claimed more land in the New World, but Great Britain had many more colonists. Expansion and overlapping land claims led to the French and Indian War. Britain's victory in the war eliminated France's presence in North America and precipitated changes in British imperial policy in North America.

Origins of the French and Indian War

The **French and Indian War** had complex origins. In the 1740s and 1750s, British colonists began to venture from Virginia to settle beyond the Appalachian Mountains in the Ohio River Valley—land claimed by France. France's land claims stretched from Quebec, Montreal, and Detroit in the north to New Orleans at the mouth of the Mississippi River in the south, and from the Appalachian Mountains in the east to the Rocky Mountains in the west. At the time, France was increasing its presence in the Ohio River area in order to build up the fur trade. France began building fortifications in the region, notably **Fort Duquesne** at present-day Pittsburgh. The British colonists built a makeshift fort of their own nearby, **Fort Necessity**. In 1754, skirmishes between the two groups led to the beginning of the French and Indian War, which brought on a shift in American Indian alliances.

British Victory in the French and Indian War

There are three distinct phases of the French and Indian War. At first (1754–1756), the war was a local affair—a continuation of the skirmishes between British colonists and French forces. Most of the American Indian tribes sided with the French, who tended to be more accommodating to native peoples than the British were. The scattered British colonists attempted, unsuccessfully, to work with one another during this period. Colonial leaders met in Albany, New York (1754), in an attempt to organize an intercolonial government. **Benjamin Franklin**'s proposed **Albany Plan** was rejected by the delegates. On the battlefield, the British colonists were in retreat.

In the second phase (1756–1758), the British government, under Prime Minister **William Pitt**, took full charge of the war. Pitt alienated many colonists with his heavy-handed tactics, including forcing colonists into the army and seizing supplies from them. The colonists resisted these moves, putting the entire British effort at risk.

In the final phase (1758–1761), Pitt tried to work with colonial assemblies and also reinforced the war effort with more British troops. These moves proved successful. In 1761, French forces surrendered at Montreal. Two years later, a formal peace treaty was signed.

> **USING HISTORICAL THINKING SKILLS: CONTEXTUALIZATION**
>
> **The Context of the French and Indian War**
>
> The French and Indian War can be contextualized in a number of ways. First, it can be seen in the context of control of the interior of North America. Spain, France, and Great Britain all had substantial and overlapping land claims in North America; in the 1750s, British and French claims in the Ohio River Valley came into conflict with one another. The war can also be seen in the context of the persistent military conflicts in Europe between Great Britain and France. Historians refer to the long period of conflict between these two powers as the Second Hundred Years' War (1689 to 1815). Students could also see the war in the context of the evolving fur trade between American Indians and Europeans. As beavers and other animals became scarcer in older trapping grounds, American Indians and their European allies moved into new areas to meet the demand for furs. This movement led to tensions between and among American Indian nations and their European allies.

The Treaty of Paris (1763)

In the **Treaty of Paris**, France surrendered virtually its entire North American empire. It ceded to Great Britain all French territory in Canada and east of the Mississippi River. France ceded to Spain all of its territory west of the Mississippi River. British North American colonists were pleased that the land beyond the Appalachians seemed ready for additional settlement. American Indians living in these lands were in an increasingly vulnerable position.

B. Debt and Taxation Following the French and Indian War

If British colonists celebrated the removal of the French from North America, their celebration was short lived. Almost immediately, the British government attempted to confront an ongoing problem—the large debt that had accumulated during almost half a century of constant warfare. The British government believed its victory in the French and Indian War had been especially beneficial to the colonists. In return, the British reasoned it was fair for the colonists to assume some of the costs of the war and of continued protection through increased taxation.

The Sugar Act

The first significant post-war tax was enacted with the **Sugar Act** (1764). The act actually lowered the existing tax on molasses imported into North America from French colonies in the West Indies. However, along with lowering the tax, the act also sought to crack down on widespread smuggling. The act strengthened the admiralty courts system, shifting prosecutions of smuggling cases from local jury trials to British maritime courts. The British hoped to generate additional income through these measures.

The Stamp Act

The **Stamp Act** (1765) provoked the most intense colonial opposition of all measures enacted by the British following the French and Indian War. It represented a departure from previous British colonial policy. Previous tax acts were aimed at regulating trade; this act was designed solely to raise revenue. It was a direct tax on the colonists rather than an indirect trade duty. The act imposed a tax on all sorts of printed matter in the colonies—court documents, books, almanacs, and deeds (see more on opposition to the Stamp Act, pages 97-98).

Quartering of British Troops

The **Quartering Act** of 1765 addressed the housing of British soldiers who were stationed in the colonies following the French and Indian War. The act stipulated that Great Britain would house soldiers in barracks, but if the number of soldiers exceeded available facilities, local inns, pubs, and even private residences could be used by British authorities to house them. Colonial assemblies were expected to shoulder the costs of housing and feeding these soldiers. Often these troops were given part-time wages, compelling them to supplement their wages by finding work in the community. The largest number of troops were stationed in Boston.

C. American Indian Resistance and Colonial Settlement Following the French and Indian War

In the aftermath of the French and Indian War, American Indians in the areas newly won by Great Britain found themselves in an increasingly precarious position—on the one hand, they wanted to maintain the lucrative fur trade with Europeans, while on the other, they hoped to resist encroachment by British colonists. At the same time, colonists continued to settle in the interior of the continent, creating tensions between backwoods settlers and governing elites.

Clashing Cultures in the Great Lakes Region

As the British made their presence felt in the lands formerly held by the French, the difference between the British and the French in their approach to American Indians became more evident. The French, for practical and cultural reasons, worked at developing harmonious relations with American Indian tribes. For instance, they negotiated with Indian leaders and participated in ceremonial exchanges of gifts with the tribes. The British, however, had little patience for gift exchanges. General **Jeffrey Amherst**, commander-in-chief of British forces in North America, saw gift exchanges as demeaning. American Indians, on the other hand, saw in generous gift-giving an expression of dominance and protection.

In the uncertain world created by the defeat of the French, some American Indians attempted to foster a greater sense of unity and cultural resistance among the often-fractious tribes of the Great Lakes and Ohio Valley regions. In 1760 and 1761, a Delaware leader named **Neolin** offered American Indians an apocalyptic vision of a future that could transpire if they did not change their ways. He encouraged American Indians to curb their contact with European fur traders; reduce the presence of guns, alcohol, and other European goods; and lessen infighting. His efforts set the stage for unified, violent resistance.

Pontiac's Rebellion

With the defeat of the French in the French and Indian War, American Indian groups that had been allied with the French found themselves in an unstable situation. The **Ottawa tribe**, for instance, in the northern Ohio region found itself without allies as British colonists set their sights on traditional Ottawa lands. After the war, British troops occupied several French-built forts. The Ottawa chief, **Pontiac**, and other Indian leaders organized resistance to British troops stationed around the Great Lakes and southward on several rivers. In the months after the 1763 signing of the Treaty of Paris, Indian warriors attacked British-held **Fort Detroit**. This attack was followed by strikes on six other forts and on colonial settlements along a swath of land from upstate New York to the area south of Lake Michigan, and along the Appalachian frontier, where settlers were entering Indian country. The attacks were initially successful; Pontiac and his allies captured several forts west of Detroit, with more than 400 British soldiers and 2,000 colonists killed or captured. Amherst was replaced by the more capable **Thomas Gage** in August 1763. Bloodshed continued into 1764. Pontiac's Rebellion was finally broken by Gage. Smaller skirmishes continued until the **American Revolution**, when many American Indian groups sided with the British.

The Proclamation Act (1763)

In response to the outbreak of Pontiac's Rebellion, Great Britain issued the **Proclamation of 1763**, which drew a line through the Appalachian Mountains. Great Britain ordered the colonists not to settle beyond the line. Colonists were disgruntled; they felt that they had made sacrifices during the French and Indian War, and they were now eager to settle in these newly claimed lands. Many had already migrated toward the foothills of the Appalachians and had begun making their way further west through mountain passes. The British government, however, did not want to provoke additional warfare with native peoples in the region and incur the costs of more campaigns in the West. Further, the British wanted to continue garnering profits from the valuable fur trade with Indians. Access to western lands was one of the first major disputes between Great Britain and the colonists.

Conflict in the Interior of the Continent Following the French and Indian War

Settlement of the interior of colonial America in the decades after the French and Indian War set the stage for ongoing tensions between the policies of ruling authorities—generally based in the cities along the Atlantic seaboard—and the poorer folk inland, remote from the commercial activity of the cosmopolitan centers. After the American Revolution, the flow of pioneers beyond the Appalachians increased dramatically. This movement frequently displaced Indians, setting the stage for a new series of battles over the vast interior of the United States. The movement was challenged by the continued presence of Spain and Great Britain along the borderlands of the newly formed United States.

The Scots-Irish

The middle colonies—Pennsylvania, New York, New Jersey, and Delaware—experienced remarkable growth in the eighteenth century. German, Scots-Irish, and other immigrants contributed to the growth of the colonies. The largest immigrant group in the eighteenth century was the **Scots-Irish**, Presbyterians originally from Scotland, who generations earlier had settled in Ireland, where they got their name. Difficult economic conditions impelled thousands to migrate to America. Immigrants from the southwestern German states were the second biggest group.

Economic Opportunity in Pennsylvania

The initial destination of the **Scots-Irish** was **Pennsylvania**, where the availability of land and the need for workers attracted immigrants, especially to Philadelphia. Many soon moved westward into the mountainous interior. Other regions of colonial North America were less hospitable. Farther south, slavery was the dominant form of labor; farther north, the legacy of Puritanism still enforced a cultural homogeneity. New York City attracted immigrants, but farmers found that the best land along the Hudson River was taken up by large estates.

The Paxton Boys

As early as the 1720s, some farmers were settling beyond the crest of the **Appalachian Mountains**, in the backcountry of Pennsylvania, Virginia (the area that would later become West Virginia), and North Carolina.

Small-scale farmers in Pennsylvania specialized in growing wheat and experienced a higher standard of living than their counterparts in Europe. The **Scots-Irish** farmers carried with them from Europe resentments toward British rule. In the aftermath of the French and Indian War and Pontiac's Rebellion, a new wave of Scots-Irish settlers encroached upon American Indian lands in violation of previously signed treaties. As tensions between American Indians and settlers increased, a vigilante group of Scots-Irish immigrants, called the **Paxton Boys**, organized raids against American Indians on the Pennsylvania frontier. In 1763, these raids included an attack on peaceful **Conestoga Indians** (many of them Christians) that resulted in twenty deaths. After the attacks on the Conestoga, in January 1764, about 250 Paxton Boys marched to Philadelphia to present their grievances to the Pennsylvania legislature. Their **"Apology"** (or explanation), presented to the legislature, reflected bitterness at the American Indians on the frontier of Pennsylvania, as well as resentment of the Quaker elite of the colony for maintaining a more lenient policy toward American Indians.

> **USING REASONING PROCESSES:**
> **CONTINUITY AND CHANGE**
>
> **A Shift in Colonial Policy**
>
> Note the shift in British policy from the "salutary neglect" approach prior to the French and Indian War to the close supervision of the postwar period. This change in Britain's imperial policy can be seen as an important cause of the resentments and protests that culminated in the American Revolution.

Topic 3.3 Taxation Without Representation

In the aftermath of the French and Indian War (1754–1763), new taxes enacted by the British and more rigorous enforcement of existing taxes generated intense resentment and resistance among many colonists. This movement culminated in the independence movement and revolution against Great Britain.

A. Colonial Resistance to British Policies in the Aftermath of the French and Indian War

After the French and Indian War, the relationship between the British colonists and Great Britain changed, as the colonists began to unite and organize around a series of threats—actual and perceived—posed by changing British policies. This changing relationship fostered a resistance movement and finally an independence movement.

The Stamp Act Congress

The first significant, coordinated protests against British policies occurred in response to the **Stamp Act** (see pages 97–98). In October 1765, delegates from nine colonies met in New York and drew up a document listing grievances, which went beyond the Stamp Act itself. The **Declarations of the Stamp Act Congress** asserted that only representatives elected by colonists could enact taxes on the colonies. **"No taxation without representation"** became a rallying cry of opponents of British policies. The declarations followed on the heels of a series of proposals, written by **Patrick Henry**, called the **Virginia Resolves**. Not all of the resolves were passed by the Virginia assembly, but they were all written up and circulated throughout the colonies. The resolves, debated in June 1765, called for a degree of colonial self-government that went beyond more moderate proposals.

The British responded to the cry of "No taxation without representation!" with the theory of **"virtual representation."** The theory held that members of Parliament represented the entire British Empire. The colonists therefore were "virtually represented" by the members of Parliament, even though the colonists did not vote for these members. The Stamp Act crisis is often considered to be the beginning of the period of the **American Revolution** (1765–1783).

Committees of Correspondence

In communities throughout the colonies, opponents of British policies organized **committees of correspondence** starting in 1764. These committees spread information and coordinated resistance actions. By the 1770s, the committees had become virtual shadow governments in the different colonies, assuming powers and challenging the legitimacy of the legislative assemblies and royal governors.

Crowd Actions

The **Stamp Act** generated a variety of crowd actions in the colonies. In cities and towns throughout the colonies, **"Sons of Liberty"** groups harassed, and occasionally attacked, Stamp Act agents. There were several incidents of stores ransacked if the proprietor did not comply with boycotts of British goods. In Boston, the home of the lieutenant governor, **Thomas Hutchinson**, was ransacked. Finally, the Stamp Act itself was rescinded (1766), but a series of British moves and colonial responses in the coming years worsened the situation.

> **USING HISTORICAL THINKING SKILLS: SOURCING AND SITUATION**
>
> **Mobs and Crowds**
>
> Many secondary historical sources refer to the street activities in protest of British policies in the period before the American Revolution as "mob actions." Of late, social historians have tended to favor the term "crowd actions." Be aware of the different implications of these two terms. "Mob actions" imply random acts of violence committed by angry groups of people, while "crowd actions" imply acts taken with a particular goal in mind by groups of people with an articulated agenda. Be aware of the distinction between the two terms in your own writing about the period.

The Townshend Acts

The **Townshend Acts** (1767), passed in the wake of the Stamp Act crisis, imposed additional taxes on the colonists. Britain's Chancellor of the Exchequer, **Charles Townshend**, made sure these new taxes—on paint, paper, lead, tea, and other goods—were "external" taxes, on imports, not "internal" sales taxes on items. Although opposition to these import duties was slow to develop, by 1768 many colonial leaders renewed their calls for **boycotts** of British goods. The boycott movement gained strength throughout the thirteen colonies. Patriotic women engaged in producing **homespun clothing**. Artisans benefited from the boycott as Americans sought locally produced goods. These simple goods were seen as virtuous substitutes for extravagant British goods.

The Boston Massacre

In 1768, Great Britain redeployed royal troops to Boston following rioting that year. The presence of these troops angered many Bostonians. Many colonists viewed **"standing armies"** as threats to liberty. They asserted that during times of war, it is appropriate for citizen regiments to be mobilized, but when peace came, these troops must be disbanded. Further, the British soldiers competed with colonists for waterfront jobs. During the winter of 1770 a deadly incident between British soldiers and a group of Bostonians reverberated throughout the colonies. The **Boston Massacre** (1770), as the incident came to be known, occurred in March as a disagreement between an on-duty British sentry and a young wigmaker's apprentice escalated into a scuffle. Angry colonists heckled and threw stones at British sentries ordered out to restore calm. Finally, the troops fired on the colonists, resulting in five deaths, including an African American named **Crispus Attucks**. In years to come, the incident would be repeatedly used as colonial propaganda to illustrate the brutality of the British troops.

Gaspee Affair

After the Boston Massacre, the early 1770s witnessed a lessening of public acts of resistance. The seeming calm broke in June 1772, when a British revenue schooner, the *Gaspee*, ran aground in shallow waters near Warwick, Rhode Island. The schooner was searching for smugglers who thrived in those waters. Local men boarded the ship, looted its contents, and torched it. The *Gaspee* affair represented a shift toward more militant tactics by colonial protestors.

The Tea Act and the Boston Tea Party

Relations between British authorities and American colonists took a dramatic turn for the worse in 1773 with the passage of the **Tea Act**. The **British East India Company** was in crisis; its stock value had virtually collapsed. To bolster the company, the British passed the Tea Act, which greatly reduced taxes on tea sold in the colonies by the British East India Company. The act enabled the company to sell massive quantities of low-priced tea directly to colonial merchants on consignment, thus bypassing local middlemen and undercutting smugglers. This act actually lowered tea prices in Boston, but it angered many colonists who accused the British of doing special favors for a large company. The colonists responded by dumping cases of tea into Boston harbor. The dumping of the tea was not just a symbolic act; its value in today's money would be nearly $2 million.

The Coercive/Intolerable Acts

The British passed a series of acts in 1774, in the wake of the Boston Tea Party, called the Coercive Acts, or Intolerable Acts.

- The **Massachusetts Government Act** brought the governance of Massachusetts under direct British control. The act limited the powers of town meetings and provided the royal governor with the power to directly appoint officials who had previously been elected.
- The **Administration of Justice Act** allowed British authorities to move trials from Massachusetts to Great Britain. British policy after the French and Indian War consistently sought to move trials away from local communities. This move struck colonists as an abridgment of a basic right of Englishmen—the right to a trial by a jury of one's peers.
- The **Boston Port Act** closed the port of Boston to trade until further notice.
- The **Quartering Act** expanded the scope of the 1765 Quartering Act and required Boston residents to house British troops upon their command.
- A fifth act, the **Quebec Act**, was passed around the same time but was unrelated to the Boston Tea Party. This act enlarged the boundaries of the province of Quebec and let Catholics in Quebec freely practice their religion. Many Protestant Bostonians saw this as an attack on their faith.

Formation of the Continental Congress

British authorities hoped that the **Coercive Acts** would make an example of Massachusetts and isolate it from the other British colonies. The opposite occurred. Colonists throughout colonial America resented the British for these acts. Colonial assemblies passed resolutions condemning the acts. In town after town, local institutions, including the **Committees of Correspondence** (see pages 97-98), organized resistance to British policies. Power was shifting from the instruments of royal governance to these extralegal colonial bodies. After the Virginia legislative assembly was dissolved by the British government, members held a special meeting to call for an intercolonial assembly. The **First Continental Congress** met in Philadelphia in September and October 1774, with representatives from each of the thirteen colonies, except Georgia.

> **USING HISTORICAL THINKING SKILLS: CONTEXTUALIZATION**
>
> **Standing Armies and the Context of Colonial Protest**
>
> The are several valid approaches to contextualizing the colonial protests before the American Revolution. Certainly, they can be seen in the context of Britain tightening its grip on the thirteen colonies in the period following the French and Indian War through new taxes and regulations. The protests can also be seen in the context of colonial ideology. There was a long-standing suspicion, in Great Britain and in the colonial world, of professional standing armies. In today's world, most people accept the existence of professional armies, even in peacetime. However, in the 1700s, many colonists agreed with the sentiments of James Madison—"The means of defense against foreign danger, have been always the instruments of tyranny at home" (1787). This suspicion can help us understand the intensity of colonial protests before the Revolution. New taxes were seen as a means to fund a standing army. The Quartering Acts (1765 and 1774), requiring the colonies to cover the costs of food and shelter of British soldiers, bolstered anger at the ongoing presence of a standing army. This anger can be seen in the harassment of British troops preceding the Boston Massacre (1770).

The Congress passed several resolutions including nonimportation, nonexportation, and nonconsumption agreements in an attempt to cut off all trade with Britain. The Congress also called for the creation of local **Committees of Safety** to enforce these agreements and recommended that the colonies begin to make military preparations in defense of a possible invasion by British troops. Finally, the Congress agreed to continue its functions and to meet again the following spring. The **Second Continental Congress** began its deliberations in May 1775 (see page 104).

B. The Resistance Movement from Above and from Below

Traditional accounts of the movement to resist British policies tend to stress the guidance of important colonial leaders, such as Benjamin Franklin, John Adams, and John Hancock. Their participation in the Committees of Correspondence and the Continental Congress, as well as their oratory and writing, played an important role in the resistance movement. However, the activism of groups of artisans, laborers, and women also pushed the movement forward.

The Role of Women in the Resistance Movement

Many women participated in the efforts to resist British policies. Women made clothing, both to honor **boycotts** of British goods and also to help supply troops once the American Revolution began. Women were also prominent in crowd actions against merchants who were thought to be holding back goods in order to profit from wartime shortages. A group of women who were active in the opposition movement formed the **Daughters of Liberty** in 1765 as protests were developing against the Stamp Act. The group continued to organize boycotts, **"spinning bees"** (see box, page 101), and public protests throughout the coming decade. During the Tea Act crisis in 1773 (see page 99), Daughters of Liberty chapters organized the production and distribution of homemade substitutes of the Chinese and Indian teas sold by the British East India Company, created using local roots and leaves. Fifty-one women in North Carolina signed a declaration vowing to give up tea and other British products—an action known as the **Edenton Tea Party** (1774). After war broke out, colonial women helped on the actual battlefield as nurses and water carriers. At least one woman enlisted in the **Continental Army**. **Deborah Sampson** disguised herself as a man and participated courageously in several battles.

Artisans and Laborers and the American Revolution

Urban **artisans** had long been active in resistance to British policies. Artisans encouraged boycotts of British goods, knowing that such boycotts would lead to a greater demand for American-made goods. However, they were driven as much by ideology as self-interest. Artisans became increasingly radicalized in the years leading up to the American Revolution. Anti-British street actions in Boston and Philadelphia needed the mobilization of artisans and workers to be effective. Colonial elites realized that these commoners were reliable allies in the struggle against the British. Boston shoemaker **Ebenezer Macintosh** was an important leader of crowd actions in the Stamp Act period. When the American Revolution began, craftsmen and laborers made up the bulk of both local militias and Continental Army units.

In Philadelphia, radicalized artisans were instrumental in the revolutionary struggle in 1776. The prewar Philadelphia political leadership, primarily members of the merchant class, opposed declaring independence and cutting ties to British trade. Artisans and laborers, with **Thomas Paine** and **Benjamin Rush** participating in the leadership, formed extralegal committees and militia groups in support of revolution. They ended up crafting the most democratic constitution among the new states (see more on the Pennsylvania constitution, page 109).

Topic 3.4 Philosophical Foundations of the American Revolution

The American Revolution occurred in the midst of a fertile period in the history of ideas. A variety of schools of thought put forth contending new ideas about society, politics, religion, and governance. Many colonists came to believe in the superiority of republican forms of government. This was evident in key documents from the period of the American Revolution, including Thomas Paine's *Common Sense* (1776) and the Declaration of Independence (1776).

A. Protestant Evangelicalism and Enlightenment Philosophy

The rise of Protestant evangelical movements shaped the worldviews of many British colonists, inspiring them to see themselves as a chosen people surrounded by the blessings of liberty. In addition, the ideas of the Enlightenment shaped American thinking about the ideal political system.

Protestant Evangelicalism and the American Revolution

Protestant evangelical thought made a significant imprint on the language and ideas of many of the supporters of American independence. One can trace the Protestant assertion of the uniqueness of America's mission in the world back to **John Winthrop's** call to build a "city set upon a hill" (1630) (see page 66), or, a generation later, to **Reverend Samuel Danforth's** "Errand in the Wilderness" sermon (1672). However, it is not until the 1700s that historians mark the beginning of **Protestant evangelicalism**—a more intense and radical form of Protestantism, more focused on individual conversion and less centered on established churches.

From the time of the Great Awakening revival movement (see page 82) through the period leading up to independence, Protestant evangelical ministers used language that complemented and contributed to ideas of republicanism. Ministers spoke of **"liberty"** and **"virtue"** delivering their congregants from **"bondage and servitude."** The French and Indian War came to be seen by many evangelicals as a battle against Roman Catholicism. After the war, evangelicals and republicanism increasingly began to share a language of opposition and resistance—likening British rule to the devil and urging colonists to resist corruption. The struggle against the British came to be seen by many as part of an ongoing struggle against godless tyranny. The influence of Protestant evangelicalism on **Patriot** sentiment can be seen in a sermon by the Boston Baptist minister, **Rev. John Allen**, *Oration Upon the Beauties of Liberty* (1772). The oration began with a condemnation of the British threat to prosecute those involved in the *Gaspee* affair (see page 98). He used the incident as a springboard for a broad and scathing attack on British governance of the colonies. It became an extremely popular address during the period before independence; it was reprinted seven times in four cities.

Enlightenment Thinking in the Age of Revolutions

Historians continue to debate the degree to which the **American Revolution** was motivated by ideology and the degree to which it was motivated by the experience of living under the thumb of restrictive British policies. Certainly, the ideas of the **Enlightenment** shaped the thinking of many patriots and helped provide them with a lens through which to perceive, and resist, British rule. This is especially evident when one views the American

---

> **USING REASONING PROCESSES:**
> **CONTINUITY AND CHANGE**
>
> **"Spinning Bees," Protest, and Gender**
>
> "Spinning bees" were public events in which colonial women produced homespun cloth. The events were a form of protest against British policies, such as the Stamp Act (1765) and the Townshend Acts (1767). The cloth they produced supported boycotts of British products and became a potent symbol of protest against the British. On the eve of the American Revolution, the entire graduating class of Harvard wore items of homespun clothing at their graduation ceremony. The "spinning bees" are part of a long tradition of women participating in public protest and reform movements. "Spinning bees" embody an innovative approach to women protesting. On the one hand, women, by playing a prominent role in public political events, were challenging traditional gender expectations. On the other hand, they were doing so in a way that, on the surface, seemed to be in keeping with gender norms—tending to a basic household chore. We see continuities in regard to gendered forms of public protest in the "maternalist" approach of many female Progressive-era reformers (1900–1920). Working on issues such as child labor and public health allowed women to work on public issues, but in fields that mainstream society found acceptable—child rearing and caring for the ill. This reform work was often framed as "social housekeeping."

Revolution within the context of what has become known as the **"age of revolutions."** The American Revolution was the first of several revolutions (including ones in France, Haiti, and a host of Spanish colonies) that, in keeping with Enlightenment thinking, broke with the past and articulated a new set of ideas about governance, individual liberty, and reason. For example, the French Enlightenment philosopher, **Montesquieu**, argued in **"The Spirit of the Laws"** (1748) that liberty could best be sustained by dividing the powers of government and maintaining a balance of power; his ideas influenced both criticism of the British monarchy and the formation of a new American government.

The Ideas of John Locke

John Locke (introduced in Period 2) was perhaps the most influential Enlightenment thinker, read widely in America during the time of the Revolution. Locke had written ***Two Treatises on Government*** in the early 1690s to defend England's **Glorious Revolution** (1688). He identified the basis of a legitimate government in his ***Second Treatise of Government*** (1689). Locke argued that a ruler gains legitimacy through the consent of the governed. The basic responsibility of government is to protect the natural rights of the people; Locke identified the most basic of these rights as **life**, **liberty**, and **property**. If a government should fail to protect these basic rights, it is the right of the citizens to overthrow that government. Locke's theory of natural rights states that power to govern belongs to the people. Locke was one of the main intellectual influences in the writing of the **Declaration of Independence**. Locke's writings challenged **Thomas Hobbes's** defense of an **absolutist monarchy** and Sir **Robert Filmer's** assertion of the **divine right of kings**.

B. *Common Sense*, the Declaration of Independence, and Republican Self-Government

Theoretical debates about the proper form of government took on urgency in the North American colonies in the 1770s as the imperial crisis intensified. Enlightenment ideas informed the writings of Thomas Paine and shaped the content of the Declaration of Independence. American thinkers and revolutionaries embraced the ideas of republican self-government based on natural rights theory.

Divided Loyalties

By 1775 and 1776, even though fighting had begun between colonists and British forces (see page 104), independence was not a foregone conclusion. Historians estimate that around 40 to 45 percent of colonists, known as **"Patriots,"** wanted independence; around 15 to 20 percent, known as **"Loyalists"** or **"Tories,"** wanted to retain ties to Great Britain. (The remainder did not strongly support either side in the conflict.) Both sides articulated reasons for their stance—whether those reasons were ideological, economic, or personal.

The Olive Branch Petition

Some members of the **Continental Congress** still hoped for reconciliation. Congress sent the **"Olive Branch Petition"** to **King George III** in July 1775, affirming loyalty to the British King and blaming the current problems on **Parliament**. The

---

USING HISTORICAL THINKING SKILLS:
SOURCING AND SITUATION

Explaining Audience: The Olive Branch Petition

In discussing audience, a particular document may have more than one intended audience. On the one hand, it is clear that the audience of the Olive Branch Petition was King George III. It is addressed to him. On the other hand, the historical situation of the document raises questions about audience. Most historians believe that the document had no real chance of opening peace talks with the British Crown. The situation had devolved into open warfare between Britain and the thirteen colonies. Further, on the day after the Olive Branch Petition was passed, Congress issued a resolution titled the Declaration of the Causes and Necessity of Taking Up Arms, explaining why the colonists had begun fighting. Ultimately, the Olive Branch Petition may have been more for internal consumption. The intended audience, therefore, would be colonial moderates. The petition would let them see that Congress had made one last attempt to arrive at a peaceful resolution with Britain and that the King rejected it.

petition proposed a structure in which the colonies would exercise greater autonomy within the British empire, and the British would enact more equitable trade and tax regulations. George rejected the Olive Branch Petition without reading it.

Common Sense

As the debate over independence ensued, **Thomas Paine** published a best-selling pamphlet called ***Common Sense***. He advocated that the American colonies declare independence from Great Britain. He wrote that he could not see a "single advantage" in "being connected with Great Britain." The revolution was well under way in January 1776 when Paine wrote *Common Sense*. He argued against the conciliatory logic of the Olive Branch Petition (see pages 102–103), plainly and forcefully putting the blame for the crisis on King George III.

The Declaration of Independence

On July 4, 1776, the delegates to the **Second Continental Congress** formally ratified the **Declaration of Independence**. The first draft of the document was written by **Thomas Jefferson** in consultation with fellow members of a five-person committee appointed by Congress; the draft subsequently underwent edits by the entire Second Continental Congress. The body of the Declaration of Independence is a list of grievances against the king of Great Britain, but the eloquent preamble contains key elements of Locke's natural rights theory. It states that **"all men are created equal"** and **"endowed by their Creator with certain unalienable Rights."** The declaration goes on to assert that government gains its legitimacy from **"the consent of the governed."** If a government violates people's natural rights, the people have the right **"to alter or abolish it."** These ideas have shaped democratic practices in the United States and beyond. (See more on the events leading up to the ratification of the Declaration of Independence in Topic 3.3 and Topic 3.5.)

Visions of Republicanism

When the United States declared, and eventually won, its independence from Great Britain, it was not immediately clear what type of government it would embrace. There was widespread agreement that America would become a **republic**—a country in which sovereignty, or power, ultimately rested with the people rather than a monarch. This was a radical move for the time; there had been virtually no republics in the world since the Roman republic two thousand years earlier.

There was, however, disagreement about what was expected of citizens in a republic. For many Americans, **republicanism** implied a particular moral stance in the world. Republican citizens, in this formulation, were independent people who embodied civic virtue, putting the interests of the community above their own self-interest. Republican citizens led industrious, simple lives. This vision of republicanism looked back to the ancient Roman republic as an ideal. Some elements of republicanism can also be traced back to the Puritan experiment, with its rejection of top-down ecclesiastical authority, its communitarian spirit, and its concern about the corrupting effects of power. In this understanding of republicanism, virtuous citizens had to be on the watch for decadent and corrupt leaders who pursued luxury and power at the expense of the common good.

At the same time, other Americans were developing a different set of ideas about republicanism. They argued that individuals pursuing their own self-interest were the ideal republican citizens. This understanding of republicanism drew inspiration from the economic ideas of **Adam Smith**. In his two important works, *The Theory of Moral Sentiments* (1759) and *The Wealth of Nations* (1776), Smith argued that rational self-interest and competition can lead to greater prosperity for all. This understanding of republicanism put more of a focus on ambition and economic freedom, while the earlier understanding put more of an emphasis on public virtue and civic-mindedness. These competing visions of republicanism shaped many of the debates during the first decades of the United States.

Topic 3.5 The American Revolution

At the onset of the American Revolution, the Patriot cause faced serious obstacles, including considerable Loyalist opposition and the overwhelming military might of Great Britain. Despite these factors, the rebellious colonists were successful. The military leadership of George Washington, the actions of colonial militias and the Continental Army, the ideological commitment of many colonists, and support from foreign powers all worked to the advantage of the Patriot cause.

A. The War for Independence—Factors in the Victory of the Patriot Cause

The American crisis reached a boiling point by 1775. Fighting between the British Army and rebellious colonists began at Lexington and Concord in that year and intensified after the Second Continental Congress declared independence in July 1776.

Lexington and Concord

In April 1775, fighting began between **colonists** and **British** troops in the Massachusetts towns of **Lexington** and **Concord**. Americans often call the first shot of this clash **"the shot heard round the world."** The event symbolized a marked shift in the colonial situation from resistance to rebellion.

Factors in the Outcome of the War

Both sides had important advantages and disadvantages in the **American Revolution**. The **British** had a highly trained, professional army; they had the strongest navy in the world; and they had substantial financial resources. The British could also count on the support of about a third of the colonial population, which remained loyal. Great Britain offered freedom to slaves who joined the British side. The British also could count on a majority of American Indian tribes for support.

However, the British troops were fighting far from home. It was difficult to maintain supply lines over the course of a long war and over a huge theater of war. Also, Great Britain had enemies, such as the French who wanted to see them defeated. The eventual entry of France into the war on the American side tipped the scales decisively against the British.

The **Patriots** had excellent leadership in **General George Washington**, who counted on several key generals, especially **Nathanael Greene** and **Henry Knox**. In addition, Washington had support from talented European volunteer officers: the **Marquis de Lafayette** (French), **Baron von Steuben** (Prussian), and **Thaddeus Kosciusko** and **Casimir Pulaski** (Polish). The Patriots had the advantage of defending their home territory; they did not have to attack Great Britain to emerge victorious. Finally, many Patriot soldiers believed deeply in the cause of independence. Colonial disadvantages included lack of financing (see page 105) and a lack of a strong central governing authority.

USING REASONING PROCESSES: CONTINUITY AND CHANGE

Defensive Versus Offensive Wars

It is easier to defend one's territory than it is to conquer another's territory. This is seen in the American Revolution (1775–1783), and it was one of the advantages of the Confederacy in the American Civil War (1861–1865). This factor helps explain the eventual victory of the Patriot cause over the more powerful British military in the American Revolution. In the case of the Civil War, Union forces—utilizing the North's material and demographic advantages—were able to subdue the Confederate rebellion on the enemy's territory.

USING HISTORICAL THINKING SKILLS: MAKING CONNECTIONS

Urban and Rural Areas in Times of War

The Battle of Saratoga demonstrated to the British that urban centers were easier to control than rural areas. Later in American history, the United States realized that same lesson in the Vietnam War (1965–1973). American forces were able to hold onto urban centers, such as Saigon, but were unable to maintain control in the rural areas and small villages of Vietnam.

The Phases of the American Revolution

Historians point to three distinct phases of the **American Revolutionary War**. The **first phase** (1775-1776) took place primarily in New England. In this phase, Great Britain did not grasp the depth of Patriot sentiment among many colonists. The British thought that the conflict was essentially brought on by an impetuous minority in New England. After the British suffered heavy losses in their victory at the **Battle of Bunker Hill** (March 1776), they abandoned **Boston** and reevaluated their strategy.

The **second phase** (1776-1778) occurred primarily in the **middle colonies**. The British thought that if they could maintain control of **New York**, they could isolate rebellious **New England**. A massive British force drove George Washington and his troops out of New York City in the summer of 1776. However, British forces coming south from Canada suffered a major defeat at the **Battle of Saratoga** in October 1777. The battle made it evident that the British might be able to hold urban centers like New York City, but that it would be very difficult to control the vast stretches of eastern and southern North America. Saratoga also showed **France** that the colonists could mount formidable forces for battle. Early in 1778, France formally recognized the United States as an independent nation and agreed to supply military assistance. France's motivation was its animosity toward Great Britain, not affinity with the ideals of the Declaration of Independence.

The **third phase** (1778-1783) took place in the **South**. Great Britain hoped to rally loyalist sentiment in the South, where it was strongest, and even tap into resentment among the slave population there. The southern strategy did not bear fruit despite British victories at **Savannah, Georgia** and **Charleston, South Carolina**. In the North, fighting had reached a stalemate, despite the aid that "turncoat" **Benedict Arnold** supplied to the British (1780). By October 1781, a joint **American-French** campaign caught British **General Cornwallis** off guard, and he surrendered at **Yorktown**, Virginia. Skirmishes continued between the two sides until the 1783 **Treaty of Paris** formally ended the American Revolution.

B. Funding the War Effort

Throughout the American Revolution, civilians attempted to provide financial and material support to the Patriot cause. However, these efforts were insufficient. The Continental Army faced economic shortages throughout the war.

Currency, Inflation, and Financial Difficulties

The **Continental Army** was persistently underfunded and frequently short of basic supplies. **Congress** lacked the power to levy taxes on the people; it had to request funds from the various states. The war was a massive undertaking in terms of organization and financing. The newly formed and disorganized Congress was not prepared for the task. Congress attempted to solve the financial problems of the war by printing money, but this currency soon lost its value amid runaway inflation. Merchants frequently sold goods to the British, who could pay in gold and silver rather than have to accept the worthless currency of the Continental Congress. This was starkly evident in the winter of 1777-1778, when Washington's troops at **Valley Forge**, Pennsylvania, experienced food shortages.

Congress turned to other measures to pay the soldiers. It began issuing certificates for frontier land in lieu of payment. These certificates were often used as currency, as soldiers had more immediate needs than procuring frontier land and used the certificates to purchase goods.

> **KEEP IN MIND**
>
> **Treaties of Paris**
>
> There are three important treaties that are each called the "Treaty of Paris" in American history—following the French and Indian War (1763), the American Revolution (1783), and the Spanish-American War (1898). Look at contextual information to understand which treaty is being discussed in a document or a question.

Topic 3.6 The Influence of Revolutionary Ideas

The American Revolution generated debates in the United States about what type of society would emerge in the new nation. An ongoing tension emerged between those who sought to expand democratic participation and those who sought to maintain traditional forms of inequality. In addition, the ideas of the American Revolution were invoked by movements for change in other countries in the decades following the birth of the United States.

A. The Call for Egalitarianism

Although the primary goal of the American Revolution was independence from Great Britain for the thirteen colonies, the rhetoric that was employed to justify the revolution inspired others to demand fundamental changes in society. Many called for the abolition of slavery and for greater political democracy in the new governing structures.

Moves to Abolish Slavery

Despite the language of equality in the **Declaration of Independence** and in many state constitutions, political leaders were reluctant to apply such language to enslaved African Americans. In several northern states, **slaves** petitioned state legislatures to grant them their **"natural rights,"** namely freedom. In 1779, petitions for **emancipation** in New Hampshire and Connecticut were rejected. In Massachusetts, seven free African Americans, including the brothers **Paul Cuffe** and **John Cuffe**, refused to pay taxes on grounds that they did not vote and were, therefore, not represented. Their actions led to the extension of voting rights to tax-paying African Americans in Massachusetts. Slaves in Massachusetts sued for their freedom, initiating several legal cases that cited the language of the Massachusetts constitution, **"all men are born free and equal."** Several such cases were decided in favor of the slaves, effectively ending slavery in Massachusetts through judicial decisions.

> **USING HISTORICAL THINKING SKILLS:**
> **CONTEXTUALIZATION**
>
> **Slavery and Its Critics**
>
> Students often assume that the unpleasant ideas of earlier eras—such as slavery or racism—were simply accepted by all of society. However, it is important to recognize that these ideas were not universally accepted. In regard to both slavery and to notions of white supremacy, important voices challenged the mainstream thinking of the day. As slavery persisted and grew in the early decades of the United States, the debate about the meaning of freedom and democracy intensified.

Several other states slowly began to take action against slavery. **Vermont**, which was a sovereign entity from 1777 to 1791 (when it was admitted as the fourteenth state), outlawed slavery in its 1777 Constitution, citing the language of the Declaration of Independence. In 1780, political leaders in **Pennsylvania** voted to end slavery by gradual emancipation. The law was not immediately beneficial to enslaved people in Pennsylvania. It stated that infants born on or after March 1, 1780, would be free, but only after they reached the age of 28. However, many slaves in Pennsylvania simply ran away, sometimes aided by sympathetic whites.

B. Evolving Ideas on Gender

The importance of women in the revolutionary struggle and the spread of Enlightenment ideas around equality set the stage for the evolution of ideas around gender. The ideal of "republican motherhood" emerged in the decades after the American Revolution.

"Remember the Ladies"

The experience of women participating in the struggle for independence, from organizing boycotts to aiding men on the battlefield (see pages 100 and 101), gave rise to a sense of **egalitarianism** among many women and men. This rethinking of traditional gender roles was evident in a private letter that **Abigail Adams** sent to her husband **John Adams** in March 1776, as he and other leaders of the Patriot cause debated independence and a new legal framework. She expressed hope that "you would **remember the ladies** and be more generous and favorable to them than your ancestors." She requested that the new legal system "not put such unlimited power into the hands of the husbands." Some historians have dismissed the letter, and John's response, as a humorous exchange between intimates. However, in the context of other writings by Abigail Adams, it is clear that gender equality was an issue she took seriously. The letter is especially significant in the context of the American Revolution. The rhetoric of the revolutionary era railed against tyrannical rule. Many found analogies between the tyranny of king over subject and the tyranny of husband over wife.

"Republican Motherhood"

The arguments deployed by the Patriot cause in the American Revolution inspired many male and female writers to challenge traditional notions of gender and to put forth new ideas about the proper role of men and women in the new nation. The concept of **"republican motherhood,"** drawing together a number of elements, asserted that women did indeed have civic responsibilities in the evolving culture of the new nation. The concept drew on **Enlightenment** thinkers, such as **John Locke**, who asserted, in his *Two Treatises on Government*, that marriage should involve a greater degree of consent, challenging traditional notions of female subordination. Further, the experience of the war itself, and women's participation in it, contributed to changing idea around gender.

The concept of "republican motherhood" did not put forth an agenda of political equality between men and women. It went only so far as to assert that women did have a role to play in civic life. The main feature of this role was to raise civic-minded republican sons and to reform the morals and manners of men. It asserted that women were active agents in maintaining public virtue—a realm traditionally associated with men. The ideas of "republican motherhood" still confined women to a largely domestic role, but these ideas did expand the possibilities for women to gain an education; after all, it was important for women to gain the literacy and knowledge needed to raise the next generation of republican leaders.

C. The Impact of the American Revolution Abroad

The ideas of the American Revolution reverberated among many different peoples struggling against oppressive regimes.

Revolution in France

In 1789, a little over a decade after the thirteen colonies declared independence, and a mere six years after the **Treaty of Paris** was signed, a revolution began in France. The French revolutionaries were inspired by some of the same Enlightenment ideas that had inspired revolutionaries in America and were inspired by the American model itself. This first phase of the **French Revolution** was begun by the national legislature against the absolutist power of the monarch. The first phase had widespread support in the United States. Soon, the revolution entered a more radical phase. In 1793, the monarchy was completely abolished, the power of the church was limited, and, during a fever of revolutionary zeal, more than 40,000 suspected enemies of the revolution were publicly executed, among them the king and queen of France. This **"reign of terror,"** carried out by the **Jacobins'** political club, peaked in 1793–1794. The leader of the Jacobins, **Maximilien Robespierre**, was himself executed in 1794. The **Directory**, a body of five men, took power in 1795 and held that power until 1799, when the French Revolution came to an end. After that, **Napoleon Bonaparte** assumed power in a coup d'état. As the revolution took its turn into a more radical and violent direction in 1793, Americans became increasingly divided about the events in France.

Rebellion in Haiti

In 1791, a revolution broke out in the western part of the Caribbean island of **Hispaniola**. The revolution occurred in the French part of the island, called **Saint Domingue**. This French colony was primarily a sugar-producing slave society, made up of half a million African slaves and 60,000 free people. Of the free people, about half were white and half were mixed-race *(gens de couleur)*. The mixed-race population of Saint Domingue owned about a third of the slaves on the island, but were barred from participation in the political system.

The revolution had three phases. First, the white colonists resisted French rule, inspired in part by the model of the American Revolution and in part by the recent French Revolution. Second, the mixed-race planters rebelled, challenging their second-class status. Finally, the slaves themselves rebelled. The slave rebellion, led by **Toussaint L'Overture** and aided by Spanish troops, occupied much of the country. The rebellion of slaves on Saint Domingue sent waves of fear among southern planters in the United States, especially after fleeing whites and mixed-race people brought stories of the rebellion to communities in the southern United States. Soon after L'Overture's death, **Haiti** established its independence (1804) as the first Black republic in the Americas.

Independence Struggles in Latin America

Of all the revolutions that followed the American Revolution, those in **Latin America** are most similar to it. In both the British North American colonies and the Spanish American colonies, colonists decided to break long-held ties with European powers. Also, both the North American and the South American struggles for independence involved deep divisions within the respective colonial societies; rebels and loyalists clashed on both continents. Both revolutionary struggles occurred in societies that included slavery. Starting in 1808, several nations in Spain's vast New World empire—which extended from Mexico in the north to Argentina in the south, Peru in the west to Venezuela in the east—rebelled against Spanish rule. The revolutionaries were inspired by a combination of ideology, geopolitics, and material interests—just as their North American predecessors were.

Topic 3.7 The Articles of Confederation

After declaring independence, Americans experimented with different forms of government, both on the state level and the national level. The Articles of Confederation established a weak central government, with the states retaining a great deal of their powers. The weaknesses of the Articles of Confederation soon became apparent as the United States faced a series of domestic and international challenges.

A. Governance on the State Level

After the Second Continental Congress declared independence, the newly established states created constitutions that placed power in the hands of the legislative branch. State constitutions varied in the extent to which they embraced democratic participation.

State Constitutions

In May 1776, even before independence had been declared, the **Second Continental Congress** urged the colonies to draft **constitutions**. By 1778, ten states had drawn up constitutions, and Connecticut, Massachusetts, and Rhode Island updated their colonial charters. All the state constitutions affirmed the republican notion that government ultimately rests on the consent of the governed. Most of these constitutions reflected the older

---

USING HISTORICAL THINKING SKILLS: CONTEXTUALIZATION

The Context of the Articles of Confederation

When analyzing the Articles of Confederation in retrospect, it is tempting to see the document as a recipe for dysfunction and its framers as misguided. However, looking at the context of the document can help students construct a fuller understanding of the Articles. The Articles of Confederation were written as the United States was attempting to divorce itself from Great Britain. Many Americans were wary of distant authority and wanted to keep decision-making close to home; they did not want to see a new central government with a free hand to do as it pleased. In addition, the Articles can be seen in the context of intellectual currents in colonial America in the 1700s. Republicanism, with its roots in both ancient Roman and Renaissance European thought, had been a central part of American political culture. It fostered a distrust of powerful governments and encouraged a virtuous citizenry to guard against corruption and greed among government officials. Keeping power on the local level, as the Articles did, made sense in this intellectual climate.

view of **republicanism** (see page 103). That is, these constitutions tended to be based on the idea that governing units should be relatively small and that distant power could become tyrannical. Some states created some form of **direct democracy.** Many states strengthened the **lower legislative house**. The lower house would be more responsive to the will of the people through more frequent elections. Some states established **annual elections** in the lower house. Pennsylvania and Georgia abolished the upper house altogether.

Pennsylvania created the most radical of the state constitutions. The older, elite leadership of the colony was marginalized after it came out strongly against independence in the summer of 1776. The power vacuum that resulted was filled by a pro-independence, democratic-minded group of activists, including **Thomas Paine** and **Benjamin Rush**. These activists gave voice to the artisan and lower-class communities of Philadelphia rather than to the merchant elite class. The constitution that was drafted abolished property qualifications for voting and also abolished the office of governor. This constitution was in effect until the 1790s. Although Pennsylvania created the most democratic constitution, many states included lists of individual liberties that government was not to abridge. **Virginia's Declaration of Rights** (1776) inspired other states to follow suit.

B. The Articles of Confederation and the Critical Period

The framers of the Articles of Confederation created a "firm league of friendship" among the states, rather than a strong, centralized nation. Before 1776 they had lived under a powerful, distant authority, and they did not want to repeat that experience. Also, many of these early leaders were fiercely loyal to their states and did not want to see state power taken away. The Articles of Confederation may have appealed to those who feared arbitrary and distant authority, but during the period of their operation, often called the "critical period," the United States faced a series of domestic and international problems that led some to call for a stronger central government. The word "critical" in this case is similar to its use in medicine. Just like a patient in critical condition, the continued existence of the United States was in question.

The Articles of Confederation

The **Articles of Confederation** were written in 1776, just as the Declaration of Independence was being written and debated. The Articles of Confederation, however, lack the philosophical grandeur of Thomas Jefferson's document. The Articles essentially put down on paper what had come to exist organically over the previous year, as the First and Second Continental Congresses began to assume more powers and responsibilities. The main concern at the time was carrying out the war against Great Britain. The document was edited and sent to the states for ratification in 1777. It took, however, an additional four years for all the states to ratify it. The issue of western land claims caused several states to initially reject the document (see page 111).

Structure of Government Under the Articles of Confederation

The Articles called for a one-house, or **unicameral**, legislature, continuing the practice of the Second Continental Congress. This Congress would have delegations from each state. States could send anywhere from two to seven delegates, but each state delegation would get one vote. Decision-making in Congress was not easy. Routine decisions required just a simple majority, or seven votes. Major decisions, however, required nine votes, allowing five states to block major legislation. Changes and amendments to the document itself required a unanimous vote in Congress and ratification by all the state legislatures.

Raising Revenue

Under the Articles of Confederation, the national government's lack of broad powers was especially problematic in regard to **raising revenue**. This was an acute problem during wartime. The central government did not have the power to tax the people directly. The idea of being taxed only by local representatives carried over from the days of the Stamp Act crisis (1765). The central government depended on voluntary contributions from the states.

Congress agreed that states would contribute revenue in proportion to their population, but the states were often tardy or resistant.

Inflation, Debt, and the Rejection of the Impost

The United States faced serious economic problems during the 1780s. The Confederation government and the states printed millions of dollars in paper money, driving up **inflation**. In addition, the government borrowed millions of dollars during the war. After the war, the government had trouble paying off these **debts**.

Robert Morris, chosen by Congress to address these issues, proposed a 5 percent impost, or import tax, to raise revenues. Since this would require a change in the Articles themselves, all thirteen states had to be on board. **Rhode Island** and **New York**, which both had thriving ports, did not want to give up the revenue stream from state duties, so they rejected the proposed **impost**. This rejection demonstrated the difficulties Congress faced in passing important reforms.

Shays's Rebellion (1786–1787)

Several of the problems associated with the **"critical period"** were evident in a farmers' uprising in Massachusetts called **Shays's Rebellion** (1786–1787). In the western part of the state, struggling farmers, many of whom were veterans of the Revolution, were troubled by several government actions. Taxes in Massachusetts were high, unlike in other states, and had to be paid in hard currency (backed by gold or silver), not cheap paper currency. Unable to pay these taxes, many farmers were losing their farms to banks. The farmers petitioned the legislature to pass **stay laws**, which would have suspended a creditors' right to foreclose on farms. This, along with petitions to lower taxes, was rejected by the Massachusetts legislature.

After being frustrated by the legislature, hundreds of Massachusetts farmers, led by veteran **Daniel Shays**, protested and finally took up arms. They were responding to a perceived injustice as they had a decade earlier when under British rule. They closed down several courts and freed farmers from debtors' prison. Local militias did not try to stop the actions, which spread to more towns in Massachusetts. After several weeks, the governor and legislature took action, calling up nearly 4,000 armed men to suppress the rebellion. The insurrection reflected ongoing tensions between coastal elites and struggling farmers in the interior. Concerns about the ability of the authorities to put down future uprisings were on the minds of the delegates to the **Philadelphia convention** (see below), which convened just three months after Shays's Rebellion ended.

> **USING REASONING PROCESSES:**
> **CAUSATION**
>
> **The Impact of Shays's Rebellion**
>
> Shays's Rebellion is considered one of important causes of the change in governing documents in the United States, from the Articles of Confederation to the Constitution. Many political leaders saw the inability of the central government to halt this rebellion as a major problem. The event convinced national leaders, such as George Washington, Alexander Hamilton, and James Madison, to push for the creation of a completely new governing document rather than simply a set of amendments to the Articles of Confederation. According to the progressive historian Charles Beard, in *An Economic Interpretation of the Constitution of the United States* (1913), these wealthy leaders created the Constitution to protect and enhance their prosperity and economic advantage over the poorer classes.

Toward a New Framework for Governance

By 1786, many Americans, especially elite property owners, began to raise concerns about the stature of the United States on the world stage and the competency of a weak central government. With these concerns in mind, in 1786 a group of **reformers** received approval from Congress to meet in **Annapolis, Maryland**, to discuss possible changes in the **Articles of Confederation**. A follow-up meeting was scheduled in **Philadelphia** for May 1787. In between these meetings, from August 1786 until February 1787, Shays's Rebellion erupted in Massachusetts (see text and box above). The rebellion was eventually put down, but it added fuel to the impetus to reform the governing structure. By the time of the Philadelphia meeting, the delegates were ready to scrap the entire Articles of Confederation and write something new (see Topic 3.8).

C. Organizing the Northwest Territory

The Confederation Congress made important progress in incorporating the country's western lands by passing the Northwest Ordinance and establishing procedures and guidelines for the incorporation of new states.

The Northwest Territory

After the United States declared independence from Great Britain, there was debate about the status of the vast swath of land between the **Appalachian Mountains** and the **Mississippi River**. Some states insisted that **western land claims** from the colonial period should be honored. Virginia, for instance, claimed all of the land north of the Ohio River. New York claimed a huge portion of the West, including land that overlapped with Virginia's claim. Some states, such as New Jersey and Maryland, had no claims. Maryland insisted that it would not ratify the **Articles of Confederation** until all states gave up their land claims and the western lands became part of a national domain. Congress persuaded the states with claims to do just that in 1781.

Land Ordinances and the Northwest Ordinance

Once the lands west of the Appalachian Mountains came under the control of the national government, Congress set about passing a series of acts to clarify the status of these lands and to encourage their settlement. The **Land Ordinance of 1784** divided the **Northwest Territory** into ten potential new states, each with the guarantee of self-government. The following year, Congress passed the **Land Ordinance of 1785**, reducing the number of states from ten to five. The ordinance also called for the creation of townships, each six by six miles; these townships were then divided into thirty-six lots, each one square mile. A lot in every town was set aside for education; four additional lots were set aside for other public and governmental uses. The remaining lots were to be sold. In 1787, Congress passed the **Northwest Ordinance**, setting up a process by which areas could become territories, and then states. Once the population of a territory reached 60,000, it could write a constitution and apply for statehood. These states would be on equal footing with the original thirteen states; they would not have a second-class, colonial status. Also, the Northwest Ordinance banned **slavery** in the territory north of the Ohio River. These acts encouraged the steady and orderly flow of settlers into the West. These policies, however, proved disastrous for American Indians. Congress's handling of the Northwest Territory is seen as one of the few major successes of the government under the Articles of Confederation.

Moving into the Northwest Territory

In the 1790s, a steady stream of migrants made their way into the southern portion of the Northwest Territory, settling along the Ohio and its tributary rivers. The process was made easier by further congressional action. Future president **William Henry Harrison**, who from 1799 to 1800 was a nonvoting congressional delegate from the Northwest Territory, successfully promoted the passage of legislation that made it easier for ordinary settlers to buy land there. The **Harrison Land Law**, which allowed for sales of smaller plots, facilitated the rapid population growth of the Northwest Territory. In 1803, the southeastern portion of the territory was incorporated as the state of **Ohio**. The remainder of the region was designated as the **Indiana Territory** in 1800. This territory later became the states of Indiana, Illinois, Michigan, and part of Wisconsin.

Topic 3.8 The Constitutional Convention and Debates over Ratification

As the limitations of the Articles of Confederation became more apparent, American political leaders drafted the Constitution, which was designed to strengthen the central government. Debates over the Constitution led to the adoption of a Bill of Rights as Americans continued to debate the proper balance between liberty and order.

A. Compromise and the Framing of the Constitution

The delegates who had been chosen to work on changes to the Articles of Confederation quickly agreed at the 1787 Philadelphia meeting to get rid of the Articles altogether and to create a new framework for government. For four months, delegates met, argued, and wrote. These deliberations resulted in a series of compromises that formed the basis of the new Constitution.

The Great Compromise

The delegates at the **Constitutional Convention** agreed that a central government with far greater powers was needed, but several contentious issues occupied much of their attention. A major source of disagreement was how the various states should be represented in the new government. Bigger states expressed dissatisfaction with the one-vote-per-state system that existed under the Articles; they argued that larger states should have a larger voice in governance. The delegates from these states rallied around the **Virginia Plan**, which would have created a **bicameral** legislature that pegged the number of representatives from each state to the population of the state. The small states feared their voices would be drowned out in such a legislature. They countered with the **New Jersey Plan**, which called for a **one-house** legislature with each state getting one vote (similar to the existing Congress under the Articles of Confederation). After much wrangling, the delegates agreed on the **Great Compromise**, which created the basic structure of **Congress** as it now exists. The plan called for a **House of Representatives**, in which representation would be determined by the population of each state, and a **Senate**, in which each state would get two members.

B. The Constitution and Slavery—Compromise and Postponement

Though many voices noted the inconsistency of slavery and the ideals put forth in the nation's founding documents, slavery continued in the United States. The framers of the Constitution were, to some degree, uneasy with the institution of slavery. This uneasiness is reflected in the fact that the word "slavery" is not used once in the entire document. Slaves are referred to as "other persons." Although the framers of the Constitution did not mention the word *slavery*, they were willing to compromise on the issue and postpone any final decision about it to the future. This postponement led to decades of debate and conflict over the issue.

The "Three-Fifths Compromise"

Once it was established that representation in the **House of Representatives** would be based on population, the question arose: Who would be counted in determining a state's population? Specifically, would a southern state be able to count its slave populations in the census? This was a major issue when one considered that for states such as South Carolina and Mississippi slaves comprised more than 50 percent of the populations. To count them in the census would more than double the size of their delegations in the House. Northern states objected on the grounds that slaves could not vote; in fact, they were considered property, not human beings. After much debate, a compromise was reached in which southern states could count three-fifths of their slave populations in the census. This **"Three-Fifths Compromise"** defied common sense, but it got the delegates through an impasse.

Tacit Approval of Slavery

Other sections of the Constitution seem to give **tacit approval** of the institution of **slavery**. The delegates voted to protect the **international slave trade** for 20 years, guaranteeing the flow of slaves into the country from Africa and the Caribbean for another generation. (The international slave trade was ended by Congress in 1808, the earliest date that the Constitution allowed.) In addition, the Constitution provided for the return of **fugitive slaves**. (A mechanism for their return was contained in the Fugitive Slave Act of 1793; the process was strengthened with the Fugitive Slave Act of 1850.) Though slavery was not mentioned by name, the inclusion of regulations around slavery made clear that the Constitution recognized its existence.

C. Federalists, Anti-Federalists, and the Adoption of the Bill of Rights

Once the Constitution was completed, it went to the states for ratification. Each state was to call a convention to vote for ratification, and only nine states were needed for approval. This was still not an easy process. Large numbers of Americans opposed the creation of a powerful central government. Public opinion in Virginia, Massachusetts, and New York was clearly against ratification. North Carolina and Rhode Island did not even hold conventions. Ultimately, all the states did vote to ratify the Constitution. Many opponents of the new Constitution came around to voting in the affirmative only after prominent supporters of the document promised to add a bill of rights to the Constitution.

The Federalists

The supporters of the Constitution labeled themselves **Federalists**. Three important Federalist theorists were **Alexander Hamilton**, **John Jay**, and **James Madison**. As the **New York** convention was debating **ratification** in late 1787 and 1788, the three wrote a series of articles that were later published in book form—*The Federalist*. This highly influential political tract outlined the failures of the Articles of Confederation and the benefits of a powerful government with checks and balances. In *Federalist Number 10*, Madison argued that, for a large and diverse population, a **complex government** was the best guarantee of liberty. With such a complex government, no one group could gain control and dominate others. This argument challenged the traditional republican notion that republics must be small in order to be democratic. In *Federalist Number 51*, he argued for a **separation of powers** within the government and a system of checks and balances.

Anti-Federalism

Opponents of the new Constitution, **Anti-Federalists**, as they were called by their Federalist adversaries, worried that the new government would be controlled by members of the elite. They saw the document as favoring the creation of a powerful, aristocratic ruling class. Leading Anti-Federalists were **Patrick Henry** and **George Mason**. They argued that officials in the national government would be, almost by definition, removed from the concerns, and the control, of ordinary people. They were distrustful of distant authority. The thirteen colonies had just emerged from under the rule of the British Empire, so many colonists were eager to see that power was exercised locally. One of the Anti-Federalists' primary concerns was that individual rights were not adequately protected by the Constitution. They noted that the document did not contain a bill of rights.

Ratification

Delaware ratified the Constitution almost immediately, in December 1787. By January 1788, four more states—Pennsylvania, New Jersey, Georgia, and Connecticut—voted for **ratification**. In January, supporters of the Constitution faced their first real test in Massachusetts. Prominent Massachusetts political leaders, including **Samuel Adams** and **Governor John Hancock**, opposed ratification. Also, many followers of Daniel Shays were active in the process and were strongly opposed to the Constitution. Federalist leaders assured the ratifying convention that they would recommend the creation of a national bill of rights in order to address Anti-Federalist concerns. In February, Massachusetts voted to approve the Constitution. By May, Maryland and South Carolina came on board. New Hampshire provided the ninth, and deciding, vote in June 1788. By May 1790, the final four states—Virginia (1788), New York (1788), North Carolina (1789), and Rhode Island (1790)—voted for ratification and joined the new Union.

The Bill of Rights

During the debate over ratification of the Constitution, seven of the states voted to ratify only on the condition that Congress would pass a list of rights of the people. Anti-Federalists in these states feared that a powerful government would step on individual liberties. As promised, one of the first acts of Congress was passage of the **Bill of**

Rights—the first ten amendments to the Constitution. Much of the language in the Bill of Rights, written by **James Madison**, comes from the various states' constitutions.

The First Through Fourth Amendments: Basic Rights of the People

The **First Amendment** contains the **"establishment clause"** prohibiting the establishment of an official religion in the United States. The remainder of the First Amendment deals with various forms of freedom of expression. The **Second Amendment** guarantees the **right to bear arms**. Some have argued that the language of the Second Amendment seems to link the right to bear arms to participation in militias; others have argued that it is an absolute individual right. The **Third Amendment** addresses a much-hated British practice—forcing colonial residents to house soldiers. Americans would not be compelled to quarter soldiers. The **Fourth Amendment** guarantees a modicum of privacy from searches by government officials. People are protected in their "persons, houses, papers and effects" from "unreasonable searches and seizures." Authorities must first obtain a warrant issued by a judge upon evidence of "probable cause."

The Fifth Through Eighth Amendments: Rights of the Accused

Several amendments in the Bill of Rights address protections people have when they are brought into the legal system. The logic of these amendments is that the legal system is powerful and well-funded, and should therefore have checks placed upon it to protect the individual. The **Fifth Amendment** calls for grand jury indictments, prohibits authorities from trying a suspect twice for the same crime (**"double jeopardy"**) and from forcing a suspect to testify against himself or herself. The Fifth Amendment also prohibits the government from seizing someone's property, unless it is for a "public use" and the owner receives "just compensation." The power of the government to seize private property under these stipulations is known as **"eminent domain."** The **Sixth Amendment** guarantees suspects the right to a **"speedy and public" trial**, with a jury, conducted in the district where the crime was committed. Also, the suspect has a right to be informed of the charges and has the right to cross-examine witnesses giving testimony. Finally, suspects have the right to call friendly witnesses to the stand and to have a lawyer. The **Seventh Amendment** guarantees the accused the right to a **trial by jury**, even in civil cases (involving conflicts between two parties over monetary damages). The **Eighth Amendment** prevents the government from inflicting **"cruel and unusual" punishments** and prevents the setting of **"excessive bail."**

The Ninth and Tenth Amendments

The last two amendments of the Bill of Rights deal with limits and parameters of rights and powers inherent in the government. The **Ninth Amendment** guarantees that additional rights, not mentioned in the Bill of Rights, shall be protected from government infringement. The **Tenth Amendment** deals with governmental powers and the relationship between the federal government and the states. It asserts that powers not delegated to the federal government, nor prohibited by the Constitution, shall be retained by the states and by the people.

The Right to Vote

The right to vote is absent from the Bill of Rights. The federal government left it to the states to formulate rules for voting. It was only later that voting would be seen as a fundamental right that needed the protection of constitutional amendments. The **Fifteenth Amendment** (1870) prohibited voting restrictions based on race, the **Nineteenth Amendment** (1920) prohibited restrictions based on gender, and the **Twenty-sixth Amendment** (1971) lowered the voting age to 18.

Topic 3.9 The Constitution

The delegates at the Constitutional Convention created a national government that was more powerful than the one that had existed under the Articles of Confederation. However, the structure of the Constitution contained safeguards against the government assuming excessive powers. Three branches were created, each with the power to check the power of other two. A system of federalism was also created, allowing state governments to retain certain powers.

A. The Structure of Government Under the Constitution

The framers of the Constitution created three separate and coequal branches of government. The legislative branch creates laws, the executive branch carries out laws, and the judicial branch interprets laws.

The Three Branches of Government, Separation of Powers, and Checks and Balances

The **Constitution** spells out the specific powers of each of the three branches of government. The powers of the **legislative branch**—**Congress**—are enumerated in **Article I**. These include the power to levy taxes, to regulate trade, to coin money, to establish post offices, to declare war, and to approve treaties. The framers of the Constitution wanted Congress to have the flexibility to deal with the needs of a changing society. Toward this goal they included the **elastic clause**, which stretched the powers of Congress by allowing it to create laws it deemed **"necessary and proper"** to carry out its listed powers. However, the definition of "necessary and proper" soon became a matter of much debate. The powers of the **executive branch**—the **president**—are included in **Article II**. These include the power to suggest legislation, to command the armed forces, and to nominate judges. The president is charged with carrying out the laws of the land. The powers of the **judiciary**, headed by the **Supreme Court**, are outlined in **Article III**. The federal judiciary has the power to hear cases involving people or entities from different states and to hear cases involving federal law. Later, in the case of ***Marbury v. Madison*** (1803), the Court assumed its most significant power—**judicial review**, the power to nullify laws that it deems inconsistent with the Constitution (see page 137).

> **USING HISTORICAL THINKING SKILLS:**
> **CLAIMS AND EVIDENCE IN SOURCES**
>
> ### *Federalist Number 51* and the Constitution
>
> In *Federalist Number 51*, James Madison argued for a government with three branches and a system of checks and balances. The document represents the rationale for and defense of the basic structural elements of the Constitution. In this essay, Madison asserted that "ambition must be made to counteract ambition"—that is, the passions, priorities, and interests of individuals in one branch would be checked, or counteracted, by members of another branch. "If men were angels," Madison wrote, such checks wouldn't be necessary; in fact, government itself wouldn't be necessary. Madison argued that the task at hand was to create a government that had the power to govern and that also had mechanisms to prevent it from becoming tyrannical. "You must first enable the government to control the governed; and the next place, oblige it to control itself."

The framers were very conscious of the problems of a government with limitless powers. After living under the British monarchy, they came to believe that a powerful government without checks was dangerous to liberty. Therefore, they created a governmental system with three separate branches, each with the ability to check the powers of the other two. The goal was to keep the three branches in balance. An example of this concept of **checks and balances** is the president's ability to veto (or reject) bills passed by Congress, or the Supreme Court's ability to strike down laws that it deems unconstitutional.

Federalism—the National Government and the States

Federalism refers to the evolving relationship between the national government and the states. The Constitution gave the national government considerably more power than had the Articles of Confederation. Under the Constitution, states still hold on to certain powers (**reserved powers**), but an expanded national government is given many new powers (**delegated powers**). These expanded national powers include the power to tax, borrow money, regulate commerce, and promote the "general welfare." At one point, Madison proposed granting Congress the power to strike down state laws, but this measure was rejected. The Constitution does make it clear, however, that the national government is the **"supreme law of the land."**

Topic 3.10 Shaping the New Republic

The United States faced a host of challenges in its first years of independence. The continued presence of European powers in North America challenged the government to find ways to safeguard the borders. At the same time, war and conflict in Europe made it difficult for the United States to pursue both free trade and neutrality. In addition, neither the Constitution nor political leaders in the early national period clarified the status of American Indians in the United States, setting the stage for future conflicts. Finally, the nation experienced heated debates over a national bank, the future economic direction of the United States, and the proper balance between security and civil liberties.

A. Spain and Great Britain Challenge American Growth

The United States continued to have difficulties with the presence of European powers in North America. The British were reluctant to abandon their holdings, including several forts in the Northwest Territory, and Spain persisted in challenging American use of the Mississippi River.

British Forces and American Indians

Americans became increasingly frustrated that the **British** seemed intent on thwarting the westward movement of Americans from the towns of the eastern seaboard. British forces had not evacuated forts in the western territories following the signing of the Treaty of Paris (1783). The British maintained a thriving **fur trade** with **American Indian** groups in the area above the Ohio River. Further, the British provided the **Shawnee**, the **Miami**, and the **Delaware** with weapons that could be used in resisting American migration. The British insisted that they would not remove their western forces until the United States repaid its war debts and allowed loyalists to recover property that had been confiscated during the war. In 1785, the United States minister to Great Britain pressed for a resolution of these issues, but to no avail.

Conflicts with Spain and Pinckney's Treaty

The United States had ongoing conflicts with Spain following the **Treaty of Paris** (1783). First, the borders between the United States and Spanish territory were in dispute. The Treaty of Paris, between the United States and Great Britain, stipulated that American territory extended south to the northern boundary of Spanish Florida. However, in a separate treaty between Great Britain and Spain, the extent of Spanish territory was not spelled out. An earlier treaty between the two countries gave Spain control of territory north of that boundary, in present-day Alabama and Mississippi. Second, although American territory abutted the Mississippi River, Spain repeatedly attempted to limit American shipping on the river. The United States was able to resolve these issues with Spain. Negotiations between the diplomats **Thomas Pinckney** of the United States and **Don Manuel de Godoy** of Spain resulted in **Pinckney's Treaty** (1795; ratified in 1796). Spain agreed to allow for American shipping on the Mississippi River. The treaty also defined the border between the United States and Spanish-held territory in western Florida.

Conflicts with Great Britain and Jay's Treaty

Tensions between the United States and **Great Britain** continued into the 1790s. Once war broke out between **France** and Great Britain in 1793, U.S. ships maintained a brisk trade with both the French West Indies and with France itself. Great Britain was none too pleased with this development and began intercepting American ships (almost 300) in or near the West Indies. In addition, southern planters wanted reimbursement from the British for slaves that had fled to British lines during the American Revolution and were never returned. Also, western settlers were resentful of the continued presence of British forces in forts in the Northwest (see above). This last issue became significant in light of the increasingly bloody clashes between U.S. forces and American Indians. Americans accused the British of aiding the Indians in order to maintain their profitable **fur trade**.

Washington sent **John Jay**, the chief justice of the **Supreme Court**, to Great Britain to seek redress of these grievances. Jay returned in 1795 with a treaty that was perceived as especially favorable to the British, who did agree to withdraw from the West, but only after eighteen months. The British would not compensate American shippers for lost cargoes, nor would they compensate American planters for lost slaves. In addition, American planters would be forced to repay debts to the British that dated from the colonial era. The one concession that Jay managed to wrest from the British was limited trading rights in the West Indies. Other issues would be addressed in the future by arbitration commissions.

Reactions to **Jay's Treaty** were decidedly mixed. **Alexander Hamilton** and his supporters saw the treaty as the best they could get at the moment. Supporters of **Thomas Jefferson**, especially from the South and the West, argued that their interests had been sold out to the mercantile interests in New England. They saw the treaty as evidence of the pro-British sympathies of the Hamiltonians. An opponent of the treaty scrawled on a wall: "Damn John Jay! Damn everyone who won't damn John Jay!"

B. Role of the United States in the Aftermath of the French Revolution

Despite America's intention to be independent of European affairs, events in Europe greatly impacted the newly formed United States. Just as Americans were ratifying the Constitution in 1789, the French Revolution was beginning. Americans were divided; their debates about the French Revolution foreshadowed ongoing debates about the role of the United States in the world.

The Question of Alliances

The debates over the role of the United States in the world took on greater significance after **France** and **Great Britain** went to war in 1793. Many Americans felt that the United States had an obligation to help France, in return for the help the United States received from France in the American Revolution, and because a 1778 treaty committed the United States to help if France were under attack. Others argued that the United States should stay out of the war. After all, the treaty was made with a French government that no longer existed and the French Revolution had devolved from a democratic movement into a bloodbath. **King Louis XVI** and thousands of his countrymen had been guillotined. Many of these neutrality-minded Americans also harbored warm feelings for the British system, despite the fact that the war with Great Britain had concluded a mere decade earlier. Already, the two nations had resumed commercial ties.

Conflict with France and the XYZ Affair

Events during the administration of **President John Adams** challenged America's commitment to **neutrality** (see pages 116–117). In 1797, in retaliation for America's favorable treaty with Great Britain (see Jay's Treaty above), **France** rescinded the 1778 alliance with the United States and allowed French privateers to seize American ships. After more than 300 ships were seized, President Adams sent a delegation of negotiators to Paris to attempt a peaceful solution. The delegation was not initially allowed to discuss the matter with the French foreign affairs minister **Charles Talleyrand**. Rather, three intermediaries approached the American delegation and informed them that they could begin negotiations if they paid $250,000 and promised a $12 million loan to France. The three French agents were never named. When word of this interchange made its way

---

USING REASONING PROCESSES:
COMPARISON

Political Parties and Foreign Policy

The Federalists and the Democratic-Republicans pursued very different foreign policies, especially in regard to France. Note that during the presidential administration of the Federalist John Adams (1797-1801), U.S. relations with France were more strained; during the administrations of Democratic–Republican presidents, from 1801 to 1815 (the end of the War of 1812), U.S. relations with Great Britain were more strained. During the Federalist period, we see the XYZ Affair and the Quasi-War with France. During the Democratic-Republican period, we see the impressment of U.S sailors by Great Britain, the *Chesapeake-Leopard* Affair (1807), and trade restrictions that led up to the War of 1812 with Britain.

into American papers, the three agents were referred to simply as X, Y, and Z. The **XYZ affair** incensed President Adams and many Americans. Congress allocated money for a military engagement against France. Warships were dispatched to the Caribbean and fought French ships in America's first undeclared war, labeled by historians the **Quasi-War** (1798–1800). This military encounter helped instill respect for the **U.S. Navy**, which had just been reestablished in 1797.

C. Spanish Missions in California

Spain encouraged migration into the northern reaches of New Spain—present-day California—by expanding mission settlements. These missions offered opportunities to Spanish soldiers and settlers, while fostering a cultural blending of Spanish and Indian peoples.

The Expansion of the Mission System

In the last decades of the eighteenth century and into the nineteenth century, Spanish Catholics of the Franciscan order established a series of **missions** in California with the goal of spreading their faith among local Indians. A Catholic priest, **Junipero Serra**, was instrumental in establishing the first missions in California; ultimately twenty-one missions were founded. These settlements were both religious missions and military outposts, and they represented an attempt by Spain to maintain a presence along the northern borderlands. The goal of the missions was not only spiritual. The Spaniards extracted labor from the native peoples.

The missions had disastrous results for the native tribes of California. Disease ravaged their populations; in 1806, a measles epidemic wiped out a quarter of the mission Indians in the San Francisco area. Further, missionaries and their employees often treated the local populations brutally, raping women and subjecting local populations to beatings and slavery-like working conditions. An Indian revolt took place at the **Mission San Diego de Alcala** in 1775, but the mission system continued to exist into the early 1800s. By the 1830s, the Mexican government abandoned the mission project, selling mission lands to private individuals.

D. American Indian Policy in the New Nation

The ratification of the Constitution did not bode well for American Indians within the boundaries of the United States. The Constitution did not precisely define the relationship between the government and the American Indians. This shortcoming set the stage for further bloody conflicts on the frontier.

American Indians and the Constitution

The **Constitution** did not clarify the status of **American Indian** tribes and nations within its borders, though the document did recognize the tribes as **legal entities**. For instance, it gave Congress the power to regulate commerce—among the states, with foreign nations, and "with the Indian tribes." However, in mentioning them separately from foreign nations, the Constitution made it clear that they did not have legal standing as foreign nations. Further, although the tribes were not foreign nations, most individual Indians were not fully citizens of the **United States** either. Members of the tribes were not entitled to representation in Congress. Finally, the central issue of control of land was not settled by the Constitution. Over time, a series of treaties, agreements, and court decisions attempted to clarify the legal status of American Indian lands. However, these measures proved to be provisional, leaving Indian lands vulnerable to incursions by white settlers.

E. Putting the Constitution into Practice

The Constitution, ratified in 1788, existed on paper. It took the first two presidential administrations, those of George Washington and John Adams, to put the principles of the Constitution into practice.

The Judiciary Act of 1789

The **Constitution** called for a federal judiciary, including a supreme court, but left it up to **Congress** to flesh out such a system. The **Judiciary Act of 1789** created thirteen federal judicial districts. Each district had a district court as well as a circuit court that could hear appeals from the district courts. The **Supreme Court** could hear appeals from the circuit courts and would have the final say. In addition, the act stipulated that the Supreme Court could hear cases on appeal from state courts if the case involved federal law. The Court would also have original jurisdiction over civil actions between states, or between a state and the United States. The act made it clear that the Supreme Court would have the last word on constitutional interpretation.

Washington and the "Unwritten Constitution"

President George Washington established several traditions and customs that have come to be known as the **"unwritten constitution."** The establishment of a **presidential cabinet** is one of these customs. Washington wisely chose capable and experienced men to run the new government's three departments—state, war, and the treasury. Washington chose **Thomas Jefferson** for the **Department of State**, **General Henry Knox** for the **Department of War**, and **Alexander Hamilton** for the **Treasury**. He also chose **Edmund Randolph** as the nation's first attorney general and **John Jay** for chief justice of the Supreme Court. Washington began meeting regularly with these men, seeking their input on important matters. This practice of meeting regularly with a presidential cabinet was subsequently followed by all American presidents. Washington's decision to run for no more than two terms was also part of the "unwritten constitution," until Congress and the states ratified the **Twenty-second Amendment** (1951), following **Franklin D. Roosevelt's** four electoral victories, making the traditional two-term limitation part of the written Constitution.

> **USING REASONING PROCESSES: CONTINUITY AND CHANGE**
>
> **Interpreting the Constitution**
>
> The debate over whether the government should charter a national bank, as Secretary of the Treasury Alexander Hamilton proposed, represents an ongoing debate in American history between strict and broad interpretations of the Constitution. The debate often revolves around the meaning of the "necessary and proper clause" (or elastic clause). A broad interpretation of the clause, Thomas Jefferson argued, would effectively create a national government with unlimited power. However, a narrow interpretation would greatly hamper the government's ability to legislate in a changing world. This debate can be seen in the decision by Jefferson, who as president took a broader view of the Constitution, to purchase the Louisiana Territory (1803). The debate is reflected in reactions to the liberal decisions of the Warren Court in the 1960s. Conservatives asserted that the "judicial activism" of the era reflected a too broad interpretation of the Constitution.

F. Policy Debates in the New Nation

A series of policy conflicts and disagreements emerged during the presidential administrations of George Washington and John Adams, reflecting a growing divide among the public. Around these divides coalesced two political groups, the Federalists and the Democratic-Republicans. These policy conflicts centered around economic policy, foreign policy, and the relationship between the federal government and the states.

Federalists and Democratic-Republicans

The first two political parties—the **Federalists** and the **Democratic-Republicans**—put forth profoundly different views in regard to public policy. At the same time, they facilitated a robust national debate on pressing issues. Federalists tended to be more pro-British, more critical of the French Revolution, more friendly to urban, commercial interests, and more ready to use the power of the federal government to influence economic activity. The leading theorist of the Federalists was **Alexander Hamilton**. The Democratic-Republicans tended to be more critical of the British, more supportive of the French Revolution (at least in its early, less violent stages), more critical of centralized authority, and more favorable to agricultural interests. **Thomas Jefferson** was a leading theorist of the Republicans. These two parties developed a strong dislike of each other, especially after the passage of the **Alien** and **Sedition Acts** in 1798 (see page 121), which seemed like thinly veiled attempts to silence and weaken the Democratic-Republicans. The passage of the acts seemed to backfire; the Democratic-Republicans gained strength and won the **presidential election of 1800.**

Hamilton's Economic Program and the National Bank

President George Washington's secretary of the treasury, **Alexander Hamilton**, proposed a series of economic measures meant to put the United States on a sound economic footing. Central to his plans was a national bank, which would hold the government's tax revenues and act as a stabilizing force on the economy. Hamilton proposed a bank that would be 20 percent publicly controlled and 80 percent privately controlled. Hamilton thought it was important to have wealthy Americans financially and psychologically invested in the new government. The proposal to create a national bank became a source of disagreement between Hamilton and **Secretary of State Thomas Jefferson**, who argued that the Constitution did not permit Congress to create a national bank. This was not among the powers listed in the Constitution. Hamilton countered that the **elastic clause**, which lets Congress do what it considered **"necessary and proper"** in carrying out its duties, implicitly allowed for the creation of a national bank. President Washington agreed and signed the bank into law in 1791.

Dealing with Debt

Alexander Hamilton's economic program included two other significant parts. He proposed an elaborate and controversial plan to deal with the new nation's substantial **debt**. He insisted that debts incurred by the national government and carried over from the war years be paid back, or funded, at full value. He believed that this would create confidence in the fiscal solvency of the new central government and would enhance its legitimacy. Many of the old **debt certificates** had been sold by their holders. The original holders had little faith that the government would ever make good on the actual loans. The certificates were changing hands at a fraction of their original value. Full funding meant that these old certificates could be redeemed at their full value—a financial windfall for speculators who had bought them up. In addition, Hamilton insisted that the government assume, or agree to pay back, state debts incurred during the war. The proposal met with strenuous opposition from states that either did not have a large debt or had already paid back their debts. To accomplish the goals of **"funding"** (paying back national debts at full value) and **"assumption"** (taking on and paying back state debts), Hamilton prodded the government to take out new loans by selling **government bonds**.

Encouragement to Manufacturing

The final piece of **Alexander Hamilton's** financial program was to encourage manufacturing by imposing tariffs on foreign-made goods and subsidizing American industry. (Congress adopted Hamilton's **"Report on Manufactures,"** except for his recommendation to subsidize industry.) He believed industrial development would be key to a balanced and self-reliant economy. At the time of Hamilton's report, the nation faced no immediate need to develop its manufacturing sector; however, the War of 1812 provided such a motivation by bringing the importance of manufacturing to the fore.

The Excise Tax and the Whiskey Rebellion (1794)

A conflict between elites and western farmers occurred in rural **Pennsylvania** in 1794. To help raise revenues to pay for his

> **USING REASONING PROCESSES:**
> ## COMPARISON
>
> ### Responses to Rebellions
>
> Be prepared to contrast the ineffective response to Shays's Rebellion, which lasted for several months in 1786 and 1787, with the massive force of troops sent to put down the Whiskey Rebellion (1794). The response to Shays's Rebellion took place in the context of a weak central government, under the Articles of Confederation. (Shays's Rebellion finally had to be put down by a privately-funded militia.) The response to the Whiskey Rebellion—13,000 federal troops sent to western Pennsylvania—took place in the context of the newly enacted Constitution. President George Washington was determined to establish federal authority and make clear that a strong national government would not tolerate unlawful challenges to its authority.

ambitious plans, Hamilton proposed enacting new taxes. The most prominent of these taxes, and most controversial, was an **excise (or sales) tax on whiskey**. This tax hit grain farmers especially hard. These hardscrabble farmers in remote rural areas were barely making ends meet. Distilling grain into whiskey allowed them to increase their meager profit. Transporting bushels of grain over primitive roads to population centers was prohibitively expensive; distilling grain into whiskey made the crop much more valuable and easier to transport.

The grain farmers of western Pennsylvania felt they could not shoulder this substantial tax. In 1794, farmers took action. Fifty men marched to the home of the local tax collector. From there the gathering swelled to 7,000 men and marched to **Pittsburgh**. At this point, the federal government took action. **Alexander Hamilton** and **George Washington** had vivid memories of **Shays's Rebellion** (1786–1787), a violent rebellion of farmers in western Massachusetts that lasted several months (see page 110 and see box, page 120). Washington nationalized nearly 13,000 militiamen into the army and marched them himself to Pennsylvania to suppress the rebellion and ensure that the laws of the land would be followed.

The Alien and Sedition Acts (1798)

In an atmosphere of animosity and distrust between the **Federalists** and the **Democratic-Republicans**, the **Alien and Sedition Acts** were passed by a Federalist-dominated Congress in order to limit criticism from the opposition Republican Party. The Alien and Sedition Acts actually were comprised of four acts. The main two acts were the **Naturalization Act**, which made it more difficult for foreigners to achieve American citizenship, and the **Sedition Act**, which made it a crime to defame the president or Congress. The broad wording of the Sedition Act was consistent with contemporary British sedition laws but seemed to challenge the free-speech guarantees of the recently ratified First Amendment. The other two acts, the **Alien Friends Act** and the **Alien Enemies Act**, allowed the president to imprison and deport noncitizens. Jeffersonians were especially troubled by the expansion of federal power that the acts represented.

The Kentucky and Virginia Resolutions

Thomas Jefferson and **James Madison** were so opposed to the Alien and Sedition Acts (see above) that they proposed the idea of nullification in their **Virginia and Kentucky Resolutions** (1798–1799). These resolutions put forth the idea that a state had the right to **nullify** a law it found to be inconsistent with the Constitution. The resolutions did not slow down enforcement of the **Alien and Sedition Acts**, but they raised issues about the relationship between the federal government and the states.

> **USING REASONING PROCESSES:**
> **CONTINUITY AND CHANGE**
>
> **State Versus Federal Power**
>
> The Kentucky and Virginia Resolutions (1798–1799), which asserted the state power to nullify federal legislation, were part of an ongoing debate over the respective powers of the federal government and state governments. The issue reemerged in the conflict over the Tariff Act of 1828, which steeply raised tariff rates on a number of items. The act, labeled by its critics the "Tariff of Abominations," led to South Carolina again arguing that states had the power to nullify federal acts. The Civil War settled a fundamental issue in regard to states' rights versus federal powers; it established that states do not have the right to secede. Southern states again invoked the rights of states to bypass federal mandates in regard to civil rights acts and decisions in the 1950s and 1960s. The issue of the powers of the respective governments still emerges in policy debates today—in regard to assisted suicide, marijuana consumption, gun control laws, mandates related to the COVID-19 pandemic, and other issues—although with less intensity than it did in the nineteenth century.

G. The Struggle for Neutrality in the 1790s

Despite attempts by the United States to remain neutral in regard to European affairs in the 1790s, the country found itself drawn into foreign conflicts. President George Washington took the opportunity in his "Farewell Address" to caution against the formation of "permanent alliances."

Washington and Neutrality

President Washington chose to remain neutral in the conflicts between Great Britain and France. He issued the **Neutrality Act** (1793) and he urged the United States to avoid permanent alliances with foreign powers. In his **Farewell Address**, he cautioned the newly independent nation against being drawn into the seemingly endless conflicts in Europe. His calls for neutrality have been invoked by isolationists throughout American history, including during debates about U.S. entrance into both twentieth-century world wars.

Topic 3.11 Developing an American Identity

The period from independence to the end of the eighteenth century witnessed the development of cultural forms that united the new country and helped it establish an identity separate from its European roots.

A. Culture and Identity in the Early National Period

In the decades following independence, a variety of cultural products were created that expressed a sense of national identity. For many Americans, political independence from Great Britain needed to be followed by cultural independence from European forms and traditions. The development of this uniquely American culture continued and flourished in the first decades of the nineteenth century (see Topic 4.9).

American Education

Noah Webster, a noted author, political thinker, and educator, asserted that American culture was separate from, and superior to, British culture. He saw the United States as a tolerant, rational, democratic nation—distinct from the superstitions, ostentatious habits, and warring history of Europe. He published a three-volume set of textbooks that were intended for American schoolchildren—*A Grammatical Institute of the English Language*. The work consisted of a speller (1783), a grammar (1784), and a reader (1785). The speller, known as the *American Spelling Book*, put forth simplified Americanized spellings—*theater* instead of *theatre*, *color* instead of *colour*. After 1800, he expanded his speller into a comprehensive dictionary: *An American Dictionary of the English Language*, completed in 1828. American schoolchildren also used *Geography Made Easy* by **Jedidiah Morse**, who insisted that American schoolchildren should use American textbooks.

American History

Within decades of independence, several writers set out to frame American history in a heroic light. **Mercy Otis Warren**, a long-time writer, political activist, and Anti-Federalist agitator, wrote a three-volume *History of the Revolution* (published in 1805). **Mason Weems** wrote a best-selling glowing biography of the nation's first president, *The Life of Washington*, first published in 1800. A later edition of the book contained the imagined story of a young George Washington admitting to his father that he had damaged a cherry tree with his hatchet, prefacing the admission with the words, "I cannot tell a lie." These volumes were intended to instill a nationalist spirit in Americans.

American Architecture

During this period, the first true American architects appeared on the scene. Among them was **Charles Bulfinch** (1763–1844) who is credited with bringing the **Federal style** to the United States after his European tour. Federalist architects were highly influenced by Scottish architect **Robert Adam** (1728–1792). Simplicity and balance characterize Federal architecture, a style indebted to ancient Greek and Roman elements, such as a triangular pediment atop large, marble columns. Americans consciously wanted to draw connections between the United States and the democratic and republican models of the ancient world; this impulse is reflected in Federal architecture.

Topic 3.12 Movement in the Early Republic

The closing decades of the eighteenth century witnessed increased migrations of white settlers into the interior of North America. These migrations led to conflicts between settlers and American Indians, tensions between backcountry farmers and coastal elites, and new forms of cultural blending. As Americans moved deeper into the interior, attitudes about slavery became more entrenched.

A. Migrations, American Indians, and Shifting Alliances

As more white settlers moved into the interior of North America in the decades after the American Revolution, various American Indian groups were forced to evaluate and adjust their alliances—with other tribes, with European powers, and with the United States. American Indians wanted to both limit the movement of settlers into the interior of the continent and to safeguard tribal lands and natural resources.

The Status of American Indian Lands After the American Revolution

After the Revolution, land struggles between white settlers and American Indian groups continued. The 1783 **Treaty of Paris** between the United States and Great Britain ignored the status of Indians in the American West. The land between the Appalachian Mountains and the Mississippi River had been set aside as an **Indian Reserve** by the British royal **Proclamation of 1763** (see page 96). In the Treaty of Paris (1783), the British agreed to withdraw their garrisons from this area, but the agreement did not make any accommodations for the Indians living there. (The British did not relinquish their last garrisons on American soil until 1795, following Jay's Treaty; see page 117.) As more Americans moved into this area after the Revolution, especially between the Ohio River and the Great Lakes, the status of the native peoples became more precarious.

Treaty of Fort Stanwix

In 1784, under the **Articles of Confederation**, the government tried to solve the problem of native land claims north of the Ohio River by working out the **Treaty of Fort Stanwix**. The negotiations occurred with the six-nation **Iroquois Confederacy**. The stated purpose of the negotiations was to formulate a peace treaty in the wake of the Revolution (in which two of the six Iroquois nations had sided with the British). The negotiations included the Iroquois ceding control of land north of the Ohio River. However, the Iroquois did not, for the most part, occupy the land in question, and their claims to it—based on the outcome of the **Beaver Wars** of the previous century (see page 76)—were dubious. The main occupants of the region, the **Shawnee, Delaware**, and **Miami**, were not part of these negotiations and protested bitterly that their land had been ceded without their consent.

Additional treaties were negotiated in the 1780s. In the **Treaty of Fort McIntosh** (1785), representatives of **Wyandotte, Delaware, Chippewa**, and **Ottawa** ceded lands in the trans-Ohio River region, in what became known as the **Northwest Territory**. Another agreement, the **Treaty of Fort Harmar** (1789), addressed the issue of control of other lands north of the Ohio. None of these treaties provided a satisfactory solution to the issue of control of the region. First, the powerful **Shawnee** were not part of the negotiations. Also, the continued presence of the British, as well as disputes about the authority of negotiators, complicated the issue.

American Defeat at the Wabash River

The situation between American Indians and white settlers grew increasingly tense after 1790. As settlers continued pushing into Indian territory, a series of military conflicts ensued in the 1790s in the region. American Indian forces, led by the **Miami** warrior

> **USING REASONING PROCESSES:**
> **CONTINUITY AND CHANGE**
>
> **Ongoing "Indian Wars"**
>
> The "Indian Wars" of the 1790s are part of an ongoing pattern of the United States breaking treaties, expanding westward, and engaging in conflicts with American Indians. The pattern stretches from the seventeenth century to the late-nineteenth century.

Little Turtle, engaged in major battles against U.S. troops in present-day Ohio. American troops led by **General Arthur St. Clair** suffered a massive defeat at the mouth of the **Wabash River** in 1791. More than 600 troops were killed in this encounter, making it the United States' single most costly battle in the entire history of wars with American Indians.

The Battle of Fallen Timbers and the Treaty of Greenville

In the aftermath of the defeat of U.S. troops at the Wabash River, **President George Washington** was determined to gain control of the region north of the Ohio. He doubled the U.S. presence in Ohio and appointed **General Anthony ("Mad Anthony") Wayne** to lead American forces. At the **Battle of Fallen Timbers** (1794), the Indians were soundly defeated by superior American firepower. The following year, 1795, native groups gave up claims to most of Ohio in the **Treaty of Greenville**. The treaty brought only a temporary peace. Within a generation, settlers would push farther into Ohio and Indiana; these incursions would become connected with the U.S. declaration of war against Britain in 1812.

B. Internal Migrations, Frontier Cultures, and Tensions in the Backcountry

The United States pursued policies to encourage migration beyond the Appalachian Mountains. Many individuals needed no encouragement; land and economic opportunity beckoned to many struggling farmers to move westward. As more people began leaving settled coastal towns and moving inland, tensions increased between coastal elites and backcountry farmers. These tensions evolved along cultural, political, and ethnic lines.

The Dynamics of Backcountry Settlements

Since the seventeenth century, tensions had existed between backcountry settlers and elite policymakers in the more established urban centers of the East. This was evident in **Bacon's Rebellion** in 1676. Backcountry Virginia settlers grew resentful of the policies of Governor **William Berkeley** and the **House of Burgesses**. They argued that they paid a disproportionate share of taxes in the colony and were not represented in the House of Burgesses. Also, they believed that the colonial government was not taking sufficient action to push native tribes farther west (see more on Bacon's Rebellion, pages 79–80).

Similar tensions surfaced in the second half of the eighteenth century, during both the colonial period and the early national period. The **Carolina Regulators** movement, composed of backcountry farmers in North and South Carolina, challenged the policies and practices of merchants, bankers, local officials, and the colonial government. The tensions came to a fore between 1765 and 1771, when the movement took up arms against colonial authorities in the **War of the Regulation**. A catalyst for the uprising was the collection of debts in these backcountry areas. After several years of drought and poor harvests, many farmers suffered income loss as well as shortages of basic supplies. They were forced to rely on local merchants and bankers to extend them credit and loans. The collection of debts was, the farmers contended, rife with corruption. The system of local court officials and sheriffs, and the political infrastructure that supported it, was perceived as an oppressive outside force. The uprising was an attempt to challenge this outside force. The uprising did not change the power structure in the Carolinas, but it did establish patterns of thought and action that became evident in the coming years in the rebellion against British rule.

Tensions between elites and backcountry farmers can be seen in the actions of the **Paxton Boys** in western **Pennsylvania** (1763–1764), as bitterness toward local Indian groups and objections to the policies of Pennsylvania's colonial government resulted in violence (see pages 96–97). Such tensions did not subside with independence. During the "critical period" of the 1780s, farmers in western Massachusetts grew resentful of both banks and the Massachusetts legislature. They found themselves burdened by crushing debt as well as steep taxes. They staged a months-long rebellion against local courts, banks, and the state government, known as **Shays's Rebellion** (1786–1787). It is seen as an important catalyst for the convening of the 1787 **Constitutional Convention** (see page 111). Several years later, the **Whiskey Rebellion**, culminating in 1794, staged by farmers in western Pennsylvania over the excise tax on whiskey, again demonstrated backcountry mistrust of the polices of elites (see pages 120–121).

C. The Expansion of Slavery and Divergent Regional Attitudes Toward Slavery

After the American Revolution, attitudes around slavery became increasingly shaped by region, as slavery became more entrenched in the South and in adjacent western lands, while it began to disappear in the North.

The North Moves Toward a Free-Labor System

Many northerners came to see unfree labor as inconsistent with the republican ideas of the **American Revolution**. Even indentured servitude disappeared from most states by 1800. In many northern states, slavery became less important to the economy. Vermont outlawed slavery altogether (in 1777, fourteen years before it became a state), Pennsylvania passed a **gradual emancipation law** (1780), and other northern states began to follow suit. Gradual emancipation laws did not free existing slaves; they provided for the freedom of the future children of slave women (often after serving their masters for a certain number of years). Such an approach respected contemporary understandings of property rights. In the years after the American Revolution, free Black communities developed in many northern states and in some states of the upper South, such as Virginia and Maryland.

The Growth of Slavery in the South

In the decades after the American Revolution, slavery became increasingly important in the South. **Eli Whitney**'s invention of the **cotton gin** in 1793 set the stage for a remarkable growth in the production of cotton, in the growth of the southern economy, and in the reliance on slavery (see pages 147 and 166). Despite gradual emancipation in the North, voluntary emancipation throughout the United States, and the escape of many slaves during the chaos of the American Revolution, the number of slaves in the United States grew from 500,000 in 1776 to 700,000 in 1790. With the ending of indentured servitude, the stark differences between the growing free-labor ideology of the North and the expanding slave-labor system of the South became more apparent. These diverging attitudes on slavery would come to shape many of the debates leading up to the Civil War.

Topic 3.13 Subject to Debate

Debating the Causes and Nature of the American Revolution

Along with the Civil War, the American Revolution is one of the most hotly debated topics among historians. The Revolution gave birth to the United States, so the stakes involved in understanding and interpreting it are especially high—one's understanding of the Revolution is shaped by, and shapes, one's understanding of the United States itself.

Historians for generations have debated the reasons the thirteen colonies declared independence. Some historians have stressed economic grievances against the mother country—colonists declared independence to be free of British mercantilist rules. These historians have emphasized the colonial cry, "No taxation without representation," as central to the struggle. This theory assumes a basic continuity in terms of values from the colonial period to the national period; the values of the market shaped both periods.

Opposing historians argue that economic issues were only part of the equation. They see a real break with the past—socially, culturally, and ideologically. Bernard Bailyn's *The Ideological Origins of the American Revolution* (1967) points to the development of a new set of ideas about politics and democracy, shaped by radical British libertarian writers.

Historians influenced by the "New Left," such as Jesse Lemisch, look at class divisions within American society, not just divisions between the colonies and Great Britain. This approach sees a class conflict in colonial America. On one side of the conflict were the colonial elites, who tried to prevent the American Revolution from becoming truly revolutionary. They wanted to maintain the colonial social structure, but without the British overlords. On the other side were dockworkers, artisans, small-scale farmers, apprentices, slaves, free Blacks, and other traditionally marginalized people who pushed for a real break with the hierarchies of the past. Their radical agenda was largely derailed by the delegates at the Constitutional Convention, who put a lid on these revolutionary impulses.

The Effectiveness of the Articles of Confederation

There are several important questions about the "critical period" that students should be aware of. The first important question examines the nature of the Articles of Confederation. Because the Articles lasted less than a decade, and because the Constitution has endured for more than 230 years, there is a tendency to elevate the historical standing of the Constitution and to denigrate the Articles of Confederation. This is to be expected, but we should be careful not to go too far. To admit to the effectiveness of the Constitution does not require us to ignore anything positive about the Articles. The thirteen colonies won the American Revolution during the Articles of Confederation period. Also, the Articles did an excellent job of dealing with the newly acquired western lands. It is true that the national government was weak while under the Articles, but even this can be seen as a positive. The Articles, we can argue, effectively protected the traditional rights of the states. Historical debate should be fair to the much-maligned Articles.

The Nature of the Constitution

The Constitutional Convention has been the subject of much debate through American history. Charles Beard, a Progressive-era historian, asserted that the men who wrote the Constitution were all men of means who made sure to protect their economic interests. This interpretation notes the undemocratic features of the Constitution (the electoral college and the method for selecting senators) and asserts that the document is essentially interested in protecting the economic interests of the propertied class at the expense of democracy. Some left-leaning historians see the ratification of the Constitution as a virtual coup d'état, checking the more revolutionary elements of the American Revolution. This view runs counter to mainstream thinking, which elevates the effectiveness of the Constitution, especially when contrasted with the perceived ineffectiveness of the Articles of Confederation.

Practice Multiple-Choice Questions

DIRECTIONS: Pick the letter that best answers the following questions.

Questions 1-3 are based on the following passage:

"And We do further declare it to be Our Royal Will and Pleasure, for the present as aforesaid, to reserve under our Sovereignty, Protection, and Dominion, for the use of the said Indians, . . . all the Lands and Territories lying to the Westward of the Sources of the Rivers which fall into the Sea from the West and North West as aforesaid.

"And We do hereby strictly forbid, on Pain of our Displeasure, all our loving Subjects from making any Purchases or Settlements whatever, or taking Possession of any of the Lands above reserved, without our especial leave and Licence for that Purpose first obtained."

—Royal Proclamation of 1763 (excerpt)

1. A primary impetus for the British king issuing the proclamation, excerpted above, was

   (A) a series of armed conflicts between colonists and an alliance of American Indian tribes, known as the Covenant Chain, led by Chief Pontiac.
   (B) raids by Cherokee and Creek warriors in the interior of Georgia and South Carolina following the "Trail of Tears."
   (C) a bloody conflict, known as King Philip's War, waged by the Narragansett against encroachments by colonists.
   (D) skirmishes between Virginia settlers and the Powhatan Confederation.

2. The Royal Proclamation of 1763 had the effect of

   (A) uniting British colonists and American Indians in mutual distrust of British intentions.
   (B) slowing down British immigration to North America.
   (C) intensifying tensions between Great Britain and France.
   (D) creating resentment by colonists toward British policies in North America.

3. The Royal Proclamation of 1763 could best be understood in the context of

   (A) Britain shifting the structure of its empire and allowing colonies more direct control of internal affairs.
   (B) Britain's attempting to consolidate imperial control over its North American colonies.
   (C) Britain attempting to prevent the spread of revolutionary sentiment.
   (D) Britain shifting its policies from a mercantilist model to a free-market capitalist model.

Questions 4–6 refer to the following image:

—Benjamin Franklin, "Magna Britannia: Her Colonies Reduc'd," 1767

4. The main point of the cartoon above is that

   (A) the thirteen British North American colonies should unite in order to better advance their grievances against Great Britain.
   (B) the North American colonists, in the aftermath of the French and Indian War, should develop a better system of defending themselves from attacks from Great Britain.
   (C) British policies in North America, notably enacting taxes, could result in fatal effects on the British Empire.
   (D) the presence of a British standing army in North America would have a detrimental effect on the liberties and rights of the British colonists.

5. The primary intended audience for this cartoon was

   (A) members of Parliament in Great Britain.
   (B) Boston merchants and traders.
   (C) backcountry settlers in Pennsylvania.
   (D) members of the Sons of Liberty.

6. The sentiment reflected in the image was also reflected in which of the following?

   (A) Paul Revere's engraving, "Boston Massacre," 1770
   (B) The Treaty of Fort Stanwix, 1768
   (C) The "Olive Branch Petition," adopted by the Continental Congress in 1775
   (D) Thomas Paine's pamphlet, *Common Sense*, 1776

Questions 7–9 are based on the following passage:

"Your sentiments, that our affairs are drawing rapidly to a crisis, accord with my own. What the event will be is also beyond the reach of my foresight. We have errors to correct. We have probably had too good an opinion of human nature in forming our confederation. Experience has taught us that men will not adopt and carry into execution measures the best calculated for their own good without the intervention of a coercive power. I do not conceive that we can exist long as a nation without having lodged somewhere a power which will pervade the whole Union in as energetic a manner as the authority of the state governments extends over the several states. . . .

"What astonishing changes a few years are capable of producing. I am told that even respectable characters speak of a monarchical form of government without horror. . . . What a triumph for our enemies to verify their predictions! What a triumph for the advocates of despotism to find that we are incapable of governing ourselves, and that systems founded on the basis of equal liberty are merely ideal and fallacious."

—George Washington, letter to John Jay, August 1, 1786

7. The sentiments in the letter by George Washington, above, reflect which of the following continuities in American history?

   (A) Debates about the proper balance between liberty and order
   (B) Debates about reconciling republicanism with the institution of slavery
   (C) Debates about the relationship among the three branches of government
   (D) Debates about the use of the military in subduing domestic disturbances

8. Based on the context of the letter, which of the following most closely describes the meaning of Washington's phrase, "We have probably had too good an opinion of human nature"?

   (A) Contemporary Deist spiritual beliefs were misguided in that they abandoned the Calvinist notions of "original sin."
   (B) The United States had overestimated the good will and honor of Great Britain in terms of following the stipulations of the Treaty of Paris (1783).
   (C) The U.S. Army misread the willingness of American Indians in the Ohio Valley and Great Lakes regions to live side-by-side with white settlers.
   (D) The framers of the Articles of Confederation made a mistake in allowing for too great a degree of democracy in the new republic.

9. In subsequent U.S. history, those who shared the sentiments George Washington expressed in the letter above would most likely have taken which of the following positions?

   (A) Support for joining France in its war with Great Britain in 1793 in honor of the 1778 Treaty of Alliance with France
   (B) Opposition to the chartering of a national bank in 1791
   (C) Support for ratification of the Constitution in 1789
   (D) Opposition to the Alien and Sedition Acts of 1798

Questions 10–12 are based on the following passage:

"We may . . . be said to have reached almost the last stage of national humiliation. There is scarcely any thing that can wound the pride or degrade the character of an independent nation which we do not experience . . . Do we owe debts to foreigners and to our citizens . . . ? There remains without any proper or satisfactory provision for their discharge. Is commerce of importance to national wealth? Ours is at the lowest point of declension."

—Alexander Hamilton, *Federalist* No. 15, 1787

10. Which of the following factors did Alexander Hamilton believe was a source for the problems in the excerpt from *Federalist* No. 15?

    (A) Economic class divisions among the American people that prevented them from forging a unified vision
    (B) A failure of American policymakers to abandon mercantilist principles and to embrace a laissez-faire approach to trade
    (C) A weak central government without the powers to address pressing issues
    (D) An unhealthy obsession among the American people with religion and individual salvation, at the expense of interest in solving practical national problems

11. Which of the following specific developments contributed to the general sentiment expressed in *Federalist* No. 15?

    (A) Great Britain refused to evacuate forts in the Great Lakes region.
    (B) Spanish forces retook Florida from the United States.
    (C) French forces aided American Indians in conducting raids on New England.
    (D) Dutch traders forced American ships to extend tribute payments in order to dock in Holland.

12. To address the problems identified in *Federalist* No. 15, Hamilton proposed

    (A) abandoning an isolationist approach to foreign policy and adopting a more aggressive and interventionist stance.
    (B) adopting a new constitution in order to create a more powerful national government.
    (C) forging alliances with American Indian nations to present a united front to European powers.
    (D) increasing spending on military forces and cutting spending on social programs.

Answers and Explanations

1. **(A)** A primary impetus for the British government issuing the Proclamation of 1763 was a series of armed conflicts between colonists and an alliance of American Indian tribes, known as the Covenant Chain, led by Chief Pontiac. The act drew a line through the Appalachian Mountains. Great Britain ordered the colonists not to settle beyond the line. The British government did not want to provoke additional warfare with native peoples in the region in the wake of the French and Indian War.

2. **(D)** The Royal Proclamation of 1763 had the effect of creating resentment among colonists toward British policies in North America. Many colonists were disgruntled because they felt that they had made sacrifices during the French and Indian War, and they were now eager to settle in these newly claimed lands.

3. **(B)** The Royal Proclamation of 1763 could best be understood in the context of Great Britain's attempting to consolidate imperial control over its North American colonies. If British colonists celebrated the removal of the French from North America following the French and Indian War, their celebration was short lived. Almost immediately, the British government attempted to confront an ongoing problem—the large debt that had accumulated during almost half a century of constant warfare. The government believed its victory in war had been especially beneficial to the colonists. In return, the British reasoned it was fair for the colonists to assume some of the costs of the war and continued protection through increased taxation. New taxes and more rigorous enforcement of existing taxes generated intense resentment and resistance among many colonists.

4. **(C)** In this cartoon, Benjamin Franklin is warning of an unfortunate future. He is predicting that British taxation policies, notably the Stamp Act, could have fatal consequences for the British Empire. A dismembered Britannia has fallen from the globe and sits surrounded by her scattered limbs, identified as different North American colonies. In the background of the cartoon we see British ships sitting idle—an allusion to the importance of Britain's trade with America. On the ground sits a rejected olive branch. The banner across Britannia's body reads *"Date Obolum Bellisario"* ("give a farthing to Bellisarius"), an allusion to a Roman military hero who was reduced to beggary after being accused of treason.

5. **(A)** The primary intended audience for this cartoon was members of Parliament in Great Britain. Franklin was living in Great Britain at the time and spent a great deal of effort trying to pressure Parliament to rescind the Stamp Act. Franklin is attempting to convey to Parliament that British taxes are not only burdensome for the colonists; the taxes could lead to a crisis that might result in the dismemberment of the empire. In order to avoid such a future, Franklin is pushing Parliament to mend bridges between Great Britain and its North American colonies before it is too late.

6. **(C)** The sentiment reflected in the image—that peace and reconciliation between Great Britain and the colonies was a desirable goal—was also reflected in the "Olive Branch Petition," adopted by the Continental Congress in 1775. Franklin himself had moved toward a more oppositional position by that point, but many colonists still held out hope that a peaceful solution could be reached.

7. **(A)** The letter by Washington reflects his position in the ongoing debate about the proper balance between liberty and order. This same debate also occurred around President Abraham Lincoln's suspension of habeas corpus during the Civil War, around the Espionage and Sedition Acts during World War I, around the Japanese internment during World War II, and around the McCarran Internal Security Act of 1950. It is occurring in the early twenty-first century over the 2001 Patriot Act.

8. **(D)** George Washington came to believe that the Articles of Confederation government erred in allowing for too great a degree of democracy. There was a heated debate in the 1780s about the appropriate degree of democratic participation in society and about the nature of the public. Many

of the political leaders who coalesced around the Federalist point of view on the Constitution came to believe that too much democracy was dangerous. Their fears would be borne out in the coming weeks when Shays's Rebellion began in Massachusetts. This was a central reason that Washington, Hamilton, and other Federalists wanted to replace the Articles of Confederation with the Constitution.

9. **(C)** George Washington is expressing great unease with the ability of the government, under the Articles of Confederation, to maintain order in the United States. He was worried about the lack of strong authority in the United States. People who shared this view would have supported the ratification of the Constitution, as Washington himself did. People who favored order over democracy would certainly not have supported the revolutionary French government in 1793 (A). Supporters of increasing the power and authority of the central government generally supported the chartering of a national bank (B). The Alien and Sedition Acts imposed greater order and restraints on the people (D); therefore, someone who shared Washington's sentiments would have supported it, not opposed it.

10. **(C)** Alexander Hamilton came to believe that many of the problems facing the United States could be traced to the inadequacy of the structure of government under the Articles of Confederation. He was instrumental in writing a new document, the Constitution, and in pushing for its ratification. He, James Madison, and John Jay wrote a series of articles under the collective pseudonym, Publius, in defense of the new Constitution. The eighty-five numbered articles, including the one excerpted in the question, were later collected as *The Federalist*. Hamilton believed that a government that allowed for more power on the national level would be more effective in carrying out an assertive agenda and would be given greater respect on the world stage.

11. **(A)** Many Americans were alarmed that Great Britain would not evacuate forts in the Great Lakes region even after the signing of the Treaty of Paris (1783). In the treaty, Great Britain recognized the independence of the United States, but it maintained that it would not leave the forts in the West until the United States compensated Loyalists for property losses. The presence of a foreign power on U.S. soil was an embarrassment to Hamilton. He came to believe that the structure of the government itself needed to be changed in order for the United States to gain respect on the world stage.

12. **(B)** A series of events in the 1780s led Hamilton to believe that a new form of government was necessary in order for the United States to thrive. He was part of a group of political leaders who met in Philadelphia from May to September, 1787, with the goal of framing a new governing document. They wrote the Constitution and then sent it to state ratifying conventions. The Constitution represented a marked departure from the Articles of Confederation. The Constitution created a centralized national government. States still retained certain powers, but the Constitution stated that the national government would be supreme.

6

Period 4: 1800–1848 The Meaning of Democracy in an Era of Economic and Territorial Expansion

TIMELINE

1800	Election of Thomas Jefferson
1803	Louisiana Purchase
	Marbury v. Madison
1804	Reelection of Jefferson
1807	*Chesapeake-Leopard* Affair
	Embargo Act
1808	Election of James Madison
1810	*Fletcher v. Peck*
1811	Battle of Tippecanoe
1812	Beginning of War of 1812
	Reelection of Madison
1814	The burning of Washington, D.C., by British forces
	Hartford Convention
	Treaty of Ghent
1815	Battle of New Orleans
1816	Election of James Monroe
	Chartering of the Second Bank of the United States
1817	Construction of Erie Canal begins
1819	Panic of 1819
	Dartmouth College v. Woodward
	McCulloch v. Maryland
1820	Missouri Compromise
	Reelection of Monroe
1821	Opening of the Lowell factories
	Cohens v. Virginia
1822	Stephen Austin establishes first American settlement in Texas
1824	*Gibbons v. Ogden*
	Election of John Quincy Adams
1825	Opening of the Erie Canal
1827	Public school movement begins in Boston

1828	Passage of the "Tariff of Abominations"
	Election of Andrew Jackson
1829	Publication of "David Walker's Appeal to the Coloured Citizens of the World"
1830	Opening of the Baltimore and Ohio Railroad
	Passage of the Indian Removal Act
	Founding of Mormonism
1831	William Lloyd Garrison begins publication of the *Liberator*
1832	Beginning of Nullification Crisis
	Jackson vetoes renewal of Second Bank of the United States
	Worcester v. Georgia
	Reelection of Jackson
1833	Founding of the American Anti-Slavery Society
1834	Whig Party organized
	First strike by the "Lowell girls"
1835	Publication of Alexis de Tocqueville's *Democracy in America*
1836	Congress passes the "gag rule"
	Jackson issues Specie Circular
	Battle of the Alamo
	Texas independence
1837	Elijah Lovejoy murdered by proslavery mob
1838	"Trail of Tears"
1840	Election of William Henry Harrison
	Formation of the Liberty Party
1841	John Tyler assumes presidency upon Harrison's death
	Brook Farm founded
1843	Dorothea Dix organizes movement for asylum reform
1844	Samuel Morse invents the telegraph
	Election of James Polk
1845	Texas annexation and statehood
	Beginning of Irish "potato famine"
1846	Creation of the Independent Treasury
	Resolution of dispute with Great Britain over Oregon Territory
	Beginning of Mexican War
1848	Seneca Falls Convention
	Treaty of Guadalupe Hidalgo ends Mexican War
	Gold found in California
1851	Herman Melville writes *Moby Dick*

Topics in Period 4

In this chapter, you will learn about:

- Topic 4.1 Contextualizing Period 4
- Topic 4.2 The rise of political parties and the era of Jefferson
- Topic 4.3 Politics and regional interests
- Topic 4.4 America on the world stage
- Topic 4.5 The market revolution: Economic transformations
- Topic 4.6 Market revolution: Society and culture
- Topic 4.7 Expanding democracy
- Topic 4.8 Jackson and federal power
- Topic 4.9 The development of an American culture
- Topic 4.10 The Second Great Awakening
- Topic 4.11 An age of reform
- Topic 4.12 African Americans in the early republic
- Topic 4.13 The society of the South in the early republic
- Topic 4.14 Subject to debate

Topic 4.1 Contextualizing Period 4

> The first half of the nineteenth century witnessed a series of economic, territorial, and demographic changes that led to struggles over the definition and limits of democratic control.

Growth and expansion were defining features of the United States in the first half of the nineteenth century. The economy was rapidly changing and growing, as an older semi-subsistence economy was giving way to a market economy with a national, and even international, reach. The "market revolution" affected various parts of the country differently. Reformers and intellectuals tried to make sense of these changes and entered into debates about the meaning and shape of democracy. The area of land claimed by the United States grew substantially during this period, as the country attempted to fulfill its professed "manifest destiny," and American Indians resisted and changed in the process. In the northern states the beginnings of industrialization appeared, while slavery grew dramatically in the South on the strength of cotton cultivation. In some ways, the regions of the United States became more interlinked as local economies were drawn into national markets, but at the same time, the issue of free labor versus slave labor pushed the country further apart.

Topic 4.2 The Rise of Political Parties and the Era of Jefferson

The first decades of the nineteenth century led to a growth in the importance of political parties, which organized debate around issues of national importance. Also during this time, Supreme Court decisions asserted federal power over state power. Finally, diplomatic actions led to the United States greatly expanding its territory.

A. Political Parties and the Rise of the First Two-Party System

Although many of the founders of the United States did not anticipate political parties, they developed in the 1790s and have been a feature of American political life ever since. These parties are often large tents built around a variety of interest groups and constituencies. The first two-party system comprised the Democratic-Republicans and the Federalists.

The Federalists, the Democratic-Republicans, and the "Revolution" of 1800

The first two-party system took shape in the 1790s and pitted the **Democratic-Republicans** against the **Federalists** (see pages 119–121). The Federalists, coalescing around the plans of Alexander Hamilton, embraced a broader national agenda, advocating the use of a national bank and import duties to promote commercial and manufacturing activities, while the **Democratic-Republicans**, following the lead of **Thomas Jefferson**, sought to limit the power of the national government and reserve greater authority at the state level.

The two parties engaged in a bitter campaign during the **presidential election of 1800**. Supporters of **President John Adams** (Federalist) and of **Thomas Jefferson** (Democratic-Republican) resorted to ugly tactics in regard to portraying the opposing candidate in a negative light. Federalist loyalists predicted that if Jefferson won the election, a reign of terror—following the example of the French Revolution—would occur in the United States. They also spread rumors about Jefferson carrying on a relationship with a slave woman. (Most historians, as well as a 2018 exhibit at Monticello organized by the Thomas Jefferson Foundation, assert the veracity of the rumors that Jefferson fathered children with one of his slaves, **Sally Hemings**, especially in light of DNA evidence; some historians continue to challenge these findings.) The Democratic-Republicans portrayed Adams as a would-be king, opposed to the most basic elements of liberty.

> **USING REASONING PROCESSES:**
> **CONTINUITY AND CHANGE**
>
> **Two-Party Systems**
>
> Two-Party systems have existed in American history from the 1790s to the present day, but the nature and approach of the parties involved has changed over time. Two-party systems persist because many voters refrain from voting for a third-party candidate, fearing their least favorite candidate will win. These voters end up voting for the "lesser of two evils." (See more on third parties in American history in box on page 238.) The first two-party system consisted of the Democratic-Republicans and the Federalists, embodying the ideas of Thomas Jefferson and Alexander Hamilton, respectively. The decline of the Federalist Party led to a brief period of one-party rule—"The Era of Good Feelings" (1817–1825). This period was followed by a second two-party system of the Jacksonian Democrats and the opposition Whig Party. This party system existed until the 1850s when the crisis over slavery destroyed the Whig Party and transformed the Democratic Party into a staunchly proslavery party. The Civil War era gave rise to the third two-party system, the Democrats and the Republicans. The positions of these two parties have changed dramatically, but organizationally, they persist until the present day.

Jefferson seemed to have won the election, but a mistake among the Democratic-Republicans in the electoral college voting resulted in a tie between Jefferson and his vice-presidential candidate, **Aaron Burr**. At that time, each elector cast two ballots, but there was no distinction between votes cast for a presidential candidate or a vice-presidential candidate. (Afterward, the **Twelfth Amendment**, ratified in 1804, changed the procedure so that the electoral vote for president is separate from the electoral vote for vice president.) The decision of who shall be president was then thrown to the Federalist-dominated House of Representatives. Some Federalists wished to embarrass Jefferson and select Burr to be president. However, Hamilton pushed for his Federalist allies to vote for Jefferson, who ultimately received enough electoral votes to win the presidency. Jefferson labeled this transfer of power from the Federalists to the Democratic-Republicans the **"revolution of 1800,"** reflecting his belief that his administration would return the United States to its founding principles.

The Decline of the Federalist Party and the "Era of Good Feelings"

Despite fears of turmoil, power peacefully changed hands in 1800 from the **Federalist Party** to the **Democratic-Republicans**. Some of the political acrimony of the 1790s died down during the first decades of the nineteenth century. The Federalist Party lost support in this time as the Republican-leaning agricultural areas of the country grew more rapidly than the commercial centers of the Northeast. The Federalists suffered a further blow because of their vigorous opposition to the popular **War of 1812** (see page 142). The decline of the Federalist Party led to the **"Era of Good Feelings"** (approximately 1815 to 1825) when only one major party, the Democratic-Republicans, continued to function on the national level.

With the Federalist Party in its death throes, the Democratic-Republican Party candidate, **James Monroe**, easily won the election of 1816. Four years later, the Federalists made even less of a challenge to Monroe. President Monroe was somewhat of a throwback to the presidents of the eighteenth century. He was the last president to consistently wear the silk stockings, knee breeches, and powdered wigs of the earlier era. He also adopted President George Washington's practice of bringing men of differing ideological bents into his administration. Many of Monroe's policies, such as promoting "internal improvements," seemed like pages out of the Federalist playbook.

The Federalist agenda also lived on in the **Supreme Court**, which was not subject to the whims of the electorate and kept alive many elements of the Federalist agenda (see below). In addition, the nation began to adopt manufacturing, just as **Alexander Hamilton** had hoped. **Henry Clay's "American System"** kept alive much of Hamilton's program (see page 139).

B. The Supreme Court Asserts Federal Power and the Power of the Judiciary

The Supreme Court, during the tenure of Chief Justice John Marshall (1801–1835), issued a series of decisions that extended the power of the federal government over state laws while establishing the primacy of the judiciary in interpreting the meaning of the Constitution.

Marbury v. Madison (1803) and the Principle of Judicial Review

The most important decision of the **Marshall Court** was in the case of *Marbury v. Madison*. The important outcome of the case was that the principle of **judicial review** was established. The details of the decision have to do with the seating of judges who had been appointed in the last days of the John Adams administration. These judges had been appointed by Adams to fill slots created by an expanded judiciary that grew out of the **Judiciary Act of 1801.** The act was passed in the final weeks of the Adams administration. Adams worked feverishly to fill these seats before his term expired, thereby solidifying Federalist power in the court system for years to come. When Thomas Jefferson assumed office, not all of the commissions had been formally delivered. Jefferson, angered at the eleventh-hour appointments, ordered his secretary of state, **James Madison**, to not deliver them. In this way, he could appoint his own judges.

One potential judge, **William Marbury**, sued to have his commission delivered. The **Supreme Court** ruled that Marbury was not entitled to his seat because the law he was basing his argument on—the Judiciary Act of 1789—was unconstitutional. Marshall established the Supreme Court's power to review laws and determine whether they are consistent with the Constitution. Laws declared unconstitutional by the Court are immediately struck down. Before *Marbury v. Madison*, the extent of the Supreme Court's power was ill-defined; its prestige and influence was limited. The power of judicial review has been the main function of the Supreme Court since then and has been instrumental in maintaining a balance among the three coequal branches of the government.

The Marshall Court and Federal Power

Several important Marshall Court decisions strengthened federal power over state power. *McCulloch v. Maryland* (1819) prohibited Maryland from taxing the Second Bank of the United States, a federal institution. *Gibbons v. Ogden* (1824) invalidated a monopoly on ferry transportation between New York and New Jersey that had been issued by New York, and asserted that only the federal government could regulate interstate trade. In the case of *Cohens v. Virginia* (1821), the Marshall Court affirmed the right of the Supreme Court to receive appeals from state courts. The case, which originated in the Virginia state court system, involved the ability of the state to prohibit the Cohen brothers from selling lottery tickets in Virginia. The Court upheld Virginia's right to forbid the sale of the tickets.

The Supreme Court again revoked a state statute in the case of *Worcester v. Georgia* (1832). The Court held that any dealings with American Indian nations be carried out by the federal government, not by state governments.

Specifically, the decision struck down a Georgia statute that forbade non-American Indians from entering American Indian territory without first obtaining a license from the state. In a larger sense, the Court upheld the autonomy of American Indian communities. The **Cherokees** were "a distinct community, occupying its own territory," the Court asserted; "the laws of Georgia can have no force." The decision was largely ignored by the United States government under Andrew Jackson as it pursued its Indian removal policy (see page 155).

C. The Louisiana Purchase and Territorial Expansion

The purchase of the Louisiana Territory marked a turning point for the United States, as the country pursued a variety of means to gain influence and control over North America. Between 1803 and 1853, the United States took a number of steps to establish the international boundaries of the future forty-eight states. The first major acquisition of territory after the defeat of the British in the American Revolution was the Louisiana Purchase. (The final two steps, acquisition of the Mexican Cession in 1848 and the Gadsden Purchase in 1853, are discussed in Period 5, pages 182-183.)

The Louisiana Purchase

In 1803, the United States was given the opportunity to purchase the vast swath of land beyond the Mississippi River known as the **Louisiana Territory**. The Louisiana Territory was long held by France, which ceded it to Spain in 1762, at the close of the **French and Indian War**. France regained the territory in 1801, but the ambitious French leader, **Napoleon Bonaparte**, in need of cash to fund war with Great Britain, soon was ready to sell the Louisiana Territory. American negotiators quickly agreed to a price of $15 million (1803).

President Thomas Jefferson was at first reluctant to approve the **Louisiana Purchase** because the Constitution did not allow for the acquisition of additional lands. Jefferson had long held a **strict constructionist** view of the Constitution, asserting that the government's power was limited to what was explicitly allowed in the Constitution (see box, page 119). However, if Jefferson waited for a constitutional amendment specifically allowing Congress to acquire new lands, Napoleon could rescind his offer. So, Jefferson violated his stated principle and quickly presented the offer to Congress, which assented and appropriated the funds.

The purchase of the Louisiana Territory was arguably the most significant act of Jefferson's presidency. The purchase was important for two reasons. First, it doubled the territory of the United States, adding the fertile **Great Plains**. This flat area west of the Mississippi would become the most important agricultural region in the United States. Second, the United States gained full control of the port of **New Orleans**. New Orleans is at the outlet of the mighty **Mississippi River**, which stretches from Minnesota down the spine of the United States. The impact of the Louisiana Purchase on economic growth was remarkable. Between the 1810s and the 1850s, the value of produce from the interior of the United States went up more than tenfold.

The Lewis and Clark Expedition

The **Lewis and Clark expedition** (1804-1806) increased understanding of the region included in the Louisiana Purchase. President Jefferson commissioned **Meriwether Lewis** and **William Clark**, army officers, to explore the territory. They explored and mapped the region, seeking practical routes through the mountains, and established the presence of the United States in the West.

Topic 4.3 Politics and Regional Interests

As the United States acquired new territories, Americans debated whether these new lands should allow slavery or not. Attempts at compromise were made in the first half of the nineteenth century with mixed results. Although efforts were made to create a more cohesive national economy, many political leaders asserted regional economic interests over national concerns.

A. The Persistence of Regional Priorities

A growing schism between northern and southern political leaders can be seen in the first half of the nineteenth century. Regional economic interests often trumped national interests.

The Market Economy and Regional Loyalties

Although the growth of the national economy was evident in the first half of the nineteenth century, regional economic and political loyalties persisted. In the **northern states**, the beginnings of **industrialization** became apparent, while **slavery** grew dramatically in the **South** on the strength of the cultivation of cotton. In some ways, the regions of the United States became more interlinked as local economies were transformed into national markets, but at the same time, the issue of free versus slave labor steadily divided the country.

B. The American System and Sectionalism

Attempts by the federal government to create linkages between the regions of the country were of limited success. The market economy ended up creating stronger links between the North and the Midwest; the South became increasingly isolated from the rest of the country.

Henry Clay's "American System"

In the nationalist mood that followed the **War of 1812**, **Henry Clay**, a leading member of the House of Representatives, put forward a series of proposals to promote economic growth that he later called the **"American System."** First, Clay realized that America needed **"internal improvements"** in transportation in order to grow economically. At the beginning of the century, the transportation system in the United States was woefully lacking. At the time of the War of 1812, the military had difficulty moving materials and men because of the nation's inadequate transportation system. Second, Clay proposed putting **high tariffs** on imported goods. He believed that high tariffs on incoming manufactured goods would promote American manufacturing. High tariffs would make foreign goods more expensive to the consumer, and American-made goods would seem cheaper by comparison. Third, Clay proposed chartering the **Second Bank of the United States** in order to stabilize the economy and make credit more readily available. These proposals were important steps taken by the government to usher in the market revolution. By the end of the **Monroe Administration**, Congress had rechartered the Second Bank of the United States and passed a protective tariff (both in 1816).

> **USING REASONING PROCESSES:**
> **CONTINUITY AND CHANGE**
>
> **Hamilton and Clay**
>
> Note the marked continuities between Alexander Hamilton's economic program (see page 120) and Henry Clay's "American System." Both supported tariffs, a central bank, and government encouragement of manufacturing. Clay also supported economic growth through government-subsidized infrastructure projects ("internal improvements"). Contemporary Republicans often support pro-business government policies, as Clay and Hamilton did; however, current pro-business Republicans tend to favor low tariffs and deregulation of the economy—not funding for "internal improvements."

The Growing Isolation of the South

Despite **Henry Clay's** attempt to foster unity among the regions of the country, the South became increasingly isolated from both the North and the Midwest. Roads and railroads connected the North and the Midwest but tended to bypass the South. Further, patterns of migration connected the North and the Midwest culturally. Farmers, artisans, and laborers living in New England, New York, or Pennsylvania were far more likely to venture toward Ohio or Illinois in the first half of the nineteenth century than they were to go to South Carolina or Mississippi. These connections isolated the South culturally from the rest of the nation and, over time, would isolate it politically.

C. A Temporary Truce on the Slavery Question in the Pre–Civil War Period

The most divisive regional issue in the first half of the nineteenth century was slavery. The Missouri Compromise (1820) created a temporary, uneasy truce over slavery in new territories. As the United States gained additional territories in the years leading up to the Civil War, this truce broke down.

The Missouri Compromise

The **"Era of Good Feelings"** (1815–1825) (see page 136) was not free of disagreements and sectional competition. The question of whether slavery would expand to the West emerged as a contentious issue in 1820. Controversy arose between the slave-holding states and the free states when **Missouri** applied for statehood as a slave state in 1818. At the time, there were eleven slave states and eleven free states. The admission of Missouri would have upset that balance. An aging Thomas Jefferson wrote in an 1820 letter that the heated controversy over the admission of Missouri was "like a fire bell in the night," and that it "filled me with terror." He and others warned that the question of slavery could threaten the Union itself. A compromise was reached in 1820 to maintain the balance between free and slave states by allowing for the admission of two new states—Missouri as a slave state and **Maine** as a free state. The **Missouri Compromise** also divided the remaining area of the Louisiana Territory at 36°30' north latitude. Above that line, slavery was not permitted (except for in Missouri); below the line, it was permitted. Throughout the coming decades, as white Americans continued to expand into the territories of the West, debates over the slavery question would continue to roil the nation.

The "Gag Rule" in the House of Representatives

Regional political differences over slavery became increasingly evident in the House of Representatives. Beginning in the 1830s, abolitionists pressed congressmen to introduce and debate antislavery resolutions on the floor of the House. **Representative John Quincy Adams** (who was elected to the House after his tenure as president) was a key House figure in attempting to bring such resolutions to the floor. In response, southern politicians successfully pushed for a series of resolutions that would automatically "table" any such resolutions, preventing them from being read or debated. Such **"gag rules"** were in effect in the House from 1836 to 1844.

> **KEEP IN MIND**
>
> **A Divided Congress in the Antebellum Period**
>
> Throughout the antebellum period, the Senate tended to be friendlier to the slave system than the House. The southern states had more power in the Senate than they did in the population-based House.

Topic 4.4 America on the World Stage

The United States pursued a foreign policy around the goals of expanding its boundaries, increasing trade, and isolating itself from European conflicts. These goals were pursued both through government actions and private initiatives.

A. Trade, Diplomacy, and the Expansion of American Influence

The desire of the United States to establish new patterns of trade and to establish a global presence, across both the Atlantic and Pacific Oceans, led to numerous economic, diplomatic, and military initiatives in both the Western Hemisphere and in Asia. Early on, the United States struggled to establish favorable trading relationships across the Atlantic; these efforts led to the War

> **USING HISTORICAL THINKING SKILLS:**
> **MAKING CONNECTIONS**
>
> **The Post-Presidency— from Adams to Carter**
>
> Most presidents have rather quiet and private retirements. John Quincy Adams did not. He is the only former president to serve in the House of Representatives, where he became an outspoken critic of slavery. Other presidents with meaningful careers after their terms in office are William Howard Taft, who became chief justice of the Supreme Court, and Jimmy Carter, who has been active in Habitat for Humanity and international issues of war and peace.

of 1812. Later, the United States sought to establish the Western Hemisphere as its sphere of influence with the announcement of the Monroe Doctrine (1823). Finally, during this period, the United States took actions to open trade with Asia.

The Barbary Wars (1801–1805, 1815)

President Thomas Jefferson's first foreign policy crisis involved U.S. trade with the Middle East. Trade in the Mediterranean was controlled by four seafaring North African states—**Morocco**, **Algiers**, **Tunis**, and **Tripoli**, whose domain was known as the **Barbary Coast**. These states demanded large payments from trading nations as "tribute." Nations that did not comply found their shipping subject to seizure and plundering by Barbary Coast pirates. Merchants during the colonial era had enjoyed the protection of Great Britain. When the United States became independent, **Presidents George Washington** and **John Adams** agreed to the terms set by the Barbary states. In 1801, Tripoli demanded a steep increase in payment from the United States. When Jefferson refused, Tripoli declared war on the United States in the **First Barbary War**. Jefferson sent warships to the region to engage in fighting and to protect American shipping. The move proved popular. The slogan **"Millions for defense, but not a cent for tribute"** became widespread in America. In the end, the United States did not achieve a decisive victory. In the peace treaty (1805), Tripoli agreed to release hostages that had been taken during the war in exchange for $60,000 and promised to stop raiding American ships. Critics of the treaty saw the payment as a form of tribute; in the coming years, Barbary pirates resumed raiding American ships. However, the war boosted America's profile on the world stage and demonstrated the cohesion of American forces fighting far from home. It took a **Second Barbary War** (1815) to finally bring an end to the American practice of paying tribute to the Barbary states.

Ongoing Troubles with European Nations

The conflicts between **Great Britain** and **France** that occupied the administrations of Washington and Adams reemerged during the administrations of **Thomas Jefferson** and **James Madison**. Both presidents Jefferson and Madison attempted to continue the policy of neutrality that Washington had set forth while, at the same time, extending foreign trade, sometimes with nations at war with one another. In 1803, French leader **Napoleon Bonaparte** declared war on Britain. At first, the United States benefited from trading with both warring partners. Soon, both countries tried to block American trade with the other. Great Britain was more aggressive in its efforts to stop American ships. British Navy warships routinely stopped and boarded American merchant ships, often seizing cargo. More irritating still for the Americans was the practice of seizing American seamen and "pressing" them into service in the British Navy. Britain claimed that these men were deserters from the British Navy, but most were not. This practice of **impressment** affected 6,000 American seamen between 1803 and 1812. The situation between the United States and Britain reached a crisis in 1807 when the fifty-gun British warship HMS *Leopard* fired on the unprepared thirty-eight-gun American Navy frigate USS *Chesapeake*. Three Americans were killed and four were abducted in the ***Chesapeake-Leopard* affair**.

"Peaceful Coercion" and Free Trade

As Great Britain continued to interfere with American shipping, Presidents Jefferson and Madison initially chose **"peaceful coercion"** over war. Jefferson passed the **Embargo Act** (1807), which cut off U.S. trade to all foreign ports. He thought that this would pressure the belligerent nations to agree to leave U.S. ships alone. However, the main effect of the embargo was to cripple America's mercantile sector. The Embargo Act proved to be very unpopular, especially in New England, whose economy depended on trade.

In the waning days of President Jefferson's administration, Congress replaced the unpopular Embargo Act with the **Non-Intercourse Act** of 1809, opening trade with all nations except for Great Britain and France. However, this act proved to be almost as unpopular, as Great Britain and France had been two of America's biggest trading partners.

Macon's Bill No. 2 (1810)

In an attempt to revive trade, Congress passed **Macon's Bill No. 2** in 1810. The bill stipulated that if either Great Britain or France agreed to respect America's rights as a neutral nation at sea, the United States would prohibit trade with that nation's enemy. Napoleon agreed to this arrangement, and consequently, the United States cut trade to Britain in 1811. However, Napoleon did not honor his commitment and France continued to seize American ships. The cutting off of trade with Britain worsened relations and pushed the two nations to the brink of war.

The War of 1812

Trade conflicts and pressure from the **"War Hawk"** congressmen (see page 155) pushed **President James Madison** to declare war against **Great Britain** in 1812. The vote on the war in Congress was divided along sectional lines. New England and some Middle Atlantic states opposed it; the South and Midwest voted for it. The vote to begin the **War of 1812** occurred just as Britain was making assurances that it would stop interfering with American shipping.

The war lasted two and a half years. Britain achieved several early victories, defeating American forces at **Fort Dearborn** and **Fort Detroit**. Madison managed to win reelection in the midst of the war, but the Federalists, who were critical of the war effort, made a strong showing. By 1813, the United States began to achieve key victories in battle. The United States burned the city of **York** (now Toronto) and won several battles at sea and on the Great Lakes. At the **Battle of the Thames** in Canada, American forces defeated British and American Indian forces and killed the Indian leader, Tecumseh. In one of the stunning episodes of the war, British forces seized **Washington, D.C.**, in 1814 and burned public buildings, including the Presidential Mansion (now called the White House) and the Capitol building. The United States achieved a major victory at **New Orleans** in early 1815, led by **General Andrew Jackson**. Jackson and his British adversaries had not realized that the United States had already signed a peace treaty, formally ending the war weeks before, in late 1814.

The Hartford Convention and Opposition to the War of 1812

The first major challenges to federal policy in the nineteenth century came not from the South but from **Federalist** politicians in New England. The **War of 1812** was unpopular among some Americans, especially among New England merchants, who saw their trade with Great Britain disappear. As diplomats were negotiating an end to the war in December 1814, Federalists from New England convened in Hartford, Connecticut, to express their displeasure with the conflict. Some of the more radical delegates suggested that New England secede from the Union, but this proposal was rejected at the convention. The **Hartford Convention** did call for several amendments to the Constitution that were intended to set limits on both the power of the federal government and the influence of the Democratic-Republican Party. One would have required a two-thirds vote in Congress for future declarations of war; another would have removed the three-fifths clause from the Constitution (see page 112).

The Treaty of Ghent

The **Treaty of Ghent** (1814) ended the War of 1812. Britain had grown weary of war after fighting Napoleon for more than a

---

USING HISTORICAL THINKING SKILLS:
CONTEXTUALIZATION

The Context of the War of 1812

The War of 1812 can be seen in the context of the ongoing bitter political conflicts between the Federalist Party (based primarily in the Northeast) and the Democratic-Republican Party (with its greatest strength in the South and West) (see pages 119–120). The Federalist Party had long favored close commercial ties with Great Britain, whereas the Democratic-Republican Party favored westward expansion and a definitive break with Great Britain. By 1812, the Federalist Party was in serious decline (see page 136). The Democratic-Republicans controlled Congress and had occupied the White House since 1801. The call to war with Great Britain reflected the strength of the Democratic-Republicans. Once the war began, the support for it was weakest in the Northeast, where Federalist politicians organized the Hartford Convention to express their opposition to the war (see this page).

decade and the United States for two years. The United States realized that it could not achieve a decisive victory over Great Britain. The treaty ended the war where it had begun. The two sides agreed to stop fighting, give back any territory seized in the war, and recognize the boundary between the United States and Canada that had been established before the war. The treaty did not mention the specific grievances the United States had against Britain—aid to American Indians, interference with American shipping, or impressments of American seamen.

"Old China Trade"

United States merchants opened a lucrative trade with **China** following the American Revolution. This commerce with China, not officially sanctioned by the United States government, is known as the **"Old China Trade."** The trade, driven by the American demand for Chinese products, such as tea, porcelain, silk, and nankeen (a coarse cotton cloth), opened new markets to the United States, but also brought to the fore cultural differences between the United States and China. From the American perspective, trade was seen as a basic right and as a means to expand national and personal wealth; it was assumed that other countries also would want to expand their trade for similar reasons. In traditional Chinese thought, however, commerce was looked down upon.

Chinese officials did allow trade with foreign countries, but they saw this trade through the lens of tradition—the trade existed by the largess of the emperor in return for tribute paid by states that acknowledged the superior position of China. Trade increased in the nineteenth century as the United States found that furs were in demand in China. These furs were obtained from American Indian groups along the Pacific Coast through the **"maritime fur trade"** from as far north as present-day Alaska and carried in increasingly large clipper ships. Seeing the growing power of Great Britain in China, the United States worked out the **Treaty of Wanghia** (1844), which ended the unofficial "Old China Trade." In the treaty, China extended to the United States the same trading privileges that had been extended to Great Britain.

Nationalist Sentiment and the Monroe Doctrine (1823)

America's newfound confidence on the international stage was evident in **President James Monroe's** foreign policy address to Congress in 1823. Monroe was alarmed at threats by the **Holy Alliance of Russia, Prussia, and Austria** to restore **Spain's** lost American colonies. He also opposed a decree by the **Russian czar** that claimed all the Pacific Northwest above the 51st parallel. Although both problems worked themselves out, Monroe issued a statement warning European nations to keep their hands off the Americas. The major purpose of the **Monroe Doctrine** was to limit European influence in the Western Hemisphere. The United States did not have the military might to enforce this pronouncement at the time, but it was an important statement of intent. The Monroe Doctrine and **Washington's Farewell Address** (see pages 121–122) became cornerstones of America's **isolationist foreign policy**.

The Adams-Onís Treaty (1819)

The United States gained control over **Florida** with the **Adams-Onís Treaty** in 1819. This treaty with **Spain** was negotiated by **John Quincy Adams**, who was then secretary of state under **President James Monroe**. The treaty transferred control of Florida to the United States, accepted Spain's claims to Texas, and settled the boundary between Louisiana (which had gained statehood in 1812) and Spanish-held territory. The status of Florida became a concern for the United States as it had become a destination for escaped slaves. The Florida issue became more pronounced during the **First Seminole War** (1814–1819) (see page 156). Americans were troubled by the so-called Negro Fort along the Apalachicola River. The fort had been British during the **War of 1812**; after the war, a British officer transferred control of the fort to fugitive slaves and Seminole Indians. General Andrew Jackson organized the capture of this fort during the First Seminole War. Following these incidents, gaining control of Florida became a goal of United States diplomats.

The Webster-Ashburton Treaty, the "Aroostook War," and the *Caroline* Incident

The United States settled a dispute in 1842 with Great Britain over the border between Maine and British-ruled Canada. The border had been vaguely drawn by the **Treaty of Paris** (1783) following the American Revolution. In 1838 and 1839, the issue of the border became more heated as Americans and Canadians began moving into the area around the Aroostook River, in Maine and New Brunswick, Canada. Although no lives were lost, brawling occurred between these two groups in what has become known as the **"Aroostook War."** The **Webster-Ashburton Treaty** roughly split the disputed territory and established a firm boundary between Maine and New Brunswick. It also settled a controversy over the border between Minnesota Territory and Canada. The treaty also addressed the *Caroline* **incident**. In 1837, British authorities had burned an American vessel, the *Caroline*, which was being used by anti-British Canadian rebels to transport supplies. In response, New York officials had arrested a Canadian sheriff and threatened to execute him for participating in the murder of an American crew member. In the treaty negotiations, both sides admitted wrongdoing.

"Fifty-four Forty or Fight": Negotiating the Oregon Border

Both Great Britain and the United States laid claim to the lands of the **Pacific Northwest**. In 1818, the two nations agreed on a **"joint occupation"** of the **Oregon Country**. In the 1830s and 1840s, adventurous Americans began traveling west along the Oregon Trail and settling in the lush valley of the Willamette River. In 1844 politicians pushed for sole U.S. ownership of the entire Oregon Country, the northern boundary of which was the north latitude line at 54°40′. **"Fifty-four forty or fight"** was the rallying call of those who wanted the United States to annex the entire territory. Great Britain balked at giving up all the territory. In 1846, the administration of **President James Polk** reached a compromise with Britain, establishing the border at the **49th parallel**. That line is the current boundary between the western United States and Canada.

Topic 4.5 The Market Revolution: Economic Transformations

A series of technological innovations dramatically altered the American economy. Old patterns of economic activity gave way to new patterns of production, distribution, and consumption, changing the nature of agriculture and manufacturing.

A. The Market Revolution

The growth of the market economy, often labeled the "market revolution" by historians, dramatically altered many aspects of American society. The market revolution linked cities and created regional interdependence. The local economies of the eighteenth century began giving way to a national, and even international, economic system.

The Expansion of Banking

Banking and credit began to play an increasingly important role in economic expansion. The **Second Bank of the United States**, chartered in 1816, extended credit, as did many newly chartered state banks. In addition, many **"wildcat" banks** had come into existence in the early 1800s. These banks typically issued currency (bank notes) in excess of the value of assets held by the bank (in gold and silver coins, as well as in bonds). Wildcat banks were known for providing easy access to credit—readily loaning these unstable notes to ordinary Americans. The easy access to credit from the different types of banks put money into circulation and fueled economic expansion, but also created economic instability, as was evident in the **Panic of 1819** (see below).

"The Panic of 1819"

The interconnected and volatile nature of the emerging "market economy" was evident in the "Panic of 1819." The origins of the economic downturn can be found in both the growing role of the United States as an exporter of farm goods and in the fevered speculation in western lands. United States agricultural exports increased during the Napoleonic Wars (1803–1815), which disrupted European agriculture. This growth in the agricultural sector stimulated a land boom in the West. The land boom was also fueled by the easy access to credit, as wildcat banks (see page 144), as well as more established banks, freely gave out loans. However, the remarkable growth of the economy following the panic demonstrated the vitality of the new economy.

The Incorporation of America

The market revolution was facilitated by the changes in laws that made it much easier to create and expand a corporate entity. In the late 1700s and early 1800s, **corporate charters** were granted to groups of individuals, but mainly on a temporary basis and mainly for a public-oriented purpose, such as building a bridge or a road. However, by the 1830s and 1840s, states began rewriting corporate laws allowing for the chartering of businesses. These laws allowed for the establishment of an entity—a corporation—in which members of the public could invest their money. Incorporation laws provided investors with **"limited liability."** Investors could only lose the amount they had invested; they were not liable for any debts beyond their investments, nor could they be held liable in any civil suits. In the following decades, the number of corporations and investors grew dramatically.

The Supreme Court and the Market Economy

Supreme Court decisions in the first half of the nineteenth century tended to uphold and define the rules of the growing market economy, especially the sanctity of contracts. The Supreme Court, in the decision of *Trustees of Dartmouth College v. Woodward* (1819), defined the charter that Dartmouth College had received during the colonial period as a contract. When the state of New Hampshire attempted to rescind Dartmouth's charter and make it a state college, the Court ruled that the original charter was valid and must stand. In *Fletcher v. Peck* (1810), the Supreme Court upheld a corrupt land deal between the state of Georgia and private individuals. The Court ruled that the deal, in effect a contract, might not have been in the public interest, but a contract should be upheld.

B. Advances in Technology

A series of technological innovations strengthened the market economy and brought efficiency to the production of goods. These innovations included the steam engine, interchangeable parts, the telegraph, agricultural implements, and machinery to produce textiles.

Agricultural Efficiency

Several new inventions improved the efficiency of agricultural work in the antebellum period. These were not yet the mechanized implements of the Gilded Age (see page 215). Rather, this period was characterized by hand-operated tools or animal-assisted implements. The **steel plow**, developed by **John Deere** in 1847, proved to be more durable and efficient than the cast-iron plow. Manufacturers developed more efficient grain drills, mowers, hay rakes, and harrows. There were two significant inventions that allowed for greater efficiency in grain production. The first, the **automatic reaper**, developed by **Cyrus McCormack** in 1831, cut and stacked wheat and other grains. The machine, operated by one farmer and pulled by horses, could harvest as much wheat as five men. After harvesting, the grain must be threshed—the individual edible kernels of grain must be loosened from the inedible chaff (the dry husks that surround the grain). This was traditionally done by hand or by animals walking on the harvested stalks. The second invention, the **thresher**, could process wheat far more quickly than previous methods. These machines were used on farms of the "Old Northwest" (as the region between the Great Lakes and the Ohio and Mississippi Rivers came to be called). They pointed the way toward the mechanized agriculture of the post–Civil War period.

Eli Whitney and Interchangeable Parts

By the 1850s, many industrial processes came to rely on the use of **interchangeable parts**. The parts of a specific item were made to exact specifications and could be rapidly assembled into standardized finished products. In the early 1800s, this technique was proposed by **Eli Whitney** (who had earlier developed the cotton gin) in the production of small firearms. Others implemented the idea of interchangeability in clock and watch making. By the time of the Civil War, it had spread to a wide variety of manufacturing operations.

The Development of Steam Power

One of the most important technological developments in the first half of the nineteenth century was the harnessing of **steam power**. Developments in Great Britain in the late eighteenth century led to high-pressure steam engines that could be used for powering ships and locomotives. In the United States, **Robert Fulton** developed a functioning steamboat, the *Clermont*, that was demonstrated on New York's Hudson River in 1807. Within twenty years, steamboats came to dominate commercial shipping, swiftly plying the major rivers and canals of the United States, as well as the Great Lakes. Soon, similar technologies were used by steam-powered locomotives. In the years leading up to the Civil War, steam power was beginning to be used in factories—replacing the water wheels that had characterized factories since the turn of the nineteenth century.

Advances in Communication

The major advance in communications in the antebellum period was the **telegraph**. **Samuel Morse** developed and patented the telegraph, and sent the first message—"What hath God wrought?"—in 1844. The first telegraph line was from Washington, D.C., to Baltimore. Telegraph messages were transmitted using long and short electrical impulses, called Morse code. By 1850, telegraph lines, usually built alongside railroad tracks, connected the country. The telegraph greatly facilitated the development of a national market for products and services. Clothing manufacturers in Massachusetts could send their orders to southern cotton growers in a matter of minutes. Previously, it could take days to send information long distances.

C. Improvements in Transportation and Regional Interdependence

Improvements in transportation made production for faraway markets possible. By 1850, the eastern half of the United States was crisscrossed by a series of roads, canals, and railroads that, along with navigable rivers, moved goods from city to city and from the interior to the coast. These improvements allowed for regional specialization—western grain and southern cotton could be rapidly transported to eastern population centers to be consumed or processed.

Canals and Roads

The first set of improvements, which occurred between 1800 and 1830, included the expansion and improvement of roads and canals and the development of the steamboat. The construction of canals and roads, called at the time *internal improvements*, did much to expand trade, especially between the Midwest (then known as the West) and eastern cities. These projects were generally built by private entities, often with support and subsidies from federal and state governments. Most significant was the **Erie Canal** (completed in 1825), which connected the Hudson River to the Great Lakes, thus connecting New York City with the interior of the country. The cost of moving a ton of freight from Buffalo to New York City dropped by approximately 90 percent with the completion of the Erie Canal. The most important road project was the building of the **National Road**, also known as the **Cumberland Road**, stretching from Maryland into the Ohio River Valley. Construction took place from 1811 to 1853. Soon, however, roads and even canals were overshadowed by a quicker and more powerful means of transportation—the railroad.

Railroads

The first railroad tracks were laid in 1829 by the **Baltimore and Ohio Railroad**. By 1860, railroads connected the far reaches of the country east of the Mississippi River and beyond. Railroads sped up the movement of goods and expanded markets. The cost of moving a ton of wheat one mile by wagon in 1800 was between 30 and 70 cents; it dropped to about 1.2 cents by railroad by 1860. Railroad construction dramatically increased in the post–Civil War era, connecting the far-reaches of the continent and increasing the nation's economic vitality (see page 216).

D. Regional Specialization

The market revolution affected the North and the South in different ways in the antebellum period. The North developed banking, manufacturing, and shipping industries, while the South focused on increasing its cotton production. Both the North and South were growing economically in the first decades of the nineteenth century. In many ways, the growth of each region reinforced the growth of the other. However, this symbiotic relationship would not persist. Political and ideological differences would emerge as America moved toward the midway point in the century. These differences would come to overshadow commonalities and lead to civil war.

Commerce, Trade, and Manufacturing in the North

Manufacturing expanded throughout the North in the 1820s and 1830s. By the early 1830s, more than 40,000 women worked in textile mills in New England (see more on textile manufacturing, pages 150–151). The **Waltham-Lowell System**—bringing all stages of textile production under one roof, with employees living in company housing—soon spread to other industries and to other parts of the country. Manufacturing operations emerged in some of the cities of the Old Northwest, including Cincinnati and Chicago. In addition, the use of interchangeable parts, a key component of mass production (see page 146), soon spread to other processes. Manufacturers of agricultural implements, tools, clocks, and ironware began to use interchangeable parts.

> **USING HISTORICAL THINKING SKILLS:**
> **CONTEXTUALIZATION**
>
> **American Manufacturing In Context**
>
> America's first steps toward manufacturing and industrial production took place in the context of strained relations with Great Britain. The Embargo Act (1807), the Non-Intercourse Act (1809), and the War of 1812 (1812–1815) all had the effect of greatly reducing imports of manufactured items from Great Britain and increasing the demand for American-made goods. These foreign policy actions contributed to the United States becoming more economically self-sufficient.

The Growth of Cotton Production in the South

In the first half of the nineteenth century, cotton replaced other staple crops as the most profitable crop throughout the South. The profitability of southern cotton contributed to a dramatic growth in slavery in the first half of the nineteenth century and an expansion of the internal slave trade. Most of the cotton used in the mills in New England was grown by slave labor in the South. The invention of the **cotton gin** by **Eli Whitney** (1793) allowed for the rapid processing of cotton. That, combined with insatiable demand in the North and in Great Britain for cotton, led to more and more acres being put under cultivation. Cotton production connected the United States to the global economy. By 1860, 58 percent of American exports consisted of cotton. Cotton production increased from about 700,000 bales in 1830 to nearly five million bales on the eve of the Civil War. This amounted to three-quarters of the world's supply of cotton. Cotton was justifiably called **"King Cotton."** As cotton production increased, the number of slaves in the South also increased (see page 167).

> **KEEP IN MIND**
>
> **King Cotton, North and South**
>
> Cotton was not only king in the South. The increase in cotton production benefited many elements in the North as well as in the South. Cotton was bought and sold in New York City and processed into cloth in New England. Northern banks lent money to plantation owners and northern insurance companies insured their slaves.

Topic 4.6 Market Revolution: Society and Culture

The market revolution led to new settlement patterns in the United States—encouraging both the movement of immigrants from abroad into the United States as well as the movement of people within the country. In addition, the market revolution dramatically changed American society, drawing more people into its orbit, altering class relations, and redefining gender and family roles.

A. Migrations and New Communities in the Age of the Market Revolution

A variety of social and economic factors contributed to native-born white citizens moving into the West and settling in new communities along the Ohio and Mississippi Rivers. At the same time, the growth of manufacturing in the United States drew immigrants from abroad into growing cities. The majority of immigrants who arrived in the United States between 1800 and 1860 came from northern and western Europe. The two largest groups came from Ireland and from the German states. Many of these immigrants stayed in the cities of the Northeast, while some ventured into the interior of the country.

Irish Immigration

The largest immigrant group into the United States during the antebellum period came from **Ireland**. The increase in Irish immigration during the 1840s was primarily the result of crop failures at home that led to mass starvation. Blight afflicted the potato crop, which was a staple for Irish people. The **"potato famine"** was partly a natural phenomenon and partly the result of British policies. Great Britain controlled Ireland and used the best land to grow wheat and other crops for export, while potato farming was pushed to marginal land. The result was weak potato plants less able to withstand disease. It is estimated that one million Irish starved to death between 1845 and 1852 (out of a population of eight million), while another two million left Ireland— with approximately one million coming to the United States and one million settling in other countries. Four-fifths of the Irish immigrants to the United States settled in port cities such as **New York** and **Boston** and in other cities and towns of the Northeast.

German Immigration

The second-largest immigrant group during the antebellum period was **German**. German immigrants to the United States tended to be financially better off than the Irish immigrants. Many were skilled craftsmen and entrepreneurs who immigrated to the United States to escape the political repression following the failed **Revolution of 1848** in the German states. German immigrants were more likely to have the resources to continue their journeys beyond their initial city of disembarkation (usually New York City). Many settled in the **"German triangle"** of western cities—Cincinnati, St. Louis, and Milwaukee.

The Movement to the West

The **West** grew rapidly in the antebellum period, especially after the **War of 1812**, as improvements in transportation—first roads and canals, and later railroads—opened new areas for settlement. More than four million Americans crossed the Appalachian Mountains between 1800 and 1840 to settle in the West. Most of these migrants to the West traveled in groups. New communities grew quickly, with migrants depending on one another to clear land, construct dwellings and barns, and create a sense of community on the frontier. Many southern planters moved into **Alabama**, **Mississippi**, **Louisiana**, **Arkansas**, and, later during this period, **Texas** (see page 167). Many of these small-scale farmers hoped to recreate the **Cotton Kingdom** of the old South, complete with slave labor, on the less expensive lands further west. From the upper South, many farmers moved into the southern portions of **Ohio**, **Indiana**, and **Illinois**. Finally, many New England and New York farm families settled in northern portions of Ohio, Indiana, and Illinois, as well as **Wisconsin** and **Michigan**. Some migrants **"squatted"** on their new land, lacking legal title or deed. Others purchased land from either the federal government or from speculators. Over time, the regional distinctiveness of the original thirteen states left its imprint on newly settled areas. The towns and churches of the Old Northwest (the current upper Midwest) began to resemble New England, while the plantations and slave-labor system of the newly settled South resembled the Old South.

B. The Market Revolution's Impact on Economic Class

The market revolution altered the nation's social fabric. The economic changes of the antebellum period fostered both a degree of social mobility for some as well as a growing middle class. At the same time, the gap between the rich and the poor widened. The period saw both the development of a wealthy business elite and the growth of a large class of laboring poor.

Social Mobility, Class, and the "Free-Labor" Ideology

Overall, the material wealth of the United States grew dramatically in the age of the **market revolution**. The average income for Americans increased, and the general standard of living improved. The economy of the United States in the first half of the nineteenth century provided for a degree of **social mobility** for many ordinary Americans. Factory workers could hope to gain greater skill and higher wages in their field of work. In addition, industrial and agrarian workers could hope to own their own land in the expanding West. This social and geographic mobility reflected—and bolstered—the **"free-labor"** ideology, which gained currency among many Americans in the nineteenth century. This ideal held that in the United States it was possible for wage earners to actually own land and become independent of others. It upheld the dignity of work and led northerners to see their society as superior to that of the South. In the South, physical labor was denigrated and associated with slaves. The "free-labor" ideology would become a central tenet of Abraham Lincoln's Republican Party in the 1850s (see page 191).

The "free-labor" ideology reflected reality for many Americans, yet large numbers of workers found themselves stuck in low-wage **factory work**. The benefits of the growing economy were certainly not equally distributed. The lion's share of the benefits went to a small percentage of Americans. Many entrepreneurs, merchants, bank owners, and industrialists were able to accrue vast fortunes. On the eve of the Civil War, approximately 5 percent of the population controlled half of the country's wealth; earlier, in the period following the American Revolution, that share of the wealth was divided among 10 percent of the population.

At the same time that the gap between the rich and the poor grew, the period also witnessed the growth of a **middle class**. The institutions of the market revolution—banks, corporations, legal offices, transportation operations—required a workforce of lawyers, clerks, bank workers, accountants, customs officials, and other white-collar professionals. These occupations provided a pathway to economic advancement for many Americans.

The Development of Unions

In many ways, the growth of manufacturing in the antebellum period slowly undermined the autonomy of workers and notions of a self-governing citizenry. As individual autonomy declined in the factory setting, workers increasingly turned to the idea of forming **unions** to advance their goals and improve their working conditions. A labor union allowed workers in a firm to bargain "collectively" with their employer. In the 1830s, the mill workers in **Lowell, Massachusetts**, organized as the **Factory Girls Association**, staged two strikes. In 1834, the women staged an unsuccessful **"turn-out"** to protest a wage cut. Two years later, they had greater success protesting a rent increase in the boardinghouses. Their limited success was soon undercut by the **Panic of 1837** and by the coming of large-scale Irish immigration (see page 148). Workers in other fields also began to organize unions in the antebellum period. The 1842 decision by the Massachusetts Supreme Judicial Court in ***Commonwealth v. Hunt*** set an important precedent by declaring that unions were lawful organizations as long as they used legal means—including striking—to achieve their goals. Successes for organized labor, however, were limited in the pre–Civil War period. Several organizations of skilled workers, including the **National Typographical Union** (1852) and the **Stone Cutters** (1853), achieved a greater degree of success in achieving their goals. The rise of the union movement signaled a shift away from the face-to-face relationships that characterized workplace settings in the eighteenth century.

C. Workers and New Methods of Production

New methods of production attracted men and women into a growing market economy and away from small-scale agricultural work.

The "Putting-out System"

In the first decades of the nineteenth century, a system of manufacturing developed in which many workers performed piecework at home. In this **"putting-out system,"** men and women would perform a task arranged by an agent and would be paid by the piece produced. Often, the task was a small part of a larger operation, such as repeatedly cutting leather forms to be sewn elsewhere into shoes. This system was suited to small-town and rural communities. Often, families might be simultaneously involved in semi-subsistence agriculture and in the "putting-out system"; the seasonal nature of farm work allowed for additional work to be taken in at various times of the year. This system was something of a bridge between the craftwork of the eighteenth century and the industrial revolution of the late nineteenth century.

Slater Mill and the Development of the Factory System

Before the Civil War, America began to move toward the industrial production of goods. This trend continued with even greater energy after the Civil War (see box, this page). The first field to industrialize was the textile industry. As early as the 1790s, **Samuel Slater** built the first factory in the United States after smuggling machinery plans out of Great Britain. This factory in Pawtucket, Rhode Island, and dozens that were built in the following years, spun cotton and wool into yarn or thread. The spinning machines in Slater's mill were powered by the fast-flowing Blackstone River. Water, human, and animal power characterized industry in the pre–Civil War era.

The Lowell System

Early elements of industrialization emerged in rural New England in the 1820s and 1830s. Extensive water-powered textile factories opened along the Merrimack River in **Lowell, Massachusetts**, starting in 1821, and drew in young women from the New England countryside to operate the machines. It was thought that these women could be paid less and would only be temporary factory operatives. At some point, it was assumed, they would get married and be replaced by new women, who would be recruited to replace them. Also, the era of mass migration from Europe had not yet begun, so it was difficult to recruit male factory operatives, especially with farmland in the United States still reasonably priced. By 1830, eight **Lowell mills** employed more than 6,000 women.

The fathers of these young women were told by factory recruiters that their daughters would be working in a **"factory in the garden"**—a clean, bucolic setting, unlike the dirty and dangerous factory cities of Great Britain. The

> **USING REASONING PROCESSES: CONTINUITY AND CHANGE**
>
> **Was There an Industrial Revolution Before the Civil War?**
>
> There is some disagreement among historians about whether the term "industrial revolution" better applies to the period before the Civil War or the period after. Some historians label the prewar steps toward industrialization "the first industrial revolution," and postwar developments "the second industrial revolution." Pre–Civil War changes in the economic sector include the development of steam power, canals and railroads, and the mechanized factory. We also see the expanding scope of markets—local production began to give way to regional, national, and international markets. Hence, this first industrial revolution is often referred to as the "market revolution." Post–Civil War changes are characterized by steel production, the development of the automobile, advances in electricity, and, most notably, mass production.

women tended to live in closely supervised boarding houses, and the work was also strictly monitored. Despite this scrutiny, both on the job and even at the boarding houses, the **"Lowell girls"** experienced a degree of freedom and autonomy unheard of for young women at the time. Many participated in producing a periodical called the *Lowell Offering*. They demonstrated their sense of solidarity and assertiveness by going on strike in 1834 and again in 1836, following announced wage cuts and rent increases in company boarding houses. The 1836 strike was successful, but by the 1840s the young farm women were being replaced by Irish immigrants who were in dire need and ready to work for lower wages.

D. Gender and Family Roles in the Age of the Market Revolution

The market revolution affected gender and family roles. During this period, many Americans came to see separate spheres in society—a male-dominated public sphere and a female-oriented private sphere. A set of domestic ideals that came to be called the "cult of domesticity" developed in the first decades of the nineteenth century.

Gentility, Domesticity, and the Middle-class Ideal

Many historians note the emergence in the first half of the nineteenth century of a new set of cultural ideas centered around the **middle class**. This culture was built around the home, nostalgia, sentimentality, and a watered-down (non-Calvinist) Christian piety. This middle-class cultural ideal assigned to women a dependent role as the "weaker sex." In an increasingly market-oriented society, women were seen as outside of the rough-and-tumble world of money and politics. The qualities that were assigned to women were timidity and disdain for competition. This culture was manifested in sermons by Protestant ministers, seeking to broaden their appeal, and by female authors of popular fiction.

The "Cult of Domesticity" and the "Proper" Role for Women

Antebellum society underwent a redefinition of women's "proper" role in society. The ideas of **"republican motherhood,"** current in the decades after the American Revolution, gave way to a less public-minded conception of a middle-class woman's "place." Commentators in the first half of the nineteenth century tended to see women as intellectually inferior and insisted that their proper role was maintaining the house and caring for children. This **"cult of domesticity"** insisted that women keep a proper Christian home—separate from the male sphere of politics, business, and competition. This ideal discouraged women from participating in public life.

The legal structure of the United States already relegated women to a second-class status. For example, women could not vote or sit on juries, nor were they entitled to protection against physical abuse by their husbands. And if women married, any property they owned became the property of their husbands. All in all, under the legal doctrine of *feme covert*, wives had no independent legal or political standing.

Topic 4.7 Expanding Democracy

In the first decades of the nineteenth century, states expanded suffrage by reducing or eliminating property qualifications for voting. This led to a growth in the importance of political parties and elections. Observers noted the development of a democratic culture in the United States during this period.

A. Participatory Democracy and an Expanding Electorate

Several developments in the first half of the nineteenth century transformed Americans politics. The older system of deference to established elites gave way to a more participatory, competitive form of politics. These changes are evident in the rise of President Andrew Jackson. The electorate in Jackson's successful bid for the presidency in 1828 was far broader than in previous elections. (See more on President Jackson in Topic 4.8.) Related to the democratization of the voting process was an increased focus on character and personality.

The Growth of Popular Politics and the Elimination of Property Qualifications

Politics changed dramatically in the period following the **"Era of Good Feelings."** In the 1820s most states reduced or removed property qualifications for voting so that most free white males had the right to vote. The impulse to expand democratic participation was strongest in the newly admitted states of the West. Ohio, admitted in 1803, initiated the move toward **eliminating property qualifications** for voting and allowed any voter to hold public office. Between 1816 and 1821, six new states admitted to the Union also provided for greater democratic participation than the state constitutions enacted in the period of the Revolutionary War. Affordable land was more widely available in the West than in the original thirteen states, so the percent of landless men was smaller there. In the 1820s, many of the older states felt pressure from popular movements to follow suit and reduce or eliminate impediments to white male suffrage. Most states reduced property qualifications for voting during this period, but many still restricted voting to taxpayers. Although it is difficult to determine the percent of adult white males who were eligible to vote in the decades following the American Revolution, historians estimate that eligibility for voting rose to about 90 percent of adult white men by 1840. Consequently, candidates had to campaign more aggressively and tailor their appeal to reach a broader audience.

The Dorr Rebellion and Resistance to the Expansion of Democracy

In many states, conservative politicians opposed the enactment of reforms designed to broaden the electorate. In Massachusetts, **Daniel Webster** led conservative opponents of democratic reform in the **Massachusetts Constitutional Convention** of 1820-1821, arguing that "power naturally and necessarily follows property." Although the **Federalist Party** suffered setbacks following the War of 1812, Federalist political leaders in Massachusetts were able to block several of the more egalitarian proposals of the convention. While Massachusetts did eliminate property requirements for voting, it did not eliminate the requirement that voters must be taxpayers.

In Rhode Island, conflict over the expansion of democracy resulted in a short-lived rebellion. Rhode Island held onto property qualifications for voting longer than any other state. In a state with a growing propertyless class of industrial wageworkers, resentment over this impediment to democracy was widespread. In 1841, democratic reformers organized a **People's Convention**, which wrote a new, more democratic, state constitution. These reformers then conducted an unsanctioned statewide referendum on their constitution, which overwhelmingly passed. They then tried to put this new constitution into effect and inaugurate a new governor, **Thomas Dorr**. However, none of these moves had official state approval; they were seen as an extralegal rebellion. Federal troops were sent by **President John Tyler**. Dorr was briefly imprisoned and the **"Dorr Rebellion"** was quickly put down, but the incident illustrated the strong popular desire for a more democratic governing structure.

Democracy in America by Alexis de Tocqueville

The French writer **Alexis de Tocqueville** visited the United States in 1831, along with the French prison reformer, **Gustave de Beaumont**, to study the American prison system. Tocqueville's travels and observations led him to produce a broader account of American society, ***Democracy in America***, published in two volumes (1835 and 1840). The book became a classic account of democracy, as well as an insightful description of the United States at the time. Tocqueville was especially interested in why representative democracy had taken hold in the United States while it failed in many other countries. He noted that democracy in the United States meant more than access to voting. He described a democratic ethos that was rooted in American culture. This was evident in the fervent belief in equality, in active participation in voluntary civic organizations, and in the perception that individual initiative (not birth) determined one's degree of success in the public sphere.

Topic 4.8 Jackson and Federal Power

The era of President Andrew Jackson (1829–1837), which occurred in the context of the expansion of democratic participation, witnessed the development of a new two-party system as well as intense debates around the extent of federal power. As the United States gained control of additional territory and more Americans migrated into the interior of the country, conflicts with American Indians expanded.

> **KEEP IN MIND**
>
> **Jackson and States' Rights**
>
> Be careful about generalizing in regard to Andrew Jackson's attitude toward states' rights. He comes from a southern states' rights tradition, and he defended Georgia against the Supreme Court decision *Worcester v. Georgia*. But he *was* the president, and when John Calhoun challenged federal tariff policy, Jackson took the side of federal power. Read Jackson's Farewell Address for a good summary of his political thought.

A. The Second Two-Party System: The Democrats and the Whigs

A second two-party system developed in the 1830s out of the contentious issues of the era of President Andrew Jackson. The tense unity of the one-party "Era of Good Feelings" broke apart as the Jacksonian branch of the Democratic-Republicans became known simply as the Democratic Party, and Jackson's opponents, led by Henry Clay, organized the Whig Party (1833).

Jacksonian Democracy

Many of the political divisions that characterized this period emerged in force during the administration of **President Andrew Jackson**. The years of his presidency (1829–1837), as well as the immediate aftermath, bear the name the **Age of Jackson**, or the **Age of Jacksonian Democracy**.

Andrew Jackson and his supporters grew bitter at the results of the **election of 1824**. Of four candidates competing for the presidency that year, none reached the required number of electoral votes to be declared president. Despite Jackson having the largest number of electoral votes, the House of Representatives elected **John Quincy Adams** to become president. It was widely believed that **Speaker of the House Henry Clay** convinced enough representatives to tilt the election toward Adams. In the following weeks, when Adams named Clay his secretary of state, Jackson's support labeled the entire episode a **"corrupt bargain."** In the election of 1828, Jackson's supporters painted John Quincy Adams as out-of-touch and elitist, while Adams's supporters portrayed Jackson as ill-tempered. Jackson's backwoods, populist appeal helped him win the election.

The **election of 1828** is considered by many historians to be the first modern election. The electorate was much broader than in previous elections. In the 1820s most states reduced or removed **property qualifications** for voting so that most free white males had the right to vote (see page 152). Consequently, candidates had to campaign more aggressively and tailor their appeal to reach a broader audience. Related to the democratization of the voting process was an increased focus on character and personality.

The "Tariff of Abominations"

Tariff rates became an extremely contentious issue in the first half of the nineteenth century. A major controversy around tariff rates occurred during the administration of **President Jackson** and reflected the escalation of regional tensions. The controversy originated with the **Tariff Act of 1828**, which revised tariff rates on a variety of imports. The act, known by its critics as the **"Tariff of Abominations,"** dramatically raised tariff rates on many items and led to a general reduction in trade between the United States and Europe. This decline in trade hit **South Carolina**, which depended on cotton exports, especially hard.

John C. Calhoun and the Nullification Crisis

In the 1830s, debates over tariff rates pitted many southern politicians against federal policy. The high tariff rates established by the **Tariff Act of 1828** (see above) especially angered southern politicians. A new tariff act, signed by **President Jackson** in 1832, lowered tariff rates but did not satisfy many politicians in South Carolina. These politicians, led by **John C. Calhoun,** who had been Jackson's vice president until he resigned in 1832, asserted the right of states to nullify federal legislation. Under this theory of **nullification**, a state could declare an objectionable federal law null and void within that state. In actuality, courts at the state and federal level, including the Supreme Court, have consistently upheld the Supremacy Clause of the Constitution, which asserts that federal law is superior to state law. Courts have also held that under Article III of the Constitution, only the federal judiciary has the final authority to judge the constitutionality of a federal act. Nonetheless, the South Carolina legislature voted to hold a Constitutional Convention in 1832; the convention voted overwhelmingly to declare the tariff acts of both 1828 and 1832 unconstitutional and unenforcible in South Carolina. Jackson was alarmed at South Carolina's flouting of federal authority and challenged the move. He pushed through Congress the 1833 **Force Bill** (quickly nullified by the South Carolina convention), which authorized military force against South Carolina for committing treason. At the same time, Congress revised tariff rates once again, providing relief for South Carolina. The Force Bill and the new tariff rates, passed by Congress on the same day, amounted to a face-saving compromise. However, the issue of states' rights versus federal power would emerge again in the coming decades in relation to the issue of slavery.

Destruction of the Second Bank of the United States

One of the fiercest battles of the Andrew Jackson presidency was over the **Second Bank of the United States**. Jackson revived the criticism of a national bank that had been part of the national discourse since Alexander Hamilton had first proposed such an institution in 1791. Despite the fact that the bank was performing its function admirably, Jackson insisted that it put too much power into the hands of a small elite. Jackson's political opponents thought that his animosity to the bank would hand them a political victory. These opponents brought the issue of rechartering the bank to Congress in 1832, four years before the bank's charter was to expire. They thought that a Jackson veto would weaken his chances for reelection. But Jackson's opponents miscalculated. He did veto the rechartering of the bank. However, the forceful and uncompromising rhetoric in his **veto message** played well with the voters and he won reelection. Jackson, encouraged by his electoral success, was not satisfied to let the bank die its natural death upon its charter running out in 1836. He took actions to kill the "monster" bank immediately. He moved federal deposits from the Second Bank of the United States to state banks in Democratic-leaning states.

The Specie Circular and the Panic of 1837

President Andrew Jackson's suspicion of bankers and credit led him to issue the **Specie Circular** (1836), mandating that government-held land be sold only for hard currency (gold or silver "specie"), not paper currency. The move resulted in falling land prices and a shortage of government funds. Both the destruction of the Second Bank of the United States and the Specie Circular contributed to the economic downturn known as the **Panic of 1837**. The Panic of 1837, which lasted five years, was the worst economic crisis in the United States up to that point. The crisis brought many canal and railroad projects to a halt, contributed to hundreds of banks and businesses folding, and led to high unemployment. The Panic of 1837 also damaged the political fortunes of the **Democrats**. Jackson's successor, **Martin Van Buren**, did little to address the economic crisis. He paid the price in the election of 1840, losing badly to the **Whig Party** candidate, **William Henry Harrison**.

> **KEEP IN MIND**
>
> **Federal Aid**
>
> The idea that the federal government should intervene to help the victims of economic downturns did not gain currency until the twentieth century. Politicians still debate the appropriate level of federal assistance.

Whigs and Democrats

The opponents of **President Andrew Jackson** and the **Democratic Party** founded the **Whig Party** in 1833. It is difficult to generalize about the constituents of each party. Northerners and southerners, for example, could be found in both parties. Irish and German Catholic immigrants tended to support the Democrats, while evangelical

Protestants were more likely to support the Whigs. Many Whigs supported government programs aimed at economic modernization, as outlined in **Henry Clay's "American System"** proposals (see page 139). The language of the Democratic Party was more populist, arguing that high tariffs would "fatten" urban commercial interests. Issues, in general, tended to be less important in this period than they had been in the formative years of the country or than they would become again during the lead-up to the Civil War. Both parties focused intently on winning elections and holding on to power.

B. Contention Between Whites and American Indians over Western Lands

White settlers and American Indians clashed on the frontier in the first half of the nineteenth century. The enthusiasm of land-hungry settlers was matched by the determination of native peoples to hold on to their traditional lands. These clashes led to wars and to federal efforts to control American Indian groups.

American Indians and the West

Westward settlers were continuing in the footsteps of early colonists—pushing into the interior of the continent and antagonizing native peoples in the process. In the early 1800s, white settlers were pouring into the region of the Ohio River and its northern tributaries, which included the state of **Ohio** (1803) and the **Indiana Territory**. Federal and state officials had extracted land agreements from the American Indian tribes for years. It was never clear if the Indian leaders who made the agreements had the authority to do so, nor was it clear that white settlers would live by these agreements. In 1809, the governor of the Indiana Territory, **William Henry Harrison**, negotiated the **Treaty of Fort Wayne**. Indians agreed to cede three million acres for a nominal fee. The most important regional native leader at the time, **Tecumseh**, was not present for this agreement. He was on a trip recruiting followers to resist encroachments by white settlers. He and his brother, **Tenskwatawa**, **"the Prophet,"** had been organizing a spiritual and political front, attempting to unite all the Indian nations east of the Mississippi River.

Battle of Tippecanoe and the War Hawks

Settlers in the **Indiana Territory** persuaded **Governor William Henry Harrison** to wage war against **Tecumseh's** confederation. The **Battle of Tippecanoe** (1811) ousted members of the confederation and was perceived as an American victory. Western congressmen, who became known as the **War Hawks**, became convinced that Britain was encouraging and funding Tecumseh's confederation. Just as relations with Britain were deteriorating over trade issues, War Hawks, led by **Henry Clay** of Kentucky and **John C. Calhoun** from South Carolina, were pushing for military action against the British. Such action, it was thought, would allow the United States to eliminate the American Indian threat and, perhaps, even allow the United States to invade **Canada**. This pro-war sentiment in the West and South was one of the causes of the **War of 1812** (see page 142).

Indian Removal Act (1830)

As the profitability of cotton production rose in the South in the first half of the nineteenth century, the value of land increased dramatically. Many whites wanted to push westward and acquire land in the interior of the South. Much of the southern territory was the traditional lands of the **"Five Civilized Tribes"**—**Cherokee**, **Chickasaw**, **Choctaw**, **Muscogee-Creek**, and **Seminole**. As far back as the **Jefferson administration**, federal policy had been to respect the rights of American Indians to inhabit this land. **President Andrew Jackson**, however, abandoned this policy and, in deference to market pressures and the call of white southerners to expand, adopted a policy of Indian removal. This policy applied to the American Indians of the South as well as the Old Northwest and, to a lesser degree, New England and New York. Jackson asserted that it was necessary for these peoples to be removed to the areas of the United States beyond the Mississippi River. He said, perhaps disingenuously, that this was in the best interests of the Indians themselves, who were being forced off their traditional lands by the encroachment of white settlers. He pushed for the **Removal Act** of 1830.

The "Trail of Tears"

The state of **Georgia**, with the support of **President Andrew Jackson** and then Jackson's successor, **President Martin Van Buren**, initiated the process of moving American Indians to the West despite the Supreme Court decision in *Worcester v. Georgia* (1832) declaring that American Indian tribes were subject to federal treaties, not to the actions of states (see pages 137–138). The decision, in effect, voided Georgia's efforts to remove the **Cherokee**. President Jackson purportedly said, "**John Marshall** has made his decision. Now let him enforce it." By 1838, the Cherokee had exhausted their legal and political challenges to removal. Some cooperated with removal and ceded their lands. However, the majority, led by the Cherokee "principal chief," **John Ross**, adopted a policy of passive resistance to remain on their land. Federal troops were dispatched to enforce Georgia's removal policy. The resulting expulsion of 18,000 American Indians to the **Oklahoma Territory**, their trek labeled the **"Trail of Tears"** (1838), resulted in the deaths of approximately one-quarter of the people on the journey.

American Indians and Florida

Americans, especially white southerners, had an ongoing history of conflict with American Indians in **Florida**, which had long been **Spanish** territory. Florida was ceded to **Great Britain** in 1763 following the French and Indian War and given back to Spain in the **Treaty of Paris** (1783), ending the American Revolution. In the late 1700s and early 1800s, white southerners grew frustrated with the number of escaped slaves who made their way into Florida. These fugitives were often given protection by American Indians in Florida. This concern led to raids by southern whites into Florida, followed by counterraids by the **Seminole** and other American Indians on communities in Georgia and Alabama.

These hostilities led to the **First Seminole War**, which began during the **War of 1812** and continued to the end of the decade. A second Seminole War occurred in the 1830s. Florida had come into American hands as a result of the **Adams-Onís Treaty** (1819) (see page 143). By the 1830s, the Seminole were being pressured by the federal government to relocate to the West. In the **Second Seminole War** (1835–1842), native warriors fought U.S. troops to a standstill in the Everglades. Many Seminole remained defiant of government removal efforts even after the capture of the Seminole leader, **Chief Osceola**.

"Indian Territory"

As part of the government's American Indian removal policy, many tribes from east of the Mississippi River were relocated to a designated **"Indian Territory"** that existed within the boundaries of present-day **Oklahoma**. This establishment of an Indian Territory was part of the **Indian Intercourse Act** of 1834. Many Indian groups resisted relocation to the Indian Territory through legal channels and through armed resistance. Once in the territory, conflicts ensued between American Indian groups indigenous to the area and those relocated there. Eventually this territory was reduced in size and finally it ceased to exist and was folded into the Oklahoma Territory in 1907.

Topic 4.9 The Development of an American Culture

During the first decades of the nineteenth century, Americans participated in a variety of cultural movements. Many Americans contributed to the development of a national culture, combining European aspects with distinctly American aspects. At the same time, groups of people in the United States developed cultural forms that reflected the particularities of their own experiences and worldviews.

A. The Emergence of a National Culture

The aftermath of the **War of 1812** (see page 142) saw not only an increase in nationalist sentiment, but also the development of a uniquely American culture. This culture borrowed elements of European culture, but also sought to create something uniquely American. **Noah Webster**, for instance, sought to codify a specifically American dictionary, separate from British English, when he published his *American Dictionary of the English Language* in 1828 (see page 122).

The American Renaissance

The antebellum period experienced a renaissance in literature. Some of the greatest literature in American history comes out of the decades before the Civil War. In the early 1850s, this literary spirit reached its peak. The literature of that period included **Herman Melville's** *Moby Dick* (1851), the first edition of **Walt Whitman's** *Leaves of Grass* (1855), **Nathaniel Hawthorne's** *The Scarlet Letter* (1850) and *The House of the Seven Gables* (1851), and **Henry David Thoreau's** *Walden* (1854). This literature is uniquely American, grappling with religious and existential questions raised by the legacy of the Puritans and focusing on the promise and the contradictions of America's experiment in building a democratic nation in the New World.

B. European Romanticism and American Culture

Romanticism, which had its origins in Europe, deeply influenced art, literature, and thought in the United States. The movement was strongest, both in Europe and the United States, during the first half of the nineteenth century.

The Romantic Perspective

In many ways, **romanticism** was a reaction to industrialization and to the market revolution—to work becoming more ordered around routines, to the increasing social value attached to wealth accumulation, and to the rationalization of nature. Romantics often harkened back to a simpler, more authentic past—or at least to their perception of this idealized past. In some ways, romanticism represented a radical, even revolutionary, response to the modern world. In other ways, it was deeply nationalistic, and even reactionary, in its embrace of a pure, uncorrupted sense of national community.

Hudson River School

The reverence for European cultural products combined with a desire to create a uniquely American form of expression can be seen in the landscape paintings that came to be known as the **"Hudson River School"** of painting. The Hudson River School, which flourished from the 1820s to the 1870s, is best represented by three artists—**Thomas Cole**, **Asher Durand**, and **Frederic Church**. These artists were inspired by the European tradition of romantic paintings of dramatic landscapes, often featuring the ruins of ancient castles or temples. The United States lacked such ancient ruins. In their place, these artists captured pristine wilderness. Many of the paintings hinted at the impending hand of civilization about to spoil virgin landscapes. Many Hudson River School painters shared transcendentalist ideas about the glory of nature. Several of the works focused, of course, on the **Hudson River**, a waterway that generated new interest in the aftermath of the opening of the **Erie Canal** (1825) (see page 146). These paintings often emphasized emotion and sentiment over accuracy.

Romanticism in American Literature

In the early 1800s, many Americans were captivated by the novels of the British writer **Sir Walter Scott**. His novels, with classical historical settings (*Ivanhoe* was set in twelfth-century England) and larger-than-life heroic figures, epitomized romanticism in literature. Soon, American authors began to create literature that drew on Scott's romanticism, but was distinctly American. **James Fenimore Cooper** was perhaps the most successful American romantic writer. His **"Leatherstocking Tales,"** including *The Last of the Mohicans* (1826), captured the danger and fascination of the frontier experience. **Washington Irving** also captured the spirit of romanticism in literature. His humorous short stories, **"Rip Van Winkle"** (1819) and **"The Legend of Sleepy Hollow"** (1820), portrayed a fanciful version of America. In an 1809 novel, he invented the fictional historian **Diedrich Knickerbocker** to tell a whimsical history of old New Amsterdam as well as to satirize the politics of then-contemporary New York City.

Both Cooper and Irving were internationally popular and set the stage for the more serious-minded authors of the American renaissance (see page 157).

Topic 4.10 The Second Great Awakening

A variety of political, economic, cultural, and demographic developments led to the "Second Great Awakening." This spiritual awakening inspired other religious movements as well as a host of reform movements.

A. Religious and Spiritual Movements in Antebellum America

Religious ferment was intense in the antebellum period. A variety of spiritual movements emerged in the period. These movements reflected the desire to create order and find meaning in a rapidly changing world.

The "Second Great Awakening"

In the first decades of the nineteenth century, American clergy members sought to revive religious sentiment among the American people. A similar situation led to the first **"Great Awakening"** of a century earlier. At the turn of the nineteenth century, many clergy members worried that Americans seemed more captivated by politics—forming and building a new nation—than by God and salvation. Many ordinary Americans also felt a yearning to get in touch with a more immediate religious experience. The result was the **"Second Great Awakening."** The movement of large **"camp meetings"** began in Kentucky early in the 1800s and soon spread to other states. It was especially strong in upstate New York and western Pennsylvania. The growing population centers along the **Erie Canal** in upstate New York came to be known as the **"burned-over district"** because of the intensity of the religious revival there.

Second Great Awakening ministers, such as **Charles Grandison Finney**, told his audiences that a person could determine his or her eternal life. This approach to the afterlife was very different from the old Puritan notion of **predestination**, which held that one's eternal life was planned out by God. This sense that redemption was in one's own hands not only encouraged individual redemption but also societal reformation. Not only could one become perfect in the eyes of God, but one could also work to perfect society as well. In this respect the Second Great Awakening acted as a springboard for a variety of reform movements.

> **USING HISTORICAL THINKING SKILLS: CONTEXTUALIZATION**
>
> **Contextualizing the Second Great Awakening**
>
> The Second Great Awakening can be seen in the context of the market revolution of the early 1800s. The religious movement spoke to many of the farmers, merchants, and businessmen and women who were brought into the larger U.S. society by new market relations. The messages of the market and of the Second Great Awakening were similar. Market relations told the individual that success or failure was in his or her hands; hard work, dedication, and self-restraint would lead to economic success. The Second Great Awakening told the individual that salvation was also in his or her hands. Righteous living, self-control, and a strong moral compass would lead to salvation.

Mormonism

The **Church of Jesus Christ of the Latter-Day Saints**, known as the **Mormons**, was founded in 1830 by **Joseph Smith**, in upstate New York. It was one of many sects that developed during the spiritual ferment of the Second Great Awakening. Several of these sects, including Mormonism, separated themselves from the larger community, developing cohesive and insular communities of their own. As the Mormons gained more adherents, the group was met by hostility for its unorthodox teachings and practices. Some mainstream Protestants mocked Mormon beliefs that, to them, appeared to be superstitious or magical. Others dismissed Mormonism for rejecting the belief in the "holy trinity." The most controversial practice was **polygamy**—allowing men to have multiple wives (subsequently renounced by the Mormon church in 1890). The group journeyed from New York to Ohio, then to Missouri, and then to Illinois. In Illinois, Smith was killed by an anti-Mormon mob (1844), and a new leader named **Brigham Young** led the majority of the Mormons to **Utah** (1847). (See more on the Mormon exodus, page 180.)

Transcendentalism

Transcendentalism was a spiritual and intellectual movement critical of the materialist direction the United States was taking in the first half of the nineteenth century. The movement put more stock in intuition than in empirical observation. **Henry David Thoreau** wrote about the importance of nature in finding meaning. He lived in relative isolation at **Walden Pond** for two years (1845–1847) and chronicled the experience in the book, *Walden; or, Life in the Woods* (1854). He wrote a famous essay called **"Resistance to Civil Government"** (1849), more commonly known as **"Civil Disobedience,"** urging individuals to not acquiesce to unfair and unjust government dictates. Another important figure in the movement was **Ralph Waldo Emerson**, who wrote a series of philosophical essays, including **"On Self-Reliance"** (1841). Although the transcendentalists were critical of the direction of mainstream society, they did not gravitate toward the reform movements of the day. Some transcendentalists separated themselves from mainstream society; several utopian communities were started by transcendentalist thinkers during this period.

> **USING HISTORICAL THINKING SKILLS: MAKING CONNECTIONS**
>
> **The Impact of Thoreau**
>
> Thoreau's book, *Walden; or, Life in the Woods* (1854), was influential in the back-to-the-land movement of the 1960s and 1970s. Thoreau's explanation for living for two years in the isolation of Walden Pond—"I went to the woods because I wished to live deliberately, to front only the essential facts of life . . ."—was echoed in the thinking of some of the young adherents of the counterculture who established rural communes or who lived on isolated homesteads in the 1960s and 1970s.

Utopian Communities

Utopian communities were experiments in communal living, usually in rural settings, and structured around a guiding principle. Many of these communities shared with transcendentalism an aversion to the materialistic direction of society. However, whereas transcendentalists focused on the cultivation of the self, utopian communities sought a more collective alternative to mainstream society. The most well-known community was **Brook Farm**, established outside of Boston in 1841. Brook Farm, started by the transcendentalist **George Ripley**, was based on the idea that all the residents would share equally in the labor of the community and would partake equally in leisure. Contrary to much antebellum thought, the adherents at Brook Farm saw leisure in a positive light—as a means of becoming fuller human beings. Writer **Nathaniel Hawthorne** (see page 157) was one of the original participants in the commune but grew disillusioned with the experiment. Inspiration for utopian communities came from thinkers such as the French socialist **Charles Fourier** and the Scottish industrialist and philanthropist **Robert Owen**. The **New Harmony** community in Indiana was founded by Owen himself in 1825 around principles of total equality.

Spiritual Developments in American Indian Communities

Many **American Indians**, in the face of warfare, disease, dispossession, and displacement, developed spiritual practices that both borrowed from their traditional religious beliefs and adapted elements from their contemporary experiences, including exposure to Christianity. In the wake of the defeat and dispossession of the **Iroquois Confederacy**, a Seneca named **Handsome Lake** developed a set of spiritual practices that came to be known as the **"Longhouse Religion."** Drawing on traditional native and Quaker motifs, he denounced the factionalism that undermined Indian resistance to white incursions, and he spoke out against alcohol consumption and the breakdown of the family. Although Handsome Lake met resistance from both Christian missionaries and native traditionalists, he offered many American Indians a sense of hope in the face of staggering setbacks.

Topic 4.11 An Age of Reform

Reform movements and voluntary organizations grew in number and importance in the first half of the nineteenth century. These movements were influenced by the Second Great Awakening religious revival, as well as by liberal European ideas. The Romantic notion of human perfectibility was central to these movements.

A. Reform Movements in the Antebellum Period

Although reform movements have existed throughout most of American history, the antebellum period saw a dramatic upswing in reform activity. Much of the reform activity was associated with the Whig Party. Democrats tended to be skeptical of the expanded scope of government functions that many of the reformers called for. (See more on the politics of the antebellum period in Topic 4.8.) The reform impulse of the antebellum period resulted in the creation of a variety of institutions that were intended to impart a set of cultural values seen as essential to the emerging market economy—self-discipline, respect for authority, punctuality.

> **KEEP IN MIND**
>
> **Periods of Reform in American History**
>
> Be familiar with the three most prominent periods of reform in American history: The reform movements of the 1830s and 1840s, the progressive reform movement of the 1900s and 1910s, and the reform movements of the 1960s and 1970s inspired by the civil rights movement.

These institutions reflected the "perfectionism" inherent in the Second Great Awakening. Reform movements attempted to transform different aspects of American society and had varying degrees of success.

The Temperance Movement

The goal of the **temperance movement** was to limit or even ban the production, sale, and consumption of alcoholic beverages. Many temperance activists focused on individual self-control; they encouraged people to voluntarily take an oath to abstain from alcohol. Others sought to use the power of government to limit or eliminate the consumption of alcoholic beverages. The temperance movement was the largest reform movement of the first half of the nineteenth century.

There were several reasons the temperance movement attracted a large following in the antebellum period. Temperance was especially popular among women. Many women were troubled by the large amount of alcohol their husbands and sons drank. Heavy alcohol consumption was part of the fabric of daily life for many men. By 1830, the average man drank almost ten gallons per year of hard liquor and about thirty gallons per year of beer, wine, and hard cider. In an era when pure water was difficult to come by, especially for urban working-class people, it made sense to drink alcoholic beverages; the alcohol killed dangerous bacteria. In addition, tavern owners were more than happy to cash men's paychecks on payday evening, knowing that much of that money would stay in the tavern. Men not only came home with little money in their pockets, but they also came home drunk. Many men in this drunken state took out their frustrations on their wives and children, with both verbal and physical abuse. As a result, many women were eager to be active in the temperance movement.

The largest temperance organization in the antebellum period was the American Temperance Society, founded in 1826. **Lyman Beecher's *Six Sermons on the Nature, Occasions, Signs, Evils, and Remedy of Intemperance*** (1827) was a guiding text of the movement, which was successful in gaining recruits. The **American Temperance Society** claimed 1.5 million members by 1835. Alcohol consumption per person in the United States dropped by about half from 1830 to 1840. The **"prohibitionist"** impulse within the movement had successes in the 1850s. **Maine** became a **"dry"** state in 1851, completely banning the sale or manufacture of all alcoholic beverages, followed by twelve other states. The 1840s and 1850s proved to be the high point of the movement in the nineteenth century. By the 1870s, the movement had lost some of its intensity; most of the "dry" states had repealed their prohibition laws.

The Asylum and Penitentiary Movement

The institution building impulse of the antebellum reform movements was reflected in new approaches in regard to people with mental illness and convicted criminals. In early America, people with mental illness were often treated as common criminals, spending years behind bars. In the 1840s, activists, including many women, spearheaded a movement to improve treatment for those with mental illness. One of the main organizers was **Dorothea Dix**, whose efforts led to the creation of the first generation of **psychiatric asylums** in the United States. Dix and other reformers also attempted to reform prisons themselves. Newly created **penitentiaries** were meant to reform and rehabilitate inmates, not simply punish them. Prisoners were given moral instruction and time to meditate on their transgressions—to develop "penitence" and remorsefulness.

Public Education

The campaign for **free public education** gained a large following in the 1840s. **Horace Mann** was among the most vocal advocates during this period. Mann was secretary of education in Massachusetts in the 1840s and 1850s, and served in the U.S. House of Representatives. The movement saw education as essential to democratic participation. Critics of the public school movement argued that moral education should be carried out by parents, not the government. Catholic families worried that instruction would include Protestant indoctrination.

B. Debating the Future of Slavery in America

Slavery became an increasingly contentious issue in the United States in the first half of the nineteenth century. After the outlawing of the international slave trade in 1808, many states restricted the citizenship possibilities of African Americans. The period witnessed a growing abolitionist movement as well as plans for emancipation, including sending freed or escaped slaves to colonize Africa.

Abolitionism

The reform spirit of the **Second Great Awakening** inspired the modern abolition movement. **Abolitionism** was a minority opinion among northern whites in the antebellum period, but it had a major impact on America, widening sectional divisions in the period before the Civil War.

> **USING REASONING PROCESSES:**
> **CAUSATION**
>
> **Reforming Society or Reforming Self**
>
> The causes of the growth of the reform impulse in antebellum America were varied. On the one hand, many reformers were alarmed at certain *societal* changes and dislocations in the United States associated with the market revolution. Public education, for example, was seen as a way of addressing the widening gap between the well-off and the working-class masses; tax-funded schools would provide the children in all classes with the means to succeed in life. On the other hand, many reformers were driven more by religious fervor and put more emphasis on *individual* morality and self-restraint. This focus on individual self-restraint is evident in the temperance movement. Such reformers might see slavery as problematic because it allows for, and even encourages, immoral violent behavior on the part of slave owners. The more socially-minded opponents of slavery would highlight the injustice of the system and the impact the system had on enslaved people.

William Lloyd Garrison and "Immediate Emancipation"

In 1831, **William Lloyd Garrison**, a white abolitionist, began publication of *The Liberator*. Garrison quickly became the key figure in the movement for the immediate and uncompensated abolition of slavery. Antislavery sentiment had existed before that, but most antislavery groups advocated a more gradual approach to ending slavery. That is, slave owners could keep their current slaves, but would not be able to enslave additional people. Slavery would therefore gradually end as the current slaves died. Additionally, many antislavery activists before Garrison advocated African colonization (see page 162). Garrison broke with both of these approaches. He said all slaves should be immediately freed, that there should be no compensation to their owners, and that freed slaves were entitled to the same rights as white people.

American Colonization Society

The **American Colonization Society** was founded in 1817 with the goal of transporting African Americans to Africa. The motives of the founders of the organization varied. Some sympathized with African Americans and urged them to leave the United States to escape from the ingrained racism of many white Americans. Other founders thought of African Americans as an inferior caste and wanted to rid America of them. Advocates of colonization believed that slaves either could not or should not receive treatment as equals in the United States. The society purchased land in West Africa and began a colony they called **Liberia**. Between 1820 and the Civil War only about 12,000 African Americans went to Africa. About 7,000 were former slaves who were freed under the condition that they leave the United States; the rest were free African Americans who believed they had a better chance to succeed in Liberia. Most African Americans, free or slave, showed very little interest in leaving their country to live in Africa. **Frederick Douglass**, for example, was very critical of colonization proposals. He saw colonization as accommodating the institution of slavery, rather than working toward its end.

C. Growing Tensions over Slavery

In the first half of the nineteenth century, antislavery efforts intensified in the North. At the same time, resistance to abolitionist activism grew in both the South and the North.

Abolitionism and Electoral Politics

A group of abolitionists formed the **Liberty Party** in 1840. This minor third party put forth the idea that the Constitution was essentially an antislavery document and that the United States should live up to the ideals contained in it. In this, the party differed from **William Lloyd Garrison**, who insisted that the Constitution protected slavery and, therefore, should be condemned (see page 161). The Liberty Party hoped to influence public opinion through the electoral arena. Garrison, on the other hand, rejected participating in electoral politics.

Racism and Resistance to the Antislavery Movement

Ideas around race differed by region in the antebellum period. Although many northerners subscribed to white supremacist views, white supremacist ideas were not central to the culture of the region because there were very few African Americans in the North (less than one percent of the population). In the South, however, **white supremacy** became central to southern white culture in the first half of the nineteenth century, especially after northern abolitionists began to actively press the cause of antislavery in the 1830s. Most white southerners held that African Americans were inferior beings. This view justified slavery as an institution both necessary and proper. White supremacy and slavery allowed the main divide in the South to be race rather than class. It allowed even the poorest whites to believe they were part of the superior caste and to feel they had something in common with the wealthiest plantation owners.

USING REASON PROCESSES:
COMPARISON

Different Approaches to the Opposition of Slavery

Be prepared to compare the different strands of thought in regard to opposition of slavery. William Lloyd Garrison was uncompromising in his call for *immediate and uncompensated emancipation*. Garrison, along with Elijah Lovejoy and other abolitionists, represented the most radical position among white opponents of slavery. *Gradual emancipation*, embodied in the rejected Tallmadge Amendment to the Missouri statehood bill (1819), would have prevented the future enslavement of individuals, but did not push for immediate abolition. In many ways, this moderate approach was compatible with the *colonization movement*. The American Colonization Society, which sought to send African Americans to Africa, might have had antislavery people (notably, Quakers) among its founders, but it came to be seen as compatible with the slave system. It had the support of some southern whites who wanted to rid the South of its free Black population. The *free-soil movement* was primarily against the spread of slavery to new territories; it wanted these areas to be populated by small-scale yeoman farmers, not large slave plantations.

The Lovejoy Incident

The abolitionist movement faced opposition in the North as well as from white southerners. A violent incident in 1837 sent a chill over the abolitionist movement. **Elijah Lovejoy**, an abolitionist newspaper publisher in Illinois, was killed by a **proslavery mob**. He had been the subject of harassment; mobs had destroyed his printing press three times before they killed him.

D. The Women's Rights Movement

A women's rights movement developed in the antebellum period, seeking to address gender inequalities and to improve opportunities for women. The movement expressed its ideals at the 1848 Seneca Falls Convention in Western New York.

> **USING REASONING PROCESS: CONTINUITY AND CHANGE**
>
> **The Women's Rights Movement Over Time**
>
> Be aware of continuities and discontinuities between the women's rights movement of the period 1848–1920 and the movement of the 1960s and 1970s. Tactics and priorities shifted as soon as the right to vote had been attained. The earlier movement grew out of the abolitionist movement; the later movement was inspired by the civil rights movement.

Women in the Public Sphere

The dictates of the **"cult of domesticity"**—that woman confine their activities to the private sphere—exerted a powerful influence on middle-class society in the antebellum period (see more on the "cult of domesticity," page 151). However, many women challenged these dictates. They followed the lead of **Dorothea Dix**, who was active in the movement for more humane treatment for those with mental illness (see page 161), to push for a variety of reforms in the 1820s and 1830s. Middle-class New York City women formed the **Female Moral Reform Society** (1834) to urge women not to engage in **prostitution**. The society targeted the men who frequented prostitutes, publishing lists of names of such men. These movements allowed women, who otherwise were excluded from politics and government, to participate in the public sphere.

Women also played an important role in the **abolitionist movement**. Two important orators and activists in the movement were the **Grimké sisters, Angelina and Sarah**. They were the daughters of a prominent South Carolina slave owner. Later in life, in the 1830s, they converted to Quakerism and to the abolitionist cause. Two other abolitionist activists, **Elizabeth Cady Stanton** and **Lucretia Mott**, were barred from attending the **World Anti-Slavery Convention** in London (1840) because of their gender. Mott and Stanton began thinking not only about the abolition of slavery but also about the conditions of women in the United States.

Seneca Falls Convention

In 1848, **Elizabeth Cady Stanton** and **Lucretia Mott** led a group of women, including many veterans of the abolitionist movement, to challenge the cultural and legal restrictions on women in the antebellum period. Their initial meeting in upstate New York, the **Seneca Falls Convention**, is often considered the birth of the women's rights movement. This was the first public gathering convened to raise the issue of women's suffrage. However, the convention went beyond advocating for voting rights for women. It called attention to the entire structure of gender inequality, including issues relating to property rights, education, wages, child custody, divorce, and the overall legal status of women. The convention issued a **Declaration of Sentiments** modeled after the **Declaration of Independence**. The document declared, "all men *and women* are created equal."

Topic 4.12 African Americans in the Early Republic

The changes brought about by the market revolution—most notably, the growth of the national and international market for cotton—led to the dramatic growth of slavery in the antebellum period. Enslaved and free African

Americans developed a variety of responses to the expansion of slavery, including rebellions, resistance, political activism, and new cultural patterns.

A. Slave Rebellions—The Limits of Antislavery Efforts in the South

Armed and organized slave rebellions were rare in North America. The conditions of slavery in the United States made outright rebellion virtually impossible to carry out. Compared with slave plantations in Brazil, Jamaica, Cuba, and other areas of the New World, American plantations were relatively small and dispersed over a wide geographic area. The ratio of whites to Black slaves was higher in the United States than in most of the Caribbean and South American slave societies. Slaves, therefore, were outnumbered by whites. In addition, the white population was well-armed and generally united in its support of the slave system. While rebellions were rare, slaves engaged in other forms of resistance (see pages 165–166). Three significant episodes of attempted rebellion in the first half of the nineteenth century are discussed below. These rebellions were not successful, but they made clear that slaves were deeply resentful of their situation.

Gabriel's Rebellion

A Virginia slave named **Gabriel** attempted to organize a rebellion in 1800. Gabriel, who was trained as a blacksmith, was frequently hired out to Richmond employers. His interactions with urban artisans, both Black and white, introduced Gabriel to discussions and debates about republicanism and democracy. He adopted the anti-elitist ideas of many of the Virginia Democratic-Republicans who were active in the political debates with the Federalists in the 1790s. Gabriel meticulously planned out a rebellion, recruiting as many as a thousand men to participate in the rebellion. He envisioned his rebellion to include poor whites and to be more of a republican revolution than a slave rebellion. However, the rebellion was quashed by the Virginia militia before it began. A major rain storm made some roads impassable, causing Gabriel to postpone the action. In addition, two slaves had alerted their owners about the planned rebellion. Twenty-seven supposed participants in the planned rebellion were hanged, including Gabriel himself.

The Denmark Vesey Conspiracy

Denmark Vesey was tried for plotting a slave rebellion in 1822. Vesey, a free Black man in Charleston, South Carolina, was one of the founders of the African Methodist Episcopal Church. He spoke to fellow congregants of deliverance and used the Bible as a source of hope for freedom. He was charged by local authorities with conspiring to organize a plot to destroy Charleston and instigate a broad slave uprising. Some historians have questioned whether a rebellion was in the works at all (see box right). In any case, Vesey and thirty-five others were hanged as punishment for the alleged conspiracy.

USING HISTORICAL THINKING SKILLS: SOURCING AND SITUATION

The Voices of Slaves in Primary Sources

It is important to examine primary documents from the period of American slavery cautiously. Some documents contain supposed words or thoughts of enslaved people but were created by and for the white community. This extra layer can add a degree of distortion or omission, raising issues of reliability in regard to understanding the mindsets of enslaved people. This difficulty can be seen in attempts to understand the Denmark Vesey conspiracy. Several historians, notably Michæl P. Johnson, assert that traditional accounts of the rebellion relied too heavily on edited and altered court transcripts of testimony by accused co-conspirators, who might have said what prosecutors wanted to hear in order to avoid serious punishment. Further, the incomplete trial testimony was woven into a cohesive narrative by local officials—perhaps to justify the severe punishments meted out or simply to show that due process had been followed. In this case, the slave-owning class, and their allies, had incentive to misrepresent the words and thoughts of the slave community. The accuracy of claims of a planned rebellion remains a source of historical debate.

Nat Turner's Rebellion

In 1831, **Nat Turner**, a slave preacher, organized a rebellion in Southampton County, Virginia. He led a band of African Americans, armed with guns and axes, on a bloody revolt that resulted in the deaths of fifty-five men, women, and children. The revolt was finally put down by state and federal troops. More than a hundred African Americans were executed by authorities, and more were attacked and killed by angry mobs in the wake of the revolt. Turner's rebellion was the largest rebellion in the nineteenth century. It led to increased fears of slave rebellions in the South and the enactment in many areas of stricter laws governing the behavior of slaves.

B. The Cultures of African-American Communities—Free and Slave

African Americans developed cultural forms that emphasized maintaining dignity and autonomy in the face of enslavement and oppression. Both free communities and slave communities developed strategies and cultural patterns that challenged their status and pointed toward a better future.

David Walker

An important early figure in the antislavery movement was the African-American writer and activist **David Walker**. In 1829, he issued a pamphlet entitled **"David Walker's Appeal to the Coloured Citizens of the World."** This radical tract called on people of African descent to resist slavery by any and every means. His praise of self-defense made southerners furious. Several southern legislatures declared the pamphlet seditious and enacted penalties against anyone caught distributing it.

Frederick Douglass

Starting in the 1840s, the towering figure in the abolitionist movement was **Frederick Douglass**. Douglass was born into slavery in 1818 and escaped to the North in 1838. He had learned to read and write, hiding his education from his master, who, like most slave masters, wanted to conceal from his slaves the instruments of learning. Douglass became a powerful speaker in the antislavery movement. His first of three autobiographies, *Narrative of the Life of Frederick Douglass* (1845), was a bestseller. One of the most well-known and important antislavery speeches is Douglass's July 5, 1852, address to the Rochester Anti-Slavery Sewing Society, **"What to the Slave Is the Fourth of July?"** The speech is critical of the United States for not abiding by its founding principles. He asserts that it is preposterous to expect enslaved African Americans to celebrate the birth of American freedom when they, themselves, are still oppressed. Douglass remained an important figure before, during, and after the Civil War, until his death in 1895.

The African Methodist Episcopal (AME) Church

Throughout American history, African Americans developed religious beliefs and practices that reflected their experiences in America. The **African Methodist Episcopal Church** (AME) reflected this tradition. The denomination was founded by **Richard Allen** in Philadelphia in 1816 from several African-American Methodist churches. The founding of the AME reflected a desire on the part of the free African-American community to have greater autonomy and to tailor religious services to the needs and experiences of the African-American community. The AME borrowed many elements from the mainstream **Methodist** church; the founder of the Methodist movement, **John Wesley**, was an outspoken critic of the slave trade. However, in contrast to mainstream Methodism, AME theology consistently touched on issues of race in its understanding of scripture and history.

Cultural Resistance to Slavery

Slaves were not passive as they endured their harsh lives. Certainly, they learned that outright rebellion would almost certainly end in failure and death (see pages 164–165). However, slaves developed cultural practices that constituted subtler forms of resistance—practices that sustained families and communities, and that attempted to carve out some degree of autonomy in the face of near total control. Slaves passed on fanciful stories from generation to generation— stories that often had a pointed message. In the **Br'er Rabbit stories**, for example, the weak often got the better of the strong. Music sustained slave communities. Slaves, for instance, might make their own fiddles and banjos, using a large gourd for the body and horsehair for the strings. These hybrids of African and American instruments helped create music that combined African traditions with the traditions of the South and provided some relief from the unremitting drudgery of slavery.

Topic 4.13 The Society of the South in the Early Republic

In many ways the South remained distinct from the rest of the country. Ideologically, politically, and culturally, the South developed a regional identity markedly different from the other regions of the country. Cotton and slavery came to be seen as defining features of Southern society.

A. Slavery and the Southern "Way of Life"

Despite the fact that the majority of white Southerners owned no slaves, slavery came to be seen as an essential element of the Southern "way of life." The defense of slavery by white Southerners became an element in the development of regional pride in the South.

Southern Defense of Slavery

As the abolitionist movement attacked the system of slavery (see pages 161–162), southern public figures emerged to give a vigorous defense of the institution. Arguments took a variety of approaches. Some contrasted the factory system of the North with the slave system of the South, arguing that **northern "wage-slaves"** were not taken care of or fed and were fired when business was slow. The most well-known defender of slavery in the 1850s was **George Fitzhugh**. He was sharply critical of the pronouncements of northern defenders of the **"free-labor" ideology** (see page 149), insisting that the system masked a heartless approach to the world. This movement went so far as to claim that slavery was a **"positive good"** for the slaves—that it provided them with skills, discipline, and "civilization."

Biblical Defense of Slavery

The southern defense of slavery frequently invoked biblical passages. Some southern clergymen argued that the **Bible** demanded the submission of the inferior classes to the superior classes—especially slave to master. They cited passages, often out of context, such as, "[T]ell slaves to be submissive to their masters and to give satisfaction in every respect" (from *The Epistle of Paul to Titus* in the New Testament). Religious defenders of slavery most frequently invoked the so-called **"curse of Ham"** to justify the institution. Noah, angry at his son, Ham, cast out Ham's son Canaan, with the words "a slave of slaves shall he be to his brothers" (from *Genesis*). The story is open to many interpretations, but it remained central to the **biblical defense of slavery**.

The "Mudsill Theory"

Some southern defenders of slavery argued that civilization—in the ancient world as well as in the contemporary South—depended on slavery. For civilization to flourish, it was necessary for a lower class of people to do the menial work so that a higher class could engage in more elevated pursuits. This lower class—in the case of the antebellum South, slaves—was analogous to the **mudsill** of a grand house. The mudsill was the lowest threshold of a building, which supported the foundation. This theory was popularized by South Carolina senator **James Henry Hammond** in a speech in 1858. He cautioned that a class of poor, landless people could threaten social harmony and undermine civilization.

B. Cotton, Slavery, and the Southern Exception

The South was distinct in its dependence on exports to the international market—by 1850 supplying approximately half of the world's cotton; by 1860, three-fourths. Slavery, which grew rapidly in the period 1800 to 1860, came to define the culture of the South.

Cotton and Slavery

Slavery became dominant in the South just as it was becoming unpopular in the eyes of the world. In 1807, Great Britain outlawed the international slave trade. The following year, the United States took the same step (the international slave trade had been protected by the Constitution until 1808). All of the northern states had voted to abolish slavery outright or gradually. Some northerners, and even some white southerners, were critical of slavery, but slavery and cotton were the main engines behind American economic growth in the first half of the nineteenth century.

Slavery and the Culture of the South

The main source of the distinctiveness of the South was, as **Alexis de Tocqueville** noted in ***Democracy in America*** (1831), slavery. Slavery grew rapidly in the decades leading up to the Civil War. By 1850, nearly a third of the southern population was African American. In 1790, there were approximately 700,000 slaves in the South. By 1830, that figure had climbed to two million and, by 1860, to four million. In **Mississippi** and **South Carolina**, African Americans were the majority of the population. In contrast, on the eve of the Civil War only one northerner in seventy-six was African American. The presence of such a large African-American population in the South played an important role in shaping southern culture. This can be seen in language, food, music, and dialect. However, the most important consequence of the presence of a large slave population in the South was the commitment of white southerners to **white supremacy**. A belief in the racial inferiority of Blacks, mixed with fear and even hatred, shaped white southern views of African Americans. Although many white northerners also held racist notions of African Americans, the white supremacist outlook lacked the intensity it held in the South.

C. Westward Expansion and the Politics of Slavery

Cotton and slavery came to dominate the economy of the South in the antebellum period. As cotton became increasingly profitable in the first half of the nineteenth century, growers often depleted the soil through over-cultivation. As a result, cotton growers sought new lands in the fertile areas of the South to the west of the Appalachian Mountains.

Expansion into Texas—From Settlement to Independence

As early as the 1820s, white Americans began moving into the Mexican territory of **Texas**. Many of these settlers were southern whites who hoped to duplicate the plantation model from the Old South. Initially, Mexico was eager to attract settlers to its northern frontier, in part to provide a buffer from incursions by Indian raiding parties. Led by **Stephen Austin**, settlers were attracted to Texas because there was an abundance of affordable land that could be used for cotton cultivation.

Mexico allowed these settlers a degree of self-government through the 1820s, but tensions began to develop in the 1830s. The Texas settlers routinely flouted Mexican law—most notably in practicing slavery, which was banned in Mexico. The new president of Mexico, **General Antonio Lopez de Santa Anna**, sought to bring the Texans into line with Mexican law and custom. In 1835, the Texans rebelled. Many rebels were Spanish-speaking **"Tejanos,"** who objected to being ruled from Mexico City. At first the rebels suffered major setbacks. Almost 200 died defending **the Alamo** in **San Antonio**, a former mission where the rebels had taken refuge. Weeks later, almost 400 were killed by Mexican forces near the town of Goliad. Under the leadership of **General Sam Houston**, the rebels regrouped and emerged victorious. Texans won independence from Mexico, establishing the independent **Republic of Texas** in 1836.

Annexation of Texas and the Politics of Slavery

Many Texans were eager for their **"Lone Star Republic,"** as the **Republic of Texas** was known, to join the United States. One of the first official acts of the Texas president, in 1836, was to send a delegation to Washington with an offer to join the United States. Democratic **President Andrew Jackson**, however, not wanting to worsen sectional tensions by admitting a large slave state, blocked annexation. His successors likewise did not want to open the contentious debate that would accompany Texas annexation. **Presidents Martin Van Buren** (1837–1841) and **William Henry Harrison** (1841) avoided the issue. **President John Tyler** (1841–1845), who assumed the presidency after Harrison's death, supported Texas annexation, but did not have the political support to make this goal a reality. As the election of 1844 approached, he did not have the backing of either the Whigs or the Democrats and contemplated a third-party run. When the Democrats nominated the expansionistic **James K. Polk** in 1844, Tyler dropped out of the race. After Polk won the election, outgoing President Tyler was able to push **Texas annexation** through Congress in early 1845 (see page 182).

Topic 4.14 Subject to Debate

Was It an "Era of Good Feelings"?

Historians have debated the nature of the "Era of Good Feelings." Consensus historians—those who deemphasize divisions in American history and focus on national commonalities—look to the era as a golden age of cooperation and growth. Other historians have noted the beginnings of divisions over the issue of slavery. These divisions were evident in the debates over the Missouri Compromise. Some historians have focused on class divisions that began to emerge in the United States as the old master-apprentice system gave way to the wage-labor system that came to dominate the economy by the post–Civil War period.

The Legacy of President Andrew Jackson

President Andrew Jackson has been a frequent topic of essay questions on the AP exam; an understanding of how he has been remembered will be useful in discussions of the period. In the latter part of the nineteenth century, he was scoffed at in historical literature. Historians of that era tend to come from the elite classes of New England. To them, Jackson seemed boorish, arrogant, ignorant, and authoritarian. By the early twentieth century, Progressive-era historians influenced by Frederick Jackson Turner's frontier thesis looked more favorably upon Jackson. Turner saw the experience of the frontier as central to the shaping of the American character. By the 1920s, the image of frontier pioneers became part of popular culture just as Americans were becoming more urban and more settled. Americans developed a sense of nostalgia for the pioneers, as is evident in the popularity of Laura Ingalls Wilder's *Little House on the Prairie* novels. In this cultural moment, Jackson was rehabilitated. He was seen as a man of the pioneer era who brought that democratic, frontier spirit with him to the White House.

More recently, the historical memory of Jackson has again taken a turn for the worse. From the 1960s onward, historians have drawn unfavorable parallels between Jackson's expansionistic impulses and American foreign adventures abroad, from Vietnam to Iraq. Further, since the 1970s many Americans have become more attuned to the historical suffering of American Indians. In this context, the Indian Removal Act and the "Trail of Tears" mark a permanent stain on the legacy of the Jackson administration.

The stature of Jackson in public memory has fallen to such a degree that a movement grew in the 2010s to remove him from the twenty-dollar bill and replace his image with that of a prominent woman. In 2016, the Treasury Department announced that Jackson would be replaced by Harriet Tubman. The proposed change was shelved by the Trump Administration (2017) and then endorsed by President Biden (2021). However, the Treasury Department has indicated that a new $20 bill would not appear before 2030.

The Antebellum Period and the Advent of Social History

The economic and social transformations of the antebellum period have become important topics in historical work recently. Social historians have become more interested in the lives of workers, women, American Indians, families on the frontier, and slaves than in the policies and acts of presidents. These social historians, active in the field since the 1970s, have done much to topple the "great, white men" from their pedestals in the historical field. In place of laws, speeches, and treaties, social historians look at letters, diaries, census records, and court records to get a better sense of what life was like for ordinary Americans. This is not to say that political history is no longer relevant or important—it is, both in the history field at large and on the AP exam. However, do not ignore the advances made in the field of social history. Be aware of the important social groups of each era and the impact they had on history.

Reform Movements—Democratic or Restrictive?

Historians have disagreed over the nature of the reform movements in the antebellum period. Some have focused on the democratic and egalitarian impulses of the movement. The women's rights movement and the abolitionist movement certainly were attempts to push America in a more democratic direction. However, other historians have focused on the more judgmental and restrictive nature of reform movements. One can see some of the Puritan dogma still present in the antebellum period. The temperance movement reflects the more restrictive aspect of reform movements. The push for public education can be seen in both lights. On the one hand, it embodies the democratic spirit of providing free education to all—a prerequisite for meaningful participation in the democratic process. At the same time, the lessons and the rote learning tended to impose a rigid set of middle-class Protestant values on a diverse working class.

The Impact of Westward Expansion

History textbooks implicitly grapple with a major issue of interpretation—how the expansion of the United States should be discussed. Territorial expansion at the expense of indigenous peoples and neighboring nations would, if carried out elsewhere, probably earn the disfavor of textbook writers. Such books, for instance, might discuss the arrogance of Napoleon's conquests or the brutality of Japanese expansion in Asia in the 1930s. By contrast, the era of manifest destiny is often shrouded in the language of idealism, democracy, adventure, and optimism. Perhaps this is to be expected; after all, contemporary Americans enjoy the fruits that early U.S. expansion provided to subsequent generations. Nevertheless, historical interpretation, to be taken seriously, should try to maintain fair and consistent criteria in evaluating parallel actions committed by different nations.

Historians and the Nature of Slavery

The nature of the slave system has long been a source of disagreement among historians. A bitter debate erupted in the 1970s over conclusions in the book *Time on the Cross* (1974), by Robert W. Fogel and Stanley Engerman. The book, relying heavily on quantitative data, asserted that while slavery was an immoral institution, it was an efficient business model that was less brutal on slaves than many other historians had asserted. Historians challenged the argument put forth by Fogel and Engerman, calling into question their use of evidence and their methods. The historian Herbert Gutman challenged their use of data on the number of whippings that occurred on a plantation; Gutman argued that *Time on the Cross* underestimated the incidence of whippings and mischaracterized the impact of the whip on slaves.

Practice Multiple-Choice Questions

DIRECTIONS: Pick the letter that best answers the following questions.

Questions 1–3 refer to the following passage:

"From whence originated the idea, that it was derogatory to a lady's dignity, or a blot upon the female character, to labor? and who was the first to say, sneeringly, 'Oh, she works for a living'? Surely, such ideas and expressions ought not to grow on republican soil. The time has been, when ladies of the first rank were accustomed to busy themselves in domestic employment.

"Homer tells us of princesses who used to draw water from the springs, and wash with their own hands the finest of the linen of their respective families. The famous Lucretia used to spin in the midst of her attendants; and the wife of Ulysses, after the siege of Troy, employed her self in weaving, until her husband returned to Ithaca. And in later times, the wife of George the Third of England, has been represented as spending a whole evening in hemming pocket-handkerchiefs, while her daughter Mary sat in the corner, darning stockings.

"Few American fortunes will support a woman who is above the calls of her family; and a man of sense, in choosing a companion to jog with him through all the up-hills and down-hills of life, would sooner choose one who had to work for a living, than one who thought it beneath her to soil her pretty hands with manual labor, although she possessed her thousands. To be able to earn one's own living by laboring with the hands, should be reckoned among female accomplishments; and I hope the time is not far distant when none of my country-women will be ashamed to have it known that they are better versed in useful, than they are in ornamental accomplishments."

—"Dignity of Labor," *The Lowell* [Massachusetts] *Offering,* 1842

1. The essay from the *Lowell Offering*, quoted above, describes the physical labors performed by important women—princesses in the time of Homer, the Roman noblewoman Lucretia, the wife of Ulysses, and the daughter of King George III of Great Britain—in order to

    (A) demonstrate the long history of women being treated as second-class citizens.
    (B) assure poor women that hard work and dedication were the keys to advancement to a higher status.
    (C) differentiate the emerging American culture from the corrupt traditions of Europe.
    (D) convince middle-class men and women that they should not look down upon women performing physical work.

2. The contributors to the *Lowell Offering* were

    (A) New England abolitionists who participated in the Second Great Awakening.
    (B) "factory operatives" at the textile mills in Lowell, Massachusetts, during the early stages of American industrialization.
    (C) Transcendentalist writers who lived at the Brook Farm utopian community.
    (D) African-American women who gained their freedom following the gradual elimination of slavery in Massachusetts.

3. The reading from the *Lowell Offering* reflects which of the following historical developments?

    (A) The popularity of the "Arts and Crafts" movement, which sought to revive traditional artisan techniques
    (B) The cultural shift that allowed for women to replace men in offices, as typists, accountants, and receptionists
    (C) The increasing number of Americans who made their living producing goods for national and foreign markets rather than relying on semi-subsistence agriculture
    (D) The movement to encourage society to see women's work in the home as actual labor that contributed to the social good

Questions 4–6 are based on the following image:

—Lithograph of the Cherokee tribal member George Guess (also known as Sequoyah), 1828

4. The image above of the Cherokee tribal member George Guess (also known as Sequoyah) demonstrates

   (A) the desire of the Cherokees to establish an independent nation in the southern portion of the United States.
   (B) the resistance of Cherokees to laws prohibiting the establishment of schools on Cherokee lands.
   (C) the revival of traditional spiritual practices among members of the Cherokee nation.
   (D) the push by many Cherokee leaders to embrace mainstream culture and to become full members of the new American nation.

5. In the decade following the publication of the previous, above, Cherokee Indians

   (A) were relocated to "Indian Territory" in the West.
   (B) established long-lasting reservations in Georgia.
   (C) were wiped out by disease and warfare.
   (D) lost their recognition as a federally protected tribe.

6. The Cherokee Indians received the strongest support in the 1830s from

   (A) President Andrew Jackson.
   (B) the United States Supreme Court.
   (C) the United States Congress.
   (D) the legislature of the state of Georgia.

Questions 7–8 refer to the following passage:

"When the churches are thus awakened and reformed, the reformation and salvation of sinners will follow, going through the same stages of conviction, repentance, and reformation. Their hearts will be broken down and changed. Very often the most abandoned profligates are among the subjects. Harlots, and drunkards, infidels, and all sorts of abandoned characters, are awakened and converted. The worst parts of human society are softened, and reclaimed, and made to appear as lovely specimens of the beauty of holiness."

—Charles G. Finney, "What a Revival of Religion Is" (excerpt), 1835

7. The message of the passage above, by Charles G. Finney, illustrates

   (A) the persistence of the Puritan idea that salvation is restricted to a predetermined "elect."
   (B) the belief that church attendance and contributing to church coffers were sufficient means for achieving salvation.
   (C) the belief that salvation was open to all members of society, even the most sinful, if they repented.
   (D) the idea that God had turned his back on the United States because of the nation's moral transgressions.

8. Which of the following developments could best be seen as an effect of the religious movement that Charles G. Finney spearheaded?

   (A) The growth of socialist utopian communities
   (B) The drive to expand to the West
   (C) The proliferation of reform movements
   (D) The elimination of American Indian communities from the American South

Questions 9–11 are based on the following passage:

"When the day of election approaches, visit your constituents far and wide. Treat liberally, and drink freely, in order to rise in their estimation, though you fall in your own. True, you may be called a drunken dog by some of the clean-shirt and silk-stocking gentry, but the real roughnecks will style you a jovial fellow. Their votes are certain, and frequently count double.

"Do all you can to appear to advantage in the eyes of the women. That's easily done. You have but to kiss and slabber their children, wipe their noses, and pat them on the head. This cannot fail to please their mothers, and you may rely on your business being done in that quarter.

"Promise all that is asked, said I, and more if you can think of anything. Offer to build a bridge or a church, to divide a county, create a batch of new offices, make a turnpike, or anything they like. Promises cost nothing; therefore, deny nobody who has a vote or sufficient influence to obtain one.

"Get up on all occasions, and sometimes on no occasion at all, and make long-winded speeches, though composed of nothing else than wind. Talk of your devotion to country, your modesty and disinterestedness, or any such fanciful subject. Rail against taxes of all kinds, officeholders, and bad harvest weather; and wind up with a flourish about the heroes who fought and bled for our liberties in the times that tried men's souls."

—Robert Penn Smith (writing as David Crockett), *Colonel Crockett's Exploits and Adventures in Texas*, 1837

9. Which of the following developments from the 1820s and 1830s is illustrated by the reading above?

    (A) Demographic shifts were giving middle-class, literate voters increased power in determining the direction of national politics.
    (B) As larger numbers of citizens participated in the electoral process, the nature of political campaigning changed.
    (C) Reform-minded political leaders played an increasingly important role in national political campaigns.
    (D) Military heroes played a larger role in politics, while lawyers and statesmen played a diminished role in electoral politics.

10. Which of the following describes an important reason for the trend illustrated by the above passage?

    (A) Naturalization laws were changed, reducing the amount of time it took for immigrants to attain citizenship.
    (B) Several important states extended voting rights to women.
    (C) Civil rights legislation paved the way for large numbers of free African Americans to vote.
    (D) Most states reduced or eliminated property qualifications for voting.

11. The political shifts, evident in the reading, were especially beneficial to

    (A) the Jacksonian Democrats.
    (B) temperance reformers.
    (C) women suffragists.
    (D) New England Federalists.

Answers and Explanations

1. **(D)** The main point of the essay in the *Lowell Offering* is that there is dignity in productive work. The writer is citing the long history of important women performing physical tasks in order to convince middle-class men and women that there is nothing inappropriate about women working. Many members of the middle class subscribed to a set of cultural ideas known as the "cult of domesticity," which insisted that women keep a proper, Christian home—separate from the male sphere of politics, business, and competition. This ideal discouraged women from participating in public life. The reading from the *Lowell Offering* challenged that norm.

2. **(B)** The contributors to the *Lowell Offering* were "factory operatives" at the textile mills in Lowell, Massachusetts, during the early stages of industry in the United States. Starting in 1821 a series of textile mills were built in Lowell, drawing in young women from the New England countryside to operate the machines. It was thought that these women could be paid less and would be only temporary factory operatives. The era of mass migration from Europe had not yet begun, so it was difficult to recruit male factory operatives. By 1830, eight mills employed more than 6,000 women.

3. **(C)** The reading from the *Lowell Offering* reflects the increasing number of women, as well as men, who were making the transition from semi-subsistence agriculture to production for distant markets. This was a key aspect of the market revolution. Although much of this work was done in factories, many people performed piecework at home as part of the "putting-out system," in which men and women would perform a particular task as part of a larger operation—such as making shoes or small firearms.

4. **(D)** The image of the Cherokee tribal member George Guess (also known as Sequoyah) demonstrates the push by many Cherokee leaders to embrace mainstream culture and to become full members of the new American nation. Guess was the inventor of the Cherokee alphabet. He was born in Taskigi, Tennessee, around 1760. He was the son of a white man and a Cherokee woman. Sequoyah is pictured in western-style dress, demonstrating the teaching of the Cherokee alphabet.

5. **(A)** Despite the efforts of the Cherokee to adapt to the cultural norms of white society, state and federal authorities took action in the 1830s to remove the Cherokee and other tribes from the South, relocating them to areas labeled "Indian Territory" in the West (primarily in the future Oklahoma). President Andrew Jackson pushed for passage of the Indian Removal Act (1830). It took several years of political and legal maneuvering, but the Indian Removal Act was eventually implemented during the presidency of Jackson's successor, Martin Van Buren. The Cherokee, unlike the other affected tribes, resisted the pressure to sign a treaty that would cede their ancestral lands. The result of their resistance was their forcible removal, leading to the deaths of thousands of Cherokee, in an episode known as the "Trail of Tears."

6. **(B)** The Cherokee received their strongest support in the 1830s from the United States Supreme Court. Before their forced removal to the West, the Cherokee won a short reprieve from the Supreme Court with the decision in *Worcester v. Georgia* (1832), which recognized the Cherokee people as a nation within the state of Georgia and ruled that they would not be subject to the Indian Removal Act. However, the state of Georgia, with the support of the federal government, began moving them to the West anyway.

7. **(C)** Charles G. Finney is asserting that salvation was open to all members of society, even the most sinful, if they repented. Finney was one of the leading lights of the Second Great Awakening, a Protestant revival movement in the first three decades of the nineteenth century. The ministers of the Second Great Awakening rejected the old Calvinist and Puritan idea that salvation was based on predestination. They held that people could try to improve themselves in order to improve their chances of getting into heaven. This was a more democratic notion of salvation; it was also a more hopeful one.

8. **(C)** The Second Great Awakening inspired a wide variety of reform movements. Participants in the awakening sought to perfect society as well as their own personal behavior. Temperance was a major issue that grew out of the movement—it involved personal improvement as well as societal improvement. Temperance advocates took a personal pledge to abstain from drinking, and they also advocated for the legal prohibition of alcohol. Other issues included prison reform, women's rights, public education, and emancipation.

9. **(B)** The reading illustrates the fact that as larger numbers of citizens participated in the electoral process, the nature of political campaigning changed. Politics became less about ideas and character and more about appearances and personality. "Crockett" humorously puts forth a formula for winning elections in this changed environment, from kissing babies to making empty promises.

10. **(D)** A primary reason for the increase in the electorate in the 1820s and 1830s was that most states reduced or eliminated property qualifications for voting. Previously, voting was restricted to property owners, effectively excluding poor and working-class men from the political process.

11. **(A)** The political shifts evident in the reading were especially beneficial to the Jacksonian Democrats. In the 1820s and 1830s, most states reduced or removed property qualifications for voting so that most free males had the right to vote. This change helped Jackson win the presidential election in 1828. His humble origins appealed to the newly enfranchised working man.

7

Period 5: 1844–1877 The Civil War and Reconstruction

TIMELINE

1846	Beginning of the Mexican-American War
1848	Treaty of Guadalupe Hidalgo ends the Mexican-American War
1850	Compromise of 1850
1852	Publication of *Uncle Tom's Cabin* by Harriet Beecher Stowe
1854	Ostend Manifesto
1856	Beginning of "Bleeding Kansas"
	The beating of Senator Charles Sumner
1857	*Dred Scott v. Sandford* decision
1859	John Brown's raid on Harper's Ferry arsenal
1860	Election of Abraham Lincoln
	South Carolina secedes from the United States
1861	Inauguration of Lincoln
	Six more states, all from the Deep South, secede
	Fighting at Fort Sumter; Civil War begins
	Four more states, from the upper South, secede
	First Confiscation Act
1862	Homestead Act
	Morrill Land Grant Act
	Second Confiscation Act
	Robert E. Lee becomes commander of Confederate army; achieves significant battlefield victories
	Dakota War
1863	The Emancipation Proclamation goes into effect
	Union victories at Gettysburg and Vicksburg
	New York City Draft Riots
1864	Grant besieges Richmond
	Reelection of Lincoln
	Sherman's March to the Sea
1865	Freedman's Bureau established
	Richmond Falls; Confederacy surrenders
	Lincoln assassinated; Andrew Johnson assumes presidency
	Southern states begin to pass Black Codes
	Thirteenth Amendment ratified

	1866	Civil Rights Act passes
		Ku Klux Klan formed
		Ex parte Milligan
	1867	Reconstruction Acts passed; beginning of Congressional Reconstruction
		Tenure of Office Act
	1868	Johnson impeached
		Fourteenth Amendment ratified
	1870	Fifteenth Amendment ratified
	1875	Civil Rights Act
	1876	Disputed election between Samuel J. Tilden (Democrat) and Rutherford B. Hayes (Republican)
	1877	Compromise ends Reconstruction; Hayes becomes president

Topics in Period 5

In this chapter, you will learn about:

- → Topic 5.1 Contextualizing Period 5
- → Topic 5.2 Manifest Destiny
- → Topic 5.3 The Mexican-American War
- → Topic 5.4 The Compromise of 1850
- → Topic 5.5 Sectional conflict: Regional differences
- → Topic 5.6 Failure to compromise
- → Topic 5.7 Election of 1860 and secession
- → Topic 5.8 Military conflict in the Civil War
- → Topic 5.9 Government policies during the Civil War
- → Topic 5.10 Reconstruction
- → Topic 5.11 Failure of Reconstruction
- → Topic 5.12 Subject to debate

Topic 5.1 Contextualizing Period 5

> As the United States expanded its borders, economy, and population, sectional tensions—most notably over slavery—led to a civil war. The war and its aftermath dramatically transformed American society, ending the institution of slavery and raising fundamental questions about the nature of American democracy.

The acquisition and settlement of new territories in the western half of the North American continent opened up a question that many politicians had sought to avoid—should these new territories allow slavery? Most northern politicians were not abolitionists; indeed, abolitionism was a minority position in the North in 1850. However, the issue of the expansion of slavery became increasingly divisive in the 1850s. Some northerners adopted the free-soil ideology—the idea that lands out West should be open to small-scale farming, without competition from large-scale plantation agriculture using slave labor. By the end of the decade, more northerners were grappling with the moral issues around slavery. Positions became decidedly more entrenched on the eve of the Civil War.

The importance of the Civil War to American history cannot be overstated. This bloody war settled one of the most vexing issues in American history—the existence of slavery in an otherwise democratic country—and opened up space for broad debates about the substance of democracy in post–Civil War America.

Topic 5.2 Manifest Destiny

As the American economy grew between the War of 1812 and the Civil War, many Americans continued the push ever farther into the continent. This westward movement had profound implications for Canada and Mexico as well as for American Indian nations within the borders of the growing United States. Finally, the acquisition of additional territory enflamed sectional tensions, as the debate over the expansion of slavery intensified in the decade before the Civil War.

A. Westward Migrations

Many Americans migrated to the West during the period leading up to the Civil War. These migrants were driven by a variety of factors including economic opportunities in the West, the desire for raw materials, and religious persecution in the East.

Americans Respond to the Call of "Manifest Destiny"

Many Americans came to believe that it was the **"manifest destiny"** of the United States to expand westward and extend its power in the Western Hemisphere. "Manifest destiny" refers to the movement of individuals to the West, but it also alludes to the political extension of United States territory. The term *manifest destiny* was coined in an 1845 newspaper column by journalist and editor **John O'Sullivan**. It captured the fervor of the westward expansion movement, implying that it was God's plan that the United States take over and populate the land from coast to coast. The idea of manifest destiny shaped many of the political debates of the era. Americans who did settle out west were probably driven more by economic factors, such as cheap land or precious metals, than they were by a desire to fulfill a divine plan.

Overland Trails

Migrants to the West traveled along one of several overland routes. The most famous was the **Oregon Trail**, a 2,000-mile route from Missouri to the Pacific Northwest (see more on the settlement of the Oregon Territory, page 144). Other trails included the **Santa Fe Trail**, which followed a more southern route, from Missouri to New Mexico, and the **California Trail**, which branched off from the Oregon Trail. It is estimated that about 300,000 people traveled these trails, usually in wagon trains, between 1840 and the Civil War. Though stories of death and desperation on these treks capture the public imagination, an accurate account of the risks involved is more difficult to come by. The story of the **Donner Party** (1846–1847) is frequently repeated. A wagon train of eighty-seven California-bound migrants became snowbound in the Sierra Nevada mountains over the winter. Only forty-eight were rescued, with some of the survivors having resorted to cannibalism. Historians note, however, that the death rate on these trails was only slightly higher than for Americans in general at the time. American Indians were far more likely to work for the migrants as guides and to engage in trade with them than they were to ambush them.

The California Gold Rush

Discoveries of mineral resources in the West were a powerful draw on westward migration. The various discoveries of gold and silver from 1848 until the 1880s led to a repeated pattern of rushes, boomtowns, and economic consolidation, as lone prospectors and crowds of fortune seekers gave way to industrial-mining operations (see more on the mining frontier, pages 217–218). The most significant strike of precious metals in the antebellum period was at **Sutter's Mill** in Coloma, California, in 1848. That year, **California**, part of the Mexican Cession, became United States territory, acquired as a result of the **Mexican War** (see page 182). As word spread, thousands of people came to California to try to strike it rich in this first gold rush. A large percentage of the 300,000 people who migrated to California came in 1849, thus their nickname, **"Forty-niners."** A few people did strike it rich. However, very soon, the easily accessible gold was panned from riverbeds. Getting access to gold beneath the surface required capital-intensive methods. The necessary machinery was beyond the reach of ordinary prospectors.

The Mormon Exodus

In 1847, the **Church of Jesus Christ of the Latter-Day Saints**, the religious group known as the **Mormons**, settled in the region of the Great Salt Lake in Utah (see more on the origins of Mormonism, pages 158–159). The land at the time was Mexican territory. When the Mormons arrived, the Mexican War had already begun. After the United States victory in the war (1848), Utah and the remainder of the Mexican Cession became United States territory. The Mormons ended up in Utah after suffering persecution in more populated areas.

> **USING REASONING PROCESSES:**
> **CAUSATION**
>
> **Competing Causes of Westward Expansion**
>
> Be aware of the variety of factors that may have caused individuals to make the decision to move to the West: Some were small farmers inspired by the "free-soil" ideal; some were drawn to Texas to find a place as slave-owning cotton growers; some were part of the Mormon exodus to Utah; some were gold seekers drawn to California.

B. The Ideological Foundations of Manifest Destiny

The drive for the United States to expand westward grew out of several important beliefs. Many Americans came to believe that the economic growth and security of the United States depended on expansion. In addition, the drive to expand was fueled by a set of beliefs around race and culture that saw nonwhites in an inferior light.

Manifest Destiny and Race

In many ways, the ideology of **manifest destiny** reinforced contemporary notions of race. Many white Americans had come to believe that the variety of peoples who inhabited the North American continent—Mexicans, American Indians, African Americans—were incapable of establishing or participating in democratic, efficient governance. This racial justification for westward expansion, which developed in the decades after 1810, drew on several sources. **European Romanticism**, which became increasingly influential in these decades (see page 157), put more emphasis on uniqueness and individual difference. In addition, there was a rise in so-called **scientific racialism** in the early 1800s. This idea held that "races" were fundamentally different from one another and that the Anglo-Saxon race was superior to nonwhites. The movement westward was seen as proof of the superiority of the so-called Anglo-Saxon race over the **"savage tribes"** of the West.

The Spread of Democratic Civilization

In addition to using racial theories, many Americans justified manifest destiny by asserting the superiority of American institutions and practices. These Americans cited the strong tradition of democratic practices in the United States. The conquest of Mexico (see pages 181–182) was seen as a victory by liberty-loving Protestants over tyrannical and anti-republican Catholics.

C. Government Promotion of Western Expansion

Groups and individuals were migrating to the West before the Civil War with little encouragement from the government. During and after the Civil War, the government passed legislation to promote Western transportation and development. With the Democrats absent from Congress during the war, the Republicans had a free hand to implement legislation that would further their vision of the United States. Congress passed the Homestead Act, the Morrill Land Grant Act, and the Pacific Railroad Act, all in 1862. These acts helped implement the "free-labor" ideology of the Republican Party.

The Morrill Land Grant Act

The **Morrill Land Grant Act** (1862) promoted secondary public education primarily in the West. Under the act, the federal government transferred substantial tracts of its lands to the states. The states could build public colleges on these lands, or they could sell the land to fund the building of educational facilities. The land-grant colleges in the West were designed to train and educate the next generations of western residents.

The Pacific Railroad Act

The **Pacific Railroad Act** (1862) and supplementary acts passed in the 1860s extended government bonds and tracts of land to companies engaged in building transcontinental railroads. These acts ended up granting 130 million acres of federally held land to railroad companies. Individual states sweetened the pot for railroad construction by extending another 50 million acres to railroad companies.

The Homestead Act

The government encouraged development of the West by passing the **Homestead Act** (1862), which provided free land in the region to settlers who were willing to farm it. The Homestead Act reflected the **"free-labor"** ideal of the **Republican Party** (see pages 149 and 191). Hundreds of thousands of people applied for and were granted homesteads. Many of these homesteaders did not have extensive farming skills and went bankrupt. Increasingly, by the late 1800s, it became difficult for small farmers, even competent ones, to compete with large-scale agricultural operations.

D. Economic Expansion Beyond the Western Hemisphere: The United States and Asia

American economic interests included opening up trade to Asia. The United States initiated economic, cultural, and diplomatic ventures toward this end.

Opening Trade with Japan

With the growth of the economy and the development of West Coast ports, the United States became increasingly interested in trading with Japan. The **Tokugawa shogunate** (1600–1868) had virtually isolated Japan from Western countries since the seventeenth century. It had allowed for limited trade with the Netherlands and with China. The Tokugawa government repeatedly resisted, occasionally by force, attempts by Americans and Europeans to establish business and diplomatic ties. The United States was determined to alter this policy and open Japan to American trade. With a letter from **President Millard Fillmore**, **Commodore Matthew C. Perry** led a naval expedition to Japan. The first journey was in 1852–1853, and a second was made in 1854. Perry, through vague threats and skillful diplomacy, was able to secure a treaty with Japan that opened Japan up to American trade.

Topic 5.3 The Mexican-American War

The Mexican-American War proved to be an important turning point in the period leading up to the Civil War. Debates over the status of slavery, American Indians, and Mexicans in these newly acquired lands became heated in the years following the war.

A. The Mexican-American War and Westward Expansion

The Mexican-American War had its origins in America's desire to expand its territory to the Pacific Ocean. The specific causes of the war can be traced back to tensions between the United States and Mexico over Texas. The war resulted in the United States gaining a large part of northern Mexico.

The Election of 1844 and the Annexation of Texas

The election of 1844 put the issue of **Texas annexation** on the national agenda. Democratic hopeful **James K. Polk** promised to push for Texas annexation as well as for a resolution to a border dispute with Great Britain over Oregon (see page 144), offering something to both southern and northern voters. By 1844, the **Democrats** were clearly emerging as more expansionistic and more proslavery than the **Whigs**. When the Democrats had difficulty agreeing on a nominee, Polk emerged as a compromise candidate, pushing aside **President John Tyler's** bid for reelection. In the general election, Polk defeated Whig candidate **Henry Clay**. Even before Polk took office, the outgoing president Tyler, who had long been an advocate of Texas annexation, saw Polk's victory as an electoral mandate for Texas annexation and was able to push it through Congress. Texas joined the United States as the fifteenth slave state in 1845. The issues raised by the annexation of Texas would reemerge in the aftermath of the Mexican-American War and assume a prominent place in the political schisms of the 1850s.

Origins of the War with Mexico

The Mexican government was furious that Texas had become part of the United States (see above). Meanwhile, **President James Polk** and American expansionists were eager to incorporate the remainder of Mexico's northern provinces into the United States. Tensions between the two nations were brought to the surface because of a dispute over the southern border of the new United States territory of Texas. Mexico said the border was at the **Nueces River**. The United States insisted it was at the **Rio Grande** (the present-day border between Texas and Mexico), 150 miles to the south. In 1846, skirmishes in the disputed area led to war between Mexico and the United States.

Victory over Mexico on the Battlefield

The United States won several early battles in the **Mexican-American War** (1846–1848). One prong of the invasion, in the area of Mexico south of Texas, was led by **General Zachary Taylor**. U.S. forces also won victories in present-day California. However, Mexico was determined not to part with its northern provinces after having lost Texas. It took the hard-fought capture of the Mexican capital, Mexico City, led by **General Winfield Scott**, to force the Mexican government to capitulate.

The Treaty of Guadalupe Hidalgo

In 1848, the Mexican government signed the **Treaty of Guadalupe Hidalgo**, giving up its claims to the disputed territory in Texas and agreeing to sell the provinces of **California** and **New Mexico**, known as the **Mexican Cession**, to the United States for $15 million. This territory includes present-day California, Nevada, Utah, and parts of Arizona, New Mexico, Colorado, and Wyoming.

Gadsden Purchase

The final land acquisition in what would become the continental United States was the **Gadsden Purchase**, acquired from Mexico in 1853, five years after the **Mexican-American War**. The Gadsden Purchase added more area to the vast swath of land obtained by the United States following the war and was sought by the United States as a possible southern route for a **transcontinental railroad**.

The Acquisition of the Mexican Cession and the Slavery Question

The **Treaty of Guadalupe Hidalgo** (1848) granted the United States a huge portion of Mexico for a mere $15 million. A week before the United States formally acquired the **Mexican Cession**, gold was discovered in California, leading to a rapid and substantial growth in the population. The question of whether the newly acquired territories would be admitted as free or slave states became a pressing issue in the years following the war. The **Wilmot Proviso** (introduced in 1846), banning slavery from the Mexican Cession, never became law (see pages

184–185). The question of whether slavery would exist in the newly acquired territories continued to generate national controversy in the 1850s (see pages 184–186 and pages 189–191).

B. Conflict on the Frontier Following the Mexican-American War

Western expansion led to conflicts on the frontier with American Indians and with Mexican Americans. As the boundaries of the United States changed and as migrants pushed west, violent conflicts ensued over the control of land. These "Indian wars" resulted in defeat for the Indians, as the last autonomous native groups came under the control of the U.S. government. The conflicts played an important role in changing the cultures and lifeways of the groups involved. As a result, questions reemerged about the legal status of these groups.

Expansion and Violence on the Frontier

In the 1830s, the federal government removed American Indians from the South and forced them to relocate to land out west known as **Indian Territory**. The most well-known episode of removal was the **Trail of Tears** (1838) (see page 156). The idea of setting aside vast areas of land in the West for use by American Indians was superseded as more and more white settlers pushed westward. Settlers were pushing beyond the Mississippi River in large numbers. Many were headed to the West Coast, following the annexation of the lush agricultural lands of the **Oregon Territory** (1848) and the discovery of gold in **California** (1848). However, the trails west went right through Indian lands, creating tension and conflict. The government began, in the 1850s, to take control of Indian land and restrict American Indians to reservations.

The Growth of the Reservation System

As early as 1851, the federal government pursued a policy of restricting American Indians to established **reservations**—confined areas that were set aside by the government. The **Indian Appropriations Act** of 1851 established reservations in present-day Oklahoma. A major goal of the reservation system was to keep American Indians off lands that white settlers wanted to settle. In exchange, American Indians were promised a degree of autonomy as well as annuities. In the following years, reservations were established in other states. After the Kansas and Nebraska territories were opened for white settlement in the 1850s (see page 189), the reservation policy reduced the land of American Indians from approximately fifteen million acres to less than 1.5 million acres. Often the lands set aside for reservations were incapable of sustaining crops, reducing the inhabitants to utter poverty. Many tribal groups resisted being put into reservations.

The Treaty of Fort Laramie (1851)

In the late 1840s and early 1850s, as more settlers made their way to the West Coast, American Indians along the **Great Plains** resisted further encroachments. In 1851, representatives of the United States government and more than 10,000 Plains Indians convened in **Fort Laramie**, in Wyoming, and came to an agreement that called for the Indians to provide a corridor for the passage of wagon trains to the Far West. In exchange, the government promised that the remaining Indian lands in the West would not be encroached upon. White settlers persistently refused to honor the Treaty of Fort Laramie and other treaties between the federal government and American Indian tribes.

The Dakota War (1862)

In the 1850s, groups of **Eastern Dakota Sioux** in **Minnesota** had been relegated, through treaties and force, to an inadequate reservation along the Minnesota River. These Dakota people were at the mercy of corrupt government agents and unscrupulous traders. In 1861 and 1862, crop failures and lack of government annuities (caused by the exigencies of the Civil War) created desperate conditions for the Dakota Sioux. In response, Dakota Sioux warriors, led by **Chief Little Crow**, initiated attacks on the white settlers who had settled on former Sioux lands in the Minnesota River Valley (1862). Over 300 settlers and approximately 100 troops were killed by the warriors, and 150 Sioux were also killed in the fighting. Soon after the fighting, a military commission tried and sentenced 303 Dakota Sioux men to death. **President Abraham Lincoln** reviewed the death sentences and commuted 264 of them (despite threats of mob violence by white settlers) and allowed 39 of them to proceed.

The Colorado War and the Sand Creek Massacre (1864)

The migration of settlers to the West continued in the period of the **Civil War** (1861–1865). One result of this migration was the **Colorado War** (1864–1865), fought by U.S. army forces, the **Colorado militia**, and white settlers against the **Southern Cheyenne**, **Arapaho**, and allied **Brulé** and **Oglala Sioux** (or Lakota) peoples in **Colorado Territory**. The war included an especially violent encounter, the **Sand Creek Massacre**. In 1864, after a settler family including two children was killed, presumably by American Indians, white settlers demanded revenge. Subsequently, **Colonel John M. Chivington** led an attack by a Colorado militia company upon a peaceful Cheyenne village, killing between 150 and 500, mostly women and children. Chivington ignored the villagers' surrender flags. A congressional investigating committee later condemned the "brutal and cowardly acts" of Chivington and his men.

American Indians in the Mexican Cession

In the aftermath of the **Mexican-American War** (1846–1848), the settlement of white Americans in California had devastating effects for Indian peoples. The Indian population of California dropped from about 150,000 in 1848, on the eve of the **gold rush**, to less than 30,000 by the beginning of the **Civil War** (see more on the gold rush, pages 179–180). California Indians were often falsely portrayed as degenerate, primitive, and idle. Disease took the lives of thousands, but systematic campaigns of extermination by white settlers against the native peoples of California contributed to what many historians have come to label a genocide. In 1853 the federal government greatly reduced the size of reservations set aside for Indians in California. In addition, farmers were eager to exploit the labor of Indians. When the framers of the California constitution prohibited slavery, they had Black slavery, not Indian slavery, in mind. As the 1850s progressed, thousands of Indians were either murdered or enslaved. The **Yuki** people of **Round Valley** in northern California were viciously targeted; their population fell from over 5,000 in 1854 to approximately 300 a decade later. Several Indian groups simply ceased to exist, with their people either killed or dispersed.

Topic 5.4 The Compromise of 1850

As the United States expanded to the West, the question of whether new territories should allow slavery or not led to heated political controversies. These controversies intensified as the United States acquired additional territory in the Mexican-American War (see pages 181–183). The Compromise of 1850 sought to address these controversies, but resulted in a widening of the sectional rift.

A. Territorial Acquisition and the Slavery Question

The issue of slavery in the new territories was one of the most divisive controversies of the antebellum period and was the catalyst that would eventually plunge the nation into civil war.

The Wilmot Proviso

Americans reached an uneasy truce on the issue of slavery in new territories with the passage of the **Missouri Compromise in 1820** (see page 140). However, the controversy came to the fore again as the United States gained additional territory following the **Mexican-American War** (1846–1848). Northern politicians tried, unsuccessfully, to ban slavery in territories that might be gained in the war by putting forth the **Wilmot Proviso** (1846). These politicians were not, for the most part, abolitionists, but they believed in the "free-labor" ideal (see page 149). They wanted additional land for white settlers to set up homesteads without competition from the slave system. The proviso was passed by the House of Representatives, where politicians from the populous northern states dominated, but failed in the Senate.

The Election of 1848 and the Free-Soil Party

In the election of 1848, both the **Whigs** and the **Democrats** avoided taking strong stands on the issue of slavery. **Senator Lewis Cass**, the Democratic candidate, lost to Whig candidate **Zachary Taylor**, one of the heroes of the **Mexican-American War.** In response to the conspicuous silence on the part of the major parties on the slavery question, antislavery men in both parties founded the **Free-Soil Party** in 1848. The party ran candidates in the presidential elections of 1848 and 1852. It garnered 10 percent of the vote in 1848, but only 5 percent in 1852. Many of its members later joined the **Republican Party**, which was founded in 1854 (see page 191).

Popular Sovereignty

Senator Lewis Cass, the Democratic candidate for president in 1848, proposed a compromise measure on the question of slavery in the newly acquired territories. He came up with the idea that the question of slavery should be left to the people of a particular territory. This idea became known as *popular sovereignty*. Cass and other proponents of popular sovereignty left the issue of timing vague. Northerners hoped that the vote on slavery in a territory would occur early on—as soon as a territorial legislature was assembled. They believed that the first settlers would be small, independent farmers from the more populous North who would immediately close the door to slavery. Southerners wanted the vote to occur later—just before a territory applied for statehood. This would give the slave system time to develop. Though Cass, who represented Michigan, thought of popular sovereignty as a compromise, it alienated many northern Democrats, some of whom voted for the Free-Soil Party in 1848 (see above). Though Congress failed to immediately act on his idea, popular sovereignty became an important issue in the 1850s (see page 192).

Cuba and the Ostend Manifesto

Southern expansionists hoped to extend their slavery empire beyond the continental United States. **Cuba**, with its profitable sugar plantations, came into their sights in the 1850s. **President James K. Polk** offered to purchase the island from Spain. When Spain balked, some American adventurers unsuccessfully tried to take it by force. Later, American diplomats, sent to Belgium by pro-southern **President Franklin Pierce**, again tried to secretly buy Cuba. Their goals, written up as the **Ostend Manifesto** (1854), provoked anger from northern politicians when the document was released to the press.

B. California Application for Statehood

In 1849, President Zachary Taylor urged California and New Mexico to apply for statehood. Both regions had antislavery majorities. California was soon ready to apply for statehood. The population of California quickly grew to more than 300,000 in the wake of the discovery of gold.

USING HISTORICAL THINKING SKILLS: MAKING CONNECTIONS

Cuba and the United States

Cuba, ninety miles off the coast of Florida, has loomed large in American diplomatic history, from the French and Indian War in the eighteenth century to the Spanish-American War in the nineteenth to the Cuban missile crisis in the twentieth. In recent decades, immigrants from Cuba to Florida have shaped that state's political landscape. In late 2014, President Barack Obama and Cuban President Raul Castro began the process of normalizing relations between the two nations and undoing travel and trade restrictions that had been in place since 1961, following the Cuban Revolution. In 2017 and 2019, President Donald Trump has undone some of the elements of the "Cuban thaw."

California and the "Compromise" of 1850

By 1850, **California** had enough of an American population to form a state (a population threshold of 60,000 was established by the 1787 Northwest Ordinance). Californians wrote up a constitution to submit to Congress in which slavery would be illegal. Southern senators objected to the admission of an additional free state. Senate negotiators, led by the aging **Henry Clay**, worked out a series of measures to resolve this extremely contentious problem. These measures became known as the **Compromise of 1850**. The most important elements of the compromise were the admittance of California as a free state, which pleased northern politicians, and a more stringent **Fugitive Slave Law**, which pleased southern politicians. Other measures included allowing the Territories of New Mexico and Utah to decide the question of slavery based on popular sovereignty, accepting a new boundary between Texas and the Territory of New Mexico, and banning the slave trade (but not slavery) in Washington, D.C. Senate negotiators put forth these measures as an omnibus bill, but it soon became clear that neither antislavery senators from the North nor proslavery "fire-eaters" from the South would vote "yes" on the Omnibus Bill. **Stephen Douglas**, a Democratic senator from Illinois, proposed "unbundling" the legislative package and voting on each measure separately. The measures all passed, and **President Millard Fillmore** (who assumed the presidency in 1850 upon the death of **President Zachary Taylor**) signed them into law. The lack of agreement on the 1850 "compromise" highlights the hardening of sectional tensions.

Topic 5.5 Sectional Conflict: Regional Differences

Sectional divisions between the North and the South intensified in the decade leading up to the Civil War. These divisions resulted from the ideological debates around slavery, along with regional economic and demographic changes. The status of slavery in new territories brought these debates to the surface.

A. The North and Immigration

Large numbers of immigrants, mainly Irish and German, entered the United States before the Civil War. Many of these groups lived in ethnic communities and retained the religions, languages, and customs of the Old World.

Irish Immigration and the Five Points

Large-scale immigration from **Ireland** in the antebellum period transformed American cities and contributed to a strong nativist movement (see more on the Irish "potato famine" and migration, page 148). The largest destination for **Irish immigrants** in the United States was the **Five Points** neighborhood of **New York City**. It was one of the most desperate urban slums in the Western world in the mid-nineteenth century, comparable to London's East End. The neighborhood was certainly the worst in the United States in terms of density, disease, infant and child mortality, unemployment, prostitution, and violent crime. At the same time, the Five Points could be seen as the original American melting pot, combining elements of the African-American community (especially as slavery gradually ended in New York in the period up to 1827) and the Irish community. Irish immigrants and African Americans, and smaller numbers of other immigrant groups, worked side-by-side, lived in the same boarding houses, intermarried, and danced and sang together at dancehalls and saloons. Intermarriages were prevalent enough that the census added the category **"mulatto"** to the 1850 census. At the same time, tensions existed between the two groups. These tensions came to the surface in the draft riots during the Civil War (see page 193). This cultural race-mixing, combined with bitter racism, became an important element of American identity into the twentieth century.

B. Anti-Immigrant Sentiment in the Antebellum Period

A strong anti-Catholic nativist movement developed in the United States. The main goal of this movement was to limit the rights, political power, and cultural influence of newly arrived immigrants.

Nativism

The first half of the nineteenth century witnessed a dramatic increase in immigration from Europe, as well as a strong xenophobic nativist movement. **Nativism** was both an emotional impulse as well as an organized movement. Many Americans thought that the new immigrants, who were mostly non-Protestant, lacked the self-control of "proper," middle-class Protestant Americans. For nativists, this lack of self-control was evident in the drinking habits of immigrants. Nativists tried to regulate and weaken the drinking culture of immigrant communities, which manifested itself in Irish pubs and German beer halls.

> **USING HISTORICAL THINKING SKILLS:**
> **MAKING CONNECTIONS**
>
> **Nativism Over Time**
>
> Anti-immigrant sentiment has surfaced several times in American history, usually targeting the most recent immigrant group: Irish immigrants in the 1840s and 1850s; Chinese immigrants in the 1870s and 1880s; the "new immigrants" of eastern and southern Europe at the turn of the twentieth century; and immigrants from Latin American countries in the twenty-first century.

The "Know-Nothings"

The nativist movement found political expression in the **Know-Nothing Party**. The party was the political wing of a growing anti-Catholic, anti-Irish movement that gained traction in the wake of the large-scale Irish immigration of the late 1840s and 1850s (see page 148). The Know-Nothing Party (formally known as the American Party) emerged in the 1840s and, by the 1850s, had achieved electoral success in several states, especially in the Northeast. Later in the 1850s, many "Know-Nothings" joined the newly formed Republican Party.

C. Differing Economic Models: The "Free-Labor" Ideal Versus the Slave System

The economies of the North and South were moving in different directions in the period leading up to the Civil War. The economy of the North was increasingly focused on a free-labor model, with manufacturing industries at its base; the economy of the South was increasingly dependent on a slave-labor, agricultural economy. The population of the North grew rapidly during this period while the South's free population growth was slow.

D. Abolitionism in the North—Strategies and Tactics

The abolitionist campaign became increasingly visible and vocal in the 1850s. Abolitionists debated the most effective strategies and tactics. Some relied on the written word and forceful arguments against the institution of slavery. Others helped fugitive slaves make their way north. A small minority advocated using violence to achieve their goals.

The Fugitive Slave Act and Personal Liberty Laws

Many northerners grew alarmed at the enforcement of the 1850 **Fugitive Slave Act**. The strict provisions of the 1850 act allowed slave catchers to bring the brutality of the slave system to the streets of northern cities. In response, many northern states passed **"personal liberty laws"** offering protection to fugitives. Many whites and free African Americans in northern cities even formed vigilance committees to prevent the slave catchers from carrying out their orders. The Supreme Court had long protected slave catchers from state restrictions on their activities. In ***Prigg v. Pennsylvania***, the Court overturned the abduction conviction of **Edward Prigg**, a slave catcher, on the grounds that federal law—the Constitution itself and the Fugitive Slave Act of 1793—was superior to state law. This approach was reinforced by the decision in ***Ableman v. Booth*** (1859). In this case, the Court overturned a Wisconsin Supreme Court ruling. The Wisconsin court had ruled that **Sherman Booth**, who had disrupted a slave catcher protected by the 1850 Fugitive Slave Act, was not guilty; the Wisconsin decision declared the Fugitive Slave Act itself unconstitutional. The United States Supreme Court reversed this decision, asserting the supremacy of federal statutes and court decisions over state courts.

Uncle Tom's Cabin

Sectional tensions were further enflamed by the publication in 1852 of the novel *Uncle Tom's Cabin*. The novel, written by **Harriet Beecher Stowe** of the antislavery Beecher family, depicted in graphic and emotional detail the brutality of slavery. For many northerners, slavery now had a human face. The novel outraged southern supporters of slavery, who attempted to ban it.

John Brown and the Raid on Harper's Ferry

In the fall of 1859, **John Brown** carried out a raid to acquire weapons from a federal armory in Harper's Ferry, Virginia (now West Virginia)—an event that pushed North–South relations to the breaking point. Brown, with ties to many of the leading abolitionists of the day, including **Frederick Douglass**, recruited a small group of men to capture the armory's weapons, intending to distribute them to slaves. Brown believed this would initiate a massive slave rebellion that would cause the collapse of slavery. The men managed to capture the armory, but were soon overwhelmed by reinforcements led by future Confederate commander **Robert E. Lee**. Brown was tried and executed later in 1859.

> **KEEP IN MIND**
>
> **Was John Brown Insane?**
>
> Traditional historical accounts of John Brown have often referred to Brown as "wild" or "insane." Be careful when making such characterizations of Brown. There is no strong evidence to support such a claim. His lawyer stated he was insane in court, but that was to prevent Brown from getting the death sentence. Brown protested his lawyer's tactics. It is safe to say that Brown was deeply religious and committed to the antislavery cause.

Although the event did not accomplish its stated goal, its impact on history is undeniable. It convinced proslavery southerners that there was a conspiracy afoot among northerners to violently interfere with the institution of slavery. The truth of the matter was that Brown's raid was roundly condemned by most northern politicians, but the perception of a united front among northerners persisted in the South.

E. The Southern Response to the Slavery Question

In the decade before the Civil War, white southerners defended slavery as a "positive good." This defense of slavery was accompanied by racist stereotyping of African Americans. The defense of slavery went hand in hand with a defense of states' rights and the theory of nullification.

Racism and the Defense of Slavery

In the first half of the nineteenth century, the defense of slavery shifted. From the revolutionary era into the nineteenth century, white southerners often defended slavery as a **"necessary evil."** Thomas Jefferson likened the institution to grabbing "the wolf by the ear, and we can neither hold him, nor safely let him go"—acknowledging that slavery was an evil, but asserting that its end would have dire consequences. **John C. Calhoun** dismissed this older, negative description of slavery; he labeled such views as "folly and delusion." By the middle of the nineteenth century, southern whites, influenced by writers such as **George Fitzhugh**, asserted that slavery was actually a **"positive good"** (see page 166). **Mary Henderson Eastman's** novel, *Aunt Phillis's Cabin: or, Southern Life as It Is* (1852), a response to *Uncle Tom's Cabin* (see above), reflected this proslavery ideology; the novel depicts benign masters and happy slaves. By the 1850s, these arguments proliferated and shaped cultural and religious practices in the South.

Racism and Culture

Racist ideas were reflected in the popular culture of the pre–Civil War period, notably in the growing popularity of **minstrel shows**. Minstrel shows have a long tradition in American history. They generally consisted of whites (and occasionally African Americans) performing variety shows in **"blackface."** The shows included skits, jokes, music, singing, and dancing. Minstrel shows presented racist caricatures of African Americans as lazy, shiftless, dim-witted, and happy-go-lucky. By the 1850s, the culture of **minstrelsy** evolved and grew; many historians see this evolution as a conscious rebuttal to abolitionist agitation. Representations of African Americans became increasingly vicious—with Black characters cooked or hunted or fished for. The shows were not restricted to the South—they reflected a broader sentiment among American whites when it came to race. Some white southerners actually objected to the shows because they brought the issues of race and slavery to the fore. The shows, however, remained popular throughout the country and reinforced political and social ideas about the position of African Americans in society.

By the 1840s and 1850s, southern slave-owners became increasingly interested in the religious practices of their slaves, often building churches on their plantations and mandating attendance. Christian views in the South evolved in this context. Ministers in the South might point out that the Hebrews owned slaves or that slavery was not condemned by Jesus. Further, these ministers often cited biblical passages about the importance of servants obeying their masters.

Topic 5.6 Failure to Compromise

Northern and southern politicians tried repeatedly to compromise on the issue of slavery in the new territories of the United States in the 1850s, but these attempts proved unsuccessful.

A. The Deterioration of Relations Between the North and the South

In the aftermath of the Compromise of 1850 (see pages 184–186), political leaders in the North and the South, as well as the Supreme Court, put forth a variety of proposals and plans for resolving the issue of slavery in the territories. These included the Kansas-Nebraska Act (1854) and the *Dred Scott* decision (1857). However, none of these moves proved to be successful in reducing sectional tensions. The physical assault of Senator Charles Sumner, on the floor of the Senate, was emblematic of the deterioration of relations between the North and the South.

The Kansas-Nebraska Act

In 1854, **Senator Stephen Douglas** of Illinois introduced the **Kansas-Nebraska Act** to the Senate. Douglas, who owned significant tracts of land in **Chicago**, hoped that the first transcontinental railroad would have a more northern route, using Chicago as a hub. Any railroad construction would have to be carried out in organized territory. The act called for dividing the **northern section** of the **Louisiana Purchase** territory into two organized territories, **Kansas** and **Nebraska**. The most contentious part of the act was allowing for the possibility of **slavery** in the territories of Kansas and Nebraska—areas that had been closed to slavery by the **Missouri Compromise** (1820). The act mandated that the question of slavery in these territories be decided by **popular sovereignty**. Many northerners, who assumed that the issue of slavery in these territories was long resolved, were angry at the act and at Douglas.

"Bleeding Kansas"

Violence erupted in **Kansas** as proslavery and antislavery men fought for control of the state. In keeping with the dictates of the 1854 **Kansas-Nebraska Act**, elections were held for a territorial legislature in 1855. Even though only 1,500 settlers were recognized as legal voters, more than 6,000 votes were cast, as thousands of proslavery **Missourians** came over the border for the day to cast votes. In response to such a clearly fraudulent election, antislavery Kansans chose their own shadow legislature. Each side wrote up a constitution for Kansas. Antislavery men wrote up the **Topeka Constitution**; proslavery men created the **Lecompton Constitution**. **President Franklin Pierce** recognized the proslavery government, and called the antislavery government traitorous. A proslavery posse of Missourians, under the auspices of a federal marshal, attacked the antislavery town of Lawrence in May 1856.

Several days after the **"sack of Lawrence,"** and just two days after the beating of **Senator Charles Sumner** in Congress (see below), **John Brown**, a deeply religious antislavery activist, initiated the killing of proslavery men along the banks of the **Pottawatomie Creek** in Kansas. Brown, his sons, and several followers killed five men with swords (see more on John Brown, page 188, including box).

Open violence continued in the Kansas Territory, on and off, for the next several years. In many respects, **"Bleeding Kansas"** can be seen as a dress rehearsal for the Civil War. The question of slavery in Kansas was unresolved when Abraham Lincoln was elected president (1860). After southern secession began, Kansas soon joined the Union as a free state in January 1861.

The Beating of Senator Charles Sumner

The growing tensions between North and South were evident in a violent incident that occurred on the floor of the Senate in 1856. **Senator Charles Sumner** from Massachusetts had given a pointed antislavery speech, called **"Crimes Against Kansas,"** in which he singled out **Senator Andrew P. Butler** of South Carolina. Butler's nephew, a South Carolina representative named **Preston Brooks**, heard about the speech and attacked Sumner at his desk in the Senate chamber, beating him viciously with a heavy cane. The injuries left Sumner incapacitated for four years. Northerners saw the beating as a further sign of southern barbarity; southerners made Brooks a hero.

> **USING REASONING PROCESSES: COMPARISON**
>
> **Was Slavery Becoming "National"?**
>
> In the 1850s, proslavery southerners and antislavery northerners perceived the political and social developments of the day in very different ways. Be prepared to compare the perceptions of these two groups. Antislavery northerner politicians perceived that Southerners were engaged in a conspiracy to make slavery a "national" rather than a "sectional" institution. The *Dred Scott* decision, for example, seemed to support the idea that slavery was a national institution and that Congress could do little to stop it. Compare that to the perceptions of proslavery southerners. They perceived that radical abolitionists had taken control of the Republican Party and were determined to end slavery immediately, by legislative or extralegal means.

The *Dred Scott* Decision

Northern and southern relations were further pushed apart by the Supreme Court decision in the case of ***Dred Scott v. Sandford*** (1857). The case involved the fate of a slave named **Dred Scott**, owned by a doctor serving in the U.S. Army. Scott and his wife, along with their owner, lived for a time in Illinois and in the Wisconsin Territory, areas where slavery had been banned by the **Northwest Ordinance**. Years after returning to Missouri, Scott sued for his and his wife's freedom on the grounds that they had lived for a time in free areas and that made them free. The Supreme Court did not find Dred Scott's arguments persuasive. First, the Court ruled that Scott was still a slave and did not even have the right to initiate a lawsuit. Next, the Court ruled that Congress had overstepped its bounds in declaring the northern portion of the Louisiana Purchase territory off-limits to slavery. The decision, therefore, invalidated the **Missouri Compromise** of 1820. Finally, the Court declared that no African Americans, not even free men and women, were entitled to citizenship in the United States because, according to the decision, they were **"beings of an inferior order."** Northerners were astounded at the sweep of the decision. The *Dred Scott* decision seemed to argue that slavery was a national, rather than a sectional, institution and that Congress could do little to stop it.

B. The Death of the Second Two-Party System

Controversies over slavery weakened the second two-party system. As the Whigs collapsed, and as the Democratic Party became stronger in the South and more explicitly proslavery, sectional parties emerged, notably the Republican Party, with strength in the North and in the Midwest.

Party Realignment

The **Kansas-Nebraska Act** became a lightning rod for sectional divisions (see pages 189–190). The **Whigs** were bitterly divided between proslavery **"Cotton Whigs"** and antislavery **"Conscience Whigs."** Meanwhile, the **Democratic Party** became increasingly a regional southern, proslavery party.

The Republican Party and the Free-Labor Ideal

In 1854, the modern **Republican Party** was born. This party was composed of many different factions—former members of the **Know-Nothing Party**, **"Conscience Whigs," free-soilers**, **abolitionists**, and **former Democrats**, to name a few. Central to the Republican Party was the **"free-labor"** ideology. This ideology upheld civic virtue and the dignity of labor and put a great deal of emphasis on economic growth and social mobility. It vigorously defended a free-labor system that allowed hard-working individuals to achieve independence and property. The economic superiority of free labor to slave labor became a major part of the Republican argument against slavery. The free-labor ideology was critical of the unchangeable nature of Southern society, dominated by an aristocracy of slaveholders. The Republican slogan in the 1856 presidential campaign of **John C. Fremont**, "Free soil, free labor, free men, Fremont," encapsulated this ideology. Though the party was critical of slavery, it did not advocate abolition. Rather, it adopted the position that slavery should not be allowed to spread to the new territories.

> **USING REASONING PROCESSES:**
> **CONTINUITY AND CHANGE**
>
> **Republicans, Then and Now**
>
> The Republican Party, started in 1854, is the same party that exists today; however, its politics have changed considerably. The party that was born in opposition to the spread of slavery now gets less than 10 percent of the African-American vote. Since the 1920s, it has become increasingly conservative and pro-business.

The Election of 1856

The election of 1856 made clear that the stability of the **Democrat-Whig** two-party system was over. With the **Whig Party** dissolved and the **Know-Nothing Party** divided over the slavery issue, the **Republican Party** emerged as a major party just two years after its birth. The **Democratic Party** won the election by shrewdly picking a northern candidate who had southern sympathies, **James Buchanan**. It was clear after the election that a new two-party system was emerging with the Democrats and the Republicans. Though these two parties have changed dramatically in the last century and a half, they remain the two main parties.

Topic 5.7 Election of 1860 and Secession

Whatever trust existed between political leaders of the North and of the South broke down by 1860. The rancorous election of 1860 resulted in the election of the Republican candidate Abraham Lincoln and the secession of the southern states.

A. The Election of 1860 and the Secession Crisis

The presidential election of 1860, with the victory of Republican Abraham Lincoln who espoused a free-labor platform, convinced many southern political leaders that they should take action to withdraw their states from the Union.

The Election of 1860

The **election of 1860** demonstrated the fractured nature of the American political system on the eve of the **Civil War**. The **Democratic Party** was divided between a northern wing and a southern wing. The **northern Democrats**, rallying around the idea of **popular sovereignty**, nominated **Stephen Douglas** for president. Douglas carried only Missouri and part of New Jersey. The **southern Democrats**, who strongly endorsed slavery, carried the Deep South. A third formation, the **Constitutional Union**, which endorsed maintaining the Union and avoided the slavery issue, won the upper South. The **Republican Party** chose **Abraham Lincoln** in 1860 as its standard bearer.

Lincoln's Electoral Victory in 1860

Abraham Lincoln had served briefly as a **Whig** congressman from Illinois, speaking out against the war with Mexico. He ran for Senate in 1858, losing to **Stephen Douglas**, but impressing the public with his oratory skills. In seven debates in different parts of Illinois, Lincoln repeatedly asked Douglas whether he favored the spread of **slavery**. Douglas avoided the issue, putting forth **popular sovereignty** as a cure-all to the slavery question, and race-baiting Lincoln. Lincoln had been opposed to the institution of slavery his entire life, and had been an advocate of the **American Colonization Society**, but, as he ran for president in 1860, he indicated that he would not nor could not tamper with slavery where it already existed. He promised, however, to block its expansion to new territories in the West. Lincoln won 40 percent of the popular vote, but carried the electoral vote, winning virtually all the states of the North, as well as California and Oregon.

> **KEEP IN MIND**
>
> **What Happened to the "United States"?**
>
> When textbooks discuss the Civil War, they often call the United States "the Union." Using this term is fine, but it is also fine to continue to use "the United States" in your essays. The United States did not disappear. Often, historians use "the Union" for the sake of clarity; however, the decision also has political overtones.

Southern Secession

Even if **President Lincoln** kept his promise not to interfere with slavery in the slave states, many southern slaveholders still would not have been satisfied. In many ways, slavery needed to grow in order to remain economically viable. Lincoln's electoral victory in 1860 alarmed southern defenders of slavery to the point that leading political figures in the South were ready to **secede**. Even before Lincoln was inaugurated, seven southern states did secede (South Carolina in late 1860; Mississippi, Florida, Alabama, Georgia, Louisiana, and Texas in early 1861). In their declarations of secession, southern states made clear that the issue of slavery was their main concern. In listing its reasons for secession, for example, Mississippi began, "Our position is thoroughly identified with the institution of slavery."

The Onset of War

Once inaugurated, **President Lincoln** made it clear that he would not permit **southern secession**, but he did not want to initiate a war with the breakaway states. The presence of U.S. troops at **Fort Sumter**, in the harbor of **Charleston, South Carolina**, proved to be the spark that ignited the war. The leadership of the nearly formed **Confederate States of America** decided that it would not tolerate the presence of the U.S. flag over Fort Sumter. In April 1861 Confederate president **Jefferson Davis** ordered bombardment of the fort, which was forced to surrender. This encounter constituted the opening shots of the **American Civil War**. Following the surrender of Fort Sumter, four additional states seceded (Virginia, Arkansas, North Carolina, and Tennessee). Lincoln reacted resolutely to this challenge. That same month, he issued a proclamation calling for 75,000 troops to "cause the laws to be duly executed." Soon, the United States and the seceded southern states were at war. (Several slave states—Maryland, Delaware, Kentucky, Missouri, and West Virginia, which was established during the war—did not formally secede; these were known as the **border states**.)

Topic 5.8 Military Conflict in the Civil War

There are several key factors in understanding the Union victory over the Confederacy. The states that stayed in the Union comprised a larger population and a larger industrial capacity than the secessionist states. Both sides had strengths and weaknesses, but as the war progressed, the strengths of the Union—notably its material and population advantages—became more significant in achieving victory.

A. Mobilizing for War

Both the Union and the Confederacy had to mobilize their entire societies and economies in order to wage war. Both sides also faced opposition on their home fronts.

Industrialization

The Civil War spurred rapid **industrialization** of the **North**. During the Civil War, the **Union** government required an enormous amount of war materials, from guns and bullets to boots and uniforms. Manufacturers rose to the occasion by rapidly modernizing production. These changes in production sped up the process of industrialization that was in its beginning stages before the war. Industrialization stimulated a long period of economic growth, turning the United States into a world economic power. The manufacturers themselves benefited from the war effort. Many of the **"captains of industry"** who came to dominate the economy during the **Gilded Age** of the last decades of the nineteenth century, such as **Andrew Carnegie**, **John D. Rockefeller**, **Jay Gould**, **J. P. Morgan**, and **Phillip D. Armour**, began their economic rise through supplying the Union war effort.

Funding the War

The United States government funded the war effort in three ways—issuing currency, borrowing money, and levying new taxes. These economic and fiscal policies greatly expanded the scope and size of the federal government. Though the federal government reduced its budget when the war ended, it did not return to the barebones condition of the antebellum period.

Congress issued three **Legal Tender Acts** in 1862 and 1863, allowing the government to issue paper currency, or **"greenbacks."** Unlike currency backed by gold or silver, greenbacks were backed only by people's faith in the government. The value of greenbacks fluctuated as the war progressed. In order to standardize the issuing of bank notes, stabilize the banking system, and stimulate economic growth, the government passed a series of **National Banks Acts** (1863–1864). These acts created a national banking system—allowing existing banks to join the system and to issue U.S. Treasury notes as currency. The system attempted to provide a degree of stability to the banking and currency system in the United States during a period when there was no central bank. (The Second Bank of the United States had expired in 1836; the Federal Reserve Bank was not created until 1913.)

For the first time, the government appealed to the public to purchase **bonds** in order to fund the war. Individuals lent the government approximately $400 million during the war by purchasing bonds. Banks and other financial institutions ended up loaning the government the vast majority of the $2.6 billion borrowed during the war.

Finally, the government created a wide array of new taxes including, for the first time, an **income tax**. Tax rates remained modest during the war in the face of widespread public opposition. The wartime income tax expired in 1872, but the call for additional income taxes became popular among socialist and populist reformers during the Gilded Age. A new income tax was enacted in 1894 but was declared unconstitutional by the Supreme Court in *Pollock v. Farmers' Loan and Trust Company* (1895). Later, the **Sixteenth Amendment** to the Constitution (1913) allowed Congress to levy income taxes (see box, page 265).

New York City Draft Riots

President Abraham Lincoln had to deal with considerable resistance to the war within the borders of the loyal states. One of the most significant episodes of resistance to Union policies involved riots against the **Enrollment Act** (1863), establishing a military draft, in New York City in July 1863. Protests initially focused on government draft offices. Protesters were particularly angry about a stipulation of the draft law that allowed men to pay a $300 commutation fee which exempted them from serving as a soldier. This substantial sum was well beyond most working-class men. In the subsequent days, the protests turned violent, and one target of the rioters was the city's African-American population, accused of taking jobs from whites. At least 120 people were killed in the **New York City Draft Riots**.

Civil Liberties and Home Front Opposition

President Abraham Lincoln suspended the **writ of habeas corpus** during the Civil War, authorizing the arrest, without due process, of rebels and traitors. Lincoln was responding to riots and threats of militia action in Maryland. (Maryland was one of the **border states**—slave states that did not join the Confederacy.) In 1863, Congress supported Lincoln's move by passing the **Habeas Corpus Suspension Act** (1863). After the war, the Supreme Court, in *Ex parte Milligan* (1866), ruled that the suspension of habeas corpus did not empower the president to try and convict citizens before military tribunals; civilians can be tried in military courts only if civilian courts are not operating.

> **USING HISTORICAL THINKING SKILLS: CONTEXTUALIZATION**
>
> **Civil Liberties During Wartime**
>
> Before condemning President Abraham Lincoln as being "authoritarian" or "heavy-handed" for suspending the writ of habeas corpus, and jailing people without a trial, keep the following in mind. In many civil wars in human history, it has been common for authorities to simply kill enemy sympathizers; arresting them without due process, it could be argued, is relatively humane for a civil war.

B. Turning the Tide: Factors in the Union Victory

The Confederacy demonstrated initiative and military skill early in the war, but a variety of factors contributed to the Union victory in a prolonged war. The Union eventually found skilled military leadership and developed effective battlefield strategies. The material advantages of the North began to play a more important role as the war progressed. The Union decision to wage "total war" on the South's infrastructure and environment also played a part in the Union victory.

Strengths and Weaknesses of the Two Sides

The Union side had some key advantages in the war. It had a far greater **population** than that of the rebellious Southern states (twenty-two million versus less than six million, excluding slaves). It also had a far greater **military capacity** than the Confederacy, a more **diverse economy**, and an extensive **railroad network**. All of these advantages would become especially significant as the war dragged on. The Union had the capability to resupply its troops and to recruit reinforcements for fallen soldiers.

The Confederacy's greatest advantage was that it could fight a **defensive war**. It did not have to invade and conquer the North in order to declare victory. The Union, on the other hand, had to fight an **offensive war** in southern territory in order to win. Another Confederate advantage was the South's rich military tradition. It had able generals and a cohort of military men to draw from.

Fighting the Civil War

The Union had a three-part strategy. First, the navy would blockade southern ports. The intent of this strategy, labeled the **Anaconda Plan**, was to prevent supplies from reaching the South and southern products from being shipped abroad. The second part was to divide Confederate territory in half by taking control of the **Mississippi River**. Finally, a contingent of troops would march on the Confederate capital of **Richmond, Virginia**, and achieve victory.

President Lincoln and much of the northern populace expected that the war would be quick and that victory would be easy. These illusions were shattered after the **First Battle of Bull Run** in Virginia. Confederate troops routed advancing U.S. troops. The Confederacy continued to hold the advantage on the battlefield for the remainder of 1861 and throughout 1862. Lincoln went through several generals-in-chief to lead the Union army before settling on **Ulysses S. Grant** (1864). Union forces suffered defeats at the

> **KEEP IN MIND**
>
> **Military History**
>
> The material in this section about the military aspects of the Civil War is, more or less, the extent of what you need to know. For this and other wars, there might be a question about strategy, diplomacy, or "turning points," but there will not be a question about the inner workings of a specific battle. However, such knowledge could certainly be used in adding complexity or nuance to an essay response.

Second Battle of Bull Run, the Battle of Fredericksburg, and other encounters. The 1862 Battle of Antietam that repelled a Confederate invasion is considered a Union victory, although a more aggressive Union general might have inflicted heavier damage. The early years also saw the first encounter between two ironclad ships, the Confederacy's *Merrimac* and the United States' *Monitor* (1862). The fighting between the two ships resulted in a draw, but it pointed the way toward the future of naval battles worldwide.

The Union **Navy** managed to maintain a successful blockade of the South. A few fast, steam-powered **"blockade runners"** managed to evade the blockade—but transporting cotton on such ships was too expensive to be profitable on the world market. At first, the Confederacy initiated an embargo on selling cotton to **Great Britain**, with the idea of bringing British factories to a standstill until Great Britain agreed to recognize the Confederacy and aid its war effort. However, this effort at **King Cotton diplomacy** simply hurt the southern economy. The Union blockade prevented the Confederacy from changing direction and selling its surplus cotton on the world market. Successful negotiating with Great Britain in 1862—by United States **Secretary of State William Seward** and **Minister to Great Britain Charles Francis Adams**—assured the Union that Great Britain would stay on the sidelines unless it were virtually certain that the Confederacy would become an independent nation.

An important turning point in the war was the **Battle of Gettysburg** (1863). This battle, in Pennsylvania, was the high-water mark for the Confederacy. After Gettysburg, the Confederacy was in retreat. An important Union victory was at **Vicksburg, Mississippi** (1863). With that victory, Union forces gained control of the Mississippi River, cutting the Confederacy in two. In 1864, **General William Tecumseh Sherman's "March to the Sea,"** from Atlanta to Charleston, shattered the South's last hope for a negotiated peace. Confederate general **Robert E. Lee** finally surrendered to **General Ulysses S. Grant** at **Appomattox Courthouse**, Virginia (1865).

Topic 5.9 Government Policies During the Civil War

The decision to shift the focus of the Civil War from maintaining national unity to also eradicating slavery played an important part in the Union victory in the Civil War.

A. The Focus of the War: From Union to Emancipation

The issuing of the Emancipation Proclamation expanded the focus of the Civil War from preserving the union to emancipating the slaves. This move proved to be decisive to northern victory; it opened up the possibility of large-scale enlistment of African Americans, and it contributed to the Confederacy remaining isolated diplomatically on the international scene.

President Lincoln and Slavery

President Abraham Lincoln's greatest wartime achievement was playing a key role in the emancipation of the slaves. Lincoln was partly motivated by the desire to keep **Great Britain** at bay during the war. The British might decide to aid the **Confederacy** to ensure the steady flow of southern cotton, but the British public would not condone joining the South to perpetuate slavery. However, Lincoln did not achieve this historic goal on his own—**abolitionists**, **Radical Republicans**, and, of course, **free Blacks** and **slaves** themselves all contributed to the effort to put the issue of

> **USING REASONING PROCESSES: CAUSATION**
>
> **From Union to Emancipation**
>
> In his First Inaugural Address (1861), Lincoln assured the South, "I have no purpose, directly or indirectly, to interfere with the institution of slavery in the States where it exists." In September 1862, Lincoln issued the Emancipation Proclamation, dramatically changing the goals of the Union in the Civil War. By 1865, in his Second Inaugural Address, Lincoln said that it was evident to everyone that a "peculiar and powerful interest [slavery] . . . was somehow the cause of the war." The evolution of Abraham Lincoln's thinking about emancipation is a complex process. Historians cite a variety of circumstances—military, diplomatic, ideological, political, ethical—that affected Lincoln's thinking. Certainly a complete understanding of the process cannot leave out the role of the slaves themselves. In large numbers, they escaped from southern plantations, journeyed to Union lines, provided information on Confederate troops' movements, helped build fortifications for the Union, and fought in the Union army. Their actions brought the question of emancipation to the top of the Union's agenda.

liberation on the wartime agenda. Lincoln ushered in this historic event of emancipation while guiding the country through a devastating civil war. He was able to convince a reluctant country that ending slavery was consistent with the most basic of American values.

The Confiscation Acts (1861)

Initially, **President Abraham Lincoln** was reluctant to take action against slavery for fear of pushing the border states toward secession. When Congress passed the **Confiscation Acts** in 1861 and 1862, Lincoln was opposed (although he did not veto them). These acts were framed as military measures. The first declared that any slaves pressed into working for the Confederacy could be taken as **"contraband of war"** and considered **"confiscated property."** The second act allowed for the seizure of the slaves owned by Confederate officials.

The Emancipation Proclamation (1862)

By the summer of 1862, **President Abraham Lincoln** had come to believe that the time was right for moving forward on the issue of emancipation. He waited until the Union had achieved a victory on the battlefield. The **Battle of Antietam** in September 1862 repelled a Confederate invasion, which was enough of a Union victory to prompt the president to issue the **Emancipation Proclamation** on September 22. The edict ordered the freeing of all slaves in rebel-held territory as of January 1, 1863. Significantly, the order did not free slaves in the loyal border states or in Union-held areas of Confederate states. Of course, orders from the United States government did not hold any weight for Confederate leaders, so the Emancipation Proclamation did not initially free any slaves. However, the order clearly changed the goals and tenor of the war, and made clear that this was as much a war for the liberation of the slaves as it was for the preservation of the Union.

The End of Slavery

President Abraham Lincoln came to see the Civil War as divine punishment on the entire nation for the sin of slavery. Perhaps it was God's will, he said in his **Second Inaugural Address** (1865), "that every drop of blood drawn with the lash shall be paid by another drawn by the sword." After years of brutal warfare, as Union troops advanced upon rebel territory, the **Emancipation Proclamation** was enforced and slavery was brought to an end. The process was completed over a month after the formal end of the Civil War. Union troops had finally advanced into the most remote of the former Confederate states, **Texas**. On June 19, 1865, in Galveston, Union General Gordon Granger and his troops announced that "in accordance with a proclamation from the Executive of the United States, **all slaves are free**." The anniversary of that announcement has long held significance in the African-American community as **"Juneteenth."** In 2021, President Joe Biden signed legislation making "Juneteenth" a federal holiday.

B. Lincoln and the Meaning of the Civil War

President Abraham Lincoln used a series of speeches, notably the Gettysburg Address (1863), to put the Civil War into a larger context and portray the elimination of slavery as part of the fulfillment of America's founding principles. Further, the Civil War, and

> **USING HISTORICAL THINKING SKILLS:**
> **CONTEXTUALIZATION**
>
> ### The Civil War in Context
>
> There are several compelling strategies for putting the Civil War in context: the breakdown of the system of two nationally-oriented political parties; the development of a free-labor, industrial economy in the North versus a slave-labor, agrarian economy in the South; the acquisition of new territories in the era of "manifest destiny" and debates over the expansion of slavery; or the intensification of ideological debates around the institution of slavery itself. Historian Eric Foner also notes that the Civil War can be seen in the context of modern nation-building processes. Such nation-building took place in different parts of the world in the nineteenth century, such as the Meiji Restoration in Japan in 1868 or the Risorgimento that resulted in the formation of Italy, completed in 1871. The unification that occurred in the United States, however, was built around a set of democratic principles rather than around a particular ethnicity. Lincoln himself saw the Civil War as ushering in "a new birth of freedom."

Lincoln's understanding of the significance of the war, represents an important step in the transition of the United States from a union of individual states to a modern unified nation.

The Gettysburg Address and the Transition Toward a Modern Nation

The **Battle of Gettysburg** (1863) was a major turning point in the Civil War. Several months after the battle, **President Abraham Lincoln** went to Gettysburg to dedicate a military cemetery at the site. His address at the ceremony succinctly framed the Civil War in the larger context of fulfilling the democratic goals that were implicit in the founding documents of the United States. He invoked the **Declaration of Independence**, which had been ratified **"four score and seven years"** before his **"Gettysburg Address"** (1863). He stated that the United States was **"conceived in Liberty,"** and that an important founding principle was that **"all men are created equal."** The Civil War was, in Lincoln's thinking, a test of whether a nation conceived around the principles of liberty and equality can last. The men who died trying to make these principles a reality had made the battlefield a sacred site. It was up to the living, Lincoln asserted, to bring those principles into fruition—to ensure that there shall be **"a new birth of freedom."**

The outcome of the Civil War, especially in light of Lincoln's understanding of the conflict, played an important role in the growth of the United States as a modern nation. The war made it clear that the states did not have the autonomy to secede—that the nation was indivisible, larger than the sum of its parts. From the time of the Civil War, the United States was increasingly referred to as a nation, rather than a union of states.

Topic 5.10 Reconstruction

The impact of the Civil War and Reconstruction on American society was profound. Broadly speaking, the war changed the relationship between the states and the federal government. Specifically, the war made it clear that the United States was indivisible; secession would not be allowed. Most important, the Civil War ended the practice of slavery in the United States. The Civil War and Reconstruction initiated debates over redefining citizenship, especially when it came to women and African Americans.

A. The Expansion of Citizenship Following the Civil War

Three constitutional amendments were ratified during the Reconstruction period, immediately following the Civil War. The Thirteenth Amendment (1865) outlawed slavery, the Fourteenth Amendment (1868) provided citizenship and due process of law to African Americans, and the Fifteenth Amendment (1870) prevented discrimination in voting based on race. These amendments were all designed to extend legal and political rights to former slaves.

The Thirteenth Amendment

Slavery had been virtually destroyed as Union troops defeated the Confederacy. Yet, by the end of the Civil War, some slaves were still not freed, especially in areas that had not been under Confederate control, such as Kentucky and Delaware. The **Thirteenth Amendment** (1865) freed the remaining slaves but, more importantly, it enshrined in the United States Constitution that **slavery** was illegal in America.

The Fourteenth Amendment

The **Fourteenth Amendment**, adopted in 1868, asserted that all people born in the United States are citizens. The United States broke with many European countries in embracing the concept of **birthright citizenship**, or *jus soli* (right of the soil). Birthright citizenship currently exists in many countries of North and South America but is less common elsewhere in the world. Further, the amendment stated that the **"privileges and immunities"** of citizens shall not be abridged by states. Also, it stated that no citizens shall be deprived of "life, liberty, or property without due process of law." In addition, the amendment limited the political power of former officials in the Confederate government. Section 3 disqualifies from federal or state office any former government official who had taken an oath to support the Constitution, and then, afterward, **"engaged in insurrection or rebellion"** against the United States or gave "aid and comfort" to its enemies.

The amendment was bitterly opposed by southern states, which were forced to approve it before they could regain representation in Congress. The amendment undid long-held custom as well as the ***Dred Scott* decision** (1857) by putting African Americans on an equal footing with whites and providing a guarantee of **equality before the law**. Although the Fourteenth Amendment extended citizenship rights to African Americans, it did not guarantee them the right to vote. The Fourteenth Amendment addresses voting rights by stating that for each male inhabitant who was denied the vote, the state would be forced to deduct a whole person from its total population count—the basis for apportioned representation. Republicans hoped that this would apply strong pressure on the states not to disenfranchise African Americans. Southern states, however, resisted extending the vote to African-American men, leading to the passage of the Fifteenth Amendment (see below). The use of the word "male" in the Fourteenth Amendment was the first time either "male" or "female" was used in the Constitution.

The Fifteenth Amendment

The **Fifteenth Amendment**, granting African-American men **voting rights**, was ratified in 1869. The amendment states that the vote may not be denied to someone based on "race, color, or previous condition of servitude." African-American women, like white women, still could not vote. Women were not guaranteed the right to vote until ratification of the **Nineteenth Amendment** (1920). The guarantee of voting rights for African-American men was a key element of the Reconstruction program of the **"radical Republicans."**

B. The Women's Rights Movement and the Constitution

Some participants in the women's rights movements welcomed the Reconstruction-era Constitutional amendments. However, other participants objected to their limited nature. Specifically, issues of gender equality were not addressed by these sweeping changes.

Debates over the Fifteenth Amendment

The proposal to ratify the **Fifteenth Amendment** generated a great deal of debate within the women's rights movement. Many activists were already disappointed with the wording of the Fourteenth Amendment, which inserted the word "male" into a discussion of voting. This was the first time that the word "male" was included in the Constitution. Before the Fourteenth Amendment, suffragists could argue that the Constitution had *implicitly* allowed women the right to vote by not *denying* it to them. It was, they argued, custom and tradition that had precluded female voting—not the Constitution itself. This was no longer the case, with the word "male" linked to the phrase "right to vote" in the Fourteenth Amendment.

The wording of the Fifteenth Amendment further alienated many women's rights advocates. **Elizabeth Cady Stanton** and **Susan B. Anthony** refused to support the Fifteenth Amendment because it did not extend the right to vote to women. Other feminists, led by **Lucy Stone** and her husband, **Henry Blackwell**, while disappointed with the wording of the Fifteenth Amendment, argued that it was important to support Reconstruction and the Republican Party. They asserted that women's suffrage could be accomplished on a state-by-state basis. These divisions led to the formation of rival organizations. Stanton and Anthony formed the **National Woman Suffrage Association** (NWSA) in 1869. Stone, Blackwell, and others established the **American Woman Suffrage Association** (AWSA), also in 1869. The AWSA and NWSA eventually reconciled and in 1890 merged to become the **National American Woman Suffrage Association** (NAWSA).

C. The Limited Successes of Reconstruction

Reconstruction refers to the process of reuniting the nation following the Civil War and restructuring the political, legal, and economic systems in the states that had seceded. The Reconstruction period resulted in some short-term successes—bringing the Union back together, extending political and leadership opportunities to former slaves, and altering the relationship between the races in the South. The period also saw a shift in power from the early phase of Reconstruction, dominated by the executive branch, to the latter phase, dominated by Congress. The successes of the Reconstruction period proved to be short lived. The Republican Party failed to establish itself as a viable political party in the South. Further, efforts at changing the culture and racial attitudes of the South proved elusive. Finally, a combination of resistance by white southerners and a lack of resolve on the part of northerners led to the end of the Reconstruction period.

Approaches to Reconstruction

As the Civil War was coming to an end, **President Abraham Lincoln** and the **Republican Party** began to address several questions regarding the postwar world. These questions included: What accommodations would be made for the freed men and women of the South? How would the secessionist South be reintegrated into the United States? What punishments, if any, would be meted out to those who had rebelled against the United States? Finally, who held responsibility for reuniting and reconstructing the country—the president or Congress? Did, as the president argued, the secessionist states still exist as political entities, simply awaiting new governing personnel, or had they committed state "suicide" and reverted back to the status of territories? Many congressional Republicans argued that the states had ceased to exist, and therefore needed to be readmitted by Congress. The answers to these questions formed the basis of competing visions of what **Reconstruction** would entail.

Wartime Reconstruction

President Lincoln was eager to quickly restore the Union. An initial goal of his was restoring southern representation in Congress. In 1863, he announced his **"ten percent" plan**. Under this plan, if 10 percent of the 1860 vote count in a southern state took an oath of allegiance to the United States and promised to abide by emancipation, then that state could establish a new government and send representatives to Congress. This was a low bar for these states to comply with. In 1864, he vetoed the **Wade-Davis Bill**, which would have established much more stringent standards for the southern states to meet. The bill would have required half of the voters in a state to sign a loyalty oath to the United States before Reconstruction could begin, and would have guaranteed equal treatment before the law for former slaves. Finally, in 1865, in his **Second Inaugural Address**, Lincoln announced that he wanted to reunite the country **"with malice toward none; with charity for all."** This approach was consistent with Lincoln's broader goal of ending the war as soon as possible. Lincoln was assassinated less than a month after his second inauguration, so it is difficult to surmise how he would have negotiated the difficulties of the Reconstruction era.

Presidential Reconstruction

After **President Lincoln's assassination** in 1865, his vice president, **Andrew Johnson**, assumed power. Johnson had been tapped for the vice presidency because he did not vacate his seat in the Senate when his native Tennessee declared secession in 1861. Although Johnson had broken with the planter class in the South, it became clear that he had no affinity for the Republican Party, nor for emancipation and equality for African Americans. He continued pursuing the lenient and rapid approach to Reconstruction that Lincoln had mapped out. Johnson quickly recognized the new southern state governments as legitimate after they renounced secession and ratified the **Thirteenth Amendment** banning slavery. In the South, many members of the old slave-owning class were now back in power. These men tried to replicate the conditions of the Old South, including passing a series of restrictive laws known as the Black Codes (see below). Southern postwar conditions were so similar to prewar conditions that many northerners wondered if they had **"won the war, but lost the peace."**

Black Codes

Immediately after the Civil War, in 1865 and 1866, Southern states passed **Black Codes**. These statutes regulated the activities of African Americans and in many ways recreated the conditions of slavery. Certain Black Codes forbade African Americans from owning land or owning a business. A central feature of these Black Codes was a broad and harsh set of vagrancy laws, which allowed for the arrest of freed people for minor infractions. Such laws often included criminalizing being on a public road without having a certain amount of money. Punishments for violations of Black Codes frequently included forcing African Americans to labor on a plantation for a period of time. In 1865, **Mississippi** was the first state to pass Black Codes—all the other ten states of the former Confederacy soon followed suit. In this atmosphere, a group of Republicans in Congress initiated a more sweeping Reconstruction program, implementing much of it by overriding President Andrew Johnson's vetoes.

Congress and the President Clash over Reconstruction

In 1866, tensions increased between **President Andrew Johnson** and congressional **Republicans**. Johnson vetoed two measures passed by Congress—an extension of the **Freedman's Bureau** and a **Civil Rights Act** that was designed to overturn the Black Codes the southern states had implemented. The biggest fight, however, between Johnson and congressional Republicans was over the ratification of the **Fourteenth Amendment** (see pages 197–198). After Congress sent the Fourteenth Amendment to the states for ratification in 1866, Johnson took an active role in urging Southerners to reject the amendment. President Johnson saw the amendment as further congressional interference in Reconstruction. He was confident that his allies would prevail in the 1866 midterm elections and the Fourteenth Amendment could be defeated.

Radical Reconstruction

President Andrew Johnson tried to mobilize skeptical white voters against the Fourteenth Amendment in the 1866 midterm elections. However, the strategy backfired. Republicans won a resounding victory in the 1866 elections and embarked on more sweeping measures. This phase of Reconstruction, known alternatively as **"Radical Reconstruction"** or **"Congressional Reconstruction,"** showed the potential of a biracial democracy in the United States while also showing the limits of federal resolve and the strength of white southern opposition.

Reconstruction Acts of 1867

Congressional Republicans were able to push through the **Reconstruction Acts** of 1867. These sweeping acts, passed over President Johnson's veto, divided the South into five military districts. These areas could rejoin the United States only if they guaranteed basic rights to African Americans. The radicals were not able to fully carry out their program. **Representative Thaddeus Stevens** introduced a bill in the spring of 1867 to redistribute land so that each **freedman** could be granted forty acres. The idea resonated with freedmen, some of the Radical Republicans in Congress, and many poor whites in the South who were eager to limit the economic clout of the large planters. However, the idea ran against the basic Republican value of protecting private property. The issue of **land reform** died in committee in the summer of 1867.

The Impeachment of President Johnson

The clash between **President Andrew Johnson** and the congressional **Republicans** degenerated to such an extent by 1868 that the Republicans voted to impeach Johnson. The House charged the president with violating the **Tenure of Office Act**, an act the Republicans had passed to protect their ally, **Secretary of War Edwin Stanton**. The act prohibited the president from firing cabinet members without Senate approval. The act itself was of questionable legality, but Johnson fired Stanton anyway, initiating the **impeachment trial**. The Senate narrowly found Johnson not guilty, but the whole procedure rendered Johnson powerless to stop Congress's Reconstruction plans.

The Composition of Reconstruction Governments

The southern state governments during Congressional Reconstruction were composed of a variety of elements. **Democrats** still served in state legislatures, often in the minority, during the Reconstruction period. The **Republicans** were composed of several different groups. Southern whites who joined the Republicans were labeled **"scalawags"** by their Democratic opponents. Many southern white Republicans were former Whigs and sought to promote economic progress for the South. In addition, many northerners came to the South to participate in Reconstruction. Some of these northern Republicans sought personal advancement in coming South; many were motivated by a desire to assist the former slaves in their adjustment to life as freed men and women. Southern Democrats labeled these northerners **"carpetbaggers,"** implying that they hurriedly threw some belongings in a carrying bag and traveled to the South to make a quick fortune.

Many of the Republican legislators were African Americans. Only in **South Carolina**, and only briefly (1873), did African Americans control the majority of seats in even one legislative chamber. They were consistently in the minority. However, the fact that African Americans were elected to public office in the South at all was a major accomplishment. In the 1870s, two African Americans were elected to the United States Senate—**Hiram Revels** and **Blanche K. Bruce**—and more than a dozen African Americans were elected to the House of Representatives.

> **USING HISTORICAL THINKING SKILLS: SOURCING AND SITUATION**
>
> **"Scalawags" and "Carpetbaggers"**
>
> The terms "scalawag" and "carpetbagger" appear frequently in primary sources of the Reconstruction period as well as in historical accounts of the period. Be aware that these are not neutral descriptors; rather, they reflect a particular point of view and historical situation. They were originally used as derogatory terms to disparage those who cooperated with Reconstruction governments and to discredit Reconstruction policies. If you use these terms in your writing, do so with caution. It may be wise to acknowledge their origins or to modify them with the phrase "so-called."

The Record of Reconstruction Governments

The record of the Reconstruction governments in the South is still a subject of controversy, over a century and a half later. White southerners at the time accused the Reconstruction government of corruption and ineptitude (see box, right). More recently, however, historians have pointed out that these governments accomplished a great deal, against great odds. The accomplishments of Reconstruction included the establishment of **schools for African Americans**. The attainment of an education was a burning desire for many of the freed African-American men and women. Schools thrived in the period despite the costs involved and despite the personal risk incurred by participants. Important African-American institutions, such as **Howard University** and **Morehouse College**, were established during the Reconstruction period. In addition, the Reconstruction governments established hospitals that served the African-American community, rewrote constitutions, updated penal codes, and began the physical rebuilding of the war-torn South.

> **USING HISTORICAL THINKING SKILLS: CONTEXTUALIZATION**
>
> **Corruption and the History of Reconstruction**
>
> White southerners at the time, and historical work afterward, frequently cited the burdens imposed by the Reconstruction governments. These accounts specifically noted rampant corruption, "gold-plated spittoons," "extravagance," and ineptitude. Examples of corruption among state Reconstruction officials (exaggerated as they may be) should be seen in the context of the American political system at the time. Corruption in American politics seemed everywhere during the post–Civil War era—from Tammany Hall and "Boss" Tweed to the White House of President Ulysses S. Grant (see pages 240–242). More recent histories of the Reconstruction period put assertions of corruption in this broader context and look at such claims with a more critical eye.

The Waning of Reconstruction

Several factors contributed to the decline of Reconstruction, after only a dozen years. Southern conservative Democrats, who called themselves **"redeemers,"** aggressively sought to regain power, state by state. The "redeemers" were aided by networks of white terrorist organizations that used violence to silence African Americans and to intimidate them from participating in public life. The bloodiest single act against African Americans during Reconstruction occurred in **Colfax, Louisiana**, in 1873, in the wake of the contested 1872 election for governor. Both a Democratic candidate and a Republican candidate claimed victory, with the Democratic candidate garnering support from a state board and the Republican candidate gaining the support of a federal judge. In early 1873, the Republican candidate and his slate of appointees, which included African Americans, occupied a courthouse in Colfax. Other African Americans, many armed, came to the courthouse to protect the Republican administration from attack by white opponents. In April, a large group of white insurgents, including many **Ku Klux Klan** members, descended upon the courthouse, killing over a hundred African Americans before taking over the building. When the violence was legally challenged, the Supreme Court, in the case of *United States v. Cruikshank*, issued a decision that greatly weakened Reconstruction. The decision held that the federal **Enforcement Act of 1870**, which enabled federal authorities to protect the constitutional rights of African Americans from vigilante violence, was unconstitutional. Congress, according to the Court, had the power to protect individuals from discrimination by *states*, but not by *individuals*. In the end, northern whites simply lost their zeal for reforming the South. By the 1870s, many whites in the North were more interested in the industrial development of the North than in the "race problem" in the South.

> **USING HISTORICAL THINKING SKILLS: MAKING CONNECTIONS**
>
> **The Electoral College Over Time**
>
> A working knowledge of the electoral college is essential to understanding some of the close elections in American history, especially those in which the winner of the national popular vote did not end up winning the presidency. Electoral voters are assigned to presidential candidates based on the results of the popular vote in each of the states. In most states, the winner of the popular vote receives *all* of that state's electoral votes. A candidate can win enough states to attain the majority of electoral votes (and be declared president-elect), while losing the overall popular vote. This occurred in 1824, 1876, 1888, 2000, and 2016. Calls to alter or abolish the electoral college are often invoked after such elections, but such a constitutional amendment would probably not attain the needed approval of three-fourths of the states. Smaller states and swing states would be more likely to support the status quo.

The Formal End of Reconstruction: The Election of 1876

The final nail in the coffin of Reconstruction was the disputed presidential election of 1876. The **Democratic** candidate, **Samuel J. Tilden**, won the majority of the popular vote, but neither he nor his **Republican** opponent, **Rutherford B. Hayes**, were able to claim enough electoral votes to be declared the winner. In three states—**South Carolina**, **Louisiana**, and **Florida**—the Democrats and the Republicans both claimed victory. A special electoral commission, with a Republican majority, declared Hayes the winner in the three contested states. Democrats protested, with some threatening to block Hayes's inauguration. Party leaders reached an informal agreement, known as the **Compromise of 1877**, which allowed Hayes to win the presidency. In return, the Republicans agreed to end Reconstruction, paving the way for rule by the Democratic Party in the South.

Topic 5.11 Failure of Reconstruction

The gains for African Americans during the Reconstruction period were short lived. After white southerners attained "home rule," they carried out a series of policies that effectively sidestepped the protections of the Fourteenth and Fifteenth Amendments. Violence, and the threat of violence, further eroded the civil rights of African Americans. In addition, economic arrangements evolved that kept African Americans in a state of debt and poverty.

A. From Slavery to Sharecropping

Even though slavery ended with the Civil War, patterns of land ownership remained unchanged. New economic arrangements emerged that would prove to be both exploitative and soil-intensive—notably, the sharecropping system.

The Development of the Sharecropping System

Economically, most African Americans were still engaged in agricultural work following the Civil War. Plantation owners sought to hire gangs of African-American workers to labor under the supervision of a white overseer. These workers chafed at this arrangement, with its stark resemblance to the slavery system. They desired a plot of their own—**"forty acres and a mule."** Some **Radical Republicans** urged the government to divide up the former slave plantations and distribute the land to freedmen. This radical proposal did not gain sufficient support to become reality (see page 200). Short of this, African Americans began to rent land. They would customarily pay "rent" with a portion of their yearly crop—usually half. This **"sharecropping" system** was somewhat of a compromise—African Americans did not have to work under the direct supervision of an overseer, and white plantation owners acquired cotton to be sold on the open market. After paying back loans for seed money and tools, sharecroppers were left with very little for basic necessities. The system created a cycle of debt, which prevented African Americans from acquiring wealth and owning land.

B. Conflicts over Notions of Citizenship and American Identity

During the Reconstruction period, amendments to the Constitution reflected a changing notion of national purpose and identity. These constitutional changes led to debates among Americans over rights for African Americans, women, and other groups. The Fourteenth and Fifteenth Amendments to the Constitution granted African Americans citizenship, equal protection of the laws, and voting rights. In the years that followed, these rights were systematically reduced by violence and political tactics. A system of segregation, with approval from the Supreme Court, became entrenched in the South.

Segregation in the South

A series of segregation laws, known as **"Jim Crow laws,"** were passed in the southern states in the years following Reconstruction. The origins of the term can perhaps be attributed to a song-and-dance routine from the 1830s called "Jump Jim Crow," which included white actors in blackface caricaturing African Americans. Later in the century, "Jim Crow" became an insulting term for African Americans; the laws that applied to African Americans, therefore, became known as Jim Crow laws. These laws segregated public facilities, such as railroad cars, bathrooms, and schools. Furthermore, they relegated African Americans to second-class status in the South. These state and local laws first appeared in the South starting in 1881.

The Supreme Court and the Narrowing of the Fourteenth Amendment

The passage of Jim Crow laws in the South after Reconstruction was aided in part by a narrow interpretation of the **Fourteenth Amendment** by the Supreme Court. Advocates of civil rights for African Africans hoped that the Fourteenth Amendment (ratified in 1868) would prevent the implementation of Jim Crow laws. The amendment prevents states from making laws that limit the **"privileges or immunities"** of any United States citizen. However, the Supreme Court interpreted this broad language in such a narrow way that it allowed for the implementation of Jim Crow laws. Earlier, in the ***Slaughterhouse Cases*** (1873), the Court made a distinction between national citizenship and

> **USING HISTORICAL THINKING SKILLS:**
> **MAKING CONNECTIONS**
>
> **The Legacy of the Fourteenth Amendment**
>
> Although the Fourteenth Amendment was largely sidestepped in the decades following Reconstruction, it established judicial principles that came to fruition in twentieth-century civil-rights decisions and legislation. The amendment, granting Congress the power to enforce the provisions of the amendment, led to the passage of landmark twentieth century legislation, including the Civil Rights Act of 1964 and the Voting Rights Act of 1965. In its decision in *Brown v. Board of Education* (1954), the Supreme Court specifically cited the amendment's assertion that "no State shall . . . deny to any person . . . the equal protection of the laws." It used this wording as the basis for declaring segregated schools unconstitutional.

state citizenship. The case was not a civil-rights case: it involved a suit by several New Orleans slaughterhouses that had been closed down by the state. The slaughterhouses asserted that their due process rights had been taken away in violation of the Fourteenth Amendment. The Court ruled that the Fourteenth Amendment applied to national citizenship rights, such as the right to vote in national elections and the right to travel between states. The Court said that the amendment did not apply to rights that derived from "state citizenship." As a result, the Fourteenth Amendment would not be of use in prohibiting state Jim Crow laws. In 1883, the Court further narrowed the Fourteenth Amendment in a series of decisions known as the *Civil Rights Cases*. These decisions struck down the 1875 Civil Rights Act, holding that the Fourteenth Amendment did not apply to privately owned "public accommodations," such as restaurants and hotels. Later, in the case of *Plessy v. Ferguson* (1896), the Supreme Court specifically asserted that racial segregation did not violate the equal protection provision of the Fourteenth Amendment (see page 223).

The Exclusion of African Americans from the Political Process

A series of actions effectively removed African Americans from the political process. **Literacy tests** and **poll taxes** limited their ability to vote. Poor whites got around these rules with the **"grandfather clause,"** guaranteeing a man the right to vote if he or his father or grandfather had the right to vote before the Civil War. In addition, the Democratic Party often held **"whites only"** primaries, thus legally excluding African Americans from the only elections that really mattered in the solidly Democratic South. African Americans who spoke out against this were targets of violence and even murder. The **Ku Klux Klan** was first organized in 1866. Thousands of African Americans were killed by **lynch mobs** as the local authorities looked the other way.

A "Second Reconstruction"

Reconstruction lasted only a decade; its accomplishments were limited and short lived. However, in many respects the failures of Reconstruction in the nineteenth century set the stage for a **"second reconstruction"** in the twentieth. The democratic spirit of the Reconstruction period inspired civil rights activists in the twentieth century (see Topic 8.6 and Topic 8.10).

Topic 5.12 Subject to Debate

Slavery and the Question of Civil War Causation

The events of the 1850s have assumed a central place in one of the most contentious historiographical discussions about American history: How should the coming of the Civil War be understood? Central to that question is the role of slavery leading up to the Civil War. Partisan historians from the South and the North have tended to blame the other side. Southern partisans blame the North for interfering with their "domestic institutions." Northern partisans blame the extreme language of the *Dred Scott* decision, the violence done to Senator Charles Sumner, and the strident defense of slavery as indicators of rigidity on the part of the South.

For decades after the war, many historians held that the war was an "irrepressible conflict." The phrase was actually coined before the war, in 1858, by Senator William H. Seward, discussing the possibility of a future conflict between the sections—one he saw as inevitable. The war was inevitable, the theory held, because of slavery, which was both at the heart of the issue and beyond compromise. The "irrepressible conflict" school has received more recent backing from contemporary historian Eric Foner, who focuses less on northern moral concerns about slavery and more on the "free-labor" ideology. This ideology, which was a central part of the culture of the North, held that the lands out west should be for small-scale farming without competition from the slave system.

Several historical schools have questioned the centrality of slavery in the conflict. Progressive historians Mary and Charles Beard, writing in the 1920s, argued that the conflict was actually between a capitalist industrial North and an agrarian, almost feudal, South. Other historians have blamed the conflict on "blundering politicians"—asserting that the politicians could have compromised on slavery and other issues. These schools of thought gained adherents from the 1920s onward but have been challenged more recently in the post–civil rights movement era.

The Myth of the "Lost Cause"

For decades, the Southern myth of the "lost cause" has influenced mainstream historical writing on the Civil War. The "lost cause" myth holds that the Confederate cause was a noble and honorable one, as the South had a rich tradition of military skill and chivalry. The only reason the South lost the Civil War was because of the overwhelming forces of the North. The North had greater industrial capacity and a larger population to draw from. However, this understanding completely ignores the centrality of the slavery question. Even among northerners in the first half of the twentieth century, the question of slavery was left out of discussions of the war. It is only in the last third of the twentieth century that the history field has fully rejected the "lost cause" myth.

Viewing the Reconstruction Period in Context

Traditional historical accounts of the Reconstruction period criticize the Republican Party for imposing crushing burdens on the South, for occupying it with troops, and for saddling it with inept and corrupt government. Recent historical accounts have moved away from this grim representation by emphasizing the real progress made by African Americans under Reconstruction. The short-lived gains made under Reconstruction helped to inspire civil rights activists in the twentieth century.

Practice Multiple-Choice Questions

> **DIRECTIONS:** Pick the letter that best answers the following questions.

Questions 1–3 are based on the following passage:

"I have directed Commodore Perry to assure your imperial majesty that I entertain the kindest feelings toward your majesty's person and government.

"The United States of America reach from ocean to ocean, and our Territory of Oregon and State of California lie directly opposite to the dominions of your imperial majesty. Our steamships can go from California to Japan in eighteen days.

"Our great State of California produces about sixty millions of dollars in gold every year... and many other valuable articles. Japan is also a rich and fertile country, and produces many very valuable articles.... I am desirous that our two countries should trade with each other, for the benefit both of Japan and the United States.

"We know that the ancient laws of your imperial majesty's government do not allow of foreign trade, except with the Chinese and the Dutch; but as the state of the world changes and new governments are formed, it seems to be wise, from time to time, to make new laws....

"These are the only objects for which I have sent Commodore Perry, with a powerful squadron, to pay a visit to your imperial majesty's renowned city of Yedo: friendship, commerce, a supply of coal and provisions, and protection for our shipwrecked people."

—President Millard Fillmore, letter to the Emperor of Japan, presented by Commodore Matthew Perry, 1853

1. A major goal of Commodore Matthew Perry's expedition was to

   (A) challenge the "spheres of influence" system in Japan that had been developed by the major European powers.
   (B) reduce tensions that had developed between Japan and the United States over competing colonial claims.
   (C) expand American trade into a country that had traditionally isolated itself from most foreign powers.
   (D) overthrow the militaristic regime of Japan and replace it with a democratic government.

2. The United States naval expeditions to Japan in the 1850s, led by Commodore Matthew Perry, resulted in

   (A) a long period of Japanese isolation from Western trade and influence.
   (B) war between the United States and Japan.
   (C) Japan becoming an American colony.
   (D) Japan opening its ports to trade with the West.

3. The expedition by Commodore Matthew Perry could best be understood in the context of

   (A) an expanding American economy.
   (B) shifting alliances among major world powers.
   (C) increased nativist sentiment in the United States.
   (D) debates over the expansion of slavery.

Questions 4–6 refer to the following table:

Occupations of Gainfully Employed Irish Immigrants in New York, 1855	Occupation # Irish-born (and % of total)
SKILLED	
Bakers	861 (23)
Blacksmiths	1,339 (50)
Brewers/Distillers	52 (14)
Carpenters	2,230 (30)
Dressmakers/Seamstresses	4,559 (46)
Ironworkers	150 (56)
Machinists	398 (23)
Masons/Bricklayers	2,203 (61)
Merchants	278 (4)
Policemen	292 (25)
Printers	519 (25)
Retail shopkeepers	916 (35)
Shoemakers	2,121 (31)
Tailors	4,171 (33)
Wine and liquor dealers	891 (55)

PROFESSIONALS	
Doctors	113 (8)
Lawyers	40 (4)

UNSKILLED	
Domestic Servants	23,386 (74)
Laundresses	1,758 (69)
Laborers	17,426 (86)
Drivers/Hackmen/Coachmen	805 (46)

Source: Robert Ernst, *Immigrant Life in New York City, 1825–1863* and *NY State Census of 1855*, 1994.

4. Which of the following factors was an important cause of the immigration trend reflected in the chart?

    (A) Great Britain had recently begun using harsh tactics against Irish dissidents, leading to large numbers of dissidents fleeing Ireland.
    (B) The Irish agricultural sector had recently undergone rapid mechanization, displacing a large percentage of the rural population of Ireland.
    (C) A large-scale famine in Ireland, caused by the failure of the potato crop, had recently occurred, driving many Irish people to flee the country.
    (D) New York State had recently passed a religious toleration act, creating a more welcoming atmosphere for Irish Catholic immigrants.

5. Which of the following conclusions is supported by the evidence in the chart?

    (A) Irish immigrants were quickly able to climb the economic ladder of New York City and gain employment in middle-class professions.
    (B) Irish immigration to New York City in the period before the Civil War did not significantly alter the economic structure of the city.
    (C) Irish workers played a prominent role in the union movement in New York City in the 1850s.
    (D) Irish immigrants comprised a majority of the workers in low-paying, unskilled occupations in New York City by the 1850s.

6. Which of the following describes a significant response to the development reflected in the chart in the 1850s?

    (A) The federal government implemented the National Origins Act, establishing a quota system to stem the flow of Irish immigrants into the United States.
    (B) Congress rewrote naturalization laws in order to expand the number of years immigrants must live in the United States before they can attain citizenship and voting rights.
    (C) The United States and Ireland reached an understanding that President Franklin Pierce would pressure New York State to end discriminatory practices against Irish immigrants, and that Ireland would pass legislation limiting immigration into the United States.
    (D) A new political party, commonly called the Know-Nothing Party, attracted large numbers of voters with a strong anti-immigrant, anti-Catholic message.

Questions 7–8 refer to the following passage:

"It is the sentiment around which all their [Republicans'] actions, all their arguments, circle, from which all their propositions radiate. They look upon it as being a moral, social, and political wrong; and while they contemplate it as such, they nevertheless have due regard for its actual existence among us, and the difficulties of getting rid of it in any satisfactory way and to all the constitutional obligations thrown about it. Yet, having a due regard for these, they desire a policy in regard to it that looks to its not creating any more danger. They insist that it should, as far as may be, *be treated* as a wrong; and one of the methods of treating it as a wrong is to *make provision that it shall grow no larger.*"

—Abraham Lincoln, from debate with Stephen Douglas, October 1858

7. The position of Abraham Lincoln in the above passage emerged most directly in response to which of the following mid-nineteenth century trends?

    (A) Large-scale immigration from Ireland
    (B) The spread of the ideas of Romanticism
    (C) Violent slave rebellions in the South
    (D) Territorial growth of the United States

8. The logic of the quotation is most consistent with

    (A) George Fitzhugh's 1857 book, *Cannibals All!*
    (B) the Wilmot Proviso, introduced in Congress in 1846, 1847, and 1848.
    (C) Frederick Douglass's 1852 oration commonly known as "What to the Slave Is the 4th of July?"
    (D) "John Brown's Last Speech," read in court in 1859.

Questions 9–10 refer to the following passage:

"No negro or freedman shall be allowed to come within the limits of the town of Opelousas without special permission from his employers. Whoever breaks this law will go to jail and work for two days on the public streets, or pay a fine of five dollars.

"No negro or freedman shall be permitted to rent or keep a house in town under any circumstances. No negro or freedman shall live within the town who does not work for some white person or former owner.

"No public meetings of negroes or freedmen shall be allowed within the town.

"No freedman shall be allowed to carry firearms, or any kind of weapons. No freedman shall sell or exchange any article of merchandise within the limits of Opelousas without permission in writing from his employer.

"Every negro is to be in the service of (work for) some white person, or former owner."

—"Black Codes," Opelousas, Louisiana, 1865

9. "Black Codes," such as the ones excerpted above, were implemented in many Southern states and localities after the Civil War in order to

    (A) establish rules for African Americans to obtain land to farm on.
    (B) extend the power of the Republican Party.
    (C) limit the rights and privileges of African Americans.
    (D) comply with the stipulations of the Fourteenth Amendment.

10. An important result of the enactment of "Black Codes," such as the ones excerpted above, was to

    (A) convince many radical and moderate Republicans that a more extensive Reconstruction program was needed.
    (B) encourage large numbers of African Americans to leave the South and move to Northern cities.
    (C) prod the Supreme Court to play a more active role in defending the constitutional rights of African Americans.
    (D) push President Andrew Johnson to replace several southern governors with former Union generals who would ensure that African-American rights were guaranteed.

Answers and Explanations

1. **(C)** A major goal of Commodore Matthew Perry's expedition was to expand American trade into a country that had traditionally isolated itself from most foreign powers. With the growth of the economy and with the acquisition of West Coast ports, the United States became increasingly interested in trading with Japan. The Tokugawa shogunate (1600–1868) had virtually isolated Japan from Western countries since the seventeenth century. The United States was determined to open Japan to American trade.

2. **(D)** The United States naval expedition in the 1850s, led by Commodore Matthew Perry, resulted in Japan opening its ports to trade with the West. The first journey was in 1852–1853 and a second occurred in 1854. Perry was able to secure a treaty with Japan that opened the country up to American trade.

3. **(A)** The expedition by Commodore Matthew Perry could best be understood in the context of an expanding American economy. Growth and expansion were defining features of the United States in the decades between 1800 and the Civil War. The economy was rapidly changing and growing, as an older semi-subsistence economy was giving way to a market economy with a national and even international reach.

4. **(C)** The chart indicates a significant Irish presence in New York City by 1855; the majority of unskilled jobs in New York City were held by the Irish. The single biggest factor contributing to this migration of people was the large-scale failure of the potato crop in Ireland and the devastating famine that following in its wake. By the 1840s, Great Britain controlled Ireland and used the best land there to grow wheat and other crops for export, while potato farming was pushed to marginal land. The result was weak potato plants less able to withstand disease. It is estimated that a million Irish starved to death between 1845 and 1850, while another million left for America.

5. **(D)** The chart shows that the Irish comprised a majority of workers in unskilled fields in New York in the 1850s. The Irish were in desperate straits and took low-paying unskilled jobs. Many were involved in building the city's Central Park in the 1850s. Irish immigrants tended to enter the labor market on a lower rung than German immigrants. The Irish immigrants tended to come from rural backgrounds and did not have the skills needed to rise in the workforce. By contrast, German immigrants tended to arrive with skills in particular trades, including carpentry, brewing, metal-work, and other crafts.

6. **(D)** The large-scale Irish immigration into the United States in the 1840s and 1850s resulted in a strong nativist movement. The most successful political manifestation of this movement was the Know-Nothing Party. The party emerged in the 1840s and, by the 1850s, achieved electoral success in several states, especially in the Northeast. Many members of the party eventually ended up joining the newly formed Republican Party.

7. **(D)** Abraham Lincoln is describing the Republican Party's position on slavery in 1858. It comes from one of several debates with Stephen Douglas during their respective campaigns for Senate that year. Lincoln was a member of the Republican Party, even though he uses the word "they," rather than "we," to describe the Republicans. In this excerpt, Lincoln notes that the Republicans were against the institution of slavery and opposed to its spread to new territories. The party felt that slavery was constitutionally protected in the states where it already existed. The territorial growth of the United States—following the acquisition of the Mexican Cession (1848)—forced public figures to take a position on the question of slavery. The Kansas-Nebraska Act (1854) further intensified debate over slavery in the United States.

8. **(B)** The logic of the Republican position—opposition to the spread of slavery—was most consistent with the Wilmot Proviso. During the Mexican-American War (1846–1848), Congressman David Wilmot and other northern politicians tried, unsuccessfully, to ban slavery in territories that might be gained in the war by putting forth the Wilmot Proviso (1846). The proviso was passed by the House of Representatives three times (1846, 1847, and 1848), where politicians from the populous northern states dominated; however, it failed to garner enough votes for passage in the Senate, where southern and northern politicians were equally represented.

9. **(C)** "Black Codes" were implemented in order to limit the rights and privileges of African Americans. These statutes regulated the activities of African Americans and in many ways recreated the conditions of slavery. Certain Black Codes forbade African Americans from owning land. Punishments for violations of Black Codes included forced labor on a plantation for a period of time.

10. **(A)** The enactment of Black Codes throughout the South demonstrated that the former slave-owning class was determined to maintain power in the post–Civil War period. These laws convinced many Republican senators, notably Thaddeus Stevens and Charles Sumner, to enact a Reconstruction plan far more extensive than the mild plan implemented by President Andrew Johnson. They pushed for the Military Reconstruction Act and three other acts in 1867 in order to reorganize the South (except for Tennessee) as a conquered territory. The act divided the South into five military zones. As the territories recognized and protected the rights of African Americans, they were readmitted into the United States as states.

8

Period 6: 1865–1898 The Challenges of the Era of Industrialization

TIMELINE

1866	Medicine Lodge Treaty establishes the reservation system
1869	Founding of the Knights of Labor
1873	Panic of 1873
1876	Alexander Graham Bell develops the telephone
	The Battle of the Little Big Horn/Custer's Last Stand
1877	Great Railroad Strike
	Munn v. Illinois
1879	Thomas A. Edison develops the light bulb
1881	Helen Hunt Jackson publishes *A Century of Dishonor*
1882	Formation of the Standard Oil Trust
	Chinese Exclusion Act
1883	Opening of the Brooklyn Bridge
1886	Founding of the American Federation of Labor
	Haymarket bombing
	Wabash, St. Louis and Pacific Railway Company v. Illinois
1887	Interstate Commerce Act
	Opening of the first subway system in the United States (Boston)
	Dawes Severalty Act
1890	Sherman Antitrust Act
	Beginning of Ghost Dance movement
	Massacre at Wounded Knee
1892	Homestead lockout
1893	World's Columbian Exposition (Chicago World's Fair)
	Panic of 1893
1894	Pullman Strike
1895	*United States v. E. C. Knight Company*
1896	*Plessy v. Ferguson*

Topics in Period 6

In this chapter, you will learn about:
- Topic 6.1 Contextualizing Period 6
- Topic 6.2 Westward expansion: Economic development
- Topic 6.3 Westward expansion: Social and cultural development
- Topic 6.4 The "New South"
- Topic 6.5 Technological innovation
- Topic 6.6 The rise of industrial capitalism
- Topic 6.7 Labor in the Gilded Age
- Topic 6.8 Immigration and migration in the Gilded Age
- Topic 6.9 Responses to immigration in the Gilded Age
- Topic 6.10 Development of the middle class
- Topic 6.11 Reform in the Gilded Age
- Topic 6.12 Controversies over the role of government in the Gilded Age
- Topic 6.13 Politics in the Gilded Age
- Topic 6.14 Subject to debate

Topic 6.1 Contextualizing Period 6

> The transformation of the United States during the last decades of the nineteenth century from an essentially rural and agrarian society to an increasingly industrial and urban one brought about a host of economic, political, diplomatic, social, cultural, and environmental changes.

The United States economy expanded tremendously in the late 1800s as the country experienced rapid industrialization. The era of industrial expansion after the Reconstruction period is known as the "Gilded Age." Although the nation as a whole enjoyed an increase in its wealth, that wealth was not equally distributed. The owners of big businesses, labeled "robber barons" by their critics, enjoyed unparalleled wealth, whereas many of the workers lived in squalid conditions in working-class slums. The contrast between the mansions of Andrew Carnegie and Henry Frick along New York City's Fifth Avenue and the tenements depicted in Jacob Riis's *How the Other Half Lives* (1890) startled many Americans.

The era of rapid industrial and economic expansion in the late nineteenth century dramatically transformed American culture and society. Americans experienced new cultural products, new patterns of work and leisure, and new class and ethnic divisions. These new aspects of American life were most evident in the growing cities. Cities became centers of industrial production and magnets for the large number of immigrants coming into the United States. At the same time, agriculture was becoming more mechanized, requiring fewer people in rural areas. New York retained its stature as the largest American city, with Chicago, Cleveland, Detroit, and other cities of the Midwest and the Northeast also growing rapidly.

In addition, during the decades between the end of the Civil War and the turn of the twentieth century, a series of important developments transformed the South and the West. White and African-American southerners both shaped the "New South," as the region left behind plantation slavery. Ultimately, white southerners were able to create a series of laws and customs that relegated African Americans to a second-class status. At the same time, government policies and economic opportunity encouraged waves of settlers to make their way west. The Midwest became a major agricultural region and the center of a politicized and determined farmers' movement. As settlers ventured farther west, clashes ensued with American Indian groups who lived on coveted lands. These clashes led to the demise of autonomous native peoples within the United States borders.

Topic 6.2 Westward Expansion: Economic Development

Economic opportunities and government policies encouraged the development of the West in the decades after the Civil War. Farmers in this period found themselves drawn into the world of mechanized agriculture. In many cases, these farmers formed local and regional organizations in order to resist the power of railroads (which controlled the price of shipping crops) and corporate interests.

A. Mechanization and the Transformation of American Agriculture

By the late 1800s, mechanization was rapidly transforming American agriculture. Mechanization had both positive and negative effects for American farmers. At the same time that it increased overall agricultural production, mechanization also led to lower prices for agricultural products.

The Impact of Mechanization

During the decades following the Civil War, expensive machines, such as the **mechanical reaper** and the **combine harvester**, replaced hand-held tools to harvest field crops. This equipment greatly expanded agricultural output and reduced the man-hours needed for agricultural tasks such as mowing, baling, and threshing. Production of corn and wheat soared, more than doubling between 1870 and 1900. The mechanical combine and the mechanical reaper allowed a farm crew to tend hundreds of acres instead of just a few. At the same time, mechanization worked to undermine small-scale family farms. First, the overall increase in production lowered the prices that farmers received per bushel of corn or wheat. Second, most farmers could not afford the new equipment. By the late 1800s, large-scale farms came to dominate agriculture in the United States. Agriculture changed from small-scale farms with laborers using hand tools into large-scale mechanized operations. Many smaller farmers went out of business because they could not compete with the large farms.

B. Agrarian Resistance in the Face of Structural Change

Farmers created local and regional organizations in response to dramatic changes in agriculture in the late 1800s.

Debt and Dependence in the Gilded Age

During the post–Civil War period, farmers felt they were being squeezed from all sides. **Railroad companies** were overcharging farmers for carrying their produce to Chicago and other destinations. Also, the **tight supply of currency** in the United States was making it difficult for farmers to pay off their debts and at the same time was driving down the commodity prices they received for their crops. Finally, **banks** were foreclosing on farms. These problems led farmers to seek solutions through forming local and regional organizations to challenge corporate power. Some of their political agitation was carried out within the two-party system but, significantly, farmers decided to also work outside of mainstream politics.

The Greenback Party

An early political formation with agrarian roots that sought an expansion of the currency supply was the **Greenback Party**. Founded in 1878—during the economic downturn following the **Panic of 1873**—the party advocated issuing paper money that was not backed by gold or silver. The issuing of currency based solely on public faith was done briefly during the Civil War (see page 193) and resulted in farmers receiving higher prices for their crops. The party received a million votes in the 1878 congressional elections. The party soon disbanded, but the call for expanding the money supply was taken up again following the **Panic of 1893**.

> **KEEP IN MIND**
>
> **The Image of the Farmer in American History**
>
> Farmers have often been represented throughout history as slow and dim-witted. Their participation in the Grange (an agricultural advocacy group founded in 1867), in farmer co-ops, and in the populist movement demonstrated a level of sophistication at odds with the image of the "hayseed." Avoid condescending stereotypes.

The Grange and Granger Laws

The National Grange of the Patrons of Husbandry, more commonly known as the **Grange**, is a farmers' organization that pushed for state laws to protect farmers' interests. Founded in 1867, it led the fight in many Midwestern states to pass laws that regulated railroad freight rates and made certain abusive corporate practices illegal. These laws came to be known as **Granger Laws**. Initially, the Supreme Court, in *Munn v. Illinois* (1877), upheld these laws, asserting that it was within the government's permissible powers to regulate private industry. Later, the Court reversed itself. In *Wabash v. Illinois* (1886), the Court ruled that individual states could not regulate railroads because they cross state lines. (See more on railroad regulation, page 237.)

Protecting Communal Lands of the Southwestern *Hispanos*

Clashes occurred in the 1880s and 1890s in the Southwest between recently arriving settlers from older states and long-time Mexican and American Indian occupants of the land. Much of the conflict occurred in northern **New Mexico**, which was federally administered land that the United States gained from Mexico following the **Mexican-American War** (1846–1848). For years newcomers had been migrating to this area and squatting on the land. The **Homestead Act** of 1862 gave these squatters a degree of legitimacy in the eyes of the federal government.

Large portions of these lands were used communally by the local *Hispano* population (the name given to the descendants of the original Spanish-speaking settlers in what would become the United States). Hispanos lived in villages and used the surrounding lands for grass, timber, water, and other resources. By the 1890s, the local Hispanos and Indians had lost more than 90 percent of their traditional lands and began organizing resistance. Attempts by the local population to regain their lands from federal authorities fell on deaf ears. The Surveyor of General Claims Office generally demanded that documentation of ownership be in English, but titles held by the Hispanos were in Spanish. Finally, groups such as **Las Gorras Blancas** (named after the white caps they wore) and **Las Manos Negras** (The Black Hands) organized resistance. This included raids on settler-held land, often cutting fences and burning property. Several members of Las Gorras Blancas formed a populist party, the **United People's Party** (in English), and successfully ran for the New Mexico legislature in 1890. Ultimately, the varied tactics of the movement failed to regain lost lands.

C. Transportation, Communication, and the Opening of New Markets in the West

The government subsidized new transportation and communications systems during the Gilded Age. These new systems opened new markets in North America.

Land Grants to Railroads

In the second half of the nineteenth century, the federal government encouraged economic growth by subsidizing improvements in transportation and communications. Most importantly, the government encouraged the building of railroad lines. Railroads connected the far reaches of the country and sped up the movement of goods and expanded markets. The cost of goods came down and the standard of living of Americans rose. The government encouraged this expansion of the railroad network by giving railroad companies wide swaths of land through which new rail lines would be built. Most of these grants occurred between 1850 and 1871. The **Pacific Railway Act** of 1862 greatly accelerated the process. Under the act, **land grants** went directly to railroad corporations rather than to states. These generous land grants totaled more than 175 million acres—which represents an area larger than the state of Texas. These land grants generated huge profits for railroad companies. The presence of railroad lines made the land on either side of the tracks more accessible and more valuable, bringing about $435 million to the railroad companies.

The Telegraph and the Telephone

The federal government aided the development of new communications systems by granting patents to protect inventions such as the **telegraph** and the **telephone**. The telegraph network, which developed before the Civil War (see page 146), continued to spread throughout the country during the Gilded Age. The first transatlantic cable was laid in 1858, ushering in an era of rapid communications between Europe and North America. The telegraph industry came under the control of **Jay Gould** in 1879, when he became the head of **Western Union**. In 1876, **Alexander Graham Bell** was granted a patent for the telephone. As is the case with many innovations, a host of individuals were working simultaneously on developing the telephone. Within a year, the **Bell Telephone Company** was established. By the end of 1880, almost 50,000 telephones were in use in the United States. These developments greatly aided the development of corporations with a national, and even international, reach.

D. Promoting Westward Expansion—Government Policies, Railroads, and Mining Operations

A series of government policies encouraged settlement of the West. The building of transcontinental railroad lines and the discovery of mineral resources drew ever more people westward after the Civil War.

Government Policies and Westward Expansion

The federal government had long made it a priority to promote settlement of the West. The government continued the policy of extending land to individual farmers that it had begun with the **Homestead Act** of 1862 (see page 181). The original Homestead Act had not proven to be as successful as its promoters had hoped. The size of the grants, 160 acres, were too small for the grazing and grain farming that characterized western agriculture. Also, although the land was free, homesteaders still needed to build homes and purchase the expensive equipment necessary for large-scale farming. The majority of land recipients sold their plots. Congress responded by increasing the size of plots granted to homesteaders. The **Timber Culture Act** (1873) allowed homesteaders to receive additional lands if they agreed to plant trees on a portion of it, and the **Desert Land Act** (1877) offered acreage for a discounted price if the recipients agreed to irrigate the land.

Government Support for Transcontinental Railroads

The **Pacific Railroad Acts**, passed in the 1860s, promoted government bonds and land grants to railroad companies to complete rail lines to the Pacific Ocean (see pages 181 and 216). The completion of the **Pacific Railroad**, the nation's first **transcontinental railroad** at **Promontory Summit, Utah**, in 1869 was a milestone in the development of a network of railroad lines that connected the far reaches of the country. In the coming decades, four additional transcontinental lines were completed. Only the last of the five lines, the **Great Northern Railway** (completed in 1893), was built without the benefit of federal land grants.

Railroad companies were anxious to sell the land they had been granted. The land in towns and cities along the transcontinental railway was valuable because of the new accessibility created by the rail lines. Western railroad companies relentlessly promoted land sales to the populations of the overcrowded cities of the East.

Mining Operations in the West

The extraction of precious metals was extremely profitable in the nineteenth century and was a major motivation in the settlement of the West. The rush for riches began with the discovery of gold in California in 1848 (see pages 179–180) and continued for the next four decades throughout the West. In 1859, the extensive silver deposits of **Nevada's Comstock Lode** were discovered, leading to the creation of a major boomtown, Virginia City (see page 219). In 1858, gold was discovered at **Pike's Peak Country**, located in the Kansas and Nebraska Territories. The influx of over 100,000 people into the region resulted in the establishment of boomtowns such as **Denver City** and **Boulder City**, and the rapid establishment of the Colorado Territory in 1861. Similar "rushes" occurred in the Dakotas, Montana, Arizona, Utah, and Idaho.

Most of the **mining operations** in the West went through similar stages. After word got out about the discovery of a precious metal, thousands of prospectors hurried to the area to attempt to be first to cash in. A few did; most did not. Soon, whatever deposits existed along the surface were quickly found by placer mining—using pans, sluice boxes, picks, and shovels along river beds. After that, a more industrial phase of mining occurred. To extract the vast deposits that lay beneath the surface required expensive hydraulic equipment. This equipment was too expensive for placer miners. Large mining firms invested in elaborate operations. Thus, mining had more in common with industrial operations in the East, with investors enjoying substantial profits, shares in operations being traded on international markets, and wage workers replacing prospectors.

Topic 6.3 Westward Expansion: Social and Cultural Development

A variety of economic opportunities drew waves of settlers to the West. As settlers moved westward, American Indians were increasingly threatened. The reservation system, the destruction of the buffalo, military actions, and assimilationist policies worked to circumscribe Indian options and culture.

A. Settling the West

A variety of economic opportunities drew people to the West, including railroad construction, mining, timbering, farming, and ranching. Migrants to the West hoped to achieve a degree of self-sufficiency and independence. Immigrants from China, Scandinavia, Germany, Canada, Ireland, Great Britain, and elsewhere mingled with native-born whites, Spanish-speaking *Hispanos* (see page 216), and African-American "Exodusters" (see page 230) in this multicultural West.

Chinese Communities in the West

Chinese immigrants were initially drawn to North America by the **gold rush** in California (see pages 179–180). By 1852, 20,000 Chinese immigrants had moved to California; by 1870, over 63,000 lived in America, with nearly 80 percent in California. White Californians pushed for laws to exclude Chinese immigrants from mining, including an 1852 **Foreign Miners' License Tax**. Discrimination, legal obstacles, and changes in the economics of mining pushed most Chinese immigrants away from mining and toward other jobs; Chinese laborers often ended up doing jobs that others avoided. Up to 12,000 Chinese workers helped complete the first **transcontinental railroad** line in 1869, representing 90 percent of the workforce.

Anti-Asian Sentiment and the Chinese Exclusion Act

Chinese immigrants faced a great deal of discrimination and outright hostility in the second half of the nineteenth century. Federal naturalization laws, altered after the Civil War to accommodate African Americans, denied citizenship to Asian immigrants. Further, an 1854 California Supreme Court decision, ***the People of the State of California v. George W. Hall***, ruled that Chinese Americans were not allowed to testify against whites in court. This decision made it virtually impossible to prosecute crimes of white violence against Chinese Americans. When the economy suffered a major downturn in the 1870s, following the **Panic of 1873**, many Californians singled out the Chinese population as the cause of the crisis. Many labeled Chinese residents, "coolie labor." This term may be derived from the word "kuli," a Tamil (South Indian language) word for wages. In the early 1800s, it came to be applied to indentured Asian workers, and later was used as a derogatory term for Chinese laborers. The **Workingmen's Party** (formed in 1876), arguing that the presence of Chinese laborers depressed wages, pushed for legislation excluding Chinese immigrants from the United States. This activism, coming as Reconstruction was ending in the South, proved to be successful. The 1882 **Chinese Exclusion Act** represents the first discriminatory federal law that targeted a particular national group. It banned Chinese immigration, with the exception of a small number of job categories, for ten years. The law was later renewed and in 1902 made permanent; it was finally repealed in 1943.

Mining Boomtowns in the West

Bustling towns seemed to grow overnight in parts of the West during the post–Civil War period. These towns were often populated by prospectors trying to strike it rich. As the towns grew, many women began to arrive, finding employment as boardinghouse owners, washerwomen, cooks, and maids. A typical **boomtown** was **Virginia City** in present-day Nevada. The town was born in the wake of the discovery of the **Comstock Lode** in 1859. By 1875, Virginia City had a population of over 25,000 people, making it one of the largest towns in the interior of the West. These boomtowns were very different from the "**Wild West**" towns portrayed in classic Western movies. For one, they were just as ethnically and racially diverse as typical cities in the East. Virginia City included Irish, Chinese, Germans, Italians, Mexicans, Scandinavians, French, Canadians, immigrants from several South and Central American countries, African Americans, American Indians, and immigrants from as far away as Morocco and the Pacific Islands. Further, as mining operations became more elaborate and industrial, the towns more closely resembled the established industrial cities in the East—complete with schools, theaters, and churches.

Ranching and the Era of the Cowboy in the West

After the completion of transcontinental rail lines, cattle-ranching operations were established on the **Great Plains**. Ranching gave rise to the era of the cowboy, romanticized in Western literature and movies. From the mid-1860s to the mid-1880s, **cowboys** drove large herds of cattle across the open plains. These cowboys, many of whom were African American and Mexican, herded the cattle to seasonal grazing areas, and then, to railroad stops, where they would be shipped to **Chicago** for slaughter. By the mid-1880s, several factors ended the era of open-range grazing. Large ranchers began to enclose grazing areas with newly-invented **barbed wire**. These enclosures ended the era of driving herds across open plains. Further, severe blizzards in the late 1880s decimated the cattle population of the Great Plains. When the herds recovered, free-spirited cowboys were replaced by wage-earning hired hands, working under managers on the giant ranches.

Farming on the Great Plains

As the promise of gold and silver drew many people to the West in the years before and after the Civil War, the promise of owning land drew many more people west. The **Homestead Act** (1862) and the completion of the **transcontinental railroad** (1869) facilitated the movement of settlers. In the last three decades of the nineteenth century, millions of native-born whites, immigrants, and African Americans settled on farms west of the Mississippi River. From the last years of the Civil War until the turn of the twentieth century, nine new states in the Great Plains region and farther west joined the United States starting with Nevada (1864) and Nebraska (1867) and ending with Wyoming (1890) and Utah (1896). The populations of Minnesota, the Dakotas, Kansas, and Nebraska all grew dramatically between the end of the Civil War and 1900: from 300,000 to 5 million.

Early pioneers drawn to the Great Plains were nicknamed **"sodbusters"** because they had to cut through the thick layer of sod to get to the topsoil needed for farming. Many of these settlers used the cut sod itself to build their houses (nicknamed "soddies").

About a fifth of the farmers who established farms in this era obtained land directly from the government through the Homestead Act and similar federal legislation. Most farmers purchased land either from railroads, which had substantial holdings as a result of land grants from the government, or from speculators who obtained land from unsuccessful homesteaders. As the century progressed, the dream of land ownership proved to be beyond the means of many people. The **family farms** of the prairie gave way to **large-scale agribusiness**. By the late 1800s, a system of agricultural production and distribution developed, drawing western grain farmers into national and international markets. The costs of mechanization and irrigation drove many farmers into debt, leading to bankruptcies and consolidation. Large-scale farming in the West followed a pattern similar to mining and ranching operations. By the end of the century, increasing numbers of residents of the West were migrant farmers, tenant farmers, sharecroppers, and hired employees as land was consolidated into fewer and fewer hands.

B. Violence on the Frontier

The period following the Civil War witnessed the most violent Indian warfare since the colonial period. Union forces had established a presence on the Great Plains during the Civil War. During the war, violent episodes included the Dakota War (1862) and the Colorado War (1864-1865). (See more on violence on the frontier in the period leading up to the Civil War, pages 183-184.) The movement of settlers in the years following the Civil War put additional pressures on land in the West held by American Indians and led the federal government to violate treaties it had made with the various tribes.

Destruction of the Buffalo

As railroads pushed westward, the herds of the **American bison** (commonly known as **buffalo**) were wiped out. Railroad workers and passengers went on a killing spree, shooting buffalo for food and (mostly) sport. Also, industrial uses for the hides of buffalo put pressure on their numbers. In a matter of decades, the buffalo herds on the Plains were virtually exterminated. This greatly weakened the Plains peoples, who depended on the buffalo for spiritual and physical sustenance.

Red Cloud's War and the Second Treaty of Fort Laramie

Violence on the frontier increased during and immediately following the **Civil War** (1861-1865). The **Homestead Act** (1863) and the development of railroad lines brought a wave of settlers into the **Great Plains** region. Between 1866 and 1868, fighting occurred in the **Wyoming** and **Montana Territories** between the **Lakota**, **Northern Cheyenne**, and **Northern Arapaho** on one side, and **U.S. troops** on the other. This fighting, known as **Red Cloud's War,** included a major defeat for U.S. forces known as **Fetterman's Massacre**. The fighting ended with the **Second Treaty of Fort Laramie** (1868), in which the United States allowed the Lakota to maintain much of the disputed territory and agreed to close the **Bozeman Trail.**

The Indian Peace Commission (1867)

In 1867, Congress tried to negotiate an end of warring on the Great Plains by establishing the **Indian Peace Commission**. The commission met in **St. Louis, Missouri**, throughout 1867 and 1868 with a number of Plains Indian tribes. Although several treaties were negotiated, Congress did not consistently fund or enforce agreements made by the commission. Further, the government did not understand nor recognize the decision-making process of the different Indian groups. A primary goal of the commission was to further confine Indian groups to reservations and pursue a policy of **assimilation**. (See more on assimilation on page 221.) The commission was seen as a failure, as fighting on the Great Plains continued over the next decade.

The Battle of the Little Big Horn and Custer's Last Stand (1876)

The discovery of gold in the **Black Hills** of the **Dakota Territory** in 1874 brought a new wave of settlers into the northern Plains region and brought tensions to a peak. These tensions resulted in the **Great Sioux War** in 1876. Sioux warriors, along with Cheyenne allies, achieved a major victory over American forces at the **Battle of the Little Big Horn**. The episode, also known as **Custer's Last Stand**, resulted in the death of **General George Custer** along with 225 of his men. Subsequently, U.S. forces led by **General Philip Sheridan** soundly defeated American Indian forces. The Lakota Sioux, the largest and most powerful tribe of the Plains Indians, were then confined to a reservation in the Dakota Territory. The defeat of the Sioux was a major turning point in the long campaign by the government of controlling the previously autonomous American Indian tribes of the Great Plains.

C. Government Policies and the Fate of American Indians

American attitudes and policies toward native peoples sometimes emphasized assimilation, sometimes removal, and sometimes extermination. All these approaches saw Indians as a problem that needed to be rectified.

President Grant and the "Peace Policy"

In 1869, **President Ulysses S. Grant** announced that the government would pursue a **"peace policy"** in regard to American Indians. The main pillar of this policy was **assimilation**. The shift involved a move away from negotiating treaties with different American Indian nations. Rather, the individual Indians would become "wards of the state" and would be "civilized" by emissaries from the government. This paternalistic arrangement would be accompanied by a move away from reservations and toward individual ownership of plots of land. Eventually, according to the policy, Indians would become citizens of the United States rather than members of Indian nations. The policy did not initially gain many adherents, but the goal of assimilation would later be reflected in the 1887 Dawes Severalty Act (see below).

Helen Hunt Jackson and the Call for Reform

By the 1880s, sympathizers of American Indians pushed for a change in government policy, away from the warfare that characterized the era. A prominent reformer was **Helen Hunt Jackson**, whose 1882 book, *A Century of Dishonor*, chronicled the abuses the U.S. government committed against native peoples. She sent a copy of the book to each member of Congress. Historians have placed the activism of Jackson and other women within the context of gender norms in the Victorian era. It was seen as the duty of white middle-class women to civilize people. This duty was evident in the call for a reduction of cruelty toward American Indians by government forces. It can also be seen in the desire to "civilize" native peoples. These women were successful in lobbying for the 1887 Dawes Severalty Act (see below).

The Dawes Severalty Act (1887)

Efforts at reform resulted in a shift in government policy toward American Indians. The **Dawes Severalty Act** (1887), also known as the General Allotment Act, abandoned the reservation system and divided tribal lands into individually owned plots ("severalty," in this case, refers to lands that are owned by individuals, not owned jointly). The goal of the policy was for American Indians to assimilate into white culture—specifically into the norms of white middle-class culture. The idea of forcing Indians to have private dwellings, with gardens and fences, reflected ideal middle-class living arrangements. This reform proved to be as damaging to American Indians as was the earlier reservation policy.

> **USING REASONING PROCESSES:**
> **CONTINUITY AND CHANGE**
>
> **Changing American Indian Policy**
>
> In the 1930s, the federal government moved away from the assimilationist Dawes Severalty Act. Rather than mandate the division of American Indian lands, the government eventually undid this destructive policy with the Indian Reorganization Act (1934), allowing autonomy for tribal lands.

Indian Boarding Schools

Beginning in the late 1870s, the **Bureau of Indian Affairs** established a series of **Indian boarding schools** that were designed to assimilate American Indian children into white culture by stripping them of their culture. The **Carlisle Institute** in Pennsylvania, established in 1879, was a model for other schools. Students were forced to cut their hair and to rid themselves of traditional clothing. They also had to practice Christianity and were trained in menial tasks. **Colonel Richard Henry Pratt**, who was the headmaster at the Carlisle Institute for twenty-five years, neatly summed up the goal of the schools—his motto was, **"Kill the Indian in him, and save the man."**

D. American Indian Resistance

By the 1880s, in the face of continued encroachments and defeats, American Indians developed different strategies to respond to threats to their land. The U.S. government responded to resistance with violence, resulting in the end of autonomous American Indian groups in the United States.

The Ghost Dance Movement

In the midst of the apocalyptic losses suffered by American Indians in the 1870s and 1880s, some tribes adopted a spiritual practice known as the **Ghost Dance**. The Ghost Dance movement was developed by a Northern Paiute prophet named **Wovoka**. He drew on traditional American Indian rituals, emphasizing cooperation among tribes and clean living and honesty. It was not successful in stopping white incursions, but it led to a spiritual revival that had a profound effect on Indian tribes into the twentieth century.

Wounded Knee and the End of Autonomous American Indian Groups

By the 1880s, the last autonomous American Indians had been defeated in the **"Indian Wars"** and brought under U.S. control through a series of military conflicts. From the earliest encounters between settlers and American Indians, settlers had encroached upon tribal lands and, using superior firepower, pushed Indians farther into the interior of the continent.

The last "battle" of the "Indian Wars" was a massacre at the Lakota reservation near **Wounded Knee Creek** in South Dakota in 1890. U.S. forces attempted to peacefully disarm a group of **Lakota Sioux Indians** camped there, but soon the U.S. troops opened fire on them. More than 200 Lakota men, women, and children were killed.

Topic 6.4 The "New South"

Promoters of a "New South" encouraged industrialization and modernization in the southern states. Although some segments of the southern economy experienced industrialization, overall the South remained predominantly agrarian, with sharecropping and tenant farming dominating the region. The limited industrial growth that occurred in the "New South" offered few opportunities for African Americans. White supremacy and "Jim Crow" policies relegated African Americans to a second-class citizenship in the post-Reconstruction South.

A. The Limited Success of Calls for a "New South"

After the Civil War, several southern public figures argued for a "New South." It was hoped that southern industrialists could join forces with northern businessmen and bankers and create a more modern South.

The Persistence of Tradition in the "New South"

The most prominent spokesmen for a **"New South"** was **Henry Grady**, an Atlanta journalist. He argued for a mixed economy in the South that would include industrialization. He wanted to move away from the single-crop plantation agriculture of the "Old South." There were pockets of industrialization in the South, especially textile production. However, for the most part, the promise of a "New South" proved to be hollow. For the remainder of the nineteenth century, and well into the twentieth century, the South remained mired in poverty and underdevelopment. African Americans continued to toil in the **sharecropping system** or as **tenant farmers** (see page 203). Both systems involved African Americans working land that they did not own. In the sharecropping system, farmers would pay "rent" with a portion—or share—of their yearly crop. Tenant farming was a slight step up the social ladder from sharecropping. Generally, tenant farmers rented land from a landowner, paying in cash. Often the tenant farmer owned his own tools and only had to rent the land itself at a fixed rate.

B. Segregation in the "New South"

Racist social theories became prominent in the Gilded Age. These theories, along with the Supreme Court decision in the *Plessy v. Ferguson* case, sanctioned discrimination, segregation, and even violence against African Americans. African-American reformers challenged white supremacy and fought for political and social equality.

The Proliferation of the "Jim Crow" System

After **Reconstruction** ended (1877), African Americans saw the gains from this era—in terms of political and economic rights—steadily erode. **Jim Crow laws** segregated public facilities such as railroad cars, restrooms, and schools. These laws further relegated African Americans to second-class status in the South. Though the **Fourteenth Amendment** (1868) guaranteed all citizens equal protection of the laws, in the *Slaughterhouse Cases* (1873), the Supreme Court had ruled that the Fourteenth Amendment applied only to national citizenship rights, such as the right to vote in national elections and the right to travel between states—not to rights derived from "state citizenship" (see pages 203–204). In this legal setting, Jim Crow laws proliferated throughout the South.

Plessy v. Ferguson and the "Separate but Equal" Doctrine

In the case of *Plessy v. Ferguson* (1896), the Supreme Court decided that racial segregation did not violate the equal protection provision of the **Fourteenth Amendment** (1868). The decision was a setback for those who sought an end to the **Jim Crow system** of racial segregation in the South. Jim Crow laws were state and local ordinances that first appeared after Reconstruction ended (1877). Typical laws called for separate schools or separate train cars for African Americans. Opponents of racial segregation argued that Jim Crow laws violated the Fourteenth Amendment. This amendment, ratified during Reconstruction, stated that no person shall be denied **"equal protection of the laws."** Jim Crow laws, opponents argued, violated the Fourteenth Amendment because the laws relegated African Americans to inferior public accommodations and had the effect of making them second-class citizens. However, the Court disagreed. The decision established the **"separate but equal" doctrine**, stating that segregation was acceptable as long as the facilities for both races were of equal quality.

Challenging Jim Crow in the Gilded Age

In the face of segregation and marginalization, African Americans did not remain passive. **Ida B. Wells** was one of the more radical African-American voices for social justice in the Gilded Age. As a young woman, she sued the Memphis and Charleston Railroad for denying her a seat in the ladies' car. Initially she won the case, but the railroad ultimately won on appeal. After three friends of hers were lynched, Wells began to write and campaign against the practice of lynching. Her journalism deconstructed many of the myths around **lynching**. In particular, she challenged the assertion of many Southern whites that sexual assault of white women by Black men was a frequent occurrence, and that lynching was therefore justifiable. "Nobody," she wrote, "in this section of the country believes the old threadbare lie that black men rape white women." She asserted that lynching was a tactic to suppress African-American political activism and to reassert white supremacy. Another important Gilded Age activist was **Booker T. Washington**, who encouraged African Americans to gain training in vocational skills. Toward this end, he was selected to be the first leader of the Tuskegee Institute (1881). He argued that confrontation with whites would end badly for African Americans; he counseled cooperation with supportive whites and collective self-improvement. Later, his conciliatory approach was challenged by the more radical **W. E. B. Du Bois** (see page 264).

Topic 6.5 Technological Innovation

Innovations in technology in the period following the Civil War allowed for greater access to natural resources. These innovations were essential for the expansion of industrial production that came to define the Gilded Age.

A. The Raw Materials of Industrialization

The rapid expansion of industrial production in the post–Civil War era was made possible by advances in technology. New forms of technology provided growing industrial operations with raw materials and new forms of fuel.

Steel and the Bessemer Process

Steel production was key to the industrialization of the United States. Iron production grew throughout the nineteenth century and was used extensively as the railroad system developed in the United States. Steel, an alloy made through the chemical bonding of iron with carbon, was far more durable, versatile, and useful than iron. Steel has existed since antiquity, but before the middle of the nineteenth century, it was too expensive to be commercially useful. The development of the **Bessemer process** by the Englishman **Henry Bessemer** greatly reduced the cost of steel and made it available to a wide variety of industrial operations. The process, which involved blowing air into molten iron, was patented by Bessemer in 1856. By the late 1860s, a more efficient production method, called the open-hearth process, replaced the Bessemer process.

Coal and Oil

The new industrial processes of the Gilded Age required new forms of fuel. The most practical fuel was a form of hard coal called **anthracite**. It was readily available in western Pennsylvania. Later, softer coal, called **bituminous**, came into wide use in industrial processes.

In the 1850s, innovators such as **George Bissell** demonstrated that oil could be refined and used for a variety of processes, such as illuminating lamps. Its most important industrial use in the nineteenth century was lubricating machinery. Bissell raised money to attempt to drill for oil in western Pennsylvania. The first oil well was established by one of Bissell's employees, **Edwin Drake**, in 1859 in Titusville, Pennsylvania. Later in the century, the demand for oil increased as it came to be refined into gasoline, a fuel for automobiles.

Topic 6.6 The Rise of Industrial Capitalism

During the last decades of the nineteenth century, the United States experienced unprecedented changes in production as large-scale industry and business consolidation replaced older forms of production. These changes were accompanied by expanding international communications networks and pro-business government policies. The age was marked by new forms of consumption and marketing.

A. The Rise of the Corporation and Mass Production

In addition to technological advances (see Topic 6.5), a variety of factors contributed to a dramatic increase in the production of goods after the Civil War. New business and managerial models, advances in marketing, and a growing labor force all contributed to the development of mass production.

The Evolution of the Corporation and the Managerial Revolution

Before the Civil War, many states made it significantly easier for an entity to **incorporate** (see more on incorporation laws, page 145). An early entity to incorporate was the **Pennsylvania Railroad** in 1846. Many companies followed suit in the period following the Civil War. Large corporations developed management systems that separated top executives from managers who were responsible for day-to-day operations. This **managerial revolution** included modern cost-accounting procedures and the division of responsibilities. A new class of middle managers evolved in the post–Civil War period, supervising the various departments, such as purchasing, accounting, marketing, and sales. The managerial revolution also created the need for secretaries and other office workers, opening up new opportunities for women in the workforce (see more on women in the workplace, page 227).

Advances in Marketing and Distribution

During the last three decades of the nineteenth century, **industrial capitalism** devised methods to distribute the large quantities of goods produced by the growing **factory system**. As the living standards of many working-class people began to show signs of growth (see page 227), patterns of consumption began to change. Many products, most notably clothing, went from home production to commercial production. Over the course of the nineteenth century, ready-made clothing replaced homemade clothing. Commercially prepared canned food made inroads with families who had been used to growing and processing their own foodstuffs.

Chain Outlets and Department Stores

During the last decades of the nineteenth century, new types of retail outlets began to supplement, and to some degree replace, traditional small-scale, locally owned stores. By the end of the nineteenth century, chains such as the **Atlantic and Pacific (A & P) Tea Company** (groceries) and **F. W. Woolworth** (manufactured dry goods) opened outlets in cities and towns throughout the United States. Opulent department stores, such as **Wanamaker's** in Philadelphia and **Macy's** in New York City, catered to middle-class residents. Companies such as **Sears, Roebuck** and **Montgomery Ward** printed **mail-order catalogs** of the products they sold and encouraged people to purchase items from the catalogs using **installment payment plans**. Being far from a metropolitan center and the actual stores was no longer an impediment to participating in the burgeoning consumer culture of the late nineteenth century because of mail-order catalogs.

The Labor Force in the Industrial Era

The expansion of industry required a growing labor force. Migrants from within the United States and abroad were drawn to America's industrial cities during the Gilded Age. Before the Civil War, **immigrants** were primarily from northern and western Europe—Great Britain, Ireland, and the Germanic states. By the 1870s, new sources of immigration included southern and eastern Europe, Mexico, and China (until passage of the Chinese Exclusion Act in 1882) (see more on the "new immigration," page 230). Employers often hired recruiters to entice Europeans to immigrate to America. Recruiters paid for the passage of these immigrants, with the money later deducted from their wages. This practice was made illegal in 1885, but the flow of immigrants continued until the first decades of the twentieth century.

B. Economic Consolidation

Consolidation, monopolies, trusts, and holding companies became defining features of the business landscape during the Gilded Age. Wealth and power became concentrated in fewer and fewer hands.

The Rise of Major Industries

During the Gilded Age of the late 1800s, the era of small, locally oriented businesses began to give way to large corporations and trusts that came to dominate entire industries. The three most important industries of the era were **railroads**, the **steel industry**, and the **oil industry**. The corporate model spread to a wide variety of industrial processes, including the production of bicycles, clothing, shoes, and paper, as well as the processing of food products.

Andrew Carnegie and Vertical Integration (or Consolidation)

Andrew Carnegie came to dominate the steel industry by investing in all aspects of steel production. **Carnegie Steel Company** (which was sold to United States Steel in 1901) controlled not only the mills where the steel was made, but also the coal mines that supplied the coal used in steel production and the iron ore mines that supplied the base metal of steel. In addition,

> **USING HISTORICAL THINKING SKILLS:**
> **CLAIMS AND EVIDENCE IN SOURCES**
>
> **Mark Twain and The Gilded Age**
>
> The term "Gilded Age" was coined by Mark Twain and Charles Dudley Warner in their novel, *The Gilded Age: A Tale of Today* (1873). The novel satirizes the greed, corruption, and excess of the late 1800s. The term alludes to gold leaf gilding on statues. These statues might be shiny like gold, but beneath the surface is often just cheap plaster or a base metal. The age had great wealth, but beneath the surface was desperate poverty. Twain and Dudley got the idea for the term from Shakespeare's *King John*: "To gild refined gold, to paint the lily... is wasteful and ridiculous excess."

Carnegie controlled transportation lines—the ships that transported the iron ore and the railroads that transported the coal to the factory. This type of organization—in which all key aspects of the business are performed by the particular company—is called **vertical integration**.

Rockefeller and Horizontal Integration (or Consolidation)

Horizontal integration entails the merging of companies that create the same or similar products. This process can lead to a monopoly if a company captures the vast majority of the market for a particular product or service. A common way that corporations gained monopoly control of an industry was by establishing trusts. A trust consisted of trustees from several companies involved in the same industry acting together rather than in competition with one another. **John D. Rockefeller** organized, in the oil-processing industry, the most well-known trust: **Standard Oil**.

Other Business Leaders of the Gilded Age

Andrew Carnegie and John D. Rockefeller were the most famous industrial and business leaders of the second half of the nineteenth century. Others included **Collis P. Huntington**, a railroad magnate; **Mark Hanna**, a coal and iron merchant who became a leading senator from Ohio; **Philip Armour**, a meat-processing giant in Chicago; and **Stephen Elkins**, a magnate in mining, railroads, and politics. Financiers, such as **J. P. Morgan**, parlayed leverage through control of various industries, including several railroad companies, into dominance of the entire U.S. economy. The power and scope of these men led reformers to call for legislation to check their influence over the economy and to reign in monopolistic practices (see page 237).

C. Corporations Look Abroad

In the last decades of the nineteenth century, American businessmen—investors, traders, and factory owners—began to realize the potential of overseas economic expansion.

The Growth of Multinational Corporations

Foreign trade was rapidly expanding in the Gilded Age. In 1870, American exports totaled just under $400 million. A decade later, the figure had more than doubled to over $850 million. By the turn of the twentieth century, it was $1.4 billion. In the 1880s and 1890s, several companies including Standard Oil, Eastman Kodak, and American Tobacco had established branches in other countries. The economic downturn following the **Panic of 1893** further encouraged businessmen to seek new markets abroad. Further, the perception that the American frontier had "closed" pushed American business to seek opportunities in foreign lands. The historian **Frederick Jackson Turner**, in his influential essay, **"The Significance of the Frontier in American History"** (1893), argued that the West was essential for American economic growth. Now that it had been settled, the next logical step for American economic expansion, many thought, was foreign lands. (See Topic 7.2 for more on economic expansion as an impetus for American imperialism.)

Topic 6.7 Labor in the Gilded Age

The United States experienced unprecedented economic growth in the last decades of the nineteenth century, but the fruits of that growth were not equally distributed. The era witnessed a growing gap between the wealthy and the poor. As the working class expanded, a series of pitched conflicts over wages and working conditions occurred at industrial worksites. Workers suffered some major setbacks in these conflicts and failed to significantly alter the distribution of wealth in the Gilded Age.

A. Poverty and Wealth in Industrializing America

As America became increasingly industrialized, communities became divided between the wealthy, living lives of opulence and "conspicuous consumption," and those living in poverty. However, despite long hours and low wages, the relative standard of living improved for many working-class Americans, as the prices of many goods and services decreased.

The Wealthy Class

The decades after the Civil War, often referred to as the **Gilded Age** (see box, page 225), saw the growth of a well-to-do class that greatly surpassed previous wealthy classes in terms of money, cohesiveness, and power. These wealthy businessmen built gaudy mansions in exclusive urban neighborhoods and equally sumptuous summer "cottages" in Newport, Rhode Island, and other exclusive enclaves. The social critic and economist **Thorstein Veblen,** in his book, *The Theory of the Leisure Class* (1899), coined the phrase "conspicuous consumption" to describe the lavish spending habits of the wealthy.

The Working Class

Wages for workers rose slightly in the decades after the Civil War, but were well below levels that economists consider necessary for a minimum degree of comfort. Further, wages could be cut during economic downturns, as is evident in the years following the **Panics of 1873 and 1893**. Also, workers were vulnerable to the seasonal nature of work. However, the individuals and families who had recently relocated to industrial cities and towns had amounts of spending money that were unimaginable in their former places of residence—whether small farms in Kansas or rural villages in southern Italy. Further, although wage increases were meager, prices were falling for mass-produced goods during the Gilded Age. These trends made a world of new goods and services available to many working-class people.

B. An Expanding Workforce

The industrial expansion of the United States in the decades following the Civil War required an ever-growing workforce. Much of the demand for new workers was met by a wave of immigration to the United States in the late 1800s (see page 230). In addition, women and children joined the labor force in growing numbers.

Women and Children in the Labor Force

As the nature of work changed from skilled craftsmanship to unskilled tasks in a mass-production system, children and women began to enter the paid workforce in large numbers. Because wages for working-class men remained relatively low, families often had to supplement their incomes with children and women entering the labor force. In turn, the influx of women and children into the labor force depressed overall wages. From the 1870s until World War I, **child labor** grew each decade. By 1900, children, aged ten to fifteen years old, made up 18 percent of the industrial workforce. The number of women in working-class communities who worked in the industrial labor force also increased in the Gilded Age. By 1900, women made up 17 percent of the industrial workforce.

C. Conflict at the Work Site

The post–Civil War period witnessed a marked increase in the number and intensity of workplace conflicts between labor and management. Workers organized local and national unions and engaged in battles with management over wages and working conditions.

The Declining Status of Work in the Age of Industrialization

Workers saw their position and status erode during the Gilded Age period, as cutthroat competition and mechanization of the production processes worsened working conditions. Wages rose incrementally for workers during this period, but gains were precarious—often erased during cyclical downturns in the economy. In addition, the increased reliance on child labor and the growing number of immigrants further eroded wages. The wealth generated by the rapid expansion of industry in the post–Civil War period was certainly not evenly distributed.

In addition, marginal gains in income were offset by a countervailing trend—the loss of control over the processes of production. Mass-production techniques entailed the breakdown of processes, so that workers would perform a specific task that did not require a great deal of training or skill. The age of the autonomous craftsman, who determined the conditions and pace of work, went by the wayside in the age of industrial capitalism. This **"de-skilling"** of the work process led not only to a loss of any sense of pride in one's work but also to an increase in unsafe and unsanitary conditions. The **loss of control** of the work process was often a root cause of worker grievances in the Gilded Age. Many workers responded by forming and joining labor organizations, or **unions**, to advance their cause through **collective bargaining** and, if all else failed, through **striking**.

An Era of Pitched Battles in the Workplace

The fierce **labor battles** of the Gilded Age were almost exclusively won by management, with its near monopoly on weaponry, the support of the government and the courts, and vast numbers of poor, working-class men willing to serve as strikebreakers. These battles often occurred in the wake of announced pay cuts during the economic downturns of the 1870s and of the 1890s.

The Knights of Labor

A significant early union was the **Knights of Labor**, founded in 1869. This union welcomed all members, regardless of race, gender, or level of skill. The Knights, led by **Terence V. Powderly** in the late 1880s, had a broad agenda that included not only improvements in wages and hours for their workers, but also social reforms such as better safety rules and an end to child labor. By 1886, the organization had approximately 800,000 members, but by the 1890s a series of circumstances, as well as organizational problems, caused a sharp decline in the Knights' membership and influence. Ethnic, linguistic, and racial barriers among members of the Knights of Labor made united action more difficult. In addition, a centralized and autocratic governing structure within the Knights of Labor prevented new leadership from expanding the organization. Finally, government repression in the wake of the Haymarket bombing in Chicago (see below) weakened the organization.

The Great Railroad Strike of 1877

In 1877, the **Baltimore and Ohio Railroad (B&O)** announced a 10 percent pay cut for its workers. Wages had already been falling during the economic depression that followed the **Panic of 1873**. Railroad workers in West Virginia went on strike. Fellow workers down the line—in Pittsburgh, Chicago, and even San Francisco—followed suit. At its height, the **Great Railroad Strike** involved more than 100,000 railroad workers and more than half a million other workers. Violence erupted in nine states. **President Rutherford B. Hayes** called out federal troops, many recently withdrawn from enforcing Reconstruction policies in the South. Many observers thought a second civil war was unfolding.

The Haymarket Incident (1886)

In 1886, a strike at the **McCormick Reaper Works** in Chicago turned violent. Unskilled workers at the McCormick works struck and their jobs were quickly given to **"scabs"** (replacement workers). The striking workers attacked several of the "scabs" on May 3, two days after a large **May Day rally** in Chicago to demand an eight-hour day. The police and Pinkerton guards opened fire on the strikers, killing or injuring six men. The strikers called for a rally on

May 4 in **Haymarket Square**. Toward the end of the rally a bomb exploded in the midst of the police ranks. Several police were killed. The police responded by opening fire on the rally. Eight strikers were tried and convicted on scanty evidence; four were executed. At the time, many Americans shied away from the perceived violence of the labor movement. The popularity of the **Knights of Labor** diminished in the aftermath of the incident.

The American Federation of Labor (1886)

The **American Federation of Labor**, formed in 1886, differed from the Knights of Labor in that it included only skilled workers, the "aristocracy of labor." It did not permit unskilled workers to join, nor did it allow African Americans or women to join. It was known as a **craft union**, in distinction from the Knights, which was an **industrial union**. Further, the AFL did not engage in any sort of political activities. It was known as a **"bread and butter"** union, in that its one goal was getting higher wages and better conditions for its members. It did not work for broader social reform. The AFL maintained a growing membership into the twentieth century. One of its founders and its first leader was a cigar maker named **Samuel Gompers**.

The Homestead Strike (1892)

A momentous labor battle took place at **Andrew Carnegie's** steelworks in **Homestead, Pennsylvania**, in 1892. Though Carnegie had the reputation of being a friend of labor, he was determined to break the union known as the **Amalgamated Association of Iron and Steel Workers**, a powerful craft union under the AFL umbrella. When the Amalgamated's contract expired in 1892, Carnegie announced that he would not renew it—in effect breaking the union. Carnegie traveled outside of the country in the summer of 1892 and left the plant under the control of manager **Henry Clay Frick**, a notorious anti-union man. Frick built a fence around the plant, locked out the workers, brought in "scabs," and hired **Pinkerton guards** to enforce his edicts. A battle ensued between the "Pinks" and the workers. The workers won a temporary victory and took over the plant, but the governor then called in 8,000 National Guard troops to retake it. Frick was able to reopen the plant, without union workers, in a devastating blow for organized labor.

The Pullman Strike: Strife in a Company Town (1894)

The **Pullman Strike** occurred during the economic downturn following the **Panic of 1893**. The **Pullman Company**, which built railroad cars, cut wages several times in 1893 and 1894. Pullman was also the name of the town in Illinois where the workers lived. The town was built by the Pullman Company in 1880 as a model company town. The housing was better than most working-class housing but was also more costly. The town exemplified the two sides of company towns—on the one hand it provided decent housing, but on the other hand it allowed the company to have a great deal of control over its workers and to deny housing to "troublemakers" (such as pro-union workers). The company owned all the housing, and rent was taken directly out of wages. When wages were cut in 1893 and 1894, rents were not cut. Workers appealed to the **American Railway Union** (ARU), led by **Eugene V. Debs**, to come to their aid. In May 1894, three union organizers were fired. In response to these firings, most of the 3,300 workers went on strike. ARU members across the nation voted to support the strike by refusing to handle trains that

---

USING REASONING PROCESSES:
CONTINUITY AND CHANGE

The Federal Government and Unions Over Time (I)

Federal actions in regard to unions changed dramatically between the Gilded Age and the era of the New Deal in the 1930s. During the Gilded Age, the federal government generally sided with management over labor. *In re Debs* (1895), for example, upheld the government's injunction against the Pullman Strike. Federal courts in the 1890s, including the Supreme Court, consistently allowed the Sherman Antitrust Act (1890) to be used by the government to outlaw many union activities. In the 1930s, however, the opposite was true—the federal government gave its support to the efforts of organized labor. Section 7(a) of the National Industrial Recovery Act (1933) guaranteed the right of workers to form unions. After the act was struck down by the Supreme Court, the Wagner Act (1935) reaffirmed the right of private sector employees to organize into unions, engage in collective bargaining, and take collective action such as strikes. (See also box on page 323.)

contained Pullman cars. Railroad traffic was brought to a standstill. Courts issued two injunctions against the strike. **President Grover Cleveland** eventually called out federal troops to put it down. Violence immediately ensued, leading to the death of twenty-five strikers. The strike ended in defeat for the union, with new workers hired by Pullman. Following the episode, the Supreme Court, in its decision in the judicial proceeding entitled *In re Debs* (1895), asserted that the government was justified in stopping the strike.

Topic 6.8 Immigration and Migration in the Gilded Age

During the age of industrial expansion, the population of urban centers grew dramatically. Migrants from abroad and from within the United States flooded into American cities and created a new urban culture.

A. Migrations and a Diverse Workforce

After 1880, immigration took on new importance in providing a steady stream of workers for American factories and in transforming American society. Cities drew immigrants from southern and eastern Europe as well as from Asia. In addition, African Americans began leaving the rural South to come to cities in the South and in the North. A number of factors propelled these migrations—religious persecution, poverty, and the lack of social mobility in the countries and regions of origin of the migrants. These migrations created a more diverse labor force.

The "New Immigration"

The large wave of immigrants who came to the United States between 1880 and 1920 was essential to the industrialization of the United States. Immigration patterns changed during the years of the Gilded Age. The Irish and German immigrations of the pre–Civil War years were supplemented by waves of immigrants from **southern and eastern Europe** and other areas. An estimated twenty million people immigrated to the United States, most settling in industrial cities such as New York, Pittsburgh, and Chicago. The label **"new immigrants"** was applied to these groups.

The bulk of these immigrants tended to come from the agricultural areas just outside the industrial core of Europe and North America as traditional economic patterns in these agrarian regions broke down in the face of capitalist development. The "new immigrants" included large numbers of people from Russia, Italy, Poland, and the Balkan region. The number of immigrants from China was growing until the government passed the Chinese Exclusion Act (1882) (see page 218). Immigrants were drawn to the economic opportunities of the United States, although many Jews left Russia to avoid anti-Semitic massacres known as **pogroms**.

The "Exoduster" Movement

As **Reconstruction** came to an end (see pages 201–202), many African Americans in the South realized that they were losing the few white political allies they had in their home states. The withdrawal of federal oversight in the South, accompanied by a rise in **Ku Klux Klan** violence and the enactment of Jim Crow laws, solidified the status of African Americans as second-class citizens. In this atmosphere, some African Americans decided to abandon the South. Starting in the late 1870s, a movement of approximately 40,000 African Americans—labeled the **"Exoduster" movement**—departed from states along the western tier of the former Confederacy, crossing the Mississippi River to settle in Kansas. Smaller numbers settled in Oklahoma and Colorado. Some "Exodusters" made it only as far as Missouri. African-American activists and white philanthropists established organizations, such as the **Colored Relief Board** and the **Kansas Freedmen's Aid Society**, to help "Exodusters" make the journey to Kansas. The most successful "Exodusters" settled in the growing towns of Kansas.

B. The New Culture of the Immigrant City

The growing cities of the Gilded Age provided new cultural opportunities for their residents, but also began to show deep social and economic divides along lines of class, race, ethnicity, and culture.

A Divided City

The **Gilded Age** is characterized by a bifurcation, or division, of the city between **working-class districts** and **wealthy enclaves**. Before the Civil War, different classes lived in close proximity to one another. An owner of a printing shop, for example, might live on the second and third stories of a building above his street-level shop. His apprentices might live in his attic—owner and workers under one roof. However, in the second half of the century, the middle class and the wealthy moved from the industrial zones, away from the noisy factories and docks and from the stench of the slaughterhouses. In **New York City**, the wealthy moved uptown; elsewhere, they moved away from the urban core. In the bifurcated city, the working-class districts tended to become utterly squalid, while the wealthier areas had the nicest amenities—wider streets, large parks, and sunlight.

Living Conditions for the Working Class and the Poor

Despite modest increases in wages, the working class and the poor were often crowded into substandard **tenement housing** in slumlike neighborhoods. The densest neighborhood in the world in the late 1800s was the **Lower East Side** of New York City. Conditions there were typical of many similar districts in other cities—lack of ventilation and light, streets thick with horse dung, and a lack of basic municipal services, such as sewer lines, running water, and garbage removal. The conditions of the poor were chronicled in photojournalist **Jacob Riis's** *How the Other Half Lives*. His grim photographs of tenement life drew many people's attention to the plight of the poor.

> **USING HISTORICAL THINKING SKILLS:**
> **SOURCING AND SITUATION**
>
> **Was Jacob Riis a Racist?**
>
> In analyzing audience in regard to Jacob Riis's book, *How the Other Half Lives,* notice how the book reflects the perceptions and prejudices that his middle-class audience tended to hold at the time. His descriptions of "hot-headed" Italians, of "senseless idolatry" among Chinese people, and of "the Jew [who] runs to real estate as soon as he can save up enough for a deposit to clinch the bargain," appear to many readers today as insensitive and reductionist, but may have been received approvingly by his audience at the time the book was written.

Working-Class Culture and Urban Life

Modest increases in wages and a slightly shorter workday provided more opportunities for **leisure-time activities** for the masses of urban residents. The large number of working-class people moving into cities transformed urban culture and changed the physical city itself. The most popular leisure-time activity for working-class men was drinking in saloons. **Saloons** were often part social hall, part political club, and part community hub. The reformist attacks on saloons, and on alcohol consumption in general (see page 242), were seen as attacks on working-class immigrant culture as much as they were on drunkenness.

Topic 6.9 Responses to Immigration in the Gilded Age

The large-scale immigration to the United States in the last decades of the nineteenth century generated a variety of responses from different individuals and groups. Immigrants themselves negotiated between the cultures of their homeland and of the United States. Americans already living in the United States debated whether immigrants should be welcomed or rejected. The ideas of Social Darwinism emerged during this era and were at odds with reformers who sought to aid recently-arrived immigrants.

A. Debates over Identity and Immigration

Immigrants often grappled with issues of assimilation—how much would they "Americanize" and how much would they seek to retain their native cultures? In addition, many Americans already living in the country expressed concerns about the identity of the United States in an era of mass immigration.

The Persistence of Ethnicity in the Gilded Age City

The large number of immigrants pouring into the United States in the late 1800s dramatically altered the social geography of American cities (see page 282). At the same time, the experience of moving to the United States remade the immigrants themselves. Immigrants from the small towns and rural areas of Europe had to adjust to life in urban America. They felt the pull of **assimilation** on one hand and the desire to maintain a sense of **ethnic solidarity** on the other. In New York, Chicago, and other large cities, foreign-language papers emerged, such as the Yiddish-language *Jewish Daily Forward* (*Forverts*) and the Italian-language *Il Progresso Italo-Americano*. Parts of New York, such as lower Manhattan's **Little Italy** and the Jewish areas of the **Lower East Side**, became increasingly defined by ethnicity. Immigrant groups established savings institutions, insurance programs, choruses, political organizations, and summer camps. The various ethnic enclaves of the Gilded Age city provided grocery stores so that immigrants could purchase foods reminiscent of their countries of origin. Some newcomers to the city did not intend to stay. Millions of immigrants, mostly young men, worked for part of the year in the United States and then spent part of the year in their home country. These young men were called **"birds of passage"** because of their seasonal migrations.

Immigration and Nativism

The new immigrant groups of the Gilded Age—primarily from southern and eastern Europe—were seen by some as markedly different from the pre–Civil War groups in terms of appearance, language, and customs. These **"new immigrants"** (see page 230) heightened fears among conservative, Protestant public figures, such as **Henry Cabot Lodge** and **Madison Grant**. These nativists feared that the Anglo-Saxon Americans were committing "race suicide" by allowing "inferior" races to enter America in large numbers.

B. Justifying the Inequities of the Gilded Age

Writers and intellectuals put forth ideas justifying the socioeconomic structure of the Gilded Age. Theories such as Social Darwinism, which saw the inequities of the era as both fitting and unavoidable, gained currency during the era.

The Waning of the "Free-Labor" Ideal

In many ways, the rise of giant corporations ran counter to traditional American ideas about the economy and society. The **"free-labor" ideology** of the pre–Civil War era put forth the idea that working for another person was a temporary condition; eventually each employee would accumulate enough money to start his own farm or shop (see page 149). However, with the army of unskilled workers flooding into the emerging factory system of the late nineteenth century, it became increasingly clear that these people, and their offspring, were not going to rise to become independent entrepreneurs. As older ideas about the nature of the American economy became outmoded, new ones gained traction. Some of these ideas unabashedly embraced the new corporate order (see below). Others challenged it (see page 236).

Social Darwinism

Social Darwinism was an attempt to defend the new industrial order of the late 1800s. Social Darwinists sought to apply **Charles**

USING HISTORICAL THINKING SKILLS: CONTEXTUALIZATION

The Appeal of Social Darwinism

To understand the appeal of Social Darwinism among many Americans, it is important to look at the context it developed in. The Gilded Age of the late 1800s saw unrivaled economic growth. Although the benefits of this growth were not equally distributed among different economic classes, many marveled at the new world that industrialization had created—enormous steel plants, an extensive railroad network, urban growth, and opulent mansions. To the owners of large corporations and to those who embraced this new industrial order, Social Darwinism made perfect sense. It both justified the wealth and power of the industrial age and warned against any type of regulation or reform.

Darwin's ideas about the natural world to social relations. The theory was popularized in the United States by **William Graham Sumner**. Sumner was attracted to Darwin's ideas about competition and **"survival of the fittest."** He argued against any attempt at government intervention into the economic and social spheres, a position that favored **laissez-faire** (or hands-off) economic policies. Interference, he argued, would hinder the evolution of the human species. The inequalities of wealth that characterized the late 1800s were part of the process of "survival of the fittest."

Horatio Alger and the Myth of the Self-Made Man

Horatio Alger wrote a series of **"dime novels"** (often as cheap as ten cents) that often featured a poor boy who achieves success in the world. The boy's success is usually the result of a bit of luck and a bit of pluck—fortunate circumstances as well as determination and perseverance. These **"rags-to-riches"** novels, such as *Ragged Dick*, put forth the idea that anyone could make it in Gilded Age America; the reality, however, was quite different.

C. The Settlement House Movement

The goal of the settlement house movement was to aid immigrants, especially immigrant women. The movement was the most visible example of an alliance between middle-class women and working-class men and women. In many ways, the movement set the template for the social activism of the Progressive era of the early twentieth century (see Topic 7.4, pages 262–271).

Jane Addams and Hull House

By 1911, more than 400 **settlement houses** existed in the United States, usually run by women. These houses offered classes, set up employment bureaus, provided childcare facilities, and helped victims of domestic abuse. **Jane Addams** founded and ran **Hull House** in Chicago. Addams challenged prevailing societal expectations around gender and family life. She wrote two autobiographical volumes, including *Twenty Years at Hull-House* (1910), and was awarded the Nobel Peace Prize in 1931. Addams is considered one of the founders of the field of **social work** in the United States.

Topic 6.10 Development of the Middle Class

The spread of the corporate model and the consolidation of major businesses led to a managerial revolution (see page 224). This revolution required a host of managers, clerical workers, salespeople, and accountants. The new urban industrial economy also required a host of support services—such as health care, education, and legal services. The expansion of the middle class and the growing amount of leisure time led to a new consumer culture. In addition, some business leaders asserted that the wealthy had an obligation to improve society through philanthropic work.

A. The Growth of the Urban Middle Class and the Expansion of Consumer Culture

Traditional accounts of the Gilded Age have often focused on the great disparities between the wealthy owners of corporations and the struggling working class—between the mansions of Newport, Rhode Island, and the tenements of the Lower East Side. Another important element of the new economy was the dramatic rise of the middle class.

The Rise of the Middle Class

In the last decades of the nineteenth century, a class of **white-collar employees** became essential to the successful functioning of industrial capitalism. White-collar employees saw their wages rise faster than working-class (blue-collar) men and women, and their average workday was shorter than that of laborers and factory workers.

Women filled many of the lower-level white-collar jobs, as more office workers were hired in the large firms of the Gilded Age. **Secretarial work** had been seen as men's work in the pre–Civil War period, as is evident in **Herman Melville's** 1853 short story, **"Bartleby, the Scrivener: A Story of Wall Street"** (the story of an office clerk who suddenly refuses to perform his duties). As the typewriter came into use, literate women learned to type and were hired to perform office duties. Women were also hired as schoolteachers, a growing field in the late 1800s. On the eve of the Civil War, there were only 100 public high schools in the United States; by 1900, that figure had climbed to 6,000.

The Commercialization of Leisure

The growth of the **middle class** went hand in hand with the commercialization of leisure-time activities. The community-sponsored town fairs and dances of rural America were replaced by for-profit ventures in the city. The most successful large-scale **amusement park** was Brooklyn's **Coney Island**. Coney Island consisted of three main amusement areas, as well as a boardwalk, vaudeville theaters, and other assorted attractions. Among the most successful entertainments was **"Buffalo Bill" Cody's Wild West show** (starting in 1883), which mythologized the "Old West," just as the "Indian Wars" of the actual West were ending (see pages 220–222). Circuses became popular in the Gilded Age. **P. T. Barnum** created the most popular circus of the era (1871), labeling it **"the greatest show on Earth."**

> **KEEP IN MIND**
>
> **The Romanticizing of the West**
>
> Be aware of the differences between the real history of the West and the romanticizing of that history. "Buffalo Bill" Cody was romanticizing the "Old West" when people still had memories of the real West.

Newspapers

As printing costs went down and literacy rates went up, **newspaper** circulation increased dramatically in the Gilded Age. In the latter decades of the nineteenth century, large-circulation papers, such as **Joseph Pulitzer's** *New York World* and **William Randolph Hearst's** *New York Journal*, gained readership through exaggerated, sensationalistic coverage of events. This **"yellow journalism"** played a role in pushing public opinion toward support for the 1898 **Spanish-American War** (see pages 257–259).

The Health of the City and the Parks Movement

As cities became denser and more disease-ridden, reformers sought to provide more opportunities for city dwellers to enjoy outdoor recreation. Older notions of disease causation—that disease, for example, was divine punishment for sinful behavior—gave way to the idea that our environment plays a significant role in our health. Later, doctors adopted the **germ theory** of disease causation, put forth by German microbiologist **Robert Koch** (who was active from the 1870s to the 1900s). **Public parks** were part of a strategy to provide an alternative to dirty streets and alleyways (as well as saloons) for healthful recreation.

> **KEEP IN MIND**
>
> **"Muckraking Journalism" Versus "Yellow Journalism"**
>
> Do not confuse these two terms. The term "yellow journalism" was first used during the newspaper circulation wars between Joseph Pulitzer and William Randolph Hearst in the late 1890s. The term was likely derived from a character, "The Yellow Kid," in a comic strip that appeared in both publishers' papers. A commentator referred to the use of exaggeration, distortion, sensationalism, and eye-catching headlines as the "school of yellow kid journalism." "Yellow journalism" is often contrasted with professional, well-researched, balanced reporting. The term "muckraker" refers to the crusading journalists and writers of the Progressive era who exposed wrongdoing by government officials, showed the negative side of industrialization, and let the world see a variety of social ills. The term dates back to the 1678 theological novel by John Bunyan, *Pilgrim's Progress*, in which one of the characters is referred to as "the Man with the Muck-rake." In 1906, President Theodore Roosevelt used the term to extend half-hearted praise to investigative journalists; they were important to society, but only if they knew "when to stop raking the muck."

Frederick Law Olmsted and New York's Central Park

The most important park project of the nineteenth century was **New York's Central Park** (1858). The design competition was won by **Frederick Law Olmsted** and **Calvert Vaux**. The park embodies some of the contradictions of the parks movement. On the one hand, Olmsted sought to create a **democratic meeting place** where the city's different classes could congregate and enjoy the benefits of nature. On the other hand, working-class advocates wondered aloud why the park was built so far from the working-class districts of the city. Also, the rules and regulations made the park seem, to some people, more about **social control** than enjoyment. As a result of his work on Central Park, Olmsted became the most prominent landscape artist in the United States, designing (along with Vaux) **Brooklyn's Prospect Park** in the early 1860s, the grounds for the 1893 **Chicago World's Fair**, and numerous other parks, campuses, and private grounds.

Recreation and Spectator Sports

Park grounds became centers for a variety of recreation activities in the late 1800s. Several of these activities went from being participatory activities to spectator sports. These include:

Baseball: Developed in 1845, baseball became the "national pastime" by the Gilded Age. The first truly professional team was the Cincinnati Red Stockings (1869).

Tennis: Lawn tennis was developed in Great Britain (1873) as mainly a women's sport. It gained popularity in America among men and women during the Gilded Age.

Croquet: Croquet was a popular activity in public parks during the last third of the nineteenth century. It was often played by mixed-gender groups.

Cycling: "Wheeling"—bicycle riding—became very popular in the Gilded Age. The difficult "penny-farthing" bicycles, with their enormous front wheel, gave way to the modern design of the "safety bicycle" in the 1880s. "Wheeling" was especially popular among women, who enjoyed the freedom from male supervision that bicycle riding offered.

Football: College football games became popular in the Gilded Age. The first contest was between Rutgers and the College of New Jersey (Princeton) in 1869.

B. The Moral Obligations of the Wealthy Class

During the Gilded Age, some members of the business elite argued that the wealthy had a moral obligation to give something back to the community. These sentiments led several wealthy business leaders to make major financial contributions that improved cities and enhanced educational opportunities.

Andrew Carnegie and "The Gospel of Wealth"

Andrew Carnegie asserted, in his essay **"Wealth"** (1899), that the rich have a duty to live responsible, modest lives and to give back to society. This **"gospel of wealth"** asserted that successful entrepreneurs should distribute their wealth so that it could be put to good use, rather than frivolously wasted. Carnegie ended up donating the majority of his fortune to charity and public-oriented projects. He believed in a laissez-faire approach to social problems. He did not want the government interfering in the social and economic spheres. That is, in part, why he urged his fellow millionaires to take action on behalf of the community. In this way, the government would not have to.

Topic 6.11 Reform in the Gilded Age

During the last decades of the nineteenth century, a variety of individuals and groups put forth ideas about the age they were living in. Reformers and intellectuals challenged the prevailing social structure of the day. Many women in this era broke with Victorian-era gender expectations to participate in social change movements.

A. Challenges to the Dominant Corporate Ethic

A variety of critics challenged the dominant corporate ethic of the day. Some of these critics offered utopian visions of the future, while others questioned the logic of the capitalist system itself.

Henry George and the "Single Tax" on Land

Henry George was a writer, economist, and politician who was critical of the persistence of poverty in a nation of such technological and industrial progress. In his bestselling book, *Progress and Poverty* (1879), he criticized the vast resources, especially land, controlled by the wealthy elite. He argued for the elimination of all taxes, except for a **"single tax"** on the value of land. Land becomes valuable, he argued, due the activities of the society around the land; the benefits of these social activities should therefore accrue to the public, not to idle landowners. The tax would be sufficiently high so as to eliminate land accumulation and speculation; in effect, it would make land the "common property" of society.

Socialism and Anarchism

Many Americans began to question the basic assumptions of capitalism and embraced alternative ideologies, such as **anarchism** and **socialism**. These radical ideas never gained the number of adherents in the United States that they did in Europe. Occasionally, conservative newspapers and politicians exaggerated the strength of these movements in the United States. Newspapers often conflated the labor movement in general with these "dangerous" movements in order to delegitimize or stigmatize the labor movement. Still, these movements had adherents in the United States. After the utter failure of the **Pullman Strike** (see pages 229–230), **Eugene V. Debs** moved away from the labor movement and toward socialism. He was one of the founders of the **Socialist Party of America** in 1901.

Edward Bellamy's *Looking Backward, 2000–1887*

The most famous American socialist tract of the nineteenth century was **Edward Bellamy's** *Looking Backward, 2000–1887* (1888). This novel imagined a man who falls asleep in 1887 and awakens in 2000 to find a socialist utopia in which the inequities and poverty of the Gilded Age have been eradicated.

Coxey's Army

In 1894, **"Coxey's Army,"** a group of disgruntled workers, many of whom were recently laid off by railroad companies, marched from Ohio, through Pennsylvania, and on to Washington, D.C., to demand that the government take action to address the economic crisis following the **Panic of 1893**. President Grover Cleveland ignored their pleas for some sort of government relief. There were other similar "armies" of populist-inspired working-class men.

> **USING HISTORICAL THINKING SKILLS:**
> **MAKING CONNECTIONS**
>
> **Was Coxey Ahead of His Time?**
>
> In 1894, the Coxeyites were ridiculed and ignored. However, a generation later, the New Deal consisted of exactly the types of programs Coxey and his men were pushing for. It shows that social movements influence government policies, but sometimes the process takes a while.

B. Gender, Voluntary Organizations, and Social Reform

Increasingly, women in the late 1800s challenged prevailing notions of gender by forming voluntary organizations, working in settlement houses to aid immigrants (see page 233), attending college, and promoting social and political reform. These women, and their male allies, pushed for a greater degree of equality in the United States.

Challenging the "Cult of Domesticity"

As the economic dislocations wrought by industrialization touched more and more families, many women became politically engaged. Many women began to challenge the rigid gender expectations embodied in the **"cult of** domesticity" (see page 151). In the 1880s and 1890s, **women's clubs** began to emerge in many towns and cities. These clubs investigated and advocated around issues of poverty, working conditions, and pollution. In 1890, women organized an umbrella organization—the **General Federation of Women's Clubs**. These clubs often used the rhetoric of domesticity to justify their activism outside the home. The organization used the term **"maternalism"** to describe the dual role of women as mothers and as social activists. Many women put their energy into the temperance campaign to curb alcohol consumption in the United States. Founded in 1874, the **Women's Christian Temperance Union** (WCTU) became a mass organization, especially under the leadership of Frances Willard. Members of the WCTU later became involved in both the populist movement of the 1890s (see page 238) and the Progressive movement of the early twentieth century (see pages 262–271). Women continued to press for voting rights in the late 1800s. The **National American Woman Suffrage Association** was formed in 1890, merging two earlier suffrage groups (see page 198).

Topic 6.12 Controversies over the Role of Government in the Gilded Age

Critics of corporate power pushed the government to take steps to rein in the massive corporations of the Gilded Age. However, these efforts at regulation were vigorously opposed by industrial leaders. Debates also ensued over calls for overseas expansion.

A. Laissez-Faire Policies Versus Reform

In the face of calls for reform and regulation of industrial capitalism in the Gilded Age, opponents of regulation argued that laissez-faire policies promoted economic growth. The French phrase *laissez-faire* means "to let alone." It describes a government policy that would take a hands-off approach to regulating economic activities.

Reform Efforts in the Gilded Age

Reformers and critics of the new industrial capitalist order pushed for government measures designed to regulate economic activities. These efforts were strenuously opposed by defenders of **laissez-faire** policies. Efforts at regulation were often hampered by the courts and by lax enforcement. Take, for example, the case of railroad regulation. In 1886 the Supreme Court, in the ***Wabash, St. Louis and Pacific Railway Company v. Illinois*** case, limited the ability of states to regulate railroads, asserting that states could not impose "direct" burdens on interstate commerce. In response, the federal government created the **Interstate Commerce Commission** (1887) to regulate railroads. However, the ICC was chronically underfunded and was, therefore, ineffective.

A similar pattern can be seen in antitrust legislation. The **Sherman Antitrust Act** (1890) was the first attempt by Congress to keep monopolistic practices in check. The act made it illegal for firms to make agreements with one another that limit competition. In addition, it became illegal for a particular firm to engage in practices that are designed to establish a monopoly in a particular field. The idea of the law was to encourage competition in the economy and to protect consumers from abusive practices. The act, however, had only limited usefulness. In the case of ***United States v. E. C. Knight Company*** (1895), the Supreme Court greatly limited the scope of the act by making a distinction between trade (which would be subject to the act) and manufacturing (which would not). Manufacturing, the Court ruled, was a local activity not subject to congressional oversight; trade, however, involved interstate commerce, and was, therefore, within the purview of congressional regulation.

B. Debates Around Pursuing an Imperialist Policy

Foreign policymakers began to look abroad—to the Pacific, Asia, and Latin America—to gain greater access and control over foreign markets and natural resources.

Industry and Empire

Not long after the major European powers began carving up Africa and Asia, the United States entered the scramble for overseas possessions. Many Americans resisted the idea of the United States embarking on overseas expansion; after all, the country had been born in a war against a major imperial power. However, the growing industrial capacity of the United States and the desire for new markets led the country to look abroad. The American acquisition of **Hawaii** and the **Spanish-American War** (both 1898) set the United States on the path of having a global presence. (The role of the United States as an imperialist power is discussed in detail in Topics 7.2 and 7.3.)

Topic 6.13 Politics in the Gilded Age

A number of political issues, mostly around economic issues, came to dominate the Gilded Age. The economic changes of the era generated political debates around tariffs and currency. Corruption seemed rife on all levels of government despite efforts of reformers. Farmers grew increasingly frustrated with the policies of the two main political parties and sought political solutions outside of the traditional two-party system.

A. Farmers and the Populist Party

The People's (Populist) Party was formed by activists to challenge the growth of corporate power over the agricultural sector. The party sought a radical redistribution of power in the United States and pushed for stronger government intervention in the economy.

Organizing the Populist Party

The **Populist Party**, which was born in 1892, was able to harness growing discontent following the **Panic of 1893** and gave a voice to a radical program for change that included increased democracy, a graduated income tax, regulation of the railroads, and currency reform. The Populists insisted that the amount of currency in circulation was insufficient. It sought to undo the **"crime of '73,"** referring to the 1873 act of Congress that put the United States on the gold standard (see page 241). The call for the **"free and unlimited coinage of silver"** became one of the main rallying cries of the Populists. Their program, the **Omaha Platform**, was written at their founding convention in 1892. The party did remarkably well in the presidential election later that year, garnering more than a million votes and twenty-two electoral votes. The party made solid gains in the midterm election of 1894, electing six senators and seven representatives from the farming regions in the South and the West. The Populists were perhaps the most successful third party in the nineteenth century, but their popularity was short lived.

The Election of 1896 and the "Cross of Gold" Speech

The election of 1896 was significant in several ways. It resulted in the demise of the **Populist Party** and helped establish the identity of the major political parties in the twentieth century. The most contentious issue in the election was the amount of currency in circulation. **William Jennings Bryan** ran for president in 1896 on the ticket of the Democratic Party. He broke with the more conservative elements in the party and endorsed the call for the unrestricted minting of silver currency. In his famous **"Cross of Gold"** speech, he promised not to let the American people be crucified "upon a cross of gold." His support for the free coinage of silver led to the Populist Party (see above) joining forces

> **USING HISTORICAL THINKING SKILLS:**
> **MAKING CONNECTIONS**
>
> **Third Parties in American History**
>
> Third-party presidential candidates have been able to highlight particular issues on the national stage even if they do not win elections. It is very difficult for third parties (such as the Populist Party) to win elections in the American political system, which favors the two main parties. The Free-Soil Party (1848–1854) focused on opposition to the expansion of slavery; the States' Rights Democrats (or Dixiecrats) ran Strom Thurmond for president in 1948 to support segregation. The Green Party ran Ralph Nader for president several times, most notably in 2000, to raise awareness of environmental and social justice concerns.

with the Democratic Party in supporting Bryan. The Republican candidate, **William McKinley**, appealed to banking and business interests by promising to keep the country on the **gold standard**. The defeat of Bryan proved to be a devastating blow to the Populists, who never fully recovered. The positions of the two main parties shaped the political landscape well into the twentieth century. The **Republican Party** continued to be more aligned with pro-business interests, and the **Democratic Party** continued to present itself as the champion of the "little guy." In addition, the two parties maintained dominance in different regions, with the South solidly Democratic and the North predominantly Republican.

B. Politics, Big Business, and Corruption in the Gilded Age

Close ties—and charges of corruption—came to define the relationship between government and business in the Gilded Age. In response to these charges, members of the public called for reform at the local, state, and national levels.

The Evolution of the Two-Party System

Neither the **Democrats** nor the **Republicans**, the two main political parties from the Civil War to the present, were able to dominate national politics during the last decades of the nineteenth century. The Republicans controlled the White House for most of the period from 1869 to the turn of the century (the one exception was the two nonconsecutive terms of **President Grover Cleveland**, 1885-1889 and 1893-1897). However, the elections were extremely close, with no presidential candidate receiving a clear majority of the popular vote in any election between 1872 and 1896. Control of Congress was split. The Republicans controlled the Senate for most of the period, and the Democrats controlled the House. Only briefly, for three different two-year periods, did one of the parties control the White House and both houses of Congress. This changed following the victory of the Republican William McKinley in the election of 1896 (see above). After that election, the Republicans held a strong majority in the country until the New Deal era of the 1930s.

In many ways, the Gilded Age saw the two main political parties, the Democrats and the Republicans, become increasingly removed from the concerns of ordinary Americans. Both parties seemed more responsive to the priorities of the newly formed trusts and industrial giants than to the needs of farmers, workers, or the urban poor. Corruption permeated political life from the backrooms of local political clubhouses to the corridors of power in Washington, D.C. A spate of reform movements developed to address this situation, most notably the People's Party, better known as the **Populist Party**, in the last decade of the nineteenth century (see page 238).

Ideology Takes a Back Seat

Neither the **Republicans** nor the **Democrats** took strong stands on most of the pressing issues of the day. Neither party showed a willingness to deal with any of the various problems associated with the industrial expansion of the age. Issues like child labor, the consolidation of industries, workplace safety, and abuses by railroad companies were either avoided or dealt with in a limited fashion. Neither party did much to protect the rights of **African Americans** (especially after the end of Reconstruction) or of **American Indians**. Neither party addressed the call of many **women** for the right to vote. One issue that consistently divided the parties was the **tariff**; Democrats wanted lower tariff rates and Republicans wanted higher tariff rates. (See page 241 for more on tariff rates.)

Owners of major companies openly curried favor with congressmen with contributions, gifts, and outright bribery. Political leaders, even presidents, seemed to shrink in importance when compared with the towering industrial figures of the day. Cornelius Vanderbilt II, John D. Rockefeller, and Andrew Carnegie are far more clearly imprinted on the national collective memory than are the **"forgotten presidents"** of the Gilded Age.

Corruption and the Grant Administration

American political life was rife with corruption during the post–Civil War period. This was true on the local level, as evidenced by the illegal schemes of **"Boss" William Marcy Tweed** in New York (see pages 241–242), as well as on the national level. The administration of **Ulysses S. Grant**, former Union commanding general in the Civil War, was tainted by corruption. Historians assess Grant's ability as a president far below his abilities on the battlefield. The Republican president was not decisive on the issue of Reconstruction (see pages 197–202). In addition, he surrounded himself with incompetent and corrupt advisors and appointees. Grant rewarded friends, army contacts, and party loyalists with jobs that required political experience, which his appointees sorely lacked. Though Grant was not directly charged with corruption, key members of his administration, including his vice president, were.

Corruption and Civil-Service Reform

Civil-service reform became a major issue in the late nineteenth century. The civil service is the workforce of government employees. Attempts were made to remove nepotism and cronyism from government hiring practices. Reformers in the 1880s pushed for civil-service jobs to be allocated to the most qualified people rather than to allies and relatives of powerful politicians.

Mugwumps, Stalwarts, and Half-Breeds

The issue of civil-service reform divided the **Republican Party** in the wake of the scandals of the Grant administration. Reform-minded Republicans, mainly from Massachusetts and New York, were nicknamed **"Mugwumps"** by their critics, after the Algonquian word for "chief." They wanted to move away from the corruption of the Grant years and create a merit-based civil service. Those most resistant to abandoning the spoils system were nicknamed **"Stalwarts."** Those loyal to the Republican leadership, but wanting some degree of reform, were known as **"Half-Breeds."** Rutherford B. Hayes, who won the disputed election of 1876, was not well liked by any of the factions and chose not to run for reelection in 1880.

The Pendleton Act

A series of events in the summer of 1881 made civil-service reform a more pressing issue and led to the passage of the **Pendleton Act**. The **Republicans** nominated **James A. Garfield** for president in 1880. He won the presidency, but was shot four months after his inauguration in 1881. Garfield died from the wound two months later. The assassin, **Charles J. Guiteau**, may have suffered from mental illness, but the reason he gave for his actions was that he was passed over when he sought a government job, despite his work on the Garfield campaign. Congress passed the Pendleton Act in 1883 to set up a merit-based federal civil service, a professional career service that allots government jobs on the basis of a competitive exam. This system still covers most of the bureaucratic jobs in the federal government. Upper-level, policy-oriented positions are still rotated when new presidential administrations come into office.

USING HISTORICAL THINKING SKILLS: DEVELOPMENTS AND PROCESSES

Currency and Inflation

Be familiar with basic economic concepts involving the currency supply because it was an important issue in the last decades of the nineteenth century. An expansion of the currency supply would have led to inflation. As more currency is added to the economy, the relative value of the money in circulation decreases because there is more of it. The prices of goods and services, in turn, effectively increase, or are inflated. The opposite is true if there is too little currency: the relative value of money increases, and prices fall, or deflate. Inflationary policies would have benefited farmers, but hurt consumers. In general, banking interests tend to support limiting the money supply so that money loaned out maintains its value. Deflationary policies can benefit workers as long as wages remain stable and do not fall.

The Politics of Tariff Rates

The rate of taxation on imported goods was a divisive political issue throughout the nineteenth century and into the twentieth. Industrialists tended to encourage higher **tariffs** to keep out foreign competition. **Republican** politicians tended to support this stance. Farming interests, and many **Democratic** politicians, tended to support a lower tariff rate. Their cotton and wheat sales to Europe benefited from increased international trade; high tariffs impeded international trade. Republicans had pushed tariffs higher during the Civil War to fund the war effort. By the 1880s, the government was awash in money from the tariff, and tariff reformers argued that lowering the tariff would put more money into circulation and stimulate economic activity. **President Chester Arthur** broke with Republican orthodoxy and looked into lowering the tariff. Tariff reform foundered in Congress; ultimately, a small decrease in tariff rates was passed.

The tariff issue remained contentious during Democratic president **Grover Cleveland's** first administration. Many Democrats, including Cleveland, began to push for lower rates. These tariff reformers became increasingly critical of the power of trusts and large corporations in dominating the economy. They saw high tariff rates as benefiting these big business interests at the expense of consumers and small producers. In 1888, the Republican Party nominated **Benjamin Harrison**, grandson of President William Henry Harrison. Business interests poured money into the Harrison campaign. In 1890, Harrison signed into law the highest tariff in the nation's history.

The Currency Issue

The vibrant economic growth that characterized much of the last decades of the nineteenth century came to a screeching halt in 1893 (see more on the **Panic of 1893**, page 286). Many observers, both contemporaries and historians, cite the inadequate amount of **currency** in circulation as one of the underlying weaknesses in the economy. The money supply in the last decades of the nineteenth century did not have the ability to grow as the economy expanded. For decades the United States used metallic money, as stipulated in the **Mint Act of 1792**. The act allowed for the coinage of gold *and* silver. However, in 1873, Congress changed this policy, allowing only for the coinage of gold. The amount of gold being coined in the 1870s and 1880s could not keep up with the growing economy. This was especially hard on farmers as it depressed the prices they received for their goods, which made it difficult to repay loans. The situation was beneficial to bankers, who wanted a relatively stable currency so that money repaid on loans retained its value (see more on the currency issue and the election of 1896, pages 238–239).

C. Politics, Power, and Reform in Urban America

The growing cities of the Gilded Age experienced changes in governance and movements for political reform. Political machines became increasingly powerful in urban America, sometimes providing social services to immigrant groups in exchange for political support. Settlement houses and self-help groups emerged in the last decades of the nineteenth century to help immigrants adapt to life in America.

Urban Politics and the Rise of Machine Politics

Politics in major cities came to be dominated by **"political machines."** In the aftermath of the Civil War, political parties on the local level created smooth-running organizations whose purpose was to achieve and maintain political power. Political ideology was barely a concern in these bare-knuckled electoral contests. New York City was dominated by the **Democratic Party** machine, run by party **"bosses"** and headquartered at **Tammany Hall**. The most famous Tammany chief was **William Marcy "Boss" Tweed. "Boss"** Tweed and other political leaders earned a reputation for corruption. Tweed's complicated schemes included the building of a courthouse that involved millions of dollars in kickbacks to Tammany

> **KEEP IN MIND**
>
> **Immigrants and Political Machines**
>
> Do not be too quick to condemn political machines for exploiting immigrants. The relationship is complicated. Political machines were corrupt, but they provided real benefits to immigrant communities.

Hall. Tweed's nefarious doings were exposed by the press, most notably by editorial cartoonist **Thomas Nast**. The Tammany Hall political machine was popular with German and Irish immigrants; under the Democratic Party, the city initiated massive municipal projects that provided jobs to thousands of immigrants.

The Campaign Against Prostitution

The issue of **prostitution** tapped into the concerns of a variety of constituencies in the late 1800s. Religious-based activists saw the practice as sinful. Campaigners for gender equality saw a double standard in society's acceptance of male extramarital sexual activities (including with prostitutes) while females involved in prostitution were subject to prosecution. Public-health advocates saw prostitution as spreading venereal disease. Anti-poverty activists saw prostitution as reinforcing a cycle of poverty for working-class women. These forces united in pressuring local authorities to close "red-light" districts. Later, in the early twentieth century, progressive reformers successfully lobbied for the **Mann Act** (1910), which cracked down on the transport of women across state lines to engage in prostitution.

The Temperance Campaign

The movement to ban alcohol from American society was one of the largest reform movements in the nineteenth century. The **Anti-Saloon League** (founded in 1895) and the **Women's Christian Temperance Union** (founded in 1874) headed the temperance campaign in the early twentieth century. The temperance movement was especially popular among women. Many women, who had the responsibility of putting food on the table, were troubled by the fact that their husbands often drank away their paychecks. Another reason for the popularity of the temperance crusade was that it complemented the growing nativist, or anti-immigrant, movement. (See more on the temperance movement, page 270.)

Topic 6.14 Subject to Debate

The Appropriateness of the Label "Robber Baron"

A central point of contention in interpretations of the Gilded Age is the place of the owners of big business. The image that has stuck is that of the bloated "robber baron." This image was promoted by many contemporaries during the Gilded Age. The unprecedented accumulation of such wealth and power seemed at odds with the ideal of a society of yeoman farmers or urban artisans. Further, the lavish spending habits of these wealthy men—illustrated by the gaudy mansions of New York's Fifth Avenue—also seemed outside of the American tradition of thrift and humility. This image of greed and excess was kept alive by Progressive-era historians and is still part of the collective memory of the era. Recently, some historians have begun to question this depiction of the Gilded Age. For one, even in the late nineteenth century, most of the big companies were incorporated and run by boards of directors. The age of an arbitrary proprietor ordering his employees around was an anachronism even in the late Gilded Age. Second, recent historical interpretations have noted the tremendous wealth generated during this period. Over time, this rising tide of wealth helped lift all boats through higher wages and better conditions. It is not by accident that so many "new immigrants" came to the United States. To the immigrants leaving wretched poverty, America truly was a land of opportunity at the turn of the twentieth century. In your essay writing, keep in mind the origins of the image of the "robber baron" and its usefulness in understanding the realities of the Gilded Age.

The Populist Movement—Reasonable or Irrational?

Historians have long debated the "revolt of the farmers" in the 1880s and 1890s. You should be familiar with the different poles in the debate. On the one hand, some historians have looked admiringly on the Populist movement. They note the dire situation farmers found themselves in and see the movement as a reasonable response. This approach also looks approvingly at the legacy of the movement; some of its goals were taken up by the Progressive movement in the early decades of the twentieth century, and even by the New Dealers in the 1930s. Other historians, notably Richard Hofstadter in his essay, "The Paranoid Style in American Politics" (1964), paint the Populist movement as an irrational, emotional rebellion against the modern world. These historians cite the racism, anti-Semitism, anti-urbanism, and anti-immigrant sentiment evident in certain corners of the movement. In this light, the Populist movement might be seen as a precursor of the revived Ku Klux Klan in the 1920s and McCarthyism in the 1950s.

Corrupt Political Bosses and Immigrant Communities

Historians have debated the impact of "machine politics" in the nineteenth century. Starting in the Progressive era, historians wrote disparagingly about the corruption of the political bosses of the Gilded Age. In this narrative, these bosses undermined democracy until reformers rose up and cleaned up the political process. There is certainly truth to this narrative. However, reality is usually more complicated. Social historians have recently examined the positive impact the political machines had on immigrant communities. The machines may have been corrupt, but they provided the only safety net and jobs programs for recently arrived immigrants. In some ways, the attacks on the political machines were attacks on the structure of the immigrant community. In your essay writing, it would be wise to exercise caution when talking about the political "bosses" of the Gilded Age.

The "Old West" in History and Memory

There has been a major disconnect between the "Old West" of popular memory and the West of the historical record. Generations of Western movies have presented a morality play between virtuous pioneers and treacherous Indians. It is only in the last generation that the popular memory of the West has shifted. Movies such as *Dances with Wolves* (1990) have served as cultural correctives. In your writing, try to avoid the stereotypes and clichés of the "Cowboy-and-Indian" genre.

Practice Multiple-Choice Questions

> **DIRECTIONS:** Pick the letter that best answers the following questions.

Questions 1–3 refer to the following passage:

"Be it enacted by the Senate and House of Representatives of the United States of America in Congress assembled, That in all cases where any tribe or band of Indians has been, or shall hereafter be, located upon any reservation created for their use, either by treaty stipulation or by virtue of an act of Congress or executive order, . . . the President of the United States [is] hereby . . . authorized, whenever in his opinion any reservation or any part thereof of such Indians is advantageous for agricultural and grazing purposes, to cause said reservation, or any part thereof, to be surveyed, . . . and to allot the lands in said reservation in severalty [separate plots of land, individually owned] to any Indian located thereon . . ."

—Dawes Severalty Act (excerpt), 1887

1. A primary goal of the Dawes Severalty Act (1887) was to

    (A) turn American Indians into property-owning, profit-oriented, individual farmers.
    (B) keep alive traditional practices and languages.
    (C) open up American Indian lands in Georgia, South Carolina, and Alabama to mining and cotton production.
    (D) compensate American Indian tribes for lands that had been taken through fraudulent treaties.

2. An important impetus for the passage of the Dawes Severalty Act was

    (A) the Supreme Court decision in the case of *Worcester v. Georgia*.
    (B) a nonviolent protest movement against existing policies led by Crazy Horse.
    (C) the success of the Freedmen's Bureau in addressing the problems of African Americans in the South.
    (D) the depiction of mistreatment of American Indians in Helen Hunt Jackson's book, *A Century of Dishonor*.

3. Which of the following developments was similar to the Dawes Severalty Act in that they both had similar goals for the future of American Indians?

    (A) The formation of the Ghost Dance movement
    (B) The establishment of Indian Boarding Schools
    (C) The passage of the Indian Reorganization Act
    (D) The founding of the American Indian Movement

Questions 4–7 refer to the following image:

—"The Grange Awakening the Sleepers," 1873.

4. The 1873 political cartoon shown makes the point that

   (A) railroads have brought prosperity to previously isolated communities.
   (B) the safety of railroad workers was being ignored by the powerful railroad corporations.
   (C) the public needed to recognize the threat that large railroad companies posed to the economic and political system.
   (D) railroad lines were undermining rural culture by bringing the vices of urban life to small-town America.

5. The Grange, represented by the standing figure in the cartoon, received its strongest support from which of the following groups?

   (A) Western farmers
   (B) Urban immigrants
   (C) Wealthy industrialists
   (D) Middle-class managers

6. The Grange emerged most directly in response to which of the following nineteenth-century developments?

   (A) The influx of migrants from Ireland in the aftermath of the "potato famine" of the 1840s and 1850s
   (B) The growing power of corporations over the economy and the political system
   (C) The development of political machines
   (D) The efforts of corporations to gain control over resources and markets in Asia and Latin America

7. Which of the following later groups or movements most fully adopted the political and economic agenda of the Grange?

   (A) The Congress of Industrial Organizations
   (B) The Populist Party
   (C) The National Association for the Advancement of Colored People
   (D) The "New Left"

Questions 8–9 refer to the following image:

—Frederick Burr Opper, "Just as dangerous now as then," 1883

8. The 1883 cartoon above makes the point that

    (A) the "new immigrants" from eastern and southern Europe, with their different customs and religious beliefs, were just as dangerous to the American way of life as the American Indians were to the Pilgrims in the seventeenth century.
    (B) the United States was filling up with people; additional immigrants would displace native-born Americans, just as the seventeenth-century Pilgrims displaced the American Indians.
    (C) among the "new immigrants" were many hard-working men and women, but also many radicals, anarchists, revolutionaries, criminals, and other "dangerous" elements.
    (D) incoming immigrants faced a gauntlet of threats when they arrived in America, just as the Pilgrims did when they arrived in the seventeenth century.

9. Which of the following best represents a continuity with the political sentiments expressed in the cartoon above?

    (A) Jane Addams and Ellen Gates Starr founding Hull House in 1889
    (B) The 1854 platform of the "Know-Nothing" Party
    (C) Attorney General A. Mitchell Palmer carrying out deportation hearings during the "Red Scare" of the 1920s
    (D) Congressmen Albert Johnson and David Reed proposing the Immigration Act of 1924

Questions 10–12 are based on the following passage:

"I am but one of many victims of Rockefeller's colossal combination . . . and my story is not essentially different from the rest. . . . I established what was known as the Ohio Oil Works. . . . I found to my surprise at first, though I afterward understood it perfectly, that the Standard Oil Company was offering the same quality of oil at much lower prices than I could do—from one to three cents a gallon less than I could possibly sell it for.

"I sought for the reason and found that the railroads were in league with the Standard Oil concern at every point, giving it discriminating rates and privileges of all kinds as against myself and all outside competitors."

—George Rice, "How I Was Ruined by Rockefeller," *New York World*, October 16, 1898

10. Rockefeller's business model as described by George Rice would best be considered an example of

    (A) global distribution.
    (B) horizontal integration.
    (C) regional planning.
    (D) vertical consolidation.

11. Attempts to rein in the power of corporations, such as the Standard Oil Company, in the 1890s and 1900s

    (A) were frequently approved by Congress but were stymied by presidential vetoes.
    (B) were largely successful, as a coalition of reformers, political leaders, and labor leaders collaborated on realigning the American economy.
    (C) were discussed by radical groups but were rejected by the vast majority of Americans as Communistic and "anti-American."
    (D) were often hindered by Supreme Court decisions that upheld the rights of business to operate without excessive government regulation.

12. Defenders of corporate actions, such as the ones described in the passage above, would find support in

    (A) Herbert Spencer and the ideas of Social Darwinism.
    (B) Henry George's proposal for a "single tax" on land.
    (C) the Omaha Platform of the Populist Party.
    (D) Upton Sinclair's novel, *The Jungle*.

Answers and Explanations

1. **(A)** A primary goal of the Dawes Severalty Act (1887) was to turn American Indians into property-owning, profit-oriented, individual farmers. This was part of a push toward assimilation as a policy for American Indians. Some reformers had come to believe that the reservation system was destructive to Indians and that the best strategy forward was to encourage them to give up traditional ways. In addition, the seeming inability or unwillingness on the part of native peoples to adopt a mainstream American lifestyle was seen by many Americans as both unacceptable and uncivilized.

2. **(D)** An important impetus for the passage of the Dawes Severalty Act was the depiction of mistreatment of American Indians in Helen Hunt Jackson's 1881 book, *A Century of Dishonor*. Her book chronicled the abuses by the U.S. government against the tribes. She hoped to awaken the conscience of the American people and their representatives to the brutal mistreatment of Indians. She sent a copy of the book to each member of Congress.

3. **(B)** American Indian boarding schools were established in the late nineteenth and early twentieth centuries as a means of educating native children according to the standards of mainstream white American culture. In this regard, they were similar to the Dawes Act in that both promoted assimilation as the solution to the "Indian problem." Children were forbidden to speak their native languages, were given European-American style haircuts, and given new names to replace their traditional names.

4. (C) The cartoon shows people sleeping under railway tracks, which normally lay on crossbeams termed "sleepers." A Granger tries to warn them of the approaching dangers—a locomotive with coaches labeled, "Consolidation Train," "extortion," "bribery," and so forth. The Grange, formally known as the National Grange of the Order of Patrons of Husbandry, was born in 1867. It initially was started to foster mutual aid among farmers and promote more efficient agricultural techniques. However, the organization soon began to focus on state and national political reforms. The Granger movement was successful in many states in regulating the railroads and grain-storage warehouses. The cartoon is titled "The Grange Awakening the Sleepers."

5. **(A)** The Grange was primarily an organization of farmers. Its agenda of subjecting the railroads to government control grew out of the concerns of farmers. It also organized cooperative businesses to help farmers market their goods directly to the public and avoid middlemen. Urban immigrants (B) might share some of the Granger bitterness toward the wealthy class, but they would not be drawn to the Granger agenda. The wealthy (C) and the rising middle class (D) of the late 1800s would not necessarily find common cause with the Granger movement.

6. **(B)** The Grange emerged in response to the unprecedented accumulation of power in the hands of a few massive corporations. Corporate power, many observers believed, was undermining the democratic system. Corporate leaders exerted a great deal of sway in the political system. Efforts to check corporate power, such as passage of the Sherman Antitrust Act (1890), often proved to be fruitless. In *United States v. E. C. Knight Company* (1895) the Supreme Court undermined the act by narrowing its scope to only trade, leaving manufacturing more or less unregulated. The Court ruled that the American Sugar Refining Company, which controlled approximately 98 percent of all sugar refining in the United States, was exempt from the antitrust law.

7. **(B)** The organization that most clearly followed in the footsteps of the Grange movement was the Populist Party, which became a formidable force in the 1890s. The movement was primarily a farmer's movement that resented the concentration of wealth and power among industrialists and bankers. It supported a national income tax so that those with higher incomes would pay more than the poor. It also supported unlimited coinage of silver in order to increase the amount of currency in circulation.

8. **(D)** The 1883 cartoon makes the point that incoming immigrants faced myriad dangers when they arrived in America, just as the Pilgrims did when they arrived in the seventeenth century. The dangers immigrants faced in the late nineteenth century included crooked money-changers, baggage handlers who stole all of the immigrant's worldly possessions, landlords renting out substandard housing, and employers looking to exploit cheap labor. This is a rare pro-immigrant cartoon. Many of the cartoons of the period depict immigrants as a threat to the values of the United States.

9. **(A)** The founding of Hull House in Chicago (1889) by Jane Addams and Ellen Gates Starr represents a continuity with the political sentiments expressed in the cartoon. Both the cartoon and the settlement house movement demonstrate empathy for the predicament that recent immigrants often found themselves in. Settlement houses, such as Hull House, were established to aid immigrants, especially immigrant women. By 1911 more than 400 settlement houses existed in the United States, usually run by women. The other choices all reflect aspects of the nativist, or anti-immigrant, movement.

10. **(B)** The business model described by George Rice could best be considered an example of horizontal integration. Horizontal integration entails creating a monopoly, or near monopoly, in a particular industry. A common way that corporations gained monopoly control of an industry was by establishing trusts. A trust consisted of trustees from several companies involved in the same industry acting together rather than in competition with one another. John D. Rockefeller organized the most well-known trust in the oil-processing industry.

11. **(D)** Attempts to rein in the power of corporations, such as the Standard Oil Company, in the 1890s and 1900s were often hindered by Supreme Court decisions that upheld the rights of business to operate without excessive government regulation. In the case of *United States v. E. C. Knight Company* (1895), for example, the Supreme Court examined the constitutionality of government attempts to check the power of large trusts. The Sherman Antitrust Act was passed in 1890 in order to curtail the power of the trusts. In the *Knight* case, the Court greatly limited the scope of the act by making a distinction between trade, which would be subject to the act under the Commerce Clause, and manufacturing, which would not.

12. **(A)** Defenders of corporate actions such as those described in the passage would find support in Herbert Spencer and the ideas of Social Darwinism. Social Darwinism was an attempt to apply Charles Darwin's ideas about the natural world to social relations. The ideas of Social Darwinism were put forth by the English philosopher Herbert Spencer, and were popularized in the United States by William Graham Sumner. Social Darwinists argued that the inequalities of the late 1800s reflected the process of the "survival of the fittest." Any attempt to intervene in the process would be counterproductive. This hands-off approach to economic activities is known by the French phrase *laissez-faire*. Social Darwinism appealed to owners of large corporations because it both justified their wealth and power and warned against any type of regulation or reform.

9

Period 7: 1890–1945 Economic Dislocation and Reform in the Age of Empire and World War

TIMELINE

1893	Queen Liliuokalani deposed by a coalition of U.S. Marines and businessmen
	Panic of 1893
1898	Spanish-American War
	United States annexation of Hawaii
	Formation of the American Anti-Imperialist League
1899–1900	Secretary of State John Hay establishes Open Door policy in China
1899–1902	Philippine-American War
1900	Hurricane and flood in Galveston, Texas
1901	Publication of *The Octopus: A California Story* by Frank Norris
1903	The United States acquires Panama Canal Zone (Canal completed, 1914)
	Elkins Act
1904	Publication of *The Shame of the Cities* by Lincoln Steffens
	Publication of *The History of the Standard Oil Company* by Ida Tarbell
	Election of Theodore Roosevelt
1905	Founding of the Niagara Movement
1906	Theodore Roosevelt wins Noble Peace Prize
	Publication of *The Jungle* by Upton Sinclair
	Meat Inspection Act
	Pure Food and Drug Act
	Hepburn Act
1908	Election of William Howard Taft
1909	Creation of the National Association for the Advancement of Colored People
1910	Mann Act
1912	Election of Woodrow Wilson
1913	Sixteenth Amendment (federal income tax) ratified
	Seventeenth Amendment (direct election of senators) ratified
	Henry Ford introduces conveyor belt to automobile production
1914	Federal Reserve Act
	Federal Trade Commission
	Clayton Antitrust Act
	Beginning of World War I

1914–1917	United States intervention in Mexico
1915	Release of D. W. Griffith's film *Birth of a Nation*
1916	Reelection of Woodrow Wilson
1917	United States enters World War I
	Espionage Act
1918	Sedition Act
	Armistice ends World War I
1919	Eighteenth Amendment (Prohibition) ratified
	Creation of the Comintern
	Senate rejects the Treaty of Versailles
1919–1920	Boston Police Strike
1920	Nineteenth Amendment (women's right to vote) ratified
	Deportation of Emma Goldman
	Schenck v. United States
	Seattle General Strike
	Height of the "Palmer raids"
	Election of Warren G. Harding
1921	Emergency Quota Act
	Beginning of Teapot Dome Scandal
1924	National Origins Act
	Election of Calvin Coolidge
1925	Scopes trial
1927	Execution of Sacco and Vanzetti
1928	Kellogg–Briand Pact
	Election of Herbert Hoover
1929	Stock market crash
	The Great Depression begins
1930	Hawley-Smoot Tariff
1931	The Marx Brothers' movie *Duck Soup* released
1932	Bonus March
	Reconstruction Finance Corporation established
	Election of Franklin D. Roosevelt
1933	The 100 Days
	"Bank holiday"
	Agricultural Adjustment Act (AAA)
	Glass–Steagall Act (Federal Depositors Insurance Corporation established)
	National Industrial Recovery Act (NIRA)
	Civilian Conservation Corps (CCC)
	Twenty-first Amendment (repeal of Prohibition) ratified
1934	Share Our Wealth clubs started by Huey Long
	Securities and Exchange Commission
	Clifford Odets writes the play *Waiting for Lefty*
1935	National Labor Relations Act (Wagner Act)
	Social Security Act

	Schechter decision strikes down NIRA
	Works Progress Administration
	First Neutrality Act
1936	Butler decision strikes down AAA
	Roosevelt's "Court packing plan"
	Roosevelt elected to a second term
	Charlie Chaplin's *Modern Times* released
1936–1939	Spanish Civil War
1937	"Roosevelt Recession"
	Farm Security Administration
1939	Cash-and-Carry Policy
	Nazi–Soviet Pact
	The movie *Mr. Smith Goes to Washington* released
	John Steinbeck's *The Grapes of Wrath* published
1940	Selective Service Act
	Tripartite Pact
	Roosevelt elected to unprecedented third term
1941	Lend-Lease Act
	Roosevelt issues Executive Order 8802, banning discrimination in war-related industries
	Japanese attack on Pearl Harbor
	United States enters World War II
1942	Battle of Midway
1943	Tehran Conference
1944	D-Day—allied invasion of Normandy
	Korematsu v. United States
	Bretton Woods Conference
	Roosevelt elected to a fourth term
1945	Yalta Conference
	Battles of Iwo Jima and Okinawa
	Death of Roosevelt
	Harry Truman becomes president
	German surrender
	Potsdam Conference
	Dropping of the atomic bomb on Hiroshima and on Nagasaki
	Japanese surrender

Topics in Period 7

In this chapter, you will learn about:

- Topic 7.1 Contextualizing Period 7
- Topic 7.2 Imperialism: Debates
- Topic 7.3 The Spanish-American War and its aftermath
- Topic 7.4 The Progressives
- Topic 7.5 World War I: Military and diplomacy
- Topic 7.6 World War I: Home front
- Topic 7.7 1920s: Innovation in communications and technology
- Topic 7.8 1920s: Cultural and political controversies
- Topic 7.9 The Great Depression
- Topic 7.10 The New Deal
- Topic 7.11 Interwar foreign policy
- Topic 7.12 World War II: Mobilization
- Topic 7.13 World War II: Military
- Topic 7.14 Postwar diplomacy
- Topic 7.15 Subject to debate

Topic 7.1 Contextualizing Period 7

> The United States faced a series of profound domestic and international challenges during the period 1890 to 1945. As the country became increasingly pluralistic, Americans debated how best to meet these challenges. Debate centered on the role of the government in the economic and social life of the country and on the role of the United States on the global stage.

After 1890, the United States began to play a more aggressive role on the world stage, intervening in Hawaii, Cuba, Panama, Mexico, and beyond, as well as acquiring possessions from Puerto Rico to the Philippines. These ventures (including building a modern U.S. Navy battle fleet) raised the profile of the United States and established it as a rising major power. When the Great War, later known as World War I, began in Europe in August 1914, most Americans were not eager to join the conflict. The war seemed to be a continuation of the age-old rivalries of the European nations. As the conflict dragged on, a number of factors pushed America toward intervention. The United States did not play a major role in World War I until the final year of the conflict, but the war ushered in some important changes in the United States. Culturally, the country became more aggressively patriotic and conservative; the reform impulse of the Progressive era was pushed to the background. The war expanded the role of the federal government and contributed to the "Great Migration" of African Americans toward the North. America's participation in the war strengthened its position on the world stage, even though the country withdrew into isolationism in the years following it.

The first decades of the twentieth century witnessed the growth of the Progressive movement. In response to the rapid industrialization, political corruption, and unplanned urbanization of the Gilded Age, the Progressive movement developed an extensive slate of proposals for reform. The movement claimed many legislative victories and ultimately influenced both the New Deal and twentieth-century liberalism.

During the 1920s, we see the development of the some of the cultural divisions that have roiled Americans ever since. Many historians note the resurgence of "traditional values" in the United States in response to the unfolding of a more modern America. This tension between tradition and modernity has shaped much of the historical work on the 1920s. Not all the elements of the 1920s fit neatly into this model of tradition versus modernity. Take, for instance, the experiment in the prohibition of alcohol—its origins were both in the Progressive movement's push for government-sponsored social engineering as well as in the religious crusade to eradicate "immoral" habits. Still, the tradition-versus-modernity model is a useful lens through which to examine the 1920s. This decade ended with the stock market crash that ushered in the Great Depression (1929–1939).

The Great Depression was the most devastating economic downturn in American history. It is one of several such economic depressions, which include downturns following the economic panics of 1819, 1837, 1857, 1873, and 1893. However, in none of these episodes did the country reach the depths of despair realized during the Great Depression. A basic understanding of introductory economic concepts, such as supply and demand, Keynesianism, and the business cycle, will come in handy in assessing the causes and responses to the Great Depression. The most significant response to the Depression, the New Deal, helped to redefine the relationship between the government and the economy and helped launch the modern welfare state.

This period ends with World War II, a cataclysmic war that profoundly transformed the nations that participated in it, including the United States. World War II set in motion a series of demographic, political, and social trends that would shape American history for the remainder of the twentieth century. A large percentage of the millions of returning soldiers soon settled down, married, and had the children who would comprise the "baby boom" generation. Moreover, the war brought the United States out of the Great Depression and set the country on a trajectory of sustained economic growth for a generation. Wartime experiences inspired both African Americans and women, setting the stage for the civil rights movement and the women's liberation movement. The United States did not retreat into an isolationist stance after the war, as it had after World War I. The wartime alliance of the United States and the Soviet Union would soon degenerate into the Cold War (1945–1991).

Topic 7.2 Imperialism: Debates

In the late 1800s, the United States entered the overseas imperialism scramble after the major European powers began carving up Africa and Asia. As America became increasingly involved in world affairs, debates ensued in the United States about the country's proper role. Many Americans resisted the idea of the United States embarking on overseas expansion.

A. The Motives of American Imperialism

A variety of motivations led America to pursue overseas possessions. These factors included economic motives, competition with the imperialist nations of Europe, and racial theories. America began to reach beyond the North American continent as the perception grew that the western frontier was closed.

Alfred Thayer Mahan and the Importance of Naval Power

Historian **Alfred Thayer Mahan**, a retired admiral, stressed the importance of naval power and colonies in achieving and maintaining influence on the world stage. This idea might seem commonplace, but the United States throughout the nineteenth century was more focused on domestic issues and expansion over the American continent. He pushed for the United States to develop a strong navy, maintain military bases and coaling stations throughout the world, and administer an overseas empire. These ideas were central to his book, *The Influence of Sea Power Upon History, 1660–1783* (1890).

> **USING REASONING PROCESSES: COMPARISON**
>
> **Imperialism Versus Colonialism**
>
> The two terms are not always interchangeable. Colonialism usually implies the effort of one country to establish settlements in another land; imperialism usually implies the effort to rule territory that is already occupied and organized without the intent of establishing significant settlements in that territory. Colonialism is generally associated with the actions of European powers in the period from the 1500s to the 1700s, in the context of mercantilist goals. Imperialist expansion, carried out by European powers, the United States, and Japan in the late 1800s and early 1900s, grew out of industrialization and strategic military concerns. In both cases, talk of a "civilizing mission" was often used.

Industrialization and the Panic of 1893

Contributing to the push for imperialism was the unprecedented growth of American industry. Some policymakers thought imperialism would become necessary if the United States were to become the world's predominant industrial power. Imperial holdings would provide American industry with important raw materials. Also, the people in these new American possessions could provide a market for the growing output of consumer products American industry was turning out. The desire for new markets intensified with the onset of the economic depression following the **Panic of 1893** (see page 286). This economic downturn left Americans unable to absorb additional consumer items. The economy did not fully recover until 1901.

"The White Man's Burden" and Racial Hierarchy

America's imperialist ventures were justified, in part, by particular assumptions about race at the time. Mainstream thinking in the United States in the late 1800s posited the superiority of the descendants of the **Anglo-Saxon people**, as well as the inferiority of the nonwhite peoples of the world. This racist notion was widely held, but it led to divergent impulses. Some white Americans felt it was the duty of the "civilized" peoples of the world to uplift the less fortunate; others felt that the "inferior" races would simply disappear in a struggle for the "survival of the fittest." The often-misguided nature of the urge to uplift the peoples of the world was made clear in British writer **Rudyard Kipling's** famous poem, **"The White Man's Burden"** (1899). **Josiah Strong**, a Protestant clergyman, argued that the "Anglo-Saxon race" had a responsibility to "civilize and Christianize" the world.

> **USING HISTORICAL THINKING SKILLS:**
> **SOURCING AND SITUATION**
>
> **Justifying Imperialism**
>
> In a document-based question about the causes of American imperialism, be careful to note the point of view and purpose of a document. The pronouncements of a president or a senator might not explain actual motivation. Often a public rationale for an event is different from the actual rationale. Look critically, for instance, at President McKinley's assertion that the war in the Philippines was motivated by a desire to "civilize" the Filipino people.

The notion of racial hierarchy accepted by most white Americans was starkly displayed at the **World's Columbian Exposition** in Chicago in 1893, as a sideshow of the "exotic" peoples of the world was presented to fairgoers. These displays of "natives" were contrasted with the industry and progress of the advanced civilizations. The obvious implication was that the advances of civilization must be made available to the rest of the world. **Frederick Douglass** and **Ida B. Wells** wrote a pamphlet critical of the fair's racist assumptions entitled, *The Reason Why the Colored American Is Not in the World's Columbian Exposition*.

Christian Missionaries

Christian missionary work went hand in hand with American expansion. **Missionaries** were eager to spread the gospel and introduce new populations to Christianity. Many of these missionaries targeted China's large population.

Hawaii

American missionaries arrived in **Hawaii** as early as the 1820s. Later in the century, American businessmen established massive sugar plantations, undermining the local economy. Discord between the businessmen and **Queen Liliuokalani**, ruler of the island, emerged after 1891. The pineapple grower, **Sanford Dole**, urged the United States to intervene. The Americans staged a coup in 1893, deposing Queen Liliuokalani. U.S. forces immediately protected the new provisional government led by Dole. The provisional government hoped for U.S. annexation of the islands, but that did not occur until 1898. (Hawaii eventually became the fiftieth state in 1959.)

B. Debate over the Role of the United States in the World

Differences of opinion about the proper role for the United States in the world occurred throughout the nineteenth century. The debate over U.S. expansion heated up in 1898, following America's victory in the Spanish-American War.

The American Anti-Imperialist League

In the aftermath of the **Spanish-American War**, as the **Treaty of Paris** (1898) was debated in the Senate (see pages 258–259), critics of American imperialism coalesced around the newly formed **American Anti-Imperialist League**. The league was a coalition that included conservative Democrats (known at the time as "Bourbon Democrats") as well as more progressive elements. The league included author **Mark Twain**, who became increasingly radical as he grew older. He was the vice president of the league from 1901 to 1910 and wrote some of its more scathing condemnations of imperialism.

A Departure from American Traditions

Some opponents of **imperialism** thought that American control over a far-flung array of island nations was markedly different from earlier acquisitions; these islands were densely populated and far from the settled parts of the United States, unlike the **Louisiana Purchase** (1803) or the **Mexican Cession** (1848). These opponents argued that earlier territorial gains of the United States were intended to absorb American citizens and eventually to achieve statehood and equal footing with the existing states. There was no expectation that the **Philippines**, for example, would absorb large numbers of American citizens. The United States would, indefinitely, rule over a foreign population, much as Great Britain had ruled over its thirteen American colonies before the Revolution. Critics saw this prospect as an immoral departure from the democratic traditions of a nation that was born in a war against a major power.

Anti-imperialist Sentiment and White Supremacy

Some critics of imperialism reflected prevailing white supremacist ideas. These critics feared that by acquiring the **Philippines**, for example, the United States would experience an influx of Filipinos. These critics, which included many southern Democrats, saw Asians as inferior to whites and worried about the "polluting" of the American population. Some anti-imperialists feared that an influx of people from American colonies would undermine the bargaining power of American workers.

Topic 7.3 The Spanish-American War and Its Aftermath

A variety of motivations factored into the United States decision to wage war against Spain in 1898. The subsequent American victory in the Spanish-American War proved to be a turning point in United States history, making it one of the world's imperialist powers.

A. The Spanish-American War

The roots of the Spanish-American War can be traced to an ongoing struggle in Cuba for independence from Spain. Three wars for independence occurred in the final decades of the nineteenth century (1868–1878, 1879–1880, and 1895–1898). At the same time, United States business interests expanded in Cuba. By 1894, 90 percent of Cuba's exports were going to the United States. A variety of factors led the United States to intervene (in 1898) in the final three months of the third Cuban war for independence.

United States Interest in Cuba

In the 1890s, the United States became increasingly concerned about Spanish actions in **Cuba**. Spain was in control of Cuba, but an independence movement was trying to end Spanish rule. Spain's governor of Cuba, **Valeriano Weyler**, used cruel tactics to suppress the rebellion. Thousands of Cubans were crowded into concentration camps. By 1898, one-quarter of Cuba's rural population (approximately 300,000 people) had died as a result of starvation and disease.

Many Americans wanted the United States to intervene on Cuba's side in its struggle against Spanish rule. Some Americans saw parallels between the Cuban struggle for independence from Spain and America's struggle for independence from Great Britain. Also, some American businessmen were angered by the interruption of the **sugar** harvest by the fighting between Cuban rebels and Spanish forces.

"Yellow Journalism" and the Call to War

Events in Cuba were brought to the attention of ordinary Americans through mass-produced **newspapers**. Industrialization and increased literacy set the groundwork for America's first mass media (see page 234). To attract customers, newspapers began printing bold, sensational headlines, often disregarding journalistic objectivity and even the truth. This sensationalist journalism came to be known as **"yellow journalism."** News organizations used these techniques of exaggeration and innuendo to build support for war with Spain. These newspapers breathlessly followed events in Cuba, with lurid accounts of Spanish wrongdoing and condemnations of **"Butcher" Valeriano Weyler**, the Spanish governor.

The Sinking of the *Maine*

The event that led directly to the **Spanish-American War** was the destruction of an American battleship, the **USS *Maine***, which blew up in the harbor of Havana, Cuba's capital. Many in the United States thought the sinking was the work of Spain, especially after American newspapers bluntly accused Spain of the crime, despite the scarcity of evidence.

> **USING REASONING PROCESSES:**
> **CONTINUITY AND CHANGE**
>
> **The Media, Public Opinion, and Foreign Policy**
>
> Media depictions of international events have frequently shaped public opinion around U.S. foreign policy. Occasionally, sober-minded investigative reporting has challenged conventional wisdom and pushed policymakers to reevaluate options. During the Vietnam War in the 1960s, for example, coverage by television journalists such as Morley Safer and Walter Cronkite led many Americans to question American involvement there. Often, however, coverage suspends critical judgment and amplifies government assumptions. The interplay between sensational journalism and the government's pro-war policies can be seen in the "yellow journalism" leading up to America initiating the Spanish-American War (1898), in film newsreels in theaters bolstering American engagement in World War II, in the twenty-four hour cable television news-cycle in the late twentieth century, and in online fringe news sources in the early twenty-first century.

United States Victory in the Spanish-American War

The **Spanish-American War** was brief. The United States declared war in April 1898 and Spain agreed to an armistice four months later, in August. American forces landed in **Cuba** on June 22, 1898, and Spanish forces surrendered there on July 17. Fighting in the **Philippines**, also a Spanish possession, lasted just days, as Admiral **George Dewey** led American naval forces in an alliance with Filipino rebels to take the capital, Manila. Theodore Roosevelt led a charge up **San Juan Hill** in a key battle for Cuba. The colorful Roosevelt and his men—known as **"Rough Riders"**—made headlines in American papers, elevating Roosevelt's status in the political realm.

The Treaty of Paris

Following the **Spanish-American War**, United States and Spain negotiated the **Treaty of Paris**, signed in 1898 and ratified in 1899. In the treaty, Spain agreed to cede the **Philippines**, **Puerto Rico**, and **Guam** to the United States; the United States agreed to pay Spain $20 million for these possessions. Ratification of the treaty was nearly quashed by the heated debates in the press and among political leaders over imperialism (see page 257).

Anti-imperialists insisted that the Constitution did not permit the American government to make rules for peoples who were not represented by lawmakers.

Cuba and the Platt Amendment

Cuba gained its independence following the **Spanish-American War**. However, in many ways, Cuba became independent in name only. The United States wanted to ensure that American economic interests would not be challenged by a future Cuban administration. The United States, therefore, insisted that the **Platt Amendment** be inserted into the Cuban Constitution. This amendment allowed the United States to militarily intervene in Cuban affairs if it deemed it necessary. The amendment limited the Cuban government's ability to conduct its own foreign policy and to manage its debts. Also, the amendment allowed the United States to lease a naval base at **Guantanamo Bay**. American troops intervened in Cuba three times between 1902 and 1920. The United States still maintains a naval base at Guantanamo Bay.

B. The United States as an Imperialist Power

The Spanish-American War was a turning point in terms of America's role in the world beyond North America. As a result of the war, the United States acquired island territories, became more involved in the Caribbean and Latin America, acquired the Philippines—after a protracted struggle that cost many thousands of Filipino lives—and became increasingly involved in Asia.

The Insular Cases

As the United States acquired imperial holdings, the question of whether constitutional provisions should be applied to people in the new American territories led to heated debates. Expansionists argued that the **Constitution** did not necessarily "**follow the flag**"—that residents of American colonies should not expect citizenship or basic constitutional rights. Anti-imperialists saw this position as hypocrisy, insisting that to deny constitutional rights to people living under the American flag would put the United States, in the words of a 1901 newspaper editorial, "into the rank of land-grabbing nations of Europe." The Supreme Court settled this issue in a series of cases in 1901 that have come to be known as the **Insular Cases** ("insular" means island-related). The Court agreed with expansionists that democracy and imperialism are not incompatible, and that the imperial power need not grant its colonial subjects constitutional rights. The decisions were based on the racist assumption that the colonial subjects were of an inferior race, and the colonial power had the responsibility to uplift these peoples before granting them autonomy.

War in the Philippines

Many Filipinos were surprised and disappointed to learn that the United States decided to hold on to the **Philippines** as a colony following the **Spanish-American War**. Filipino rebels had been fighting against Spain since 1896 and had initially seen the United States as a liberating force that would help them rid the nation of Spanish rule and usher in independence. However, this was not the intent of the United States. Following the ratification of the **Treaty of Paris** in 1899, a bitter, three-year long war ensued. The **Philippine-American War** was far more lengthy and deadly than the Spanish-American War itself (Filipino forces continued to resist American control for another decade). The Filipino insurgency was led by **Emilio Aguinaldo**. The United States held on to the Philippines until after World War II (1946).

> **USING REASONING PROCESSES:**
> **COMPARISON**
>
> **A Tale of Two Wars**
>
> In writing about American imperialism, do not forget about the war in the Philippines. The Philippine-American War lasted longer (three years) and resulted in more casualties (more than 4,000 American deaths; possibly 200,000 or more Filipino deaths) than the better-known Spanish-American War (four months; fewer than 400 American deaths; fewer than 15,000 combined Cuban and Spanish deaths).

China and the Open Door Policy

The bitter conflict in the Philippines was in many ways designed to provide the United States with a stepping-stone to an even greater prize—trade with **China**. Its large population and natural resources made China a target for the imperialist nations. The major powers of Europe had begun carving up China earlier in the nineteenth century. Britain, Japan, Germany, Russia, and France each proclaimed a **"sphere of influence"**—a port city and surrounding territory—from which other nations would be excluded. The United States asserted that all of China should be open to trade with all nations. **Secretary of State John Hay** enunciated this goal in a note to the major powers, asserting an **"open door"** policy for China. The United States claimed to be concerned for the territorial integrity of China, but actually was more interested in gaining a foothold in trade with China. The "open door" policy was begrudgingly accepted by the major powers.

The Boxer Rebellion

Following the end of the **Second Opium War** in 1860, **Christian missionaries** came to China in large numbers but met with little success there. The number of converts was small, and the presence of the missionaries inspired the growth of militant anti-foreign secret societies among Chinese citizens. The most well-known of these societies was the **"Boxers,"** or the **Society of Righteous and Harmonious Fists**. The Boxers led a rebellion that resulted in the death of more than 30,000 Chinese converts as well as 250 foreign nuns and approximately 200 Western missionaries. The United States participated in a multination force to rescue Westerners held hostage by the Boxers (1900).

Theodore Roosevelt and the "Big Stick"

In September 1901, just six months into his second term as president, **William McKinley** was fatally shot while attending the Pan-American Exposition in Buffalo, New York, by the anarchist Leon Czolgosz. McKinley's vice president, **Theodore Roosevelt**, became president. (See more on President Roosevelt's domestic agenda, page 268.) Roosevelt was an adventurer, an expansionist, and a hero of the Spanish-American War. His foreign policy approach is neatly summed up in his famous adage that the United States should **"speak softly, but carry a big stick"** when dealing with other nations (Roosevelt borrowed the phrase from an African proverb). The "big stick" implied the threat of military force. He envisioned the United States acting as the world's policeman, punishing wrongdoers. He asserted that the "civilized nations" had a duty to police the "backward" countries of the world. He claimed that the United States had the right to militarily intervene in the nations of Latin America. This assertion of American might is known as the **Roosevelt Corollary to the Monroe Doctrine**. In 1902, he sternly warned Germany to stay out of the Americas after Venezuela failed to repay a loan to Germany and Germany threatened military intervention.

Panama and the Panama Canal

President Theodore Roosevelt's aggressive approach to Latin America is clearly evident in regard to American actions in **Panama**. With the acquisition of overseas Pacific territories and with increased interest in trade with China, American policymakers wanted a shortcut to Asia. Merchant ships and naval vessels had to travel around the southern tip of South America to reach the Pacific Ocean. The building of a **canal** through Panama, therefore, became a major goal for Roosevelt.

Before 1903, Panama was a region of **Colombia**. American investors picked this narrow piece of land as an ideal location for a canal to facilitate shipping between the Atlantic and Pacific Oceans. When Colombia refused the U.S. offer of $10 million to build a canal, American investors, with the backing of President Roosevelt and the U.S. military, instigated a "rebellion" in Panama against Colombia. Panama became an independent country and immediately agreed to the **Hay–Bunau-Varilla Treaty** (1903) with the United States to build the canal. The building of the canal was carried out by 60,000 workers over ten years, opening in 1914. Roosevelt later boasted that he "took the Canal Zone."

Roosevelt, Diplomacy, and the Nobel Peace Prize

President Theodore Roosevelt was interested in establishing the United States as a major player in world diplomacy. Toward this end, he acted as mediator between France and Germany in their conflict over Morocco (1905). Roosevelt was also interested in maintaining a balance of power among the other world powers. That same year, Roosevelt offered to mediate an end to the **Russo-Japanese War** (1904–1905). A peace conference was held in Portsmouth, New Hampshire, with Roosevelt presiding. Despite Roosevelt's aggressive actions in Latin America, he was granted the **Nobel Peace Prize** (1906) for these diplomatic efforts.

The "Gentleman's Agreement"

In 1907, the diplomatic gains **President Theodore Roosevelt** had achieved with **Japan** (see above) were threatened by discriminatory legislation passed in **California**, restricting the rights of "Orientals." In 1906, the San Francisco Board of Education decided that the small number of Japanese-American students in the system would no longer be able to attend school with white students. They would be segregated and sent to racially specific schools, similar to segregated schools established for Chinese-American students. The move reflected a strong nativist sentiment in California at the time. Roosevelt quietly worked out a **"Gentleman's Agreement"** in which Japan agreed to limit immigration to the United States and Roosevelt agreed to pressure California authorities to end discriminatory practices.

President Taft and "Dollar Diplomacy"

President William Howard Taft (1909–1913) pursued an aggressive foreign policy, as his predecessor, President Theodore Roosevelt, did. However, Taft put more emphasis on expanding and securing American commercial interests than on pursuing the global strategic goals that Roosevelt had championed. Taft's foreign policy has come to be known as **"dollar diplomacy."** He sent troops to **Nicaragua** and the **Dominican Republic** to coerce them into signing commercial treaties with the United States. In general, he tried to substitute "dollars for bullets" in pursuing American interests. However, he failed to stem the **Mexican Revolution** in 1911 (see more on the Mexican Revolution, page 262).

President Wilson's Foreign Policy

The initial focus of the presidency of **Woodrow Wilson** was on domestic concerns (see pages 269–270). However, his administration (1913–1921) became increasingly drawn into foreign policy matters, from problems in the Americas to war in Europe (see pages 271–276). Wilson was driven by both a desire to secure American economic interests abroad and by a strong moral compass; often these impulses clashed with one another.

Wilson immediately signaled a break with his Republican predecessors by appointing the anti-imperialist **William Jennings Bryan** to be secretary of state. Bryan sought peaceful

> **USING HISTORICAL THINKING SKILLS:**
> **CONTEXTUALIZATION**
>
> **Foreign Policy and Economic Priorities**
>
> Often in American history, one can better understand foreign policy decisions by viewing them in the context of economic trends. The decision to build the Panama Canal was driven by strategic concerns, but the decision can also be seen within the context of economic priorities—namely, the growing industrial capacity of the United States following the Civil War, the desire for raw materials to fuel the manufacturing sector, and the mandate to increase global trade.

> **USING HISTORICAL THINKING SKILLS:**
> **CLAIMS AND EVIDENCE IN SOURCES**
>
> **Imperialism and Historians**
>
> Historical writing often reflects the times that the historian is writing in as much as it reflects evidence from the past. This is true of historical writing on the subject of American imperialistic ventures in the period following the Spanish-American War. Historians writing during the World War II and early Cold War era often saw these early twentieth-century imperialistic ventures (in the Philippines, Puerto Rico, Cuba, Panama, and elsewhere) in a positive, even heroic, light. Historians writing a generation later, during the aftermath of the controversial Vietnam War, often saw the earlier American interventions abroad as misguided impositions of American economic priorities on weaker nations. In comparing historical writings, be sure to note the year that each historian was writing in.

accommodations with many nations, but he and Wilson were not above flexing America's military muscle in the Americas. Wilson authorized the continued occupation of **Nicaragua** by American Marines to suppress a rebellion against the American-backed president of the country. He sent troops to **Haiti** in 1915 and to the **Dominican Republic** in 1916 to ensure that American business interests were not challenged.

Wilson and the Mexican Revolution

President Woodrow Wilson became enmeshed in the twists and turns of the **Mexican Revolution**, which lasted through the 1910s. The revolution began with the ousting of an autocratic leader in 1910. The revolution soon degenerated into a civil war that left nearly a million Mexicans dead. In 1914, Wilson challenged the legitimacy of the new Mexican leader, **General Victoriano Huerta**. He sent marines to Mexico to overthrow the regime. Huerta fled the country, and a new, more pro-American government came to power. This new government was challenged by an uprising led by the rebel leader **Francisco "Pancho" Villa**, who successfully intercepted a train carrying American gold and led a raid into American territory that left eighteen Americans dead. Wilson authorized more than 12,000 troops to invade Mexico to capture Villa, who eluded the American forces. By early 1917, the United States turned its attention away from Mexico as it began preparations for World War I.

Topic 7.4 The Progressives

The Progressive movement developed in the late 1890s and continued through the first decades of the twentieth century. Reformers and journalists addressed a host of issues associated with the growth of an industrial society.

A. The Progressive Movement

The reformers who propelled the Progressive movement were largely urban and middle class; women were disproportionately represented in their ranks. They worked on reform at the local, state, and national levels.

The Making of the Progressive Movement

The **Progressive movement** was essentially a middle-class response to the excesses of rapid industrialization, political corruption, and unplanned urbanization. Not only were middle-class college graduates the primary activists in the movement, but also the tone and tenor of the movement was decidedly middle class. Progressivism existed at the grass-roots level as well as in the corridors of power. Two influential presidents, **Theodore Roosevelt** and **Woodrow Wilson**, took on the progressive mantle. However, the movement was more an amalgam of interests, ideas, groups, and individuals, rather than a tight-knit cohort of activists with a cohesive ideology and a clearly articulated vision of the future. The movement was a bundle of contradictions. The leaders of the movement championed reforms to benefit the working class but looked at the actual working class with a mix of paternalism and suspicion. The movement challenged women's exclusion from the political process but largely accepted the prevailing racist social views of African Americans. To some degree, progressivism challenged the abuses of unbridled capitalism, yet many industrialists embraced progressive legislation in order to tame the freewheeling nature of the capitalist system and to create a more rational, predictable economic order.

Women and the Progressive Movement

A large percentage of progressive activists were women. The Progressive movement provided a means for women to become engaged in public issues in an era when most states restricted the vote to men. Women often framed their participation in the movement as **"social housekeeping."** In this way, it did not seem like such a radical break from the traditional domestic activities in which women were expected to find fulfillment. Prominent women in the Progressive movement included **Florence Kelly**, an activist for the reform of factories and chief factory inspector for Illinois (1893); **Frances Perkins**, head of the New York Consumers' League (1910) and, later, secretary of labor under President Franklin Roosevelt (1933–1945); and **Jane Addams**, founder of Hull House in Chicago (1897) (see page 233).

Pragmatism

Progressives gravitated toward the **pragmatist** philosophical ideas of **William James** and **John Dewey**. Pragmatists questioned the philosophical quest for eternal truths. Rather, they argued, the value of an idea lay in its ability to positively impact the world. Experimentation was central to the pragmatists' work. Dewey put this idea into practice at the **University of Chicago Laboratory Schools**, an experimental institution he started in Chicago in 1896 that put much more of an emphasis on the process of learning and on student participation than on the content of the curriculum.

Reform Darwinism

Progressive activists rejected the ethos of **Social Darwinism**, which applied Charles Darwin's ideas about the natural world to the world of human interactions (see pages 232–233). Progressives embraced the Darwinian idea of evolution but thought that the evolution of human society to its highest ideals required active intervention and cooperation rather than a laissez-faire approach. This call to active intervention in the evolution of the social order is called **Reform Darwinism**.

Muckrakers and the Birth of Investigative Journalism

Progressives believed in the power of the newly developed mass print media to shed light on social ills and to inspire action. The practitioners of a new investigative form of journalism were known as **"muckrakers."** *McClure's*, *Harper's*, *Cosmopolitan*, and several other magazines became staples in middle-class homes by the turn of the twentieth century, their readers increasingly drawn to articles detailing the corruption and scandals of the modern world. Many muckrakers saw themselves on a mission to shine a light on sordid business and political practices of the day. Important muckrakers included **Upton Sinclair**, **Ida Tarbell**, **Lincoln Steffens**, and **Frank Norris** (discussed below in the context of the topics they wrote about).

Progressives and Municipal Reform

Progressive activists were alarmed at the inefficiency and corruption of municipal government. The **political machines** that developed in large American cities in the nineteenth century continued to dominate cities in the early twentieth century. The most famous nineteenth-century political machine was the Democratic Party machine in New York City—headquartered in **Tammany Hall** and dominated by **"Boss" William Marcy Tweed** (see pages 241–242). The inefficiencies of urban governance were also highlighted in **Lincoln Steffens's** 1904 muckraking book, *The Shame of the Cities*. This book is a collection of pieces he had written for *McClure's* magazine.

Progressivism and Moral Reform

The progressive zeal to attack social ills led many to campaign against "sin" and "vice." These middle-class reformers were more than ready to impose their notions of "proper" behavior on the society as a whole. Reformers tackled excessive drinking, prostitution, rowdy behavior, and bawdy entertainment in their attempt to **"civilize"** the urban environment (see more on Prohibition, page 270).

The Progressive Response to the Triangle Factory Fire

In 1911, the Progressive movement was spurred to take action after a tragic fire swept through the **Triangle Shirtwaist Factory**. The factory, which produced women's blouses (then known as "shirtwaists"), was located in the upper floors of a factory building in the Greenwich Village section of **New York City**. Most of the employees were young women, many of whom were recent Italian or Jewish immigrants. A fire began in one of the scrap bins and soon spread. Trying to flee, the workers discovered that one of the entrances was blocked by flames and another was locked (perhaps to keep the workers in, or to keep union organizers out). Some escaped by elevator, some by a fire escape before it collapsed. Ultimately, 146 workers died. The tragedy led to the creation of fire safety laws in New York and to the rapid growth of the **International Ladies Garment Workers' Union**.

B. Divisions Within the Progressive Movement

The Progressive movement consisted of a broad constellation of individuals and groups. While progressivism is associated with certain goals and principles, the individuals and groups involved often held divergent views on particular issues—including race and segregation, popular participation in government, and immigration restrictions.

The Progressive Movement, Race, and Segregation

White progressives generally accepted prevailing notions around race. As discussed in Period 5, a rigid system of segregation developed in the South following the end of Reconstruction (1877). Southern states had passed a series of **Jim Crow laws**, segregating African Americans from whites in public facilities. Further, voting laws and intimidation had virtually excluded African Americans from voting, despite passage of the **Fifteenth Amendment** (1870). Violence by the **Ku Klux Klan** and others had become the backdrop to life in the South for African Americans. In the beginning of the twentieth century, eugenics tried to justify segregation and racist attitudes with scientific backing by holding that different races had distinctly different mental characteristics and capabilities. This pseudo-scientific theory also contributed to the growing anti-immigrant sentiment in the United States (see more on nativism, page 278).

Many progressive activists and writers simply ignored the conditions of African Americans. Some endorsed the segregation system that had developed in the South. Progressive president **Woodrow Wilson**, for example, was an outspoken racist. He ordered the segregation of government offices, including post offices, throughout the country. His advocacy of white supremacy went even further than contemporary social attitudes. He praised the racist film, *Birth of a Nation* (1916) by **D. W. Griffith**, with its positive portrayal of the Ku Klux Klan during the Reconstruction period.

Fighting Segregation in the Progressive Era

A small number of white progressives challenged the Jim Crow system. **Lillian Wald**, the director of the **Henry Street Settlement** in New York City, was active in the fight for racial integration. However, the principal voices for social justice for African Americans came from African-American activists who attempted to put the issue of race and racism on the national agenda. **W. E. B. Du Bois** was a militant civil-rights activist who wrote about the injustices carried out against African Americans in the South. He was one of the founders of the **National Association for the Advancement of Colored People (NAACP)** in 1909. The leadership of the organization had first met in 1905 on the Canadian side of Niagara Falls, where they formed the **Niagara Movement**.

Different Directions Among African-American Leaders

African-American activists in the Progressive era put forth different, and often competing, approaches to social change. **W. E. B. Du Bois's** call for full political equality and civil rights for African Americans (see above) was in marked contrast to the more conciliatory approach of **Booker T. Washington** (see page 223). A third important figure in the African-American community was **Marcus Garvey**, best known for urging African Americans to return to their ancestral homelands in Africa. Not many African Americans made the journey, but Garvey was influential in instilling a sense of pride among many African Americans; in this he is seen as an important figure in the Black-nationalist movement.

Democracy Versus Expertise in Progressive Governance

As discussed earlier in this chapter, progressive reformers were troubled by corruption and cronyism in government. **Lincoln Steffens's** book, *The Shame of Our Cities* (1904), turned a spotlight on municipal corruption, but corruption was rampant on all levels of government. Progressive reformers were of two minds when it came to challenging the power of corrupt **political machines**. One progressive impulse was to empower professional managers and planners, while the other impulse was to empower the citizenry through democratic reforms.

Expertise, Efficiency, and Mastery

Many progressive reformers embraced the goals of expertise and efficiency in regard to reforming the structures of governance. A system of expert managers would, reformers argued, be far superior to systems based on cronyism, nepotism, and favoritism. Many progressives looked favorably to the **"scientific management"** techniques developed by **Frederick Winslow Taylor** (see more on Taylor, page 280). The movement held the optimistic belief that experts in government could address a variety of social ills using scientific and rational criteria. Many of these ideas are articulated in **Walter Lippmann's** book, ***Drift and Mastery*** (1914). Lippmann argued that governance based on rational scientific ideas could overcome forces contributing to societal drift. By "drift," he meant a society lacking direction and discipline.

Efficiency and Municipal Government in the Wake of the Galveston Flood

The issue of municipal inefficiency and corruption came to the fore in the aftermath of a devastating hurricane and flood that struck **Galveston, Texas,** in 1900. Upwards of 8,000 people, approximately 20 percent of the population of Galveston, died in the deadliest natural disaster in United States history. Given the ineffective response by the city government, local leaders quickly took steps to create commissions to spearhead the cleanup and to rebuild the city. These commissions created a model for the **commission form of government** that soon spread from Galveston to other cities. Elected commissioners in this form of government run the city and head various departments, such as public works, fire, and sanitation. The purpose of the commission form of government is to prevent city officials from being under the sway of powerful political bosses.

The Push for Expanded Participation in Democracy

While many progressive reformers looked to experts and managers to counteract governmental corruption, a large segment of the movement pushed for **democratic empowerment** of the citizenry. This push did not address the most obvious impediment to democratic participation—laws and practices preventing the majority of African Americans from voting. However, a host of reforms, as discussed below, were advocated to make local, state, and national governments more responsive to the popular will.

Women's Suffrage

Perhaps the most important reform to come out of the Progressive era was the ratification of the **Nineteenth Amendment** to the Constitution (1920), which gave women the right to vote. The push for women's suffrage dates back to at least the **1848 Seneca Falls Convention** (see more on the origins of the women's suffrage movement, pages 163, 198, and 237). The **National American Woman Suffrage Association**, which formed in 1890 out of two earlier organizations, grew to over two million

---

USING HISTORICAL THINKING SKILLS:
CONTEXTUALIZATION

Progressive-Era Amendments

The ratification of amendments to the Constitution occurs in a particular historical context and reflects particular social and political currents. Students should be able to contextualize these changes to the Constitution. Four important amendments to the Constitution can be seen in the context of the Progressive movement. The Sixteenth Amendment (allowing for a federal income tax), the Seventeenth Amendment (providing for the direct election of senators), and the Nineteenth Amendment (extending the vote to women) reflect the Progressive call for a more equitable and democratic society. The Eighteenth Amendment (calling for prohibition) reflects the Progressive push for moral reform.

members by 1917. A more radical **National Woman's Party** was founded by **Alice Paul** in 1916. Men and women in the movement organized hundreds of parades, raised millions of dollars, and engaged in hunger strikes and civil disobedience. **President Woodrow Wilson** came to support women's suffrage in 1918, recognizing the "suffering and sacrifice" that women had experienced during World War I.

The Referendum, the Recall, and the Initiative

Reformers hoped that by expanding democracy, the power of **political machines** would be lessened. In states across the United States, progressives proposed, and often implemented, reforms to expand democracy. The **referendum** was a Progressive-era reform that allowed people to vote directly on proposed legislation. A proposed referendum item would appear on the ballot on election day; voters would either vote "yes" or "no" on the referendum. Several states still have the referendum. The **recall** empowered the people of a city or state to remove an elected official before his or her term ended. Several states still have the recall. In 2003, Californians recalled Governor Gray Davis and replaced him with Arnold Schwarzenegger. The **initiative** allowed citizens to introduce a bill to the local or state legislature by petition.

Direct Primaries

In the nineteenth century, political party leaders usually picked the candidates who would run in the general election. This practice removed a key element of the electoral process from public participation. In some districts, where one political party dominated the general elections, the only meaningful input into the political process occurred at the primary stage. The Progressive movement, therefore, pushed for the adoption of **direct primaries**, which empowered voters to choose party candidates to run for elected public office. Minnesota was the first state to adopt a direct primary in 1899. Most other states had also adopted direct primaries by 1916.

Direct Election of Senators

Progressives pushed for the **direct election of senators**. Previously, senators were chosen by state legislatures. The framers to the Constitution had envisioned the Senate as an august body of even-tempered men, who would counterbalance the enthusiasms and rash decisions of the House of Representatives—the "people's chamber." Such thinking was deemed elitist by many progressive activists. The **Seventeenth Amendment**, ratified in 1913, allowed voters to cast direct votes for U.S. senators.

The Australian Ballot

In the nineteenth century, **political machines** routinely printed ballots with their candidates on them. Voters would then deposit these ballots, which were often printed on different colored paper, in voting boxes, allowing anyone who was interested to see which ballot a voter deposited. Some states used voice voting—voters would state their preference to an official, who would then record their vote in a poll book. These systems allowed for voter intimidation. In 1888, Massachusetts adopted a **secret ballot**, which was already in use in **Australia**. These ballots, printed by the state instead of the parties and filled out by voters in curtained booths, became the norm in America by 1910.

C. Progressive Reform on the National Level

The Progressive movement had a profound impact on national politics. Progressives pushed for federal legislation to expand democratic participation and to protect both the economy and the environment from abuses.

Progressivism and Industrial Capitalism

During the Gilded Age of the late nineteenth century, America's industrial output grew exponentially with virtually no government regulation. Industrialists and their allies championed **laissez-faire** economics—the idea that government should stay out of economic activities (see page 237). By the early twentieth century, many Americans came to believe that unregulated industry could be harmful to individuals, communities, and even to the health of industrial capitalism itself. If people lost confidence in the products of the industrial system, sales would suffer.

The Jungle and the Meat-packing Industry

A public outcry about the conditions of the **meat-processing industry** was generated by **Upton Sinclair's** 1906 novel, *The Jungle*, which vividly depicts the horrible conditions in the meat-packing industry. The novel takes place in Chicago and follows a Lithuanian immigrant family through the stockyards of Chicago. Based on extensive research by Sinclair, the novel brought to light the unsanitary and dangerous conditions of the meat-packing industry. While the socialist message of the book was largely ignored by the public, the depiction of meat processing was not. The public uproar that followed the book's publication led Congress to pass the **Meat Inspection Act** (1906) and the **Pure Food and Drug Act** (also 1906), which established the **Food and Drug Administration**.

The History of the Standard Oil Company

The **Standard Oil Company**, a giant trust assembled by **John D. Rockefeller**, had come to dominate the petroleum-processing industry by the end of the nineteenth century (see page 226). Journalist and teacher **Ida Tarbell** detailed the rise of Standard Oil in a series of articles in *McClure's Magazine* and then in her book, *The History of the Standard Oil Company* (1904). Her research exposed the ruthlessness of Rockefeller's oil company and contributed to the government invoking the Sherman Antitrust Act (see page 237) to break up the Standard Oil Trust in 1911.

Regulating Workplace Practices—*Muller v. Oregon* and the "Brandeis Brief"

Progressives tackled the dual issues of **long working hours** and **child labor**. In the late nineteenth century, workdays of twelve hours or more were not uncommon, and child labor had become a normal practice in large factories, where children as young as ten years old worked daily. The movement to reform the workplace suffered a setback in 1905, when, in the case of *Lochner v. New York*, the Supreme Court ruled a New York State law restricting hours for bakers unconstitutional. The Court cited the sanctity of private contracts between employers and employees. However, the Progressive movement achieved a major boost in another Supreme Court decision just three years later, *Muller v. Oregon* (1908). That decision upheld an Oregon law limiting the number of hours women could work. The decision cited the supposed physical limitations of women and the threat to their health that long workdays posed. It specifically cited women's role as child bearers. The case is significant because of the brief written by future Supreme Court justice **Louis Brandeis** on behalf of the state of Oregon. Brandeis cited copious scientific, psychological, and sociological studies to bolster the case for limiting women's hours of work. This type of legal argument has come to be known as a **"Brandeis brief."** The use of non-legal information in legal matters would become increasingly common in the twentieth century, including in the case of *Brown v. Board of Education of Topeka* (1954) (see page 330).

> **USING HISTORICAL THINKING SKILLS: CONTEXTUALIZATION**
>
> ***Muller*, the Progressive Movement, and Gender**
>
> The decision in *Muller v. Oregon* (1908), a major victory for the Progressive movement, can be examined in the context of changing and competing views about gender. As activists in the women's rights movement challenged unequal treatment in American society, the Progressive movement exhibited differing approaches to gender. Although many progressives challenged ingrained understandings of gender, the *Muller* decision reinforced traditional notions of female frailty.

Challenging Child Labor

Progressive reformers challenged the pervasive practice of **child labor** (see page 227). An effective tactic of the movement was publishing photographs of children working in industrial settings. **Lewis Hine's** photographs were especially effective in bringing the issue to greater public attention. In 1916, the Progressive movement had a short-lived success with the issue of child labor, when Congress passed the **Keating-Owen Child Labor Act**. Realizing that local factory rules were under the domain of state law, Congress addressed the issue of child labor by prohibiting the sale, across state lines, of goods produced by factories that employed children under fourteen years of age. Congress used its power to regulate interstate commerce. Less than a year later, in the case of ***Hammer v. Dagenhart*** (1917), the Supreme Court found the act unconstitutional. The Court asserted that the goods being regulated were not inherently "immoral," as prostitution or liquor might be. Therefore, what was being addressed by the law was manufacturing practices, and manufacturing practices were subject to state, not federal, law. Child labor was not effectively addressed until federal fair-labor standards were established during the **New Deal** era of the 1930s.

Progressivism in the White House

The Progressive movement was primarily a grassroots movement of thousands of activists, but in the early twentieth century, progressivism entered the discourse of the national political parties. **President Theodore Roosevelt**, a Republican, embraced many progressive reforms, but his handpicked successor, **President William H. Taft**, proved to be a disappointment to the Progressive movement. The divisions within the Republican Party over President Taft contributed to the electoral victory in 1912 of Democrat **Woodrow Wilson**. The pervasiveness of progressive ideology crossed party lines, with Wilson implementing some important progressive reforms.

Theodore Roosevelt and the "Square Deal"

Theodore Roosevelt assumed the presidency following the assassination of **William McKinley** in 1901 and quickly began to move the Republican Party and the nation itself in a progressive direction. His domestic agenda was known as the **"Square Deal."** Moreover, he championed the cause of conservation of natural resources and came to be known as the **"trust buster."**

Roosevelt and the Regulation of Business

President Theodore Roosevelt's "Square Deal" approach to public issues is reflected in his handling of the **anthracite coal strike** in 1902. He called representatives from both management and labor to the White House, threatening to take over the mines if owners did not negotiate in good faith. Ultimately, the miners received a 10 percent wage increase, but not union recognition. Roosevelt also pushed for important consumer protections in the wake of the publication of *The Jungle* (see page 267), and stronger measures to protect the environment (see pages 270–271). Also, Roosevelt wanted stronger regulation of the powerful railroad industry. The coercive and even violent tactics of the railroad industry (in its dealings with California wheat farmers) were depicted in Frank Norris's novel, ***The Octopus: A California Story*** (1901). Roosevelt strengthened the **Interstate Commerce Commission** (ICC, created in 1887) with the **Elkins Act** (1903), which targeted the railroad practice of granting rebates to favored customers, and the **Hepburn Act** (1906), which gave the ICC greater latitude to set railroad rates.

Roosevelt as "Trust Buster"

President Theodore Roosevelt saw the concentration of economic power in a few hands as potentially dangerous to the economy as a whole. Although the **Sherman Antitrust Act** (1890) was passed to limit monopolistic practices, the act was not enforced with a great deal of enthusiasm (see page 270). Roosevelt made a point of using the act to pursue **"bad trusts"**—ones that interfered with commerce—not necessarily the biggest trusts. One of his first targets was the Northern Securities Company, a railroad holding company, which grew out of a merger of several major railroad companies in 1901. By controlling all railroad traffic in the Northwest, from Chicago to Washington, it had eliminated competition in this region. His efforts were challenged in court. In ***Northern Securities Co. v. United States*** (1904), the Supreme Court upheld the power of the government to break up Northern Securities under the Sherman Antitrust Act. The case was a victory for Roosevelt, whose efforts at challenging monopolies earned him the nickname **"trust buster."**

The Administration of William Howard Taft

After **President Theodore Roosevelt's** nearly two terms in office, he picked his secretary of war, **William Howard Taft**, to succeed him. Taft readily won the nomination of the Republican Party and defeated the Democratic candidate, **William Jennings Bryan**, in the 1908 election.

Progressives were repeatedly disappointed by Taft, who was not a skillful politician and failed to develop a base of support. He agreed to higher tariff rates by signing the **Payne-Aldrich Tariff** into law (1909), despite the progressive goal of lowering tariff rates to reduce consumer prices. In addition, he ended up firing **Gifford Pinchot** as chief of the United States Forest Service after Pinchot's clashes with Taft's development-minded secretary of the interior, **Richard Ballinger**. Taft did pursue antitrust suits, even though his public rhetoric did not emphasize this. He initiated ninety antitrust cases, including a major case against **U.S. Steel** (see page 286).

Taft, Roosevelt, and the Election of 1912

Theodore Roosevelt came to regret his decision to throw his support behind President **William Howard Taft**. After 1910, a wide rift developed within the **Republican Party** between Taft and Roosevelt. By 1912, this rift became a virtual civil war within the party. Roosevelt and his supporters walked out of the Republican Party nominating convention in 1912 after the party chose Taft to run for reelection. Roosevelt and his loyalists founded the **Progressive Party** (more commonly known by its nickname, the **Bull Moose Party**), and nominated Roosevelt to run as a third-party candidate in the general election. The election was further complicated by the candidacy of **Eugene V. Debs** of the **Socialist Party** (see page 236). The split within the Republican Party allowed the Democratic Party candidate, **Woodrow Wilson**, to win the presidency. He won the majority of the electoral votes, despite winning only 41 percent of the popular vote, to Roosevelt's 27 percent, Taft's 23 percent, and Debs's 6 percent.

Progressivism and Woodrow Wilson

Woodrow Wilson was an anomaly in the White House. He was only the second Democrat to serve since Andrew Johnson (1865–1869). In the decades following the Civil War, Republicans had repeatedly **"waved the bloody shirt"**—invoking the memory of the **Democratic Party's** role in secession and war—and won several close presidential elections during the Gilded Age. Wilson was also the first southerner elected to the White House since Johnson (he was born in Virginia). Wilson, a historian and a scholar, had been governor of New Jersey and president of Princeton University before assuming the presidency. He had established a track record as a progressive reformer when he entered the White House.

Wilson and the Federal Reserve Act

During his presidency, **President Wilson** grew increasingly suspicious of the banking industry. He argued that it was inflexible and in the service of the stock market more than in the service of the American public. In addition, concerns over the banking system had been raised following the **Panic of 1907**, which threatened several major banks. With no central bank in place, it took the intervention of the financier, **J.P. Morgan**, to avert a more serious crisis (see more on the Panic of 1907, pages 286–287). Many economists and reformers grew apprehensive that the viability of the nation's financial system was in the hands of a private banker. To address these concerns, Wilson pushed for passage of the **Federal Reserve Act**, which created a central banking system in 1913. The **Federal Reserve System**, which is partly privately controlled and partly publicly controlled, is comprised of twelve regional Federal Reserve Banks. One of its main functions is to regulate economic growth. Its policies can expand or contract the currency supply. If the economy is sluggish, the Fed attempts to stimulate economic growth by expanding the currency supply. If inflation occurs, the Fed attempts to slow down economic activity by reducing the currency supply. An important mechanism for regulating economic growth is raising or lowering the interest rate at which the Fed loans money to other banks. Other banks follow suit, raising or lowering the interest rates at which they loan money to the public. For example, by lowering interest rates, the Fed stimulates economic activity by making it more attractive for people to make major purchases. On the other hand, the Fed might raise interest rates if it wants to cool economic activity in order to prevent inflation.

Regulation of Business

President Wilson was a strong supporter of small business and took a dim view of the growing power of big business. He readily took on the mantle of business regulation that had been central to the agenda of the Progressive movement from its inception. Progressives had become increasingly alarmed at the power of unregulated business during the era of rapid industrialization in the late nineteenth century. In 1890, the **Sherman Antitrust Act** had been passed, but was used with limited success (see page 237). Wilson strengthened the antitrust powers of the federal government with the **Clayton Antitrust Act** (1914). A key difference in the new act was that it specifically exempted **labor unions** from being targeted by antitrust actions. The Sherman Act had often been used to break up strikes.

President Wilson also pushed for the creation of the **Federal Trade Commission** (1914) to regulate business practices and enforce provisions of the Clayton Antitrust Act. The legislation that created the FTC enumerated a host of powers and responsibilities, including guarding against "unfair or deceptive acts or practices in or affecting commerce."

The Prohibition Movement and the Eighteenth Amendment

The movement to limit or eliminate **alcohol consumption** in American society had been one of the largest reform movements in the nineteenth century. (See more on the temperance movement, pages 160 and 242.) It gained new enthusiasts among progressives who sought to harness the power of the government to change social behavior. In the first decades of the twentieth century, saloons were seen as parasites on working-class communities, fleecing their patrons. The **Anti-Saloon League** (founded in 1893) saw the saloon industry as profiteering off alcohol abuse.

The final victory for the **prohibition movement** came in 1919, the year after World War I drew to a close. The movement equated the prohibition of alcohol with the quest to bring democracy to the world. The United States would purify the world of undemocratic forces and purify its citizens of corrupting alcohol. Furthermore, the anti-German sentiment that developed during World War I also played a role; many American breweries had been founded by German immigrants and had German names. All these factors led to the ratification of the **Eighteenth Amendment**, which banned the production, sale, and transportation of alcohol as of January 1, 1920. Congress passed the Volstead Act in 1918 to set up the legal mechanisms to enforce the amendment.

D. Addressing Environmental Issues in the Progressive Era

By the late nineteenth century, many observers began to note the toll that industrial processes began to take on the natural environment. Debates ensued during the Progressive era over appropriate strategies to address environmental degradation.

Concern for Disappearing Wilderness

By the last decades of the nineteenth century, some Americans were beginning to note the disappearance of wilderness and the toll that rapid industrialization was taking on the **environment**. Logging and mining operations were destroying vast forested areas. Sportsmen were early advocates of environmental protection. For example, the sportsman, zoologist, and adventurer **George Bird Grinnell** and **Theodore Roosevelt** organized the **Boone and**

USING HISTORICAL THINKING SKILLS:
CONTEXTUALIZATION

The Environment and Romanticism

Growing concern for environmental degradation took place within the context of romanticism, a dominant intellectual and artistic movement in the nineteenth century. Romanticism (see page 157) had generated interest in untouched natural environments. Romantics worried about the corrupting influences of civilization and championed the restorative powers of nature. Paintings of the West by Albert Bierstadt, depicting awe-inspiring landscapes and hinting at the storm clouds of modern civilization on the horizon, generated interest in "unspoiled" landscapes.

Crockett Club (1887)—named after the two prominent American backwoodsmen—not only to promote outdoor activities but also to lobby for environmental protection.

Roosevelt and Conservation

As president, **Theodore Roosevelt** embraced the cause of **environmental conservation**. In keeping with the progressive reliance on expertise, he appointed the scientifically trained **Gifford Pinchot** to head the **U.S. Forest Service** and to lead the government's conservation efforts. The roots of the Forest Service date back to the 1870s, as concerns grew about the clear-cutting of forests. In 1876, Congress appointed a special agent in the Department of Agriculture to assess the condition of forested land. This office became the Division of Forestry in 1881 and was renamed the Forest Service in 1905.

Expansion of the National Park System

The federal government began the **National Park System** in 1872 when it created **Yellowstone Park**, primarily in Wyoming. In 1890, California's **Yosemite Valley** and the surrounding area were designated a national park (it had been granted federal protection in 1864). **President Roosevelt** expanded the system, creating five additional national parks. He also established 150 national forests, including **Shoshone National Forest**, the nation's first national forest. Ultimately, Roosevelt put over 200 million acres under public protection.

Conservationism and Preservationism

President Theodore Roosevelt endorsed the view that the nation's natural resources should be used in a responsible way so they would continue to exist for future generations. This view, labeled **conservationism**, can be contrasted with the views of environmental preservationists. **Preservationists** want society to have a hands-off approach to the remaining relatively untouched natural areas. An early preservationist was **John Muir**, one of the founders of the **Sierra Club** (1892), an organization dedicated to preserving wilderness and to monitoring the federal government's oversight of protected lands. Conservationism, by contrast, with its emphasis on regulation and responsible economic utilization of resources, tapped into major strands of progressive thinking—efficiency, expertise, scientific management, and government intervention.

The Controversy over the Hetch Hetchy Valley

Both **conservationists** and **preservationists** (see above) were concerned about the rapid disappearance of natural areas in the United States and both endorsed the establishment of national parks. However, the two positions were often at odds. The destruction of the **Hetch Hetchy Valley** in California illustrates divergent approaches to the environment during the Progressive era. The spectacular Hetch Hetchy Valley, within the borders of **Yosemite National Park**, was targeted by San Francisco officials as a possible water source for the growing city. Officials sought to dam the Tuolumne River and turn Hetch Hetchy into a giant reservoir. Although federal officials initially balked at destroying the valley, they reversed themselves after a devastating earthquake and fire destroyed much of San Francisco in 1906. The fire highlighted the inadequacy of **San Francisco's** existing water supply and the need for a municipally controlled water system. Preservationists, led by John Muir and the Sierra Club, fought a seven-year battle against what they saw as the destruction of a sacred natural site. The plan was given final approval by the Woodrow Wilson administration in 1913 and was completed a decade later.

Topic 7.5 World War I: Military and Diplomacy

As World War I (1914–1918) began in Europe, Americans began to debate the proper role of the United States in the world. The aftermath of the war led to debates about how the United States could best pursue its international interests.

A. The United States Enters World War I

When World War I began in 1914, the United States initially proclaimed neutrality in the conflict. A variety of factors, including President Woodrow Wilson's call to make the world "safe for democracy," led the United States to enter the conflict.

The Context of World War I

Historians cite several developments that created an unstable, even dangerous, situation in Europe in the years before **World War I**. History teachers often graphically represent these factors as sticks of dynamite; the sticks, in such a drawing, are labeled **"nationalism," "imperialism," "militarism,"** and **"the alliance system."** By the end of the nineteenth century, a rise in nationalism among the European powers was clearly evident. The nations of Europe began to see themselves as actors in a Darwinian struggle to be the "fittest." Inexpensive newspapers and rising literacy rates allowed for the dissemination of patriotic sentiments to an entire nation. This sense of nationalism was fueled by a competition to imperialize the remaining independent areas of Asia and Africa. A scramble occurred among the major powers, setting the stage for tensions and conflict. The situation was made more dangerous by an ominous arms buildup among the European nations, especially the rival maritime nations of **Great Britain** and **Germany**. The two nations built larger and larger warships, typified by Great Britain's **HMS Dreadnought**, which ushered in an era of similarly massive Dreadnought-class battleships. Finally, the situation was made more volatile by a dangerous series of alliances. Essentially, a conflict between any two belligerents would soon degenerate into a broad European-wide war as mutual-defense treaties would drag more nations into the conflict.

The Onset of War

If the long-term causes of **World War I** (see above) are presented as sticks of dynamite, then the spark that ignited them was the assassination of the heir to the throne of the **Austro-Hungarian empire**, **Archduke Franz Ferdinand**. While visiting the city of **Sarajevo** in Bosnia and Herzogovina, part of Austria-Hungary, the archduke was assassinated by a pan-Slavic nationalist in 1914. The assassination resulted in Austria-Hungary declaring war on Serbia. The alliance system brought **Germany** into the conflict on the side of Austria-Hungary, while **Russia**, and then **France** and **Great Britain**, were brought into the conflict on the opposing side. As the war began, Russia, France, and Great Britain, who had previously formed an informal understanding known as the **Triple Entente**, formed the core of the **Allied Powers,** which also included Serbia, Belgium, Montenegro, Japan, and several other nations as the war progressed. Austria-Hungary, Germany, and Italy, known as the **Triple Alliance**, formed the core of the **Central Powers,** which grew to include the Ottoman Empire, Bulgaria, and several other co-belligerents; Italy switched sides, joining the Allied Powers in 1915. The conflict would last four years and result in the deaths of an astounding 8.7 million military personnel.

United States Neutrality

The United States initially assumed that it could stay neutral during **World War I**. Several factors kept the United States neutral in the war for the first three years. The United States, from the time of **President Washington's Farewell Address,** had attempted to stay aloof from the ongoing conflicts of Europe. That had not always been easy. The United States went to war with Great Britain at the beginning of the nineteenth century (1812) and with Spain at the end of the century (1898). These wars, however, were not fought in Europe. **Isolationism**, when it came to affairs on the European continent, remained strong. Neutrality also allowed the United States to trade with both sides in the conflict.

Immigration Patterns and Public Opinion Around World War I

Immigration patterns did not immediately predispose the United States toward support for either side in World War I. The United States was home to millions of people from belligerent nations on both sides of the conflict. On the one hand, **German** and **Irish** immigrants tended to favor the Central Powers. Many German Americans favored their country of ancestry while many Irish Americans had a longstanding resentment of Great Britain. On the other hand, Americans had ties to **Great Britain**. Despite the two wars that they had fought (the **American Revolution** and the **War of 1812**), the United States and Great Britain shared a language and strong cultural ties.

From Neutrality to Intervention

Although several factors initially kept America out of World War I, important developments propelled the United States toward intervention. **President Woodrow Wilson** had emphasized the principle of **freedom of the seas**. He indicated that the United States would trade and sell weaponry to either side in the conflict, but Great Britain had effectively blockaded Germany. Trade, therefore, shifted to Great Britain as the war progressed. Between 1914 (when the war began) and 1917, U.S. trade with Britain increased by 300 percent, while trade with Germany shrank to almost nothing.

Germany responded by warning that U.S. ships in the waters off Great Britain would be subject to attack by **U-boats** (submarines). The sinking of the British ocean liner, *Lusitania*, in May 1915 infuriated many Americans (128 Americans were among the dead). In response to American and British protests of the action, Germany responded (accurately) that the ship was listed as an auxiliary war ship and that it was openly carrying munitions. Another British passenger ship, the *Arabic*, was sunk by a German U-boat attack in August 1915 (two Americans were among the dead). Germany, however, wanted to keep the United States out of the war and, in response to American protests, agreed in the ***Arabic* Pledge** (1915) to make no attacks on passenger ships without prior warning. The following year, a French ferry named the *Sussex*, carrying passengers from England to France, was torpedoed by a German U-boat, resulting in eighty deaths and hundreds of injuries (several Americans were among the injured). Wilson, angry at the attack on innocent civilians (including Americans), threatened to break off relations with Germany. In response, Germany issued the ***Sussex* Pledge** (1916) to appease the United States, reaffirming the promise of the *Arabic* Pledge and extending it to include merchant ships (unless the presence of war materials had been established). The United States took advantage of this pledge and traded extensively with Great Britain, much to the consternation of Germany.

Progressives and the War

Progressives were initially divided about American participation in World War I. At the beginning of the war, many progressives were leery about American involvement. They predicted that participation in a major war would distract the nation from domestic reform. However, many progressives saw great possibilities in American participation in the war. **John Dewey**, in an essay in the *New Republic*, encouraged progressives to see the "**social possibilities of war.**" These possibilities included an expansion of the federal government, a sense of unity and national purpose, and a renewed focus on issues of social justice.

President Woodrow Wilson and the War

As the war dragged on in Europe, public opinion began to shift toward the **Allied Powers** of **Great Britain**, **France**, and **Russia**. This was partly brought about by wartime news coverage, which

---

USING HISTORICAL THINKING SKILLS:
SOURCING AND SITUATION

President Wilson's "War Message"

It is important to carefully analyze high stakes public announcements—such as presidential calls for war—with special attention toward purpose and audience. In regard to President Woodrow Wilson's 1917 "War Message to Congress" calling for intervention in World War I, you should be able to interrogate Wilson's claims that the United States was entering the war to make "the world . . . safe for democracy." Be prepared to discuss the purpose of such a document—rallying a reluctant public to participate in a major war—rather than simply recounting information contained within it as fact.

tended to present **Germany** and the **Central Powers** as aggressive, and even barbaric, in their prosecution of the war. Also, the Allied Powers seemed to be more clearly the democratic side of the war after czarist Russia was no longer part of the alliance. (The czar was toppled in February 1917 and Russia later withdrew from the war.) **President Wilson's** approach to the conflict changed rapidly. During his bid for reelection in 1916, Wilson's campaign repeatedly reminded voters that **"he kept us out of war."** However, after his reelection, Wilson became increasingly convinced that U.S. participation in World War I was necessary to make the world **"safe for democracy."**

Wilson's shift to a pro-war stance divided Americans. Some joined Wilson on his intellectual journey; they too began to think of participation in the war as an idealistic crusade to create a new world order based on peace and autonomy. However, many opposed the drive for war. The government went to great lengths to alter public opinion (see below).

The Zimmerman Note and Unrestricted German Submarine Warfare

Many Americans moved toward a pro-war position after the secret **"Zimmerman Note"** became public in March 1917. The intercepted telegram from German foreign secretary Arthur Zimmerman indicated that Germany would help Mexico regain territory it had lost to the United States if Mexico joined the war on Germany's side. Americans took this as a threat to their territory.

Finally, in early 1917, Germany announced it would rescind the *Sussex* Pledge and would resume **unrestricted submarine warfare** against Great Britain and its allies, including the United States. In February and March of 1917, hundreds of American ships were sunk by German submarine attacks. This proved to be the final straw for the United States. In April 1917, the United States declared war on Germany.

> **USING HISTORICAL THINKING SKILLS: MAKING CONNECTIONS**
>
> **World War I and Modern Advertising**
>
> The campaign organized by the Committee on Public Information could be considered one of the first major national advertising campaigns in United States history. The lessons about shaping public opinion during the war were used in commercial advertising campaigns in the 1920s. The staff of the CPI included Edward Bernays, a pioneer in public relations (see page 280). Bernays created a famous campaign in 1929 to promote female smoking. He branded cigarettes as feminist "Torches of Freedom" and hired women to march, while smoking cigarettes, in New York City's Easter Sunday Parade.

Shaping Public Opinion

In the aftermath of the United States' **declaration of war**, the government worked hard to shape public opinion. **President Wilson** established the **Committee on Public Information** (CPI) in 1917 to organize pro-war propaganda. It was led by **George Creel**, a former muckraking journalist. The CPI sent **"Four-Minute Men"** around the country to give brief, impassioned speeches in favor of the war effort to schools, civic groups, churches, and any gathering that would have them. The CPI also produced a series of evocative posters to convince Americans to support the war. Several of these posters specifically targeted the supposed ruthless actions of German soldiers, often labeled the "Huns," a derogatory term that alludes to the nomadic tribes of the ancient world that plundered Europe. One of the posters, created by the American artist and illustrator **James Montgomery Flagg**, featured the image of Uncle Sam pointing directly at the viewer of the poster with the famous tag line, **"I Want You for U.S. Army."**

Funding the War

The mission of the Committee on Public Information was not simply to garner moral support for the war. It also focused on raising funds for it. Many of the committee's posters encouraged Americans to purchase **bonds** to fund the war's costs. One poster called on Americans to "Beat Back the Hun with Liberty Bonds"; another told Americans, "If you can't enlist—invest." The government, in an attempt to avoid excessive tax increases, ended up raising two-thirds of the war's costs from war bonds.

Federal Agencies and War Production

Several government agencies were created during World War I to ensure a smooth transition to a war economy. The **War Industries Board** was created by the government to direct industrial production. The agency was led by **Bernard Baruch**. He sought to bring together labor and management in order to ensure uninterrupted production of armaments, uniforms, and other needed items. The **Food Administration**, with future president **Herbert Hoover** at the helm, was created to ensure sufficient food production to feed the troops as well as the civilian population. The **National War Labor Policies Board** dealt with labor disputes. This constellation of government agencies was exactly what progressive reformers had hoped to create on a permanent basis.

B. The Role of the United States in World War I

The United States played an important role during the final year of World War I. The role of American troops, organized as the American Expeditionary Forces, was relatively limited. However, the infusion of fresh American troops helped tip the balance of World War I in favor of the Allies.

American Participation in World War I

The United States entered World War I late in the conflict. It did provide the Allies—Great Britain and France—with much needed reinforcement. France and Great Britain had been at war for nearly three years when the United States joined the conflict. The two million soldiers of the **American Expeditionary Forces** proved to be crucial in Allied offensives that led to victory.

By the time the United States entered, the war had bogged down into a unrelenting stalemate. Both sides had dug into trenches separated by a strip of **"no-man's land."** When one side attempted a frontal attack on the other, as soon as the soldiers were ordered out of their trenches they were subjected to machine gun fire, barbed wire, and poison gas. Such fighting might result in one side or the other capturing a few hundred yards of desolate land, but more decisive victories were difficult to achieve. The five-month-long **Battle of the Somme** (1916), for example, resulted in more than a million casualties and no substantial gains for either side.

In June and July 1918, American troops joined French troops in repelling German advances, fighting at **Chateau-Thierry** and **Rheims**. In September, American troops began to participate in assaults on German-held territory. By October, the Allies' advances toward the German border led German military leaders to seek a ceasefire. An **armistice** was signed on November 11, 1918, bringing World War I to a close. American troops suffered over 300,000 casualties, including over 50,000 battlefield deaths and over 60,000 non-combat deaths (many from the deadly "Spanish flu" epidemic that soon raged around the world).

C. The United States and the Postwar World

Following World War I, President Woodrow Wilson was active in the negotiations for a peace treaty. His involvement was important in proposals to create the League of Nations, an institution formed to maintain world peace. However, the question of American participation in the League caused strenuous debates in the United States. Ultimately, the U.S. Senate refused to ratify the Treaty of Versailles and rejected American involvement in the League of Nations.

Wilson's Fourteen Points

President Wilson was determined to shape the structure of the postwar world. He felt strongly that the causes of the war should be identified, addressed, and alleviated. Wilson put forth a document, known as the **Fourteen Points** (1918), which emphasized international cooperation. He envisioned a world order based on freedom of the seas, removal of barriers to trade, self-determination for European peoples, and an international organization to resolve conflicts. These ideas were rejected by the victorious European powers, with the exception of the creation of the **League of Nations**.

United States Rejection of the Treaty of Versailles

Ironically, the United States did not join the **League of Nations**. This international body was the one component of **President Wilson's Fourteen Points** document that was embraced by the victorious European nations. The United States would have had to approve the **Treaty of Versailles** in order to join the League. Despite Wilson's enthusiasm for passage of the treaty, some **isolationist** Republican senators vowed to reject it. This group, labeled **"irreconcilables,"** included **isolationists** determined to withdraw the United States from world affairs. Some of these Republican senators were also eager to humiliate Wilson for perceived political slights, including his exclusion of Republicans from the recent Paris peace conference. Other senators took a middle position: this group, labeled **"reservationists,"** would agree to vote to approve the treaty if the Senate put certain conditions on American participation in the League of Nations. Wilson refused to compromise on this and urged his allies in the Senate to reject any amendments (or reservations). Without the senators in the middle, the Treaty of Versailles was rejected by the Senate in 1919. In many ways, the debates around the Treaty of Versailles and the victory of isolationist sentiment shaped American foreign policy for the next decade.

Topic 7.6 World War I: Home Front

World War I opened opportunities for employment in war-related industries, leading to significant internal migrations to urban centers. At the same time, the years during and immediately following World War I saw a backlash against the experimentation of the Progressive era and a rise in patriotism and xenophobia.

A. World War I and the Conservative Rejection of Progressive Reform

Government restrictions on freedom of speech during World War I were followed by the Red Scare and government attacks on organized labor after the war.

Civil Liberties During Wartime

Despite the hopes of many progressives, World War I ushered in a repressive atmosphere that stymied progressive reform and led to the curtailment of civil liberties. The **Espionage and Sedition Acts** were passed during World War I to put limits on public expressions of antiwar sentiment. The Espionage Act (1917) made it a crime to interfere with the draft or with the sale of war bonds, or to say anything "disloyal" about the war effort. The Sedition Act (1918) extended the reach of the Espionage Act.

The Espionage Act was upheld by the Supreme Court in the decision in *Schenck v. United States* (1919). **Charles Schenck** and other members of the Socialist Party had been arrested for printing and distributing flyers opposing the war and urging young men to resist the draft. The Court asserted that freedom of speech is not absolute and that the government is justified in limiting certain forms of speech during wartime. The Court argued that certain utterances pose a **"clear and present danger."** By analogy, the Court reasoned that one is not allowed to falsely shout "Fire!" in a crowded theater.

> **USING REASONING PROCESSES:**
> **CONTINUITY AND CHANGE**
>
> **Civil Liberties and War Over Time**
>
> The debate over civil liberties during wartime is an ongoing issue. Be prepared to compare restrictions on civil liberties at different crisis points in history: The Alien and Sedition Acts during the "Quasi-war" with France in the 1790s, the suspension of the writ of habeas corpus during the Civil War, the Espionage and Sedition Acts during World War I, the internment of Japanese-Americans during World War II, and the enactment of the Patriot Act following the terrorist attacks of 2001.

The Crusade Against Organized Labor and Dissent

Attacks on organized labor occurred amidst a dramatic increase in union activism in the immediate aftermath of **World War I**. Labor conflict and the increased visibility of radical movements led to an atmosphere of repression against radicals and immigrants.

When World War I ended, the government disbanded the agencies that it had created to regulate economic activity during the war. Workers, for instance, no longer had the protections of the **National War Labor Policies Board**. In addition, inflation was no longer kept in check by the government. In 1919, prices rose nearly 75 percent. In these conditions, workers across America organized and fought to protect wartime gains. The year 1919 saw the second largest strike wave in American history (the largest strike wave was in 1945–1946). There were more than 4,500 strikes, involving four million workers. The biggest strike was the **Seattle General Strike** in February. The radical **Industrial Workers of the World** and the more moderate **American Federation of Labor** worked together to virtually close down Seattle. In September, more than 340,000 steelworkers went on strike. Late in 1919 and into 1920, the police force in Boston went on strike. In all three of these strikes, and in countless others, the workers were soundly defeated.

Management used a variety of techniques to maintain the upper hand in dealing with organized labor. First, management was able to paint striking workers as subversives and would-be **Bolsheviks**. Second, corporate leaders strenuously pushed for **open shops**—workplaces in which the union could not require workers to join the union. Finally, the government intervened on behalf of management. The Supreme Court, for instance, held that picketing was not protected by the First Amendment. It was not until the New Deal era of the 1930s that the labor movement was able to regain momentum.

The Red Scare

The backlash against the strike wave of 1919, combined with the virulent strain of patriotism unleashed by World War I, set the groundwork for the **Red Scare** of the late 1910s and early 1920s. The Red Scare, a campaign against Communists, anarchists, and other radicals, also targeted labor leaders, attempting to portray the labor movement as a front for radical organizing. The Red Scare was both a grassroots response of ordinary Americans as well as a government-orchestrated campaign. The scare can be traced to the successful Bolshevik revolution in Russia that brought the **Communist Party** to power and led to the establishment of the **Soviet Union**. In 1919, the **Bolsheviks** created the **Comintern**, an international organization of Communist Party leaders determined to duplicate the success of the Bolsheviks in other countries. Conservative Americans took the pronouncements of the Comintern at face value, even though the Communist movement in the United States was small.

In December 1919, the Russian-born anarchist and activist **Emma Goldman** was deported by the Justice Department. Later, in January 1920, **Attorney General A. Mitchell Palmer** began a broad hunt for suspected radicals. Palmer's Justice Department carried out unwarranted raids, known as **"Palmer Raids,"** of suspected radicals' homes. Six thousand alleged radicals were identified by Palmer's men. Although Palmer did not uncover the makings of an uprising, he did end up deporting more than 500 noncitizens. The movement spread to the local level as radical newspapers were shut down, libraries were purged of allegedly radical books, and accused elected officials were removed from office. The Supreme Court decision in *Schenck v. United States*, which established the "clear and present danger" guideline for limiting free speech, gave cover to such excessive restrictions on civil liberties (see page 276). Soon, Americans began to question Palmer's aggressive tactics, but suspicion of "reds" persisted throughout the 1920s.

The Trial of Sacco and Vanzetti

The repressive atmosphere of the Red Scare era can be seen in the trial of **Nicola Sacco** and **Bartolomeo Vanzetti**. Their trial for robbery and murder illustrated the intolerance that many Americans had toward immigrants and toward alleged radicals in the 1920s. The two men were accused of robbing and killing a payroll clerk in Massachusetts in 1920. The evidence against them was sketchy, but the judge was openly hostile to the men, who were not only immigrants but also anarchists. After they were found guilty, many Americans protested the verdict and wondered if an immigrant, especially with radical ideas, could get a fair trial in the United States. Despite protests, the two men were executed in 1927.

B. World War I and the Rise of Nativism

During World War I, many Americans became increasingly critical of immigrant groups. This nativist sentiment culminated in legislation in the 1920s restricting the number of immigrants allowed to come into the United States (see pages 282-283).

Anti-Immigrant Sentiment

Nativism, or opposition to immigration, rose sharply during World War I. Government propaganda designed to prod Americans to support the war effort frequently vilified Germans, labeling then "Huns" and portraying them as ruthless killers (see page 274). Some publications by the government's public opinion agency, the **Committee for Public Information**, encouraged people to report neighbors who they thought were undermining the war effort. These efforts contributed to popular hatred toward German Americans. In 1917, the German-born director of the Boston Symphony Orchestra, **Karl Muck**, endured relentless hounding by the public, which questioned whether his loyalties lay with Germany or the United States. He was eventually forced to resign. In 1918, in a suburb of St. Louis, a German immigrant, **Robert Prager**, was lynched by an anti-German mob. Similar violent incidents occurred in many communities during the war years. Libraries banned German books and schools prohibited the teaching of German. Anti-German sentiment spread to a broader anti-immigrant crusade during the war. In 1917, Congress passed the **Immigration Restriction Act**, which established a reading test requirement for admission to the U.S. and barred immigrant laborers from several countries that were designated as the **"Asiatic Barred Zone."**

C. War, Opportunity, and Migration

Wartime job opportunities brought about by industrialization and war led to migrations during World War I and the years immediately following the war. The "Great Migration" involved the migration of African Americans out of the rural South. Segregation and racial violence also contributed to this migration. In many cases, white residents of cities reacted to the arrival of African Americans with hostility and violence.

The Great Migration

The needs of industry for labor during World War I led to the **Great Migration** of **African Americans** out of the South, which lasted until the onset of the Great Depression (a second wave of the migration occurred during and after World War II). There are several important reasons for the migration of African Americans from the **rural South** to the **urban North**. A basic factor was the mistreatment African Americans received in the South. White southerners created a series of **Jim Crow laws** that separated African Americans from whites in schools, buses, trains, and other facilities. A rigid system of segregation persisted in the South well into the twentieth century and constantly reminded African Americans of their second-class citizenship. In addition, African Americans were excluded from the political system in the South. A series of obstacles, such as **literacy tests** and **poll taxes**, limited their ability to vote. (See more on the Jim Crow era, pages 203-204.)

The main factor that drew African Americans to the North was jobs. By the turn of the twentieth century **industrialization** was in full swing in northern cities such as New York and Chicago. Factories using new mass production techniques were able, at first, to fill the jobs with local people and European immigrants. But World War I created a labor crisis for these factories, which were producing goods around the clock. Even before the United States entered the war in 1917, American factories were turning out war materials for Great Britain. After the United States entered the war, demand for these goods increased. In addition, European immigration to the United States dropped significantly because of the war. Also, almost three million potential factory hands were drafted into the U.S. military. Factory agents from the North frequently made recruiting trips to the South, offering immediate employment and free passage to the North.

Racial Violence—Chicago, Washington, Tulsa, and Beyond

As many African Americans made the journey from the rural South to the urban North (see page 278), racial violence ensued in many cities. There were at least twenty-five significant race riots in 1919 alone. This racial antagonism was, in part, an offshoot of the reactionary political backlash against progressivism following World War I and in part a reaction to the demographic changes brought about by the **Great Migration**. The rise of the **Ku Klux Klan** in the 1920s (see page 285) was fueled by these political and demographic changes and, in turn, provided ideological ballast to the racial violence of the era. In July 1919, a riot against African Americans occurred in **Washington, D.C.**, and an even more violent riot in **Chicago** left thirty-eight people dead and more than 500 injured. Racial violence also occurred in the South, including at Longview, Texas and Elaine, Arkansas.

The deadliest race riot in American history occurred in **Tulsa, Oklahoma**, in 1921. The immediate cause of the rioting was an encounter in an elevator between a young white female elevator operator and a young African-American male shoeshiner. The details of the encounter are murky—evidence suggests that the young man tripped or fell on the young woman. Rumors of rape quickly spread, and a white mob attempted to lynch the young man. A group of African-American veterans intervened to try to prevent the lynching. A maelstrom of violence ensued, as white residents, including police and National Guardsmen, rioted through the **Greenwood District** of Tulsa, which was the center of the African-American community. Greenwood was known as the **"Black Wall Street,"** and was considered the wealthiest African-American community in the United States at the time. The district was destroyed by the rioting, with over 10,000 people left homeless and more than 300 African Americans killed.

Topic 7.7 1920s: Innovation in Communications and Technology

In many ways, the 1920s witnessed the beginnings of many elements of the modern age. Large corporations came to dominate the American economy. Improvements in technology and new manufacturing techniques led to increased production of consumer goods, greater mobility, and improved standards of living. Finally, new forms of media paved the way for a mass-media culture, while also introducing Americans to a variety of regional cultural products.

A. Technological Advances, Corporate Growth, and the Consumer Economy

The Gilded Age saw the advent of the modern corporate economy, as mergers, holding companies, and trusts led to fewer entities controlling larger segments of the economy (see pages 225–226). This trend continued into the twentieth century, as the assembly line, mass production, and new management techniques brought about a further consolidation of the economy. In addition, the production and consumption of consumer goods stimulated the American economy for much of the 1920s. New products, such as automobiles and radios, captured the public's imagination, and new production techniques increased industrial output.

USING REASONING PROCESSES: CAUSATION

The Declining Power of Workers in the 1920s

The bargaining power of factory workers in the 1920s declined, as workers found it increasingly difficult to obtain better wages and conditions. There are several reasons for this development. First, the changing nature of work—characterized by the shift from craft work to mass production—undermined workers' position. Unskilled assembly-line workers were far easier to replace than skilled workers. In addition, mass immigration in the late 1800s and early 1900s contributed to the weakening of the bargaining position of workers. Further, labor unions were weakened in the 1920s. Employers led a broad campaign against unions called the "American Plan." The campaign depicted union activity as alien to the nation's tradition of individualism. Finally, government policies undermined unionization efforts. The "Red Scare" of the early years of the decade sought to portray unionists as subversive Communists and anarchists. Also, the courts readily issued injunctions against strikes and other union activities.

Henry Ford and Mass Production

The most important figure in the development of new production techniques was automaker **Henry Ford**. In 1913 he opened a plant with a continuous conveyor belt. The belt moved the chassis of the car from worker to worker so that each did a small task in the process of assembling the final product. Although this **mass-production** technique reduced the price of his Model T car and made it affordable to the middle class, the **assembly line** dealt a blow to the skilled mechanics who had previously built automobiles.

The Impact of the Automobile

Americans embraced the **automobile** more rapidly and more thoroughly than people in other nations. By the end of the 1920s, Americans owned 80 percent of the world's automobiles. Approximately twenty-three million cars were on the roads. Automobiles rapidly became more affordable. When the Model T was first introduced in 1908, an average American worker would have had to work approximately twenty months to earn enough money to purchase an automobile. By 1924, a Ford car cost about the equivalent of two to three months' salary.

The automobile changed American society in profound ways. The growth of the automobile industry—using mass-production techniques developed early in the twentieth century by Henry Ford (see above)—stimulated the growth of the steel, chemical, oil, and glass-production industries, employing nearly four million Americans. The automobile led to a reshaping of demographic patterns, as more Americans began to settle in suburban communities (see more on the rise of suburbs, pages 326–327). Although automobiles reduced rural isolation, they also contributed to **"urban sprawl."** The growing cities that developed in the twentieth century, such as Los Angeles and Houston, were designed to accommodate the automobile.

Scientific Management

The **scientific-management techniques** developed by **Frederick Winslow Taylor** were key to mass production. Taylor carefully watched workers, noted the most efficient techniques, and wrote down in exacting detail how a particular task was to be done. The resulting instructions, which broke down the production process into specialized repetitive tasks, would then be used to reconfigure work on the shop floor. Work became more efficient, but also more monotonous. Many workers, especially those with a degree of skill, resisted the loss of control and autonomy that scientific-management techniques entailed.

Advertising and Mass Consumption

If the quality of the work experience deteriorated for factory workers in the 1920s, the availability of **consumer goods** to average families greatly increased. Cars, radios, toasters, health and beauty aids, and other consumer goods filled showrooms and stores. Easy credit and layaway plans helped move merchandise. The **advertising** industry also changed a great deal in the 1920s. Advertising and public relations men tapped into the ideas of **Freudian psychology** and emerging ideas around crowd psychology. Many ads in this period attempted to reach the public on a subconscious level, rather than just presenting products and services in a straightforward manner. Public relations pioneer **Edward Bernays**, a nephew of Sigmund Freud, was a key figure in the shift in marketing toward elaborate corporate advertising campaigns. The values of advertising and promotion seeped into the broader culture—even into religion. **Bruce Barton** wrote a best-selling book, *The Man Nobody Knows* (1925), portraying Jesus Christ as a "super-salesman" and the spread of Christianity as a marketing triumph.

B. New Media and National and Regional Cultures

New technologies, such as radio and cinema, emerged during the first decades of the twentieth century. On the one hand, these new technologies helped usher in a national, mass-media oriented culture. On the other hand, the experiences of particular groups—based around race, ethnicity, and region—produced a variety of other cultural expressions.

Radio and the Development of Mass Culture

Radio grew from being virtually nonexistent at the beginning of the 1920s to becoming an extremely popular medium by the end of the decade. Early radio programming was initiated by amateurs who sent out music or sermons to the few scattered people who had "wireless receivers." Soon, **Westinghouse** and other corporations saw the potential to reach the masses with radio. By 1923, there were almost 600 licensed radio stations. Early successful programs included *The Amos 'n' Andy Show* (1928), a holdover from "blackface" minstrel shows of the nineteenth and early twentieth centuries.

Radio continued its popularity in the 1930s. Americans listened to weekly serials such as *The Shadow* and *The Lone Ranger*, to comedians such as **Jack Benny** and **George Burns**, and to soap operas such as *Painted Dreams* and *Clara, Lu, 'n Em'*. In addition, big-band swing music became very popular. Americans listened to orchestras led by **Duke Ellington**, **Tommy Dorsey**, and **Glenn Miller**.

Movies and the Development of Mass Media

Movie attendance achieved staggering levels in the 1920s. By the end of the decade, three-fourths of the American people (roughly ninety million) were going to the movies every week. The first "talkie," *The Jazz Singer*, came out in 1927.

> **KEEP IN MIND**
>
> **The Fate of Movies in the Television Era**
>
> Movies would never again draw as large a percentage of the public as they did in the 1930s and 1940s. Some thought that television would destroy the movie industry. The predictions did not come true, but television certainly made deep cuts into the movie industry's audience.

The movie industry continued to thrive during the Great Depression. Escapist musicals such as *Gold Diggers of 1933* and *42nd Street* (1933), with lavish sets and spectacular numbers, proved popular. In *The Wizard of Oz* (1939), Dorothy, played by **Judy Garland**, escapes a Kansas farm, shown in black-and-white, and is transported, along with the audience, to the magical land of Oz, shot in Technicolor. The **Marx Brothers** produced and starred in anarchic comedies, such as *Monkey Business* (1931) and *Duck Soup* (1933), which mocked authority figures and the pretensions of the wealthy. **Charlie Chaplin's** comedy *Modern Times* (1936) satirized the entire capitalist system, from the drudgery of assembly-line work to the corruption of the law enforcement system. Some movies attempted to grapple with the wrenching public issues of the time. *The Grapes of Wrath* (1940), the film version of **John Steinbeck's** novel, chronicled the conditions of "Dust Bowl" farmers migrating to California, while **Frank Capra's** *Mr. Smith Goes to Washington* (1939) depicted the triumph of a decent, "everyman" politician. Radio and movies tended to create a more homogeneous culture in the United States in the 1930s.

Modern Media and Regional Culture

The spread of new technologies in the 1920s—notably, recorded music and radio—did not only facilitate the development of a mass culture (see pages 280–281). These new inventions also provided the technical means to record local and regional cultural forms and transmit them to wider audiences. Musical traditions that would eventually coalesce into **country music** enjoyed broader appeal in the 1920s. In 1923 and 1924, record companies began issuing records of "hillbilly" songs, including "Arkansas Traveler" and "Turkey in the Straw." Record producer **Ralph Peer** traveled through the South in 1927 to locate and record local string bands, balladeers, and other musicians in traditional genres such as gospel, blues, and ragtime. Sessions held in Bristol, Tennessee, are considered to be uniquely significant in the origins of country music. Pioneering nationally-known country performers **Jimmie Rogers** and the **Carter Family** emerged from the Bristol sessions.

Topic 7.8 1920s: Cultural and Political Controversies

The 1920s witnessed a startling array of cultural and political controversies. Conflicts around national identity, immigration reform, control of the workplace, and morality pitted Americans against one another.

A. The Growth of the City

The forces of change that began in the Gilded Age continued to transform the United States in the twentieth century. America continued its transition from a rural, agrarian society to an urban, industrial one. The new society offered new opportunities to women and to migrants—both from abroad and from within the United States.

The Social Geography of the City

Immigrants from abroad poured into American cities in the first two decades of the twentieth century, continuing a trend that had begun during the **Gilded Age** (see page 230). Between the turn of the century and the beginning of World War I in 1914, approximately thirteen million European immigrants made their way to the United States. By 1920, immigrants and their children comprised 76 percent of the population of **New York City**, 71 percent of **Chicago**, and 64 percent of **San Francisco**. At the same time, the mechanization of agriculture lowered the demand for labor in rural areas of the United States, contributing to the internal migration of people into cities. By 1920, the majority (51 percent) of Americans lived in cities.

New Opportunities for Women

From the late 1800s into the twentieth century, **urbanization** and **industrialization** provided new opportunities for women in the workforce. The most common occupation for women in the mid-nineteenth century was in the field of domestic service; in the late nineteenth century, more women were working in factories and, by the first decades of the twentieth century, office work became their primary occupation.

New opportunities for women were not confined to the workplace. The **"new woman"** of the 1920s was engaged in public issues. Women often participated in the political struggles of the **Progressive movement** and gained a new sense of confidence in public issues, especially after they achieved the right to vote in 1920 (see page 265). These economic and political changes for women were reflected in changing ideas around gender. Many young women of the 1920s, often labeled "flappers," insisted on greater personal freedom in regard to sexuality, appearance, and behavior. In their embrace of new birth control methods, shorter dresses, "bobbed" haircuts, and greater public assertiveness, they rejected the Victorian moral codes of earlier generations.

> **KEEP IN MIND**
>
> **Women and Public Life**
>
> When traditional history texts discuss women and gender, they often discuss fashion and appearance—such as "bobbed" hair and shorter dresses in the 1920s. By focusing on fashion and appearance, whether of First Ladies or of ordinary women, historians might be subtly reinforcing gender expectations. Although fashion and style are certainly legitimate topics for historical inquiry, try to avoid limiting your discussions of gender to such topics.

B. Nativism and the Quota System

Congress passed restrictive immigration quota acts in the 1920s, responding to a rise in xenophobia in America in the late 1910s and 1920s. These acts greatly reduced immigration into the United States for the next several decades.

The Growth of Nativism

A large wave of immigrants from southern and eastern Europe had arrived in the United States between 1880 and 1920 (see page 230). Many Americans came to resent this wave of immigrants, fueling a popular **nativist movement**. There are several reasons nativists resented this new wave of immigration. Some nativists focused on the fact that most of the new immigrants were not **Protestant**. Poles and Italians tended to be Catholic, Russians and Greeks tended to be Eastern Orthodox, and Jews came from several countries in Eastern Europe. The cacophony of languages heard on the streets of New York or Chicago repelled many nativists. Many nativists associated immigrants with either radical movements or drunkenness. Working-class people feared that low-wage immigrant laborers would take jobs from native-born American workers. Finally, **World War I** itself contributed to the rise of nativist sentiments toward Germans and other ethnic groups (see page 278).

The Quota System

The nativist sentiment that characterized the postwar period led to passage of legislation that greatly reduced the number of immigrants allowed into the United States. The **Emergency Quota Act** (1921) and the **National Origins Act** (1924) set quotas for new immigrants based on nationality. The first act set the quota for each nationality at 3 percent of the total number of that nationality that was present in the United States in 1910. The second act reduced the percentage to 2 percent and moved the year back to 1890. This had the effect of setting very low quotas for many of the **"new immigrants"**—from eastern and southern Europe. The acts did not set limits on immigration for natives of countries within the Americas.

The Supreme Court and Restrictions on Naturalization

The Supreme Court, in two separate decisions, reflected nativist sentiments when it effectively excluded Asian immigrants from attaining U.S. citizenship. In *Takao Ozawa v. United States* (1922), the Court asserted that naturalization was available to "free white persons" (as well as people of African birth or descent). When Takao Ozawa claimed that Japanese people should be considered "free white persons," the Court disagreed, asserting that "white person" indicates a person of the "Caucasian race." Several months later, an Indian man argued before the Court that, based on the *Ozawa* decision, he should be eligible for naturalization because he was of the "Caucasian race." In *United States v. Bhagat Singh Thind* (1923), the Court used different reasoning in denying Thind citizenship. It asserted that "whiteness" was determined by "common sense" understandings of what it meant to be white, and that Indian Americans were not Caucasian "as that word is popularly understood."

C. Migration Patterns and Cultural Production

Migration patterns and urbanization contributed to the emergence of new forms of art and literature. Some of these cultural products can be seen as responses to the advent of the modern world. Much of this art and literature reflects ethnic and regional identities.

The Harlem Renaissance

The **Great Migration** of African Americans from the rural South to the urban North (see page 278) contributed to the **Harlem Renaissance**, a literary, artistic, and intellectual movement centered in the primarily Black neighborhood of Harlem, in New York City. A key goal of the movement was to increase pride in Black culture by celebrating African-American life and forging a new cultural identity among African-American people. Contributions included the writings of **Langston Hughes**, **Claude McKay**, **Countee Cullen**, **Zora Neale Hurston**, and **James Weldon Johnson**, and the jazz music of **Louis Armstrong**, **Duke Ellington**, and **Bessie Smith**. Langston Hughes's poems include "Harlem," "The Negro Speaks of Rivers," and "I, Too, Sing America." He wrote an essay that became a manifesto for Harlem Renaissance writers and artists, entitled "The Negro Artist and the Racial Mountain." Some of Duke Ellington's important compositions are "Mood Indigo," "Don't Get Around Much Anymore," and "It Don't Mean a Thing (If It Ain't Got That Swing)." James Weldon Johnson, a civil rights activist as well as a writer, wrote the poem, "Lift Ev'ry Voice and Sing," which was set to music by his brother and is often considered the African-American national anthem.

The Literature of Dissent

The **"Lost Generation"** literary movement of the 1920s expressed a general disillusionment with society, commenting on everything from the narrowness of small-town life to the rampant materialism of American society. Several writers were troubled by the destruction and seeming meaningless of World War I. *The Great Gatsby* (1925) by **F. Scott Fitzgerald** exposed the shallowness of the lives of the wealthy and privileged of the era. **Sinclair Lewis's** novels, such as *Main Street* (1920) and *Babbitt* (1924), mocked the narrowness and emptiness of middle-class life. **Ernest Hemingway's** *A Farewell to Arms* (1929) critiqued the glorification of war. Several novels of the 1930s reflected the influence of the Communist Party on American culture. Anti-fascist novels included *It Can't Happen Here* (1935) by Sinclair Lewis. Proletarian literature included the novel *The Disinherited* (1933) by **Jack Conroy** and the play *Waiting for Lefty* (1935) by **Clifford Odets**.

Regionalism in the Context of Modernity

As a national culture emerged in the first decades of the twentieth century, abetted by new forms of mass media, **regional cultures** also flourished. To some degree, regionalism in art and literature can be seen as the persistence of local mores and lifeways—a continuity of the folk traditions of small-town American life of the nineteenth century. However, many historians and literary critics see the regionalism of the 1920s and 1930s as a conscious response to, and a rejection of, the homogenizing forces of modern media and mass culture.

Regionalist literature has its roots in the nineteenth century, most famously with **Mark Twain**. His novels, *The Adventures of Tom Sawyer* (1876) and *The Adventures of Huckleberry Finn* (1884), depicted—in both setting and language—life along the Mississippi River. Regionalist writers of the late nineteenth and early twentieth centuries include **Willa Cather** (Nebraska and the surrounding Great Plains) and **Sarah Orne Jewett** (Maine). **Sui Sin Far** captured life in the Chinese-American community in San Francisco and the Pacific Northwest. Regionalism is most evident in literature of the South. The most important southern writer is **William Faulkner**, many of whose works are set in a fictional county in Mississippi. Important works by Faulkner include the novels *The Sound and the Fury* (1929) and *As I Lay Dying* (1930). Other important writers of the **"Southern Renaissance"** of the 1920s and 1930s include **Tennessee Williams**, **Katherine Anne Porter**, **Thomas Wolfe**, and **Robert Penn Warren**. One of the best-selling American novels of the period between the world wars was **Margaret Mitchell's** *Gone with the Wind* (1936), which looked back sentimentally on southern plantation life in the slavery era.

Regionalism can also be seen in the art of the 1930s, especially in much of the work of the **Works Progress Administration**. Known also as **"American Scene"** painting, regionalist art can be seen in WPA murals and paintings in post offices and other public buildings. Two important regionalist painters, **Grant Wood** and **Thomas Hart Benton**, both depicted scenes from the Midwest, most notably Wood's *American Gothic*.

The "Okie" Migration and the Culture of Displacement

The movement of thousands of displaced people from the southern **Great Plains** to **California** gave rise to several cultural developments (see more on the causes of the **"Dust Bowl,"** page 294). Okies fleeing the Dust Bowl brought the culture of the southern plains with them to California. The attitudes, politics, religious denominations, and even dialects of Oklahoma, Texas, Missouri, and Arkansas shaped the culture of agricultural centers in California's Central Valley, most notably Bakersfield. Country music artists **Buck Owens** and **Merle Haggard** both had roots in the Dust Bowl and both ended up in Bakersfield (Owens was born in 1929 in Texas, eight years before his family fled the Dust Bowl; Haggard's parents moved from Oklahoma to California in 1934, three years before Haggard's birth). The two contributed to a style of country music that was more mournful and rough-edged than the more slickly produced country music that originated in Nashville in the 1950s.

Yiddish Theater

The migration of **Eastern European Jews** to the United States from the 1880s to the 1920s gave rise to several cultural developments. The most notable contribution of this immigrant group was the flourishing **Yiddish theater**, which often rivaled Broadway in scale and quality. Yiddish theater was a major cultural force in the United States between 1890 and 1940, with over 200 venues or touring performing groups. The center of Yiddish theater in the United States was New York City. The Yiddish theater district—which contained up to twenty full-time Yiddish theaters at its height—was centered on Second Avenue in what was then considered part of the **Jewish Lower East Side**. From the 1890s, dedicated Yiddish playwrights sought to capture the immigrant experience as well as present works of Shakespeare, Strindberg, and Ibsen to the newly arrived Yiddish-speaking community. By the 1900s, the classical tradition of Yiddish theater began to compete with a more populist approach, characterized by a flamboyant style of acting, overstated pageantry, and audience participation. After World War I, many playwrights—some from the socialist movement—sought to capture more serious themes. *The Dybbuk* (1919), by Shloyme Rappoport (pen name **S. Ansky**), is considered one of the more important Yiddish dramas of this period. Yiddish theatrical presentations, such as *Der Yidisher Yenki Dudl* ("The Jewish Yankee Doodle") (1905), often explored ways of holding onto Old-World traditions while assimilating into American culture.

D. Culture Clashes in the 1920s

The advent of modernity—embodied in new technologies, mass culture, and changing demographics—gave rise to a culturally conservative backlash.

The Resurgence of the Ku Klux Klan

The original **Ku Klux Klan**, a violent, racist group with its roots in the immediate aftermath of the Civil War, had declined by the 1870s. A second Ku Klux Klan was born in 1915, and, by the 1920s, it had become a genuine mass movement. By 1925, it had grown to three million members, according to its own estimate. The Klan was devoted to white supremacy and "**100 percent Americanism**." The white supremacist ideology of the Ku Klux Klan was evident in a number of race riots in the United States in the late 1910s and 1920s (see page 279).

The Bible Versus Science

During the 1920s, a large number of Americans, especially in the South, adopted a **fundamentalist**, literalist approach to the Bible and to religion. The roots of this Protestant fundamentalist movement can be seen in several developments in the late nineteenth and early twentieth centuries, including the **Holiness Movement** of the nineteenth century; the **Azusa Street Revival** in Los Angeles (starting in 1906) and the modern **Pentecostal movement**; the popular sermons of the evangelists **Billy Sunday** and **Aimee Semple McPherson**; and the religious dimensions of the anti-alcohol movement (see page 286). Many fundamentalists at this time questioned certain assertions of modern science, especially those that came in conflict with their faith.

The conflict between Protestant fundamentalism and modern science can be seen in the Scopes trial of 1925. The trial involved the teaching of evolution in public schools. **John Scopes**, a Tennessee biology teacher, was arrested for violating the **Butler Act**, a state law forbidding the teaching of evolution. The case turned into a national spectacle, with the famous lawyer **Clarence Darrow** representing Scopes and **William Jennings Bryan** representing the state. Scopes was found guilty and fined $100. This trial is one of several important events that highlighted cultural divisions in the 1920s.

> **USING HISTORICAL THINKING SKILLS:**
> **MAKING CONNECTIONS**
>
> **A Third Great Awakening**
>
> The rise of fundamentalism in the 1920s is sometimes referred to as a "third great awakening," preceded by the First Great Awakening of the 1730s and 1740s, and the Second Great Awakening of the first decades of the 1800s. Both the Second Great Awakening and the rise of fundamentalism in the 1920s resulted in the growth of activism around social and political issues. The Second Great Awakening inspired a host of reform movements, from abolitionism to prison reform; the fundamentalist movement of the 1920s dovetailed with anti-immigrant sentiment and the "red scare." Both embraced the crusade against alcohol.

Rural and Urban Responses to Prohibition

The movement to ban alcohol from American society was one of the largest movements in the nineteenth and early twentieth centuries. It finally achieved success in 1919 when **prohibition** became national policy with the ratification of the **Eighteenth Amendment** to the Constitution (see page 270). The amendment called for a ban on the manufacture, sale, and transportation of alcoholic beverages. However, the victory of the movement proved to be hollow. Although per capita consumption of alcohol dropped dramatically in the early 1920s, it increased as the decade progressed, approaching pre-Prohibition levels by 1925. Further, the amount of lawlessness in America went up as **bootleggers**, **speakeasies**, and **organized crime** filled the gap left by the end of the legitimate alcoholic beverage industry. Criminal activity became so widespread that Congress ratified the **Twenty-first Amendment** (1933), which repealed Prohibition.

Topic 7.9 The Great Depression

The United States economy became increasingly volatile, with major downturns following the Panic of 1893 and the Panic of 1907. The most severe downturn was the Great Depression (1929–1939). These economic downturns led to calls for greater federal regulation of the economy.

A. The Transition of the American Economy and Economic Instability

The United States economy continued to grow in the late 1800s and early 1900s. In addition, it continued its transition from a rural, agricultural economy to an urban, industrial economy. As large corporations began to dominate the economy, fluctuations in the business cycle became increasingly common and increasingly severe.

The Panic of 1893

Throughout American history, business activity has moved in cycles. In the nineteenth century, the economy experienced several economic downturns, often triggered by **"panics."** Notable panics had occurred in 1819, 1837, 1857, and 1873. As the economy became more consolidated in the post–Civil War era, with only a handful of corporations controlling larger and larger segments of the economy, the potential for more severe downturns intensified. If a few large corporations experienced downturns, the potential for a large-scale disruption to the economy became increasingly likely. Such a scenario played out in 1893, and again in 1907.

The **Panic of 1893** signaled the beginning of the worst economic depression in American history before the **Great Depression** of the 1930s. The crisis began when the Philadelphia and Reading Railroad went bankrupt; two months later the National Cordage Company also failed. These bankruptcies led to a major decline in stock prices. Because many leading banks had invested their assets in the stock market, a wave of bank failures soon followed. With over 500 bank collapses, credit became hard to come by. This contraction of credit led to the subsequent collapse of approximately 15,000 businesses. By 1894, the unemployment rate had reached 20 percent of the workforce and approximately a million workers had lost their jobs. The economy did not fully recover until 1901.

The Panic of 1907

The economy took a serious downturn following the **Panic of 1907**. This panic involved a major fall in stock prices, which was caused by a lack of confidence in major New York banks. Several banks had invested in a scheme to gain control of the United Copper Company. When the scheme unraveled, there were runs on several of the banks that had invested large sums of money. Such bank runs occur when a large number of bank customers withdraw their deposits simultaneously over concerns of the bank's solvency. One major New York bank, Knickerbocker Trust Company, collapsed, sending ripples of fear through the banking world and leading to a withdrawal of reserves. The panic was partly calmed by the action of **J. P. Morgan**, who offered to have **U.S. Steel** take over a struggling steel-industry rival that a major New York bank had invested in. However, the deal could not proceed until Morgan got assurances from **President Theodore Roosevelt** that the government would not initiate antitrust action. The entire episode demonstrated the lack of control the U.S. government had over the industrial and financial worlds.

B. Causes of the Great Depression

The economic crises following the Panics of 1893 and 1907 paled in comparison to the economic downturn of the 1930s. On the surface, the economy of the 1920s seemed strong, but there were structural weaknesses that became more apparent as the decade progressed. The precise reasons for the Great Depression are still debated by historians; the following explanations are frequently cited.

Overproduction and Underconsumption

Industrial production greatly expanded in the 1920s. New products, such as automobiles and radios, captured the public's imagination, and new production techniques, such as the **assembly line** and **"scientific management"** (see pages 279-280), vastly increased industrial output. For much of the 1920s, the public was induced by easy credit and seductive advertising to absorb this increased output of consumer goods. However, by 1927 manufacturers noticed that warehouse inventories were on the rise. **Consumption** just could not keep up with **production**. A weak labor movement in the twenties led to stagnant wages. Since ordinary Americans did not share in the economic expansion of the 1920s, the gap between the wealthy and the poor grew. During the 1920s, income for the top 1 percent of the population increased by nearly 75 percent, while the bottom 90 percent of the population saw their income rise by less than 10 percent. By the late 1920s, manufacturers made the logical decision to begin laying off workers, worsening a bad situation.

Problems on the Farm

Throughout the 1920s, the **agricultural sector** lagged behind the rest of the economy. Farmers had put more acres under cultivation during World War I to meet increased demand for agricultural production. By the twenties, Europe was back on its feet, yet American farmers did not cut back on production. Mechanization and expansion left the farmers of the 1920s in a cycle of debt, overproduction, and falling commodity prices. Increased tariff rates and an isolationist foreign policy further reduced the international market for American agricultural goods.

An Inflated Stock Market

Investing in the **stock market** is always something of a gamble, but in the 1920s people gambled recklessly with borrowed money. They increasingly bought stocks on margin, paying only a small percentage of the purchase price up front, with the promise of paying the remainder in the future. This practice worked as long as stock prices rose, which they did throughout most of the 1920s. By the late 1920s, however, serious investors began to see that stock prices were reaching new heights as the actual earnings of major corporations were declining. This discrepancy between the price per share and the actual earnings of corporations led investors to begin selling stocks, which stimulated panic selling. Starting on October 24, 1929, **"Black Thursday,"** and continuing the following week, the stock market crashed, destroying many individuals' investments.

C. Hoover and the Great Depression

President Herbert Hoover was very reluctant to harness the power of the central government to intervene in economic matters. He feared that government intervention into the Depression would stifle individual initiative.

"Rugged Individualism" and Limited Government Intervention

Rather than expand federal intervention into the economy to address the dislocations of the **Great Depression**, **President Hoover** (1929-1933) invoked the idea of **"rugged individualism"**—the belief that the problems of the nation could best be solved by the determination and resolve of the American people. When people were unable to help themselves, Hoover encouraged voluntary cooperation and private charities to step in. By 1932, seeing that voluntary cooperation was not reviving the economy, Hoover signed into law the **Reconstruction Finance Corporation**. This government agency extended loans to struggling railroads, banks, insurance companies, and other firms. In addition, the agency oversaw $2 billion in appropriations to fund local projects. He refused, however, to extend direct relief to individuals.

The Bonus March and the Erosion of Confidence in Hoover

President Herbert Hoover's handling of the **Bonus March** protest in 1932 further eroded confidence in his ability to lead the United States through a period of crisis. In June 1932, a group of **World War I** veterans, who called themselves the **Bonus Expeditionary Force**, marched into Washington, D.C., to demand a bonus that they had been promised for their service in the military. About 15,000 men, mostly unemployed and poor, set up an encampment in the nation's capital. By the end of July, Hoover ordered the secretary of war to evacuate the Bonus Marchers' camp. The evacuation resulted in the deaths of several veterans and in hundreds of injuries. The image of current members of the military taking up arms against former members of the military angered many Americans. Although the handling of the Bonus Marchers reflected poorly on Hoover in the run-up to the 1932 presidential election, it should be noted that the most aggressive acts against the protestors were carried out by **General Douglas MacArthur**, against the orders of President Hoover.

> **USING REASONING PROCESSES:**
> **COMPARISON**
>
> **Hoover and Reagan**
>
> President Hoover's approach to the economy and his rhetoric set a template for Republican economic policy for much of the twentieth century. Hoover's economic policies can be compared to Reaganomics of the 1980s; both Hoover and Reagan emphasized limiting taxes and rolling back government intervention in economic affairs.

Topic 7.10 The New Deal

During the depths of the 1930s Great Depression, President Franklin D. Roosevelt pushed for a series of reforms to address both the causes and effects of the economic crisis. These reforms, known as the "New Deal," set a precedent for the federal government to play a more active role in the economic and social affairs of the nation.

A. The Creation of the "New Deal"

President Franklin D. Roosevelt and his advisors drew on Progressive-era ideas in the creation of the New Deal. The focus of the New Deal was three-pronged—extend relief to the poor, stimulate economic recovery, and create long-term reform of the American economy.

From Hoover to Roosevelt

In the presidential election of 1932, **Franklin Delano Roosevelt** offered the public a marked contrast to **President Herbert Hoover**. Roosevelt, a distant cousin of Theodore Roosevelt, was from a wealthy New York family. In 1928, Roosevelt won the governorship in New York and introduced a number of innovative programs to help New Yorkers as the **Great Depression** deepened. Though Roosevelt was from an affluent background, he was able to convey to the public a sense of empathy and

> **USING REASONING PROCESSES:**
> **CONTINUITY AND CHANGE**
>
> **The New Deal and the Progressive Movement**
>
> Be prepared to discuss the intellectual and political origins of the New Deal. In some ways, the array of New Deal government programs can be seen as a continuation of the progressive reforms enacted under Presidents Theodore Roosevelt and Woodrow Wilson. Both the Progressive movement and the New Deal challenged the traditional *laissez-faire* approach of government policy throughout the 1800s. However, the New Deal differed from the Progressive movement in key ways. The progressives were mostly middle-class men and women, imposing their values on society. The New Deal, some argue, was driven more by working-class concerns.

personal warmth. Further, his openness to experimentation allowed for a more flexible response to the Depression than Hoover's more ideological approach. Roosevelt won the **election of 1932** easily, garnering 57 percent of the popular vote and 472 out of 529 electoral votes.

Roosevelt moved the federal government in a new direction by asserting that it should take some responsibility for the welfare of the people. The Roosevelt administration developed a series of programs known collectively as the **New Deal**. Previously, people received assistance in times of need from churches, settlement houses, and other private charities. However, the levels of poverty and unemployment during the Great Depression were unprecedented. Roosevelt believed that the government needed to take action. The New Deal provided relief to individuals through a variety of agencies.

The First New Deal

The **Roosevelt administration** developed a remarkable array of programs during its **first hundred days** in 1933 and in the months immediately following. These programs, which comprised the **First New Deal**, reflected both Roosevelt's willingness to experiment and the scope of problems that faced the nation. Below are some of the more important programs.

Glass-Steagall Act (1933)

One of the most pressing problems President Roosevelt faced was the instability of the banking industry. Many people had lost confidence in the **banking system** and withdrew their money in fear that their banks might fold. With thousands of people withdrawing their money at the same time, many banks actually did close, turning collective fears into a self-fulfilling prophecy. The **Federal Deposit Insurance Corporation**, created by the **Glass-Steagall Act**, insures deposits so that if a bank does fold, people do not lose their savings.

National Industrial Recovery Act (1933)

The **National Industrial Recovery Act** was designed to stabilize the **industrial sector** of the economy. It called for representatives from labor and competing corporations to draw up a set of codes. These codes were designed to shorten hours for workers, guarantee trade union rights, establish minimum wage levels, regulate the price of certain petroleum products, and promote fair business practices. The idea was that cutthroat competition hurt the economy and pushed workers' wages down and limited their ability to purchase goods.

Agricultural Adjustment Act (1933)

The Roosevelt administration created the **Agricultural Adjustment Act** (AAA) to strengthen the agricultural sector. It quickly tackled two related problems—overproduction and falling prices of farm goods—by adopting the counterintuitive measure of paying farmers to grow fewer crops. Commodity prices did increase, but AAA policies had an unintended negative effect. In order to reduce output, landowners often evicted sharecroppers and took that land out of cultivation. This hurt many of the nation's poorest farmers, including numerous African-American farmers.

Tennessee Valley Authority (1933)

The **Tennessee Valley Authority** (TVA), still in existence, was the federal government's first experiment in **regional planning**. The TVA built dams, generated electricity, manufactured fertilizer, provided technical assistance to farmers, and fostered economic development in the Tennessee Valley.

Federal Emergency Relief Act (1933)

The **Federal Emergency Relief Act** was created to distribute more than $500 million to state and local governments, which would, in turn, distribute aid to the poor. FERA was intended to provide temporary relief for people in need.

Civilian Conservation Corps (1933)

Roosevelt created the **Civilian Conservation Corps** (CCC) to provide outdoor work for young men between the ages of 18 and 24. Projects initiated by the CCC included soil conservation, flood control, trail and road building, bridges, and forest projects. During the 1930s, approximately 2.75 million men worked on CCC projects.

Securities and Exchange Commission (1934)

Many individuals had lost confidence in the **stock market** after the 1929 crash, which was partly caused by unsound market practices. The **Securities and Exchange Commission** was created to oversee stock market operations by monitoring transactions, licensing brokers, limiting buying on margin, and prohibiting insider trading.

B. Critics of the New Deal and the Second New Deal

President Franklin D. Roosevelt had to guide the New Deal through the tumultuous political currents of the 1930s. A variety of social and political movements emerged, each offering different solutions to the economic crisis. To some degree, these movements hindered the New Deal, and to some degree, they influenced it. From the left, union activists, radicals, and populist leaders pushed for more extensive reforms. From the right, conservatives—in the media, in Congress, and on the Supreme Court—attempted to limit the scope and influence of the New Deal. The left critique of the New Deal ultimately led to a second set of reforms, which went beyond the scope of the programs of Roosevelt's first year in office.

The Growth of the Communist Party

Although the **Communist Party** never attracted a large following in the United States, it did gain new members and exerted influence beyond its numbers in the 1930s. Some Americans came to believe that the Great Depression was evidence that the capitalist system was simply not working. Others were impressed with the reported achievements of the Soviet Union. (Many Americans were not yet fully aware of the extent of the brutality of the Stalinist regime in regard to purges of Communist Party members, the catastrophic Ukrainian famine, the repressive police apparatus, or the network of camps for political prisoners, or gulags.) The Communist Party in the United States attracted members by adopting the **"Popular Front"** strategy (1934–1939); the strategy called for the Party to drop talk of an impending revolution and to cooperate with a spectrum of anti-fascist groups and governments, including Roosevelt's New Deal administration.

Populist Opposition to the New Deal

A variety of voices on the left criticized the New Deal as being overly cautious. **Upton Sinclair** (author of *The Jungle*) ran for governor of California in 1934 under the banner **"End Poverty in California,"** proposing sweeping, often socialistic solutions. **Francis Townsend**, also from California, proposed a tax to generate enough money to give everyone over sixty years of age a monthly stipend. The most serious threat to Roosevelt from the left came from **Huey Long**, the flamboyant populist governor, then senator, from Louisiana. Beginning in 1934, he organized a national network of clubs under the **"Share Our Wealth Society"** banner; the movement proposed breaking up the fortunes of the rich and distributing them to everyone else. His slogan was **"Every Man a King."** He talked of running against Roosevelt in 1936, but was assassinated in 1935.

The Growth of Organized Labor

President Roosevelt encouraged union membership in order to increase the purchasing power of workers. **Organized labor**, in turn, pushed Roosevelt to adopt more extensive reform measures. The **National Industrial Recovery Act** (1933) and the **Wagner Act** (1935) legalized union membership in the United States. Union membership, which had been falling in the 1920s and early 1930s, rose from 3 million in 1933 to 10.5 million by 1941. By the end of World War II, 36 percent of nonagricultural American workers were in unions.

The Congress of Industrial Organizations

The drive to organize workers in the 1930s led to tensions within the labor movement. The fifty-year-old **American Federation of Labor (AFL)**, a coalition of craft unions, had never shown much interest in organizing unskilled assembly-line workers. Labor leaders such as John L. Lewis of the United Mine Workers wanted the AFL to do more organizing in this growing sector of the labor force. In 1935, he and other leaders from primarily unskilled unions organized the **Committee for Industrial Organization** within the AFL. The committee's task of organizing basic industries met the ire of AFL leadership, which ordered the committee to disband in 1936, and when the committee refused, the AFL expelled the committee's unions in 1937. In 1938, the committee reconstituted itself as the independent **Congress of Industrial Organizations** (CIO). It grew rapidly, surpassing the AFL in 1941; the CIO had about 5 million members compared to the AFL's 4.6 million. (Later, in 1955, the two groups merged to form the AFL-CIO.)

The Sit-down Strike

Although unions were legal in America, employers were still under no compulsion to accept union demands. In the late 1930s, a wave of strikes ensued. A new, militant tactic of unions under the **Congress of Industrial Organizations** umbrella was the **sit-down strike**, in which employees stopped work and refused to leave the shop floor, thus preventing the employer from reopening with replacement workers (or "scabs"). The most famous sit-down strike took place at the **General Motors** plant in Flint, Michigan, in the winter of 1936–1937.

Conservative Critics Denounce "Creeping Socialism"

Some conservative critics saw the New Deal as socialism in disguise. The New Deal, they argued, had pushed the government too far into new realms. President Roosevelt's **"Court-packing plan"** (see page 292) seemed especially heavy-handed to many Americans. Congressional critics of the New Deal in both parties formulated the **"Conservative Manifesto"** in 1937, with an emphasis on lower taxes and reduced spending. The most prominent group on the right was the **American Liberty League** (founded in 1934), which consisted primarily of conservative businessmen and political figures. This group supported conservative politicians of both parties, and promoted the "open shop"—a business in which the employees are not required to join a union. Catholic priest **Father Charles Coughlin**, using his popular national radio show, attacked Roosevelt, labeling him a Communist and a dictator. Coughlin had initially supported Roosevelt in 1932 but grew increasingly critical of the New Deal, adding anti-Semitic and even fascistic elements to his broadcast.

The Second New Deal

By 1935, **President Roosevelt** was facing several problems, although the economy had improved slightly during his first two years in office. Average weekly earnings had increased for workers and unemployment had dropped from about 25 percent to 20 percent. But with more than ten million people out of work, Roosevelt could not claim that the New Deal had resolved the nation's economic woes. In addition, the Supreme Court had declared key New Deal acts unconstitutional. In *A.L.A. Schechter Poultry Corp. v. United States* (1935), the Court declared the **National Industrial Recovery Act** unconstitutional because it violated the constitutional separation of powers by delegating legislative powers to the executive branch. Several months later, the Court declared the **Agricultural Adjustment Act** unconstitutional in the *United States v. Butler* decision (1936). The Court held that taxes enacted by the AAA amounted to statutory regulations; such actions, therefore, fell under state powers, not federal powers.

With mounting pressure from a variety of populist and leftwing forces, and with a presidential election looming in 1936, Roosevelt introduced a second set of programs known as the **Second New Deal**. This second phase of the New Deal was less about shaping the different sectors of the economy and more about providing assistance and support to the working class.

Works Progress Administration (1935)

The **Works Progress Administration** (WPA) was a massive initiative that created jobs for millions of unemployed men and women. The jobs ranged from construction work to theatrical productions to writing guidebooks about each of the states. Earlier jobs programs, such as the Civilian Conservation Corps, were piecemeal compared with the immense WPA. At its peak in 1938, over three million people worked for the WPA; over eight million people in total worked for it by the time it was shut down in 1943.

Social Security Act (1935)

Social Security is perhaps the initiative that has had the largest long-term impact on American society. The **Social Security Act** was designed to help the unemployed, the elderly, and the disabled. The most important element of the plan was retirement benefits, funded by taxes on workers and employers, which workers collected after they turned sixty-five years old. The **Social Security Agency** is still in existence and has remained popular with large segments of the public.

The Wagner Act (1935)

The **Wagner Act** encouraged the formation of unions. The act established the **National Labor Relations Board**, which still exists, to oversee union elections and to arbitrate conflicts between workers and owners. It also prohibited owners from taking punitive actions against workers who sought to organize unions. As a result, the act led to a tremendous increase in union activity.

The Second New Deal and the "Court-Packing Plan"

President Roosevelt feared that the Supreme Court would invalidate key elements of the **Second New Deal**, as it had earlier New Deal acts. In 1937, he proposed a bill to alter the composition of the Supreme Court by allowing him to appoint six additional justices. This **"Court-packing"** bill generated a great deal of opposition. Congress rejected this plan, but the Court became friendlier to the president anyway. Over the next few years, some of the more conservative justices retired, and Roosevelt was able to appoint seven new justices, including the liberal **Hugo Black**.

> **USING HISTORICAL THINKING SKILLS: CONTEXTUALIZATION**
>
> **The Context of Supreme Court Decisions**
>
> Throughout history, note the political and social context of Supreme Court decisions. The justices are products of their society; they do not make their decisions in a vacuum. This can be seen in the *Plessy v. Ferguson* (1896) decision, made during the rise of Jim Crow policies, and in the *Brown v. Board of Education of Topeka* (1954) decision, delivered as the civil rights movement was gaining national attention. Likewise, the Court's rejection of important New Deal programs can be seen in the context of the conservative backlash against President Roosevelt's initiatives.

The Rollback of the New Deal

In late 1937 and 1938, **President Roosevelt** took the New Deal in a new direction that, many historians believe, hurt the economy. By 1937, the economy was showing signs of improvement. Unemployment was going down and banks and businesses were showing signs of stability. Roosevelt took the advice of some of the more conservative members of his cabinet and cut back on spending with the goal of balancing the budget.

The "Roosevelt Recession"

President Roosevelt's move to cut spending on New Deal programs contributed in 1938 to a further downturn in economic activity, known as the **"Roosevelt Recession."** Later in 1938, Roosevelt shifted direction again and increased government spending. The economy did show signs of growth, but the real boost came in 1939 as the United States began producing armaments and supplies in the looming shadow of World War II.

Keynesian Economics

When President Roosevelt cut back spending to balance the budget in the middle of the Great Depression (see page 292), he was rejecting the advice of the economist **John Maynard Keynes**. Keynes's most important book, *General Theory of Employment, Interest and Money* (1936), argued that deficit spending by the government was acceptable, even desirable, as a means of increasing overall demand and stimulating economic activity. This idea of using the tools of the government—the Federal Reserve Bank, and spending and taxation polices—to influence economic activity is known as **Keynesian economics**. John Maynard Keynes's theories have influenced government policy in the twentieth century, especially during Democratic administrations. Republican administrations have focused more on cutting government spending.

C. The Legacy of the New Deal

The New Deal did not solve the economic crisis of the 1930s, but it did profoundly change the United States. It left a legacy of agencies and laws aimed at economic security, and it ushered in a major political realignment, as a new coalition of ethnic groups, African Americans, and working-class communities identified with the goals of the Democratic Party.

Political Realignment

The 1930s witnessed the emergence of the political and ideological alignment that has existed, to some extent, into the twenty-first century. **President Herbert Hoover's** generally conservative laissez-faire approach has been echoed in the policies of **Republican** presidents Ronald Reagan, George H. W. Bush, and George W. Bush, while **President Franklin D. Roosevelt's** generally liberal interventionist approach inspired **Democratic** president Lyndon Johnson's "Great Society." Today, Democratic leaders debate how closely their party should be associated with **New Deal liberalism**, while Republicans brand their opponents "tax and spend" liberals. The debates of the 1930s are still part of the political culture.

D. The Depression, the New Deal, and Affected Groups

The various sectors of society were affected differently by the Great Depression and the New Deal. Although the 1930s was certainly a dismal time economically, some groups in the United States were better able to put forth agendas for change and to achieve gains than others.

African Americans

African Americans, already in a vulnerable position in U.S. society before the Great Depression, were especially hard hit by the economic difficulties of the 1930s. Many New Deal programs ignored African Americans—such as the Agricultural Adjustment Act, which did not help tenant farmers or sharecroppers. Roosevelt was wary of losing the support of the southern wing of the Democratic Party, so he did not push for **civil rights legislation**, nor did he endorse federal **anti-lynching legislation** (which Congress never passed).

Despite President Roosevelt's reluctance to take the lead in civil rights legislation, African Americans switched their allegiance from the party of Lincoln (the Republicans) to the Democratic Party. There are several reasons for this

> **USING REASONING PROCESSES:**
> **CONTINUITY AND CHANGE**
>
> ### The Democratic Party and Civil Rights
>
> President Franklin D. Roosevelt and the Democratic Party were just beginning to shift toward support for civil rights in the 1930s. This was a major shift for a party that in the 1860s initiated southern secession in order to defend slavery. In the 1930s, the Democratic Party still maintained a solid base among white voters in the South, so it was reluctant to fully embrace the struggle for civil rights. In the 1960s, the Democratic president, Lyndon Johnson, pushed for passage of major civil rights legislation; he even adopted the refrain of a prominent civil rights anthem in a 1965 speech, proclaiming "we shall overcome." Many of the southern whites who had made the South solidly Democratic abandoned the party in the 1960s and shifted allegiance to the Republican Party.

historic shift. **First Lady Eleanor Roosevelt** and **Interior Secretary Harold Ickes** did champion civil rights causes. The most dramatic gesture by Eleanor Roosevelt was organizing a concert by **Marian Anderson** in 1935 on the steps of the Lincoln Memorial after Anderson was blocked by the Daughters of the American Revolution from performing at their concert hall. Also, the president met periodically with a group of African-American advisors to the president, called the **"Black Cabinet."** In 1941, Roosevelt issued an executive order banning discrimination in the defense industry (see page 299). Finally, African Americans believed that Roosevelt, despite his shortcomings, was attempting to improve conditions for poor and working-class people.

The "Scottsboro Boys" Case

The racial biases of the justice system were demonstrated in the highly publicized **"Scottsboro Boys"** case (1931–1935). Nine African-American youths were convicted of rape in **Alabama** on flimsy evidence. In 1932, the Supreme Court reversed most of the convictions on the grounds that the defendants' due process rights had been violated because they were denied effective counsel. The cases were then sent back to state court for retrial. The defendants were again found guilty, even after one of the alleged victims admitted fabricating her story. Charges were later dropped for four out of the nine defendants. The remaining five served prison time.

Women

Women suffered a double burden during the Depression: on the one hand, they were responsible for putting food on the table during difficult times, while on the other hand, they were frequently scorned if they "**took a job away from a man**" by working outside the home. Further, New Deal programs tended to slight women; the Civilian Conservation Corps (1933), a New Deal program that sent young men from urban areas to work on federal lands, excluded women, and the National Industrial Recovery Act (1933) set lower wage levels for women than for men. Nonetheless, individual women such as **Frances Perkins**, the first female cabinet member (secretary of labor), and **Eleanor Roosevelt**, one of the most active and public first ladies in American history, opened doors for women. Despite criticism, more women were working outside the home in 1940 than in 1930.

American Indians

New Deal legislation profoundly affected **American Indians**. The **Indian Reorganization Act** (1934) largely undid the **Dawes Severalty Act** (1887), which had attempted to assimilate American Indians into mainstream society by breaking up reservations and dividing the land into small plots for individual American Indians (see page 221). The Indian Reorganization Act reversed this policy by restoring tribal ownership of reservation lands and recognizing the legitimacy of tribal governments. The act also extended loans to American Indian groups for economic development.

E. Economic Dislocation and Migrations in the Era of the New Deal

Large numbers of people moved within the United States (as well as out of the country) because of the economic dislocation caused by the Great Depression.

The Migration from the Dust Bowl to California

From 1934 to 1937, parts of **Texas**, **Oklahoma**, and surrounding areas of the Great Plains suffered from a major drought. The area was so dry that it became known as the **"Dust Bowl."** The Dust Bowl was caused by unsustainable over-farming coupled with a devastating drought. The natural grass cover of the region had been removed in the years leading up to the Dust Bowl, as wheat farmers increased the number of acres under cultivation. With this natural root system gone, the fertile topsoil simply blew away when drought struck from 1934 to 1937.

Approximately 3.5 million people left their homes in the areas affected by the Dust Bowl. Perhaps as many as 400,000 ended up in **California**, with about 40 percent making their way to the fertile San Joaquin Valley. Many

Dust Bowl refugees became migrant farmers, working on large farms growing cotton, grapes, and an assortment of other fruits and nuts. The plight of Dust Bowl refugees was captured in **John Steinbeck's** novel, *The Grapes of Wrath* (1939), which chronicled the travails of the Joads, an Oklahoma, or **"Okie,"** family of Dust Bowl refugees who suffered additional indignities and setbacks once they made it to California. The difficulties faced by migrant farmers in California were also captured in photographs by **Dorothea Lange**, notably *Migrant Mother*. As folk guitarist and radical activist **Woody Guthrie** sang in one of his many **"Dust Bowl Ballads,"** California may have looked like a "garden of Eden," but it was a difficult place to survive without enough money—"But believe it or not, you won't find it so hot, if you ain't got the do-re-mi."

Mexican Americans and the Great Depression

Mexican-American workers saw their wages plummet in the 1930s. Companies often fired Mexican-American workers to create job opportunities for white workers. **New Deal** programs did little to help. For instance, the Civilian Conservation Corps and the Works Progress Administration excluded migrant farm workers by requiring a permanent address. Also, local administrators would frequently remove Mexican Americans from relief programs. Further, Mexican Americans were subject to large-scale **deportations** during the Great Depression. The federal government formally deported over 80,000 Mexican Americans. However, local officials and private individuals carried out many more informal deportations, pressuring Mexican Americans to leave on their own as well as rounding up and transporting groups of Mexican Americans over the border into Mexico. Historians estimate that over 400,000 Mexican Americans were removed from the United States; the vast majority of these removals had no legal basis. Approximately 40 to 60 percent of these individuals were American citizens. The Mexican-American population decreased by almost 40 percent during the Great Depression.

Topic 7.11 Interwar Foreign Policy

The United States largely maintained a position of neutrality in the years between the two world wars. It did, however, play an increasingly large role in international treaties and investment. International events in the 1930s increasingly drew the United States into world affairs.

A. The Politics of Isolationism

Isolationist sentiment ran high in the United States in the 1920s. Many Americans were disillusioned by World War I, while others had grown resentful of the wave of "new immigrants" who had come to America. Isolationism was reflected in higher tariff rates and in treaties to reduce armament levels. Isolationism did not prevent the United States from engaging in military interventions, mostly in the Western Hemisphere, with the goal of advancing its vision of international order. However, by the 1930s, President Franklin D. Roosevelt pursued a more conciliatory approach in regard to Latin America.

> **USING REASONING PROCESSES:**
> **CONTINUITY AND CHANGE**
>
> **Tariffs in American History**
>
> Higher tariff rates ended up further dampening international trade and worsening the effects of the Great Depression. The tariff rates of the Hawley-Smoot Act of 1930 were exceeded in American history only by the "Tariff of Abominations" of 1828. Debates about tariff rates have existed throughout American history, from Alexander Hamilton's "Report on Manufactures" (1791) to President Donald Trump's trade war with China (starting in 2017).

Higher Tariff Rates—From Fordney-McCumber to Smoot-Hawley

The **isolationist** Republican presidents of the 1920s enacted higher tariffs to keep out foreign goods. The 1922 **Fordney-McCumber Act** dramatically raised tariff rates. In 1930, in the midst of the Great Depression, isolationist legislators pushed through the **Smoot-Hawley Tariff Act**, which increased tariffs to their second-highest rate in United States history; only the **Tariff Act of 1828** enacted higher average tariff rates.

The Washington Naval Conference

The presidents of the 1920s attempted to isolate the United States from world affairs and reduce spending on war materials. **President Warren Harding** successfully pressed for a reduction of naval power among Britain, France, Japan, Italy, and the United States at the **Washington Naval Conference** (1921–1922).

The Kellogg-Briand Pact

The United States was one of sixty-three nations to sign the **Kellogg-Briand Pact**, renouncing war in principle. Because the pact was negotiated outside of the **League of Nations**, it was unenforceable. While the pact has been referred to as a "worthless piece of paper," scholars and historians have noted that it provided a legal basis for the **Nuremberg trials** following World War II (see page 305) and has encouraged the use of economic sanctions rather than interstate warfare in the post–World War II world.

The Good Neighbor Policy

Into the 1920s, the United States continued **President Theodore Roosevelt's "Big Stick" approach** in regard to **Latin America**, engaging in several military interventions, including in Cuba, Nicaragua, and Haiti. Upon taking office in 1933, **President Franklin D. Roosevelt** began to pursue a more conciliatory policy in Latin America. FDR's **Good Neighbor policy** was, he said, designed to create "more order in this hemisphere and less dislike." In 1933, Secretary of State Cordell Hull signed a formal declaration, at the **Inter-American Conference** in Uruguay, that no nation had the right to interfere in the internal affairs of another nation. In 1934, Roosevelt rejected an interventionist approach in regard to Cuba by abrogating a 1903 treaty (based on the 1901 Platt Amendment; see page 259) and working out a new treaty between the United States and Cuba. At the same time, Roosevelt worked to expand trade with Latin America through the **Reciprocal Trade Agreements Act** (1934).

B. From Isolationism to Intervention

The United States existed in an increasingly dangerous world in the 1930s, creating new debates around the isolationist stance that had shaped foreign policy in the 1920s. These debates ended with the Japanese attack on Pearl Harbor, which drew the United States into World War II.

> **USING HISTORICAL THINKING SKILLS:**
> **CONTEXTUALIZATION**
>
> ### Europe in the 1930S
>
> Even though it is not American history, the series of crises in Europe in the 1930s should be familiar to you. Events abroad can provide a sense of context for actions by the United States—war between France and Britain at the turn of the nineteenth century, European imperialism in the late nineteenth century, the two world wars, and the Cold War, to name just a few.

The Challenges of Isolationism in the 1930s

The traditional **isolationism** of the United States was severely tested by developments in Europe in the 1930s. The **Fascist Party**, led by **Benito Mussolini**, had taken power in **Italy** in 1922. **Adolf Hitler** and his **Nazi** followers came to power in **Germany** in 1933. A civil war in **Spain** led to the rise of a government run by the fascist dictator **Francisco Franco** in 1939. In **Japan**, militaristic leaders set the country on an aggressive course. These dictatorial governments all took aggressive actions in the 1930s: Japan invaded Manchuria, China, in 1931; Germany occupied the demilitarized Rhineland in 1936, annexed Austria in 1937, and occupied Czechoslovakia in 1939; and Italy conquered Ethiopia in 1936. The **League of Nations** protested, and Great Britain and France objected, but it was not until Germany attacked Poland in September 1939 that Hitler met decisive opposition. Great Britain and France declared war on Germany, beginning World War II. Germany, Italy, and Japan formed the **Axis Powers** with the signing of the **Tripartite Pact** (1940).

The Continued Pull of Isolationism

As events degenerated into armed conflicts in Europe and Asia in the 1930s, a debate occurred in the United States about America's role. **Isolationists** argued strongly that the United States should stay out of world affairs. Many isolationists looked back to **World War I** as a lesson in the futility of getting involved in European affairs. The United States had lost over 100,000 men in World War I for no apparent reason, they argued. World War I had not made the world safe for democracy. Almost as soon as the war ended, antidemocratic forces emerged and set Europe once again on the path toward war. In addition, the Senate's **Nye Committee** (1934–1937) uncovered evidence that certain American corporations had profited greatly from U.S. participation in World War I. Americans wondered if the so-called **merchants of death** had pushed the country into the war.

The Argument for Intervention

While the pull of **isolationism** remained strong in the 1930s, many Americans believed it would be a mistake for the United States to isolate itself from world affairs on the eve of World War II. They mocked the idea that the Atlantic Ocean would indefinitely protect the United States from dangerous trends in Europe. **Interventionists** believed that the United States could no longer stand apart. Airplanes and submarines could bring the war to the United States very quickly. If Britain were defeated, there would be nothing standing between Hitler and America. Also, many interventionists believed the war in Europe was different from earlier European quarrels over territory or national pride. They believed that if Hitler was successful, civilization itself would be threatened. They were convinced that the Axis Powers were determined to defeat democratic forces all over the world.

> **KEEP IN MIND**
>
> **Politics and Literature**
>
> Some of the antiwar novels written in the wake of World War I, such as *All Quiet on the Western Front* (1929) by the German writer Erich Maria Remarque, and *A Farewell to Arms* (1929) by Ernest Hemingway, added fuel to the isolationist sentiment of the 1930s.

The Quarantine Speech and the *Panay* Incident

President Franklin D. Roosevelt was sympathetic to the countries defending themselves against fascism, but he knew he could not commit the United States to an interventionist position without the support of the public. After Japan broadened its invasion of China in the summer of 1937, Roosevelt delivered a speech in Chicago in which he warned of the dangers posed by aggressive nations. He argued that such nations should be "quarantined" by the international community. Roosevelt did not specify which nations he was referring to, but his meaning was clear. The public response to the **Quarantine Speech** was generally negative. Roosevelt saw that **isolationist sentiment** was still strong in the United States. This was evident several weeks later when Japan warplanes attacked and sank an American gunboat, the **USS *Panay***, on the Yangtze River in China. Even such a blatant attack on an American naval vessel was brushed aside by isolationist political leaders in the United States. They urged Roosevelt to accept Japanese apologies for the incident. This made it clear to Roosevelt that he would have to proceed with caution in global affairs. Subsequently, he did not take decisive steps toward intervention, but he also did not pretend that the United States could isolate itself from the affairs of the world.

The Onset of World War II

The question of the role of the United States grew more intense in 1939 as **World War II** formally began. The war started after German dictator **Adolf Hitler** ordered an attack on Poland. **Britain** and **France** quickly declared war on **Germany**. Soon after, **President Roosevelt** pushed for legislation allowing the United States to send armaments to Britain with the condition that Britain pay for the weapons first and transport them in their own ships. This **"cash-and-carry"** policy allowed the United States to support Britain without the risk of U.S. ships being destroyed.

Steps Toward Engagement in World War II

By mid-1940, the American public began to shift toward a more **interventionist** stance. The situation in Europe grew dire. Americans were shaken by the defeat of France at the hands of the Nazis in mid-1940. They saw how one of the great democratic powers was easily defeated by the Nazi war machine. Would Britain fall next? Would the United States be Hitler's next target? In 1940, the United States ratified the **Selective Service Act**, requiring compulsory military service for males between twenty-one and thirty-five years of age. By 1941, 70 percent of the American people were ready to help Britain directly, even if it risked getting involved in World War II. With this shift in public opinion and with his victory in the presidential election of 1940, Roosevelt was ready to take more direct action. In March 1941, Congress approved his **Lend-Lease Act**, which allowed the United States to send armaments to Britain in American ships. The Lend-Lease Act was extended to the Soviet Union after Hitler broke the **Nazi-Soviet Pact** (1939) and launched an invasion of the Soviet Union in June 1941. In July of that year, Roosevelt and British prime minister Winston Churchill solidified the alliance between their two countries by releasing a statement of "common principles" known as the **Atlantic Charter**. Though officially neutral, the United States was moving steadily toward intervening on the side of Great Britain.

Pearl Harbor and American Intervention

As World War II intensified in 1940 and 1941, the American public was not yet unified in its support of intervention. **Isolationists**, such as the renowned aviator **Charles Lindbergh**, continued to argue against any U.S. steps toward helping Britain. Lindbergh was a leader of the **America First Committee** and, historians argue, a Nazi sympathizer. Even late in 1941, it was clear that many Americans still had major reservations about America entering World War II. Debates about intervention ended abruptly on December 7, 1941, when Japanese warplanes attacked **Pearl Harbor**, the U.S. naval base in Hawaii. Almost immediately, the United States entered World War II. With American involvement in the war, the isolationist position was largely silenced.

Topic 7.12 World War II: Mobilization

In many ways, World War II required the participation of the entire American public, not simply members of the military. These efforts created a sense of unity and common cause in the country.

A. Mobilizing for World War II

The massive effort by the United States to mobilize for World War II led to an expansion of federal power and to a rapid end of the Great Depression.

Rationing and Recycling

During the war, there were shortages of consumer goods because of the needs of the military. Starting in 1942, the **Office of Price Administration** began rationing key commodities to civilians, such as gasoline and tires. Next, the government began rationing food—sugar, meat, coffee, lard, butter, and many other items. Families received **ration books** and used their ration stamps, along with cash, when they purchased these items. In addition, children organized **Tin Can Clubs** to collect scrap metal to be melted down for use in weapons and for ammunition production.

Funding the War Effort

The **Roosevelt administration** paid for the war effort through the sale of **war bonds** and increases in taxes. The government went into massive **debt** during the war, with the debt rising by a factor of six between 1940 and 1949. The experience of World War II demonstrates that massive government spending, and ensuing deficits, can play a significant role in stimulating a sluggish economy.

War Production—Becoming the "Arsenal of Democracy"

If the United States were to become the **"arsenal of democracy,"** as **President Franklin D. Roosevelt** promised in a speech in 1940, it would have to dramatically and rapidly step up the production of war-related materials. In 1942, Roosevelt created the **War Production Board**, and later the **Office of War Mobilization**, to oversee the conversion from civilian industry to war production. Almost overnight, the persistent unemployment of the **Great Depression** ended. After the United States entered World War II in December 1941, the country faced the opposite problem—labor shortages. With millions of men and women in the armed forces, the Roosevelt administration took several important steps to ensure a sufficient supply of factory workers. Women were heavily recruited to work in industry (see "Rosie the Riveter," below). To ensure uninterrupted production, labor unions agreed to refrain from striking during the war. This promise was kept, with the exception of a few strikes in the coal industry.

B. World War II and American Values

A series of debates and decisions during World War II—including the decision related to the internment of Japanese Americans and debates over race and segregation—raised fundamental questions about American values.

"Rosie the Riveter"

The government made a concerted effort to recruit **women** to participate in the war effort. Women were needed because factories were working around the clock producing military goods, and much of the male workforce was in the military. Many recruiting posters were produced by the government, usually through the **Office of War Information**, showing women in industrial settings. The fictional **"Rosie the Riveter"** character was often featured in this public relations campaign. Female workers were presented in a positive light—helping the nation as well as supporting the men in combat abroad. Such a campaign was needed because prewar societal mores discouraged women from doing industrial work. During the Great Depression of the 1930s, women were encouraged to leave the job market so that there would be enough jobs available for male "breadwinners." The World War II recruiting campaign was successful. By 1945, a third of the workforce was female.

World War II and the Status of African Americans in American Society

A series of developments during World War II led many Americans to reevaluate long-held attitudes and practices around race. **African Americans** mounted a direct challenge to the system of **Jim Crow segregation**, both through their participation in the armed forces and in war-related industries (see below and pages 301–302). In many ways, this challenge continued into the postwar world, with the growth of the civil rights movement. It also put the issues of race and segregation on the national agenda.

African Americans and War Production

Initially, many war-related industrial plants were reluctant to hire African Americans. An important African-American labor leader, **A. Phillip Randolph**, the president of the **Brotherhood of Sleeping Car Porters**, planned a public demonstration in Washington, D.C., in 1941 to protest discrimination in war-related industries. When the Roosevelt administration heard of these plans, it worked out an agreement. Roosevelt issued **Executive Order 8802**, banning discrimination in war-related industries, and Randolph called off the march.

African Americans joined millions of other Americans in moving toward industrial centers. The **Great Migration** that

---

USING REASONING PRACTICES:
CONTINUITY AND CHANGE

The Supreme Court and Wartime Liberties

The *Korematsu* decision is one of several rulings by the Supreme Court that have curtailed civil liberties in times of war. The Court upheld restrictions on free speech during World War I in the *Schenck v. United States* decision (1919). On the other hand, the Court upheld civil liberties during the Civil War. It declared President Abraham Lincoln's suspension of habeas corpus unconstitutional in *Ex Parte Merryman* (1861); later it set limits on wartime presidential powers in *Ex Parte Milligan* (1866).

began in World War I continued, with African Americans moving to the West Coast in addition to moving to northern industrial cities (see more on the Great Migration, page 283).

The Japanese Relocation

In 1942, **President Roosevelt** issued **Executive Order 9066** authorizing the government to remove more than 100,000 **Japanese Americans** from West Coast states and relocate them to distant camps in more than a dozen western states. The order applied to both **Issei** (Japanese Americans who had emigrated from Japan) and **Nisei** (native-born Japanese Americans). Most of their property was confiscated by the government. In *Korematsu v. United States* (1944), the Supreme Court ruled that the relocation was acceptable on the grounds of national security. Years later, in 1988, the U.S. government publicly apologized to the surviving victims and extended $20,000 in reparations to each one. The federal law that granted the reparations acknowledged that the Japanese relocation was based on "race prejudice, war hysteria, and a failure of political leadership," not on national security.

C. Migration and Mobilization

Wartime job opportunities led to migrations from Mexico and elsewhere in the Western Hemisphere. These migrations helped the United States meet its demands for defense workers, but they also generated resentment among some Americans.

Mexicans and World War II

The administration of **Franklin D. Roosevelt** initiated the ***Bracero* program** in 1942 to bring into the United States temporary contract workers from **Mexico**. The Mexican government pushed the United States to guarantee that these temporary workers would not be drafted. More than 200,000 Mexicans participated in the program, and it is estimated that at least that number came into the United States as undocumented workers.

Mexicans and Mexican Americans were the object of discrimination, harassment, and violence during World War II. In California, whites frequently targeted Mexican Americans for physical attacks. White teenagers and servicemen especially targeted Latinos wearing colorful "zoot-suits," then in style among Latinos and African Americans. A series of violent **"zoot-suit riots"** occurred in Los Angeles in June 1943, resulting in over 150 injuries and over 500 arrests.

Topic 7.13 World War II: Military

The United States, seeing participation in World War II as part of a global struggle against militarism and fascism, played an important role in the Allied victory over the Axis powers in World War II. At the same time, American participation in the war effort led to a reevaluation of ideas around race and gender.

A. The Stakes Involved in World War II

Americans came to see World War II as more than a conventional military conflict. As details of Japanese wartime atrocities and of the Holocaust began to emerge, many Americans came to see the war as a desperate fight for freedom and democracy against powerful militarist and fascist forces.

The Nazi Regime and the Holocaust

The **Holocaust** was the systematic murder of six million European Jews and millions of other "undesirables" by the Nazis. The roots of the Holocaust pre-date World War II, with Nazi persecution of the Jews in Germany and in territories it took over in the 1930s. The anti-Semitic and racist **Nuremberg Laws** were enacted in 1935. **Kristallnacht**, or Night of Broken Glass, a series of violent raids on Jewish homes, businesses, and institutions, carried out by Nazi paramilitary groups and civilians, occurred in 1937. In 1939, **Adolf Hitler** and other leading Nazis developed plans for a "**final solution** of the Jewish question," with the object of eliminating Europe's Jewish populations. After the Germans took over most of continental Europe, this plan went from being the scheming of a madman to a horrible, deadly reality. The plan also included other groups such as Slavic people, Roma and Sinti people, the disabled, and homosexuals, as well as political opponents. Nazis first ordered Jews into crowded urban areas called **ghettos**, then moved them to concentration or labor camps, and finally to death camps, where gas chambers and incineration ovens were built to carry out Hitler's "final solution." Reports of Nazi **death camps** began to trickle out of German-occupied Europe by 1942. As the war in Europe was ending, the Allies found these camps, revealing the full extent of the barbaric crimes against civilians committed by the Nazis during the war.

The American Response to the Holocaust

While news of the **Holocaust** put the nature of the Nazi regime into sharp focus, Americans were of different minds about what actions, beyond pursuing military victory, the United States might take in response. American officials, for instance, had resisted pleas to admit large numbers of **Jewish refugees** fleeing Europe. In 1939, the German passenger ship *St. Louis*, carrying nearly a thousand escaped German Jews, was turned away by the United States when it was off the coast of Florida, after having been turned away by Cuban authorities. **Secretary of State Cordell Hull** advised Roosevelt not to let the Jewish passengers disembark. Such resistance to admitting refugees continued during the war. (See more on the *St. Louis* episode, page 307.)

Japanese Wartime Atrocities

Many Americans also saw Japanese wartime actions as representative of a militarist ideology that threatened to undermine democratic traditions. The most notorious episode of Japanese atrocities occurred before the beginning of World War II in Europe. In 1937, **Japan** widened its military campaign against **China**, overrunning most of China's port cities. In the city of Nanjing, Japanese troops killed thousands of civilians. While the exact number of people killed is in dispute, the **Nanjing Massacre**, also referred to as the **Rape of Nanjing,** resulted in at least 80,000 deaths and perhaps as many as 300,000.

B. Staffing the Military During World War II—Opportunities and Debate

The efforts to supply troops for the armed forces and to produce war-related materials led to opportunities for women and minorities to improve their positions in society.

Staffing the Military

The **Roosevelt administration** began a push to enlarge the size of the military even before the attack on Pearl Harbor brought the United States into the war in December 1941. The **Selective Service Act**, passed in September 1940, created the first peacetime draft in American history. By the summer of 1941, almost a million and a half men were in the armed forces. In the course of the war, more than fifteen million men and women would serve in the military.

Women in the Military

World War II opened many new opportunities for **women**, both in war-time production (see page 299) and in the military itself. Many women served as nurses. In addition, more than 150,000 women joined the **Women's Army Auxiliary Corps (WAAC)**, later designated the **Women's Army Corps (WAC)**, and the **Women Accepted for Volunteer Emergency Service (WAVES)**, the women's branch of the Navy.

African Americans in the Armed Forces—The "Double V Campaign"

African Americans participated in the war effort, in part, with the expectation of raising their status at home. The **National Association for the Advancement of Colored People** encouraged African Americans to take part in the **"Double V" campaign**—promoting victory against fascism abroad and victory against racism in their home country. Ultimately 1.2 million African Americans served in the military during World War II. The most famous segregated African-American units were the **Tuskegee Airmen** and the **761st Tank Battalion**. African-American effectiveness on the battlefield encouraged President Truman to desegregate the armed services in 1948 with **Executive Order 9981**.

C. The Allied Victory over the Axis Powers in World War II

The United States participated in joint political and military efforts with the other Allied countries and helped achieve the Allied victory in World War II. In addition, American industrial production and advances in technology and science played important parts in the war effort. Finally, the commitment of large sections of the American public to victory and to the advancement of democratic ideals helped the overall war effort.

War in the Pacific Theater

Through the first year of the war, the United States sent more of its troops to the **Pacific theater** than to Europe. Even though the defeat of Hitler was a top priority for the United States, it was **Japan** that had directly attacked the United States. The United States suffered several setbacks at the hands of the Japanese military in the first few months of the war. Japan took over **the Philippines** at the end of December 1941. By May 1942, Japan controlled a massive Pacific empire and had Australia in its sights.

The Battles of Coral Sea and Midway

The United States turned the tide of the war in the Pacific in two naval battles in 1942. In May, in the **Battle of the Coral Sea**, the U.S. Navy stopped a Japanese fleet headed to New Guinea. In June, the United States achieved a victory over the Japanese fleet in the **Battle of Midway**. After Midway, the United States steadily began to push Japanese forces back toward the Japanese home islands.

> **USING HISTORICAL THINKING SKILLS:**
> **MAKING CONNECTIONS**
>
> **Turning Points in War**
>
> Although extensive knowledge of battles is not required for the AP exam, be aware of key turning points in wars, such as the Battle of Saratoga in the American Revolution, the capture of Vicksburg and the Battle of Gettysburg in the Civil War, and the Battle of Midway in World War II.

"Island Hopping"

By the end of 1943, the United States began employing a strategy called **"island hopping"** (also known as "leapfrogging") to capture key Japanese-held islands in the Pacific. The basic idea of island hopping was that the United States and the Allies would avoid attacking some of the most heavily fortified islands. Instead, they would focus on islands that were most important—perhaps as airfields or as key positions to block or attack enemy naval movements. The United States cut off the Japanese-held islands it had "hopped" over by blockading supply ships. Japanese forces on these islands would then **"wither on the vine."**

War in Europe

Before June 1944, most of the fighting against Germany was carried out by the Soviet Union in Eastern Europe. **Joseph Stalin**, the Soviet dictator, had been urging the United States and Britain to open a second front in Western Europe against Germany. At a top-secret meeting in **Tehran**, **Iran** (see more on the Tehran Conference, page 304), in November 1943, **President Franklin Roosevelt** and **Prime Minister Winston Churchill** assured Stalin that they would open up a **second European front**.

The Washington and Casablanca Conferences

In June 1942, **President Franklin Roosevelt** and **Prime Minister Winston Churchill** met in **Washington, D.C.**, to discuss strategy. In January 1943, they met again in **Casablanca, Morocco**. Stalin did not attend either meeting, but he let it be known that he hoped the other Allies would soon open up a major second front in Europe. Although there was warfare in North Africa, the brunt of the fighting against Hitler's forces had been carried out by the **Red Army**. Nearly 90 percent of German casualties in World War II came at the hands of Soviet troops. At both meetings, Churchill opposed the idea of immediately invading France; the British did not want to prematurely initiate a repeat of the trench warfare of World War I. Churchill and Roosevelt agreed to open a front in North Africa, followed by an attack on Italy. Churchill described Italy as the **"soft underbelly"** of the Axis—the part of Axis-controlled Europe most vulnerable to attack.

Fighting in North Africa

The first offensive involving American troops fighting in Nazi-occupied areas occurred in **North Africa** in November 1942. American forces, led by **General Dwight D. Eisenhower**, landed in **Morocco** and **Algeria** and pushed back the forces of **France's Vichy government**, which collaborated with the Nazis. Americans moved eastward to attack German troops in **Tunisia** and **Libya**, while British forces drove westward to trap the enemy. By May 1943, North Africa was in Allied hands.

The "Soft Underbelly" of the Axis

Approximately one-quarter of a million Allied troops landed in **Sicily** in June 1943. The Allies captured Sicily by August, which led to the Italian king dismissing **Mussolini** as prime minister (Mussolini was killed by partisans in 1945). A new Italian government left the Axis and eventually joined the Allies. Germany, however, was not ready to accept an Allied-occupation of Italy. Hitler sent reinforcements into Italy. After ferocious fighting, the Allies finally marched into **Rome** in June 1944, but the rest of the advance up the Italian peninsula was by German troops every step of the way. Italy was no "soft underbelly."

"D-Day" and the Allied Assault on Europe

In June 1944, the Allies stormed the beaches of **Normandy**, **France**, and began pushing Hitler's forces back toward Germany. On **"D-Day"** itself, June 6, nearly 200,000 Allied troops landed. Over the next several weeks, more than one million additional troops arrived. By August 1944, after heavy fighting and great loss, Allied forces under the command of **General Dwight D. Eisenhower** had liberated Paris from Nazi occupation.

V-E Day

Hitler made a last attempt to stop the Allied assault in the winter of 1944–1945. German forces counterattacked Allied lines in **Belgium** in the **Battle of the Bulge**, but eventually were stopped and driven back. American and British troops approached Germany from the west as Soviet troops approached from the east. By April 1945, the Soviets were on the outskirts of Hitler's capital, Berlin, which was under devastating bombardment. On April 30, Hitler committed suicide; on May 7, Germany surrendered: **"Victory in Europe Day."**

Victory in the Pacific

By February 1945, American forces had taken control of most of Japan's Pacific empire. **Iwo Jima** and **Okinawa**, two small, heavily fortified islands, stood between American forces and the Japanese homeland. Capturing these two islands proved to be an onerous task for American forces. The battle for Iwo Jima lasted six weeks in February and March 1945. Approximately 7,000 Americans died in the battle. The struggle for Okinawa was even more deadly. The island of Okinawa was to be a staging area for an attack on the Japanese home islands. Fighting there lasted from early April until mid-June 1945. The United States mobilized 300,000 troops for the battle.

Approximately 12,000 Americans died, while Japan lost approximately 140,000. After these bloody battles, Japan's sphere of control was reduced to its home islands.

The Decision to Drop the Atomic Bomb, and the Japanese Surrender

In April 1945, **President Franklin D. Roosevelt** died suddenly. He was succeeded by his vice president, **Harry S. Truman**. In July, just as preparations were under way for a final offensive against Japan, President Truman learned that the United States (in collaboration with Britain and Canada) had successfully tested an atomic bomb and that more bombs were ready for use. Since 1942, scientists in the top-secret **Manhattan Project** had been working on this terrifying and deadly weapon. The project involved several research labs at different sites. The facility at **Los Alamos**, New Mexico, headed by physicist **J. Robert Oppenheimer**, was charged with construction of the bomb.

The United States used this new weapon twice on Japan. On August 6, 1945, the United States dropped an atomic bomb on **Hiroshima**; on August 9, a second bomb was dropped on **Nagasaki**. As many as 226,000 people died. Soon after, on September 2, Japan officially surrendered, ending World War II. At the time, the decision to drop the atomic bomb did not generate much public debate. The atomic bombing swiftly ended a bloody conflict that had consumed fifty million lives. However, in the decades since the war, some Americans have raised questions about the decision. Critics argue that it was morally wrong for the United States to have targeted civilian populations and that the Japanese were ready to surrender. Others stand by the decision to drop the bomb. They claim it was not clear that the Japanese were on the verge of surrendering. Some of the Japanese military leadership had argued against surrender, even after the second bomb was dropped.

Topic 7.14 Postwar Diplomacy

With Europe and Asia ravaged from World War II, the United States emerged as the dominant power in the world. U.S. engagement in world affairs after the war was in marked contrast to its withdrawal from the international community following World War I.

A. The United States and the Postwar World

After World War II the United States played a lead role in shaping the postwar world through conferences and peace settlements.

Tehran Conference

Soviet Premier Joseph Stalin, **British Prime Minister Winston Churchill**, and **President Franklin D. Roosevelt** met in **Tehran, Iran**, in November 1943. The Allies agreed that the **D-Day invasion** would coincide with a major Soviet offensive. Also, Stalin pledged that the Soviet Union would join the war in Asia following the defeat of Germany. The Allies agreed in theory to forming an international peacekeeping organization.

Bretton Woods Conference

In July 1944, forty-four nations met at **Bretton Woods**, New Hampshire, to discuss the basis of the global economy following the war. The **International Monetary Fund** was established at this meeting.

> **USING REASONING PROCESSES: COMPARISON**
>
> **Post-War American Engagement**
>
> Note the marked difference between American disengagement following World War I and American engagement following World War II. Following World War I, United States policymakers pursued a policy of isolationism, evident in the Senate rejection of the Treaty of Versailles (1919), the Washington Disarmament Conference (1922), and increased tariff rates (1922 and 1930). Following World War II, however, the United States played a dominant role in containing Communism and opposing the Soviet Union in the Cold War.

Yalta Conference

The **Yalta Conference**, held in February 1945, was the most significant, and last, meeting of Churchill, Stalin, and Roosevelt. At Yalta, a coastal city in Crimea, the **"big three"** agreed to divide **Germany** into four military zones of occupation (the fourth zone would be occupied by France). Also, Stalin agreed to allow free elections in **Poland** in the future, with a Soviet-dominated interim government assuming power immediately following the war. Also at the meeting, secret agreements were made allowing for Soviet control of Outer Mongolia, the Kuril Islands, and part of Sakhalin Island, as well as Soviet railroad rights in Manchuria. Critics later faulted Roosevelt and Churchill for "abandoning" Poland and the rest of Eastern Europe to Communist forces. But there was little the United States and Britain could do to dislodge the Red Army from Eastern Europe, short of starting a third world war.

Potsdam Conference

In the summer of 1945, the final meeting of the United States, the Soviet Union, and Great Britain took place in **Potsdam, Germany.** The meeting was attended by **President Harry S. Truman**, **Joseph Stalin**, and British **Prime Minister Clement Atlee** (successor to Churchill). These leaders hammered out the details of the administration of occupied Germany. The details included the process of **"denazification"** of Germany, which led to the **Nuremberg trials.** The victorious nations set up this international tribunal to try leading Nazis for waging aggressive war and for crimes against humanity. At these trials, about thirty American judges participated. **Associate Supreme Court Justice Robert H. Jackson** was the chief prosecutor at the Nuremberg trials. Many of the Nazis defended themselves by claiming that they were merely following orders.

Topic 7.15 Subject to Debate

The Nature of American Imperialism

History textbooks can take one of several approaches to discussions of American imperialism. You should be familiar with these approaches in order to write about events and documents from this period within a broader intellectual framework.

James Loewen, in his survey of American history textbooks, identifies three approaches to talking about American imperialism. Critics of American imperialism often discuss the United States as if it were a "colossus," imposing its will on the world. This "American colossus" approach asserts that any talk of spreading democracy around the world is cynical window-dressing to hide the actual motives of American imperialism: economic exploitation. A competing view acknowledges that economic motives drive foreign policy, but is not troubled by that fact. This hard-nosed "realpolitik" approach holds that America must expand if it wants to maintain the standard of living that Americans have come to appreciate. A third view, which Loewen calls the "international good guy" approach, ignores economic motives altogether. It asserts that American motives in the world are altruistic and noble. This view takes the words of public figures at face value.[1]

The Progressive Movement and the Business Community

Some historians, such as Gabriel Kolko and James Weinstein, cast doubt on the traditional notion of progressive reformers as noble crusaders waging war on a corrupt and greedy business class. They contend that much of the impetus to reform business either originated with the business community or was shaped by it. Members of the business community were interested in reining in the worst elements of the business world. The example of the meat-packing industry demonstrates this point well. After the publication of *The Jungle*, the public's confidence in the entire industry declined. Industry leaders wanted to reform their world—rationalize and standardize it—so that people would continue to buy meat. Rather than resisting reform, industry leaders initiated it in order to restore confidence in their industry.

---

[1] James Loewen, *Lies My Teacher Told Me: Everything Your American History Textbook Got Wrong* (New York: New Press, 1995).

A second avenue of criticism of the movement had to do with the attitude of the Progressive movement toward the poor. This critique painted the Progressive movement as elitist and condescending toward the working class it was trying to help. The movement was ready to impose its idea of proper behavior on others. This is most evident in the prohibition movement—in which middle-class activists told working-class people that they should not drink. The crusade against "immoral" behavior—gambling, prostitution, smoking—also raises this issue of elitism. The nature of reform movements in general continues to divide historians.

World War I in Public Memory

World War I is often relegated to a backseat in standard history curricula—with World War II much more prominent. The perception of World War II is of a war imbued with a sense of mission—it was a "good fight" carried out by the "greatest generation." On the National Mall in Washington, D.C., a large World War II memorial occupies a prominent place between the Washington Monument and the Lincoln Memorial. The World War I monument, by contrast, is a modest gazebo tucked away to the side of the mall. It is not even a national monument—it commemorates local residents who perished in the conflict. One reason World War I has been largely ignored is that there is no clearly identifiable "evil" that the United States was trying to defeat. The history of World War I does not read like a morality play.

That said, it would be unwise for a student preparing for the AP exam to ignore World War I. There are several crucial questions to consider. For instance, how do we account for the fact that the American political landscape changed completely from the beginning of the war to the end of the war? In 1914, on the eve of the war, the Progressive movement was enjoying its heyday; in 1919, as the war ended, America had become violently conservative. The "Red Scare" was paving the way for the resurgence of the Ku Klux Klan, restrictions on immigration, and attacks on secularism. Students should be aware of the role war plays in changing the political climate.

Consensus Historians and Intolerance in the 1920s

The decade of the 1920s poses problems for historians in the "consensus" tradition. Consensus history asserts that there is a broad agreement among Americans, today and in the past, around basic ideas and feelings. According to consensus historians, Americans share a belief in democracy and individual liberties; they believe that hard work leads to advancement; they believe in God, but do not try to impose their beliefs on others or on society as a whole; and they are a tolerant, welcoming people. Consensus history gained traction in the 1950s. This broad set of ideas set America apart from the Soviet Union—an essentially different system developed by people from an essentially different background. True, as consensus historians acknowledge, there have been conflicts in American history, but they have not been over essential values. Take the labor battles of the Gilded Age. Consensus historians would argue that these disagreements do not represent fundamental differences. The strikers were not revolutionaries trying to overthrow the economic or political system of the United States; they simply wanted a greater share of the wealth that the capitalist economy was generating for the country.

Consensus historians have a great deal of difficulty explaining the 1920s. Here is a decade in which the Ku Klux Klan claimed to have 3 million members in a country of 100 million people. Even if the membership figures are inflated, the Ku Klux Klan was a huge organization. Up to three million Americans joined a violent, racist, intolerant, anti-Semitic organization. In addition, there were many cases of German-American residents being beaten in their homes by mobs of Americans in the early 1920s. These violent episodes challenge the assumptions of the consensus historians. Some historians have tried to minimize the importance of these facts or focus on the diversions of the "jazz age." Others have seen the reactionary impulses of the decade as responses to rapid social change. However, the undercurrent of intolerance and violence in the 1920s is difficult to fit into the traditional consensus model of American history.

Handling the Great Depression: Hoover Versus Roosevelt

Historians have debated the legacy of President Herbert Hoover in recent years. History textbooks tend to disparage Hoover. He is presented as aloof and rigid in the face of economic disaster. Hoover is remembered for what he did not do (provide direct relief to the poor) rather than what he did do.

Hoover's legacy in historical work tells us a great deal about historical writing. Many historians have come to lionize Hoover's successor, President Franklin D. Roosevelt, who both saved the country from the worst ravages of the Great Depression at home and from the fascist menace abroad. In the process, he created the modern liberal welfare state. This adoration of Roosevelt, in turn, has influenced historical writing about Hoover. In this context, Hoover has become the "anti-Roosevelt," representing the negative side of the coin. Hoover is lumped in with the other two Republican presidents of the 1920s, Warren Harding and Calvin Coolidge. However, a brief look at the record would indicate that Hoover was not as incompetent as he is often portrayed. He was an exceptionally competent administrator, running the successful Food Administration during World War I. When the Depression hit, he did not sit idly by. He implemented the far-reaching Reconstruction Finance Corporation, which provided needed funds to key sectors of the economy. Later he implemented public works programs.

The New Deal—Successful or Ineffective?

Was the New Deal successful or not? Some historians have noted that the New Deal did not solve the problems of the Depression. They see the creation of a bloated government bureaucracy that was too large and impersonal to address the concerns of ordinary people. These historians note that the Depression ended only when the United States began producing materials for World War II. Other historians, more sympathetic to Roosevelt and the New Deal, argue that the New Deal restored hope among the American people and prevented more widespread suffering. Defenders of the New Deal also note that organized labor made great strides because of New Deal legislation. Historians often have in mind contemporary debates about government intervention in the economy—such as debates about government health care programs or about raising the minimum wage—when they are looking at the New Deal.

Morality and Justice in the World War II Era

Two of the most heated historical questions involving the World War II era both have to do with issues of morality, justice, and war. Historians have recently had heated debates over both the Holocaust and the dropping of the atomic bombs on Japan. Some historians have insisted that the United States could have done more to save European Jews. These historians cite prewar immigration restrictions that prevented Jewish refugees from coming into the United States. In 1939, the State Department did not allow the passenger ship *St. Louis*, with more than 900 Jewish refugees seeking asylum, to dock in Florida (see page 301). The ship was forced to return to Antwerp, Belgium, where the Jews aboard were dispersed to several countries. It is estimated that 255 of them died during the war, many in Nazi concentration camps. The question as to why this happened has resonated in the contemporary world, as Americans have debated how much their country should intervene in human rights crises abroad, such as in Kosovo (1998-1999) or Darfur (2003-2020) or Syria (2011-the present).

The debate over the use of the atomic bomb has also generated a great deal of controversy in the historical world. In 1994, the Smithsonian Museum announced plans for an exhibit to open the following year to commemorate the fiftieth anniversary of the dropping of the atom bomb on Hiroshima and Nagasaki. When the floor plans and the text of the proposed exhibit were released to the public, there was a firestorm of controversy. Veterans groups and conservative historians accused the Smithsonian of "revisionism" by portraying the United States in a bad light. The plans revealed a balanced exhibit, but it was not the heroic exhibit that critics had hoped for. The text asked troubling questions, such as whether Japan was actually ready to surrender. The exhibit also showed scenes of death and destruction, which one would expect at an exhibit about a nuclear explosion. Ultimately, the entire exhibit was scrapped. The museum ended up displaying the Enola Gay (the plane that dropped the bomb on Hiroshima), but it left out any context or thought-provoking questions.

Practice Multiple-Choice Questions

DIRECTIONS: Pick the letter that best answers the following questions.

Questions 1–2 refer to the following image:

—Victor Gillam, "Overlooked - or The Folly of Foreign Missions," *Judge Magazine*, 1895

1. The point of view of the cartoon above is that

   (A) Christian missionaries were overly concerned with gaining converts in other lands while they ignored poverty at home.
   (B) open immigration policies were undermining the economic stability of the United States.
   (C) the United States should look beyond its borders and become an imperialist power.
   (D) the widening gap between the wealthy and the poor was creating a potentially revolutionary situation in the United States.

2. A reader who supported the sentiment of the cartoon above would most likely have been in support of which of the following?

   (A) The Chinese Exclusion Act
   (B) The Spanish-American War
   (C) The Supreme Court decision in the Insular Cases
   (D) The settlement house movement

Questions 3–5 are based on the following image:

—Rollin Kirby, "Until Women Vote," *Woman's Journal*, 1915

3. The main point of the 1915 cartoon above is that

   (A) women should gain the right to vote because their contribution to the economy is comparable to that of men.
   (B) women should not gain the right to vote because they are too meek to enter the fray of male-dominated politics.
   (C) women should gain the right to vote because male-dominated legislatures would not eradicate child labor and long hours for female workers.
   (D) women should not gain the right to vote because their varied duties—in the home and in the workplace—rendered them too busy to participate in politics.

4. Which of the following groups would be most likely to support the perspective of the cartoon?

   (A) Members of the New York State legislature
   (B) Advocates of the "cult of domesticity"
   (C) Members of the Progressive movement
   (D) Believers in Social Darwinist theories

5. The ideas expressed in the cartoon above most directly reflect which of the following continuities in United States history?

   (A) Debates about the role of federal, state, and local governments in the economy
   (B) Debates about the proper role of political parties
   (C) Debates about the power of the state governments to challenge federal actions
   (D) Debates about the appropriateness of limiting behavior that is deemed immoral by community standards

Questions 6–8 refer to the following passage:

"This book tells the story of how industrial workers in one American city made sense of an era in our recent history [the 1930s] when the nation moved from a commitment to welfare capitalism to a welfare state [and] from a determination to resist the organization of its industrial work force to tolerating it."

—Lizabeth Cohen, *Making a New Deal: Industrial Workers in Chicago, 1919–1939*, 1990

6. The changes described in the excerpt could best be attributed to

    (A) changes in the composition of the Supreme Court.
    (B) an increase in the power of local and state governments.
    (C) a renewed commitment to a laissez-faire approach to economic policy.
    (D) an expansion to the powers of the federal government.

7. Which of the following most strongly sought to limit or reverse the changes described in the excerpt?

    (A) Political radicals, such as members of the Communist Party
    (B) Organizations advocating on behalf of senior citizens
    (C) Civil rights organizations such as the Congress of Racial Equality
    (D) Conservatives in Congress and on the Supreme Court

8. The changes described in the excerpt were later reinforced by initiatives associated with

    (A) Senator Joseph McCarthy and the anti-Communist crusade of the 1950s.
    (B) the "Great Society" agenda of President Lyndon Johnson in the 1960s.
    (C) the domestic agenda of President Ronald Reagan in the 1980s.
    (D) Representative Newt Gingrich and the "Contract with America" in the 1990s.

Questions 9–10 refer to the following passage.

"To cast this case into outlines of racial prejudice, without reference to the real military dangers which were presented, merely confuses the issue. Korematsu was not excluded from the Military Area because of hostility to him or his race. He was excluded because we are at war with the Japanese Empire, because the properly constituted military authorities feared an invasion of our West Coast and felt constrained to take proper security measures, because they decided that the military urgency of the situation demanded that all citizens of Japanese ancestry be segregated from the West Coast temporarily, and, finally, because Congress, reposing its confidence in this time of war in our military leaders—as inevitably it must—determined that they should have the power to do just this."

—Justice Hugo Black, writing for the majority opinion of the United States Supreme Court in *Korematsu v. United States*, 1944

9. The idea expressed in the excerpt demonstrates continuity with which of the following earlier Supreme Court decisions?

    (A) Decisions allowing for "separate but equal" public facilities, such as *Plessy v. Ferguson*
    (B) Decisions limiting the powers of the executive branch, such as *Schechter Poultry Corp. v. United States*
    (C) Decisions limiting the citizenship rights of certain groups, such as *Dred Scott v. Sandford*
    (D) Decisions limiting civil liberties during times of national emergency, such as *Schenck v. United States*

10. Which of the following was the most immediate result of the decision excerpted?

    (A) The United States military was forced to compensate Japanese Americans for land they had lost during World War II.
    (B) The United States military was forced to close detention centers for Italian Americans and German Americans who had been living in East Coast cities and towns.
    (C) The United States military was permitted to keep over 100,000 Japanese Americans in internment centers for the duration of World War II.
    (D) President Franklin D. Roosevelt introduced a proposal to add additional members to the Supreme Court.

Answers and Explanations

1. **(A)** The central figure, with the telescope, represents a Protestant missionary worker. In the cartoon, the missionary worker is looking abroad to see which lands would be fruitful for missionary work. He seems to be ignoring the people in need right at his feet. The cartoon is not critical of immigration policies (B); the people at his feet are not shown to be recent immigrants. In any case, they are presented in a sympathetic light. The cartoon does not allude to imperialist ventures (C), nor does it depict a growing gap in wealth in the United States (D).

2. **(D)** Supporters of the point of view of the cartoon would also support the work of the settlement house movement because the movement was addressing the issue that the cartoonist asserted was being ignored by Protestant missionaries—poverty at home. Settlement houses were established to aid immigrants, especially immigrant women. By the 1910s more than 400 settlement houses existed in the United States, usually run by women. Jane Addams ran Hull House in Chicago.

3. **(C)** The main point of the cartoon, "Until Women Vote," by Rollin Kirby (1915), is that women should gain the right to vote because male-dominated legislatures would not eradicate child labor or long hours for female workers. The image depicts bedraggled women and despondent children entering a cannery. They are being ordered to work by a male figure labeled "New York State Legislature." The end of the male figure's whip spells out the phrase, "72 hours a week." Suffragists often argued that giving women the right to vote would lead to the passage of important social legislation.

4. **(C)** Members of the Progressive movement would support the perspective of the cartoon. The cartoon embraces two issues that were important to the Progressive movement—women's suffrage and improvements in conditions at the workplace. The Progressive movement was a broad coalition of reform-minded individuals and groups who sought to improve society. They focused on issues such as unhygienic workplaces, corruption in government, democratic participation, child labor, unfair business practices, and poverty.

5. **(A)** The ideas expressed in the cartoon most directly reflect ongoing debates about the role of federal, state, and local governments in the economy. The Progressive movement challenged the laissez-faire policies that characterized the Gilded Age. These debates were seen in the 1930s around New Deal programs and in the 1960s around Great Society programs. Debates about the role of the government in economic issues continue to occur to the present day.

6. **(D)** The excerpt is describing the impact of the New Deal, a series of programs and agencies that sought to address the Great Depression. President Franklin D. Roosevelt took the federal government in a new direction by asserting that it should take some responsibility for the welfare of the people. Previously, churches, settlement houses, and other private charities helped people in times of need.

7. **(D)** The New Deal was most strongly challenged by a series of Supreme Court decisions. Roosevelt grew increasingly frustrated with the Supreme Court after it shot down the National Industrial Recovery Act in *Schechter v. United States* (1935) and the Agricultural Adjustment Act in *Butler v. United States* (1936). In 1936, he announced a plan to increase the number of justices on the Supreme Court to as many as fifteen. He said that some of the older justices had difficulty keeping up with the heavy workload. But it was clear that he was trying to create a Supreme Court friendlier to his New Deal programs. Roosevelt's "Court-packing plan" was widely criticized and ultimately abandoned.

8. **(B)** The general thrust of the New Deal was later reinforced by the "Great Society" agenda of President Lyndon Johnson in the 1960s. The main components of Johnson's Great Society were landmark civil rights acts as well as a comprehensive "war on poverty." An important program was Medicare, which was created to provide health care for every American of sixty-five years of age

and older. The program is still in effect today. Many aspects of Johnson's Great Society were underfunded as the federal government increased spending on the war in Vietnam.

9. **(D)** The *Korematsu v. United States* decision demonstrates continuity with several other Supreme Court decisions that allowed for the limiting of civil liberties during times of national emergency. The *Korematsu* decision upheld Executive Order 9066, issued by President Franklin Roosevelt during World War II, authorizing the government to remove over 100,000 Japanese Americans from West Coast cities and relocate them to camps in the western United States. The *Schenck* decision (1919) upheld the Espionage Act, passed (along with the Sedition Act) during World War I to put limits on public expressions of antiwar sentiment. The Supreme Court argued that freedom of speech is not absolute and that the government is justified in limiting certain forms of speech during wartime.

10. **(C)** The *Korematsu* decision allowed the government to keep over 100,000 Japanese Americans in internment centers for the remainder of World War II. Of these individuals, two-thirds of them were citizens. After they were sent to the centers, most of their property was confiscated by the government. The Supreme Court ruled that the relocation was acceptable on the grounds of national security. Years later, in 1988, the United States government publicly apologized to the surviving victims and extended $20,000 in reparations to each one.

10

Period 8: 1945–1980 Redefining Democracy in the Era of Cold War and Liberal Ascendancy

TIMELINE

1944	G.I. Bill passed
1946	*Baby and Child Care* by Dr. Benjamin Spock published
	Largest strike wave in U.S. history
1947	Publication of the "X Article" ("Sources of Soviet Conduct") by George Kennan
	Truman Doctrine (Communist containment) announced $400 million in military aid to Greece and Turkey
	House Un-American Activities Committee begins Hollywood investigations
	Taft-Hartley Act
1948	Founding of the state of Israel
	Beginning of the Berlin Blockade
	President Truman issues Executive Order 9981 desegregating the military
	Election of Harry S. Truman
1949	Formation of North Atlantic Treaty Organization (NATO)
	Chinese Communist Party and Mao Zedong proclaim the People's Republic of China
1950	Senator Joseph McCarthy gains public spotlight on issue of anti-Communism
	NSC-68 adopted
	Korean War begins
	Passage of McCarran Internal Security Act
1951	Truman fires General Douglas MacArthur
	United States tests world's first hydrogen bomb
1952	Execution of Julius and Ethel Rosenberg
	Army-McCarthy hearings
	Election of Dwight D. Eisenhower
1954	Interstate Highway Act
	Brown v. Board of Education of Topeka
1955	Creation of Warsaw Pact
1956	Rosa Parks arrested for not giving up her seat; Montgomery Bus Boycott
	Reelection of Eisenhower
1957	Soviet launch of the *Sputnik* satellite
	Crisis in Little Rock, Arkansas over school desegregation
	On the Road by Jack Kerouac published

1960	Soviet Union shoots down U-2 spy plane
	Lunch counter sit-in movement begins
	Election of John F. Kennedy
1961	Bay of Pigs invasion in Cuba
1961	The Freedom Rides begin
1962	Cuban Missile Crisis
1963	Campaign to desegregate Birmingham, Alabama
	President John F. Kennedy assassinated
	March on Washington, D.C., where Martin Luther King Jr. delivers "I Have a Dream" speech
1964	Civil Rights Acts passed
	Murder of Michael Schwerner, James Chaney, and Andrew Goodman, participants in Mississippi "Freedom Summer"
	Gulf of Tonkin Resolution
	Election of Lyndon Johnson
1965	Malcolm X assassinated
	Marches from Selma to Montgomery (Alabama)
1966	Founding of the Black Panthers
1967	"Summer of Love"
	Rioting in Detroit, Newark, and other cities
1968	Tet Offensive
	Assassination of Martin Luther King Jr.
	Assassination of Robert F. Kennedy
	Violence at Democratic Convention in Chicago
	Election of Richard Nixon
	Founding of American Indian Movement
1969	Woodstock Festival
	Stonewall Riot in New York City, sparking birth of the gay liberation movement
	Apollo 11 lands on the moon
1970	President Nixon widens Vietnam War to Cambodia
	Four students killed by Ohio National Guard at Kent State protest
1971	Publication of Pentagon Papers in *The New York Times*
1972	President Nixon visits both the People's Republic of China and the Soviet Union
	Arrest of burglars at the Watergate Complex
	Reelection of Richard Nixon
1973	Congressional hearings on Watergate
1974	Nixon resigns presidency; Gerald Ford assumes presidency
	Ford grants Nixon complete pardon
1976	Election of Jimmy Carter
1977	Supreme Court decision in *Bakke v. University of California*
1978	Panama Canal Treaty
	Camp David Accords
1979	Three Mile Island nuclear accident

Topics in Period 8

In this chapter, you will learn about:

- → Topic 8.1 Contextualizing Period 8
- → Topic 8.2 The Cold War from 1945 to 1980
- → Topic 8.3 The Red Scare
- → Topic 8.4 The economy after 1945
- → Topic 8.5 Culture after 1945
- → Topic 8.6 Early steps in the civil rights movement (1940s and 1950s)
- → Topic 8.7 America as a world power
- → Topic 8.8 The Vietnam War
- → Topic 8.9 The Great Society
- → Topic 8.10 The African-American civil rights movement (1960s)
- → Topic 8.11 The civil rights movement expands
- → Topic 8.12 Youth culture of the 1960s
- → Topic 8.13 The environment and natural resources from 1968 to 1980
- → Topic 8.14 Society in transition
- → Topic 8.15 Subject to debate

Topic 8.1 Contextualizing Period 8

> In the post–World War II period, the United States assumed a position of global leadership and experienced unprecedented prosperity. At the same time, the country grappled with domestic and international issues as it sought to define itself and struggled with living up to its stated values.

The Cold War began after World War II, when two former allies, the United States and the Soviet Union, emerged as rival superpowers. The perceived threat of Communist aggression presented several challenges to the United States. The country changed in many ways as a result of the Cold War. It became much more engaged in the affairs of the world and assumed a leading role in the opposition to Communism. In addition, the nation changed domestically. New governmental initiatives—from loyalty oaths to civil defense programs—were initiated during the Cold War. Some of these programs helped allay people's concerns about the threat of Communism, though some initiatives added to people's fears.

In many ways, World War II was a turning point for American society. The postwar world was markedly different from the prewar world. A more modern, more affluent society emerged in the postwar era—one unimaginable in the depths of the Great Depression.

This period also witnessed the high tide of American liberalism, with the election of the youthful John F. Kennedy, a series of liberal decisions by the Warren Court, the implementation of President Johnson's "Great Society" programs, and the successful passage of landmark civil rights legislation.

Finally, the 1960s and 1970s saw the unraveling of the liberal agenda as the war in Vietnam sucked valuable resources from social programs, and urban rioting highlighted the limits of the federal government's ability to address the problems of the African-American underclass. These years saw violence in the streets of American cities, a widening and eventual abandonment of the war in Vietnam, assassinations of major public figures, a nationwide energy crisis, and a major political scandal that brought down a sitting president. The roots of a resurgent conservative movement can be seen toward the end of this period.

Topic 8.2 The Cold War from 1945 to 1980

Emerging as the preeminent international power after World War II, the United States engaged in the Cold War with the Soviet Union. The United States attempted to maintain a leadership position in an increasingly uncertain and unstable world.

A. Forging a New Foreign Policy in the Postwar World

After World War II, the United States pursued a foreign policy that emphasized collective security and the establishment of a multinational economic framework. As the Cold War developed between the United States and the Soviet Union, the United States adopted a policy of containment, attempting to limit the influence of the Soviet Union and Communism internationally. The United States sought to contain Communism by building a system of international security, maintaining a stable global economy, and bolstering non-Communist states.

Origins of the Cold War

Tensions existed between the **United States** and the **Soviet Union** from the time of the **Russian Revolution** (1917), when America opposed the **Bolsheviks**. The U.S.-Soviet World War II alliance against the Nazis brought them briefly together. Historians date the beginning of the **Cold War** from the close of **World War II**. The United States believed the Soviets were intent upon extending their control over Europe. As the war ended, the Soviet Union left its **Red Army** troops occupying Eastern Europe, turning these countries into **Soviet satellites**. The Soviets indicated they would allow free elections in **Poland**, but instead they installed a puppet regime. The United States worried the Soviets would try to push into Western Europe. The leader of the Soviet Union, **Joseph Stalin**, insisted that he only wanted to have friendly nations on his borders. After a history of attacks from Western powers on Russia and the Soviet Union, from Napoleon to Hitler, Stalin was wary of the West.

Containment and the Truman Doctrine

In order to block aggressive actions by the Soviet Union, **President Harry S. Truman** issued the **Truman Doctrine** (1947), in which he said that the goal of the United States would be to contain Communism. The **containment** approach to the Soviet Union had been spelled out in an article entitled **"Sources of Soviet Conduct,"** published in *Foreign Affairs* (1947). The article was also known as the **"X Article"** because it was published using the pseudonym, "X." Later it was learned that the author was **George Kennan**, a diplomat who had served in the U.S. embassy in Moscow (1944–1946). Although Kennan later lamented the militaristic approach of American foreign policy and recommended dialogue with the Soviets, the Cold War had begun. Military containment of Communism remained the cornerstone of American foreign policy for decades to come.

Military Aid to Greece and Turkey

As part of the policy of containment, the United States extended military aid to **Greece** and **Turkey** in 1947. The aid helped the Greek monarchy put down a Communist-influenced rebel movement. Further, the move quieted Republican criticism of President Harry S. Truman and improved the president's standing in public-opinion polls; he won reelection the following year. The United States demonstrated that it was committed to a policy of containment.

The Marshall Plan

The United States demonstrated its global commitment with the massive **Marshall Plan**. Developed by **Secretary of State George Marshall**, the plan allocated almost $13 billion for war-torn Europe to rebuild. A total of seventeen nations received aid between 1948 and 1951, with West Germany, France, and Britain receiving the bulk of it. The plan stabilized the capitalist economies of Western Europe and contributed to remarkable growth as the standard of living there improved. The goal was to provide a viable alternative to Soviet-style Communism; ultimately, the plan was successful in creating a strong Western Europe, allied with American interests.

The Berlin Blockade and the Berlin Airlift

In 1948, the United States decided to challenge the **Soviet blockade** of the Western-occupied section of **Berlin**, a free enclave deep within Soviet-occupied East Germany. This enclave, occupied by Allied troops after World War II, was cut off from the West within Communist-controlled **East Germany**. In 1948, the Soviet Union decided to prevent food and other supplies from entering the western section of Berlin. The goal was for the Soviet Union to take over western Berlin and make it part of East Germany. The United States did not stand by idly in the face of the **Berlin blockade**. Over the next year, **President Truman** sent more than 278,000 flights (American and Allied aircraft) to supply western Berlin. This action, known as the **"Berlin Airlift,"** prevented the Soviet Union from taking over the city. Afterward, the city was formally divided and western Berlin became part of West Germany.

The Formation of NATO

The crisis over the fate of **Berlin** (see above) solidified the commitment of leaders in the United States, Canada, and Western Europe to form a mutual defense pact. In April 1949, twelve nations—the United States, Canada, and ten Western European nations—signed an agreement creating the **North Atlantic Treaty Organization (NATO)**. The organization vowed to collectively resist any aggressive actions by the Soviet Union and created a standing army for this purpose. This marked the first time that the United States joined a formal peacetime alliance. In response to the formation of NATO, the Soviet Union formed an alliance with the Communist countries of Eastern Europe—the **Warsaw Pact**—in 1955. NATO played an important role in resisting Soviet advances throughout the Cold War period. It admitted Greece and Turkey in 1952, and West Germany in 1955. It continues to exist in the post–Cold War period, admitting many countries that had been part of the Warsaw Pact during the Cold War.

B. Carrying Out the Policy of Containment

In the 1950s and 1960s, the United States pursued containment in several different ways, including direct military engagements in Korea and Vietnam, a robust nuclear weapons program, and a space race with the Soviet Union.

NSC-68

A National Security Council Paper, known as **NSC-68**, called for a more aggressive defense policy for the United States. Written in 1950, the document asserted that the United States must assume a sole leadership position among the non-Communist nations. It went beyond the approach to containment outlined earlier by **George Kennan** (see page 318), which focused on a more collective approach to resisting Soviet aggression. The paper recommended raising taxes and devoting more funds to military spending. NSC-68 was drafted by a committee chaired by State Department official, **Paul Nitze**, who argued that the United States should attempt to **"roll back"** Communism, not simply contain it. This document largely shaped U.S. foreign policy during the Cold War through the 1960s.

The Cold War in Asia

The initial conflicts of the Cold War occurred in Europe, but, by the late 1940s, American policymakers became increasingly concerned about events in Asia. America's Cold War policies had mixed results in Asia. The United States successfully ushered **Japan** toward democracy and economic self-sufficiency. The U.S. also granted independence to **the Philippines** in 1946. But the Communist-ruled People's Republic of China proved to be a difficult problem for President Harry S. Truman.

Communism in China

In the 1930s, **China** had been roiled by an ongoing civil war. The conflict abated during the Japanese invasion of World War II, but began again after the war. The United States supported the Nationalist side, led by **Jiang Jieshi** (Chiang Kai-shek). However, the **Communist Party**, led by **Mao Zedong** (Mao Tse-tung), amassed a huge following among the poor, rural population of China. Mao's forces won in 1949 and the **People's Republic of China** was established. The news that China, the most populous nation in the world, had become Communist shocked many Americans. Republicans accused Truman of "losing" China, although in reality there was little that could have been done to prevent the eventual outcome.

The Korean War (1950–1953)

Less than a year after Mao Zedong and the Communist Party emerged victorious in China, hostilities erupted on the Korean peninsula. **Korea** had been divided at the **38th parallel** after World War II, with the United States administering the southern half and the Soviet Union administering the northern half (similar to the division of Germany). In 1948, this arrangement was formalized with the creation of two nations—**North Korea**, a Communist country, and **South Korea**, an American ally. In June 1950, North Korean troops, using Soviet equipment, invaded South Korea. President Truman decided to commit troops to support South Korea and managed to secure United Nations sponsorship. United Nations forces, led by U.S. **General Douglas MacArthur**, pushed the North Korean troops back to the 38th parallel and then marched into North Korea. When the UN forces got within forty miles of the border between North Korea and China, **China** sent large numbers of troops (estimates range from 150,000 to one million) over the Yalu River to push them back. After intense fighting, the two sides settled into defensive positions on either side of the 38th parallel.

The Firing of General MacArthur

During the Korean War, **General Douglas MacArthur** made it clear that he thought the United States could successfully invade China and roll back Communism there. Truman was convinced that initiating a wider war, so soon after World War II, would be disastrous. MacArthur made public pronouncements about strategy, arguing that **"There is no substitute for victory."** Truman fired MacArthur for insubordination and other unauthorized activities.

Armistice in Korea

The **Korean War** ended as it began—with North Korea and South Korea divided at the 38th parallel. By 1953, an armistice was reached, although a formal treaty ending the war was never signed.

President Eisenhower, the "New Look" in Foreign Policy, and "Massive Retaliation"

Faced with the competing priorities of balancing the federal budget on the one hand and continuing the policy of containment on the other, **President Dwight D. Eisenhower** pursued a policy labeled the **"New Look."** The policy emphasized the development of strategic nuclear weapons as a deterrent to potential threats from the Soviet Union. The increased reliance on nuclear weaponry was accompanied by a shift away from maintaining costly

---

USING HISTORICAL THINKING SKILLS: MAKING CONNECTIONS

"Soft on Communism"

Foreign policy is often intimately linked with domestic political considerations. Frequently, presidents make foreign policy decisions in order to bolster domestic political support or to distract from political turbulence at home. In addition, foreign policy actions often impact domestic political developments. After Communism triumphed in China (1949), Republicans accused Truman of being "soft on Communism." These accusations damaged Truman and the Democrats. The Democrats lost congressional seats in the midterm elections of 1950 and lost the White House in 1952. In addition, starting in 1950, Republican Senator Joseph McCarthy gained a wider audience in his campaign to root out domestic Communism. Noting connections between foreign policy and domestic politics in your writing can strengthen an argument.

ground forces. A strong nuclear arsenal, Defense Secretary Charles Wilson argued, would provide the United States with a **"bigger bang for the buck."**

Central to the strategy of increasing the American nuclear arsenal was the policy of **"massive retaliation."** The idea of "massive retaliation," put forth by **Secretary of State John Foster Dulles** in a 1954 speech, is that the United States would maintain a nuclear arsenal capable of retaliating with overwhelming force against aggressive moves by any enemy. The threat of massive retaliation was designed to deter conventional as well as nuclear strikes by the Soviet Union. Dulles also put forth the idea of **"brinksmanship"**—the Soviet Union needed to be aware that the United States was willing to "go to the brink" of war with its nuclear arsenal. As the Soviet Union developed a similarly powerful nuclear force, the ensuing nuclear standoff between the Soviet Union and the United States came to be known as **"mutually assured destruction."**

The Launching of *Sputnik*

Starting in the late 1950s, the Cold War expanded to a race for supremacy in terms of exploration of outer space. The **space race** began in earnest with the 1957 launching of the unmanned Soviet satellite, *Sputnik*, into space. The launch caught many Americans off guard and led to several important domestic developments. *Sputnik* alarmed U.S. government officials because the same type of rocket that launched the satellite could also be used to deliver atomic weapons to any location on Earth.

The Space Race

After the launch of *Sputnik*, the United States created the **National Aeronautics and Space Administration (NASA)** in 1958 to carry out the nation's space program. In 1961, **President John F. Kennedy** announced the goal of landing a **man on the moon** before the close of the 1960s. The budget for NASA grew under Kennedy. The goal was accomplished in 1969, when the United States was the first nation to successfully land a spacecraft and men on the moon.

Espionage and the U-2 Incident

During the Cold War, the United States maintained an extensive program of spying on the military capabilities of the Soviet Union. At first, the government denied the program existed, but in 1960 a high-altitude **U-2 spy plane** was shot down over Soviet territory. **President Dwight D. Eisenhower** admitted the program existed and defended its goals. These actions all demonstrated that the United States would take a more active role in challenging the Soviet Union.

Cuban Missile Crisis

The **Cuban Missile Crisis** occurred in 1962 when a U-2 spy plane discovered that Cuba was preparing bases for installing Soviet nuclear missiles. **President John F. Kennedy** declared that these missiles, in such close proximity to the United States, amounted to an unacceptable provocation and demanded that the Soviet premier, **Nikita Khrushchev**, halt the operation and withdraw the missiles. Khrushchev insisted on the right

> **USING HISTORICAL THINKING SKILLS:**
> **ARGUMENTATION**
>
> **The Legacy of President Nixon**
>
> In 1978, Richard Nixon speculated about his place in history. He acknowledged his mistakes in regard to Watergate, but added, "Now, let's get on to my achievements. You'll be here in the year 2000, and we'll see how I am regarded then." Historians have not developed a consensus around the legacy of President Richard Nixon. Historian and journalist Rick Perlstein, in *Nixonland* (2008), argues that Nixon's resentments and destructive politics fractured the nation for the coming decades, making consensus on basic issues nearly impossible. Although Nixon is most vividly remembered for the Watergate scandal, Nixon has his defenders. His defenders, as Nixon had hoped, focus on his achievements: environmental legislation, Title IX (gender equity in education), SALT (Strategic Arms Limitation Talks), and détente. British Conservative politician Jonathan Aitken's *Nixon: A Life* (1993) is an example of historical work in this latter vein. Nixon's legacy has even been the subject of a well-known American opera—John Adams's *Nixon in China* (1987)—which examined the process of myth-building through the lens of Nixon's historical visit to China in 1972.

of the Soviet Union to install the missiles. For days, the world stood on the brink of nuclear war. Finally, a deal was reached in which the Soviet Union would abandon its Cuban missile program and the United States would agree to honor the sovereignty of Cuba. Quietly, the United States also agreed to remove missiles from Turkey.

C. The Cold War—from Confrontation to Détente

At times the Cold War involved military confrontations—both direct and indirect—while at other times it involved mutual coexistence or détente.

Eisenhower and Khrushchev Pursue Coexistence

After the death in 1953 of Soviet leader **Joseph Stalin** and the emergence of the more moderate **Nikita Khrushchev, President Dwight D. Eisenhower** held out hope for a warming of relations with the Soviet Union and a reduction in the threat of nuclear war. Eisenhower and Khrushchev, along with leaders from France and Britain, held a summit meeting in Geneva (1955), but no substantive agreements came out of it. The launching of *Sputnik* (see page 321) and the first Soviet test of an **intercontinental ballistic missile** (ICBM), both in 1957, pushed the two nations further apart. However, a new round of meetings between Khrushchev and **Vice President Richard Nixon** occurred in 1959. Nixon's trip to the Soviet Union included the famous **"kitchen debate"** with Khrushchev while they toured an American model-home display at an international exhibition in Moscow. The two were photographed next to modern kitchen appliances as they debated the merits of Communism versus capitalism. Later in 1959, Khrushchev visited the United States and met with Eisenhower at Camp David. The following year, the two countries were on the verge of signing a nuclear test ban. Khrushchev and Eisenhower had scheduled a summit in Paris to finalize the treaty, but just before they met, an American U-2 spy plane was shot down (see page 321), scuttling any potential agreement.

U.S.-Soviet Relations Under Kennedy

President John F. Kennedy made attempts to ease tensions between the Soviet Union and the United States. In the wake of the Cuban Missile Crisis, the **Partial Test Ban Treaty** was signed by the United States, the Soviet Union, and Britain in 1963. The ban exempted underground nuclear tests. Although the treaty did not halt the arms race, it did greatly reduce atmospheric testing. Concerns about radioactive fallout from above-ground testing had intensified after the massive **Castle Bravo** hydrogen bomb test by the United States at Bikini Atoll (1954) led to incidences of radiation sickness over a wide area.

Détente with China and the Soviet Union

President Richard Nixon's policy of **détente** represented a thawing in the Cold War and an improvement of relations with the **Soviet Union**. In 1971, Nixon initiated an agreement with the Soviets whereby they accepted the independence of West Berlin and the United States recognized East Germany. Also, the 1972 **Strategic Arms Limitation Talks (SALT)** led to two arms-control agreements. Tensions still existed, but détente led to discussions between the two sides, to nominal arms-control agreements, and to cultural exchanges. In 1972, Nixon visited China, making it the first time an American president visited the **People's Republic of China**. The visit was an important step in normalizing relations with the Communist government of China.

Topic 8.3 The Red Scare

As the United States pursued international and domestic goals during the Cold War, disagreements emerged about the appropriateness of its actions. Americans continued to debate the proper balance between liberty and order as a second "red scare" took hold in the late 1940s and 1950s. In addition, some Americans questioned the growing power of the federal government.

A. Containment and the Domestic Red Scare

Though there was consensus between the major parties in regard to the policy of containing Communism, Americans debated the increasingly aggressive methods of the federal and state governments in terms of identifying and applying sanctions to suspected Communists in the United States.

The Strike Wave of 1946 and the Taft-Hartley Act (1947)

The "red scare" of the post–World War II period targeted organized labor as well as supposed Communists. Conservative political leaders frequently sought to portray union leaders as covert participants in the Communist movement. This was evident during the largest strike wave in American history (1946), as five million workers walked off their jobs. Unions, which had refrained from striking during the war, feared that the gains they had made during the war would be taken away. The strike wave was largely successful, boosting wages for factory workers and allowing them to partake in the consumer culture of the era.

The **Taft-Hartley Act (1947)**, which passed over President Truman's veto, was designed to monitor and restrict the activities of organized labor. The law was passed by a conservative, Republican-dominated Congress that had been elected in 1946. The law imposed restrictions on unions that made it more difficult to strike. It allowed states to pass **"right to work" laws**, banning **union shops** (a union shop is a workplace in which all the workers are required to join the union after a majority had voted to do so). The law also required union leaders to pledge that they were not members of the Communist Party.

> **USING REASONING PROCESSES:**
> **CONTINUITY AND CHANGE**
>
> **The Federal Government and Unions Over Time (II)**
>
> Note the rapid changes in the government's attitude toward organized labor from the New Deal era of the 1930s to the Cold War era. In the 1930s, President Franklin D. Roosevelt pushed for the recognition of unions with Section 7(a) of the National Industrial Recovery Act (1933) and with the Wagner Act (1935). Just over a decade later, the Taft-Hartley Act (1947) which passed over President Harry Truman's veto, restricted the ability of workers to form unions and to strike. Labor unions labeled the act the "Tuff-Heartless" Act and likened it to a "slave-labor" law. Also note continuities between the Taft-Hartley Act and President Ronald Reagan's handling of the strike of air traffic controllers in 1981. He had them all fired, breaking their union. This action was a major setback for organized labor. (See also box on page 229.)

Federal Employee Loyalty and Security Program (1947)

The **Federal Employee Loyalty and Security Program**, passed in 1947, barred Communists and fascists from serving in federal government positions. Created by President Harry S. Truman with **Executive Order 9835**, the program also allowed for investigations into the political affiliations of current employees. Employees had to promise to uphold the Constitution and swear they were not members of the **Communist Party** or other "subversive" organizations.

The McCarran Internal Security Act (1950)

The **McCarran Internal Security Act** mandated that Communist groups in the United States register with the government. It also allowed for the arrest of suspected security risks during national emergencies. Truman saw this act as a grave threat to civil liberties and vetoed it. However, Congress passed it over his veto.

Senator Joseph McCarthy

The most prominent elected figure in the anti-Communist movement of the 1950s was **Senator Joseph McCarthy**, a Republican from Wisconsin. McCarthy rose to national prominence in 1950 when he announced that he had a list of 205 "known Communists" who were working in the **State Department**. He later reduced that figure to fifty-seven, but he encouraged a mindset whereby people began to suspect those around them of being secret Communists. This and similar claims, mostly baseless, created a name for McCarthy and set the stage for a host of measures to halt this perceived threat. The anti-Communist movement of the 1950s is often referred to as **McCarthyism** because Senator McCarthy was so closely identified with it.

The Attack on Hollywood

Senate and House anti-Communists put a great deal of effort into investigating the film and broadcast industries, fearing that Communists would subtly get their messages out via radio, television, and movies. In 1947, several prominent directors and writers, later known as the **"Hollywood Ten,"** were summoned to testify in Washington. They refused, citing their First Amendment rights to freedom of speech and assembly. These ten and others who refused to cooperate were **"blacklisted"** in the 1950s, preventing them from finding work in Hollywood.

The Threat of Nuclear War

The threat of nuclear war was a constant presence in American life during the Cold War. Both sides invested large sums of money in nuclear weapons programs. Americans were never sure whether a conventional conflict, such as the Korean War, would turn into a **nuclear war**. Many Americans built bomb shelters in their basements or backyards. Local authorities established civil defense programs to build bomb shelters in public buildings and prepare the population for a nuclear emergency.

> **USING HISTORICAL THINKING SKILLS:**
> **CONTEXTUALIZATION**
>
> **McCarthyism in Context**
>
> There are several ways to contextualize McCarthyism. Clearly, McCarthyism developed in the context of the larger anti-Communist movement of the 1940s and 1950s. Some elements of the movement were more liberal and were critical of the excesses of McCarthy. McCarthyism can also be seen in the context of foreign policy—the Cold War generally, and the Korean War specifically. More broadly, McCarthyism can be seen in the context of what historian Richard Hofstadter called the "paranoid style" in American politics. He saw this tendency in movements that exhibit three habits: "heated exaggeration," "suspiciousness," and "conspiratorial fantasy." This style can be seen in a variety of other movements in American history, from the Anti-Masonic Party of the 1820s and 1830s to the anti-Catholic "Know-Nothings" of the 1850s to the Ku Klux Klan in the 1920s.

"Duck and Cover"

The government took a series of actions in regard to the threat of nuclear war. One action taken by the government was **air-raid drills** in public schools. When an alarm sounded, students would either be ushered to a fallout shelter in the basement of the school or would be ordered to **"duck and cover"** under their desks.

Accusations of Espionage

Many anti-Communists in the post–World War II era asserted that American Communists were more loyal to the Soviet Union than they were to their own country. Such assertions gained traction in 1948, when **Whittaker Chambers**, an admitted former Communist, told the House Un-American Activities Committee that a high-ranking official in the State Department, **Alger Hiss**, had passed secrets to the Soviet Union in the 1930s. The case made headlines when a first-term Republican congressman, **Richard Nixon**, successfully pursued perjury charges against Hiss. When the United States learned that the Soviet Union had built and tested a **nuclear bomb** (1949), many were convinced that American Communists had provided the Soviets with essential information about the bomb. **Ethel and Julius Rosenberg**, an American couple, were accused of passing secrets of the nuclear bomb to the Soviet Union. The Rosenbergs, who were members of the Communist Party, insisted on their innocence but were sent to the electric chair in 1953. Evidence has emerged since the end of the Cold War that strongly suggests that Julius had been involved in some sort of espionage on behalf of the Soviet Union.

The Smith Act and the Communist Party

Government prosecutors used the World War II–era **Smith Act** to arrest leading members of the **Communist Party** in several states on the grounds that they "conspired" to "organize" and "advocate" the overthrow of the government by force. Between 1949 and 1957, more than 140 Communists were arrested, including the leader of the party, **Eugene Dennis**.

The Fall of McCarthyism

Eventually, critics began to assert that some of the harshest anti-Communist measures of the 1950s violated people's constitutional right to freedom of speech. Criticism became more common after the conclusion of hostilities in the Korean War (1953). Finally, **Senator Joseph McCarthy** himself went too far, accusing members of the military establishment of being members of the Communist Party. After finding his accusations were baseless, the Senate voted to censure McCarthy in 1954, ending the worst excesses of what largely became known as a witch-hunt. In the case of ***Yates v. United States* (1957)**, the Supreme Court overturned the convictions of members of the Communist Party under the Smith Act.

Topic 8.4 The Economy After 1945

The United States experienced a series of demographic, economic, and technological changes in the decades following World War II. These changes profoundly impacted American society, politics, and the environment. Many Americans were optimistic about the rapid economic and social changes that were occurring in society in the period after World War II. This period witnessed the growth of the middle class, the growth of suburbia, and the decline of older urban areas.

A. The Growth of the Middle Class

The postwar period witnessed the growth of the middle class and demographic shifts toward the suburbs and toward the Sunbelt. A variety of factors stimulated these trends, including strong economic growth, federal spending, a "baby boom," the expansion of higher education, and new technological developments.

The G.I. Bill

The federal government helped returning veterans adjust to the peacetime economy with the **Servicemen's Readjustment Act (1944)**, more commonly known as the **G.I. Bill**. The act provided low-interest loans for veterans to purchase homes and attend college. By the time the original G.I. Bill expired, in 1956, nearly eight million veterans had used the bill's educational benefits (out of a total of sixteen million veterans). By 1955, the Veterans Administration backed over 4.3 million home loans under the G.I. Bill. The program was less successful in extending benefits to African-American veterans. One of the bill's sponsors, Representative John Rankin of Mississippi, made sure that states, rather than the federal government, set rules for extending benefits. Southern states set high barriers for African Americans to receive benefits. In Mississippi in 1947, for example, only two of the 3,200 Veterans Administration–backed home loans went to African-American veterans.

The Baby Boom

For several years before 1946, birthrates in the United States had remained relatively low. Couples tended to have fewer children during the lean years of the Great Depression; further, the dislocation and physical separation caused by World War II kept the birthrate low. However, when the war ended, the return of veterans soon led to many more families having many more children. The spike in birthrates from 1946 through the early 1960s produced a **baby boom** that would have lasting repercussions in American society. The baby boom required states to spend more money on public education in the 1950s and 1960s and on expanded college enrollment in the 1960s and 1970s.

Childrearing in the 1950s

The parents of the baby-boom generation were enthusiastic readers of child-rearing guides. The most influential was **Benjamin Spock's *Baby and Child Care*** (1946). Spock urged parents to treat their children as individuals, to let them develop at their own pace, and to focus less on discipline and more on affection. When baby boomers joined the counterculture in the 1960s, conservative critics cited Spock's book as having stimulated what they saw as antisocial behavior.

B. Suburban Growth and the Rise of the Sunbelt

A series of demographic shifts occurred in the post–World War II period. Many middle-class Americans abandoned urban centers and moved to newly built suburbs. At the same time, large numbers of Americans moved to the Sunbelt states of the South and the West. These changes were facilitated by technological developments, expanded higher education opportunities, and an increased degree of social mobility in the United States.

The Growth of Suburbia

An important postwar trend was the growth of suburbs. **Suburbs** were not a new phenomenon in the postwar period—indeed, the earliest residential suburbs were built around commuter railroad stations in the late nineteenth century. But a series of factors contributed to the unprecedented growth of these communities. New suburban communities were built just outside major American cities to meet the housing crunch created by all the returning World War II soldiers. Huge numbers of these soldiers quickly married, had children, and looked for affordable housing. Race also played a factor in the development of suburbia. Many white people did not want to live in the urban neighborhoods that had become racially integrated after many southern, rural African Americans had moved north to work in war industries. The movement of middle-class white Americans from urban centers to suburbs is often labeled **"white flight."** Further, African Americans were frequently barred from moving to the suburbs by restrictive racial covenants. "None of said land may be conveyed to, used, owned, or occupied by negroes as owners or tenants," read a typical 1940s covenant from a suburban development outside of Kansas City, Kansas. The federal government encouraged racial discrimination through Federal Housing Administration guidelines. The FHA, established in 1934, subsidized builders and guaranteed loans for veterans with the requirement that none of the homes be sold to African Americans.

Levittown and Suburban Development

Real estate developers facilitated the move to the suburbs. Real estate developer **William Levitt**, president of Levitt & Sons, took large tracts of land outside major cities (often farmland) and built huge developments of nearly identical, modest houses. His company applied the techniques of **mass production** to these houses, building them rapidly and cheaply. **Levittown**, on Long Island, New York, became synonymous with these mass-produced communities. These developments were not without their critics. Songwriter **Malvina Reynolds** skewered the monotony of life in these developments in the song **"Little Boxes"** (1962). In addition, Levitt followed the practice of excluding African Americans from these developments with restrictive covenants (see above).

The Interstate Highway Act

Federal and local highway initiatives made the move to the suburbs more attractive. One could now drive into cities from the suburbs quickly and easily. With the **National Interstate and Defense Highways Act** (1956), the federal government initiated a massive highway-building project that resulted in the interstate highway system. The act was also promoted as a defense measure, allowing for the rapid movement of military equipment and personnel. Americans could now feasibly leave cities and enjoy a small piece of land to call their own.

"White Flight" and the Decline of Older Cities

Not everyone shared equally in the abundance of the 1950s. As middle-class families left urban centers to move to the **suburbs** (see above), they took with them their ability to pay local taxes. Cities saw their **tax bases** shrink dramatically. With funds scarce, cities had to cut back on basic services such as policing and education. Crime became an unavoidable urban reality and city schools deteriorated. This decline in city services put more pressure on middle-class people to make the move to the suburbs. In addition, the practice of **"redlining"** blocked the flow of federally-backed loan money from reaching many African-American neighborhoods. Banks created maps with red lines drawn around such neighborhoods and labeled them "investment hazards." The **Federal**

Housing Administration, which guaranteed millions of loans for suburban homes, contributed to housing segregation by refusing to insure mortgages in "redlined" neighborhoods. By the 1960s, entire sections of cities had become **slums**.

Urban Renewal

To address the decline of older cities, the federal government developed a set of initiatives known as the **urban renewal program**. A central piece of the program was the **Housing Act of 1949**, which represented a dramatic expansion of federal money and power in the area of urban housing. **Title I** of the act provided federal financing for **slum clearance** programs, encouraging city administrations to declare areas blighted and then to demolish vast swaths of inner cities. The program displaced thousands of urban residents. In Boston, almost a third of the old city was demolished. Frequently, nothing was built to replace the demolished neighborhoods. In many cases low-income urban housing projects were built with Title I funds. However, because federal funds were not used for maintenance and upkeep, these projects often fell into disrepair. Title I was often used to clear land to build highways rather than additional housing. Urban renewal programs often left cities in worse shape than before the programs were initiated.

Topic 8.5 Culture After 1945

While American culture appeared to be increasingly conformist in the post–World War II period, some Americans challenged many of the assumptions of postwar society.

A. Cultural Conformity and Its Discontents

American culture moved in distinctly different directions in the postwar period. On the one hand, an increasingly homogenous mass culture developed; on the other hand, many artists, intellectuals, and rebellious young people challenged the pressure toward conformity that marked postwar culture.

Conformity in a Conservative Decade

Many Americans were reluctant to appear to be nonconformist in the 1950s. Part of this push toward **conformity** can be attributed to the domestic Cold War and the dictates of **McCarthyism** (see pages 323–324). Sociologists **David Riesman**, **Nathan Glazer**, and **Reuel Denney**, in their book *The Lonely Crowd* (1950), noted that Americans were more eager to mold their ideas to societal standards than they were to think independently. **William H. Whyte's** book, *The Organization Man* (1956), described the stultifying atmosphere of the modern corporation in which employees were expected to think like the group. The novel *The Man in the Gray Flannel Suit* (1955), by **Sloan Wilson**, depicted a businessman trapped in the materialistic commercial world of the 1950s. **J. D. Salinger's** bestselling novel, *The Catcher in the Rye* (1951), railed at the "phonies" who had achieved success in mainstream 1950s society.

Television

Widely available for the first time in the postwar period, **television** became an extremely popular medium. By the end of the 1950s nearly 90 percent of American homes owned a television set. After an initial burst of creativity in the late 1940s and early 1950s, television programming settled into safe, predictable genres. The most emblematic genre of the 1950s was the suburban situation comedy (sitcom), complete with a wise father figure, a stay-at-home mother, and obedient children, as in *Leave It to Beaver* and *Father Knows Best*. Westerns, such as *Bonanza* and *Gunsmoke*, and daytime dramas (labeled "soap operas" because of sponsorship by soap manufacturers), such as *The Guiding Light* and *Search for Tomorrow*, dominated the airwaves. Many of these genres were carryovers from radio (see page 281). *The Ed Sullivan Show*, a variety show which aired from 1948 to 1971, became a cultural touchstone that was watched by over ten million Americans every Sunday evening.

Rock 'n' Roll Music

Rock 'n' roll music became extremely popular among young people in the 1950s. Rock 'n' roll developed primarily in the African-American community. It was frequently dubbed "race music" and was deemed dangerous by mainstream white commentators. Many of these critics feared that the music would encourage racial mixing as well as sexually suggestive dancing. **Elvis Presley**, a white singer from Memphis, Tennessee, became a huge cultural force in America. He followed in the footsteps of numerous African-American performers, some famous (**Chuck Berry**) and some largely forgotten (**"Big Mama" Thornton**). Rock 'n' roll music was part of a distinct youth culture ushering in a generational divide in American society.

Beat Generation Literature

The **beat literary movement** represented a subversive undercurrent in the 1950s. The beats represented a rejection of mainstream social values—the suburban lifestyle, the consumer society, patriotism. The most important text of the beat movement is *On the Road* by **Jack Kerouac** (1957). Initially typed on paper taped together in a scroll, the book is a stream-of-consciousness screed. It depicts a life of spontaneity and freedom. Also important is **Allen Ginsberg's** book, *Howl and Other Poems* (1956). The poem "Howl," which began with the iconic line, "I saw the best minds of my generation destroyed by madness, starving hysterical naked," took direct aim at the foundations of Cold War American society.

Abstract Expressionism

An important artistic movement of the 1950s came to be called **"abstract expressionism."** Centered in New York City, the movement elevated the "process" of painting—emphasizing spontaneity, emotion, and intensity over studied, realistic reproductions of the visible world. The most well-known practitioner of abstract expressionism was **Jackson Pollock**, who splattered, poured, and dripped paint onto his canvasses. **Willem de Kooning** and **Mark Rothko** are also associated with abstract expressionism.

Topic 8.6 Early Steps in the Civil Rights Movement (1940s and 1950s)

An influential civil rights movement emerged in the years following World War II. Civil rights activists sought to press America to fulfill the promises of the Reconstruction era.

A. Origins, Strategies, and Tactics of the Civil Rights Movement

After World War II, civil rights activists used a variety of strategies and tactics, including legal challenges, civil disobedience, nonviolent protests, and direct action, to press for an end to racial discrimination.

The Civil Rights Movement in the 1950s

One of the most significant reform movements in American history blossomed in the 1950s—the **civil rights movement**. The movement challenged both the legal basis of the segregation of **African Americans** in the United States and the pervasive racism of American society. This racism had justified the existence of slavery and the persistence of **Jim Crow segregation**. The civil rights movement was the product of years of organizing on the local level combined with effective leadership. It influenced the federal government to take action—most notably in the Supreme Court decision in the *Brown v. Board of Education of Topeka* case (1954) (see page 330). A more receptive federal government, in turn, gave support and backing to civil rights activism on the local level. The movement forced America to examine its most cherished institutions and also to reevaluate ingrained patterns of thought. At the same time, it generated an intense backlash among whites in the South and, beyond that, shaped political discourse in the decades to come.

World War II and the Origins of the Civil Rights Movement

World War II was a transformative experience for many African-American men and women. Many returning soldiers felt a sense of empowerment and engagement they had not previously felt. Many of these veterans had taken part in the **National Association for the Advancement of Colored People's "Double V" campaign** during the war—victory against fascism abroad and victory against racism at home (see pages 301–302). The injustices of American life seemed especially reprehensible to men who had just risked their lives serving their country. In addition, the migration of many African-American men and women from the familiar patterns of rural southern life to the new challenges of urban, industrial America whetted their appetite for change and justice. This was the generation that would become the leaders of the civil rights movement in the decades after the war.

Rosa Parks and the Montgomery Bus Boycott (1955–1956)

The civil rights movement gained national attention with the **Montgomery, Alabama**, **bus boycott** of 1955 and 1956. The catalyst for the boycott was the arrest of **Rosa Parks**, a local civil rights activist who refused to give up her seat to a white person on a Montgomery city bus in December 1955. Parks had been active in the Montgomery branch of the **National Association for the Advancement of Colored People** (NAACP) for several years and was its secretary at the time of her arrest. Earlier, in 1944, she was sent by the NAACP to investigate the rape of an African-American woman, **Recy Taylor**, by six white men in the small Alabama town of Abbeville. Parks was not the first person to defy segregationist bus rules in Montgomery. Several others, including **Claudette Colvin**, had preceded Parks. However, local civil rights leaders thought the time was right and that Parks had an ideal public persona for a campaign against segregation.

Following Parks's arrest, a boycott was quickly organized. The groundwork for this undertaking was already in place. Local organizers, such as **Jo Ann Robinson** of the **Women's Political Council**, had worked on establishing networks of activists throughout the city. The movement created the Montgomery Improvement Association to direct the campaign and selected **Martin Luther King Jr.** to head the organization (see below). The boycott was widely supported by the African-American community throughout most of 1956 and led to the bus company ending its policy of making African Americans give up their seats to whites.

Martin Luther King Jr. and Nonviolent Civil Disobedience

The Montgomery bus boycott was led by a young reverend, **Martin Luther King Jr.**, from Atlanta. King's leadership during the boycott made him a well-known figure. He soon became the central figure in the civil rights movement of the 1950s and 1960s. King advocated the tactic of **nonviolent civil disobedience** to directly challenge unjust practices.

B. Government Responses to Civil Rights Activism

The three branches of the federal government made several important policy shifts on race in the 1940s and 1950s. These shifts included the 1948 desegregation of the armed forces and the Supreme Court's 1954 decision in the case of *Brown v. Board of Education*. These measures, prompted in large part by civil rights activism, were intended to promote greater racial justice.

Truman and Civil Rights

President Harry S. Truman, the Democratic president from Missouri who took office when **President Franklin D. Roosevelt** died in 1945, was an early supporter of civil rights. He created the **Committee on Civil Rights** in 1946 and pushed Congress to enact the committee's recommendations in 1948. That year, Truman issued **Executive Order 9981** to ban segregation in the military, but he failed to implement it until the Korean War (when the military was in need of additional personnel). Truman was motivated to take these steps both out of personal conviction and in response to actions by civil rights activists. Truman felt that he should not go too far because he would lose the support of southern Democrats.

A Favorable Supreme Court

Early civil rights activists pressed their cause in a number of ways, and many longed to bring the issue of segregation before the **Supreme Court**. The Supreme Court in 1954 was far more liberal than the 1896 Supreme Court, which had issued the infamous *Plessy v. Ferguson* decision. In 1953, **President Dwight Eisenhower** appointed a new, more liberal chief justice: **Earl Warren**. (See more on the Warren Court, pages 341–342.) The NAACP and its lead lawyer, **Thurgood Marshall**, thought the time was right to bring a key civil rights case to the Court.

The Case of *Brown v. Board of Education of Topeka* (1954)

In the case of ***Brown v. Board of Education of Topeka***, the Supreme Court combined five similar cases, all dealing with school segregation. The Brown in the case was the Reverend Oliver Brown, whose eight-year-old daughter, **Linda Brown**, had to go to an African-American school more than a mile from her house rather than attend a white school nearby. The Court heard a variety of types of evidence, including studies on the psychological impact of segregation on young people. This type of argument was modeled after the "**Brandeis Brief**," presented by Louis Brandeis, in the 1908 Supreme Court case, *Muller v. Oregon* (see page 267). In *Brown*, the Court ruled unanimously that the "separate but equal" doctrine established by the *Plessy* decision had to end; "separate educational facilities," the Court ruled, "are inherently unequal." The *Brown* decision set in motion a major upheaval in American society. It gave great encouragement to the civil rights movement, which believed that the federal government was in favor of civil rights; however, violence soon erupted from southern whites who tried to prevent school integration.

C. Challenges for the Civil Rights Movement

A series of challenges confronted the civil rights movement as the 1960s progressed. White resistance to desegregation grew more intense and slowed the progress of the movement.

"Massive Resistance"— Little Rock and Beyond

Many southern whites engaged in a violent backlash against the civil rights movement. These people vowed to engage in **"massive resistance"** against efforts toward integration. An example of the backlash was evident in the reaction of white southerners to segregation in **Little Rock**, **Arkansas**, in 1957 and 1958. The conflict in Little Rock began in 1957 when local authorities decided to begin the process of desegregation and allow nine African-American students to enroll in **Central High School** at the beginning of the school year. **Governor Orville Faubus** refused to cooperate with the plan, leading to mob action and violence outside the high school. Faubus initially mobilized the National Guard to block the African-American students from entering the school. Later he removed all state authorities, leaving local police to deal with a combustible situation. The violence and the national news coverage of the flouting of federal authority convinced **President Dwight D. Eisenhower** to send federal troops. Although Eisenhower was decisive in Little Rock, his administration was otherwise very reluctant to take action in regard to civil rights for African Americans.

> **USING HISTORICAL THINKING SKILLS:**
> **CONTEXTUALIZATION**
>
> **The Context of the Little Rock Crisis**
>
> The crisis in Little Rock can be seen in the context of ongoing conflicts over the relationship of federal power to state power. This was a central issue in the Civil War, almost a hundred years earlier. Governor Orville Faubus, in decrying President Dwight Eisenhower's decision to send troops to enforce desegregation, used language that was purposely evocative of the period of the Civil War and Reconstruction. He condemned the presence of "Yankee troops" in Little Rock in a press conference, adding, "We are now an occupied territory." The reaction of Faubus brings to mind William Faulkner's quotation: "The past is not dead. In fact, it's not even past."

Topic 8.7 America as a World Power

The United States became increasingly engaged with events in different parts of the world as one of the two superpowers in the post–World War II era. Debates emerged over the proper role for the United States to play in carrying out its Cold War priorities, including what policy the United States should pursue in regard to the nuclear arms race.

A. United States Actions in Latin America

During the Cold War, the United States supported a variety of non-Communist regimes in Latin America. These regimes had varying levels of commitment to democratic practices.

Regime Change in Guatemala

In pursuing its Cold War goals, the United States orchestrated the ouster of the democratically elected government of **Jacobo Árbenz** in **Guatemala** (1954). Árbenz, who had been elected president in 1951, was a reform-minded leader who began a land redistribution program. He moved to nationalize some of the vast landholdings of the American-owned **United Fruit Company**, growers of Chiquita bananas. He intended to nationalize lands that were not under cultivation and distribute them to poverty-stricken peasants. He offered to buy the land from United Fruit Company at the value the company had declared the land for tax purposes, but the company refused. The CIA then organized a plan to overthrow the Árbenz government. It trained and armed an opposition army that ousted Árbenz and installed a military dictatorship in his place. The bitter feelings left in the wake of the coup contributed to civil war in Guatemala that lasted into the 1990s.

Hostilities with Cuba

Events in **Cuba** occupied much of President **John F. Kennedy's** brief tenure as president, as Cuba became a hotspot in the **Cold War**, starting in 1959. Cuba had been run as a military dictatorship with close ties with the United States from 1933 until 1959, when **Fidel Castro** led a successful guerrilla movement to overthrow the dictatorship. By 1960, the relationship between the United States and Cuba had become hostile, while the relationship between the **Soviet Union** and Cuba grew increasingly friendly. In the final months of the Eisenhower administration, advisors planned for the United States to train, arm, and aid a group of Cuban exiles opposed to the **Communist** government of Fidel Castro.

Kennedy adopted the plan and green-lighted its implementation in 1961. The exiles landed at the **Bay of Pigs** in Cuba in April 1961 but were quickly captured by Cuban forces. The Bay of Pigs incident was the first of several attempts to oust the Communist regime from Cuba.

Intervention in the Dominican Republic

Just before the United States became heavily engaged in the conflict in Vietnam in 1965, **President Lyndon Johnson** intervened in the affairs of **the Dominican Republic**. Earlier, in 1961, the repressive military ruler, **General Rafael Trujillo**, had been assassinated and his regime collapsed. For four years, different groups struggled for control of the country. In 1965, it appeared that the left-of-center nationalist leader, **Juan Bosch**, might ascend to power in a revolt against the government. Johnson dispatched 30,000 Marines to the Dominican Republic, claiming, without evidence, that Bosch was a Communist in the mold of Cuba's Fidel Castro (see above).

B. The "Military–Industrial Complex" and the Arms Race

A series of debates occurred during the Cold War about the priorities and repercussions of American, foreign, and military policies. Many Americans became increasingly concerned about the power of what President Eisenhower termed the "military-industrial complex." In addition, debates occurred around the expansion of America's nuclear arsenal.

The "Military-Industrial Complex"

The term **"military-industrial complex"** was popularized after **President Dwight D. Eisenhower** used it in his televised Farewell Address (1961). The term implies a close-knit relationship between government officials, leaders of the military, and corporate interests, especially those involved in the production of military material and services. The implication is that important decisions about policy—including decisions about military interventions—are made, in part, to advance the interests of the military-industrial complex, which might be at odds with other foreign policy goals.

Challenging America's Nuclear Policy

Starting in the 1950s and 1960s, many Americans began challenging the country's military priorities. In the 1960s, many protested military involvement in **Vietnam** (see pages 333–335). Even before that, there were those who were critical of America's **nuclear weapons policy**. By the early 1960s, it had become evident that the United States had produced enough nuclear weapons to destroy the world several times over. The policy of **"massive retaliation"** implied, to many people, a dangerous readiness to use nuclear weapons (see pages 320–321). With both the United States and Soviet Union possessing such powerful nuclear arsenals, policymakers accepted the policy of **mutually assured destruction**, or MAD. For some policymakers, MAD created a powerful deterrent to the use of nuclear weapons; to critics, it represented a dangerous precipice on which the world was perched. The 1964 dark comedy, *Dr. Strangelove or: How I Learned to Stop Worrying and Love the Bomb*, directed by Stanley Kubrick, depicted the policy of mutually assured destruction going terribly wrong. Critics of nuclear proliferation formed the **Committee for a Sane Nuclear Policy** (often referred to as **SANE**) in 1957 to challenge the ongoing nuclear tests being conducted by the Eisenhower administration. In 1961, the newly formed **Women's Strike for Peace** resonated broadly and inspired more than 50,000 women in sixty cities to march for peace.

C. Decolonization, Nationalism, and U.S. Policy in the Middle East and Africa

In the post–World War II period, nationalist movements developed in many colonized countries in Asia, Africa, and the Middle East, setting off a wave of decolonization struggles. Both of the major powers in the Cold War attempted to gain the allegiance of these newly independent countries. However, many of these countries remained politically nonaligned.

Decolonization and U.S. Foreign Policy

In the two decades after World War II, many of the colonies of the European powers struggled to gain independence. A wave of **nationalist movements** developed throughout **Asia** and **Africa**. **India**, for example, gained independence from British rule in 1947 after a prolonged struggle led by **Mohandas Gandhi**; in **Algeria** an eight-year war preceded independence from France in 1962. U.S. foreign policy evolved in the face of these movements. On the one hand, the United States professed support for the concept of self-determination—granting **the Philippines** independence in 1946—and, on the other hand, it had strong ties with many of the European powers.

As the Cold War intensified, the **Truman** and **Eisenhower** administrations became increasingly concerned that the newly independent countries would end up in the orbit of the **Soviet Union**. The United States encouraged the European powers to negotiate with their colonies to ensure peaceful paths to independence. It also took a number of measures to keep these newly independent countries from aligning with the Soviet Union. The United States extended aid packages and technical assistance to many of these countries. The **Peace Corps**, established in 1961, served this goal. The United States also resorted to military force and covert operations to install regimes favorable to U.S. interests.

Iran and the CIA

During the **Cold War**, the United States engaged in a number of covert operations designed to oust regimes (often democratically elected) that were deemed insufficiently friendly to American interests. An early covert operation occurred in **Iran** in 1953. Earlier, in 1951, the left-leaning, reform-minded **Mohammad Mosaddegh** had been elected prime minister of Iran. Mosaddegh nationalized oil fields and refineries, angering Western oil interests. In addition, he challenged the power of Iran's hereditary ruler, **Mohammad Reza Shah Pahlavi**, who was close to the Iranian elite and to Western oil interests. President **Dwight D. Eisenhower**, stressing the importance of having regimes friendly to American interests in the oil-rich Middle East, authorized the CIA, with the support of British M16 agents, to instigate a coup against Mosaddegh. The Iranian army took Mosaddegh prisoner and restored the Shah's power. Although the United States accomplished its goal of establishing a friendly regime in Iran, the events of 1953 came back to haunt the United States a generation later in the aftermath of the 1979 **Iranian Revolution** (see page 349).

The Eisenhower Doctrine

President Dwight D. Eisenhower became increasingly concerned about events in the **Middle East** after **Colonel Gamal Abdel Nasser** took power in **Egypt** in 1954. Earlier, in 1952, Nasser had been one of the leaders of the movement to topple the corrupt, ineffectual, and pro-Western King Farouk. Nasser established close relations with the Soviets. Events became more tense after Nasser seized control of the **Suez Canal**, which was jointly owned by French and British shareholders. When **France**, **Great Britain**, and **Israel** invaded Egypt to retake control of the canal, Eisenhower and the leaders of the U.N. and the Soviet Union pressured the three powers to withdraw. Afterward, Eisenhower took a more active role in the Middle East. In a 1957 speech, he pledged the United States would support any Middle Eastern countries threatened by "any nation controlled by international Communism." The **Eisenhower Doctrine** was invoked in 1958 when a rebel movement friendly to Nasser emerged in **Lebanon**; U.S. Marines were quickly dispatched to support the Lebanese president, **Camille Chamoun**.

Topic 8.8 The Vietnam War

The United States, following the dictates of the policy of containment and the "domino theory," focused its attention on events in Vietnam in the 1950s. As France, which had controlled the region since the mid-nineteenth century, suffered setbacks, the United States began to play a more prominent role in what some observers saw as a civil conflict. U.S. involvement in the Vietnam War intensified in the 1960s and lasted until the early 1970s. The war became increasingly divisive among Americans as it progressed.

A. The War in Vietnam

The United States became involved in Vietnam in the 1950s, but did not become fully engaged in war until the Gulf of Tonkin Resolution (1964). Direct American involvement in the war ended in 1973.

Background to American Involvement in Vietnam

Vietnam is a small country along the eastern edge of the Indochina peninsula in Southeast Asia. From the mid-nineteenth century to the mid-twentieth century, Indochina, including what would become Vietnam, was a **French** possession. French Indochina was occupied by Japan during World War II; when the war ended, many Vietnamese hoped to finally be free of foreign control. However, France reoccupied the peninsula when the Japanese left. A resistance movement, led by **Ho Chi Minh**, intensified in the 1950s. In 1954, French forces were defeated at the northern town of **Dien Bien Phu**, and France withdrew. Vietnam soon was divided at the 17th parallel between a Communist-controlled **North Vietnam**, led by Ho Chi Minh, and a Western-allied **South Vietnam**. Rebel fighters, known as the National Liberation Front of South Vietnam, or **Vietcong**, fought to defeat a corrupt and dictatorial South Vietnamese government headed by Ngo Din Diem. The Vietcong frequently used brutal tactics, including assassinations and bombings, against South Vietnamese village leaders in the early 1960s. American observers concluded that, without outside help, the government of South Vietnam could very likely fall to the Communists. This conclusion led American presidents—from Eisenhower through Nixon—to prioritize American involvement in Vietnam.

The "Domino Theory"

American involvement in Vietnam was influenced by a belief in the **"domino theory."** This theory asserts that when a nation adopts a Communist form of government, its neighbors are likely to become Communist as well. President Dwight D. Eisenhower had described the "falling domino" principle in a 1954 speech. The theory presumes that Communism is imposed on a country from the outside—that it does not develop as a result of internal conditions.

The United States Sends Advisors to Vietnam

United States interest in Vietnam began during World War II, when it sent **military advisors** and assistance to support anti-Japanese fighters. After the country was divided in 1954, U.S. aid went to South Vietnam to fight anti-government rebels. The United States feared that South Vietnam would become a Communist nation like North Vietnam. By 1963, the U.S. government became increasingly concerned about the viability of the government of South Vietnam, headed by **Ngo Din Diem**. In 1963, the Diem regime brought about a crisis by moving to repress the Buddhist community. Large protests were held, including incidences of **Buddhist monks** publicly ending their lives by self-immolation. In 1963, the Kennedy administration gave quiet approval to a plot by a group of generals to kill Diem and stage a coup. However, the subsequent governing regimes remained unstable, leading the United States to increase its military presence in South Vietnam.

The Gulf of Tonkin Resolution

The United States became heavily involved in the Vietnam War after Congress passed the **Gulf of Tonkin Resolution** (1964), which gave **President Lyndon Johnson** broad latitude to pursue "conventional" military actions in Southeast Asia. In August 1964, Johnson announced that American destroyers had been fired upon by North Vietnamese gunboats in the Gulf of Tonkin, off the coast of **North Vietnam**. Later, reports questioned the accuracy of the announcement, but the incident led Congress to give Johnson a **"blank check"** to engage in military operations in Southeast Asia without a formal declaration of war. The Gulf of Tonkin Resolution can be considered the beginning of the Vietnam War.

The Escalation of the Vietnam War

American military actions in Vietnam escalated rapidly in the aftermath of the Gulf of Tonkin Resolution. In early 1965, the United States engaged in bombing raids in North Vietnam after seven marines were killed at an American base in Pleiku. Within a month, the U.S. had sent more than 100,000 troops to Vietnam; that number rose to 385,000 by the end of 1967, and nearly 500,000 by the end of 1968. During these years, the **bombing campaign** of North Vietnam intensified. In South Vietnam, the U.S. military pursued a policy of **"pacification"** of villages—that is, of pushing Vietcong rebels out of villages and of attempting to win the **"hearts and minds"** of the villagers. Frequently, however, U.S. actions resulted in the uprooting of entire villages, creating millions of refugees. As the war continued, a pathway to an American victory seemed increasingly remote. In addition, domestic opposition to the war grew more intense as Americans began to question the wisdom and morality of American action in Vietnam (see pages 346–347).

The Tet Offensive

In January 1968, the Vietcong and North Vietnamese forces launched the **Tet Offensive**, a major attack on South Vietnamese, U.S., and allied bases and towns. This offensive left over 9,000 U.S., South Vietnamese, and allied troops dead (1,600 Americans), while the North Vietnamese and Vietcong suffered more than 40,000 deaths. The offensive was defeated, but it demonstrated the ability of the Vietnamese to organize a coordinated strike throughout South Vietnamese territory.

The My Lai Massacre

In 1968, a company of American troops killed nearly every inhabitant of the Vietnamese village of **My Lai**, despite finding no enemy forces there. The U.S. Army covered up the massacre for more than a year. In 1971, a U.S. military court found the commander of the company, **Lieutenant William Calley**, guilty of the massacre. The incident led many Americans to question the morality of the war in Vietnam.

"Vietnamization" of the Vietnam War

President Richard Nixon assured the American people that he had a plan for **"peace with honor"** in the Vietnam War when he ran for president in 1968. However, instead of seeking peace, Nixon widened the war to **Cambodia** and **Laos**. Starting in 1969, Nixon began the policy known as **"Vietnamization."** This involved replacing American troops with South Vietnamese troops. However, all the measures that Nixon took would not lead to American victory. The United States pulled out of Vietnam in 1973. By 1975, South Vietnam was defeated. Vietnam was then reunited as a Communist country.

B. Debates over Executive Power

The Vietnam War generated debate about checks and balances and the extent of presidential power during times of war.

The War Powers Act

During the Vietnam War, many members of Congress grew increasingly frustrated with the actions of both of the presidents who carried out the war—**Lyndon Johnson** and **Richard Nixon**. When Nixon expanded the war into **Cambodia** and **Laos**, many congressional critics believed the president was abusing his powers and taking away Congress's authority to declare war. The **War Powers Act** (1973), which passed over President Nixon's veto just after the United States had withdrawn from Vietnam, was an attempt to check presidential power and strengthen the legislative branch in matters of war. The act requires the president to report any troop deployments to Congress within forty-eight hours, and it gave Congress the ability to force the withdrawal of U.S. troops after sixty days.

Topic 8.9 The Great Society

Liberalism—an approach to politics that embraced anti-Communism abroad and an activist federal government at home—reached its high point in the mid-1960s. President Lyndon Johnson's Great Society legislative agenda put this liberal approach to politics into practice.

A. Poverty Amid Affluence

The post–World War II period was marked by a growing middle class and the perception of overall affluence. However, writers and activists raised awareness of the persistence of poverty among large sectors of the population, which resulted in efforts to address the issue of poverty in America.

Abundance in Postwar America

Perhaps the most remarkable development of the post–World War II years was the unprecedented growth of the economy and the rising living standard for millions of Americans. The **gross domestic product** of the country—the total value of goods and services produced in the United States in a year—rose dramatically between 1945 and 1960, from $200 billion to $500 billion. Such growth is unprecedented in American society. In this period we see a dramatic rise in the **middle class**, as millions of Americans from working-class backgrounds were able to achieve many of the markers of middle-class life—home and car ownership, a college education, and a comfortable income.

The Other America

Large pockets of poverty persisted despite the growth of the postwar economy. Many Americans, including **President John F. Kennedy**, were made aware of the extent and tenacity of poverty in American society by **Michael Harrington's** book, *The Other America: Poverty in the United States* (1962). Harrington, a writer and socialist activist, noted that forty to fifty million Americans lived in poverty, many in decaying urban slums and many in isolated rural towns. He noted that many of the technological developments associated with economic growth, such as mechanization of agriculture and automation of factory work, resulted in job displacement and bitter poverty. Harrington's work helped shape the domestic agendas of Kennedy and his successor, **President Lyndon Johnson**.

B. The Liberal Agenda in the 1960s

Liberalism reached a high point in the mid-1960s, with its focus on an interventionist government at home and an anti-Communist foreign policy.

The Elements of 1960s Liberalism

The high point of 1960s **liberalism** was the domestic agenda of **President Lyndon Johnson**, called the **"Great Society"** (see page 337). However, 1960s liberalism has deep roots and drew its inspiration and strength from a number of sources.

At home, a key element of 1960s liberalism was the belief in the efficacy of government initiatives in addressing a series of social problems. This belief can be traced back to the **Progressive movement** of the 1900s and 1910s, as well as to the **New Deal** of the 1930s. Liberals looked favorably upon the thinking of the economist **John Maynard Keynes**, who encouraged government expenditures both to stimulate economic activity as well as to address broader social and economic goals. The liberal coalition that coalesced in the mid-century included moderates within the labor movement, such as **Walter Reuther** of the United Automobile Workers. These moderate labor leaders had purged the labor movement of Communists and radicals in the years after World War II. The coalition also included civil-society groups, such as the **American Civil Liberties Union**, the **National Association for the Advancement of Colored People**, and **Americans for Democratic Action**.

> **USING REASONING PROCESSES:**
> **CONTINUITY AND CHANGE**
>
> **Changing Definition of Liberalism**
>
> Note that the definition of "liberalism" has changed considerably over time. In the nineteenth century, liberalism implied unfettered individual rights; since the New Deal, liberalism has entailed support for government programs to rectify social ills.

In terms of foreign policy, mid-century liberalism was decidedly **anti-Communist**. Although liberals condemned the excesses of the anti-Communist **"witch-hunt"** of the 1950s, it nonetheless embraced the cause of containing international Communism. Some of the liberal intellectuals of the 1950s and 1960s had earlier allied themselves with the Communist movement of the 1930s. Over time, however, the violence and deceitfulness of **Stalinism** pushed them toward an anti-Communist position. Liberal anti-Communism was articulated in a book by Harvard historian **Arthur Schlesinger**, *The Vital Center: The Politics of Freedom* (1949).

Liberalism in the White House—From Kennedy to Johnson

In many ways, **John F. Kennedy's** election in 1960 symbolized a break with the conservatism of the 1950s and an embrace of liberalism. Kennedy's domestic agenda was called the **"New Frontier."** Kennedy's presidency, however, was cut short when he was assassinated in Dallas, Texas, less than three years into his presidency.

President Kennedy's sense of idealism and his commitment to service are embodied in the **Peace Corps**. The program was established by Kennedy in 1961 to assist underdeveloped countries in **Africa**, **Latin America**, and **Asia**. Under the program, American volunteers work for two years at a particular site, serving as teachers, health workers, or agricultural advisors. The program remains popular.

To mend frayed relations with the developing world, Kennedy created the **Agency for International Development** to coordinate aid to foreign countries, and the **Alliance for Progress**, a program designed to provide funds for development projects in Latin America.

Lyndon B. Johnson took office following the assassination of President Kennedy in November 1963. Johnson, a Texas Democrat, proved to be a remarkably effective president, passing a host of domestic programs that rivaled the New Deal in scope. However, Johnson's administration took a tragic turn, as his hopes for a **"Great Society"** were damaged by a costly and unpopular **war in Vietnam** (see pages 333–335).

C. The Great Society Advances the Liberal Agenda

President Lyndon B. Johnson's Great Society programs represented the high point of the liberal agenda. Johnson spearheaded a series of programs that sought to end racial discrimination, alleviate poverty, and address other social issues.

The Great Society

A major goal of **President Lyndon B. Johnson's Great Society** program was to end poverty in the United States. Great Society programs included the development of **Medicare** and **Medicaid**, welfare programs, and public housing. Johnson created the **Office of Economic Opportunity**, which oversaw many of the Great Society initiatives. These programs had limited success. The cycle of poverty proved to be too difficult to break in a short period of time. Further, the **war in Vietnam** became increasingly costly, diverting hundreds of billions of dollars that could have been used for antipoverty programs. Part of the Great Society included reforming the restrictive immigration policies that had been put into effect in the 1920s. The **Immigration and Nationality Act** of 1965 continued to limit the number of immigrants in the United States, but it eliminated the quota system based on national origins (see more on immigration reform, below).

D. Immigration Reform and the Great Society

In the period following World War II, large numbers of immigrants were drawn to the political, economic, and social opportunities offered by the United States. Migrations from abroad increased dramatically after the passage of the Immigration and Nationality Act of 1965.

Immigration and Nationality Act of 1965

The **Immigration and Nationality Act** of 1965 (also known as the Hart-Celler Act) changed the approach to immigration that had been in place since the 1920s (see pages 282–283). It abolished the national **quota system** and replaced it with overall limits on immigration into the United States. There was, for the first time, a limitation of 120,000 per year placed on Western Hemisphere immigration; the limit for immigration from the Eastern Hemisphere was set at 170,000. Exemptions were set for those who had family members already in the United States, allowing for **"chain immigration"** outside the limits established by the act. Preference was also given to immigrants with particular skills that were needed in the United States. The act opened the door to increased immigration and has altered the demographic composition of the United States (see more on the impact of the act, pages 387–388).

Topic 8.10 The African-American Civil Rights Movement (1960s)

The civil rights movement in the 1960s achieved some marked successes in ending legal segregation. However, progress toward achieving full racial equality in the United States proved to be a more daunting task.

A. Civil Rights Activism in the 1960s

The civil rights movement, which coalesced in the 1950s, continued and grew in the 1960s. As the 1960s began, a younger generation of activists began to play a prominent role in the movement. Over time, rifts developed between the older church-based leadership of the movement and a younger cadre of activists.

The Lunch Counter Sit-ins (1960)

In 1960, students in Tennessee and North Carolina began a campaign of **"sit-ins" at lunch counters** to protest segregation. The sit-ins occurred as some members of the movement grew frustrated with simply protesting and pushed the movement to take **direct action** to challenge and defy racist practices. The lunch counter sit-ins began in **Greensboro**, **North Carolina**, when four African-American students challenged the "whites only" policy of a **Woolworth's lunch counter** and sat at the counter. The lunch counter sit-ins spread to other cities, including **Nashville**. They put segregation on the front pages of newspapers and eventually pressured companies to end the practice.

The Freedom Rides (1961)

The **Freedom Rides** occurred in 1961, the year after the Supreme Court ruled that state laws separating the races on interstate transportation facilities were unconstitutional. Despite this, states maintained **Jim Crow** segregation laws that separated African-American passengers from white passengers. In 1961, the **Congress on Racial Equality** (CORE) organized a series of bus rides through the South, with African-American passengers riding alongside white passengers, to challenge these local codes. These "Freedom Rides" met a great deal of resistance in the South. In Alabama, a mob slashed the tires of one bus and then firebombed it. President **John F. Kennedy** finally sent federal marshals to Alabama to protect the Freedom Riders and to enforce federal law.

"Bull" Connor and the Birmingham Campaign (1963)

In the spring of 1963, **Martin Luther King Jr.** and the **Southern Christian Leadership Conference** decided to launch a major campaign in **Birmingham**, **Alabama**, to protest racial segregation. The campaign proved to be a turning point in the push for federal legislation. The public safety commissioner of Birmingham, **Eugene "Bull" Connor**, would not tolerate public demonstrations. He used fire hoses, police dogs, and other forms of physical force to put down the campaign. The campaign included a children's march, sometimes called the **"children's crusade,"** in May 1963. Connor used violent tactics to break up the children's march. Images of police brutality brought the Birmingham campaign to the attention of the nation and helped to bring public sympathy to the side of the civil rights movement. During the Birmingham campaign, King was arrested and wrote his famous **"Letter from a Birmingham Jail."** This letter responded to an open letter, written by white clergy members, critiquing the civil rights movement and arguing that it should let the local political system address the issue of racial injustice. King insisted that the Black community had waited long enough for change to happen. "'Wait' has almost always meant 'Never'," he wrote. The Birmingham campaign paved the way for the passage of the **Civil Rights Act**, a year later.

The March on Washington (1963)

In August 1963, the civil rights movement held one of the most significant demonstrations in American history. More than 200,000 people gathered in Washington, D.C. to march, sing, and hear speeches, including **Martin Luther King Jr.'s "I Have a Dream."** Some of the tensions that would divide the civil rights movement in the years to come were evident at the **March on Washington**. The leader of the **Student Nonviolent Coordinating Committee**, **John Lewis**, was told by some of the older organizers of the event to tone down his fiery rhetoric. The original draft of his speech, which urged the movement to march "through the heart of Dixie the way Sherman did... and burn Jim Crow to the ground," anticipated the growth of a more militant, direct-action-oriented tendency within the civil rights movement in the coming years.

The Selma to Montgomery March (1965)

Following passage of the **Civil Rights Act** (1964) (see page 341), the movement increasingly focused on **voting rights**. In 1964 and 1965, a prolonged effort to challenge restrictions on African-American voter registration took place in Selma, Alabama. Local organizers with the **Student Nonviolent Coordinating Committee** worked with the **Southern Christian Leadership Conference** on this campaign. **Martin Luther King Jr.** put himself in a position to get arrested in February, 1965, in an effort to gain publicity for the campaign. A few days later, **President Lyndon Johnson** spoke in favor of the Selma voting rights campaign. Two weeks after that, a protester, Jimmie Lee Jackson, was shot and killed by police. In response to the shooting, movement leaders organized a major march in Alabama, from **Selma to Montgomery**, that took place in March 1965, despite orders from **Governor George Wallace** to prevent the march from happening. As the marchers crossed the **Edmund Pettus Bridge** over the Alabama River, county and state police blocked their path and, after ordering them to turn back, attacked them with clubs and tear gas. The incident, known as **"Bloody Sunday,"** was broadcast on national television and aroused indignation among many Americans. The march was finally completed later in the month.

B. Debate Within the Civil Rights Movement

As the 1960s progressed, and as the civil rights movement achieved majored legislative victories (see pages 340–341), a series of debates occurred within the movement over philosophy and tactics.

From "Freedom Now!" to "Black Power!"

As the **civil rights movement** achieved success in ending legal segregation (*de jure* **segregation**) and removing barriers to voting, pervasive problems continued to plague the African-American community. Patterns of segregation enforced by custom rather than law (*de facto* **segregation**) persisted. Also, the bitter realities of poverty, substandard housing, and lack of decent jobs continued to plague large sections of the African-American community. A younger generation of activists continued to push the movement in a more militant direction and to demand power, not just rights. After 1964, a central rallying cry of the movement, **"Freedom now!"** was often replaced by the call for **"Black Power!"**

In 1966, the **Black Panther Party** took up the call for a "Black Power" movement, embracing self-defense and militant rhetoric. Initially, the Black Panthers focused on community organizing; however, their activities grew increasingly confrontational.

Malcolm X

By the mid-1960s, many African-American activists were attempting to push civil rights activism in a more militant direction. **Malcolm X** was a central figure in the more militant turn the civil rights movement took. Between 1952 and 1964 he was a member and then a leader of the **Nation of Islam**, an African-American group that shares certain practices with mainstream Islam, but differs in several important respects. The organization advocated that African Americans organize among themselves, separate from whites. After making a pilgrimage to **Mecca** in 1964 and seeing Muslims of different races interacting as equals, Malcolm X revised his views about Black separatism. He also left the Nation of Islam. In 1965, he was killed by assassins from the Nation of Islam, but his words continued to inspire the civil rights movement.

Urban Rioting

Frustrations within the African-American community reached a boiling point in the 1960s, as many cities experienced rioting between African-American residents and predominantly white police forces. The first major disturbances of the decade occurred in **Harlem** in 1964 after a police officer fatally shot a fifteen-year-old African-American boy. In the following years, major rioting occurred in **Watts**, **Los Angeles** (1965), **Detroit** (1967), and **Newark**, **New Jersey** (1967). A series of riots occurred in several American cities following the assassination of **Martin Luther King Jr.** in 1968 (see below). An estimated 50,000 people took part in the riots in Watts; 15,000 police and members of the **National Guard** were deployed to quell the rebellion. When it finally ended, thirty-five people had been killed in the conflict. The riots in Detroit in 1967 left forty-three people dead. The Detroit riots were the deadliest of over 150 race riots that occurred in what has become known as "the long, hot summer of 1967." Following the Detroit riots, **President Lyndon Johnson** formed the **Kerner Commission** to investigate the causes of rioting in African-American communities. The commission issued its report in 1968, citing poverty and segregation as root causes of the unrest. The report noted that America was moving toward separate societies, "**one black, one white—separate and unequal.**"

The Assassination of King (1968)

Martin Luther King Jr. was killed by an assassin on April 4, 1968, in Memphis, Tennessee. King's assassination was both a source of national mourning and a harbinger of the decline of the African-American civil rights movement of the era. The movement had accomplished much, but was unable to provide a solution for many of the problems facing the African-American community.

> **USING HISTORICAL THINKING SKILLS:**
> **DEVELOPMENTS AND PROCESSES**
>
> ### The Grassroots and the Government
>
> The civil rights movement vividly illustrates the complex relationship between the grassroots movement and government policy. The movement pushed the government to take action; support from the government emboldened the movement.

C. Major Federal Legislative Victories for the Civil Rights Movement

The persistence and growing strength of the civil rights movement eventually forced the hand of the federal government. Presidents John F. Kennedy and Lyndon Johnson both embraced the call for change, paving the way for passage of the Civil Rights Act and the Voting Rights Act. These acts represented the culmination of the movement.

Kennedy, Johnson, and the Politics of Civil Rights

For years the **Democratic Party** had walked a fine line when it came to **civil rights** for **African Americans**. On the one hand, many Democratic leaders since the **Franklin D. Roosevelt** administration believed that extending civil rights to African Americans was the correct and just thing to do, but on the other hand, the party did not want to alienate its southern wing. As the civil rights movement put the issue on the national agenda and as violence by white southerners put the issue on the nightly news, Democratic leaders had to react. In June 1963, the same month that civil rights leader **Medgar Evers** was murdered in front of his house in Jackson, Mississippi, **President John F. Kennedy** gave a national address in which he called civil rights a "moral issue" and pledged to support civil rights legislation. After Kennedy's assassination in November 1963, **President Lyndon B. Johnson**, himself a southerner from Texas, took up the cause of civil rights legislation with vigor, pressuring reluctant Democratic legislators to support it.

This embrace of civil rights legislation by the leadership of the Democratic Party contributed to an exodus of many white southern Democrats out of the party. Some of these individuals supported the presidential candidacy of **George Wallace**, who ran under the banner of a far-right, segregationist third-party in 1968. The vast majority of southern white Democrats who left the party in the 1960s (and since) ended up in the **Republican Party**.

The Civil Rights Act (1964)

The **Civil Rights Act** was passed by Congress and signed by **President Lyndon Johnson** in the summer of 1964. The act was intended to end discrimination based on race and gender. The Civil Rights Act guaranteed all Americans equal access to public accommodations, public education, and voting. Another section banned discrimination in employment based on race or gender.

The Voting Rights Act (1965)

The **Voting Rights Act**, passed in August 1965, authorized the federal government to oversee voter registration in counties with low African-American registration. The act also outlawed **literacy tests** and **poll taxes**—means of preventing African Americans from voting. By 1968, the number of southern African-American voters jumped from one million to more than three million. In 2013, the Supreme Court greatly limited the scope of the act. In *Shelby County v. Holder*, it weakened Section 5 of the act, which required certain states (with a history of discrimination) to obtain federal "preclearance," or approval, before implementing any changes to their voting laws.

D. The Warren Court and the Expansion of Civil Rights

A series of important Supreme Court decisions from the 1950s to the 1960s expanded democracy, civil rights, and individual liberties. These decisions occurred under the leadership of Chief Justice Earl Warren.

The Warren Court

Earl Warren was chief justice of the Supreme Court from 1953 to 1969. The Court under his leadership moved in a decidedly **liberal** direction. The first case Warren dealt with as chief justice was the landmark *Brown* case (see page 330). Through the 1960s, the Warren Court continued to protect the rights of minorities, reinforced the separation of church and state, established an individual's right to privacy, and protected the rights of those accused of crimes. Liberals have generally welcomed Warren Court decisions, while conservatives have accused Warren of practicing judicial activism.

Expanding the Rights of the Accused

Several important Warren Court decisions expanded the rights of those accused of crimes. In *Mapp v. Ohio* (1961), the Supreme Court ruled that evidence obtained in violation of the Fourth Amendment protection against "unreasonable searches and seizures" must be excluded from criminal prosecutions in state courts as well as federal courts. In *Gideon v. Wainwright* (1963), the Supreme Court ruled that the states must provide impoverished defendants with court-appointed attorneys. Previously, this stipulation applied only to federal court procedures. In the 1964 case, *Escobedo v. Illinois*, the Court ruled that defendants had a right

> **USING HISTORICAL THINKING SKILLS: MAKING CONNECTIONS**
>
> **Chief Justices—John Marshall and Earl Warren**
>
> The AP exam does not require you to know all the chief justices of the Supreme Court, but you should be familiar with John Marshall (1801–1835) and Earl Warren (1953–1969). Both the Marshall Court and the Warren Court maintained a consistent ideological approach that is evident in the respective decisions of each. The Marshall Court consistently strengthened the powers of the federal government over state powers. It also upheld the legitimacy of contracts, promoting economic growth during the era of the market revolution. Warren Court decisions upheld the rights of those accused of crimes and protected the rights of minorities. It reflected broader societal trends of the 1950s and 1960s—the rise of the civil rights movements and the embrace of liberalism by policymakers on the federal level.

to have a lawyer present during police interrogations. In *Miranda v. Arizona* (1966), the Court ruled that arrested people must be read basic rights, now known as *Miranda Rights*, including the right to remain silent and the right to have a lawyer.

The Right to Privacy

Although the right to privacy is not specifically mentioned in the Constitution, the Warren Court asserted that this right is implicit in it. In *Griswold v. Connecticut* (1965), the Court ruled that laws forbidding the use of birth-control devices were unconstitutional. The right to privacy would become important in the case of *Roe v. Wade* (1973, after the retirement of Earl Warren), which insisted that states allow abortions during the first two trimesters of pregnancy (see page 345).

Free Speech

In *Tinker v. Des Moines* (1969), the Supreme Court ruled that a school board prohibition against students wearing black armbands in protest of the **Vietnam War** was unconstitutional. The Court ruled that students in school had the right to free speech, including symbolic speech, as long as their actions did not interfere with the educational process.

In *Brandenberg v. Ohio* (1969), the Court ruled that the government cannot restrict inflammatory speech unless that speech is likely to directly incite imminent unlawful action. The case revolved around an incendiary interview with a **Ku Klux Klan** leader. Local authorities arrested him under a criminal syndicalism statute. The decision set the precedent of protecting anti-government and provocative speech.

Freedom of the Press

In *New York Times v. Sullivan* (1964), the Supreme Court overturned a lower court libel award of $500,000 to **L. B. Sullivan**, a public safety commissioner in **Montgomery, Alabama**. Sullivan had sued *The New York Times* for running an ad calling attention to the violence being committed in the South against civil-rights demonstrators. Sullivan contended that the ad libeled him, even if it did not mention him by name. White southern officials frequently used plaintiff-friendly libel laws to curb reporting of civil rights issues. The Court found such laws were detrimental to a free press. The Court set a higher standard for libel—insisting that in order to prove libel public officials must show that a publication exhibited "**actual malice.**" Specifically, a public official filing suit must show that a publication knew a statement was false and/or recklessly disregarded the truth. The *Sullivan* decision has been the Court's most forceful defense of press freedom.

Reapportionment and "One-person, One-vote"

In *Baker v. Carr* (1966), the Supreme Court ruled that states must periodically redraw legislative districts so that districts have roughly equal numbers of people. At the time, Tennessee had not redrawn its legislative districts for more than sixty years. Urban areas such as Memphis had grown much faster than rural districts. Without **reapportionment**, urban areas would be underrepresented, violating the principle of **"one-person, one-vote."**

Prayer in Public Schools and the Separation of Church and State

In *Engel v. Vitale* (1962), the Supreme Court ruled that the **Regents' Prayer**, a state-mandated prayer that was recited by public school children in New York State, was unconstitutional because it violated the doctrine of separation of church and state.

> **USING HISTORICAL THINKING SKILLS:**
> **MAKING CONNECTIONS**
>
> **Church and State in American History**
>
> The relationship between church and state has been a contentious issue throughout American history, from Roger Williams and the founding of Rhode Island in the 1630s to recent controversies over the teaching of evolution in public schools.

Topic 8.11 The Civil Rights Movement Expands

The visibility and successes of the civil rights movement inspired other movements for social change. These movements, focused on gender, sexuality, and ethnicity, addressed a host of inequalities and issues of identity.

A. Latinos, American Indians, and Asian Americans Press for Justice

In the wake of the African-American civil rights movement, various ethnic groups, including Latinos, American Indians, and Asian Americans, pushed for a redress of past injustices as well as economic and social equality.

American Indians Resistance to "Termination"

American Indians in the post–World War II period became increasingly bitter toward federal policies in regard to American Indian tribes. In 1953, the federal government passed legislation that established a policy known as **"termination."** Over time, the government would encourage American Indians to assimilate into white culture and would then terminate recognition of tribes as legal entities. Members of tribes were expected to then live in communities with non-Indians, under the same laws as all other citizens of the United States. The policy weakened the influence of tribal authorities and led to resistance on the part of many American Indians. Even though President Dwight D. Eisenhower moved away from active enforcement of the policy in the late 1950s, an active and militant resistance movement continued after the 1950s. In 1961, representatives of sixty-seven tribes met in Chicago to address common concerns. They wrote a manifesto called the **"Declaration of Indian Purpose."**

The American Indian Movement

American Indian activism continued into the 1960s. Activists were responding to a history of subjugation and to contemporary injustices; many gained inspiration from the African-American civil rights movement.

The **American Indian Movement** (AIM) was founded in 1968. The following year, the movement made headlines when several dozen activists seized control of **Alcatraz Island**, in the San Francisco Bay, claiming the former prison belonged to the first inhabitants of the area—American Indians. Protests by AIM continued in the 1970s. In 1972, nearly a thousand American Indians occupied the headquarters of the federal Bureau of Indian Affairs in Washington, D.C. The following year, **Oglala Lakota** members of AIM staged the most significant protest of this period at **Wounded Knee**, **South Dakota**, the site of the massacre of Lakota (Sioux) Indians in 1890 (see page 222). The occupation, which lasted for two months, called for a change in the administration of the **Pine Ridge Indian Reservation** and demanded that the United States government honor its treaty obligations.

AIM was successful in pressing the government to make certain changes. In 1972, **President Richard M. Nixon** promised to allow American Indians to have greater autonomy over tribal lands and affairs. In 1978, the Supreme Court, in *United States v. Wheeler*, affirmed the legal status of American Indian tribes and ruled that Congress could not "terminate" tribes. Many of the goals of the movement, however, were not achieved.

Political Activism in the Latino Community

In the 1960s, Latinos became more active in fighting for their civil rights. In the post–World War II period, Latinos became the fastest-growing segment of the United States population. Large numbers of **Puerto Ricans**, **Cubans**, and **Mexicans** immigrated into the United States in the post-war period. Many young Mexican Americans, calling themselves **"Chicanos,"** pushed for a greater sense of solidarity and for social change. In Texas, Chicanos organized **La Raza Unida** political party in 1970. The party, emphasizing Chicano nationalism, grew out of dissatisfaction with the Democratic Party in regard to fighting for greater equality. It organized throughout the Southwest in the 1970s, disbanding in 1978. A more visible organizing effort was begun by **Cesar Chavez** and **Delores Huerta**, who founded the **United Farm Workers** in 1962 in California to protect the interests of **migrant farmers**, including many **Mexican Americans**. The UFW organized a nationwide boycott of grapes in 1965 to pressure farm owners to pay their workers a decent wage. The boycott resulted in a significant victory in 1970, when several major growers in California signed a contract with the UFW and agreed to raise farm wages.

The Asian-American Civil Rights Movement

Many **Asian Americans** became increasingly active in fighting for civil rights in the 1960s and 1970s. The Asian-American civil rights movement focused on several issues—the creation of ethnic studies programs in universities, an end to the Vietnam War, and reparations for Japanese Americans forced into **internment camps** during **World War II** (see page 300). In 1969, **Amy Uyematsu** wrote an influential essay, **"The Emergence of Yellow Power,"** in which she cites the "Black Power" movement as a catalyst for Asian Americans to examine the conditions of their own lives and to fight to redress injustices. Student strikes at San Francisco State University and the University of California, Berkeley in 1968 and 1969 by Asian-American students and other students of color led to the implementation of extensive **ethnic-studies programs**. The movement dissipated somewhat after the end of the Vietnam War but, by 1988, President Ronald Reagan signed legislation in which the federal government formally apologized for the internment of Japanese Americans during World War II and distributed $20,000 in **reparations** to each internee or his or her family, totaling $1.2 billion.

B. Movements for Women's Rights and Gay Liberation

Activists began to challenge ingrained assumptions around gender. Movements developed in the 1960s to push for greater social and economic equality for women and for gays and lesbians.

The Women's Liberation Movement

In the 1960s, a **women's liberation movement** developed, challenging inequities in the job market, representations of women in the media, violence against women, and an ingrained set of social values. Women joined with others through consciousness-raising groups and realized that their contributions to society historically and within their own families were deemed less important than those of men. They saw connections to the larger society, giving rise to the motto, **"the personal is political."** Many women were inspired by **Betty Friedan's** 1963 book, *The Feminine Mystique*, which challenged the traditional options in life offered to middle-class women. Friedan was one of several women to found the **National Organization for Women** (1966), the leading liberal organization supporting women's rights. The movement gave birth to the nationally circulated magazine, *Ms.*, founded by **Gloria Steinem**, **Letty Cottin Pogrebin**, and others. Many women in the movement had come out of **New Left** activist organizations (see page 347), empowered to fight for a better world, but frustrated with the treatment women received in these organizations.

Protest at the Miss America Pageant

Many Americans heard about the women's liberation movement for the first time from news reports of a protest at the 1968 **Miss America pageant**. The pageant exemplified, to the protesters, society's attitude toward women in which women were valued for their looks above all else. Women were expected to parade in bathing suits and give vacuous answers to questions in order to win male approval.

Title IX (1972)

An important success of the women's liberation movement was Congress's passage of **Title IX of the Educational Amendments** of 1972. Title IX banned gender discrimination in all aspects of education, such as faculty hiring and admissions. It has had a major impact on funding for female sports activities at the high school and college levels.

The Gay Liberation Movement

The **gay liberation movement** was born in 1969 when patrons at the **Stonewall Inn**, a gay bar in New York's **Greenwich Village**, resisted a raid by the police and fought back. The event brought a series of grievances into the open. Gay men and women had suffered discrimination in many walks of life, including in government civil-service jobs. Many gays attempted to avoid such discrimination by concealing their sexual identity and remaining "in the closet." In the weeks after the Stonewall riots, activists in the gay community in New York City formed the **Gay Liberation Front**. The group's activities included protesting coverage of the gay community in the press, supporting gay prisoners, and challenging the American Psychiatric Association's classification of homosexuality as a mental disorder. A protest by the Gay Liberation Front and other groups at the San Francisco Examiner in 1969 became violent when employees dumped a barrel of printing ink on the protesters.

C. Feminism, the Counterculture, and the Rethinking of Gender Norms

Feminists and participants in the counterculture rejected many of the mainstream values that characterized their parents' generation. This counterculture initiated a sexual revolution in American society, greater informality in everyday life, and a rethinking of the traditional family structure in America. Although popular culture continued to portray idealized nuclear families, the increase in the number of working women and new social attitudes eroded the reality of this image.

The Sexual Revolution

The 1960s witnessed the development of more tolerant attitudes toward sexual behavior. In 1960, the **birth control pill** was introduced to the market, allowing women more control over reproduction and over their sexual lives. Many states impeded the distribution of information and products related to birth control. The Supreme Court invalidated such repressive laws in the case of *Griswold v. Connecticut* (1965), in which the Court ruled that laws forbidding the use of birth control devices were unconstitutional because they violated the privacy rights of individuals (see page 342).

Roe v. Wade (1973)

An important issue of the women's liberation movement was a woman's right to control reproduction, including whether to have an abortion. One of the major successes of the women's liberation movement was the Supreme Court decision in the case of *Roe v. Wade* (1973). The Court declared that states shall not prohibit women from having an abortion during the first two trimesters of pregnancy. Previously the decision had been left to the states, and many states forbade abortions. The Supreme Court reasoned that the Constitution guaranteed people the right to privacy. Abortion, they argued, was a decision that should be left to the woman with the advice of her physician. This decision echoed the reasoning of the earlier decision, *Griswold v. Connecticut* (1965) (see page 342), in affirming an individual's right to privacy. The issue of abortion proved to be one of the most contentious issues in America in the late twentieth and early twenty-first centuries. The Supreme Court overturned the *Roe v. Wade* decision in the 2022 *Dobbs v. Jackson Women's Health Organization* decision (see page 376).

The "Quiet Revolution"

From the 1970s to the present, the percentage of women engaged in the workforce has grown. There are several reasons for this. The **women's liberation movement** (see page 344) challenged traditional gender expectations—many women felt less pressure to marry at a young age, have children, and work at home. Also, the availability of the **birth control pill** and of **abortions** allowed women to have greater control over their reproductive lives (see above). Many women made the decision to focus on a career first, putting off decisions about whether to have children. Historians note a **"quiet revolution"** of women entering the workplace from the late 1970s until the present.

Topic 8.12 Youth Culture of the 1960s

The liberal agenda of the 1960s came under attack from groups and individuals on the left who insisted that the steps being taken were insufficient to create a truly just and equitable world. This critique, often voiced by students and other young people, found expression in the movement against the Vietnam War and in the counterculture of the 1960s.

A. Youth Culture and the Movement Against the Vietnam War

As the Vietnam War dragged on through the latter half of the 1960s, many Americans began to see the war as an unwinnable quagmire. Americans began to grow impatient with the war effort, and many questioned the wisdom and morality of the war. The war generated a sizable and passionate antiwar movement, which used a variety of tactics as the war escalated.

The Draft

In 1964, the **Selective Service System** began increasing the number of young men drafted to serve in the armed forces. By the following year, the monthly totals of draftees doubled. The draft made the **Vietnam War** an immediate concern for millions of young men and contributed to the number of young people participating in the antiwar movement.

"Living Room War"

The **Vietnam War** was the first American war to occur in an era when the vast majority of Americans owned television sets (90 percent by 1960). Americans were able to see graphic images of warfare in their living rooms for the first time. Many were shocked at what they saw. A report by **Morley Safer** in 1965 showed Marines evacuating Vietnamese civilians from their homes in the village of **Cam Ne** and then setting the village on fire. More disturbing images followed and contributed to public opinion questioning the wisdom and justness of the war.

The War and the Working Class

In many ways, the war in Vietnam was a **working-class war**. Eighty percent of the troops in Vietnam were working class and poor. Middle-class youths often managed to get college deferments or had connections to get a stateside (in the United States) position in the National Guard. In 1967, **Martin Luther King Jr.** gave a speech entitled **"Beyond Vietnam,"** condemning the war and its impact on the underclass in the United States.

The Unraveling of the Vietnam War

By 1968, the war in Vietnam increasingly seemed unwinnable. The **Vietcong** and **North Vietnamese** forces launched the **Tet Offensive** in January (see page 335), shocking the American public with their suicidal determination. Further, extensive media coverage of the war had left many Americans questioning its morality and purpose. In 1969, the horrific 1968 **My Lai Massacre** (see page 335) became known to the American public, further eroding faith in the war effort. Opponents of the war became increasingly vocal by the final years of the 1960s.

> **USING HISTORICAL THINKING SKILLS: MAKING CONNECTIONS**
>
> **The Media and War—Vietnam Era and Post-9/11**
>
> During the Vietnam War, Americans saw uncensored images of the horrors of war. This contributed to antiwar sentiment among many Americans. Later, during the Iraq War (2003–2011), the government kept a tight rein on media coverage. If reporters wanted access to the military, they had to agree to be embedded with a unit. The military would then have great control over what was reported. President George W. Bush had taken a lesson from the Vietnam War.

> **USING REASONING PROCESSES: CONTINUITY AND CHANGE**
>
> **The Supreme Court and a Free Press**
>
> The Supreme Court has been fairly consistent in the twentieth century in upholding and expanding freedom of the press. In *Near v. Minnesota* (1931), the Court ruled states cannot exercise "prior restraint" on newspapers. In *New York Times Co. v. Sullivan* (1964), the Court limited the ability of public officials to sue publications for defamation. In *New York Times Co. v. United States* (1971), the Supreme Court upheld the rights of the press by allowing for the publication of the Pentagon Papers and rejecting the government's assertion of a need to maintain the secrecy of information. Yet, in *Hazelwood v. Kuhlmeier* (1988), the Court allowed for administrators to censor student newspapers.

The Antiwar Movement

The **antiwar movement** can be traced back to the early 1960s as small peace groups questioned the purpose of the armed advisors who were sent to Vietnam. An important antiwar group on college campuses was **Students for a Democratic Society**, founded in 1960 (see more, below). By the late 1960s, several important antiwar groups had emerged out of the growing protest movement. The **National Mobilization Committee to End the War in Vietnam** was formed in 1967 to organize large national protests against the war. The movement organized several large demonstrations against the war in Washington, D.C., including two massive gatherings—in November 1969 and in April 1971—that each brought approximately half a million people to the nation's capital.

Vietnam Veterans Against the War

An influential antiwar group was the **Vietnam Veterans Against the War**. Formed in 1967, the organization harnessed the frustrations of returning veterans of the conflict. Many front-line soldiers grew to question the tactics, and even the purpose, of the war. There were several incidents of soldiers attacking commanding officers, including **"fragging"**—tossing live grenades at them during action in the field.

The Shootings at Kent State and Jackson State

The antiwar movement was stunned when students were fired upon at **Kent State University** in Ohio in May 1970, during a demonstration against President Richard Nixon's decision to invade Cambodia (see page 335). Ohio **National Guardsmen** opened fire, killing four students and wounding ten; some victims were part of the protest, some were bystanders. Eleven days later, two African-American student demonstrators were shot and killed by state police at **Jackson State University** in Mississippi.

Publication of the Pentagon Papers

Many of the antiwar movements's suspicions about the Vietnam War were borne out with the publication of the **Pentagon Papers**, a secret Department of Defense study of U.S. political and military involvement in Vietnam. The study revealed a pattern of official deception and secrecy. It was leaked to the press by **Daniel Ellsberg**, a Pentagon official critical of the direction the Vietnam War was taking. The Nixon administration tried to block *The New York Times* and the *Washington Post* from publishing the papers. Initially, the Nixon administration obtained an injunction against publication, but the Supreme Court, in the case of *New York Times Co. v. United States* (1971), overruled the injunction and upheld the right of the newspapers to publish the information.

B. The New Left

Individuals and groups on the left criticized the liberal agenda of the 1960s for doing too little to significantly challenge the economic and racial inequalities at home and for pursuing an immoral foreign policy.

Students for a Democratic Society and the Rise of the New Left

One of the most significant organizations in the antiwar movement of the 1960s was **Students for a Democratic Society** (SDS), with chapters at major college campuses across the country. The name was coined in 1960, with SDS developing out of an earlier organization. SDS held its first national convention at Port Huron, Michigan, in 1962. At this convention the organization adopted a guiding manifesto, known as the **Port Huron Statement**, which became an important document in the development of the **New Left** (see box).

> **USING REASONING PROCESSES:**
> **COMPARISON**
>
> **New Left Versus Old Left**
>
> The New Left of the 1960s can be contrasted to the worker-oriented, top-down Old Left movement that developed in the 1930s. The Old Left focused more on workplace issues, while the New Left focused on "participatory democracy" and cultural and social, as well as economic and political, issues. The New Left developed on college campuses rather than in factories. The Old Left was closely associated with the Communist Party, while the New Left was less sectarian. Both left movements embraced the struggle for African-American civil rights.

The document, written by **Tom Hayden**, stressed participatory democracy and direct action. SDS continued to grow throughout the 1960s, but splintered into factions amid intense infighting in 1969 before formally disbanding in 1974.

C. Countercultural Values and American Culture

A vibrant counterculture developed among young people in the 1960s. As the baby-boom generation came of age in the 1960s, a large portion grew increasingly weary of the cultural products of the previous generation. Mainstream culture seemed inauthentic, shallow, and corporate controlled.

Bob Dylan and the Folk Revival

Bob Dylan was able to verbalize many of the fears and hopes of the younger generation in the 1960s. Even his initial musical choices—simple, acoustic instrumentation—attracted listeners who found the pop songs of the era to be repetitive and overproduced creations of the record industry. He cultivated a vocal approach that paid homage to the untrained, indigenous music of rural America, rather than to the smooth crooners of his parents' generation. Some of his early songs became anthems of the protest movements of the 1960s, including "The Times They Are a-Changin" and "With God on Our Side" (both released in 1964). Dylan soon "went electric" (1965)—to the dismay of folk purists—finding an enormous worldwide following. His wide-ranging poetic lyrics earned him the 2016 Nobel Prize in Literature.

The British Invasion

In the 1960s, a series of British bands, most notably the **Beatles** and the **Rolling Stones**, transformed American culture. These bands took inspiration from the rich tradition of **African-American music**—from **rhythm and blues** to **rock 'n' roll**—and infused it with a youthful energy. The Beatles inspired a manic following in the United States known as "Beatlemania." If one event symbolized the beginning of the British invasion, it was the first appearance by the Beatles on the *Ed Sullivan Show* in February 1964. The Beatles also generated a backlash in the United States. Conservatives were troubled by their long hair, veiled allusions to drug use, interest in Eastern religions, and challenges to traditional notions of propriety. A comment by one of the Beatles, John Lennon, that the band had become more popular than Jesus Christ, added to the backlash.

The "Hippie Movement" and Haight-Ashbury

The **"hippie" movement** became visible in the late 1960s in neighborhoods such as **San Francisco's Haight-Ashbury** and **New York's Greenwich Village**. The apogee of the movement was perhaps the **"Summer of Love"** (1967). In many ways, this counterculture represented a complete rejection of the materialistic conformity that many young people grew up with in the 1950s (see pages 327–328). A variety of activities came to be associated with the hippie movement—urban and rural communal living, a "do-it-yourself" approach to the varied tasks of life, mystic spiritual experiences, drug use, experimental music, and avant-garde art. Taking inspiration from the sit-ins of the civil rights movement, the counterculture organized **"be-ins"**—gatherings of young people in San Francisco's Golden Gate Park or New York's Central Park that were part political protest and part spiritual and artistic festival.

Woodstock and Altamont

The **counterculture** of the 1960s reached its peak and showed its limits in two important events, months apart from each other, in 1969. The **Woodstock Festival**, in August, attracted half a million attendees to a massive weekend concert at a farm in upstate New York, and for many participants seemed to provide a glimpse of a utopian future. In December, promoters tried to duplicate the success of Woodstock with a giant music festival at the **Altamont Speedway** in California. However, the Altamont event was marred by incidents of violence; one concertgoer, armed and apparently crazed, was stopped and stabbed to death by a member of the **Hell's Angels Motorcycle Club** (the concert's security detail) as the **Rolling Stones** performed.

Topic 8.13 The Environment and Natural Resources from 1968 to 1980

In the 1960s and 1970s, Americans began to grapple with the effects of unchecked industrial and economic growth. The impacts of such growth—including energy shortages, tensions with oil-producing countries in the Middle East, and growing awareness of the long-term impact of economic growth on the environment—shaped debates in the late twentieth century and beyond.

A. The Middle East, Oil, and National Energy Policy

United States policy in the Middle East during the Cold War was driven by several, sometimes conflicting, priorities. Ideological, military, and economic concerns shaped American policy in the Middle East. After several oil crises at home, the United States attempted to create a policy for its energy future.

The United States, Israel, and the Arab World

Tensions have existed between Israel and its Middle East neighbors since the founding of Israel in 1948. The Arab nations refused to recognize Israel's right to exist. Four wars occurred between Israel and its neighbors between 1948 and 1973. The United States has remained a strong ally of Israel.

In 1973, the Arab oil-producing nations—the **Organization of Petroleum Exporting Countries** (OPEC)—cut off exports to the United States and increased the price of oil. These moves were largely in retaliation for U.S. support of Israel in the 1973 **Yom Kippur War** between Israel and its Arab neighbors.

The Camp David Accords (1978)

President Jimmy Carter succeeded in providing a foundation for a peace treaty between **Egypt** and **Israel**. The **Camp David Accords** are considered one of the few triumphs for President Carter's troubled presidency. In 1977 Egyptian president **Anwar Sadat** broke with the other leaders of the Arab world and flew to Israel to meet with Israeli prime minister **Menachem Begin**. Negotiations ensued between the two leaders, but they were unable to come up with a peace treaty. President Carter invited them to the Camp David presidential retreat in Maryland. The three men met for thirteen days and emerged with the basis for a peace treaty. The treaty resulted in an end to hostilities between Israel and Egypt, but tensions continued to exist between Israel and its other neighbors.

The Energy Crisis and the Limits of Growth

In the wake of the **OPEC oil embargo** in 1973 (see above), fuel prices rose dramatically through the 1970s. America had to confront a stark reality—there were limits to the amount of fossil fuels, particularly petroleum, available in the world, and much of it came from the volatile Middle East. Until the 1970s, Americans assumed petroleum was a cheap, inexhaustible commodity. The 1970s saw a dramatic spike in petroleum prices and higher prices at gas pumps.

The Iranian Revolution and the Iran Hostage Crisis

In 1979, the U.S.-supported leader of **Iran**, **Mohammad Reza Shah Pahlavi**, was ousted by a revolution led by the Muslim religious leader, the **Ayatollah Ruhollah Khomeini**. The United States supported the Shah to the end. Later in 1979, when the United States admitted the deposed Shah to the United States for medical treatment, angry Iranian students took over the U.S. embassy and kept the personnel there hostage. **President Jimmy Carter** finally secured their release after the U.S. presidential election in late 1980, but they were not actually released until thirty-three minutes into the administration of **President Ronald Reagan** in January 1981.

The Carter Doctrine

President Jimmy Carter asserted a more active role for the United States in the Middle East in 1980. The **Carter Doctrine** stated that the United States would repel any outside force that attempted to gain control of the Persian Gulf region. The doctrine reflects concerns about protecting United States oil interests, with an eye on halting any steps by the Soviet Union toward expanding its influence in the region. This more aggressive stance in the Middle East was brought about by the **Iranian Revolution** (1979) (see page 349) and Soviet intervention of **Afghanistan**, which also began in 1979. The Soviets sent troops into Afghanistan initially to prop up a pro-Soviet government in the face of a concerted rebellion led by the Afghani **Mujahideen** rebel group. Soviet forces initiated a coup, installed a new government, and remained in the country for a decade. Carter saw the presence of Soviet forces near the Middle East as a threat to American interests in the region.

Toward a National Energy Policy

While many policymakers were trying to find alternative sources of power to Middle East **petroleum**, some were looking for ways the United States could reduce its consumption of energy. Americans are by far the largest consumers of energy, consuming nearly twice the amount as the average resident of the United Kingdom or France. **President Jimmy Carter**, through the newly created **Department of Energy** (1977), encouraged **conservation measures**, such as turning down thermostats and turning off lights when not in use. He also encouraged investment in renewable sources of energy, such as solar power. Americans, however, were remarkably resistant to adopting conservation measures.

The Fifty-five Miles Per Hour Speed Limit and the Truckers' Rebellion

In response to the energy crisis, **President Richard Nixon** proposed a reduced national speed limit for highways in late 1973. Speed limits had previously been set only by the states. Congress passed the **National Maximum Speed Law** in January 1974, requiring states to cap speed limits on highways at **fifty-five miles per hour**. States would lose federal highway funds if they failed to comply with the new law.

The law was unpopular with many drivers. Several studies in the 1980s showed a non-compliance rate as high as 85 percent. The lower speed limit, coupled with rising fuel prices, hit **truckers** especially hard. In December 1973, as the fifty-five miles per hour speed limit was being debated in Congress, a trucker in Pennsylvania stopped his rig in the slow lane of the highway. Soon a fellow trucker stopped next to him, in the fast lane, blocking traffic on the highway. A more widespread truckers' strike occurred in January and February of the following year. Truckers, organized in ad hoc groups such as the **Owner-Operator and Independent Drivers Association of America**, using **citizen band (CB) radios**, spread the word of stoppages to other truckers. The actions by truckers showed their power to bring commerce to a standstill, but the national speed limit stayed in place until 1995 (although Congress amended it earlier, in 1987, to allow for a sixty-five miles per hour limit on rural highways).

Nuclear Energy

As the availability of petroleum from the Middle East came into question in the 1970s, some Americans put faith in **nuclear energy** as an alternative to fossil fuels. In a nuclear power plant, a nuclear reaction produces heat to drive steam turbines that, in turn, run electric generators (rather than using water power or burning coal or oil to run the turbines). The material needed for nuclear power, such as uranium, is relatively cheap and plentiful, and the reaction does not produce the greenhouse gas, carbon dioxide. However, there are problems associated with nuclear power. The waste product of a nuclear reaction is radioactive and must be safely disposed of. Further, nuclear power brings with it the possibility of catastrophic accidents (see more on the accident at Three Mile Island, Pennsylvania, pages 351–352). Nuclear power did not achieve the level of energy generation that planners had hoped for. Amid concerns about cost overruns and the safety of nuclear energy, only about half of the planned 253 generators in the United States were ever built. Currently, just under 20 percent of U.S. electricity is generated by nuclear power.

B. The Growth of the Environmental Movement

As the American economy expanded dramatically in the postwar period, critics began to question the growing exploitation of the country's natural resources. In the 1960s, writers and activists began to call attention to the abuse of the natural environment. They spearheaded an environmental movement that pushed for measures intended to address these problems.

The Environmental Movement

An important movement for change in the 1960s and 1970s was the **environmental movement**. The movement became a national phenomenon and led to some important changes in laws and social awareness. An important precursor to the rise of environmental activism in the 1960s was a controversy in the 1950s over federal plans to dam the **Green River** and flood a spectacular and ecologically significant section of the **Echo Park Valley** in the Dinosaur National Monument along the border of Utah and Colorado. A revived **Sierra Club** and other organizations pressured Congress to block the plan, which it did in 1956. Environmental issues were further brought to the public's attention by **Rachel Carson's** 1962 book *Silent Spring*, which vividly described how modern society was poisoning the Earth. Carson described the environmental impact of the agricultural pesticide **DDT**.

> **USING REASONING PROCESSES:**
> **COMPARISON**
>
> **Environmental Concerns in Different Time Periods**
>
> The environmental movement of the 1960s can be compared to the conservation movement of the late 1800s and early 1900s championed by Theodore Roosevelt. Both were connected to broader movements for change—the Progressive movement in the earlier period, and the New Left and the counterculture in the latter period. Both movements witnessed struggles over tactics and philosophy. In the early 1900s, the conservation movement advocated efficiency and "wise use" in regard to natural resources; this approach was challenged by the preservationism of John Muir (see page 271). In the more recent period, environmentalists have struggled with a variety of disputes—whether to engage in local action or focus on challenging corporate growth, how to engage with working-class and poor communities, and whether to work through political channels or to focus on building a mass movement.

Many participants in the environmental movement were veterans of the **New Left** and of the movement to end the **Vietnam War**; these New Left activists had developed a broad critique of corporate power and influence. In addition, many environmental activists were connected to the counterculture of the 1960s. The so-called **hippies** of the 1960s encouraged people to rid themselves of material possessions and live a more simple life. The environmental movement gained national exposure when the first **Earth Day** was celebrated in April 1970. That same year, the **Nixon administration** created the **Environmental Protection Agency** (EPA) to oversee regulatory and clean-up efforts and approved the **Clean Air Act** to set standards for air quality.

Love Canal and the Establishment of the Superfund

Calls for greater federal environmental regulation of the environment crystalized in the late 1970s, as evidence emerged of deadly toxic pollutants at **Love Canal**, a waterway near **Niagara Falls**, **New York**. The canal had been used in the 1940s and early 1950s by Hooker Chemical Company as a dumpsite for toxic chemicals. After housing was built on the site, residents complained for years of foul odors and black fluids emanating from the canal. More alarmingly, residents noticed unusually high levels of **birth defects** and **miscarriages**. Initially, the New York State Health Department disputed the assertion that the area was dangerous. Finally, federal authorities intervened. **President Jimmy Carter** declared a state of emergency at Love Canal in 1978. The disaster contributed to the creation of the federal **Superfund** program, within the **Environmental Protection Agency**, to investigate and clean up sites contaminated with hazardous substances. Love Canal was the first Superfund site.

The Dangers of Nuclear Energy and Three Mile Island

The environmental movement focused increasingly on the dangers of nuclear energy as the decade of the 1970s progressed (see more on the growth of nuclear energy, page 350). Groups such as the **Clamshell Alliance** in New England and the **Abalone Alliance** in California attracted thousands of activists. The movement gained strength in the wake of the worst nuclear-industry accident in U.S. history. In 1979, a partial meltdown of the core in one of the reactors at the **Three Mile Island** power plant in Pennsylvania resulted in the release of radioactive gases and radioactive materials into the environment. The accident was one of several that have dampened enthusiasm for nuclear energy. In 1986, a catastrophic accident occurred at a nuclear plant in **Chernobyl, Ukraine** (part of the Soviet Union at the time). An explosion led to the release of large quantities of radioactive material into the environment over much of the western portion of the Soviet Union and parts of Europe. More recently, in 2011, an earthquake and tsunami led to three nuclear meltdowns at the **Fukushima nuclear plant** in Japan. The Chernobyl and Fukushima disasters are the first and second worst, respectively, of over one hundred serious accidents or incidents at nuclear power plants around the world.

Topic 8.14 Society in Transition

A variety of demographic and social developments, along with anxieties about the Cold War and the threat of nuclear war, led to bitter debates in the 1960s and 1970s that divided many Americans. These debates revolved around culture, social and political values, family structure and sexual norms, and religion. Out of these debates, the gains of liberalism would come under attack from a resurgent conservative movement that showed signs of life in the 1960s and 1970s, but did not come to fruition until the last decades of the twentieth century.

A. The Conservative Response to Rapid Social and Economic Change

Conservatives perceived that society was under threat from many of the transformations that occurred in the post-war period. They grew concerned over several trends in the 1960s and 1970s: urban unrest, a perceived increase in juvenile delinquency, and new ideas about family structures.

The Origins of the Conservative Movement

The modern **conservative movement** came of age and became a powerful force with the victory of Ronald Reagan in the presidential election of 1980 (see more on the modern conservative movement, pages 365–368). However, the origins of this movement can be seen in the 1960s. Many Americans were dismayed by the street protests against the Vietnam War and the permissive attitudes of the counterculture. They also reacted negatively to the changing nature of the American family and the rise in divorce rates. In addition, many white southerners grew hostile toward the tactics and the gains of the civil rights movement.

As early as the 1960s, we begin to see divisions within the conservative movement that have persisted within the movement down to the present. On the one hand, we see the growth of an angry, paranoid conservatism, evident in the **"massive resistance"** movement in the South, the John Birch Society, and the 1968 candidacy of **George Wallace** for president. On the other hand, we see the growth of a more mainstream conservatism, evident in the influential magazine, *National Review*, edited by **William F. Buckley** and the candidacy of **Barry Goldwater** for president in 1964.

Young Americans for Freedom

Conservatives founded **Young Americans for Freedom** in the 1960s. YAF developed its founding document, the **Sharon Statement**, at a meeting at the estate of the conservative intellectual William F. Buckley in Sharon, Connecticut (1960). The organization brought together several strands of conservative thought—a correlation between free markets and "personal freedom," an emphasis on a muscular anti-Communism, and a push toward limiting the size and scope of government.

Barry Goldwater and the Origins of the "New Right"

Activists associated with Young Americans for Freedom became active in the campaign of Republican **Senator Barry Goldwater** for president in 1964. **President Lyndon Johnson** ended up winning reelection, capturing 61 percent of the popular vote. However, despite losing, the Goldwater campaign generated a great deal of grassroots enthusiasm. In many ways, Goldwater's campaign represented the beginning of the ascendency of a conservative movement that would become a force to reckon with later in the twentieth century (see pages 365–368).

B. The Decline of Public Trust in the 1970s

A series of events and trends in the 1970s—economic decline and dislocation, major political scandals, a sense of moral decay, and a perception of misguided foreign policy priorities—contributed to a decline in public trust and confidence in the government.

"Stagflation"

The economy of the United States had remained strong throughout the 1960s, despite the costs of the war in Vietnam. As the 1970s began, however, the economy began to contract. In the early 1970s, economists noted an unusual set of phenomena—both **unemployment** and **inflation** were at high levels (both over 6 percent). High unemployment is a sign of a stagnant economy but high inflation is usually a sign of an active economy. After all, it is consumer demand that pushes prices up. The incidence of both occurring simultaneously was dubbed **"stagflation."** Stagflation continued throughout the 1970s.

"Whip Inflation Now"

President Gerald Ford attempted to address the economic malaise of the 1970s, but his solutions struck the public as inadequate. Ford's most public initiative was the promotion of the **Whip Inflation Now** (WIN) campaign. The campaign encouraged people to curtail unnecessary spending and consumption. Supporters were encouraged to wear **"WIN" buttons**. After initially proposing a tax increase on corporations and the wealthy, he signed a series of tax and spending cuts into law (1975). The economy began to improve in 1976, but Ford's approval rating remained low and he lost his bid for reelection to the Democratic candidate, **Jimmy Carter**.

Foreign Policy "Failures" of the 1970s

President Jimmy Carter (1977–1981) faced a number of foreign policy challenges with mixed results. In one area, pursuing peace in the Middle East, Carter achieved a major victory (see page 349). When it came to the Panama Canal Zone (see below) and the Iran hostage crisis (1979–1981) (see page 349), the results of Carter's foreign policy were more mixed, and they provided an opening for Republicans to assert that Carter had left the United States in a weaker position.

The Panama Canal (1977)

President Jimmy Carter negotiated two treaties with Panama in 1977—the **Torrijos-Carter Treaties**, which turned the **Panama Canal Zone** over to **Panama**. One agreement, known as the **Panama Canal Treaty**, called for the United States to turn over control of the canal to Panama by December 31, 1999. The other agreement asserted that the canal shall remain neutral and open to shipping of all nations; if any country challenged this neutrality, the United States reserved the right to intervene. The treaties were ratified by the Senate in 1978. Many conservatives, notably Senators **Strom Thurmond** and **Jesse Helms**, were harshly critical of the treaties for surrendering direct control of a major strategic asset.

C. Clashing Political Values

The postwar period was marked by a number of political and social clashes between conservatives and liberals about the power of the presidency and the federal government, and about movements that sought to expand individual rights.

Watergate, the Undoing of President Nixon, and the Limits of Presidential Power

The **Watergate scandal** began in June 1972, when five men were caught breaking into the headquarters of the Democratic Party at the **Watergate Hotel** in Washington, D.C. Persistent reporting by **Carl Bernstein** and **Bob Woodward** of the *Washington Post* drew connections between the burglars and **President Richard Nixon's reelection committee** and ultimately the White House. When it became known that Nixon secretly taped his conversations in the White House Oval Office, investigators demanded that the tapes be turned over. Nixon argued that executive privilege allowed him to keep the tapes. In *United States v. Nixon* (1974), the Supreme Court ordered Nixon to turn over the tapes.

Also in 1974, the House Judiciary Committee voted in favor of three **articles of impeachment** against President Nixon—obstruction of justice, abuse of power, and contempt of Congress. The next step would have been for the entire House of Representatives to vote on whether to impeach Nixon. If the House had approved the articles of impeachment, the Senate would have tried Nixon; if found guilty of the articles of impeachment, he would have been removed from office. However, before the question of impeachment could be addressed by the entire House, **Nixon resigned**. The entire episode had the effect of eroding people's trust in governing institutions. This was reflected in opinion polls and in a decline in voter turnout rates in the last decades of the twentieth century.

Clashes over Equal Rights

The culture clashes that would come to epitomize the last decades of the twentieth century can be seen in the push to add an **Equal Rights Amendment** (ERA) to the Constitution in 1972. The ERA would have prohibited the abridgment of "equality of rights under the law…on account of sex" either by the federal government or by the state governments. The push for the ERA galvanized the **women's liberation movement** (see page 344). It also led to a conservative backlash against the proposal. Conservatives argued that passage of the amendment would destroy the traditional American family unit. The movement against the proposal was led by conservative activist **Phyllis Schlafly**. She organized a powerful coalition, urging "positive women" to embrace femininity. The amendment was approved by both the House and the Senate in 1972 but failed to get the required thirty-eight states to ratify it, even after the deadline for ratification had been moved forward to 1982. It therefore did not become part of the Constitution.

Clashing Views of Affirmative Action

The push for **affirmative action** grew out of the civil rights movement. Activists hoped not only to end segregation but also to take affirmative action to rectify past discrimination by taking race into consideration in hiring, college admissions, and other areas. In 1961, **President John F. Kennedy** issued an executive order mandating that projects using federal funds take "affirmative action" to make sure that employers do not discriminate based on race. In 1965, **President Lyndon Johnson** went further, mandating that federal contractors and subcontractors make efforts to hire "protected class, underutilized" candidates. Many public universities began taking race into consideration when looking at applicants. Some schools set aside a certain number of seats for underrepresented groups.

Affirmative action policies generated a great deal of resentment among some white applicants for university admission and for jobs. They felt they were being punished for wrongs done by others. The issue came to a head when an applicant to the University of California, Davis, School of Medicine, **Allan Bakke**, a white student, was denied admission. The school had set aside 16 percent of the places in each entering class for minority applicants. Bakke, arguing that he was discriminated against, sued and took the case to the Supreme Court. In *Bakke v. University of California* (1978), the Court decided that specific quotas for underrepresented minorities violated the equal protection clause of the **Fourteenth Amendment**. However, Justice Lewis Powell's decision asserted that race could be one of the many factors that universities may look at in the admissions process, since diversity in higher education was a "compelling interest."

D. Christian Fundamentalism and the Religious Right

The rapid growth of the Christian fundamentalist movement fueled a resurgence of the New Right. This fundamentalist movement started in churches but soon entered the political sphere, organizing opposition to liberal and progressive social trends.

Opposition to *Roe v. Wade*

The issue that propelled the cultural conservatives from the margins to prominence was abortion. In the wake of the 1973 ***Roe v. Wade*** decision, religious conservatives found their voice. The issue convinced evangelical Protestants to put aside their long-held suspicions of Catholicism and create a broad Christian conservative movement. The focus on abortion bore fruit for religious conservatives in 2022 with the overturning of *Roe v. Wade* by the Supreme Court (see page 376).

The "Moral Majority" and Focus on the Family

The religious and cultural wing of the **New Right** found voice in several grassroots organizations. The **"Moral Majority"** was founded by **Reverend Jerry Falwell**, a Southern Baptist pastor, in 1979. In the mid-1970s, Falwell embarked on a series of **"I Love America"** rallies. These rallies broke a traditional Baptist principle of separating religion from politics. Falwell asserted that this separation was at the heart of the moral decay that was afflicting America.

Focus on the Family was founded in 1977 by psychologist **James Dobson**. The organization is interdenominational, bridging the traditional divide between Catholics and Protestants. It promotes an abstinence-only approach to sex education, the reintroduction of prayer into the schools, and reinforcement of traditional gender roles. The organization has stood against the expansion of rights for gay, lesbian, bisexual, and transgendered people; it has been vocal in its opposition to same-sex marriage. Focus on the Family is one of the leading voices in the movement against abortion.

Topic 8.15 Subject to Debate

Assessing American and Soviet Actions in the Cold War

Many of our understandings of the Cold War were developed by American historians during its height in the 1950s and 1960s. As might be expected, these historians saw American actions in a positive light and Soviet actions in a negative light. "Our" side stood for democracy, freedom, and progress; "their" side stood for repression, aggression, and coercion. Since the fall of the Soviet Union in 1991, historians have reevaluated this standard narrative. Some historians have put renewed emphasis on covert operations by the United States during the Cold War, such as the 1954 CIA-backed coup in Iraq that deposed Mohammad Mosaddegh and installed the Shah. These covert operations complicate the story. In addition, historians have also looked at Soviet moves in a slightly different light. Stalin's occupation of Eastern Europe following World War II is still seen as an aggressive move, but some historians have begun to put his actions in a larger historical context. After all, perhaps the moves are less reprehensible when looked at in the context of the history of attacks on Russia that had come through Eastern Europe.

Evaluating American Communism

Historians of the Cold War period have revisited debates about the nature of the American Communist movement in the 1940s and 1950s. For many years, historians looked at Communist Party members as victims of an irrational witch-hunt. More recently, since the fall of the Soviet Union, a group of historians, led by Harvey Klehr and John Earl Haynes, have scoured old Soviet archives and found some damning evidence against the Communist Party in the United States. Klehr and Haynes have found, for instance, transcriptions that seem to implicate Julius Rosenberg in spying for the Soviet Union. Their findings have forced a reevaluation of the assumption that members of the Communist Party were innocent victims.

Avoiding Reductionism—1920s and 1950s

When writing history, beware of clichés. Mainstream media and popular memory often reduce a complex time period to a single phrase or image. When many of us hear the "Roaring Twenties," the first thing that pops into our heads might be the "jazz age." We think of *The Great Gatsby*, martinis, flappers, and speakeasies. But this image has become somewhat of a cliché, obscuring the complex societal tensions of the 1920s. Yes, people went to speakeasies, but they also joined Ku Klux Klan rallies. The more we read about the 1920s, the harder it becomes to reduce it to a catchphrase.

The same is true of the 1950s. For many Americans, the image of the 1950s can be reduced to the word "conformity." We look condescendingly at the naïve suburbanites of the decade, blithely watching bland television programs. However, as students of history, we should be wary of such easy generalizations. As in the 1920s, complex social factors were at work. Many trends in the 1950s flew in the face of conformity—the most obvious being the civil rights movement. The 1950s also saw the birth of the beat movement, the popularity of rock 'n' roll, and the beginnings of the folk music revival.

The Civil Rights Movement: "Top-Down" or "Grassroots"?

There has been much historical discussion about the origins of the civil rights movement. One key division in the discussion is between those who stress grassroots activism and those who focus on the actions of the government. Historians who favor a more "top-down" interpretation elevate the importance of powerful institutions—the courts, the police, elected officials—in shaping events. This top-down approach is the more traditional approach. Revisionist historians, many of whom come out of a New Left tradition, focus on the agency of ordinary people in shaping historical change. Of late, historians have looked at the interaction between the grassroots level and the halls of power. We see this at play with the Birmingham civil rights campaign in 1963. The campaign, which ignited a violent reaction from police (broadcast on the evening news), prompted the Kennedy and Johnson administrations to take action and to push for the 1964 Civil Rights Act. This act might not have been passed were it not for the violent events in Birmingham. And the act might not have been passed without presidential leadership, either.

The Nature of the Vietnam War

The legacy of the war in Vietnam has been hotly debated. Historians have argued about whether the conflict in Vietnam was essentially a civil war or an international Cold War struggle. One narrative sees the war as a rebellion by the indigenous Vietcong and its peasant supporters against an oppressive regime. A competing narrative sees the war as North Vietnam and China using savage tactics in attempting to impose an authoritarian regime on South Vietnam. If we accept the first scenario, then American intervention seems misguided and bound for failure. If we accept the second scenario, then American intervention seems entirely reasonable. A related question is whether the war was winnable. To some, the United States was fighting a hopeless war—additional years of extensive bombing would simply steel the resolve of the populace to resist the American occupation. To others, victory was both possible and within sight, but President Nixon abandoned the fight at just the wrong moment. Domestic political considerations and the Watergate scandal caused Nixon to make a hasty exit from Southeast Asia.

Debating Nixon

Historians have also debated the overall legacy of the Nixon presidency. In the popular imagination, the Watergate scandal looms large. However, historians point out, the scandal should not overshadow some of Nixon's real accomplishments, including promoting détente with China and the Soviet Union. Historians have also praised Nixon for avoiding the divisive social and religious issues that characterized subsequent Republican administrations. Other historians insist that Nixon's legacy is irreparably tarnished by the bombing of civilians in Southeast Asia.

Practice Multiple-Choice Questions

DIRECTIONS: Pick the letter that best answers the following questions.

Questions 1–3 refer to the following cartoon

(Note: In the cartoon, the figure on the left is intended to be Senator Joseph McCarthy; the figure on the right is intended to be President Dwight D. Eisenhower):

—Herblock, "Have a care, sir," *Washington Post*, 1954

1. The 1954 cartoon shown above makes the point that

    (A) Senator Joseph McCarthy and President Dwight D. Eisenhower successfully worked in tandem in the 1950s to slow the spread of Communism in the United States.

    (B) Senator Joseph McCarthy went too far when he accused President Dwight D. Eisenhower of sympathizing with the Communist movement.

    (C) Senator Joseph McCarthy had the foresight to guard America's borders from Communist aggression, but President Dwight D. Eisenhower failed to perceive threats to national security.

    (D) President Dwight D. Eisenhower's criticisms of Senator Joseph McCarthy's anti-Communist crusade were weak and ineffective.

2. The height of Senator Joseph McCarthy's power and influence coincided with

    (A) the wave of labor strikes immediately following World War II.

    (B) the Korean War.

    (C) the "massive resistance" campaign among white southerners.

    (D) the Cuban Missile Crisis.

3. The ideas expressed in the cartoon most directly reflect which of the following continuities in twentieth-century United States history?

    (A) Debates about the proper role of political parties

    (B) Debates about acceptable means for pursuing domestic goals

    (C) Debates about the relationship between the executive branch and the legislative branch

    (D) Debates about the role of the federal government in economic regulation

Questions 4–6 are based on the following passage.

"Now, I ask you to consider: if this is a firm, and if the Board of Regents are the board of directors, and if President Kerr in fact is the manager, then I'll tell you something: the faculty are a bunch of employees, and we're the raw material! But we're a bunch of raw material[s] that don't mean to have any process upon us, don't mean to be made into any product, don't mean to end up being bought by some clients of the University, be they the government, be they industry, be they organized labor, be they anyone! We're human beings!

"There is a time when the operation of the machine becomes so odious, makes you so sick at heart, that you can't take part; you can't even passively take part, and you've got to put your bodies upon the gears and upon the wheels, upon the levers, upon all the apparatus, and you've got to make it stop. And you've got to indicate to the people who run it, to the people who own it, that unless you're free, the machine will be prevented from working at all!"

—Mario Savio, "Sit-in Address" (excerpt),
the University of California at Berkeley, 1964

4. The address by Mario Savio, above, is an important text in which of the following movements?

    (A) The migration to the Sunbelt
    (B) The New Left
    (C) The labor movement
    (D) The New Right

5. Which of the following trends in the 1960s does the above speech best reflect?

    (A) Conservatives, fearing juvenile delinquency and challenges to the traditional family, promoted their own values and ideology.
    (B) Artists and writers increasingly rejected political activity, turning instead to more abstract forms of expression.
    (C) Groups on the left assailed liberals, claiming they did too little to transform the racial and economic status quo at home.
    (D) Working-class activists rebelled against unresponsive unions and took militant direct action against employers.

6. Which of the following economic or demographic shifts is most closely related to the movement that Mario Savio's speech exemplified?

    (A) The growth of employment opportunities in heavy industry
    (B) The decline of the family farm and the rise of corporate agriculture
    (C) The spread of social mobility and the expansion of higher education
    (D) The increased visibility of immigrant communities in major urban areas

Questions 7–8 refer to the following excerpt.

"The pursuit of this widened war has narrowed domestic welfare programs, making the poor, white and Negro, bear the heaviest burdens both at the front and at home.... It is estimated that we spend $322,000 for each enemy we kill, while we spend in the so-called war on poverty in America only about $53.00 for each person classified as 'poor.'... We have escalated the war in Viet Nam and deescalated the skirmish against poverty. It challenges the imagination to contemplate what lives we could transform if we were to cease killing."

—Martin Luther King Jr.,
"The Casualties of War in Vietnam," speech (excerpt), 1967

7. The speech was written most directly in response to which of the following?

   (A) The refusal of the federal government to desegregate the military
   (B) The failure of the Great Society to significantly reduce poverty in the United States
   (C) The focus of the Republican Party on international issues at the expense of domestic issues
   (D) Frustrations over the inability of the civil rights movement to persuade Congress to pass meaningful civil rights legislation

8. The excerpt reflects which of the following trends?

   (A) The growth of the antiwar movement in the 1960s as the Vietnam War escalated
   (B) The refusal of protest movements in the 1960s to draw connections between economic and foreign policy issues
   (C) The success of anti-Communist propaganda in silencing opposition to government policies
   (D) The shift in tactics of the civil rights movement from civil disobedience to violent resistance

Answers and Explanations

1. **(D)** The cartoon is suggesting that President Eisenhower did not take a strong enough stand in opposition to the tactics of Senator Joseph McCarthy. "McCarthyism" is the name given to the extreme anti-Communist movement in the early 1950s. Senator McCarthy became the central figure in this movement. In 1950 he announced that he had a list of "known Communists" who had infiltrated the State Department. This and similar claims, mostly baseless, created a name for McCarthy and set the stage for a host of measures to halt this perceived threat. Congress established committees to investigate Communist Party infiltration in different sectors of society. Eisenhower walked a fine line in regard to McCarthy. On the one hand, he found McCarthy's tactics reprehensible. He once said of McCarthy, "I just won't get down in the gutter with that man." However, he also welcomed the benefits that McCarthyism brought to the Republican Party. The cartoon notes Eisenhower's reluctance to challenge McCarthy publicly.

2. **(B)** Senator Joseph McCarthy had the greatest influence during the period of the Korean War. Often, in American history, periods of war opened up political space for more extreme, jingoistic political movements. This can be seen in the anti-German sentiment that accompanied World War I. In 1950, the year the Korean War began, McCarthy gained a great deal of publicity for himself by announcing that he had a list of employees in the State Department who were also members of the Communist Party. The war ended in 1953; by 1954, political leaders were publicly challenging Senator McCarthy.

3. **(B)** The differences between McCarthy and Eisenhower reflect an ongoing debate about the acceptable means of pursing domestic goals. These debates can be seen in differences over the tactics of the "Red Scare" of the 1920s, in debates over President Franklin Roosevelt's "Court-packing plan" in the 1930s, and in debates about the Patriot Act in the 2000s, which allowed the National Security Agency, the Federal Bureau of Investigation, and other government agencies to surveil U.S. citizens without a warrant. In many cases, political leaders might agree about broad goals—challenging the influence of radical groups, advancing the New Deal agenda, eliminating domestic terrorism—but might disagree on whether specific means are acceptable.

4. **(B)** The address by Mario Savio is an important text in the history of the New Left. Savio was part of the Free Speech Movement at the University of California at Berkeley. The movement grew on campus after the administration banned political activity on campus. In the fall of 1964, student activists, some of whom had participated in the Freedom Riders and worked to register African-American voters in the South in the Freedom Summer project, set up information tables on campus and were soliciting donations for civil rights causes. The university allowed only the campus's Democratic and Republican clubs to engage in such practices. The demonstrations, which continued throughout the 1964–1965 school year, were part of the growing New Left movement. Student demonstrations in the 1960s were not in opposition to the Vietnam War only, but the war became the focus of much of the campus activism.

5. **(C)** The growth of the New Left in the 1960s represented a broader trend in the 1960s: groups on the left increasingly criticized liberals, claiming they did too little to transform the racial and economic status quo in the United States. In many ways, the 1960s represented a high point in American liberalism. The Supreme Court, under Chief Justice Earl Warren, issued a host of decisions moving the legal system in a more liberal direction, and President Lyndon Johnson's "Great Society" programs expanded the nation's social-welfare safety net and extended basic civil rights to African Americans. However, members of the New Left and the Black Power movement argued that more fundamental changes in society were needed.

6. **(C)** The growth of the Free Speech Movement and the New Left in general occurred in the context of

the spread of social mobility and the expansion of higher education. Campus-based organizations thrived at a time when the size of the college-aged demographic ballooned as baby boomers reached their upper teens. In addition, the growth of the middle class contributed to a large increase in the number of students enrolled in four-year universities in the 1960s.

7. **(B)** By 1967, Martin Luther King Jr. and members of the civil rights movement were growing increasingly frustrated by the lack of progress being made by the government in regard to reducing poverty in America. King came to make explicit connections between the war in Vietnam and the failures of domestic social programs. In 1967, he said in a speech: "The promises of the Great Society have been shot down on the battlefields of Vietnam." King's antiwar stance created a major rift between him and President Johnson.

8. **(A)** Martin Luther King Jr. was certainly not alone in his opposition to the war in Vietnam. By the late 1960s, a vocal and active antiwar movement developed in the United States. As the war dragged on, and as the United States suffered more casualties, many Americans began to question the wisdom of American policies in Vietnam. The fact that images from the war were transmitted into people's living rooms also contributed to antiwar sentiment. United States involvement in Vietnam continued until 1973, when President Richard Nixon withdrew the last American troops. In 1975, the government of South Vietnam was defeated and, in 1976, it united with North Vietnam as the Socialist Republic of Vietnam.

11

Period 9: 1980–Present Political and Foreign Policy Adjustments in a Globalized World

TIMELINE

1976	Election of Jimmy Carter
1978	Panama Canal Treaty
	Camp David Accords
1979	Three Mile Island nuclear accident
	Formation of the Moral Majority
	Soviet invasion of Afghanistan
	Iranian students seize U.S. embassy; hold staff hostage for over a year
1980	United States boycotts Olympic games held in Moscow
	Election of Ronald Reagan
1981	Release of American hostages held in Iran
	Reagan fires striking air traffic controllers
1984	Reelection of Ronald Reagan
1985	Founding of the Democratic Leadership Council
1987	Iran-Contra hearings
1988	Election of George H. W. Bush
1989	Collapse of Communism in Central and Eastern Europe
1991	Operation Desert Storm
	Collapse of the Soviet Union
1992	Election of Bill Clinton
1993	Fighting in Mogadishu, Somalia
	Ratification of the North American Free Trade Agreement (NAFTA)
1994	House Republicans issue the "Contract with America"
	Both houses of Congress shift from Democratic to Republican control
1995	Peace treaty signed in Ohio between Serbian, Bosnian, and Croatian leaders
1996	Welfare Reform Act
	Reelection of Bill Clinton
1998	Impeachment of President Clinton
1999	NATO bombing of Serbia in response to violence in Kosovo
2000	Election of George W. Bush

2001	Terrorist attacks on the World Trade Center and the Pentagon
	Passage of the Patriot Act
	United States overthrow of the Taliban in Afghanistan
2003	Creation of the Department of Homeland Security
	Operation Iraqi Freedom
2007	Beginning of Subprime Mortgage Crisis and Great Recession
2008	Troubled Asset Relief Program (TARP)
	Election of Barack Obama
2009	Escalation of United States drone attacks against suspected terrorist targets
	Birth of the Tea Party movement
2010	Passage of Affordable Care Act
	Dodd-Frank Act
2011	Raid and killing of Osama bin Laden
	Repeal of "Don't Ask, Don't Tell" policy
	Beginning of Occupy Wall Street protests
2012	Reelection of Barack Obama
2013	Birth of the Black Lives Matter movement
	Edward Snowden reveals secret National Security Agency surveillance programs
2015	*Obergefell v. Hodges* decision establishes marriage equality
	Joint Comprehensive Plan of Action (Iran nuclear deal)
2016	Election of Donald Trump
2019	First impeachment of President Donald Trump
	Beginning of the COVID-19 pandemic
2020	Widespread racial justice protests
	Election of Joseph Biden
2021	United States Capitol attack
	Second impeachment of President Donald Trump
2022	Russian invasion of Ukraine
	Dobbs v. Jackson Women's Health Organization decision overturns *Roe v. Wade*
2024	*Trump v. United States* decision expands presidential immunity
	Reelection of Donald Trump

Topics in Period 9

In this chapter, you will learn about:
- → Topic 9.1 Contextualizing Period 9
- → Topic 9.2 Reagan, conservatism, and partisan divisions
- → Topic 9.3 The end of the Cold War
- → Topic 9.4 A changing economy
- → Topic 9.5 Migration and immigration, 1980 to the present
- → Topic 9.6 Defining America's role in the world in the twenty-first century
- → Topic 9.7 Subject to debate

Topic 9.1 Contextualizing Period 9

> The United States has had to adapt to a changing world in the late twentieth and early twenty-first centuries. The world of the recent past has been filled with challenges and possibilities. The United States faces divisions at home along ideological and cultural lines and has been compelled to adjust its foreign policy to meet changing global dynamics. The United States has also had to adapt to new technological and scientific advances and to economic globalization.

The late twentieth century saw the growth of a powerful conservative movement. There had been signs of a growing conservative movement in the United States since the 1964 campaign of Barry Goldwater. This movement celebrated the election of Ronald Reagan in 1980 and has been successful in redefining the terms of political debate in the late twentieth and early twenty-first centuries. Recent decades have seen an intensification of partisan divisions—from the "Contract with America" in the 1990s to the presidency of Donald Trump (2017–2021, 2025–present). The era has also seen a series of adjustments, in both domestic and foreign policy, in the aftermath of the terrorist attacks of 2001.

Topic 9.2 Reagan, Conservatism, and Partisan Divisions

During the 1980s, a renewed conservative movement rose in prominence and achieved several political goals. This movement rejected liberal views on the role of the government and embraced "traditional" social values. It continued to exert influence in regard to public discourse over the following decades.

A. The Ascendancy of the New Right

The conservative movement achieved electoral successes in the 1980s, 1990s, 2000s, and 2010s and witnessed the implementation of some of its policy and political goals. The growth of the New Right reflected a variety of economic, political, and social concerns. The movement achieved notable victories in terms of lowering taxes and deregulating business. However, this period also made evident the limits of conservative reform—many of the government programs it sought to curtail or eliminate enjoyed broad public support. In the decades following the administration of President Ronald Reagan, the New Right has continued to exert influence over the political process.

Anatomy of the New Right

The **conservative movement** has always had three distinct tendencies that sometimes have worked in unison and sometimes have been in conflict. First, there are **Cold War conservatives**, focused on containing or rolling back Communist regimes abroad. In the post–Cold War era, interventionists have argued for continued U.S. military actions abroad, notably in the Middle East. The second tendency is made up of the **pro-business economic conservatives**. These conservatives argue for lower corporate taxes, deregulation, and an economic atmosphere friendly to the priorities of big business.

The third tendency within the conservative movement is the **religious and cultural wing**. It is this group that has had the greatest grassroots support, fueling electoral victories for **Ronald Reagan**, **George H. W. Bush**, **George W. Bush**, and **Donald Trump**. This movement gained steam as tradition-minded people grew frustrated with what they saw as the excesses of the counterculture of the 1960s. They railed against the women's liberation movement for challenging traditional gender roles and against the gay liberation movement. Many conservatives had ambivalent feelings about the civil rights movement. On the one hand, some rejected the assumptions and goals of the movement outright. On the other hand, many conservatives accepted the overall goals of racial justice and enfranchisement, but rejected the more militant and, at times, violent elements within the civil rights movement. Finally, the public nature of illegal drug use in the 1960s also angered many cultural conservatives.

The New Right and the Election of Ronald Reagan

The **New Right** achieved a remarkable victory in the election of **Ronald Reagan** in 1980. Reagan had been a well-known actor in B-movies from the 1930s to the 1960s and was president of the Screen Actors Guild in the 1940s and 1950s. He became increasingly interested in politics, first as a **New Deal Democrat**. In the 1950s, he grew increasingly **anti-Communist** and became an active Republican in the 1960s. He served as governor of California from 1967 to 1975.

The election of the conservative Ronald Reagan in 1980 has been seen by many historians as a repudiation of the political and social movements of the 1960s. Reagan's victory can, in part, be attributed to more immediate causes. **President Jimmy Carter** was seen as ineffective in not securing the quick release of hostages held at the American embassy in Tehran by Iranian militants (see page 349). However, Reagan projected a sense of hope and optimism that promised to move the United States beyond the scandals and doubts of the 1970s. He promised a new "morning in America," and Americans listened. Reagan's tenure as president saw a tremendous military build up and the beginning of the end for the **Soviet Union** and the Communist Bloc, which could not match U.S. arms spending. He also gave voice to the rising New Right movement.

Reaganomics

President Ronald Reagan advanced a series of economic initiatives that bear the name **"Reaganomics."** He was not the first conservative politician to advance such policies—Reaganomics brings to mind **Herbert Hoover's** approach to the **Great Depression**. Reagan supported economic policies that favored big business. He based this on a belief in the effectiveness of **supply-side economics**. This approach to the economy stressed stimulating the supply side of the economy—manufacturers, banks, insurance corporations. The idea is that if there is growth in the supply side, there will be general economic growth, and the benefits of that growth will reach everyone. The alternative approach is to stimulate the demand side—consumers. **Demand-side economics** would emphasize government policies designed to increase workers' wages and would expand social programs such as welfare and unemployment benefits. As a believer in supply-side economics, Reagan implemented policies he thought would stimulate business. He cut taxes for corporations and greatly reduced regulations on industry. Reagan was a staunch proponent of deregulation. He and his secretary of the interior, **James Watt**, were criticized by environmental advocates for dismantling or weakening much of the environmental legislation of the 1970s.

"Contract with America" (1994)

During the administration of **President Bill Clinton** (1993–2001), the **Republican Party**, energized by conservative activists, made significant gains in both the House of Representatives and the Senate. The opposition party traditionally does well in the congressional elections that occur between presidential elections. In the 1994 midterm elections, the Republican Party gained control of both the House and the Senate. The Republicans had not controlled the House since 1954. House Republicans, led by minority leader **Newt Gingrich**, had signed and publicly issued the **"Contract with America"** six weeks before the 1994 election. It was a call to arms for Republicans and a specific blueprint for legislative action. The document called for action on a number of fronts, such as tougher anti-crime measures, tort reform, and welfare reform. Many of the House's initiatives died in the Senate, some were vetoed by President Clinton, some were implemented, and some were reworked by both parties before being passed. The success of the Republican Party in 1994 put President Clinton on the defensive in his dealings with Congress.

The Impeachment of President Clinton

Impeachment proceedings against **President Bill Clinton** constituted an important turning point in the deterioration of relations between the two main political parties. The proceedings demonstrated the growing strength of the more conservative elements within the Republican Party. Those elements doggedly pursued evidence of scandal relating to President Clinton. During Clinton's first term, Senate Republicans appointed **Kenneth Starr** as an independent council to investigate the Clintons' participation in a failed and fraudulent real estate project in Arkansas that dated back to 1978, when Bill Clinton was governor. Starr pursued the so-named **Whitewater case** relentlessly, but never tied the Clintons to the fraud.

President Clinton, however, was not able to avoid implication in a more salacious scandal. Clinton was accused of having an affair with **Monica Lewinsky,** a White House intern. Clinton denied the accusations publicly and also before a federal grand jury. When Clinton was later forced to admit the affair, Congressional Republicans felt they had evidence of impeachable crimes—**lying to a grand jury** and **obstruction of justice**. Clinton was impeached by the House of Representatives in 1998. He was found "not guilty" by the Senate (two-thirds are needed for conviction). The entire incident reflected the tense relationship between the two major political parties. Clinton emerged from the affair largely unscathed. Many Americans disapproved of his personal misconduct, but resented the attempt by Republicans to remove him from office.

The Election of 2000

The **2000 election for president** reflected political divisions in the United States and was one of the most contentious in American history. As votes were counted in **Florida**, it became evident that the tally was split almost evenly between the Democratic candidate, **Vice President Al Gore**, and the Republican candidate, **George W. Bush**. This would not have been such a problem beyond Florida but, based on the electoral votes of the other forty-nine states, neither candidate had 270 electoral votes, the number needed to be declared the winner, without Florida's electoral votes. After several weeks of legal wrangling in Florida, the **U.S. Supreme Court** reversed an order by the Florida Supreme Court to do a hand recount of several counties in Florida. The decision in *Bush v. Gore* was five to four. By overturning a state decision, the conservative members of the Court broke with their tendency in the 1990s to assert the power of states within the federal system. Critics contend that the partisan concerns of the justices might have shaped the decision. The Supreme Court ended the dispute with Bush slightly ahead of Gore in Florida, securing the presidency for Bush.

> **USING HISTORICAL THINKING SKILLS:**
> **MAKING CONNECTIONS**
>
> **Impeachment—1868, 1998, 2019, 2021**
>
> Impeachment is not synonymous with removal from office. Impeachment is the act of bringing charges against the president (or other federal official). It is parallel to indictment in the criminal court system. After impeachment by the House, the Senate conducts a trial, based on the charges listed in the "articles of impeachment." If found guilty of these charges, the president is removed from office. Three presidents have been impeached—President Andrew Johnson (1868) (see page 200), President Bill Clinton (1998) (see pages 366–367), and President Donald Trump (2019 and 2021) (see page 369 and page 370). All three avoided removal from office. President Richard Nixon resigned before the House could formally impeach him (1974).

The Presidency of George W. Bush

The **New Right** achieved a major victory with the election of **George W. Bush** in 2000. Bush, the son of the forty-first president, **George H. W. Bush**, was governor of Texas and had little national exposure. He ushered the country through the aftermath of one of the most traumatic events on American soil since the Civil War—the **terrorist attacks on 2001** (see pages 388–389). By the end of Bush's second term, public approval of his presidency was at a historic low, hampering the chances of the Republicans to hold on to the White House.

"No Child Left Behind"

One of President George W. Bush's major accomplishments was the **No Child Left Behind Act** (2002), which called for a series of reforms in public education. The law extended the reach of the federal government into education—traditionally a state responsibility. The law mandated that states set learning standards, that students attain "proficiency" in reading and math by 2014, and that teachers be "highly qualified" in the subject area. The law allowed students to transfer to other schools if they were attending a school that fell short of meeting new guidelines. The law also allowed the state to take over schools and school districts that did not meet new guidelines. The program was criticized by many states for its lack of funding to help schools reach these new goals. Also, many educators questioned the increased reliance on standardized tests in judging schools and school districts. The law was later replaced by the **Every Child Succeeds Act** (2015), which gave states flexibility in developing systems of standards and accountability.

B. The Deepening of Partisanship in the Twenty-first Century

Many of the political and cultural divisions that characterized public debate during the last decades of the twentieth century persisted, and intensified, in the twenty-first.

The Election of Barack Obama (2008)

The election of 2008 resulted in a profound milestone in American history—the election of the first African American to the presidency. Such an event was virtually unthinkable a generation earlier. As late as the 1960s, **Jim Crow segregation** was still the law of the land throughout the South and informal, de facto segregation existed throughout the nation. The civil rights movement challenged and altered many of these practices, but racist attitudes persisted among large segments of the population. **Barack Obama's** victory was the result of a series of factors. First, his campaign successfully held off a strong challenge for the Democratic nomination by **Senator Hillary Clinton**. Clinton's bid for the nomination, if successful, could have resulted in a different historic milestone—the first female president in the United States. The Obama campaign was able to harness the power of the internet, as well as the candidate's charisma, to build a large base.

The Rise of the Tea Party Movement

The election of Barack Obama to the presidency in 2008 and his reelection in 2012 generated a vocal opposition movement known as the **Tea Party**, harkening back to the American colonists' action against perceived British tyranny. To some extent the movement was a creation of the media, heavily promoted by the **Fox News Channel**, and to some extent it represented a grassroots sense of discontent with big government.

The Election of Donald Trump (2016)

The election of **Donald Trump** to the presidency in 2016 demonstrated the continued strength of the conservative movement. At the same time, the candidacy and presidency of Trump opened up fissures within the conservative movement that, in turn, have led to much soul-searching in regard to the direction of the Republican Party. Divisions around issues of immigration and trade developed as more mainstream Republicans began to grow uneasy with the anti-establishment, populist wing of the party.

Trump focused his campaign speeches on immigration, border security, and trade deals. The phrase, "Build That Wall," frequently chanted at his rallies, reflected his ability to tap into concerns over the effects of large-scale immigration. His message resonated with many Americans who felt the economic impact of the loss of manufacturing jobs (see page 384). Trump's blunt, unpolished, and aggressive style of speaking appealed to many voters. He was perceived as "speaking his mind," unencumbered by what his supporters often called **"political correctness"** or **"wokeness."** At the same time, many voters—Democrats and Republicans—were stunned by some of his comments, including comments from a 2005 recording of Trump, released weeks before the 2016 election, that seemed to excuse sexual harassment of women. Such comments, however, did not seem to diminish his support.

In the general election, Trump ran against the Democratic candidate, **Hillary Clinton**, who was the first woman to head the presidential ticket of one of the major political parties. Trump carried enough states to win a majority of the electoral college. For the second time since 2000, the winner of the electoral college vote, Trump, failed to win the overall popular vote.

The First Presidential Term of Donald Trump

President Donald Trump's first tenure in office was marked by both missteps and accomplishments. His unorthodox approach to governing was welcomed by many of his supporters, who hoped he would shake up the political establishment of Washington, D.C. His attempts to undo the **Affordable Care Act** failed to win congressional support. Trump pushed for a temporary travel ban on individuals coming into the United States from primarily Muslim countries; after setbacks in the court system, the Supreme Court (2018) permitted a version of the ban to go into effect (see page 388). At the end of 2017, the Trump administration achieved its first major legislative victory with a major **overhaul of the tax code**, enacting major cuts in corporate taxes and significant reductions in the tax rates of individual taxpayers. In addition, he issued several executive orders rolling back **environmental regulations** put in place during the **Obama administration** and undoing several measures designed to regulate the financial industry. Trump was able to reshape the ideological balance of the Supreme Court by appointing three conservative judges to the Court: Neil Gorsuch, Brett Kavanaugh, and Amy Coney Barrett.

The First Impeachment of President Trump

In 2019, the Democratic-controlled House of Representatives passed **articles of impeachment** against **President Donald Trump**, making him the third president in United States history to be impeached (see box, page 367). Impeachment grew out of the long-simmering tensions between the two major political parties. The Democrats accused him of putting his personal political interests above those of the country by enlisting Ukraine to announce investigations into a political rival.

The Election of Joe Biden (2020) and the U.S. Capitol Attack

The election of 2020 witnessed the Democratic candidate, **Joe Biden,** defeating the sitting president, **Donald Trump.** The election took place during first year of the COVID-19 pandemic (see page 379) and amidst ongoing protests around race and policing (see pages 378–379). This was the first time a sitting president was not reelected since 1992. Biden had been a long-serving senator from Delaware (1973–2009) before serving as vice president under **President Barack Obama** (2009–2017).

The general election saw the highest voter turnout (over 66 percent) since 1900. Both Biden and Trump received more votes than any previous presidential candidate. The election was marked by accusations of voter **fraud** by Trump and his supporters and by an unprecedented refusal by the sitting president to accept the results of the election. In the weeks after the election, the president and his campaign, aided by proxies, political allies, and many of his supporters, attempted to overturn the election results. Trump's claims were refuted in the mainstream media as well as by government entities. Trump's **Attorney General William Barr** said that U.S. attorneys and FBI agents found no evidence of substantial fraud. Over sixty lawsuits were filed in several states to challenge the outcome of the election, but none were successful. In the aftermath of the election in at least nineteen Republican-controlled states, political leaders cited these assertions of fraud as a rationale for changing voting procedures. Critics argue that the changes are designed to restrict access to voting by groups more likely to vote Democratic, including African Americans.

The efforts of President Trump and his supporters to overturn the results of the 2020 election culminated in a rally in Washington, D.C., on January 6, 2021, the day that Congress, with **Vice President Mike Pence** presiding, would count the electoral votes and formalize Joe Biden's victory. Following the rally, approximately 2,000 to 2,500 of the protestors marched to the Capitol. Many participated in an attack on the Capitol building, breaking through police lines. Members of Congress and Pence were evacuated from the building. After delays, additional law enforcement officers and National Guard troops were deployed to the Capitol. After the building had been cleared of protestors, Pence and Congress reconvened and certified the electoral count in the early hours of January 7.

Aftermath of the Capitol Attack: Impeachment and Immunity

In the aftermath of the January 2021 **Capitol attack** (see page 369), Democratic members of Congress took action to try to hold Trump accountable for his role in inciting the violence at the Capitol. On January 13, the House of Representatives adopted one **article of impeachment** against President Trump—**incitement of insurrection**. Supporters of the measure argued that Trump incited the January 2021 Capitol attack through his campaign to overturn the results of the 2020 election and through his words at the **"Save America" rally** in Washington, D.C., earlier on the day of the attack, including his statement, "And if you don't fight like hell, you're not going to have a country anymore." Trump's lawyers insisted those words were meant figuratively, not literally. The Senate trial occurred in February 2021, after Trump had left office. The vote was 57–43 in favor of convicting Trump, short of the two-thirds necessary for conviction. Seven Republicans voted with the fifty Democrats and independents.

In 2023, federal prosecutors completed an investigation into the aftermath of the 2020 election (including the Capitol attack) and presented their findings to a grand jury, which indicted Trump on four counts related to election interference. The case was quickly addressed by the Supreme Court, which issued a decision, in *Trump v. United States* (2024), granting presidents broad immunity from criminal prosecution. The Court ruled that a president has **"absolute immunity"** from criminal prosecution in regard to acts carried out under the president's "core constitutional powers." Other, non-core, "official acts" are subject to "presumptive immunity," and non-official acts are not subject to immunity.

The Presidency of Joe Biden

Several important accomplishments and several major setbacks characterized **President Joe Biden's** single term in office. He helped to usher in a "soft landing" for the U.S. economy following the economic crisis associated with the COVID-19 pandemic (see page 379). The unemployment rate reached a 50-year low during his term as hourly wages increased. In addition, Biden signed into law the $1 trillion **Infrastructure Investment and Jobs Act** (2021), a historic investment in the nation's crumbling infrastructure. The **Inflation Reduction Act** (2022) was a budget reconciliation measure that included provisions to lower prescription drug costs and to address domestic energy production and climate change. Following the Russian invasion of Ukraine (2022), Biden initiated sanctions against Russia and pushed for military support for Ukraine (see page 394). The chaotic exit of United States forces from Afghanistan in 2021 was a setback for the Biden administration (see page 389). Biden's approval rating fell as his term progressed, fueled by concerns about his age and fitness, along with high inflation rates in 2022 and 2023.

The Reelection of Donald Trump (2024)

President Joe Biden initially sought reelection in 2024. Some supporters expressed concern about his age (he would have begun a second term at the age of 82) and fitness for office. These concerns were amplified by the Republican nominee, former president **Donald Trump** (himself 78 at the time of the 2024 election). Following pressure from several leading Democratic leaders, Biden dropped out of the race in July 2024. He was quickly replaced on the Democratic ticket by **Vice-President Kamala Harris**. The Trump campaign focused on concerns about inflation, crime, and the flow of migrants into the United States. He won the election in November, turning several swing states that had voted Democratic four years earlier. He is the first president to serve two nonconsecutive terms since Grover Cleveland (1885–1889 and 1893–1897).

C. Reducing "Big Government": Rhetoric and Reality

During the late twentieth and early twenty-first centuries, Republican leaders often declared their intention to bring the era of "big government" to an end. However, Republican administrations witnessed an increase in the size and scope of the government, as it became evident that eliminating or reducing popular programs would be politically dangerous.

The Expansion of Medicare and Medicaid

Since the creation of **Medicare** and **Medicaid** in 1965, as part of President Lyndon Johnson's "Great Society" (see Topic 8.9), both programs have expanded. Medicare provides health insurance to those over sixty-five years old, who have worked and paid into the system, and to those with disabilities. Medicaid is a government insurance program for low-income people. Both programs have, over the years, added conditions and situations that would qualify for coverage. In addition, as people live longer—the **"graying of America"**—the costs to the Medicare program have increased despite conservative efforts to reduce the program. In the 1980s, **President Ronald Reagan** led the effort to pass a Social Security reform bill designed to ensure the long-term solvency of the program and supported the expansion of the Medicare program to protect the elderly and disabled against "catastrophic" health costs.

Growth of the Federal Deficit

The pro-business economic policies of **President Ronald Reagan**, labeled **"Reaganomics"** (see page 366), had mixed results. By cutting corporate taxes and taxes on wealthy individuals, he cut government revenues. However, at the same time, he increased spending on armaments. This combination of increased spending and decreased revenues led to a doubling of the **national debt** from around $900 billion in 1980 to over $2 trillion in 1986. A large debt is a problem because it requires large interest payments. By 1988, the interest on the national debt had reached 14 percent of total annual government expenditures. This huge debt has hindered economic growth to some degree since and forced future administrations to make difficult decisions about keeping the debt under control.

D. Debates over the Scope of Government and International Trade

A number of heated policy debates have occurred during the period from 1980 to the present about the role of the government social safety net, regulation of the financial system, and international trade.

NAFTA and the Push Toward Free Trade

A heated debate occurred in the 1990s over free trade and the globalization of the world economy. **President Bill Clinton** broke with organized labor and environmental groups by embracing the **North American Free Trade Agreement** (NAFTA). NAFTA was ratified by Congress in 1993. The agreement eliminated all trade barriers and tariffs among the **United States**, **Canada**, and **Mexico**. NAFTA was the subject of much controversy when it was promoted by President Clinton. Free-trade supporters promised global prosperity as more nations participated in the global economy. Opponents worried that nations would no longer be able to implement environmental regulations, ensure workers' rights, or protect fledgling industries from foreign competition. Clinton's championing of NAFTA represents his conscious decision to try to move the Democratic Party away from its liberal traditions and toward a more centrist approach.

The General Agreement on Trade and Tariffs (GATT)

The **General Agreement of Trade and Tariffs** is an international trade agreement that sought to encourage countries to participate in the global economy by reducing barriers to trade. GATT had existed since 1948, but the 1994 agreement

> **USING REASONING PROCESSES:**
> **CONTINUITY AND CHANGE**
>
> **The Democratic Party From Johnson to Clinton**
>
> Between the 1960s and the 1990s, the approach of the Democratic Party changed on several important issues. President Bill Clinton moved away from the liberalism of President Lyndon B. Johnson's Great Society program. Where Johnson (1963–1969) created and expanded different welfare programs, Clinton (1993–2001) moved to "end welfare as we know it," ending federal guarantees and allowing states to establish their own rules, including "workfare" requirements (see page 372). Clinton frustrated Republicans, especially his opponent in the 1996 election, Bob Dole, by moving in a rightward direction. His embrace of NAFTA, welfare reform, and criminal justice reform stole Republican thunder and assured his reelection. The more liberal wing of the Democratic Party and its more moderate wing continue to battle for the soul of the party.

was far-reaching in its commitment to free trade. The 1994 GATT agreement called into being the **World Trade Organization** (1995), which has served as a global trade referee, committed to reducing barriers to trade. Issues of globalization and free trade have inspired vocal protests. The legacy of GATT and other free-trade agreements continues to shape political debates in the twenty-first century. Some political leaders blame the decline of industrial jobs in the Midwest on these agreements; others cite the ready availability of inexpensive consumer products as evidence of the success of the free-trade ethos (see more on the deindustrialization of America, page 384).

Challenges to Globalization

President Bill Clinton's embrace of **NAFTA** was part of a broader push toward the removal of trade barriers. Proponents of **globalization** argue that the elimination of trade barriers will lower prices of products and stimulate the global economy. However, the movement toward free trade has generated much debate. Labor organizations argue that eliminating trade barriers will lead to the loss of American manufacturing jobs as businesses gravitate to countries where the going wages are the lowest. Also, environmentalists worry that free-trade treaties will prevent the participating countries from enacting strong environmental protections. These opponents came together in **Seattle**, Washington, in November 1999 to protest at a meeting of the **World Trade Organization**, an international body charged with reducing trade barriers.

Changes in the Welfare System

In 1996, **President Bill Clinton** adopted one of the planks of the Republican **"Contract with America"** by **ending welfare as a federal program** and shifting its administration to the state level. Clinton's embrace of welfare reform shocked many liberal Democrats. The Democratic Party had pushed for federal entitlement programs since the New Deal of President Roosevelt in the 1930s. Clinton perceived that many Americans were growing weary of programs that cost taxpayers money and did not seem to lessen poverty. Some Americans argued that welfare fostered a sense of dependency among recipients of welfare payments and stifled individual initiative. The reform required welfare recipients to begin work after two years—a stipulation known as **"workfare."**

Toward Health Care Reform

One of **President Bill Clinton's** first major domestic policy initiatives was reform of the country's **health care system**. Clinton put forth the idea of a federal health insurance plan that would provide subsidized insurance to many of the thirty-nine million uncovered Americans, and would, according to the plan, bring down health insurance costs for everyone. The president's wife, **Hillary Clinton**, chaired a task force on the issue. The idea of a federal health insurance plan had been proposed as early as the 1930s. It came to the fore again in the late-twentieth century as health care costs spiraled out of control and more and more people could not afford insurance. The plan was vigorously opposed by the pharmaceutical and insurance industries and was ultimately shot down by a Republican filibuster in the Senate.

Debates over Social Security Reform

With the percentage of Americans over the age of sixty-five growing, by 2030 there will be a substantial increase in the number of people receiving **Social Security**. The **"graying of America"** and its impact on the Social Security system have been concerns of politicians recently. One reason for the growing percentage of senior citizens is the large number of **"baby boomers,"** born in the period after World War II, reaching retirement age. Many people worry that when such a large percentage of the American public is retired, programs extending benefits to the elderly, notably Medicare and Social Security, will be unable to stay financially solvent. The issue of reforming the Social Security system has divided Democrats and Republicans, with Republicans pushing for some degree of privatization of the system, and Democrats pushing for increased funding streams to ensure its viability in the future. **President George W. Bush**, for example, pushed unsuccessfully for a combination of a government-funded program and personal accounts.

Reform of the Financial Sector

Heated debates have occurred from the 1980s to the present about the role of the government in regard to regulating the United States financial system. Republicans have generally argued for **deregulation** of major industries, including financial firms, and have resisted calls for increased government oversight. They have argued that excessive regulation impedes risk-taking, competition, and economic growth. Democrats, on the other hand, argue that regulation is necessary to check reckless behavior on the part of the financial industry and to protect the economy from rapid fluctuations that can result from crises in the financial sector.

The Savings and Loan Crisis and Bailout

The issue of deregulation of the financial sector came into stark relief in the 1980s with the near collapse of the savings and loan industry. In the 1980s, the nation's **savings and loan associations** (S&Ls) suffered from a spate of irresponsible and risky investments and a downturn in the housing market. Their situation was made worse by the deregulation of the industry in 1980. Legislation had widened the options for S&Ls to invest their financial holdings, paving the way for riskier speculative investments. By 1989, more than 700 S&Ls had become insolvent. In response to this crisis, **President George H. W. Bush** signed a **bailout** bill that extended billions of dollars to the industry. Taxpayers ultimately paid more than $120 billion for the bailout. Some economists believe that the bailout of the S&L industry created a **moral hazard** for other lenders—that is, it created a situation in which actors are more willing to take risks knowing that the potential costs of such risks will be borne by others. Thus, these economists see a connection between the S&L crisis and the **subprime mortgage crisis** of 2007 (see below).

The Housing Crisis and the Great Recession

Starting in late 2007, the country faced its most severe economic crisis since the Great Depression. The **Great Recession**, as the economic crisis of late 2007 to 2009 has been labeled, led to high unemployment, falling wages, and a housing crisis characterized by widespread foreclosures. It began during the 2008 campaign for the presidency. Despite actions taken by the **George W. Bush** administration in 2008, many voters came to see the financial crisis and President Bush's response as additional reasons to give the Democratic Party the chance to take the helm.

Many economists see the **crisis in the housing market** as an important cause of the Great Recession. In the 2000s, lending institutions had been devising new methods of making borrowing money cheaper and easier. Many of these practices became widespread after Congress repealed most of the provisions of the 1933 **Glass-Steagall Act** in 1999, removing regulatory constraints on the banking industry. Banks lured first-time home buyers to take out mortgages for home purchases that were beyond their means. These risky loans—characterized by high interest rates and less than favorable terms—were referred to as "subprime mortgages" because they were extended to people with low credit ratings (less than prime). By 2008, almost 30 percent of mortgages were rated as **"subprime."** Frequently, lenders would then sell these subprime mortgages to investment banks and other **Wall Street** financial institutions. In turn, Wall Street would bundle these mortgages into stock offerings. Finally, pension funds, mutual funds, foreign banks, and individuals invested in these offerings. Therefore, the risk entailed in the original mortgages was spread broadly throughout the economy.

In 2007, the housing bubble burst as the real-estate market weakened and interest rates increased. Many subprime borrowers found themselves **"underwater"**—that is, the market value of their homes sank below the amount they owed on their mortgages. In many such situations, individuals could neither sell their homes nor afford to pay their monthly mortgage payments. Their only option was to walk away from their homes and default on their loans, leading to widespread **foreclosures**.

The collapse of the housing market and the high rate of foreclosures rippled throughout the economy. Major financial institutions that had invested in risky mortgages found themselves in desperate straits when foreclosure rates reached crisis proportions. Investors were left holding **"toxic assets."** Major banks cut back on lending money, business activity slowed, and consumer spending was drastically reduced. Businesses laid off workers in large numbers; 2.8 million workers lost their jobs in 2008, pushing unemployment to 9.8 percent by September 2009. By the fall of 2008, the **Dow Jones Industrial Average**—the major indicator of the health of the stock market—had lost half its value. The crisis was devastating to millions of Americans.

Government Responses to the Great Recession

The **George W. Bush** administration and the **Federal Reserve Bank** (the Fed) took a number of steps to address the economic crisis and to prevent a collapse of major economic institutions. The Fed outlined a loan program for the country's largest banks to borrow Treasury securities at discounted rates. The Bush administration and Congress enacted legislation that extended up to $700 billion for the government purchase of "troubled mortgage-related assets" from financial firms. The goal of the **Troubled Asset Relief Program** (TARP) (2008) was to strengthen the financial sector and restore confidence in the securities market. Critics claimed that the government did not tie this money to new rules and guidelines to ensure that the money would be used for recovery and not irresponsible practices, such as giving CEOs large bonuses.

Bailout of the Automobile Industry

The **automobile industry** also went into financial crisis in 2008, partly as a result of reduced consumer spending and partly as a result of rising fuel prices. As fuel prices rose, sales of sport utility vehicles, a mainstay of Detroit, declined. **President George W. Bush** agreed in December 2008 to lend $17.4 billion to General Motors and Chrysler to keep them afloat (these funds came from the Troubled Asset Relief Program). **President Barack Obama**, elected in 2008 (see page 368), continued to extend loans to General Motors and Chrysler. Eventually these loans totaled $82 billion. The **bailout** was successful; the American automobile industry recovered and paid back $71 billion of the $82 billion that was used in the bailout.

The Stimulus Package

President Barack Obama addressed the Great Recession with a major stimulus bill—the **American Recovery and Reinvestment Act** (2009). The act provided almost $800 billion to state and local governments to be used for infrastructure projects, schools, and hospitals. The act reflected the thinking of the economist **John Maynard Keynes**, who wrote the book, *The General Theory of Employment, Interest and Money* (1936), during the depths of the Great Depression. He argued that during times of recession, the government should increase spending, taking up the slack caused by a decrease in private spending. His theory was influential in shaping President Franklin D. Roosevelt's New Deal (see pages 288–295). The impact of the stimulus package has been debated by economists. Unemployment went down during Obama's time in office—it was at 10 percent in October 2009 and 4.7 percent when he left office in 2017. However, it is not clear how much of that drop was because of the stimulus package and how much of it was the result of a generally improving economy.

The Dodd-Frank Wall Street Reform and Consumer Protection Act

The **Obama administration** pushed for measures to add regulations to the financial industry in order to rein in some of the risky practices that led to the recession of 2008. The **Dodd-Frank Wall Street Reform and Consumer Protection Act** was designed to regulate financial markets and protect consumers. It constituted the most comprehensive financial reform act since the **Glass-Steagall Act** of 1933, which established regulations for the banking industry (the Glass-Steagall Act was largely repealed in 1999).

The Dodd-Frank act was designed, in part, to end the concept of **"too big to fail."** Certain financial institutions were described as being "too big to fail" when it became evident that their failure would have had devastating consequences on the U.S. economy. To avert such failure, the government felt forced to intervene and prop up such institutions in order to prevent economic catastrophe. Many economists are critical of a situation in which certain financial institutions are perceived as too big to fail. These economists fear that "too big to fail" creates a

moral hazard (see page 373); if the leaders of massive financial institutions believe that the government will not let them fail, they are more likely to engage in risky behavior. It was precisely this type of risky behavior by major financial institutions that resulted in the Great Recession (see pages 373–374). Critics argue that the Dodd-Frank Act is not strong enough to end the "too big to fail" moral hazard. After the election of **President Donald Trump** in 2016 (see page 368), congressional Republicans began pushing to roll back many of the provisions of the Dodd-Frank Act. In 2018, President Trump signed legislation to exempt dozens of U.S. banks from the act's banking regulations.

President Obama and Health Care Reform

Like President Clinton, **President Barack Obama** chose health care reform as one of his first major domestic initiatives. The issues that motivated Clinton in 1993—spiraling health care costs, large numbers of uninsured Americans—had become more pronounced in the ensuing years. Proposals for creating a **"public option"** in regard to health insurance generated enthusiasm among many Democrats but met fierce opposition from the pharmaceutical and insurance industries and from the Republican Party. Many Republicans likened such a proposal to "socialism." Democrats were able to pass a watered-down version of health care reform in March 2010.

The **Patient Protection and Affordable Care Act** was challenged in several federal courts. Ultimately, the Supreme Court upheld the major aspects of the act. Still, the act has generated opposition from Republicans, even as more Americans have begun participating in the health insurance exchanges established by the act.

Impact of the Affordable Care Act

The **Affordable Care Act** has dramatically reduced the number of uninsured Americans. According to a 2021 report by the Department of Health and Human Services, over thirty-one million Americans have attained health insurance as a result of the Affordable Care Act—approximately eleven million people acquired coverage through the federal and state exchanges, nearly fifteen million were made eligible for Medicaid by the act, over one million were covered by the act's **"Basic Health Program,"** and over four million previously eligible adults enrolled under expanded Medicaid provisions. The uninsured rate for non-elderly people in the United States went down from 18 percent of the population in 2010 to 10 percent in 2016. At the same time, premium costs for some individuals increased, especially those middle- and upper-income individuals who do not receive federal subsidies for their insurance plans.

E. Debates Around Identity and Social Issues

In the late twentieth and early twenty-first centuries a number of social and political issues have divided Americans. Specifically, debates have occurred around the status of gays and lesbians, gender roles and family structures, race, and gun control.

Redefining Family Structures

The last decades of the twentieth century witnessed major changes in **family structures** in the United States. These changes, in turn, generated intense debate about the identity of the American family. An important trend was the growth of nontraditional families. In 1972, nonmarried households (either with or without children) stood at 26 percent of all families; that figure had risen to 47 percent by 1998. This trend has divided liberals and conservatives, with liberals pushing for measures to extend rights and services to such households, and conservatives calling for a return to traditional family values.

Women in Professions

The **"quiet revolution,"** beginning in the 1970s, of women entering the workplace in larger numbers continued through the end of the twentieth century (see page 345). The push for government-funded day care and for greater participation by men in child-rearing has encouraged this revolution. Though women have made advances in the workplace, many note that disparities still exist. In the 1970s, women earned on average fifty-nine cents for each dollar that men earned doing comparable work. That gap has closed somewhat (to approximately seventy cents for each dollar earned by men) but still exists. In addition, women argued that they were often barred from higher positions in the corporate world. They claimed a **"glass ceiling"** existed that prevented them from climbing higher. The **feminist movement** has also pushed for government-funded day care and greater participation by men in childcare.

Activism by Women

The **feminist movement**, which was prominent in 1960s and 1970s (see page 344), was at the lead of the opposition movement to the policies and pronouncements of **President Donald Trump**. On the day following President Trump's first inauguration in 2017, the **Women's March on Washington** and protest marches in other cities drew between three and five million participants.

The women's rights movement has also called attention to sexual harassment and assault through the **#MeToo Movement**. Activist Tarana Burke used the phrase "Me Too" in 2006 to highlight the magnitude of the problem. The movement has shed new light on workplace dynamics and has empowered women to break the silence around these issues. The movement gained prominence in the aftermath of accusations of sexual abuse by movie producer **Harvey Weinstein**. In 2020 and 2022, Weinstein was found guilty of a total of five felonies in two separate trials, and sentenced to a total of thirty-nine years in prison.

Abortion and the Overturning of *Roe v. Wade*

The issue of abortion has been one of the most divisive issues in the United States in the decades since the Supreme Court issued the ***Roe v. Wade*** decision in 1973. Opposition to abortion brought together fundamentalist Christians and helped fuel the rise of the New Right (see pages 355 and 365–366). In 2022, the anti-abortion movement achieved a major victory. The Supreme Court took up the case of ***Dobbs v. Jackson Women's Health Organization***, a challenge to an extremely restrictive abortion law in Mississippi. The Court used the case to reverse the *Roe* decision and to return to the states the power to regulate aspects of abortion that are not protected by federal law. The majority opinion in the case found that abortion was not a protected right under the Constitution. By 2023, at least seventeen Republican-controlled states had passed near-total bans on abortions.

The Gay Rights Movement and Changing Public Perceptions

The **gay rights movement** grew in intensity after the **Stonewall riots** of 1969 (see pages 344–345). The growth and development of the movement, coupled with a strong conservative backlash against gay rights and against public acceptance of homosexuality, has shaped debates around gay, lesbian, bisexual, and transgender identity, acceptance, and rights.

The AIDS Crisis

In the 1980s, the **gay community** faced a major health crisis that brought the public divide around homosexuality into stark relief. Starting in 1981, news reports began to appear about a mysterious disease that seemed to disproportionately affect gay men, causing anxiety and sorrow in the gay community, but also resolve and action. The Centers for Disease Control and Prevention (CDC) identified the disease that would become known as **acquired immunodeficiency syndrome** (AIDS) in 1981. Soon, it also found that the cause of the disease was infection by the **human immunodeficiency virus** (HIV), present in bodily fluids such as semen and blood. The National

Institutes of Health (NIH), a government body within the U.S. Department of Health and Human Services, was slow to acknowledge and address the crisis. It was not until 1987 that the NIH established a committee to research the impact of HIV.

AIDS swept through gay communities in New York, San Francisco, Los Angeles, and elsewhere. On the one hand, AIDS became a lightning rod in the culture wars of the 1980s and beyond. Many Christian fundamentalists saw AIDS as God's punishment for sinful behavior. On the other hand, the crisis galvanized the gay community and led to an outpouring of both grief and activism. The group **ACT-UP** popularized the slogan **"silence = death"** and staged militant protests in New York and San Francisco.

"Don't Ask, Don't Tell"

The armed forces of the United States has historically discriminated against gays serving in the military. In 1982, the **Department of Defense** issued a policy that stated, "Homosexuality is incompatible with military service." In the following years, gay and lesbian members of the military, and those excluded from the military, began a campaign to change the policy. The **Gay and Lesbian Military Freedom Project** was founded in 1988. Finally, in 1994, the military implemented a policy that allowed gay and lesbian members of the military to serve, as long as they remained "closeted," keeping their sexual identity hidden from public view. Advocates for gays and lesbians insisted that the policy, called **"Don't Ask, Don't Tell,"** was discriminatory and that it limited the freedom of speech and expression of gays and lesbians in the service. The policy was repealed by an act of Congress, signed by **President Obama** in 2011.

Same-Sex Marriage

Perhaps the clearest indicator of the rapid changes in societal attitudes toward homosexuality can be seen in the changing legal status of marriage between same-sex couples. Although gay rights proponents have long demanded that the right to legally marry be extended to same-sex couples, the issue became part of the national dialogue in 1993 when the **Hawaii Supreme Court**, in the case of *Baehr v. Lewin*, ruled that the state ban on **same-sex marriage** was discriminatory under the state constitution. The decision had the effect of galvanizing social conservatives to mobilize against same-sex marriage and to defend "traditional" marriage. Many states amended their constitutions so as to prevent the legalization of same-sex marriage. These amendments usually limited the definition of marriage as an act between a man and a woman. Further, Congress passed the **Defense of Marriage Act** (DOMA) in 1996, which allowed states to not recognize same-sex marriages performed in other states and also defined, for federal purposes, marriage as an act between one man and one woman.

The tide against same-sex marriage began to turn in 2003, when the **Massachusetts Supreme Judicial Court** ruled that the state may not forbid same-sex couples from legally marrying; it asserted that "the Massachusetts Constitution affirms the dignity and equality of all individuals. It forbids the creation of second-class citizens." Several other state high courts followed suit in the 2000s. In 2009, **Vermont** became the first state in the United States to legalize same-sex marriage through legislative means rather than through the court system. Public opinion moved rapidly on this issue. According to the Gallup organization, the aggregate of polls taken in 1996 showed 68 percent of Americans opposed extending legal recognition to same-sex couples. By 2015, the aggregate of polls showed that nearly 60 percent of Americans favored legalized same-sex marriage. In 2015, in the case of *Obergefell v. Hodges*, the Supreme Court ruled that marriage is a fundamental right that must be guaranteed to same-sex couples. The decision cited the due process clause and the equal protection clause of the Fourteenth Amendment to the Constitution.

Race and Economics in the Post–Civil Rights Era

The African-American community has experienced both major advances and significant setbacks in the decades since the civil rights movement. On the one hand, opportunities in housing and employment have opened up. High school graduation rates have risen dramatically for African Americans since the 1970s, as have rates for attending college. African Americans have entered many fields—academia, medicine, law, finance—that were virtually closed to them before the **civil rights movement**. In addition, many African Americans now live in middle-class and suburban communities that were also closed to them in an earlier era.

On the other hand, bitter poverty continues to be the reality for a large segment of the African-American population. Although **poverty rates** have declined for African Americans in the twenty-first century, as they have overall, a large segment of the African-American community remains mired in poverty. A declining industrial sector and reductions in government services have hit this segment of the African-American community especially hard. A 2018 U.S. Census Bureau study notes that 22 percent of African Americans live in poverty, while only 13 percent of all Americans do. Further, poverty for African Americans tends to be more isolating and concentrated than for whites. African Americans below the poverty line are much more likely to live in neighborhoods with overall high poverty rates. Consequently, services in these neighborhoods, such as grocery stores and schools, tend to also be substandard, intensifying the effects of poverty.

Policing, Incarceration, and Race

Changes in the criminal justice system have disproportionately impacted the African-American community. The United States has seen an unprecedented increase in its overall jail and prison population in recent decades—from less than 200,000 in 1972 to nearly 2 million today. Although the United States has only 5 percent of the world's population, it has nearly 25 percent of its prisoners. This trend has deep roots.

From the 1960s into the twenty-first century, political leaders pushed for tougher policies in regard to crime and illegal drug use. In 1965, **President Lyndon Johnson** urged Congress to engage in "an effective war against crime." The Nixon administration's **"tough on crime"** policies further criminalized the possession and use of illegal drugs. The **drug war** became a major policy goal of **President Ronald Reagan** in the 1980s. The **Anti-Drug Abuse Act** (1986) took a punitive stance toward drugs and enacted new mandatory minimum sentences for drug possession, including marijuana. **First Lady Nancy Reagan** was active in the anti-drug campaign, promoting the slogan **"Just say no"** in regard to drug use. In addition, the 1994 anti-crime bill signed into law by **President Bill Clinton** is seen by many as contributing to the increase in the prison population. The dramatic increase in the prison population has hit the African-American community especially hard. African Americans are incarcerated at more than five times the rate of whites.

In the 2010s and 2020s, several high-profile violent incidents between police officers and African Americans made headlines and focused scrutiny of the racial dynamics of policing. The ubiquity of cell phones with video capability led to several of these instances being recorded by civilians; some incidents were recorded by the police themselves. In 2014, protests erupted in Ferguson, Missouri, in the aftermath of the shooting of an unarmed 18-year-old African-American male. Many of the protests around these incidents were organized by the **Black Lives Matter** movement, which emerged in 2013. A larger and more sustained wave of protests began in the spring of 2020 in the aftermath of the murder of **George Floyd** by a police officer. Other incidents in 2020 and 2021 added fuel to the largest movement for racial justice since the civil rights movement of the 1960s. The movement was largely peaceful, but rioting, property damage, and violence occurred at several events in different cities.

Under **President Obama** (2009–2017), the Justice Department often intervened in conflicts between local police departments and the community. In Ferguson, the Justice Department found a longtime pattern of discrimination against African-American residents and violations of constitutional protections. The first **Trump administration** (2017–2021), by contrast, was generally critical of racial justice protests, focusing on incidents of violence at protests and dismissing calls made by some protesters to **"defund the police."** The protests have led many police departments to revise policies and procedures in regard to the use of force. In many ways, the protests have led to a national reckoning around broader issues of racism and racial justice, past and present.

The Debate Around Gun Violence and Gun Control

Several horrific mass shootings in the first decades of the twenty-first century have renewed debates around gun violence and gun control. In 2012, a shooting at Sandy Hook Elementary School in **Newtown, Connecticut** left twenty-seven dead and one injured, including twenty children between six and seven years old. In 2015, a mass shooting took place at the Mother Emanuel A.M.E. church in **Charleston, South Carolina**. Nine people were killed during a Bible study group at the historic Black church. In 2017, a gunman opened fire from a hotel window during a concert in **Las Vegas**, killing fifty-eight people and wounding 413. In 2018, a shooting at Marjory Stoneman Douglas High School in **Parkland, Florida**, left seventeen dead. In 2013, Congress debated two significant bills related to guns—one banning assault weapons and one calling for expanded background checks for gun purchasers. Neither bill passed. In the months after the Sandy Hook shooting, New York passed the **Secure Ammunition and Firearms Enforcement (SAFE) Act**, and Connecticut and Maryland both expanded existing gun laws. Young people, including survivors of the Parkland shooting, have been in the forefront of the movement to take measures to address gun violence. The **National Rifle Association** (NRA) has lobbied strenuously against any type of gun control legislation, citing the importance of the **Second Amendment**. An armed citizenry, gun rights advocates assert, serves as a deterrent to violent crime and will provide an important defense against tyrannical government.

Public Heath Debates in the Age of the COVID-19 Pandemic

Heated debates have occurred in the United States over public health policies in response to the **COVID-19 pandemic**. The pandemic—or global disease outbreak—began in late 2019, as officials in China reported clusters of pneumonia in the city of Wuhan. Scientists soon linked the disease outbreak to a novel (not previously identified) virus, labeled severe acute respiratory syndrome coronavirus 2 (SARS-CoV-2). Within months, the disease caused by the virus—COVID-19—had spread around the world and had given rise to worldwide health, economic, social, and political crises. The highest numbers of recorded cases and deaths have occurred in the United States, with over 110 million recorded cases and over 1.2 million deaths as of 2024.

In 2020, officials in states and cities throughout the United States instituted a variety of measures in order to stem the rapid spread of the disease. **Mitigation measures** included lockdowns and curfews, closures of nonessential businesses and schools, limits on public gatherings, the wearing of face masks, remote work, contact tracing, and physical distancing. Lockdowns and closures contributed to a major contraction of economic activity in the United States in 2020. **Vaccines**, developed in late 2020, offered a glimmer of hope; they lessened the incidence of serious illness, but they did not stop the spread of the disease. Debates on COVID-19 measures—notably mask mandates, business closures, and vaccine mandates—tended to divide Americans between those generally in support of such measures in the name of safety and collective responsibility and those who see such measures as infringements on individual liberties or as excessive or ineffective. Though the transmission of the disease continues, in May 2023, the federal government declared that COVID-19 was no longer a public health emergency.

Topic 9.3 The End of the Cold War

President Ronald Reagan had gained prominence earlier in his career as a strong anti-Communist. He brought this rhetoric to the White House and pursued an aggressive anti-Communist agenda. His interventionist approach to foreign policy set the tone for the following administrations. The United States redefined its role in the world in the 1990s in response to the ending of the Cold War.

A. The United States and the World During the Reagan Administration

In the post–Vietnam War years, debates ensued about the proper role of the United States in the world. President Ronald Reagan, who served as president from 1981 to 1989, asserted opposition to Communism through diplomatic efforts, military interventions, and a buildup of nuclear and conventional weapons.

Soviet-American Relations from Détente to Confrontation

Relations between the **Soviet Union** and the **United States**, which had been improving since **Nixon's détente** overtures in the 1970s (see page 322), soured after the Soviet Union invaded **Afghanistan** (1979). **President Jimmy Carter** suspended grain sales to the Soviets in protest of the invasion. He also successfully pushed for a U.S. boycott of the 1980 Summer Olympics in Moscow.

President Reagan continued to confront the Soviet Union. He roundly denounced the Soviet Union, using pointedly ideological language. In a 1982 speech to the British Parliament, Reagan said, "[T]he forward march of freedom and democracy will leave Marxism-Leninism on the ash heap of history." In 1983, he predicted the collapse of the Soviet system. Later that year, in another speech, he labeled the Soviet Union **"an evil empire."**

Increased Military Spending

President Reagan was determined to challenge the Soviet "evil empire." He initiated several weapons programs, vowing to close what he called a **"window of vulnerability"**—the ability of Soviet missiles to attack and decimate American missile locations before the United States could adequately respond. He began research on the **Strategic Defense Initiative**, dubbed **"Star Wars"** by critics, and initiated the costly **MX missile** program.

The Reagan Doctrine

The Reagan administration supported governments that were anti-Communist, including regimes that were undemocratic or repressive. This foreign policy came to be known as the **Reagan Doctrine**. Reagan sent troops to the island of **Grenada** in 1983 to topple the Marxist leaders of the country. He continued to support the dictatorial regime of **the Philippines** led by **Ferdinand Marcos** despite reports of electoral fraud. The regime was finally ousted in 1986, with **Corazon Aquino** replacing Marcos.

Central America and the Iran-Contra Scandal

As part of the Reagan Doctrine, his administration consistently tried to undermine the left-wing **Sandinista** government in **Nicaragua**. The Sandinistas took power in 1979 after overthrowing the U.S.-backed dictatorship of **Anastasio Somoza**. The United States funded and trained an anti-Sandinista military group known as the **Contras**. In 1982, Congress, alarmed at reports of human rights abuses by the Contras, passed the **Boland Amendment** to halt U.S. aid to the group.

Congressional action did not deter members of the Reagan administration from covertly funding the Contras. An elaborate scheme was developed to secretly sell weapons to Iran and use funds from these sales to support the Contras. In 1986, details of the **Iran-Contra affair** became public. Ultimately fourteen members of the **Reagan administration** were tried for violating U.S. law, and eleven were convicted. Among the indicted was **Secretary of Defense Caspar Weinberger**. **Oliver North**, of the **National Security Council**, an architect of the program, was also initially convicted. The convictions were overturned on appeal. Reagan himself claimed to have had no direct knowledge of the program. Critics labeled him the **"Teflon president"** because accusations of wrongdoing did not stick to him.

B. The Fall of the Soviet Union and the Collapse of Communism

President Ronald Reagan is often given credit for helping precipitate the fall of the Communist governments of the **Eastern Bloc**. It is true that an accelerated arms race taxed the Soviet economy more than it did the American economy, but one must also look at the internal dynamics of Soviet society—economic stagnation, political dissatisfaction—to understand this major development.

The Fall of the Berlin Wall and the End of the Cold War

Beginning in the 1980s, especially in the aftermath of the 1986 Chernobyl nuclear disaster (see page 352), Soviet leader **Mikhail Gorbachev** began to enact a series of political and economic reforms in the **Soviet Union**. In many ways these reforms opened the way for protests and challenges to Soviet power that ultimately undid Soviet Communism. He initiated a shift away from Communist orthodoxy with the introduction of *glasnost,* a dismantling of the repressive apparatus of the Soviet government, and *perestroika,* the introduction of elements of capitalism to the sluggish Soviet economy. In 1989, mass public protests had begun to weaken the governments in **Poland** and **East Germany**. It was clear that Gorbachev would not intervene militarily to halt this development, as previous Soviet leaders had. By the end of 1989, every Communist government in Europe—Poland, East Germany, **Hungary**, **Czechoslovakia**, **Bulgaria**, **Romania**, **Yugoslavia**, and **Albania**—was either toppled or transformed into a non-Communist regime. The iconic image of the movement was the November 1989 demolition of the **Berlin Wall** by Berliners from both sides. The wall, separating **West Berlin** from **East Berlin**, was a symbol of the rift between the Communist Bloc countries and the Western countries. By 1991, the Soviet Union itself had collapsed, ending Communism in Europe.

C. The United States in the Post–Cold War World

Debates continued about the U.S. role in the world after the end of the Cold War, as the United States engaged in a number of military and peacekeeping interventions, including the Persian Gulf War of 1990–1991.

President George Bush and the Persian Gulf War

President George H. W. Bush's main accomplishments were in the field of foreign affairs. It was during Bush's presidency (1989–1993) that the **Berlin Wall** came down and the Soviet Union collapsed. After **Iraq**, under the leadership of **Saddam Hussein**, invaded neighboring **Kuwait** in 1990 in an attempt to gain more control over the region's oil reserves, Bush organized a thirty-four-nation coalition to challenge the move. In late 1990, after fruitless negotiations, President Bush gave Hussein approximately six weeks (until January 15, 1991) to withdraw from Kuwait. When Hussein did not act, the coalition initiated **"Operation Desert Storm,"** defeating Iraqi forces and driving them from Kuwait by February 1991. During the **Persian Gulf War**, significant numbers of women served in combat roles for the first time.

Chaos in Somalia

The administration of **President Bill Clinton** deployed U.S. forces to aid a United Nations humanitarian mission in **Somalia** in 1993. Troubles in Somalia had begun earlier, in 1991, after the government was overthrown and fighting broke out between competing factions. The civil war in Somalia resulted in widespread famine, which led to more than a half million deaths. The U.N. took the initiative to deliver food to Somalia, but much of it was stolen by the warring factions and sold for weapons. In December 1992, President Bush approved the use of U.S. troops to aid U.N. relief activities. By 1993, these troops were under attack, resulting in intense fighting in the capital, **Mogadishu**. American forces suffered nineteen deaths. The mission soon ended with a U.S. withdrawal.

Democracy in Haiti

President Bill Clinton took the lead in ensuring a transition to democracy in **Haiti** in 1994. After decades of dictatorship, a democratic election had brought **Jean-Bertrand Aristide** to power in 1990. Subsequently, a Haitian general ousted him. Clinton announced American intentions to use force, if necessary, to return Aristide to power. The United Nations authorized such a move, but former **President Jimmy Carter** was dispatched to Haiti to try to negotiate an end to military rule. He was successful, and Aristide returned to power in 1995.

Intervention in the Former Yugoslavia

President Bill Clinton became increasingly concerned about violence in the former **Yugoslavia**. Under Communism, Yugoslavia had been a patchwork of different ethnicities. After Communism fell in 1989, the country split into several smaller nations. Ethnic violence developed as **Serbian** forces attempted to gain control of areas of **Bosnia** with large Serbian populations. In the process, Serbian forces initiated a campaign to remove Bosnians, by force if necessary, from these areas. This **"ethnic cleansing"** campaign resulted in atrocities against the civilian population and became a focus of concern in the media and among foreign countries. The United States and other countries decided to take action as reports of Serbian brutality became known. President Clinton brought leaders from Bosnia, Serbia, and Croatia together in 1995 in Dayton, Ohio. A peace treaty was signed, known as the **Dayton Agreement**, and 60,000 NATO troops were dispatched to enforce it.

The United States again became concerned about violence in the region in 1998 when reports emerged of Serbian attacks against ethnic Albanians in the Serbian province of Kosovo. President Clinton approved the use of U.S. forces, under NATO auspices, to engage in a bombing campaign against Serbia in 1999.

President Clinton and the Conflict in the Middle East

Toward the end of his second term, **President Bill Clinton** put a great deal of effort into attempting to broker a peace agreement between **Israel** and the **Palestinians**. From the **Six-Day War** in 1967 to the present day, Israel has occupied adjacent lands where large numbers of Palestinians live. These lands currently include the **West Bank** of the Jordan River, the **Gaza Strip**, and **Eastern Jerusalem**. Palestinians have insisted these lands should comprise a Palestinian state. Israel has resisted agreeing to the formation of a Palestinian state as long as Palestinians launched attacks on Israel. The continued growth of Jewish **settlements** in the West Bank complicated the situation. In 2000, President Bill Clinton invited Palestinian leader **Yasser Arafat** and Israeli prime minister **Ehud Barak** to **Camp David**. The goal was to work out a "final status settlement" to the Israeli-Palestinian conflict. The discussions at Camp David in 2000 did not lead to a resolution of the conflict, which still remains unresolved (see more on the Israeli-Palestinian conflict, pages 349 and 392–393).

United States Relations with China

In the late twentieth century, the United States tried to maintain cordial relations with an important trading partner while, at the same time, challenging China's human rights record as well as checking its growing influence on the world stage.

China embarked on a path of economic reform in the 1970s and 1980 under the leadership of **Deng Xiaoping**. The country moved from a planned economy to a mixed economy, allowing elements of an open or market economy to take hold. In the 1980s, there were social reforms that allowed for a degree of democratization in China. These social and political reforms ended abruptly with the brutal suppression of demonstrations in **Tiananmen**

Square in Beijing in 1989. After weeks of pro-democracy demonstrations in the square, the government declared martial law and mobilized up to 300,000 troops to suppress the demonstrations. It is estimated that the suppression of the demonstrators resulted in the deaths of several hundred to several thousand people. **President George H. W. Bush** (1989–1993) protested the massacre but did not significantly alter American policy, nor did he enforce economic sanctions passed by Congress. By 1990 China had become the fastest-growing economy in the world and the largest trading nation in the world. **President Bill Clinton** (1993–2001) continued the policy of maintaining friendly relations with China, despite the continued arrest of political dissidents in China.

Topic 9.4 A Changing Economy

Scientific and technological developments have transformed contemporary American society. While new technologies have transformed daily life, they have had varied effects on the American economy. On the one hand, productivity in many sectors has increased as the United States has become more enmeshed in the global economy. On the other hand, the country has seen the gap between the wealthy and the poor dramatically widen as wages have stagnated in many sectors.

A. The Economy in the Digital Age

The American economy adapted to the age of digital communications. Economic productivity growth has risen in the United States as participation in the global economy has grown.

The Digital Revolution

The use of **computers** has transformed the American workplace. The principles behind modern computing developed in the 1930s, and the first general-purpose computer is considered to be the **ENIAC**, developed in the United States in 1946. Two years later, transistors were developed, allowing for the replacement of bulky vacuum tubes. An important breakthrough in computing occurred twenty-five years later with the microprocessor (1971), allowing for the development of smaller computers that had formidable processing powers. **Apple** launched a **personal computer** in 1977, and **IBM** followed a few years later. In the early 1980s, **Microsoft** developed operating systems for IBM "PCs" (and, later, for the PCs of rival companies). Through the course of the 1980s, personal computers became ubiquitous in workplaces.

Economic Productivity in the Digital Age

The impact of the **digital revolution** on the American economy has been the subject of a great deal of debate. Generally, economists cite an increase in **productivity growth**—a useful measure of an economy's overall health and efficiency—starting in 1995, after years of slow growth from 1973 to 1995. This increase in productivity is generally attributed to the widespread use of information technologies, which enabled workers to perform many functions with computers and to the increase in the speed of communications across the globe. However, economists have noted that the increase in overall economic productivity has not led to the expected increases in standards of living. Some economists cite the costs of replacing outdated equipment as a countervailing factor. Others cite the changing nature of work in the digital age and the **growing income gap** as factors that prevent many ordinary Americans from enjoying the fruits of the digital revolution. Economists are currently observing and debating the economic impact of new **artificial intelligence** (AI) technologies. The AI field experienced a boom in the early 2020s, with the release of the generative chatbot, **ChatGBT**, in 2022.

B. New Technologies, New Behaviors

The late twentieth and early twenty-first centuries have witnessed the spread of computer technology. The internet has dramatically altered daily life, increasing access to information and fostering new social behaviors.

The Development and Spread of the Internet

The origins of the **internet** date from the 1960s as the **Department of Defense** sought to create a computer system that would allow far-flung military installations to exchange computer information. In the late 1980s, universities in the United States created a computer network to facilitate the sharing of research while, in Switzerland, engineers developed the **World Wide Web**—a system of interlinked hypertext documents that organizes electronic information transmitted and accessed via the internet.

Internet use grew rapidly in the 1990s and has reshaped many aspects of daily life in the twenty-first century. **Email** communications quickly rendered letter writing obsolete. File sharing of music and video has forced the entertainment industry to rethink its business model. Traditional news outlets—newspapers, magazines, and even television—have been forced to compete with the instantaneous information available on the internet. The internet has changed practices in the workplace, allowing for virtual business meetings and telecommuting (working from home or a cafe). This push toward remote work was given added urgency by the **COVID-19 pandemic**, starting in 2020, as working from home became part of the strategy of slowing the spread of the virus (see page 379). The internet has also altered the world of commerce, allowing users to browse merchandise on their personal computers and purchase items without leaving their homes. This has made shopping easier in many ways, but has driven many brick-and-mortar stores out of business.

Although the internet had become a popular fixture in American life by the mid-1990s, it was not fully utilized by political campaigns until the 2000s. The 2008 campaign of **Barack Obama** fully embraced the internet, building a grassroots network of activists and contributors that helped carry Obama to victory. Twitter (now known as X) served as a primary method for **President Donald Trump** to communicate with the public. Today, websites and social media are central to political campaigns.

The internet became more mobile with the introduction of **smartphones** in the early 2000s. Critics note the tendency of smartphones to distract users from tasks (such as driving) and social interactions in front of them, while enthusiasts marvel that the world of information on the internet is now accessible in the palm of one's hand.

C. Economic Shifts: The Decline of Manufacturing and the Rise of the Service Sector

The United States has undergone profound economic changes in the period from 1980 to the present. Most significantly, manufacturing jobs have dramatically declined, while the service sector has grown.

The Deindustrialization of America

From the 1960s onward, large numbers of factories have closed in northeastern cities such as New York and Philadelphia, as well as in Midwestern **"rust belt"** cities such as Pittsburgh, Cleveland, Detroit, and Chicago. Some firms have relocated to the South and other areas within the United States where they can take advantage of lower-wage expectations and a weak labor movement. Since the 1980s, there has been a rapid shift of the manufacturing sector out of the United States and other developed countries and to the less-developed parts of the world. **Free-trade agreements** have accelerated this trend (see page 371). The rise of the private manufacturing sector in **China** has also played a major role. Because firms in China are able to produce goods at lower costs—a result of considerably lower labor costs and an exchange rate that is favorable to China—American imports from China grew dramatically in the late twentieth and early twenty-first century. In 2019, the U.S. trade deficit with China was $345 billion (see pages 382–383).

Decline of Union Membership

The decline of manufacturing jobs in the United States has contributed to a drop in **union membership**. In 1954, union membership (as a percentage of the total workforce) peaked in the United States at 35 percent; currently, it is just over 10 percent. Another contributing factor in the decline of unionized workers was the ability of the New Right to press an agenda that values deregulation and free-market economics. A major turning point in government policy toward unionized workers came in 1981 under **President Ronald Reagan**. When air traffic controllers went on strike in 1981, he had them all fired. This action broke their union, the **Professional Air Traffic Controllers' Organization** (PATCO), and was consistent with helping big business (the airline industry), rather than the working class (the unionized air traffic controllers). The destruction of PATCO was a major blow to organized labor in the late twentieth century. In such an environment, and with a falling membership, there has been a marked decline in the militancy of the union movement. In 1970, there were more than 380 major strikes or lockouts in the United States; by 2019, that figure dropped to 25.

More recently, several states, including **Michigan** (2012) and **Wisconsin** (2015), have passed so-called **right-to-work laws** (bringing the total to twenty-eight states). These laws, enabled by the 1947 **Taft-Hartley Act** (see page 323), undermined the strength of the union movement. In right-to-work states, workers can opt out of paying union dues, even while being represented by the union. Unions argue that they negotiate on behalf of all the workers, and therefore all should be required to pay dues (even workers who decide that they do not want to join the union). In addition, unions representing public workers have come under attack in several states.

The Growth of the Service Sector

The **service sector** grew significantly in the period of 1980 to the present. The service sector of the economy is also called the "tertiary sector." The primary sector includes the extraction and production of raw materials—such as mining, lumber operations, agriculture, and fishing. The secondary sector is generally considered manufacturing—the processes involved in transforming raw materials into finished products available to the public. The tertiary, or service, sector involves the production of services rather than end products. Such services enable and enhance other sectors of the economy. The service sector includes shipping and trucking, banking services, information technology, waste disposal, education, government, health care, legal services, and a whole host of retail and food-service operations. Throughout the Western world, service-sector employment, as a percentage of overall employment, has grown over the last century, with the pace of growth accelerating since 1980. Currently, 70 percent of jobs in the United States are in the service sector. The growth of the service sector illustrates a profound shift in the American economy from the production of things to the providing of services.

While the service sector includes a wide variety of jobs, the growth of low-wage jobs in the retail and fast-food fields has contributed to the stagnation of wages and to a growing **income gap** (see page 386). The three largest employers in the United States are currently **Wal-Mart**, Yum! Brands (which includes **Taco Bell**, **KFC**, and other fast-food outlets), and **McDonald's**. Efforts to unionize workers in these fields have had limited success due to vigorous anti-union activities by the corporations and to structural difficulties in organizing a decentralized workforce with a high turn-over rate. Unions and worker-advocacy groups have pushed state legislatures to raise the minimum hourly wage allowed by law. The goal of a fifteen-dollar minimum hourly wage has been a rallying cry of this movement.

The Growth of the "Gig Economy"

The decline of traditional wage labor and the growth of the internet have contributed to a growing number of Americans participating in the "gig economy." A gig is a temporary work engagement, with the worker being paid only for that specific job. DoorDash and Uber are prominent companies within the gig economy. It is estimated that, as of 2024, 36 percent of American workers are involved in the gig economy, either as a primary or a secondary source of income. For some, gig work supplements their current income; others join the gig economy simply because they cannot find traditional, full-time, salaried employment. The gig economy provides flexibility to workers; a gig worker can accept or reject a particular assignment, depending on scheduling issues. However, the gig economy does not provide employee benefits or worker protections and often results in low pay, irregular hours, social isolation, and physical exhaustion.

D. Increasing Wealth Inequality

At the close of the twentieth century, the gap between the wealthy and the rest of the population widened in the United States. Workers experienced stagnation in terms of real wages.

The Growth of the Income Gap

Since the 1970s, economists have noted that the **income gap** between the wealthy and the middle class has grown increasingly wide. The incomes for the top-earning one percent of households increased by about 275 percent between 1979 and 2007, while the middle 60 percent of wage-earners saw their incomes rise by just under 40 percent during the same period. The flattening of wages for the middle class and the poor has meant an increase in debt for many Americans and, for many population groups, a decrease in consumer spending. A variety of political and economic factors can help explain this growing gap. Many economists cite factors mentioned above—the disappearance of higher-paying manufacturing jobs and the growth of low-wage service-sector jobs and of "gig" work. Other factors include the decline of the union movement and changes in the tax code, including the massive tax cuts initiated by President George W. Bush (implemented in 2001 and 2003). The **Great Recession** (2007–2009), which sent thousands of working-class homeowners into foreclosure, also contributed to the growing gap in wealth (see page 373). Finally, the growth of the "gig economy" has tended to depress income for workers (see page 386). In the 2010s, calls for a fundamental restructuring of the economy in order to challenge economic inequality have resonated with growing numbers of Americans. Such calls formed the basis of the **Occupy Wall Street** movement in 2011 and the campaigns of **Senator Bernie Sanders** for president in 2016 and 2020.

Topic 9.5 Migration and Immigration, 1980 to the Present

The United States experienced major demographic shifts in the late twentieth and early twenty-first centuries, contributing to significant cultural and political consequences.

A. Immigration and the Growth of the Sunbelt

Since 1980, there has been a significant shift in the population toward the states of the South and the West. The growth of these regions was partly the result of increased immigration from Latin America and Asia.

Growth of the Sunbelt

The states of the **Sunbelt**—notably California, Texas, Arizona, Nevada, and Florida—have seen remarkable growth in recent decades. This trend was seen as early as World War II when defense-related industries there attracted large numbers of workers. Affordable air conditioning also played a role in attracting migrants from within the United States to the Sunbelt. Florida has become a prime destination for retirees from colder parts of the country.

Immigration from **Latin America** accounts for much of the growth of the region. Many immigrants have been drawn to agricultural work in California and to the cities of the Sunbelt. Consequently, the political power of the South and the West has grown significantly since 1980. This has generally augured well for the **Republican Party** as national politics have come to reflect the more conservative views of those in the West and South. As a result of the most recent census (2020), North Carolina, Florida, Montana, Oregon, and Colorado each gained one member of Congress; Texas added two seats. By contrast, states in the Midwest and Northeast lost power in Congress. Pennsylvania, Illinois, Michigan, Ohio, New York, and West Virginia each lost a House seat. In addition, California, experiencing a slowdown in population growth, lost a House seat for the first time.

B. Asian and Latin American Immigration

One of the most significant demographic changes in the late twentieth and early twenty-first centuries is the influx of Asian and Latin American immigrants into the United States.

Post-1965 Immigration Patterns

After passage of the **Immigration and Nationality Act of 1965** (see pages 337–338), immigration increased significantly—especially from **Asia**, **Latin America**, **Africa**, and the **Middle East**. Although the act added limits for migration from the **Western Hemisphere** for the first time, overall the impact of the act has been profound. It has altered the demographics of the United States. Before the act, immigration accounted for less than 10 percent of population growth into the United States. Currently it accounts for approximately a third of population growth. In the thirty-five years before the act was passed, approximately 5 million immigrants came into the United States; in the 1970s alone, that number was 4.5 million, rising to more than 7 million in the 1980s and more than 9 million in the 1990s. These numbers include a rise in illegal immigration as well. Immigration has been an important factor in the growth of the **southwestern** states (see pages 386–387).

The Changing Ethnic Makeup of the United States

As the percentage of the American population composed of **Asian**, **African**, **Middle Eastern**, and **Latin American** immigrants and their children has grown, the percentage of the American population composed of non-Hispanic whites has declined—from 75 percent of the overall U.S. population in 1990 to 58 percent in 2023. It is estimated that by the year 2042, non-Hispanic whites will no longer constitute a majority of the population of the United States.

C. Immigration Policy

Since the 1970s, immigration into the United States has increased dramatically, supplying workers to the workforce while also leading to intense political, economic, and social debates.

Debates Around Immigration

The changing profile of the population of the United States has raised concerns among some Americans and has generated a broad debate around **immigration policy**. Some Americans have a more welcoming attitude toward immigration into the United States, focusing on its positive social and economic impacts; others fear that large numbers of immigrants, many entering the country illegally, will take jobs from Americans and draw on public resources. Members of the New Right expressed concern about the cultural impact of large-scale immigration. The **Republican Party** has generally argued for a more secure border with Mexico and for deportations of immigrants without proper immigration papers. The **Immigration Reform and Control Act of 1986** reflected some of these concerns. Although the act enabled some immigrants without proper papers to achieve legal status, it also forced employers to ensure that their workforce was composed of only legal immigrants.

Immigration Policy Under President Obama

President Barack Obama pushed for comprehensive immigration reform but was met with opposition in the Republican-controlled House of Representatives. In 2012, he issued an executive branch memorandum establishing the **Deferred Action for Childhood Arrivals** (DACA) policy. The policy allows individuals who had been brought into the country illegally as minors to apply for deferred action from deportation and to be eligible for work permits. At the same time that he tried to create pathways to legal status for undocumented immigrants, Obama also increased the number of deportations of undocumented immigrants, focusing on those who had recently crossed the border and those with criminal records.

Immigration Policy Under President Trump

Immigration remains a contentious issue in the United States. The issue was central to **Donald Trump's** successful campaign for the presidency in 2016. He promised to a build a wall between the United States and Mexico to prevent people from illegally crossing the border, and to temporarily block immigration from certain Muslim majority nations. His pointed comments about undocumented immigrants were greeted with dismay by many, but with enthusiastic support by others. In January 2017, Trump issued an executive order temporarily banning entry into the United States of people from seven predominantly Muslim countries, as well as indefinitely suspending the entry of **Syrian refugees**. The order was criticized by members of both political parties as constituting a **"Muslim ban"** and led to widespread protests. It stalled in the court system and subsequently was replaced by a different executive order in March 2017, which maintained a travel ban but made exceptions for green card holders and people who received visas before the ban went into effect. The Supreme Court upheld President Trump's revised travel ban in June 2018.

Immigration Policy Under President Biden

In 2021, **President Joe Biden** reversed many of the initiatives of President Donald Trump in regard to immigration. He quickly stopped construction of the border wall between the United States and Mexico. He also undid Trump's 2017 travel ban on people from predominantly Muslim countries. Finally, Biden revived the protections offered to individuals who qualified for the **Deferred Action for Childhood Arrivals** program (see page 388).

Topic 9.6 Defining America's Role in the World in the 21st Century

As the United States moved into the twenty-first century, it faced a series of challenges related to its role in the world. The terrorist attacks on the United States in 2001 caused the United States to focus its foreign policy on the war on terrorism. The actions taken by the United States, both at home and abroad, have generated debate about security and civil liberties. In addition, different presidents have taken markedly different approaches in regard to America's relationship with the international community.

A. The Terrorist Attacks of 2001 and the U.S. Response

Following the terrorist attacks on the World Trade Center and the Pentagon, a series of foreign policy and military initiatives aimed at preventing future terrorist attacks were enacted. These initiatives included prolonged and controversial military campaigns in Afghanistan and Iraq.

Terrorist Attacks Against the United States

On the morning of **September 11, 2001**, nineteen terrorists affiliated with the **al-Qaeda** network hijacked four domestic airplanes. The plan was to turn the airplanes into missiles that would destroy symbols of American power. One plane was flown into the **Pentagon**, inflicting heavy damage, and one plane crashed in a field near Shanksville, Pennsylvania, after the hijackers were overwhelmed by passengers. The other two airplanes did the most damage, crashing into the two towers of the **World Trade Center** in New York City. The damage inflicted on each building weakened their structures so that both collapsed within two hours. Approximately 3,000 people died in the four incidents, with the vast majority of the deaths occurring at the World Trade Center.

War in Afghanistan

The terrorist attacks of 2001 were soon followed by **President George W. Bush** initiating military action on two fronts—**Afghanistan** and **Iraq**. The United States initiated military actions in Afghanistan in 2001, less than a month after the September 11 terrorist attacks. American forces overthrew the **Taliban**, the government that had given refuge to **al-Qaeda**. The United States hoped to find the leader of al-Qaeda, **Osama bin Laden**, who was still at large at the end of President Bush's presidency. Even though the administration of **President Barack Obama** was able to find and kill bin Laden (see page 390), it was not able to end the war in Afghanistan despite Obama's campaign promises. Under **President Donald Trump**, the United States and the Taliban signed a conditional peace agreement in 2020, without the participation of the Afghan government. However, military conflicts continued in the country through the end of Trump's term. In April 2021, **President Joe Biden**, citing stipulations in the 2020 agreement, announced that all U.S. troops would be withdrawn by September. Taliban fighters began a final offensive in May and achieved military victories across the country. As Taliban forces began closing in on the capital, Kabul, in August, the United States military began an evacuation of American personnel and certain Afghani citizens from the country. The chaotic exit of the United States from Afghanistan was roundly criticized and proved to be an early setback for the Biden administration. Biden stood by his decision to end America's two-decade engagement in Afghanistan.

War with Iraq

"Operation Iraqi Freedom," begun in 2003, was the U.S. military campaign to remove Iraq's president, **Saddam Hussein**, from power and create a less belligerent and more democratic government in Iraq. **President George W. Bush** insisted that Hussein was developing **weapons of mass destruction** that could be used against the United States and its allies, even though it became known later that U.S. forces had failed to find any evidence of such weapons. The administration also asserted that there was a connection between Hussein and the terrorist attacks of 2001. No evidence of such a link was uncovered, and the administration moved away from that rationale.

Defeating the Iraqi army and overthrowing Saddam Hussein was relatively easy. After these goals were accomplished, President George W. Bush declared **"mission accomplished"** in May 2003. However, this operation proved to be more difficult and costly than "Operation Desert Storm" in 1991 (see page 381). Creating stability in Iraq proved to be an elusive goal for the Bush administration. Attacks by insurgents continued, both against U.S. forces and between various factions within Iraq. Operation Iraqi Freedom hurt President Bush's approval ratings in the United States and created tension between the United States and some European nations.

B. Liberty, Security, and Human Rights in the War on Terrorism

The war on terrorism has fostered a series of intense debates among the American people about the proper methods of carrying out a global war on terrorism. While some argued that destroying terrorist organizations was the only method for securing safety and seeking justice in the aftermath of the atrocities committed in September 2001, many Americans became increasingly concerned about issues of human rights and civil liberties in this campaign against terrorism.

The Patriot Act

The **Patriot Act** was passed in 2001, six weeks after the September 11 terrorist attacks. It greatly expanded the government's authority in the fight against terrorism. **President George W. Bush** argued that such measures were necessary to safeguard the nation against future terrorist attacks. Some critics have said that the act impinges on people's civil liberties. Perhaps one of the biggest controversies around the Patriot Act is the use of **National Security Letters**, or NSLs, by the Federal Bureau of Investigation. These NSLs allow the FBI to search telephone, email, and financial records without a court order, raising constitutional concerns for many people.

Department of Homeland Security

The creation of the **Department of Homeland Security** was a result of the September 11, 2001, terrorist attacks. It was created in 2003, absorbing the Immigration and Naturalization Service. It is a cabinet-level department, with the responsibility of protecting the United States from terrorist attacks and natural disasters.

Tactics in the War on Terrorism

In 2004, the release of photographs of United States Army personnel humiliating and, apparently, abusing prisoners at the **Abu Ghraib prison** in Iraq cast light on new tactics used by the United States in its handling of prisoners in the aftermath of the 2001 terrorist attacks. Army personnel at detention camps in Iraq, Afghanistan, and Guantanamo Bay, Cuba, were given permission to use **"enhanced interrogation"** techniques. Critics said these techniques, which included **"waterboarding,"** amounted to torture. The government also began to hold suspects at these facilities indefinitely, classifying them as "enemy combatants" and denying them due process rights. The Supreme Court, in *Hamdan v. Rumsfeld* (2006), ruled that the **George W. Bush** administration could not hold detainees indefinitely without due process and without the protection of the **Geneva Accords**.

President Obama and the War on Terrorism

Some of the concerns about the way the war on terrorism was being carried out under the administration of **President George W. Bush** helped elevate **Barack Obama** to the White House in 2008 over Republican **John McCain**. In 2011, the Obama administration was able to report that a Navy **"SEAL Team Six"** had killed **Osama bin Laden**. However, to the disappointment of many of Obama's supporters, the president continued many of the controversial antiterrorism policies begun during the Bush administration. In 2011, Obama allowed for the extension of three controversial measures within the **Patriot Act** that were set to expire. During the election campaign in 2008, he called the reports of prisoner abuse at the **Guantanamo Bay** detention camp "a sad chapter in American history" and promised to close it down by 2009. At the time, there were 242 prisoners at the camp. By the time Obama left office in 2017, the number of prisoners at Guantanamo Bay had been reduced to forty-one, but he had not closed the facility. During his first term in office, **President Donald Trump** spoke in favor of maintaining the detention camp. **President Joe Biden**, like Obama, expressed a desire to close it, but as of 2025, the detention camp is still operating.

In addition, President Obama generated a great deal of debate over the increased use of unmanned drone attacks on suspected terrorist targets. The program, begun under President George W. Bush, was greatly expanded under the Obama administration, despite it being criticized by the United Nations as **"extrajudicial killings,"** and **"summary justice."** Finally, President Obama renewed a clandestine program known as **PRISM**, which allows the **National Security Agency** to conduct mass data mining of phone, internet, and other communications—including, under certain circumstances, those of United States citizens. The clandestine program was exposed by computer specialist and former NSA contractor **Edward Snowden** in 2013. The revelations revived the ongoing debate among Americans around the protection of civil liberties in the age of global terrorism.

C. Energy Policy, Consumption, and the Limits to Growth

A series of developments have generated debates in the United States around energy use and policy. Ongoing conflicts in the Middle East and overwhelming evidence of long-term human-produced climate change have generated concern about continued reliance on fossil fuels. In addition, many Americans have become increasingly concerned about the overall impact of mass consumption on the environment.

Climate Change and Energy Policy

Americans are by far the world's largest consumers of energy. In the aftermath of the **Arab oil embargo** of 1973 and the energy crisis that followed the 1979 **Iranian Revolution**, some American policymakers began to look for ways for the United States to reduce its consumption of energy (see pages 349–350). This push toward a reduction in energy consumption has been augmented in recent decades by growing concerns over climate change.

Since the early 1970s, scientists have become aware of a trend toward warmer global temperatures. Some became convinced that this warming trend was caused by trapped greenhouse gases, which were in turn caused by human activities, primarily the burning of fossil fuels. In the 1990s and 2000s, a virtual consensus emerged in the scientific community around the connection between **global warming** and the emissions generated by the burning of fossil fuels. Calls were made to limit the human activities linked to global warming. The 1992 **"Earth Summit"** in Brazil led to the adoption by most of the countries in the world of the **United Nations Framework Convention on Climate Change**. The 1997 **Kyoto Protocol** set binding obligations on industrialized countries to reduce the emission of greenhouse gases. The United States signed, but did not ratify, the protocol.

More recently, the United States played in important role in the negotiations that led to the **Paris Agreement** (2015), which called for broad carbon dioxide reduction measures. By 2017, 195 parties, including the United States, China, and the European Union, had signed the agreement. In 2017, **President Donald Trump** announced that the United States would end its participation in the Paris Agreement (effective 2020).

President Joe Biden officially rejoined the Paris climate accord on his first day in office in 2021. In addition, his trillion-dollar infrastructure bill, passed in 2021, included the largest investment to date ($47 billion) in measures designed to help communities withstand the devastating impacts of climate change. He did not, however, embrace the proposal for the **Green New Deal**, a sweeping environmental agenda formally introduced by progressive members of Congress in 2019. In 2021, the United States was one of nearly 200 countries to adopt the **Glasgow Climate Pact**. Critics of the plan hoped the agreement would have included more aggressive actions in regard to moving away from fossil fuels.

To some degree, American society is making changes. California passed legislation in 2006 that would reduce greenhouse-gas emissions from all sources, including automobiles. Other communities are taking steps that include encouraging bicycling and mass transit. However, piecemeal steps, many observers argue, will not be enough. The scientific community is virtually unanimous in urging the world's nations to take dramatic steps immediately. A 2020 report from the **Intergovernmental Panel on Climate Change** said that governments have perhaps twelve years to cut global emissions by 45 percent. Such steps are necessary, the report argued, to prevent an increase in average global temperatures of more than 1.5 degrees Celsius, or 2.7 degrees Fahrenheit. If such steps are not taken, scientists predict fundamental and irreversible changes to global climate and an intensification of phenomena that have already begun—rising sea levels, drought, famine, extreme heat waves, stronger hurricanes, larger wildfires, and displacement of hundreds of thousands (perhaps millions) of people.

D. United States Foreign Policy in the Twenty-first Century

The United States remains the world's leading superpower in the twenty-first century. Debates have continued about U.S. goals and actions on the global stage.

President George W. Bush and the Withdrawal from the International Community

The debate over the role of the United States in the world continued during the administration of **President George W. Bush**. Although President Bush worked with a coalition of nations in the **invasion of Iraq** in the aftermath of the terrorist attacks of 2001 (see pages 388–389), he distrusted many of the multilateral entities in which the United States had previously participated. Bush withdrew the United States from the **Kyoto Protocol**, an international agreement on environmental goals. Also, the administration violated international guidelines in regard to the treatment of military prisoners. Bush withdrew from the **Anti-Ballistic Missile Treaty**, in effect since 1972, in late 2001 so that the United States could develop a space-based missile-defense system. In 2002, the United States withdrew from the treaty creating the **United Nation's International Criminal Court**, which went into effect later that year.

The Bush Doctrine

Debates about military interventions continued during the presidency of **George W. Bush**. These debates took on added urgency in the aftermath of the terrorist attacks of 2001. Bush shifted American foreign policy away from its traditional reliance on **deterrence** and **containment**. He put forth a more aggressive approach in the fall of 2002 that called for **pre-emptive strikes** against nations perceived as threats to the United States. In a speech at West Point Military Academy, Bush identified an **"axis of evil"** consisting of **Iraq**, **Iran**, and **North Korea**. This reliance on pre-emptive warfare is known as the **Bush Doctrine**.

United States Policy in the Middle East

Upon assuming office in 2009, **President Barack Obama** pledged to increase engagement with the predominantly Muslim nations in the Middle East and surrounding region. In January 2009, he said in an interview that, in regard to the Muslim world, he was eager to initiate a "new partnership based on mutual respect and mutual interest." He made a major speech in **Cairo**, **Egypt**, pledging to mend relations between the U.S and the Muslim world. Toward this end, he committed additional forces to **Afghanistan** while withdrawing troops from Iraq by 2011. An American presence remained in Afghanistan until **President Joe Biden** withdrew the last troops in 2021 (see page 389).

Obama spoke favorably of the changes brought about by the **Arab Spring** protests in the Middle East and North Africa. These protests and rebellions, which began in Tunisia in late 2010, channeled popular anger against oppressive regimes and low living standards. In several countries, the Arab Spring protests led to promises of institutional reform and even to regime change, but in most of these countries, authoritarian regimes subsequently reasserted power in a development known as the **Arab Winter**. In 2011, President Obama also committed United States forces, working with European allies, to challenge forces loyal to **Libyan** dictator **Muammar Gaddafi**. Gaddafi was ousted and killed in 2011, but Libya has experienced instability and civil war in the years since then.

The Iran Nuclear Deal

President Barack Obama prioritized preventing **Iran** from acquiring **nuclear weapons**. Negotiations between the United States and Iran began in 2013 and, after several setbacks, resulted in a deal entitled the **Joint Comprehensive Plan of Action** (2015). The main components of the Iran nuclear deal involved removing sanctions against Iran in exchange for measures to ensure that Iran would not produce a nuclear bomb. The deal was endorsed by ninety nations that applauded the move toward bringing Iran into the broader community of nations. Many saw the deal as an important step toward making the world safer and toward opening up economic opportunities with Iran. The deal was roundly condemned by Republican and conservative observers and by Israeli prime minister **Benjamin Netanyahu**. Many conservatives saw the deal as capitulation to a dangerous regime with ties to terrorist organizations. In 2018, **President Donald Trump** signed a Presidential Memorandum officially withdrawing the United States from the agreement and reinstating sanctions against Iran. Under **President Joe Biden**, American and Iranian negotiators began meeting in 2021 with the goal of the U.S. rejoining the agreement; however, by 2024, the deal appeared to be effectively dead.

Relations Between the United States and Israel

The United States has continued to push for a resolution of the conflict between **Israel** and the **Palestinians** in the twenty-first century, while also maintaining a strong alliance with Israel (see page 349). **President Barack Obama** increased military support for Israel and described America's alliance with Israel as "sacrosanct." However, in 2016, **Secretary of State John Kerry** strongly criticized Israeli policy in regard to the building of settlements in the West

Bank. **President Donald Trump** angered many Palestinian leaders when, in 2017, he seemed to move away from the long-held American commitment to a two-state solution to the conflict between Israel and the Palestinians. In addition, he recognized **Jerusalem** as the Israeli capital and moved the American embassy there in 2018. In 2020, Trump successfully mediated the **Abraham Accords**—bilateral agreements to normalize relations between Israel and two predominantly Arab nations, United Arab Emirates and Bahrain. A similar agreement was later reached between Israel and Morocco. Negotiations for a normalization agreement between Israel and Saudi Arabia were begun soon after, but were not finalized.

Upon taking office in 2021, **President Joe Biden** asserted strong support for Israel. He also reestablished diplomatic relations with the **Palestinian Authority**, which had ceased during the Trump administration, and reasserted American support for a two-state solution. After the October 7, 2023, attack by the Palestinian group, **Hamas**, on Israeli civilians and security personnel, Biden strongly condemned the attack and pledged to assist Israel in responding to the attack. Hamas is a militant political and military group that has controlled the **Gaza Strip** of the Palestinian territories since 2007. As of early 2025, the **Israel-Hamas War** has resulted in over 1,800 Israeli deaths and over 40,000 Palestinian deaths.

Tensions with Russia

The **United States** and **Russia** have had a tense relationship in the post–**Cold War** world. As discussed previously, in 2002 the United States withdrew from the 1971 **Anti-Ballistic Missile Treaty** with Russia. In addition, Russian president **Vladimir Putin** was opposed to both the 2003 U.S.-led Iraq War (see page 389) and the expansion of NATO into Eastern Europe. He saw both events as an expansion of American and Western influence. During this period, the United States grew concerned over Putin's rejection of democratic reforms in Russia and the establishment of limits on free expression. Many people in the United States and Europe have become increasingly concerned about a resurgence of **homophobia** in Russia and the passage of legislation discriminating against gay, lesbian, bisexual, and transgender people and the censoring of materials related to "nontraditional" relationships.

Russia's actions against neighboring countries have led to criticism by the American government and have contributed to increased tensions between the two countries. In 2008, for example, Russia sent troops and carried out air strikes in support of two regions of the country of **Georgia** that had declared an intention to break away from Georgia. There was a minor improvement in relations between Russia and the United States in 2010 with the signing of a new arms-control agreement, the **New START Treaty**. The agreement called for a reduction of nuclear warheads and launchers, as well as for on-site inspections.

Relations again took a turn for the worse starting in 2012. It became increasingly apparent that Russia and the West had very different priorities with respect to the **Syrian Civil War**. Russia made clear its support for Syrian leader **Bashar al-Assad**, despite Assad's brutal treatment of his opposition—both fighters and civilians. The Arab League, the United States, and the European Union, on the other hand, called for the removal of Assad. The fall of the Assad regime in 2024 dealt a blow to Russia's geopolitical goals in the Middle East.

Bitterness between Putin and **President Obama** (see below) became apparent in Putin's embrace of Donald Trump in the 2016 presidential campaign. The U.S. **Office of the Director of National Intelligence** declassified a report in January 2017 that described actions by Russia to interfere in the 2016 election as "denigrat[ing]" Democratic candidate **Hillary Clinton** and "show[ing] a clear preference" for **Donald Trump**. The controversy was investigated by a special counsel authorized by the Department of Justice and headed by former FBI director **Robert Mueller.** The **Mueller Report** resulted in thirty-four indictments, including against several former members of the Trump campaign.

The United States and the Russo-Ukrainian War

The most significant source of tensions between **Russia** and the United States since the end of the Cold War has been the Russian invasion of **Ukraine** in 2022. Russian aggression against Ukraine began in 2014. That year, protests in Ukraine against its pro-Russian president led the establishment of a pro-Western interim government. This turn of events coincided with unrest in **Crimea**, a region in southern Ukraine with a Russian-majority population. Russian president **Vladimir Putin** then occupied the region with Russian troops, and soon after, a referendum in Crimea was hastily held, with the majority calling for annexation by Russia. These moves were seen as illegal by the United States and the United Nations General Assembly. **President Barack Obama** imposed sanctions on several wealthy businessmen and advisors close to Putin. Conflict continued as separatists, again aided by Russia, engaged in fighting in eastern Ukraine.

After amassing over 100,000 troops on the border, Russia invaded Ukraine in February 2022, leading to condemnations and economic sanctions by the United States and other countries. The **Russo-Ukrainian War** has been extremely costly for both sides, with Russian troops suffering at least 150,000 deaths. It is estimated that Ukraine has suffered at least 12,000 civilian deaths and at least 70,000 troop deaths. **President Biden** took a leading role in opposing Russia's invasion. He labeled Putin a "war criminal" and condemned him for destabilizing global food and fuel production. As of 2025, the United States has provided the Ukrainian government, led by **Volodymyr Zelenskyy**, with over $64 billion in military aid, allowing Ukraine to fight back against Russia more effectively than many observers expected.

Normalizing Relations with Cuba

The United States has had a fraught relationship with **Cuba** over the years. After the **Cuban Revolution** (1959), Cuba became a Communist country under the leadership of Fidel Castro. It was allied with the **Soviet Union** during the **Cold War** (see page 331). Tensions increased following America's failed Bay of Pigs invasion in 1961 and the **Cuban Missile Crisis** (1963) (see pages 321–322). For years, the United States refused to recognize the government of Cuba and enforced an economic boycott of the country. However, **President Obama** announced, in 2015, that the United States and Cuba would resume diplomatic relations and that the United States would open an embassy in Havana. In 2017, **President Trump** suspended the Obama-era policy of granting Cuba relief from sanctions, but he did not rescind diplomatic relations between the two countries. **President Biden** kept economic sanctions in place, and criticized Cuba's handling of political dissidents.

> **USING HISTORICAL THINKING SKILLS:**
> **CONTEXTUALIZATION**
>
> **Relations with Cuba and Domestic Politics**
>
> Hostile relations between the United States and Cuba persisted from the 1960s until 2015. This hostility occurred in the context of the Cold War. However, the hostile relationship continued even after the Cold War came to an end in 1991. Publicly, American policymakers cited human rights violations in Cuba as the reason for the continued hostility toward Cuba. However, United States–Cuban relations can also be seen in the context of domestic politics. For years, U.S. presidents refused to normalize relations with Cuba for fear of alienating the Cuban-American community in Florida, and losing Florida in the presidential election. Florida, the home of large numbers of anti-Castro Cuban Americans, has proven to be an important swing state, most notably in the presidential election of 2000 (see page 367).

Increasing Tensions with China

Perhaps the most significant foreign relations challenge of the United States in the past decade has been managing its relationship with **China**. American leaders have continued to try to navigate ongoing tensions over trade, technology, and human rights concerns (see more on relations between the United States and China, pages 382–383).

Relations between the two nations were stable under **President George W. Bush** (2001–2009). Despite ongoing concerns over human rights abuses by the Chinese government, China offered support for the war on terrorism following the September 11, 2001, terrorist attacks. China also challenged the growing nuclear capabilities of North

Korea. **President Barack Obama** (2009–2017) also pursued a cooperative relationship with China, although he expressed concerns in regard to the imbalance in trade between the United States and China. He asserted that the value of China's currency was being intentionally set low to benefit China's exporters. Obama met for two days of talks with Chinese leader **Xi Jinping** in 2013. The two leaders found common ground in regard to combatting climate change and in regard to checking North Korea's nuclear program. However, contentious issues remained between the two leaders, including cyber espionage and U.S. arms sales to Taiwan.

Tensions between China and the United States deteriorated under **President Donald Trump** (2017–2021). A variety of issues divided the two countries, including American relations with the government of **Taiwan,** Chinese claims of sovereignty over islands in the South China Sea, and Chinese treatment of Uyghur people. The biggest rift occurred over trade, with Trump imposing levies on imported Chinese steel and aluminum in 2018, and China retaliating with tariffs on over a hundred American items. As China began to play a more assertive role in regard to global leadership, many observers noted that, by 2019, the two countries have seemed to be engaged in a new **"cold war."** Tensions between the two countries remained high during the administration of **President Joe Biden** (2021). The administration raised concerns in regard to several issues including human rights abuses by China, the treatment of minorities in China, and Chinese policy in regard to Hong Kong, as well as conflicts over trade and technology.

Topic 9.7 Subject to Debate

The Legacy of President Ronald Reagan

With Ronald Reagan's passing away in 2004, his legacy has increasingly been the subject of historical work. Much of that work is highly partisan. On the one side, critics cite rising budget deficits, an increase in homelessness along with cuts to social services that served vulnerable populations, an increase in the wealth gap resulting from tax cuts for the wealthy, and attacks on unionized workers. Critics also note that Reagan seemed aloof from issues. He napped during meetings while important policy matters were discussed and claimed ignorance of the complicated schemes that comprised the Iran-Contra scandal. Reagan's defenders focus on one of the major events of the Reagan-Bush years—the fall of Communism in Europe. Reagan initiated a massive military buildup that the Soviet Union could not keep up with. The Soviets' attempt to keep pace broke their bank and led to the opening of the floodgates of change. In addition, his defenders also cite his efforts at deregulating business activity as a major victory. In much of the recent work on Reagan's legacy, these poles dominate discussion.

Causes of the Rise of the New Right

Historians of social movements have tried to understand the rise of the New Right. Some historians have drawn comparisons to previous conservative movements—the "Red Scare" of the 1920s or McCarthyism in the 1950s. Others have connected it to religious movements of the past, such as the Second Great Awakening of the early nineteenth century. Historians have also looked at the movement in the context of a backlash against the social movements and protest culture of the 1960s. If the legacy of the 1960s is "free love," protest, and multiculturalism, the New Right stands for its opposites—conservative approaches to sexuality, respect for authority and discipline, and a unifying patriotism. The persistence of this movement into the age of Presidents Barack Obama and Donald Trump ensures that it will remain a topic of debate.

Putting the Recent Past into Context

It is very difficult to debate the legacy of the very recent past. One topic that historians have begun to wrestle with is the origins of the toxic partisan atmosphere in Washington, D.C. Some historians look to the impeachment process against President Clinton as a turning point in recent political history. The Republican-initiated inquest went beyond the usual jockeying between parties and made compromise between the parties increasingly difficult. Historians also note the unusual closeness in public appeal of the two major parties in recent elections and in opinion polls. This was evident in the 2000 election, which was finally settled by the Supreme Court in *Bush v. Gore*. As a result, both parties always feel as if victory is within reach and seek to press any advantage they can to win points with the electorate. Future historians will have to assess this partisan divide also in terms of the legacy of the nation's first African-American president and in terms of President Trump's unorthodox approach to the presidency.

Practice Multiple-Choice Questions

DIRECTIONS: Pick the letter that best answers the following questions.

Questions 1–2 refer to the following passage:

"[As] Members of the House of Representatives and as citizens seeking to join that body we propose not just to change its policies, but even more important, to restore the bonds of trust between the people and their elected representatives.

"That is why in this era of official evasion and posturing, we offer instead a detailed agenda for national renewal, a written commitment with no fine print.

"This year's election offers the chance, after four decades of one-party control, to bring to the House a new majority that will transform the way Congress works. That historic change would be the end of government that is too big, too intrusive, and too easy with the public's money. It can be the beginning of a Congress that respects the values and shares the faith of the American family.

"To restore accountability to Congress. To end its cycle of scandal and disgrace. To make us all proud again of the way free people govern themselves."

—Contract with America (excerpt), 1994

1. The writing of the Contract with America, excerpted, demonstrates which of the following?

    (A) The growth and influence of the conservative movement in the United States in the 1980s and 1990s
    (B) The ability of the Democratic Party and the Republican Party to forge alliances in the 1980s and 1990s
    (C) The importance of "third-party" movements in terms of shaping political debate in the United States in the 1980s and 1990s
    (D) The growing importance of social and religious issues, such as gay marriage and abortion, in public discourse

2. Which of the following generalizations is illustrated by the impact of the Contract with America?

    (A) The Republican Party experienced electoral setbacks, being shut out from control of the House of Representatives, the Senate, and the White House for the decade after the Contract with America appeared.
    (B) The Republican Party was able to roll back or eliminate key elements of the Great Society agenda of President Lyndon Johnson.
    (C) Although Republicans continued to denounce "big government," the size and scope of the federal government continued to grow in the 1990s, as many programs remained popular with voters and difficult to reform or eliminate.
    (D) Many Congressional Republicans quit the Republican Party and joined the Democratic Party in protest of the divisive tone of the Contract with America.

Questions 3–4 are based on the following passage:

"As citizens of global society, recognizing that the World Trade Organization is unjustly dominated by corporate interests and run for the enrichment of the few at the expense of all others, we demand:

"Representatives from all sectors of society must be included in all levels of trade policy formulations. All global citizens must be democratically represented in the formulation, implementation, and evaluation of all global social and economic policies.

"Global trade and investment must not be ends in themselves, but rather the instruments for achieving equitable and sustainable development including protection for workers and the environment.

"Global trade agreements must not undermine the ability of each nation-state or local community to meet its citizens' social, environmental, cultural or economic needs.

"The World Trade Organization must be replaced by a democratic and transparent body accountable to citizens—not to corporations.

—Global Exchange (Seattle), "Declaration for Global Democracy," 1999

3. The "Declaration for Global Democracy," excerpted, reflects

    (A) opposition to free-trade agreements in the late twentieth century.
    (B) concerns about punitive steps taken by the United States government as part of the war on international terrorism.
    (C) the desire of Congressional leaders to expand global trade and to reduce trade barriers.
    (D) fears that environmental regulations will stifle economic growth.

4. The political sentiments reflected in the "Declaration for Global Democracy" are most similar to which of the following?

    (A) President Woodrow Wilson's "Fourteen Points" document (1918)
    (B) Agreements at the Bretton Woods (New Hampshire) Conference (1944) that led to the formation of the International Monetary Fund
    (C) New Left critiques of the Vietnam War in the 1960s
    (D) The Republican Party's "Contract with America" (1994)

Answers and Explanations

1. **(A)** The Contract with America demonstrates the growth and influence of the conservative movement in the United States in the 1980s and 1990s. By 1994, the Republicans had not controlled the House in more than four decades. In an effort to create a national campaign in the congressional elections of 1994, House Republicans, led by minority leader Newt Gingrich, had signed and publicly issued the Contract with America six weeks before the election. The document called for action on a number of fronts, such as tougher anti-crime measures, tort reform, and welfare reform. The Republican Party made significant gains in the Senate and gained control of the House of Representatives. Many of the House's initiatives died in the Senate, some were vetoed by President Bill Clinton, some were implemented, and some were reworked by both parties before implementation.

2. **(C)** Although Republicans gained control of the House in 1994, Republican legislative successes were limited. The party continued to denounce "big government," but the size, scope, and budget of the federal government continued to grow in the 1990s and even grew in the first decade of the twenty-first century, with a Republican president, George W. Bush, in the White House.

3. **(A)** The "Declaration for Global Democracy" reflects opposition to free-trade agreements in the late twentieth century. The major powers of the world have taken measures to reduce tariffs on imports, thus making the movement of goods and companies across the globe easier. The United States approved the North American Free Trade Agreement (NAFTA) in 1993 and joined the new World Trade Organization in 1994 with the goal of reducing or eliminating tariffs. Free trade and economic globalization is defended by many, such as columnist Thomas Friedman, as a positive development that will create greater understanding in the world and will raise living standards in developing countries. Others, such as protestors at the 1999 meeting of the World Trade Organization in Seattle, condemn globalization as reducing environmental protections and shifting manufacturing jobs to sweatshops in poor countries.

4. **(C)** The political sentiments reflected in the "Declaration for Global Democracy" are most similar to New Left critiques of the Vietnam War in the 1960s. Both the anti-globalization movement and the antiwar movement made connections between foreign policy decisions and corporate domination. Both movements also focused on increasing democratic participation in decision making. Additionally, both movements used street demonstrations to put forth their agendas.

PART 3
Practice Tests

ANSWER SHEET
Practice Test 1

Section I: Part A—Mutiple-Choice

1. Ⓐ Ⓑ Ⓒ Ⓓ
2. Ⓐ Ⓑ Ⓒ Ⓓ
3. Ⓐ Ⓑ Ⓒ Ⓓ
4. Ⓐ Ⓑ Ⓒ Ⓓ
5. Ⓐ Ⓑ Ⓒ Ⓓ
6. Ⓐ Ⓑ Ⓒ Ⓓ
7. Ⓐ Ⓑ Ⓒ Ⓓ
8. Ⓐ Ⓑ Ⓒ Ⓓ
9. Ⓐ Ⓑ Ⓒ Ⓓ
10. Ⓐ Ⓑ Ⓒ Ⓓ
11. Ⓐ Ⓑ Ⓒ Ⓓ
12. Ⓐ Ⓑ Ⓒ Ⓓ
13. Ⓐ Ⓑ Ⓒ Ⓓ
14. Ⓐ Ⓑ Ⓒ Ⓓ
15. Ⓐ Ⓑ Ⓒ Ⓓ
16. Ⓐ Ⓑ Ⓒ Ⓓ
17. Ⓐ Ⓑ Ⓒ Ⓓ
18. Ⓐ Ⓑ Ⓒ Ⓓ
19. Ⓐ Ⓑ Ⓒ Ⓓ
20. Ⓐ Ⓑ Ⓒ Ⓓ
21. Ⓐ Ⓑ Ⓒ Ⓓ
22. Ⓐ Ⓑ Ⓒ Ⓓ
23. Ⓐ Ⓑ Ⓒ Ⓓ
24. Ⓐ Ⓑ Ⓒ Ⓓ
25. Ⓐ Ⓑ Ⓒ Ⓓ
26. Ⓐ Ⓑ Ⓒ Ⓓ
27. Ⓐ Ⓑ Ⓒ Ⓓ
28. Ⓐ Ⓑ Ⓒ Ⓓ
29. Ⓐ Ⓑ Ⓒ Ⓓ
30. Ⓐ Ⓑ Ⓒ Ⓓ
31. Ⓐ Ⓑ Ⓒ Ⓓ
32. Ⓐ Ⓑ Ⓒ Ⓓ
33. Ⓐ Ⓑ Ⓒ Ⓓ
34. Ⓐ Ⓑ Ⓒ Ⓓ
35. Ⓐ Ⓑ Ⓒ Ⓓ
36. Ⓐ Ⓑ Ⓒ Ⓓ
37. Ⓐ Ⓑ Ⓒ Ⓓ
38. Ⓐ Ⓑ Ⓒ Ⓓ
39. Ⓐ Ⓑ Ⓒ Ⓓ
40. Ⓐ Ⓑ Ⓒ Ⓓ
41. Ⓐ Ⓑ Ⓒ Ⓓ
42. Ⓐ Ⓑ Ⓒ Ⓓ
43. Ⓐ Ⓑ Ⓒ Ⓓ
44. Ⓐ Ⓑ Ⓒ Ⓓ
45. Ⓐ Ⓑ Ⓒ Ⓓ
46. Ⓐ Ⓑ Ⓒ Ⓓ
47. Ⓐ Ⓑ Ⓒ Ⓓ
48. Ⓐ Ⓑ Ⓒ Ⓓ
49. Ⓐ Ⓑ Ⓒ Ⓓ
50. Ⓐ Ⓑ Ⓒ Ⓓ
51. Ⓐ Ⓑ Ⓒ Ⓓ
52. Ⓐ Ⓑ Ⓒ Ⓓ
53. Ⓐ Ⓑ Ⓒ Ⓓ
54. Ⓐ Ⓑ Ⓒ Ⓓ
55. Ⓐ Ⓑ Ⓒ Ⓓ

Practice Test 1

Section I

Part A: Multiple-Choice Questions

DIRECTIONS: The questions in this section are grouped in sets of 2–4. Each set is organized around a primary source, secondary source, or historical issue. Select the best answer for each of the questions in this section. (55 minutes)

Questions 1–3 refer to the following passage:

"The question, therefore, should be quickly settled, whether free colored persons, born and naturalized in this country, are not American citizens, and justly entitled to all the rights, privileges and immunities of citizens of the several states; and whether the Constitution of the United States makes or authorizes any invidious distinction with regard to the color or condition of free inhabitants.

"For myself, I have not the shadow of doubt on the subject. I believe that the rights of the free colored persons need only to be vindicated before the U.S. Supreme Court, to be obtained; that no prejudice or sophistry . . . can prevent their acknowledgement . . . and that the present laws, affecting your condition, are clearly unconstitutional. The fact that you have been treated, by common consent and common usage, as aliens and brutes, is not proof that such treatment is legal, but only shows the strength, the bitterness, and the blindness of prejudice."

—William Lloyd Garrison, "To the Free People of Color of the United States," *The Liberator*, January 15, 1831

1. The approach of William Lloyd Garrison and *The Liberator* can best be seen as

    (A) an outgrowth of the Second Great Awakening.
    (B) an expression of Transcendentalist individualism.
    (C) a reflection of literary romanticism.
    (D) a rejection of the idea of "Republican motherhood."

2. The argument put forth by William Lloyd Garrison in the passage was later contradicted in which of the following Supreme Court decisions?

    (A) *Dred Scott v. Sandford* (1857)
    (B) *Ex parte Milligan* (1866)
    (C) *Plessy v. Ferguson* (1896)
    (D) *Brown v. Board of Education of Topeka* (1954)

3. The reform that William Lloyd Garrison is advocating in the passage was later enacted as a result of the

    (A) issuing of the Emancipation Proclamation (1863).
    (B) passage of the Reconstruction Act of 1867.
    (C) ratification of the Fourteenth Amendment (1868).
    (D) passage of the Civil Rights Act of 1875.

Questions 4–5 refer to the following images:

4. The differences in the two maps shown above illustrate which of the following?

    (A) The result of the Articles of Confederation government successfully handling the question of western lands
    (B) Territorial transfers that were brought about by the treaty ending the French and Indian War
    (C) The evolving status of slavery in the newly acquired territories of the United States
    (D) The impact of the "Quasi-War" with France on competing land claims in the American West

5. The establishment of the Northwest Territory (visible in the second map) by the Northwest Ordinance of 1787 contributed to problems in the subsequent decades of American history because the ordinance

    (A) ignored the earlier designation of that land as an "Indian Reserve" by the British, setting the stage for violent conflict in the region.
    (B) failed to address the issue of slavery in the Northwest Territory, leading to violence between proslavery and antislavery forces.
    (C) called for any political entities carved out of the Northwest Territory to be treated as inferior bodies to the original thirteen states, leading to a constitutional conflict that was eventually resolved by the Supreme Court.
    (D) made no provisions for individuals to gain title to land in the Northwest Territory, setting off a series of violent skirmishes among people with competing land claims.

Questions 6–8 refer to the following image:

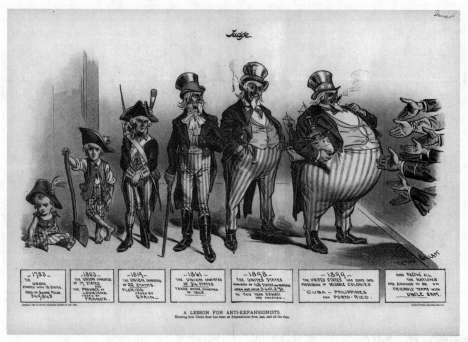

—Victor Gillam, "A Lesson for Anti-Expansionists,"
Judge Magazine, 1899

6. The circumstances depicted in the cartoon suggest that the cartoon was published in the immediate aftermath of

   (A) the War of 1812.
   (B) the Mexican-American War.
   (C) the Spanish-American War.
   (D) World War I.

7. Which of the following reflects a main point of the cartoon?

   (A) The United States' acquisition of overseas colonies represents a break from the democratic traditions that had guided America since its founding.
   (B) The United States' acquisition of overseas colonies is part of the natural progression for the country and will gain the approval of foreign powers.
   (C) The United States' acquisition of overseas territories is dangerous and could lead to war with other imperialist powers.
   (D) The United States' acquisition of overseas territories is necessary to bring civilization to the natives of the newly acquired territories.

8. In the period following the events depicted in the cartoon, the United States

   (A) formed multilateral agreements and regional alliances with developing nations.
   (B) withdrew from global affairs in the face of opposition at home and abroad to imperialistic ventures.
   (C) expanded its economic and military presence in the Caribbean, Latin America, and Asia.
   (D) insisted that the countries referred to in the cartoon improve their human rights records or suffer a reduction of foreign aid.

Questions 9–10 refer to the following passage:

"The power . . . given to the commanding officer over all the people of each district is that of an absolute monarch. His mere will is to take the place of all law. . . . It reduces the whole population of the ten states—all persons, of every color, sex, and condition, and every stranger within their limits—to the most abject and degrading slavery."

—President Andrew Johnson's veto message of the First Reconstruction Act of 1867

9. President Andrew Johnson's veto message would most likely have had the support of

    (A) Radical Republicans
    (B) freedman and freedwomen
    (C) Northern Whigs
    (D) Southern Democrats

10. The political sentiment of the veto message above is most similar to which of the following political positions taken in the twentieth century?

    (A) Justice Frank Murphy's dissent in the Supreme Court case *Korematsu v. United States* in 1944
    (B) U.S. Army lawyer Joseph Welsh's opposition to Senator Joseph McCarthy in the Army-McCarthy hearings in 1954
    (C) Governor Orval Faubus's response to the steps taken by President Dwight Eisenhower to resolve the Little Rock crisis in 1957
    (D) Student Nonviolent Coordinating Committee leader John Lewis's endorsement of the Voting Rights Act in 1965

Questions 11–12 refer to the following passage:

"In 1680, Popé, a Tewa medicine man from San Juan, synchronized an uprising of the different Pueblos that drove out the Spaniards for a dozen years. The Indians killed and mutilated many of the friars who had been trying to stamp out their religion and desecrated the alien paraphernalia of Catholicism.

"The Spaniards returned [after Popé's rebellion of 1680], but they had learned from their experience. Where their predecessors had tried to eradicate all Native practices, friars now more often turned a blind eye to such practices. . . . When Diego de Vargas returned on his campaign of conquest in 1692, Luis, a Picuri Pueblo leader, appeared before him dressed in animal skins and wearing bands of palm shell around his head; but he also wore a rosary around his neck and carried a silver cross."

—Colin G. Calloway, *New World for All: Indians, Europeans, and the Remaking of Early America*, 1997

11. The process described in the excerpt reflects which of the following developments in the seventeenth century?

    (A) Over time, Europeans developed a more accommodating attitude toward Native American cultural practices.
    (B) By the end of the seventeenth century, the Spanish developed harsher techniques for suppressing Native American resistance.
    (C) The Spanish Crown became increasingly critical of the *encomenderos*, who oversaw Spain's New World empire.
    (D) Native Americans were so devastated by European diseases in the first years of contact that they were unable to mount resistance to Spanish encroachments.

12. The excerpt demonstrates that American Indian societies most commonly reacted to the presence of Spaniards by

    (A) readily shedding traditional ways and adopting the cultural practices of the Spanish.
    (B) adapting some elements of Spanish culture while attempting to preserve a degree of cultural autonomy.
    (C) rejecting European cultural practices but accepting European political structures.
    (D) successfully using Spanish military technology and strategy against Spanish encroachments on Native American lands.

Questions 13–14 refer to the following image:

—C. D. Batchelor, *New York Daily News*, April 25, 1936

13. The 1936 cartoon above, from the *New York Daily News*, is making the point that

    (A) although European individuals and countries might be seduced into waging another major war, the United States would be wise to avoid participating.
    (B) the policy of appeasement is a bankrupt policy that can only lead to more death and destruction.
    (C) munitions manufacturers, the so-called merchants of death, were pushing the world toward war in the name of profits.
    (D) the weaponry of modern warfare had advanced to such a degree that future military engagements would result in unprecedented carnage.

14. Which of the following political positions most closely parallels the political position reflected in the cartoon?

    (A) Newspaper publisher William Randolph Hearst's position on declaring war on Spain in 1898
    (B) The Abraham Lincoln Brigade position on American intervention in the Spanish Civil War in 1937
    (C) Secretary of State Dean Acheson's position on U.S. intervention in the Korean War in 1950
    (D) Civil rights leader Martin Luther King Jr.'s position on the Vietnam War in 1967

Questions 15–17 refer to the following passage:

"The seeds of totalitarian regimes are nurtured by misery and want. They spread and grow in the evil soil of poverty and strife. They reach their full growth when the hope of a people for a better life has died. We must keep that hope alive. . . . Great responsibilities have been placed upon us by the swift movement of events. . . . I am confident that the Congress will face these responsibilities squarely."

—President Harry S. Truman, Address to Congress, 1947

15. The passage above is part of President Truman's argument to Congress in favor of

    (A) the Servicemen's Readjustment Act (G.I. Bill).
    (B) development of the hydrogen bomb.
    (C) the McCarran Internal Security Act.
    (D) an extension of aid to Greece and Turkey.

16. The passage above can best be seen as providing a rationale for

    (A) the policy of containment.
    (B) the principle of "massive retaliation."
    (C) participation in the Atlantic Charter.
    (D) embarking on a "roll-back" of Communism.

17. The ideas expressed in the passage above most directly reflect which of the following continuities in U.S. history?

    (A) Debates about the relationship between Congress and the president
    (B) Debates about the use of military force in volatile situations
    (C) Debates about the role of the United States in world affairs
    (D) Debates about the proper role of political parties

Questions 18–19 refer to the following image:

—"Your Honor, this woman gave birth to a naked child" (the figure speaking is Anthony Comstock, United States Postal Inspector), *The Masses*, September 1915

18. The political cartoon above is making the point that

    (A) government officials were taking their crusade against immoral behavior to extreme lengths.
    (B) unregulated immigration was leading to an increase in crime among men and women in urban centers.
    (C) "flappers" were imposing their standards of moral behavior on an unsuspecting public.
    (D) the court system was bogged down with insignificant complaints while perpetrators of major crimes were left untouched by the law.

19. The cartoon reflects a point of view about which of the following continuities in U.S. history?

    (A) Debates about immigration policy
    (B) Debates about the role of the federal government in regulating morality
    (C) Debates about access to health care for working-class women
    (D) Debates about the rights of the individuals accused of crimes

Questions 20–22 refer to the following passage:

"If it be conceded, as it must be by every one who is the least conversant with our institutions, that the sovereign powers delegated are divided between the General and State Governments, and that the latter hold their portion by the same tenure as the former, it would seem impossible to deny to the States the right of deciding on the infractions of their powers, and the proper remedy to be applied for their correction. The right of judging, in such cases, is an essential attribute of sovereignty, of which the States cannot be divested without losing their sovereignty itself, and being reduced to a subordinate corporate condition. In fact, to divide power, and to give to one of the parties the exclusive right of judging of the portion allotted to each, is, in reality, not to divide it at all; and to reserve such exclusive right to the General Government (it matters not by what department to be exercised), is to convert it, in fact, into a great consolidated government, with unlimited powers, and to divest the States, in reality, of all their rights, It is impossible to understand the force of terms, and to deny so plain a conclusion."

—John C. Calhoun, "South Carolina Exposition and Protest," 1828

20. The issue that precipitated the passage excerpted above was

    (A) the removal of American Indians from the South.
    (B) the rechartering of the Second Bank of the United States.
    (C) the passage of an act creating higher tariff rates.
    (D) the funding of "internal improvements."

21. The argument put forth by John C. Calhoun in the passage above states a position in a debate that is most similar to which of the following debates from earlier in U.S. history?

    (A) The debate over whether to count slaves in the census for purposes of representation
    (B) The debate over the constitutionality of acquiring the Louisiana Purchase
    (C) The debate over disestablishment of the Episcopal Church in several states
    (D) The debate over replacing the Articles of Confederation with the Constitution

22. The language of "protest" that Calhoun used in his "Exposition and Protest" was similar to the language of which of the following political positions?

    (A) The response of supporters of Andrew Jackson to the "corrupt bargain" of 1824
    (B) The response of New England Federalists to the War of 1812
    (C) The response of the Jefferson administration to the actions of the "Barbary pirates"
    (D) The response of Daniel Shays to fiscal policies of the Massachusetts legislature in the 1780s

Questions 23–25 refer to the following image:

—Carey Orr, "The Trojan Horse At Our Gate,"
September 17, 1935

23. The 1935 political cartoon shown above makes the point that

    (A) the New Deal's proposals for open immigration would threaten American democracy.
    (B) the New Deal would be ineffective in addressing the problems of the Great Depression.
    (C) the Supreme Court acted in a tyrannical way in declaring certain New Deal measures unconstitutional.
    (D) New Deal programs would usher in unconstitutional restrictions on American freedoms and liberties.

24. The sentiment expressed in the cartoon above most directly reflects which of the following continuities in U.S. history?

    (A) Debates about the proper role of the federal government in the economy
    (B) Debates about the power of the Supreme Court to "legislate from the bench"
    (C) Debates about the proper relationship between the federal government and the states
    (D) Debates about individual liberties during times of war

25. The sentiment reflected in the cartoon was similar to which of the following political expressions?

    (A) Support by the feminists for the Equal Rights Amendment in 1972
    (B) Opposition by the Republican Party to the creation of Great Society programs in the 1960s
    (C) Opposition by environmentalists to passage of the North American Free Trade Agreement in 1994
    (D) Opposition by Korean War veterans to the firing of General Douglas MacArthur by President Eisenhower in 1951

Questions 26–27 refer to the following passage:

"A drunkard in the gutter is just where he ought to be.... The law of survival of the fittest was not made by man, and it cannot be abrogated by man. We can only, by interfering with it, produce the survival of the unfittest.... The millionaires are a product of natural selection, acting on the whole body of men to pick out those who can meet the requirement of certain work to be done. In this respect they are just like the great statesmen, or scientific men, or military men. It is because they are thus selected that wealth—both their own and that entrusted to them—aggregates under their hands. Let one of them make a mistake and see how quickly the concentration gives way to dispersion."

—William Graham Sumner, *What Social Classes Owe to Each Other*, 1883

26. During the late 1800s, those who followed the ideas of William Graham Sumner in his book, *What Social Classes Owe to Each Other* (excerpted above), would most likely have advocated

    (A) government ownership of major banks and railroad companies.
    (B) a social welfare "safety net" to help people get through difficult economic times.
    (C) government efforts to curb alcohol consumption.
    (D) a laissez-faire approach to the economy.

27. The sociological ideas of William Graham Sumner reflect the idea that during the late 1800s

    (A) cultural and intellectual arguments justified the success of those at the top of the socioeconomic structure as both appropriate and inevitable.
    (B) popular writers rejected ideas from the sciences and based their arguments on faith.
    (C) intellectuals were critical of the cut-throat competition of the time and proposed radical alternatives based on creating a cooperative economy.
    (D) cultural products of the era tended to ignore the economic direction of society and looked back wistfully to the past.

Questions 28–30 refer to the following passage:

"If any person or persons shall, from and after the passing of this act, by force and violence, take and carry away, or cause to be taken or carried away, and shall, by fraud or false pretense, seduce, or cause to be seduced, or shall attempt so to take, carry away or seduce, any negro or mulatto, from any part or parts of this commonwealth, to any other place or places whatsoever, out of this commonwealth, with a design and intention of selling and disposing of, or of causing to be sold, or of keeping and detaining, or of causing to be kept and detained, such negro or mulatto, as a slave or servant for life, or for any term whatsoever, every such person or persons, his or their aiders or abettors, shall on conviction thereof, in any court of this commonwealth having competent jurisdiction, be deemed guilty of a felony."

—Excerpt from Pennsylvania law, 1826

28. Critics challenged the constitutionality of this 1826 law in the Supreme Court on the grounds that it

    (A) violated the constitutional injunction against bills of attainder.
    (B) undermined the intent of the fugitive slave clause of the Constitution.
    (C) circumvented the three-fifths clause of the Constitution.
    (D) was inconsistent with the "eminent domain" clause of the Fifth Amendment of the Constitution.

29. The passage and implementation of this Pennsylvania law reflected an ongoing conflict between

    (A) rural and urban interests.
    (B) federal law and state law.
    (C) those who favored gradual emancipation and those who favored immediate emancipation.
    (D) supporters and opponents of government regulation of commerce.

30. Debate and conflict over the Pennsylvania law, excerpted above, reflected the fact that the framers of the Constitution

    (A) specifically declared that the institution of slavery would be protected "in perpetuity" in the original thirteen states.
    (B) allowed for a state to be exempt from federal laws that went against that state's constitution.
    (C) postponed a solution to the problems of slavery.
    (D) declared that slaves could be both citizens and property.

Questions 31–32 refer to the following passage:

"I come to present the strong claims of suffering humanity. I come to place before the Legislature of Massachusetts the condition of the miserable, the desolate, the outcast. I come as the advocate of helpless, forgotten, insane and idiotic men and women; of beings, sunk to a condition from which the most unconcerned would start with real horror; of beings wretched in our Prisons, and more wretched in our Alms-Houses. . . .

"If my pictures are displeasing, coarse, and severe, my subjects, it must be recollected, offer no tranquil, refined, or composing features. The condition of human beings, reduced to the extremest states of degradation and misery, cannot be exhibited in softened language, or adorn a polished page.

"I proceed, Gentlemen, briefly to call your attention to the present state of Insane Persons confined within this Commonwealth, *in cages, closets, cellars, stalls, pens! Chained, naked, beaten with rods,* and *lashed* into obedience!"

—Dorothea Dix, "Memorial to the Massachusetts Legislature," 1843

31. Dorothea Dix's testimony to the Massachusetts legislature reflects the influence of which of the following?

    (A) Social Darwinism
    (B) The Second Great Awakening
    (C) Second-wave feminism
    (D) The Christian Science movement

32. Dorothea Dix's research and testimony is best understood in the context of

    (A) women gaining the right to vote in many states.
    (B) an economic downturn that was responsible for the closure of many state institutions.
    (C) an evolving relationship between the federal government and issues of health and poverty.
    (D) the rise of voluntary organizations to promote religious and secular reforms.

Questions 33–35 refer to the following passage:

"I was once a tool of oppression
And as green as a sucker could be
And monopolies banded together
To beat a poor hayseed like me.

"The railroads and old party bosses
Together did sweetly agree;
And they thought there would be little trouble
In working a hayseed like me...."

—"The Hayseed," song lyric, 1890

33. The song lyrics above would most likely have appeared in

    (A) an abolitionist newspaper.
    (B) a Republican leaflet.
    (C) a populist newspaper.
    (D) a civil rights pamphlet.

34. Which of the following is an accomplishment of the political movement that was organized around sentiments similar to the one in the song lyrics above?

    (A) Establishment of the minimum wage law
    (B) Enactment of laws regulating railroads
    (C) Shift in U.S. currency from the gold standard to the silver standard
    (D) Creation of a price-support system for small-scale farmers

35. The song, and the movement that it was connected to, highlight which of the following developments in the broader society in the late 1800s?

    (A) Corruption in government—especially as it related to big business—energized the public to demand increased popular control and reform of local, state, and national governments.
    (B) A large-scale movement of struggling African-American and white farmers, as well as urban factory workers, was able to exert a great deal of leverage over federal legislation.
    (C) The two-party system of the era broke down and led to the emergence of an additional major party that was able to win control of Congress within ten years of its founding.
    (D) Continued skirmishes on the frontier in the 1890s with American Indians created a sense of fear and bitterness among western farmers.

Questions 36–37 refer to the following passage:

"We are men; we have souls, we have passions, we have feelings, we have hopes, we have desires, like any other race in the world. The cry is raised all over the world today of Canada for the Canadians, of America for the Americans, of England for the English, of France for the French, of Germany for the Germans—do you think it is unreasonable that we, the Blacks of the world, should raise the cry of Africa for the Africans?"

—Marcus Garvey, "Look for me in the whirlwind," speech (excerpt), circa 1924

36. The passage could best be understood as

    (A) an argument in favor of restrictions on immigration into the United States.
    (B) an attempt to unite working-class African Americans and white men and women.
    (C) an expression of Black nationalism.
    (D) a pamphlet designed to promote the advancement of African Americans in industry.

37. The passage above presents a position in which of the following ongoing debates in American history?

    (A) The debate between interventionism and isolationism in foreign policy
    (B) The debate between separatism and integration in regard to African Americans in American society
    (C) The debate between exclusion and inclusion when it came to immigration policy
    (D) The debate between laissez-faire policies and government intervention in economic affairs

Questions 38–39 refer to the following passage:

"But even if southern progressivism included women, was it reserved for whites? The answer is that whites intended for it to be, and it would have been even more racist, more exclusive, and more oppressive if there had been no black women progressives. . . . As much as southern whites plotted to reserve progressivism for themselves, and as much as they schemed to alter the ill-fitting northern version accordingly, they failed. African-American women embraced southern white progressivism, reshaped it, and sent back a new model that included black power brokers and grass roots activists. Evidence of southern African-American progressivism is not to be found in public laws, electoral politics, or the establishment of mothers' aid programs at the state level. It rarely appears in documents that white progressives, male or female, left behind. Since black men could not speak out in politics and black women did not want to be seen, it has remained invisible in virtually every discussion of southern progressivism. Nonetheless, southern black women initiated every progressive reform that southern white women initiated, a feat they accomplished without financial resources, without the civic protection of their husbands, and without publicity."

—Glenda Elizabeth Gilmore, "Diplomatic Women," from *Gender and Jim Crow: Women and the Politics of White Supremacy in North Carolina, 1896–1920*

38. The excerpt above, from the essay by Glenda Elizabeth Gilmore, implies that historians of the Progressive movement have

   (A) failed to adequately explain why the agenda and goals of the Progressive movement never resonated with the African-American community.
   (B) ignored the latent racism and white supremacy inherent in the Progressive movement.
   (C) not written extensively on the contributions of Black women to progressivism in the South because of a scarcity of documentary evidence.
   (D) overemphasized the extent of African-American participation in the Progressive movement in order to improve the public perception of the movement.

39. The efforts described in the reading above occurred in the context of

   (A) increased federal support for civil rights measures in the United States, as American political leaders sought to bolster the democratic image of the United States on a global stage.
   (B) rapid industrialization in the South, which brought African-American working-class activists in closer contact with whites.
   (C) successful efforts by the U.S. military to segregate units fighting in the Spanish-American War and World War I, but resistance by state governments to follow the lead of the military.
   (D) a low point in race relations in the United States as "scientific" ideas about race, inaction by the federal government, and rigid segregation in the South relegated African Americans to a second-class status in the United States.

Questions 40–42 refer to the following passage:

"Observe good faith and justice towards all nations; cultivate peace and harmony with all. . . . It will be worthy of a free, enlightened, and at no distant period, a great nation, to give to mankind the . . . example of a people always guided by an exalted justice. . . .

"In the execution of such a plan, nothing is more essential than that permanent and inveterate antipathies against particular nations, and passionate attachments for others, should be excluded; and that in place of them, just and amicable feelings towards all should be cultivated. The nation which indulges towards another a habitual hatred or a habitual fondness is in some degree a slave. It is a slave to its animosity or to its affection. . . .

"The great rule of conduct for us in regard to foreign nations is in extending our commercial relations, to have with them as little political connection as possible. . . . Europe has a set of primary interests which to us have none; or a very remote relation. Hence, she must be engaged in frequent controversies, the causes of which are essentially foreign to our concerns."

—President George Washington, "Farewell Address" (excerpt), 1793

40. The ideas expressed in the passage above most directly reflect which of the following continuities in U.S. history?

    (A) Debates about the proper role of the United States in international politics
    (B) Debates about tariffs and trade
    (C) Debates about the power of the executive to establish foreign policy
    (D) Debates about the wisdom of imperialistic ventures

41. The sentiments of President Washington in his "Farewell Address" can most clearly be seen in which of the following?

    (A) President James Monroe in enunciating the Monroe Doctrine
    (B) President William McKinley declaring war on Spain
    (C) President Woodrow Wilson in writing the "Fourteen Points" document
    (D) President Franklin Roosevelt in signing the Lend-Lease Act

42. Which of the following most clearly represents a break with the approach to foreign policy that President Washington advocated in his "Farewell Address?"

    (A) Passage of the Smoot-Hawley Tariff Act (1930)
    (B) Passage of the Neutrality Act of 1935
    (C) Joining the North Atlantic Treaty Organization (1949)
    (D) Creation of the Peace Corps (1961)

Questions 43–44 refer to the following passage:

"As our late Conduct at the Conestoga Manor and Lancaster have occasioned much Speculation & a great diversity of Sentiments in this and neighboring Governments; some vindicating & others condemning it; some charitably alleviating the Crime, & others maliciously painting it in the most odious & detestable Colours, we think it our duty to lay before the Publick, the whole Matter as it appeared, & still appears, to us. . . .

"If these things are not sufficient to prove an unjustifiable Attachment in the Quakers to the Indians Savages, a fixed Resolution to befriend them & an utter insensibility to human Distresses, let us consider a few more recent Facts. When we found the last Summer that we were likely to get no Assistance from the Government, some Volunteers went out at our own Expense, determined to drive our Enemies from our Borders; & when we came near to the great Island, we understood that a Number of their Warriors had gone out against our Frontiers. Upon this we returned and came up with them and fought with them at the Munsey Hill where we lost some of our Men & killed some of their Warriors & thereby saved our Frontiers from this Story in another Expedition. But no sooner had we destroyed their Provisions on the great Island, & ruined their trade with the good People at Bethlehem, but these very Indians, who were justly suspected of having murdered our Friends in Northampton County, were by the Influence of some Quakers taken under the Protection of the Government to screen them from the Resentments of the Friends and Relations of the Murdered, & to support them thro the Winter."

—"Apology of the Paxton Boys" (pamphlet), 1764
(Note: "Apology" in this context should be read as a defense, not an admission of guilt or regret.)

43. The sentiments expressed in the explanation above reflect which of the ongoing tensions during the colonial period of American history?

    (A) Tensions between British policies and the aspirations of North American colonists
    (B) Tensions between American Indians allied with the French and those allied with the British
    (C) Tensions between freed African Americans and white planters
    (D) Tensions between backcountry settlers and elites within colonial America

44. Which of the following events from either earlier or later in the colonial period can best be seen as being part of a continuity with the events described in the passage above?

    (A) The expulsion of Anne Hutchinson from Massachusetts Bay Colony
    (B) Bacon's Rebellion in colonial Virginia
    (C) The Boston Tea Party
    (D) The trial of John Peter Zenger

Questions 45–48 refer to the following passage:

"When we were kids the United States was the wealthiest and strongest country in the world; the only one with the atom bomb, the least scarred by modern war, an initiator of the United Nations that we thought would distribute Western influence throughout the world. Freedom and equality for each individual, government of, by, and for the people—these American values we found good, principles by which we could live as men. Many of us began maturing in complacency.

"As we grew, however, our comfort was penetrated by events too troubling to dismiss. First, the permeating and victimizing fact of human degradation, symbolized by the Southern struggle against racial bigotry, compelled most of us from silence to activism. Second, the enclosing fact of the Cold War, symbolized by the presence of the Bomb, brought awareness that we ourselves, and our friends, and millions of abstract 'others' we knew more directly because of our common peril, might die at any time."

—Port Huron Statement, 1962

45. The Port Huron Statement, excerpted above, can most clearly be seen as an important document in which of the following movements?

    (A) The labor union movement
    (B) The civil rights movement
    (C) The New Right
    (D) The New Left

46. The language of this document can be seen as a repudiation of which of the following policies or actions from the Eisenhower years?

    (A) The "New Look" foreign policy
    (B) Increases in funding for the United Nations
    (C) Intervention in the Little Rock, Arkansas crisis
    (D) Renewed focus on education

47. The primary intended audience for the Port Huron Statement was

    (A) African Americans in the South.
    (B) government officials.
    (C) middle-class college students.
    (D) factory workers.

48. Through the remainder of the 1960s, the growth of the organization that published the Port Huron Statement can best be understood in the context of

    (A) rapid industrialization, urban growth and congestion, and corporate consolidation.
    (B) the baby boom, economic growth, and a rapid expansion of higher education.
    (C) economic polarization, supply-side economic policies, and the disappearance of the middle class.
    (D) the proliferation of personal computer technologies, the rise of Christian fundamentalism, and an increase in student apathy.

Questions 49–51 refer to the following passage:

"An act for the more effectual protection of the property of married women:

"§1. The real property of any female who may hereafter marry, and which she shall own at the time of marriage, and the rents, issues, and profits thereof, shall not be subject to the sole disposal of her husband, nor be liable for his debts, and shall continue her sole and separate property, as if she were a single female.

"§2. The real and personal property, and the rents, issues, and profits thereof, of any female now married, shall not be subject to the disposal of her husband; but shall be her sole and separate property, as if she were a single female, except so far as the same may be liable for the debts of her husband heretofore contracted.

"§3. Any married female may take by inheritance, or by gift, grant, devise, or bequest, from any person other than her husband, and hold to her sole and separate use, and convey and devise real and personal property, and any interest or estate therein, and the rents, issues, and profits thereof, in the same manner and with like effect as if she were unmarried, and the same shall not be subject to the disposal of her husband nor be liable for his debts."

—Married Women's Property Act, New York State, 1848

49. The Married Women's Property Act was significant in that it

   (A) expanded women's participation in the political sphere.
   (B) challenged a traditional view of women and property embodied in the legal concept of *feme covert*.
   (C) codified the cultural assumptions implicit in the concept of "Republican motherhood."
   (D) relegated women to a second-class status in regard to citizenship.

50. Which of the following groups would be most likely to support the perspective of the Married Women's Property Act?

   (A) Participants in the Seneca Falls Convention
   (B) Southern supporters of the concept of "female virtue"
   (C) Proponents of the "cult of domesticity" value system
   (D) Congregational ministers

51. The ideas expressed in the passage above most directly reflect which of the following continuities in U.S. history?

   (A) Debates about access to voting rights
   (B) Debates about the role of federal government in marriage law
   (C) Debates about discrimination in employment
   (D) Debates about the legal status of women

Questions 52–53 refer to the following passage:

"The law of love, peace and liberty in the states extending to Jews, Turks and Egyptians, as they are considered sonnes of Adam, which is the glory of the outward state of Holland, soe love, peace and liberty, extending to all in Christ Jesus, condemns hatred, war and bondage. And because our Saviour sayeth it is impossible but that offences will come, but woe unto him by whom they cometh, our desire is not to offend one of his little ones, in whatsoever form, name or title hee appears in, whether Presbyterian, Independent, Baptist or Quaker, but shall be glad to see anything of God in any of them, desiring to doe unto all men as we desire all men should doe unto us, which is the true law both of Church and State; for our Saviour sayeth this is the law and the prophets.

"Therefore if any of these said persons come in love unto us, we cannot in conscience lay violent hands upon them, but give them free egresse and regresse unto our Town, and houses, as God shall persuade our consciences, for we are bounde by the law of God and man to doe good unto all men and evil to noe man. And this is according to the patent and charter of our Towne, given unto us in the name of the States General, which we are not willing to infringe, and violate, but shall houlde to our patent and shall remaine, your humble subjects, the inhabitants of Vlishing (Flushing, part of the colony of New Netherlands)."

—The Flushing Remonstrance, 1657

52. Which of the following most accurately describes the context in which the above document was written?

   (A) The Dutch West India Company had sought to establish a model community in the New World, based on Enlightenment principles; the document grew out of this mandate.
   (B) The policies of the Dutch West Indian company had discouraged non-Dutch immigrants from settling in New Netherlands; the document was an attempt to diversify the colony.
   (C) Religious toleration had become the norm in the neighboring New England colonies in the seventeenth century; the document was an attempt to bring New Amsterdam to the same levels of toleration.
   (D) The director-general of the colony of New Netherlands, Peter Stuyvesant, was attempting to enforce conformity in New Netherlands despite the multiethnic makeup of the colony; the document was an attempt to accommodate the diverse population.

53. Which of the following was most significant in enshrining into the U.S. legal structure the ideas contained in the Flushing Remonstrance?

   (A) The preamble of the Declaration of Independence
   (B) The enumeration of congressional powers in the Constitution
   (C) The "Free Exercise Clause" of the First Amendment
   (D) The "Establishment Clause" of the First Amendment

Questions 54–55 refer to the following passage:

"The petition of several poor negroes and mulattoes, who are inhabitants of the town of Dartmouth, humbly showeth,—

"That we being chiefly of the African extract, and by reason of long bondage and hard slavery, we have been deprived of enjoying the profits of our labor or the advantage of inheriting estates from our parents, as our neighbors the white people do, having some of us not long enjoyed our own freedom; yet of late, contrary to the invariable custom and practice of the country, we have been, and now are, taxed both in our polls and that small pittance of estate which, through much hard labor and industry, we have got together to sustain ourselves and families withall. We apprehend it, therefore, to be hard usage, and will doubtless (if continued) reduce us to a state of beggary, whereby we shall become a burthen to others, if not timely prevented by the interposition of your justice and your power.

"Your petitioners further show, that we apprehend ourselves to be aggrieved, in that, while we are not allowed the privilege of freemen of the State, having no vote or influence in the election of those that tax us, yet many of our colour (as is well known) have cheerfully entered the field of battle in the defence of the common cause, and that (as we conceive) against a similar exertion of power (in regard to taxation), too well known to need a recital in this place."

—Paul Cuffe's Petition, Massachusetts, 1780

54. The main purpose of the petition by Paul Cuffe, excerpted above, was to demand

    (A) that the petitioners be released from slavery because slavery was incompatible with the Massachusetts constitution.
    (B) that the Massachusetts legislature extend reparations to the petitioners as compensation for their time in slavery.
    (C) that the petitioners receive land that had been expropriated from loyalists in order to reward them for their service to the Continental Army during the American Revolution.
    (D) that the Massachusetts legislature either grant the petitioners the right to vote or that it excuse them from paying taxes.

55. The petition by Paul Cuffe, above, best illustrates which of the following developments?

    (A) The rhetoric of the American Revolution raised awareness of social inequalities and inspired groups and individuals to call for greater political democracy.
    (B) Slave rebellions, such as the Stono Rebellion, inspired enslaved Americans throughout North America to engage in similar behavior.
    (C) African Americans who had fought alongside the British during the American Revolution felt doubly vulnerable—as African Americans and as traitors to the Patriot cause—after the British defeat.
    (D) African Americans received worse treatment under the state government of Massachusetts than they had under British law during the colonial period.

STOP If there is still time remaining, you may review your answers.

Part B: Short-Answer Questions

DIRECTIONS: Answer Question 1 *and* Question 2. Answer either Question 3 *or* Question 4.

During the AP exam, a Short-Answer Response booklet will be distributed. You must write your response to each question on the lined page designated for that response. Each response is expected to fit within the space provided.

In your responses, be sure to address all parts of the questions you answer. Use complete sentences; an outline or bulleted list alone is not acceptable. You may plan your answers in this exam booklet, but no credit will be given for notes written in this booklet. (40 minutes)

Question 1

"The events of 1763–1775 can have no meaning unless we understand that the character of English imperial policy never really changed: that Pitt and his successors at [Whitehall] were following exactly the same line that Cromwell had laid down more than a century before. The purpose of their general program was to protect the English capitalist interests which now were being jeopardized as a result of the intensification of colonial capitalist competition, and English statesmen yielded quickly when no fundamental principle was at stake, but became insistent only when one was being threatened. . . . The struggle was not over high-sounding political and constitutional concepts: over the power of taxation or even, in the final analysis, over natural rights. It was over . . . the survival or collapse of English mercantile capitalism within the imperial-colonial framework of the mercantilist system."

Andrew Hacker, historian, The Triumph of American Capitalism, 1940

"It was in the context of the sources and patterns of ideas . . . that I began to see a new meaning in phrases that I, like most historians, had readily dismissed as mere rhetoric and propaganda: "slavery," "corruption," "conspiracy." These inflammatory words were used so forcefully by writers of so great a variety of social statuses, political positions, and religious persuasions; they fitted so logically into the pattern of radical and opposition thought . . . that I began to suspect that they meant something very real to both the writers and their readers: that there were real fears, real anxieties, a sense of real danger behind these phrases, and not merely the desire to influence by rhetoric and propaganda the inert minds of an otherwise passive populace. . . . In the end I was convinced that the fear of a comprehensive conspiracy against liberty throughout the English-speaking world—a conspiracy believed to have been nourished in corruption, and of which, it was felt, oppression in America was only the most immediately visible part—lay at the heart of the Revolutionary movement."

Bernard Bailyn, historian, The Ideological Origins of the American Revolution, 1967

1. Using the excerpts above, answer (a), (b), and (c).

    (a) Briefly describe ONE major difference between Hacker's and Bailyn's historical interpretations of the American Revolution.

    (b) Briefly explain how ONE specific historical event or development during the period 1754 to 1783 that is not explicitly mentioned in the excerpts could be used to support Hacker's interpretation.

    (c) Briefly explain how ONE specific historical event or development during the period 1754 to 1783 that is not explicitly mentioned in the excerpts could be used to support Bailyn's interpretation.

Question 2

F. Graetz, "The Tournament of To-Day.—A Set-To Between Labor and Monopoly," *Puck*, 1883

2. Using the image above, answer (a), (b), and (c).

   (a) Briefly describe ONE perspective about economics and politics in the 1880s expressed in the image.

   (b) Briefly explain ONE specific event or development that led to the perspective expressed in the image.

   (c) Briefly explain ONE specific effect of the historical development referenced by the image.

DIRECTIONS: Answer either Question 3 or Question 4.

Question 3 or 4

3. Answer (a), (b), and (c). Confine your response to the period from 1530 to 1690.

   (a) Briefly describe ONE specific historical similarity between French colonization efforts in North America and British colonization efforts in North America.

   (b) Briefly describe ONE specific historical difference between French colonization efforts in North America and British colonization efforts in North America.

   (c) Briefly explain ONE specific historical reason for the difference between French colonization efforts in North America and British colonization efforts in North America that you indicated in (b).

4. Answer (a), (b), and (c).

   (a) Briefly describe ONE specific historical similarity between the immigration of Europeans to the United States from 1880 to 1920 and the "Great Migration" of African Americans from 1910 to 1930.

   (b) Briefly describe ONE specific historical difference between the immigration of Europeans to the United States from 1880 to 1920 and the "Great Migration" of African Americans from 1910 to 1930.

   (c) Briefly explain ONE specific historical reason for a difference between the immigration of Europeans to the United States from 1880 to 1920 and the "Great Migration" of African Americans from 1910 to 1930.

Section II

TOTAL TIME—1 HOUR AND 40 MINUTES

Part A: Document-Based Question

SUGGESTED READING AND WRITING TIME: 1 HOUR

It is suggested that you spend 15 minutes reading the documents and 45 minutes writing your response.
Note: You may begin writing your response before the reading period is over.

> **DIRECTIONS:** Question 1 is based on the accompanying documents. The documents have been edited for the purpose of this exercise.
>
> In your response, you should do the following:
>
> - Respond to the prompt with a historically defensible thesis or claim that establishes a line of reasoning.
> - Describe a broader historical context relevant to the prompt.
> - Support an argument in response to the prompt using at least four documents.
> - Use at least one additional piece of specific historical evidence (beyond that found in the documents) relevant to an argument about the prompt.
> - For at least two documents, explain how or why each document's point of view, purpose, historical situation, and/or audience are relevant to an argument.
> - Demonstrate a complex understanding of a historical development related to the prompt through sophisticated argumentation and/or effective use of evidence.

Question 1

1. Evaluate the relative importance of causes of the conflict between congressional Republicans and President Andrew Johnson over plans for Reconstruction in the South in the period 1865 to 1869.

> **DOCUMENT 1**
>
> **Source:** Abraham Lincoln, "Second Inaugural Address," March 4, 1865.
>
> With malice toward none, with charity for all, with firmness in the right as God gives us to see the right, let us strive on to finish the work we are in, to bind up the nation's wounds, to care for him who shall have borne the battle and for his widow and his orphan, to do all which may achieve and cherish a just and lasting peace among ourselves and with all nations.

DOCUMENT 2

Source: Mississippi legal codes, "An Act to Confer Civil Rights on Freedmen, and for other Purposes," 1865.

An Act to Amend the Vagrant Laws of the State

Section 1. All rogues and vagabonds, idle and dissipated persons, beggars, jugglers, or persons practicing unlawful games or plays, runaways, common drunkards, common night-walkers, pilferers, lewd, wanton, or lascivious persons, in speech or behavior, common railers and brawlers, persons who neglect their calling or employment, misspend what they earn, or do not provide for the support of themselves or their families, or dependents, and all other idle and disorderly persons, including all who neglect all lawful business, habitually misspend their time by frequenting houses of ill-fame, gaming-houses, or tippling shops, shall be deemed and considered vagrants, under the provisions of this act, and upon conviction thereof shall be fined not exceeding one hundred dollars, with all accruing costs, and be imprisoned, at the discretion of the court, not exceeding ten days.

Section 2. All freedmen, free negroes and mulattoes in this State, over the age of eighteen years, found on the second Monday in January, 1866, or thereafter, with no lawful employment or business, or found unlawful assembling themselves together, either in the day or night time, and all white persons assembling themselves with freedmen, free negroes or mulattoes, or usually associating with freedmen, free negroes or mulattoes, on terms of equality, or living in adultery or fornication with a freed woman, freed negro or mulatto, shall be deemed vagrants.

DOCUMENT 3

Source: "Acts of the General Assembly of Louisiana Regulating Labor, Extra Session," 1865.

[Each laborer] shall not be allowed to leave his place of employment, until the fulfillment of his contract, unless by consent of his employer, or on account of harsh treatment, or breach of contraction the part of the employer; and if they do so leave, without cause of permission, they shall forfeit all wages earned to the time of abandonment. . . .

In cases of sickness of the laborer, wages for the time lost shall be deducted, and where the sickness is feigned for purpose of idleness, . . . and also should refusal to work be continued beyond three days, the offender shall be reported to a justice of the peace, and shall be forced to labor on roads, levee, and other public works, without pay, until the offender consents to return to his labor.

When in health, the laborer shall work ten hours during the day in the summer, and nine hours during the day in winter, unless otherwise stipulated in the labor contract; he shall obey all proper orders of his employer or his agent. . . . Failure to obey reasonable orders, neglect of duty, and leaving home without permission will be deemed disobedience; impudence, swearing, or indecent language to or in the presence of the employer, his family or agent . . . shall be deemed disobedience. . . . For all absence from home without leave, the laborer will be fined at the rate of two dollars per day.

DOCUMENT 4

Source: "Selling a Freeman to Pay His Fine at Monticello, Florida," *Frank Leslie's Illustrated Newspaper*, January 19, 1867.

DOCUMENT 5

Source: "Petition to U.S. Congress, South Carolina Colored People's Convention," November 1865.

We simply desire that we shall be recognized as men; that we have no obstructions placed in our way; that the same laws which govern white men shall direct colored men; that we have the right of trial by a jury of our peers, that schools be opened or established for our children; that we be permitted to acquire homesteads for ourselves and children; that we be dealt with as others, in equity and justice.

We claim the confidence and good-will of all classes of men; we ask that the same chances be extended to us that freemen should demand at the hands of their fellow-citizens. We desire the prosperity and growth of this State and the well-being of all men, and shall be found ever struggling to elevate ourselves and add to the national character; and we trust the day will not be distant when you will acknowledge that by our rapid progress in moral, social, religious and intellectual development that you will cheerfully accord to us the high commendation that we are worthy, with you, to enjoy all political emoluments—when we shall realize the truth that "all men are endowed by their Creator with inalienable rights," and that on the American continent this is the right of all, whether he come from east, west, north or south; and, although complexions may differ, "a man's a man for all that."

DOCUMENT 6

Source: Speech, Samuel J. Tilden, leader of the Democratic Party, New York, 1868.

[The Republican Party] resolved to make the black race the governing power in those States, and by means of them to bring into Congress twenty senators and fifty representatives practically appointed by itself in Washington. . . .

The effect of a gain to the Republican party of twenty senators and fifty representatives is to strengthen its hold on the Federal Government. . . . Nor is there the slightest doubt that the paramount object and motive of the Republican party is by these means to secure itself against a reaction of opinion adverse to it in our great populous Northern commonwealths. The effect of its system and its own real purpose is to establish a domination over us of the Northern states.

DOCUMENT 7

Source: Thaddeus Stevens, speech in Congress, January 3, 1867.

Since the surrender of the armies of the confederate States of America a little has been done toward establishing this Government upon the true principles of liberty and justice; and but a little if we stop here. We have broken the material shackles of four million slaves. We have unchained them from the stake so as to allow them locomotion, provided they do not walk in paths which are trod by white men. We have allowed them the privilege of attending church, if they can do so without offending the sight of their former masters. We have imposed on them the privilege of fighting our battles, of dying in defense of freedom, and of bearing their equal portion of taxes; but where have we given them the privilege of ever participating in the formation of the laws for the government of their native land?

What is negro equality, about which so much is said by knaves and some of which is believed by men who are not fools? It means, as understood by honest Republicans, just this much, and no more: every man, no matter what his race or colour; every earthly being who has an immortal soul, has an equal right to justice, honesty, and fair play with every other man; and the law should secure him those rights. The same law, which condemns or acquits an African, should condemn or acquit a white man.

Part B: Long Essay (Question 2, 3, or 4)

SUGGESTED WRITING TIME: 40 MINUTES

> **DIRECTIONS:** Answer Question 2 or Question 3 or Question 4.
>
> In your response, you should do the following:
>
> - Respond to the prompt with a historically defensible thesis or claim that establishes a line of reasoning.
> - Describe a broader historical context relevant to the prompt.
> - Support an argument in response to the prompt using at least two pieces of specific and relevant evidence.
> - Use historical reasoning (e.g., comparison, causation, continuity or change) to frame or structure an argument that addresses the prompt.
> - Demonstrate a complex understanding of a historical development related to the prompt through sophisticated argumentation and/or effective use of evidence.

2. Evaluate the extent to which the development of the New England colonies differed from the development of the colonies of the Chesapeake Bay region in the seventeenth century.

3. Evaluate the extent to which the development of the states of the Southeast differed from the development of the states of the Northeast in the period 1865–1900.

4. Evaluate the extent to which the development of the states of the upper Midwest differed from the development of the states of the Southwest in the period 1970–2000.

Answers and Explanations

Section I

PART A: MULTIPLE-CHOICE QUESTIONS

1. **(A)** William Lloyd Garrison was a central figure in the abolitionist movement that developed in the 1830s. The movement, and other reform movements, grew out of the Second Great Awakening. This spiritual movement conveyed the message that salvation was also in each individual's hands. If one lived a moral life and practiced self-control, one could feel confident about going to heaven. In this respect the Second Great Awakening acted as a springboard for a variety of reform movements, such as abolitionism.

2. **(A)** Garrison is specifically calling for equality and citizenship for free African Americans in the United States. The decision in the *Dred Scott* case asserted the exact opposite; it stipulated that African Americans, whether slave or free, could not be American citizens and therefore had no standing to sue in federal court. *Ex parte Milligan* (1866) (B) held that military tribunals, used on occasion during the Civil War, were unconstitutional when civilian courts were functioning. *Plessy v. Ferguson* (1896) (C) allowed for segregated facilities, using the principle "separate but equal." *Brown v. Board of Education of Topeka* (1954) (D) reversed the *Plessy* decision, declaring that segregated schools were "inherently unequal."

3. **(C)** With ratification of the Fourteenth Amendment (1868), African Americans were granted citizenship in the United States. This amendment, ratified during Reconstruction, also stated that no person shall be denied "equal protection of the laws." This was a vindication of the position that Garrison took a generation earlier. "Garrisonians" would have endorsed the developments in the other three choices, but those choices did not specifically bestow citizenship on African Americans.

4. **(A)** The differences in the two maps illustrate the result of the Articles of Confederation government successfully handling the question of western lands. After the American victory in the Revolution, there was a great deal of debate about the status of the area between the Appalachian Mountains and the Mississippi River. Some states insisted that their western land claims from the colonial period should be honored, while other states had no claims on this land. Maryland, a state with no western land claims, insisted that it would not ratify the Articles until all states gave up their land claims and the western lands became part of a national domain. Congress persuaded the states with claims to do just that. The handling of western lands was considered one of the major successes of the Articles of Confederation government. The maps do not indicate any French land claims (B), nor do they refer to slavery (C). By the time of the "Quasi-War" (1798–1800) (D), western land claims by the various states had long been settled.

5. **(A)** The Northwest Ordinance did not recognize the land claims of the American Indians in the region that dated from the period of British rule. The act encouraged fair treatment of native peoples, but it did not recognize their earlier claims to the land, setting the stage for a series of clashes between whites and American Indians during the 1780s and 1790s in the Ohio River Valley and Great Lakes region. In general, the Northwest Ordinance is considered an important piece of legislation from the "critical period." It divided up the land and provided a plot in every town for public schools. The Northwest Ordinance spelled out the steps that these areas would have to go through in order to become states on equal footing with the original thirteen states (C). In addition, the Northwest Ordinance banned slavery in the Northwest Territory (B).

6. **(C)** In many ways, the Spanish-American War can be seen as a turning point in American history. After the war, the United States became a colonial power like Britain, the nation America had defeated in order to establish its own independence. The United States and Spain negotiated the Treaty of Paris (1898) following the war. In the treaty, Spain agreed to cede the Philippines,

Puerto Rico, and Guam to the United States; the United States agreed to pay Spain $20 million for these possessions. The political cartoon is expressing approval for the American acquisition of these new territories.

7. **(B)** Following the Spanish-American War in 1898, the United States gained control of the Philippines, Puerto Rico, and Cuba, as is indicated in the note labeled "1899." The acquisition of new territories generated a great deal of debate in the United States. The cartoon expresses approval for America's acquisition of these new territories. It is implying that the United States has been growing for its entire history, and that this growth is as natural as a person maturing into adulthood. Uncle Sam is portrayed as confident and increasingly powerful in the successive images. In the final iteration, Uncle Sam is holding a warship in his arm. Further, the cartoonist is asserting that the United States will gain the approval and respect of the powerful nations of Europe now that it has joined the club of imperialist nations. Choice (D) also includes an approving attitude toward American imperialism, but the cartoon does not allude to "civilizing" the peoples of the new American territories.

8. **(C)** In the period following the Spanish-American War (1898), the United States expanded its economic and military presence in the Caribbean and Latin America and increased its involvement in Asia. America's more active role in the world was due, in large part, to the aggressive foreign policy of President Theodore Roosevelt (1901–1909). Roosevelt's aggressive approach to Latin America is clearly evident in regard to Panama, where Roosevelt engineered a coup and quickly made a deal with the new Panamanian government to build a canal.

9. **(D)** President Andrew Johnson's veto message would most likely have had the support of Southern Democrats. The message alludes to treating the former Confederate states (Tennessee was excluded) as military districts, which was a central aspect of the Reconstruction Acts of 1867 and 1868. These sweeping acts divided the South into five military districts. These areas could only rejoin the United States if they guaranteed basic rights to African Americans. The Radical Republicans, who initiated the acts, were not able to fully carry out their program. They were not able to extend land ownership to African Americans, nor did they carry out mass arrests of former Confederates.

10. **(C)** Governor Orval Faubus's response to the steps taken by President Dwight Eisenhower to resolve the Little Rock crisis in 1957 echoes the sentiment of President Andrew Johnson in 1867. Faubus knew that alluding to the Reconstruction period would resonate among white southerners; bitterness over that period was still present in the collective memory of white southerners almost 100 years later. The conflict began when local authorities had decided to allow nine African-American students to enroll in Central High School at the beginning of the school year in 1957. Governor Orval Faubus refused to cooperate with the plan, leading to mob action and violence outside of the high school. The violence and the national news coverage of the flouting of federal authority convinced Eisenhower to send federal troops. The use of federal troops in a southern state provided Faubus with a metaphor that aroused bitterness almost a century after Reconstruction.

11. **(A)** The passage shows that the Spanish realized they had to accommodate Native American practices to some degree in order to maintain a presence among the Pueblo Indians. Popé's rebellion of 1680, centered in Santa Fe, resulted in attacks on Spanish Franciscan priests as well as on ordinary Spaniards. It was one of the most successful native uprisings against European conquerors.

12. **(B)** The events described in the excerpt show that the Pueblo Indians ended up adapting some elements of Spanish culture, just as the Spaniards had to accommodate some elements of Native American culture. The religious practice of the Pueblo Indians resembled Catholicism in many outward ways, but it retained many traditional Pueblo beliefs and rituals. This degree of adaptation and accommodation was more common in Spanish and French interactions with native peoples than in British interactions with American Indians.

13. **(A)** The 1936 cartoon is making the point that although European individuals and countries might be seduced into waging another major war, the United States would be wise to avoid participating. The cartoon is an expression of isolationism, which became a common sentiment among many Americans between the two world wars. The cartoon is implying that war may be seductive, but it is also brutal and deadly. Many Americans had vivid memories of World War I, and many had lost friends and loved ones. Ultimately, many asked, was it worth it? In addition, the Senate's Nye Committee (1934–1937) uncovered evidence that certain American corporations greatly profited from World War I. Americans wondered if the so-called merchants of death had pushed the country into World War I.

14. **(D)** In many ways, the position of Martin Luther King Jr. in 1967 paralleled the sentiment of the cartoon. Both argued against military involvement in foreign conflicts, and both held that the conflicts in question—World War I and the Vietnam War—did not have the potential to significantly advance American interests in the world. Initially, King did not take a position on the Vietnam War, focusing instead on domestic civil rights issues. However, King began to see the disproportionate role that African Americans played on the front lines of Vietnam, and he began to see the war as a question of morality and justice. In 1965 King began to publicly express doubts about the Vietnam War. In a 1967 appearance at the Riverside Church in New York City, King delivered a speech titled "Beyond Vietnam: A Time to Break Silence."

15. **(D)** The passage is part of President Truman's argument to Congress in favor of an extension of aid to Greece and Turkey. As part of the policy of containment, the United States extended military aid to Greece and Turkey in 1947. The aid was successful. It helped the Greek monarchy put down a Communist-influenced rebel movement. Further, the move quieted Republican criticism of Truman and improved the president's standing in public opinion polls; he won reelection the following year.

16. **(A)** The passage can best be seen as providing a rationale for the policy of containment. In order to block any further aggression by the Soviet Union, Truman issued the Truman Doctrine (1947), in which he said that the goal of the United States would be to contain Communism. The containment approach to the Soviet Union had been spelled out in an article entitled "Sources of Soviet Conduct," published in *Foreign Affairs* (1947). Containment remained the cornerstone of American foreign policy for decades to come.

17. **(C)** The ideas expressed in the passage most directly reflect a continuity with debates about the role of the United States in world affairs. This debate emerged as early as President George Washington's "Proclamation of Neutrality" (1793) as war broke out between France and Great Britain. It can be seen in the aftermath of the American victory in the Spanish-American War (1898) and in the lead-up to both world wars.

18. **(A)** The political cartoon is making the point that government officials were taking their crusade against immoral behavior to extreme lengths. The cartoon is depicting Anthony Comstock, a former U.S. postal inspector and the public face of the moral reform movement, dragging a woman into court and, absurdly, accusing her of giving birth to a "naked child." Although the cartoon is satirical, Comstock's actual actions were only slightly less outrageous. For example, he prohibited certain anatomy textbooks from being sent to medical students. The 1873 Comstock Law outlawed the distribution of information or devices related to contraception. Comstock repeatedly clashed with birth-control advocate Margaret Sanger.

19. **(B)** The cartoon reflects a point of view in the ongoing debate about the role of the federal government in regulating morality. This debate can be seen in the lead-up to the ratification of the Eighteenth Amendment in 1919. This amendment called for a ban on the manufacture, sale, and transportation of alcoholic beverages. The movement to ban alcohol from American society was one of the largest movements in the nineteenth and early twentieth centuries. The debate can also be seen in the 1960s in

discussions of various forms of birth control, including "the pill," as well as in recent debates around gay marriage and marijuana policy.

20. **(C)** The issue that precipitated the speech was the passage of an act creating higher tariff rates. The act, known by its critics as the "Tariff of Abominations," dramatically raised tariff rates on many items, and led to a general reduction in trade between the United States and Europe. This decline in trade hit South Carolina's cotton plantations especially hard. By 1832, John C. Calhoun and other South Carolina political leaders asserted the right of states to nullify federal legislation. Under the theory of nullification, a state could declare an objectionable law null and void within that state. President Jackson, a defender of states' rights, was, nonetheless, alarmed at this blatant flouting of federal authority. He pushed for passage of the Force Bill, which authorized military force against South Carolina for committing treason. At the same time, Congress revised tariff rates, providing relief for South Carolina. The Force Bill and the new tariff rates, passed by Congress on the same day, amounted to a face-saving compromise.

21. **(D)** The debate over nullification and the debate over ratifying the Constitution are similar in that in both, the issue of the power of the states was at stake. Under the Articles of Confederation, the states had a great deal more power. Those who defended the Articles—the Anti-Federalists—used language strikingly similar to Calhoun's. In the excerpt, Calhoun argues, "to reserve such exclusive right to the General Government . . . is to convert it, in fact, into a great consolidated government, with unlimited powers, and to divest the States, in reality, of all their rights. . . ." Such an argument echoes the arguments of the Anti-Federalists against the Constitution.

22. **(B)** Calhoun's protest included the threat of state nullification of federal decisions. He even threatened to consider secession if other measures did not work. This form of protest can also be seen in the response of New England Federalists to the War of 1812. The Hartford Convention (1814) raised the very real possibility that New England would secede from the United States in order to protect their economic and maritime trade interests. Although talk of nullification and secession is more associated with southern political leaders, these issues were also brought up in the intense debates about the War of 1812. The war ended before the Federalists could follow through on their threat.

23. **(D)** The main purpose of the cartoon is to point out that President Franklin D. Roosevelt had a secret agenda. In this view, Roosevelt claimed he was creating programs to help people, but secretly he was attempting to consolidate power by taking away people's freedom. The cartoon reflects conservative criticisms of the New Deal. Note that the presence of a "Trojan horse" in a political cartoon implies that someone has a sinister agenda different from a stated agenda.

24. **(A)** This cartoon is taking a position in the debate about the proper role of the federal government in the economy. This debate first became part of the national agenda during the Progressive era of the early decades of the twentieth century when reformers insisted that the federal government should play a greater role in regulating economic activity in the United States. The debate continued through the New Deal, the Great Society, and into the debates in recent decades about the federal government playing a role in reforming the health care system. Some conservatives accused the Supreme Court of legislating from the bench in the 1950s and 1960s under Chief Justice Earl Warren (B). Conservative opposition to the New Deal did not center on issues of states' rights or the power of the states (C). The country was not at war in 1933 (D).

25. **(B)** The sentiment reflected in the cartoon is similar to opposition by the Republican Party to the creation of Great Society programs in the 1960s. Johnson's Great Society programs included Medicare and Medicaid. The Medicare program provides health care for every American once each reaches the age of sixty-five. The main components of Johnson's Great Society were landmark civil rights acts as well as a comprehensive "war on poverty." Many aspects of Johnson's Great Society were underfunded as

the federal government spent more and more on the Vietnam War. In both the 1930s and the 1960s, conservatives argued that the federal government's reach was extending beyond its traditional limits and threatening individual liberty and the Constitution.

26. **(D)** William Graham Sumner is associated with the intellectual movement known as Social Darwinism. Followers of Sumner and his book, *What Social Classes Owe to Each Other*, would most likely have advocated a laissez-faire approach to the economy. The French phrase *laissez-faire* means "to let alone." It describes a government policy that would take a hands-off approach when it comes to economic activities. Social Darwinism was an attempt to apply Charles Darwin's ideas about the natural world to social relations. Sumner was attracted to Darwin's ideas about competition and Herbert Spencer's term, "survival of the fittest." He argued against any attempt at government intervention into the economic and social spheres. Interference, he argued, would hinder the social evolution of the human species. The inequalities of wealth that characterized the late 1800s were part of the process of "survival of the fittest." Social Darwinism appealed to owners of large corporations because it both justified their wealth and power and warned against any type of regulation or reform.

27. **(A)** The ideas of Social Darwinism justified the success of those at the top of the socioeconomic structure as both appropriate and inevitable. Sumner argues that we should let nature run its course; to do otherwise could lead to disaster. He argues, "We can only, by interfering with [the natural order], produce the survival of the unfittest. . . ." He therefore was against government regulations of economic activity.

28. **(B)** The law, excerpted in the question, mandated that citizens in Pennsylvania do not cooperate with slave-catchers seeking to capture fugitive slaves. The fugitive slave clause of the Constitution was present from the drafting of the Constitution, but it was given teeth later in history, with the passage of the Fugitive Slave Act, as part of the Compromise of 1850. Even before that act was passed, states were not allowed to pass laws that went directly against returning slaves to their owners. In the case of *Prigg v. Pennsylvania* (1842), the Supreme Court declared the Pennsylvania law invalid.

29. **(B)** The existence of the Pennsylvania law, excerpted in the question, demonstrates an ongoing tension between federal and state law. The Supremacy Clause of the Constitution states that the Constitution and federal laws and treaties are the "supreme law of the land." Therefore, state laws must operate within the bounds of the Constitution as defined by the Supreme Court. However, states repeatedly asserted their right to do as they pleased in the antebellum period, hoping the federal government would not try to enforce the Constitution. This tension persisted into the twentieth century, with many white southerners vowing "massive resistance" to federal edicts against segregation.

30. **(C)** The conflict around the Pennsylvania law reflected the ambiguous nature of slavery in the Constitution. The framers of the Constitution were, to some degree, uneasy with the institution. This uneasiness is reflected in the fact that the word "slavery" is not mentioned in the entire document. Slaves are often referred to as "other persons." Although the framers of the Constitution did not mention the word *slavery*, they were willing to compromise on the issue and postpone any final decision about slavery to the future. This postponement led to decades of debate and conflict over the issue.

31. **(B)** Dorothea Dix's testimony to the Massachusetts legislature reflects the influence of the Second Great Awakening. The movement spoke to many of the men and women who were brought into the larger society by the "market revolution." The Second Great Awakening told the individual that salvation was also in his or her hands. Righteous living, self-control, and a strong moral compass would lead to salvation. This idea that one could determine his or her eternal life was very different from the old Calvinist notion of predestination, which held that one's eternal life was planned out by God. The Second

Great Awakening not only encouraged individual redemption, but also societal reformation. Not only could one become perfect in the eyes of God, but also one could work to perfect society as well. In this respect the Second Great Awakening acted as a springboard for a variety of reform movements.

32. **(D)** Dorothea Dix's research and testimony is best understood in the context of the rise of voluntary organizations to promote religious and secular reforms. This activism was inspired in part by the Second Great Awakening. The era also saw the rise of the abolitionist movement, the women's rights movement, and the temperance movement. Women did gain the right to vote in state and local elections in several states, but that was not until the late 1800s; women were guaranteed the right to vote in all elections with the passage of the Nineteenth Amendment (1920) (A). Dix's activism was not motivated by an economic downturn (B); on the contrary, many historians note that the Second Great Awakening and the market revolution went hand in hand, suggesting such activism tends to occur in an expanding economy. Dix was making her argument to the Massachusetts state government, not the federal government (C). It is not until the twentieth century that the federal government began to play a role in issues of health and poverty.

33. **(C)** These song lyrics appeared in a populist newspaper in the 1890s. The allusions to monopolies, railroads, and party bosses indicate that this song was meant to publicize the plight of farmers in the late 1800s. The populist movement tapped into growing discontent among farmers in the West about the economic bind they found themselves in, and became a formidable force in the 1890s. The populists grew angry at the concentration of wealth and power by eastern industrialists. They supported a national income tax so that those with higher incomes would pay more than the poor. They also supported free and unlimited coinage of silver. Populists wanted the United States to get off the gold standard and to issue money backed by silver as well. This would increase the amount of money in circulation and would lead to inflation. Farmers supported inflationary policies so that the prices they received for their foodstuffs would increase.

34. **(B)** The farmers' movement pushed state governments to pass laws regulating railroad rates and practices. These laws, known as Granger Laws, had limited effectiveness. In the 1886 *Wabash* case, the Supreme Court limited the ability of states to regulate railroads. In response, the federal government created the Interstate Commerce Commission (1887) to regulate railroads. However, the ICC was chronically underfunded and was, therefore, ineffective.

35. **(A)** The era saw widespread corruption in government; this is hinted at in the allusion to old party bosses. As the extent of corruption in government became more widely known, from the Grant administration in Washington to Tammany Hall in New York City, activists demanded reform of local, state, and national governments. Some activists hoped for the formation of the broad coalition described in choice (B), but differences in race, ethnicity, and location made such a coalition untenable. The farmers did create a third party, the Populist Party, but it remained just that—a third party; it did not rise in prominence on a national level to compete with the two main political parties (C). The "Indian Wars" of the West were over by the 1890s (D).

36. **(C)** The passage from Marcus Garvey is best understood as an expression of Black nationalism. Garvey is best known for urging African Americans to return to their ancestral homelands in Africa. Not many African Americans made the journey, but Garvey instilled a sense of pride among many African Americans; in this he is seen as an important figure in the movement for Black nationalism.

37. **(B)** Marcus Garvey argued for African Americans to build separate institutions to demand greater power. His activism highlights the ongoing debate between separatism and integration of African Americans in American society. There are echoes of this tension in the 1960s between King's call for integration and the rise of the "Black Power" movement.

38. **(C)** The excerpt from the essay by Glenda Elizabeth Gilmore implies that historians of the Progressive movement have not written extensively on the contributions of Black women to progressivism in the South because of a scarcity of documentary evidence. She argues that African-American women "remained invisible in virtually every discussion of southern progressivism" because they did not have access to the public expressions of activism that white women did. She implies that it is the job of the historian to recognize this limitation and to figure out other ways of studying the activities of Black women in the Progressive movement.

39. **(D)** The efforts by Black women to participate in the southern Progressive movement occurred in the context of a dismal point in race relations in the United States as "scientific" ideas about race, inaction by the federal government, and rigid segregation in the South relegated African Americans to a second-class status in the United States. The year 1896, the beginning of Gilmore's study, was also the year the Supreme Court issued the *Plessy v. Ferguson* decision, giving sanction to segregation on a "separate but equal" basis.

40. **(A)** Washington's "Farewell Address" is often cited in the ongoing debates about the proper role of the United States in international politics. President Washington is closely identified with the idea of neutrality. In his "Farewell Address," he urged the United States to avoid "permanent alliances" with foreign powers. In addition, he issued the 1793 Neutrality Act after France and Great Britain went to war. He did not want the newly independent nation, on a precarious footing, to be drawn into the seemingly endless conflicts of Europe.

41. **(A)** Washington's call for neutrality can be most clearly seen in the Monroe Doctrine. The Monroe Doctrine has the same goal as Washington's "Farewell Address"—avoidance of conflicts with European powers. The Monroe Doctrine (1823) was an attempt to limit European influence in the Western Hemisphere. President Monroe was alarmed by the threats made by the Holy Alliance of Russia, Prussia, and Austria to restore Spain's lost American colonies. He also opposed a decree by the Russian czar that claimed all the Pacific Northwest above the 51st parallel. Although both problems worked themselves out, Monroe issued a statement warning European nations not to attempt to set up new colonies in the Americas. The United States did not have the military might to enforce this pronouncement at the time, but it was an important statement of intent. The other choices all involve greater involvement in European affairs.

42. **(C)** American participation in the North Atlantic Treaty Organization (1949) represents a break with the approach to foreign policy that President Washington advocated in his "Farewell Address." In his address, Washington called for the United States to avoid permanent alliances. Up until the creation of NATO, the United States did just that. However, after World War II, American policymakers thought it was important for the United States to play a more important role in global affairs. The realities of the Cold War led the United States to abandon the policies advocated by George Washington.

43. **(D)** The actions of the Paxton Boys represent ongoing tensions between backcountry settlers and elites within colonial America. In the aftermath of the French and Indian War, during Pontiac's Rebellion, a vigilante group of these Scots-Irish settlers organized raids against American Indians on the Pennsylvania frontier. These raids included an attack on Conestoga Indians in 1763 that resulted in twenty deaths. After the attacks on the Conestoga, in January 1764, about 250 Paxton Boys marched to Philadelphia to present their grievances to the Pennsylvania legislature. Tensions began to develop around this time between colonists and British authorities (A), but the Paxton Boys were citing resentment at local elites, not British authorities. Tensions among Indian groups allied with different European powers (B) is evident in the Beaver Wars of the 1600s, not the Paxton Boys. Tensions existed in colonial America between freed African Americans and white planters (C), as evidenced in court proceedings, changing atti-

tudes of whites, and legislative acts, but this was not central to the grievances of the Paxton Boys.

44. **(B)** Bacon's Rebellion and the march of the Paxton Boys form a clear continuity in colonial American history. Both events were precipitated by tensions on the frontier between backcountry settlers and American Indians; both events reflected resentment by the western backcountry settlers against the eastern colonial elites; both events reflected differing opinions around policies in regard to American Indians; and both involved extralegal violence. The other events reflected tensions in colonial America but do not represent as clear a continuity as does Bacon's Rebellion.

45. **(D)** The Port Huron Statement, written by Students for a Democratic Society, was an important foundational document of the emerging New Left of the 1960s. It raised a host of concerns that shaped the New Left of the 1960s—poverty, racism, the misguided priorities of an affluent society, the proliferation of nuclear bombs, and the paranoia of the anti-Communist crusade. The New Left was supportive of the civil rights movement (B); however, this document reflects the concerns of middle-class students, "bred in at least modest comfort." The New Left was generally supportive of workers' rights and just wages for working-class people, but it was often at odds with some of the more conservative political positions of large unions—including anti-Communism and support for the war in Vietnam (A). The concerns in the Port Huron Statement are far different from the agenda of the New Right (D). In some ways, the New Right can be seen as a reaction to the rise of the New Left.

46. **(A)** The "New Look" foreign policy shifted American military priorities away from conventional forces and toward increased reliance on nuclear weapons. The Port Huron Statement expressed concern about the proliferation of nuclear weapons that occurred, in part, as a result of the "New Look" foreign policy. U.S. funding for the United Nations increased in the 1950s (B); however, the sentiments in the Port Huron Statement are not critical of the United Nations. The Port Huron Statement expressly embraces the "southern struggle" for racial justice; as such, it would have supported Eisenhower's intervention in the Little Rock crisis (C). The United States devoted additional resources to education, especially in math and science, in the wake of the *Sputnik* launch (D); the Port Huron Statement contains no repudiation of funding for education.

47. **(C)** The primary intended audience for the Port Huron Statement was middle-class college students. The statement was written at the founding convention of Students for a Democratic Society, and was intended to be a recruiting tool as SDS tried to attract support on college campuses. The statement refers to having grown up in "comfort," not poverty. The statement expressed solidarity with African Americans in the South, but it was not meant as a recruiting tool for African Americans (A). SDS made many appeals and petitions to government officials (B), but this was not one of them. The "Old Left" of the 1930s attempted to recruit factory workers (D); the "New Left" focused more on recruiting college students.

48. **(B)** The growth of Students for a Democratic Society—the organization that published the Port Huron Statement—can best be understood in the context of the baby boom, economic growth, and a rapid expansion of higher education. The campus-based organization thrived at a time when the size of the college-aged demographic ballooned as baby boomers reached their upper teens. In addition, the growth of the middle class contributed to a large increase in the number of students enrolled in four-year universities in the 1960s.

49. **(B)** The New York law, cited in the question, allowed married women to own their own property and to keep money they might inherit. This challenged traditional understandings of women and property embodied in the legal concept of *feme covert*. Under the legal doctrine of *feme covert*, wives had no independent legal or political standing.

50. **(A)** Participants in the Seneca Falls Convention, which occurred in New York State just weeks after the New York legislature passed the Married Women's Property Act (1848), would certainly have supported the act as a step forward for the

women's rights movement. The Seneca Falls Declaration, written at the Convention, specifically cites unequal property rights as an injustice to be rectified.

51. **(D)** The passage of the Married Women's Property Act directly reflects the ongoing debate around the legal status of women. From the colonial period until the contemporary period, the legal status of women has changed so that women currently enjoy the same legal rights and responsibilities as men. These debates have involved divorce, custody, property, voting, serving on juries, serving in the military, and other issues. The passage does not address voting rights (A), or employment (C). Generally, marriage rules are established by the various states, not by the federal government; the passage does not reflect an intrusion of federal power into marriage law (B).

52. **(D)** The Flushing Remonstrance (1657) was written by English residents of the village of Flushing in the Dutch colony of New Netherland. The director-general of the colony, Peter Stuyvesant, was attempting to enforce conformity in New Netherland despite its multiethnic makeup. The authors were protesting a ban on Quaker worship in New Netherland, even though the authors themselves were not Quakers.

53. **(C)** The main idea of the Flushing Remonstrance—that government should not interfere with or limit different religious practices—was enshrined into the U.S. legal structure by the "Free Exercise Clause" of the First Amendment. The First Amendment mentions religion in two contexts. The "Establishment Clause" (D) prohibits the establishment of an official religion in the United States. The "Free Exercise Clause" asserts that Congress shall make no laws limiting the right to worship freely.

54. **(D)** The main purpose of the petition by Paul Cuffe was to demand that the Massachusetts legislature either grant the petitioners the right to vote or excuse them from paying taxes. Cuffe and his brother were free African Americans. They paid taxes, but they were not permitted to vote. The petition was based on the oft-repeated principle of the Patriot cause—no taxation without representation.

55. **(A)** The petition by Paul Cuffe illustrates the fact that the rhetoric of the American Revolution raised awareness of social inequalities and inspired groups and individuals to call for greater political democracy. The documents and publications of the Revolutionary era are filled with the language of inequality, injustice, and enslavement. The Declaration of Independence contains the idea that all men have certain basic rights, as expressed in the phrase, "life, liberty, and the pursuit of happiness." Many groups—African Americans (free and enslaved), indentured servants, women, American Indians—were inspired by this language and insisted that the new government abide by its principles.

PART B: SHORT-ANSWER QUESTIONS

Good responses to question 1

(a) A good response would describe a major difference between Hacker's and Bailyn's historical interpretations of the American Revolution, such as:

Hacker believes that the most important cause of the American Revolution was economic in nature. He argues that Great Britain was trying to enforce rules that would allow it to continue to profit from the thirteen colonies within a mercantilist framework. The colonies, on the other hand, were developing an economy independent of, and in competition with, that of Great Britain. The colonies saw British enforcement of mercantilist rules as a direct threat to their economic well-being. Bailyn, however, believes that the cause of the American Revolution was primarily political. He argues that rebellious colonists came to believe that British authorities were determined to undermine the liberty in the thirteen colonies and beyond. The colonists saw Great Britain as coming under the control of a corrupt group of leaders who needed to be overthrown so that liberty could continue to exist. Hacker might see this talk of "corruption" and "conspiracy" as rhetorical devices, but Bailyn takes them as heartfelt concerns.

(b) A good response would explain a specific historical event or development during the period 1754 to 1783 that is not explicitly mentioned in the excerpts and could be used to support Hacker's interpretation, such as:

* *The British enactment of taxes on the colonists in the aftermath of the French and Indian War led to immediate and vociferous protests. Taxes such as the Stamp Act (1765) were seen as a financial burden on the colonies and an impediment to their economic well-being.*

* *British attempts to crack down on colonial smuggling in the aftermath of the French and Indian War led to denunciations by colonial leaders. The Sugar Act (1764), for example, called for more stringent enforcement of trade rules than the earlier Molasses Act (1733).*

(c) A good response would explain a specific historical event or development during the period 1754 to 1783 that is not explicitly mentioned in the excerpts and could be used to support Bailyn's interpretation, such as:

* *Rebellious colonists were consistent in their insistence that British policies were designed to undermine liberty. This is evident in documents from the 1765 Declarations of the Stamp Act Congress to the 1776 Declaration of Independence. These documents resonated with large numbers of colonists throughout the decade before independence.*

* *Many of the British actions that the colonists protested against were not related to economic policies. The protests against standing armies in Boston and against the Quebec Act (1774) were not related to economics or trade. Even the protests against the Tea Act (1773) were not primarily driven by economic concerns; the price of tea in the colonies fell as a result of the act.*

Good responses to question 2

(a) A good response would explain a perspective about economics and politics in the 1880s expressed in the image, such as:

* *The cartoon is expressing sympathy for working people in the Gilded Age. It represents the working class as a scrawny man on a feeble horse (with "Labor" on his cap). The owners are represented by the medieval jouster, clad in a suit of armor, sitting on a steam engine. Labor does not stand a chance in workplace conflicts; the deck, according to the point of view of the cartoonist, is stacked in favor of the era's corporate owners.*

* *The cartoon is commenting on the power of the "robber barons" of the late nineteenth century. That power is represented by the jouster. He has the power of a locomotive beneath him. He is engaged in a contest with laborers, represented by a weak man on a horse. The jouster, labeled "monopoly," has power and money on his side. The worker, presented empathetically, has no way to defend his interests.*

(b) A good response would explain a specific event or development that led to the perspective expressed in the image, such as:

* *The rise of monopolies, trusts, and other large corporate entities, such as U.S. Steel, which exercised monopoly control over particular industries, increased the power of management over labor. Trusts came to dominate fields such as petroleum refining and sugar processing. The Northern Securities Company attempted to control the railway industry until it was broken up by the government. These trusts were able to pressure the government to support their efforts to defeat striking workers.*

* *Unionized workers were defeated in some of the major labor battles of the late nineteenth century, such as the Great Railroad Strike of 1877. Major corporations were able to employ replacement workers (or "scabs"), gain the support of local and federal authorities, and use security firms in the labor battles of the era.*

(c) A good response would explain a specific effect of the historical development referenced by the image, such as:

* *Organized labor continued to experience defeat at the hands of major corporations throughout the remainder of the nineteenth century. Unionized*

workers were defeated in the Homestead Strike (1892) and in the Pullman Strike (1894). Unions were no match for the power of major corporations. This situation changed in the twentieth century with passage of the Wagner Act, which guarantees the rights of private-sector employees to organize unions and engage in collective bargaining.

* Some workers began to reject the union movement altogether. Some of these workers came to believe that the only way they could effect meaningful change was to dismantle the capitalist system. They joined the Socialist Party, which formed in 1901. One noteworthy convert to the Socialist Party was Eugene V. Debs, who had previously been the founder and president of the American Railway Union.

Good responses to question 3

(a) Good responses would explain a specific historical similarity between French colonization efforts in North America and English colonization efforts in North America in the period of the period 1530 to 1690, such as:

* Both the English and French colonization efforts grew out of the dictates of the mercantilist system. Both nations hoped to acquire raw materials and goods from their North American colonies to be sent back to Europe to profit the "mother country."

* Both the English and the French established their early North American colonies adjacent to waterways that would facilitate trade and travel between the colonies and Europe. The French colony of Quebec was founded in 1608 along the St. Lawrence River, as was the city of Montreal in 1642. The English colony of Jamestown was founded along Virginia's James River in 1607; later, the colonies of Plymouth (1620) and Massachusetts Bay (1630) were founded on the Atlantic seacoast.

(b) Good responses would explain a specific historical difference between French and English colonization efforts in North America in the period between 1530 to 1690, such as:

* French colonization efforts in North America attracted relatively few French people. This led to a greater incidence of intermarriage between French colonists and American Indians. Conversely, English colonization efforts attracted large numbers of English people. There was very little intermarriage between the English and American Indians.

* While both French and English colonists had a variety of encounters at different times with American Indians—from warfare to the formation of alliances—French colonists tended to have better relationships with American Indian groups than the English did. The French were more likely to rely on diplomacy and on the exchange of gifts with American Indians than were the English. Also, the French were more likely to learn native languages and to develop interpersonal relationships with American Indians.

(c) Good responses would explain a specific historical reason for a difference between French and English colonization efforts in North America in the period between 1530 to 1690, such as:

* Population pressures were different in England and France. In England, in the 1500s and 1600s, the enclosure movement and the growth of the wool industry made much of the English countryside inaccessible to rural people. Cities were able to absorb a portion of these displaced people, but migration to the New World colonies proved to be a viable solution to many poor and displaced English men and women. There was not a comparable displacement of rural people in France at the time. Population growth and the growth of industry and commercial agriculture were slower in France in the 1500s and 1600s, resulting in far less pressure on the land. Consequently, far fewer people had a pressing economic incentive to migrate to the New World.

* The specific economic activities of the English and the French colonies in North America were different, resulting in different patterns of settlement. The English focused on developing staple crops, such as tobacco, and extracting resources, such as lumber and fish. The French, on the other hand, focused on fur trading with American Indians. Fur trading required the French to

maintain civil relations with American Indian groups. The English needed land for many of their activities, which led to encroachments upon American Indian lands and resulted in hostile relations between the English and the American Indians.

Good responses to question 4

(a) Good responses would explain a specific historical similarity between the immigration of Europeans to the United States from 1880 to 1920 and the "Great Migration" of African Americans from 1910 to 1930, such as:

* Both groups of migrants tended to come from rural, agricultural areas. Most of the southern Italians, Russians, Greeks, Poles, and others—the "new immigrants" of the late 1800s and early 1900s—were from a vast agricultural domain that was experiencing alterations in its traditional economic patterns. Likewise, the vast majority of participants in the "Great Migration" were from rural areas of the South. Large numbers of these migrants had been engaged in the sharecropping system, notably in the "Cotton Belt" of the South.

* Both migrations—from Europe and from the American South—were drawn to the North and the Midwest of the United States in search of industrial jobs. The U.S. industry was rapidly expanding in the late 1800s and early 1900s and was in need of laborers to work as factory and mill hands.

* Migrants from Europe as well as from the American South tended to live in urban neighborhoods defined by race or ethnicity. For example, many of the Russian and Polish Jews settled in the Lower East Side of New York City; many Italians settled in New York's Little Italy section. In Chicago, many African-American migrants settled in the South Side, and many who went to New York City moved to Harlem.

(b) Good responses would explain a specific historical difference between the immigration of Europeans to the United States from 1880 to 1920 and the "Great Migration" of African Americans from 1910 to 1930, such as:

* Patterns of discrimination for the various migrant groups differed from each other. While eastern and southern Europeans were subject to discrimination and hostility by nativists, they were more likely to gain acceptance into mainstream society over time than African Americans were. This move from the margins of society toward the mainstream bypassed many of the African-American participants in the Great Migration. They were more likely to remain isolated in poor neighborhoods—that came to be known as ghettos—than were European immigrants.

* Migration from Europe was subject to federal legislation, while internal migrations were not. In 1921 and 1924, the federal government passed immigration laws that set low quotas on many of the countries of origin of the "new immigrants." Such laws provided additional economic opportunities for African-American migrants to the North in the 1920s and later during World War II.

(c) Good responses would explain a specific historical reason for a difference between the immigration of Europeans to the United States from 1880 to 1920 and the Great Migration of African Americans from 1910 to 1930, such as:

* Long-standing attitudes around race in the United States made the experience of the African-American participants in the Great Migration different from that of the European "new immigrants." The Great Migration occurred in the context of the rebirth and rise of the Ku Klux Klan in the United States, of legal segregation in the post–Plessy v. Ferguson era, and of pseudoscientific ideas that created racial hierarchies. Though this racial ideology impacted European immigrants as well, over time, mainstream American society came to accept Italians, Russians, Greeks, Poles, and other eastern Europeans as "white."

Section II

PART A: DOCUMENT-BASED QUESTION

Question 1

What good responses will include:

A good response would draw on at least four of the documents to present an analysis of each of the elements mentioned in the question: the relative importance of causes of the conflict between congressional Republicans and President Andrew Johnson in regard to plans for Reconstruction in the South in the years 1864 to 1877.

Thesis (1 point)

Students will earn one point for presenting a historically defensible thesis or claim that establishes a line of reasoning. The thesis, which must consist of one or more sentences and must be located in either the introduction or the conclusion, must be more than a restatement of the prompt. Given the nature of the question, the thesis should focus on the historical reasoning process of causation. It should address the factors that contributed to the tensions between the legislative and executive branches and assess the most important causes. The thesis should make a claim about the cause or causes of the tensions—the lenient attitude of the president in regard to the former slaves in the South; the aggressiveness of the former slave-owning class following the war; the persistent mistreatment of African Americans in the immediate aftermath of the war; and/or the insistence of African Americans that a more sweeping restructuring of the South take place.

Examples of acceptable thesis statements:

* *The conflict between President Andrew Johnson and congressional Republicans over Reconstruction was caused by several factors. On one level, it was simply a manifestation of the bitter distrust between Democrats and Republicans. However, on a more significant level, the conflict was caused by divergent attitudes around racial injustice; Johnson rejected the idea of a biracial democracy, while Republicans came to see it as the most important outcome of the Civil War.*

* *Disagreements around Reconstruction plans had several causes. The long-term cause of the conflict was philosophical disagreement over the extent of federal authority in society; President Andrew Johnson embraced the idea of limited government, while congressional Republicans supported a more expansive federal role. However, it was more short-term causes that were most significant in understanding the fight over Reconstruction—specifically, aggressive moves by former slaveholders and grassroots activism by former slaves.*

Contextualization (1 point)

Students will earn one point if they describe a broader historical context relevant to the prompt. Students could contextualize this question by discussing the heated political controversies between the Democrats and the Republicans in the years leading up to the Civil War. This response can be illustrated with mention of one or more of the following: the lack of compromise evident in the Compromise of 1850, the caning of Senator Charles Sumner, the fiery rhetoric of John C. Calhoun, or the events of "Bleeding Kansas." Another option would be to place the events of the era into the larger context of the treatment of African Americans from before the Civil War through the end of the nineteenth century. Such contextualization could discuss slave codes and the lack of autonomy implicit in the slave system.

Evidence (3 points)

Evidence from the Documents (2 points)

In order to receive credit for the first point, the essay should draw from at least three documents to *address* the topic of the prompt. For the second point the student must use at least four of the documents to *support* an argument in response to the prompt. A good essay will not simply describe the contents of the documents one after another. Rather, a good essay should make connections between documents or sections of documents in crafting them into a convincing argument.

The attitude of President Abraham Lincoln toward eventual Reconstruction is illustrated in Document 1. Lincoln is urging the nation to "bind up" its wounds, and to do this "with charity to all." These recommendations can be interpreted as a call for a quick and lenient approach to southerners after their defeat. Such an approach was evident in Lincoln's "ten percent plan" and was evident in President Andrew Johnson's Proclamation of Amnesty and Reconstruction. Students can contrast this attitude with the more sweeping approach of Thaddeus Stevens, who notes how little has been done in the South in terms of creating new governments "based on principles of liberty and justice" (Document 7). Documents 2 and 3 show different aspects of life in the South in the immediate aftermath of the Civil War, specifically the nature of the "Black Codes" implemented throughout the South. Restrictions were put on African Americans with laws on "vagrancy," "idleness," and "labor contracts." Document 4 depicts the punishment for a freeman who cannot pay a fine. Students should see the resemblance to a slave auction. The student should be able to note comparisons between life for African Americans under the Black Codes and life under slavery. Document 5 illustrates action taken by African Americans to challenge the injustices that were rampant under presidential Reconstruction. The South Carolina Colored People's Convention sets forth many of the elements of a more sweeping plan—one that is embodied in Document 7, Thaddeus Stevens's speech. Document 6, a speech by a Democratic leader of Congress, can be used to complicate the motivations of congressional Republicans, asserting that their goal was political domination.

Evidence Beyond the Documents (1 point)
Students will earn one point if they use at least one piece of historical evidence (beyond that found in the documents) relevant to an argument about the prompt. The specific evidence students use will depend on the approach of the essay. Students might cite President Abraham Lincoln's "ten percent plan," the Wade–Davis Bill, the impeachment of President Andrew Johnson, the rise of the Ku Klux Klan, the Civil Rights Act of 1867, or the Military Reconstruction Act.

Analysis and Reasoning (2 points)

Sourcing (1 point)
For at least two of the documents, students must explain how or why the document's point of view, purpose, historical situation, and/or audience is relevant to an argument. To earn this point, it is not enough simply to identify an element of sourcing. A discussion of a document's point of view, purpose, historical situation, and/or audience should explain how that aspect of the document influences its meaning and sheds light on its credibility and/or on its limitations in regard to the argument of the essay. For instance, the historical situation of Lincoln's Second Inaugural Address (Document 1) was the concluding days of the Civil War, as the nation is contemplating what the post–Civil War United States will look like. Lincoln wanted both to frame the meaning of the war as it was coming to an end and to unite the country by not assigning blame to one side. This desire for unity shaped the tone and content of the speech. In regard to Document 4—the image "Selling a Freedman to Pay His Fine"—students could note that the audience for the image was probably national, rather than regional. *Frank Leslie's Illustrated Newspaper* was published in New York City. The point of the image—exposing the unjust nature of the Black Codes—becomes clearer if the audience is noted. Students could also earn the point for sourcing by discussing the purpose of the document. The image was designed to not simply illustrate an injustice. The artist wants to incite readers to take action and support a more sweeping plan for Reconstruction.

Historical Complexity (1 point)
Students must develop their argument by expanding upon the thesis. Students can earn this point if they can demonstrate a complex understanding of the historical development that is the focus of the prompt through sophisticated argumentation and/or effective use of evidence. If the essay explores the clash between Congress and the president, students can explain a relevant connection in another time period, such as clashes between Congress and President Nixon over the Vietnam War and the Watergate scandal in the early 1970s.

Students could also choose to make connections across time periods by focusing on the interplay between actions on the grassroots level and initiatives on the governmental level. In this case, on the local level we see violence by white southerners and activism by African Africans for social change; on the national level, we see implementation of a sweeping Reconstruction plan. The student could point to similar dynamics in the Progressive era, with activism on the local level and reform legislation on the national level. Also, this dynamic is at play in regard to the civil rights movement of the 1950s and 1960s. In addition, the complex understanding point can be earned by effectively using **seven** of the documents to support your argument, or by sourcing at least **four** of the documents. Finally, the point can be earned by demonstrating a sophisticated understanding of different perspectives relevant to the prompt. In this case, an essay could use evidence to note differing perspectives within the Republican Party. Such an argument might note the idealism of radical Republicans in challenging the president, while acknowledging the more pragmatic desire of Republicans to limit the power of their Democratic rival in the White House.

PART B: LONG ESSAY QUESTIONS

Question 2

What good responses will include:

A good response to long essay question 2 will compare the development of the New England colonies and the colonies of the Chesapeake Bay region in the seventeenth century, analyzing the extent to which they differed from one another.

Thesis (1 point)

Students will earn one point for presenting a historically defensible thesis or claim that establishes a line of reasoning. The thesis, which must consist of one or more sentences and must be located in either the introduction or the conclusion, must be more than a restatement of the prompt. The thesis should make a convincing claim about the relative historical significance of similarities and/or differences between two different historical developments or processes—in this case, the development of the New England colonies and the colonies of the Chesapeake Bay region in the seventeenth century. A convincing thesis can, for example, argue that geographic differences were most important in understanding differences in development, or that the backgrounds and motivations of the different groups of colonists were the key factors in understanding different development patterns. Also, a claim could acknowledge significant similarities between the regions, such as relations with American Indians or operating within the British mercantilist system.

Examples of acceptable thesis statements:

* *A comparison of the colonies of New England and the Chesapeake region in the 1600s reveals important similarities; colonists in both regions fought with American Indians to secure land claims and struggled to establish economic systems within the bounds of British mercantilism. However, their diverging paths are more historically significant. New England developed a diverse economy based on commerce, trade, agriculture, and small-scale manufacturing, while the Chesapeake region focused on the production of export crops grown by slave labor.*

* *The colonies of New England and the Chesapeake seemed very different from each other in the early decades of their existence in the 1600s. New England Puritans built tight-knit communities around shared spiritual beliefs and practices, while residents of the Chesapeake sought immediate enrichment in developing export crops. However, over time, the similarities between the two regions became more prominent. Both had to obey British laws, both struggled against American Indians, and both participated in the growing Atlantic trade.*

Contextualization (1 point)

Students will earn one point if they describe a broader historical context relevant to the prompt. Contextualizing the establishment and growth of Britain's North American colonies in the early 1600s could include a discussion of the broader trend of European exploration and colonization in the New World—including Spain's conquest of

American Indian empires in Central and South America, France's founding of colonies along the St. Lawrence River and the Great Lakes region, and efforts by the Netherlands to establish a New World presence in what would become New York and New Jersey. This discussion could describe developments in Europe that spurred exploration and colonization of the Americas. Another approach to contextualization could focus on particular developments in England in the 1500s and 1600s that set the stage for colonization of North America. These developments could include English manifestation of the Protestant Reformation, the development of dissenting religious movements in England.

Evidence (2 points)
Students will earn one point for *providing* specific examples of at least two pieces of evidence relevant to the topic of the prompt—similarities and differences in the development of the New England colonies and the colonies of the Chesapeake Bay region in the seventeenth century. Students earn a second point if they use this evidence to *support* their argument. Students could focus on the initial settlers in each region and the motivation—mostly men, in search of obtaining precious metals, tobacco (Chesapeake); Puritans practices, Calvinism, creating a "city upon a hill," theocracy (New England). An essay could discuss geographic differences—well-irrigated, relatively flat land in the Tidewater region of the Chesapeake versus the rocky soil and cold winters of New England. Conditions in the Chesapeake favored plantation agriculture and the growth of staple crops for export and, in New England, a variety of economic pursuits (fishing, lumber). Within a comparison of economic features of each region, students could focus on labor—the development of indentured servitude and slavery in Virginia, and family-based production in New England. An essay could also focus on commonalities, such as fraught relations between colonists and American Indians in the two regions—warfare with the Powhatan Confederation in 1622 (Chesapeake), and the Pequot War in 1637 and King Philip's War from 1675 to 1678 (New England). Also, both regions had to operate under mercantilist rules, including the Navigation Acts of the 1660s.

Analysis and Reasoning (2 points)
Students must develop their argument by expanding upon the thesis. Students can earn up to two points in this section. One point will be granted if the student successfully uses historical reasoning (in this case, comparison) to frame or structure an argument that addresses the prompt. Students can earn a second point if they can demonstrate a complex understanding of the historical development that is the focus of the prompt through sophisticated argumentation and/or effective use of evidence. For the first point, an essay could develop several categories of comparison. The essay should be able to argue the relative importance of particular similarities and differences. The second point, for historical complexity, could be earned in several ways, including looking at similarities as well as differences and developing an argument assessing both. Or, students could qualify or modify their argument by considering diverse or alternative views or evidence, such as the perspective of American Indians in regard to encroachments on their land. An alternative strategy could involve explaining relevant and insightful connections within and across periods. In this case, students could look at the increasing sectional tensions in the 1840s and 1850s, culminating in the Civil War, and draw connections back to differing regional developments in the 1600s. For this final point, students can also incorporate additional evidence (at least four pieces) that supports a nuanced or complex argument relevant to the prompt.

Question 3

What good responses will include:

A good response to long essay question 3 will compare the development of the states of the Southeast and the states of the Northeast in the period 1865 to 1900, analyzing the extent to which they differed from one another.

Thesis (1 point)
Students will earn one point for presenting a historically defensible thesis or claim that establishes a line of reasoning. The thesis, which must consist of one or more sentences and must be

located in either the introduction or the conclusion, must be more than a restatement of the prompt. The thesis should make a convincing claim about the relative historical significance of similarities and/or differences between two different historical developments or processes—in this case, the development of the states of the Southeast and the states of the Northeast in the period 1865 to 1900. A convincing thesis can, for example, focus on economic differences, noting the remarkable industrial expansion of the Northeast and the failure of the Southeast to achieve the goals of the "New South." Students could compare the persistence of small-town life in much of the South with the rapid urbanization in cities such as Boston, New York, and Philadelphia. A comparison of the regions could focus on the small number of "new immigrants" who ended up settling in the states of the Southeast compared to the growth of ethnic enclaves in the Northeastern cities. Similarities between the two regions could note the growing acceptance of racism and the Jim Crow system in both regions. Many white northerners accepted and even endorsed the racial hierarchy that characterized southern life, as demonstrated by the Supreme Court's decision in *Plessy v. Ferguson* (1896).

Examples of acceptable thesis statements:

* *The states of the Southeast and the states of the Northeast developed in dramatically different directions in the period between the end of the Civil War and the turn of the twentieth century. Though both regions sought to rebuild after the Civil War, the Northeast was more successful in developing an industrial economy that drew immigrants who propelled the United States to global prominence. In contrast, the states of the South remained underdeveloped, continuing old agrarian economic patterns and resisting modernization.*

* *A comparison of the states of the Southeast and the Northeast in the period 1865 to 1900 shows both differences and similarities. It is true that the economies of the two regions developed in very different directions, with the Southeast remaining agrarian and the Northeast developing the most modern industrial economy in the world. However, more importantly, the two regions showed a great deal of similarity in regard to attitudes around race. Although the Jim Crow system of racial segregation developed in the South, white people of the Northeast largely came to accept the system and the attitudes around race that it embodied.*

Contextualization (1 point)

Students will earn one point if they describe a broader historical context relevant to the prompt. Contextualizing a comparison between the development of the states of the Southeast and the states of the Northeast in the period 1865 to 1900 would almost certainly include a discussion of the Civil War. The outcome of the war affected the two regions under discussion in markedly different ways. The war unleashed the industrial capacity of the Northeast. The growth of mass-produced goods helped the Union win the war and then fueled the economic growth of the Northeast. The physical devastation of the Southeast set back economic growth by generations. An essay could go further back in history, tracing different development paths in the antebellum period and, even earlier, in the colonial period.

Evidence (2 points)

Students will earn one point for *providing* specific examples of at least two pieces of evidence relevant to the topic of the prompt—similarities and differences in the development of the states of the Southeast and the states of the Northeast in the period 1865 to 1900. Students earn a second point if they use this evidence to *support* their argument. Students could describe the remarkable economic growth of the Northeast, mentioning railroad expansion, the Bessemer process, Andrew Carnegie and the steel industry, John D. Rockefeller and the oil-processing industry, the increased availability of consumer products, or new patterns of management and ownership, including trusts. In discussing the slow pace of economic growth in the states of the Southeast, students could discuss the persistence of sharecropping and reliance on a few agricultural commodities. In addition, students could discuss the arguments put forth by journalist Henry Grady for the development of a "New South." The arguments did not gain many adherents in the South, as the region continued to be hampered by underdevelopment.

Analysis and Reasoning (2 points)

Students must develop their argument by expanding upon the thesis. Students can earn up to two points in this section. One point will be granted if the student successfully uses historical reasoning (in this case, comparison) to frame or structure an argument that addresses the prompt. Students can earn a second point if they can demonstrate a complex understanding of the historical development that is the focus of the prompt through sophisticated argumentation and/or effective use of evidence. For the first point, an essay could develop several categories of comparison. The essay should be able to argue the relative importance of particular similarities and differences. The second point for historical complexity could be earned in several ways, including looking at similarities as well as differences and developing an argument assessing both. Or, students could qualify or modify their argument by considering diverse or alternative views or evidence, such as the perspective of American Indians in regard to encroachments on their land. An alternative strategy could involve explaining relevant and insightful connections within and across periods. In this case, students could look at the increasing sectional tensions in the 1840s and 1850s, culminating in the Civil War, and draw connections back further to differing regional developments in the 1600s and 1700s. However, please note than an analysis of connections to an earlier time period cannot also be used to earn the contextualization point; one particular historical example cannot be used to fulfill the requirements of two different elements of the scoring rubric. For this final point, students can also incorporate additional evidence (at least four pieces) that supports a nuanced or complex argument relevant to the prompt.

Question 4

What good responses will include:

A good response to long essay question 4 will compare the development of the states of the upper Midwest with the states of the Southwest in the period 1970 to 2000, analyzing the extent to which they differed from one another.

Thesis (1 point)

Students will earn one point for presenting a historically defensible thesis or claim that establishes a line of reasoning. The thesis, which must consist of one or more sentences and must be located in either the introduction or the conclusion, must be more than a restatement of the prompt. The thesis should make a convincing claim about the relative historical significance of similarities and/or differences between two different historical developments or processes—in this case, the development of the states of the upper Midwest and the states of the Southwest in the period 1970 to 2000. A convincing thesis can, for example, focus on economic changes, noting the declining position of the "Rust Belt" states of the upper Midwest. By the early 1970s, this area experienced a decline in factory production and high unemployment, earning its nickname, the Rust Belt. On the other hand, the fortunes of the Sunbelt states of the Southwest improved. Military installations, high-tech industry, the oil industry, recreation, and retirement communities have all led to a growing population and a thriving economy. A thesis could also compare political trends in each region. The Sunbelt nurtured the rise of the New Right, while the Rust Belt witnessed the decline of its pro-union Democratic constituency. These trends help explain the growth of the Republican Party and the success of conservativism in the United States in the period from 1980 onward.

Examples of acceptable thesis statements:

* *In the period 1970 to 2000, the economic and demographic differences between the upper Midwest and the Southwest are more significant than similarities between the regions. The states of the upper Midwest struggled economically as the region lost much of its manufacturing base, leading to its nickname, the Rust Belt. The Southwest, by contrast, thrived, drawing in new residents and new industries. The changing demographics of the regions are reflected in the growth of the power of the Sunbelt in the House of Representatives and the diminished voice of the Rust Belt.*

* *A comparison of the states of the southwestern Sunbelt and the upper midwestern Rust Belt*

between 1970 and 2000 shows major economic differences, as the Rust Belt lost people and jobs, while the Sunbelt grew economically and in population. However, the more profound difference can be seen in politics. The rise of the Sunbelt at the expense of the Rust Belt helps us understand the growth and success of the New Right, which was nurtured in the communities of the Sunbelt before gaining national ascendency. These differences overshadow similarities between the regions.

Contextualization (1 point)
Students will earn one point if they describe a broader historical context relevant to the prompt. Contextualizing a comparison between the development of the states of the upper Midwest and the states of the Southwest in the period 1970 to 2000 could include a discussion of globalization. Globalization refers to several related trends—the reduction of tariffs and other trade barriers, the easier movement of goods and production facilities around the globe, the growth of communications networks, most notably the internet, and the growing cultural reach of mass media products. Globalization is defended by many as a positive development that will create greater understanding in the world and will raise living standards in developing countries. Others, such as protestors at the 1999 meeting of the World Trade Organization in Seattle, condemn globalization as reducing environmental protections and shifting manufacturing jobs to areas with few protections for workers. The changes in both the Rust Belt and the Sunbelt can be related to globalization.

Evidence (2 points)
Students will earn one point for *providing* specific examples of at least two pieces of evidence relevant to the topic of the prompt—similarities and differences in the development of the states of the upper Midwest and the states of the Southwest in the period 1970 to 2000. Students will earn a second point if they use this evidence to *support* their argument. In terms of the economic decline of the Rust Belt states of the upper Midwest—including western Pennsylvania, West Virginia, Ohio, Indiana, Illinois, Michigan, and Wisconsin—students could discuss the outsourcing of manufacturing jobs and the growth of automation in many industries. Between 1979 and 1983 over eleven million workers lost jobs to plant closings and downsizing of firms. In addition, trade agreements, such as the North American Free Trade Agreement (NAFTA), embraced by President Bill Clinton and ratified by Congress in 1993, eliminated all trade barriers and tariffs among the United States, Canada, and Mexico, contributing, many economists argue, to the decline of manufacturing in the Rust Belt. A discussion of the rise of the Sunbelt could include the dramatic growth of cities such as Phoenix, Houston, and Las Vegas. Students could also mention crises in many Sunbelt states around supplying water to the region's growing population. Students could also focus on politics, noting the presidential campaign of Republican senator Barry Goldwater in 1964 as both a precursor of the growth of the New Right and of the growing importance of the Sunbelt. Essays could also note the shift in political power of the two regions. As a result of the 2000 census, Arizona, Florida, Georgia, and Texas each gained two members of Congress, while California, Colorado, Nevada, and North Carolina each gained one seat. By contrast, some of the Rust Belt states lost seats—Illinois, Michigan, Ohio, and Wisconsin each lost a House seat. In terms of similarities, students could explore the growing importance of immigrant communities in both regions. Although the Southwest has been impacted by immigration, more significantly, the cities of the Midwest have also experienced the growth of immigrant communities.

Analysis and Reasoning (2 points)
Students must develop their argument by expanding upon the thesis. Students can earn up to two points in this section. One point will be granted if the student successfully uses historical reasoning (in this case, comparison) to frame or structure an argument that addresses the prompt. Students can earn a second point if they can demonstrate a complex understanding of the historical development that is the focus of the prompt through sophisticated argumentation and/or effective use of evidence. For the first point, an essay could develop several categories of comparison and could examine the connections between economic changes and

political changes. The essay should be able to argue the relative importance of particular similarities and differences. The second point for historical complexity could be earned in several ways, such as drawing connections to earlier time periods. In terms of the Southwest, students could discuss the settlement of the West in the late 1800s and the "closing of the frontier," as argued by historian Frederick Jackson Turner; the essay could also explore the development of industry in the Midwest—from the meat packing industry in Chicago to the automobile industry in Detroit. For this final point, students can also incorporate additional evidence (at least four pieces) that supports a nuanced or complex argument relevant to the prompt.

Scoring the Test

The AP U.S. History test is composed of four parts grouped into two sections. The multiple-choice test is scored with one point given for each correct answer.

- *There is no penalty for guessing*, so you should answer every question on the test.
- The Document-Based Question is given a score from 0 to 7.
- The Long Essay is given a score from 0 to 6.

To attain your final AP score, the following method should be used:

Multiple-Choice Score × 1.31 = _____

\+

Short-Answer Score × 4.0 = _____

\+

DBQ Score × 6.43 = _____

\+

Long Essay Score × 4.5 = _____

Total of all above scores is composite score = _____ **(round it)**

Score Range	AP Score
111–180	5
91–110	4
76–90	3
57–75	2
>56	1

To get a final score for the test, compare your composite score to the chart directly above.

Once you have scored each section of the test, place the score on the appropriate line above. When you are done, do the computations to get your final score. Remember that this test is designed to mimic the AP exam, but the conditions of taking a practice exam are very different from the conditions of taking the actual exam. Further, keep in mind that your scoring of the written sections may differ from the scoring of the professional readers who score the actual exam. This test is only an approximate predictor of success on the actual exam. Do not stop studying just because you got a good score here.

ANSWER SHEET
Practice Test 2

Section I: Part A—Mutiple-Choice

1. Ⓐ Ⓑ Ⓒ Ⓓ
2. Ⓐ Ⓑ Ⓒ Ⓓ
3. Ⓐ Ⓑ Ⓒ Ⓓ
4. Ⓐ Ⓑ Ⓒ Ⓓ
5. Ⓐ Ⓑ Ⓒ Ⓓ
6. Ⓐ Ⓑ Ⓒ Ⓓ
7. Ⓐ Ⓑ Ⓒ Ⓓ
8. Ⓐ Ⓑ Ⓒ Ⓓ
9. Ⓐ Ⓑ Ⓒ Ⓓ
10. Ⓐ Ⓑ Ⓒ Ⓓ
11. Ⓐ Ⓑ Ⓒ Ⓓ
12. Ⓐ Ⓑ Ⓒ Ⓓ
13. Ⓐ Ⓑ Ⓒ Ⓓ
14. Ⓐ Ⓑ Ⓒ Ⓓ
15. Ⓐ Ⓑ Ⓒ Ⓓ
16. Ⓐ Ⓑ Ⓒ Ⓓ
17. Ⓐ Ⓑ Ⓒ Ⓓ
18. Ⓐ Ⓑ Ⓒ Ⓓ
19. Ⓐ Ⓑ Ⓒ Ⓓ
20. Ⓐ Ⓑ Ⓒ Ⓓ
21. Ⓐ Ⓑ Ⓒ Ⓓ
22. Ⓐ Ⓑ Ⓒ Ⓓ
23. Ⓐ Ⓑ Ⓒ Ⓓ
24. Ⓐ Ⓑ Ⓒ Ⓓ
25. Ⓐ Ⓑ Ⓒ Ⓓ
26. Ⓐ Ⓑ Ⓒ Ⓓ
27. Ⓐ Ⓑ Ⓒ Ⓓ
28. Ⓐ Ⓑ Ⓒ Ⓓ
29. Ⓐ Ⓑ Ⓒ Ⓓ
30. Ⓐ Ⓑ Ⓒ Ⓓ
31. Ⓐ Ⓑ Ⓒ Ⓓ
32. Ⓐ Ⓑ Ⓒ Ⓓ
33. Ⓐ Ⓑ Ⓒ Ⓓ
34. Ⓐ Ⓑ Ⓒ Ⓓ
35. Ⓐ Ⓑ Ⓒ Ⓓ
36. Ⓐ Ⓑ Ⓒ Ⓓ
37. Ⓐ Ⓑ Ⓒ Ⓓ
38. Ⓐ Ⓑ Ⓒ Ⓓ
39. Ⓐ Ⓑ Ⓒ Ⓓ
40. Ⓐ Ⓑ Ⓒ Ⓓ
41. Ⓐ Ⓑ Ⓒ Ⓓ
42. Ⓐ Ⓑ Ⓒ Ⓓ
43. Ⓐ Ⓑ Ⓒ Ⓓ
44. Ⓐ Ⓑ Ⓒ Ⓓ
45. Ⓐ Ⓑ Ⓒ Ⓓ
46. Ⓐ Ⓑ Ⓒ Ⓓ
47. Ⓐ Ⓑ Ⓒ Ⓓ
48. Ⓐ Ⓑ Ⓒ Ⓓ
49. Ⓐ Ⓑ Ⓒ Ⓓ
50. Ⓐ Ⓑ Ⓒ Ⓓ
51. Ⓐ Ⓑ Ⓒ Ⓓ
52. Ⓐ Ⓑ Ⓒ Ⓓ
53. Ⓐ Ⓑ Ⓒ Ⓓ
54. Ⓐ Ⓑ Ⓒ Ⓓ
55. Ⓐ Ⓑ Ⓒ Ⓓ

Practice Test 2

Section I

Part A: Multiple-Choice Questions

DIRECTIONS: The questions in this section are grouped in sets of 2–4. Each set is organized around a primary source, secondary source, or historical issue. Select the best answer for each of the questions in this section. (55 minutes)

Questions 1–3 refer to the following image:

—Herblock, "Fire," *Washington Post*, 1949

1. Which of the following statements most accurately describes the main point of this cartoon?

    (A) The need to extinguish the Communist threat justified swift and severe government action.
    (B) The freedoms of Americans were at risk because of an overreaction to the perceived threat of Communism after World War II.
    (C) The existence of Communists in the United States was a simple problem to solve.
    (D) There was no need to panic in the face of the Communist threat.

2. Which other historical time period could have elicited a similar political cartoon?

    (A) The Panic of 1873
    (B) The Progressive Era
    (C) The Second Great Awakening
    (D) The Quasi-War with France in 1798

3. Which of the following actions would this cartoonist most likely have criticized?

    (A) Congressional passage of the McCarran Internal Security Act (over President Harry S. Truman's veto)
    (B) President Dwight D. Eisenhower's warning in regard to the "military-industrial complex" in his Farewell Address
    (C) Vice President Richard Nixon's "Kitchen Debate" with Soviet Premier Khrushchev in Moscow
    (D) The implementation of the Truman Doctrine to contain Soviet expansion

Questions 4–6 refer to the following passage:

"I know that whenever the subject has occurred in conversation where I have been present, it has appeared to be the opinion of every one that we could not be taxed by a Parliament wherein we were not represented. But the payment of duties laid by an act of Parliament as regulations of commerce was never disputed.... An *external* tax is a duty laid on commodities imported; that duty is added to the first cost and other charges on the commodity, and, when it is offered for sale, makes a part of the price. If the people do not like it at that price, they refuse it; they are not obliged to pay it. But an *internal* tax is forced from the people without their consent if not laid by their own representatives. The Stamp Act says we shall have no commerce, make no exchange of property with each other, neither purchase nor grant, nor recover debts; we shall neither marry nor make our wills, unless we pay such and such sums; and thus it is intended to extort our money from us or ruin us by the consequence of refusing to pay it."

—Benjamin Franklin, *Examination before Parliament*, 1766

4. Which Enlightenment political ideal is best represented in this passage?

    (A) Governments derive their powers from the consent of the governed.
    (B) Governmental power should be divided among three branches.
    (C) The general will, or majority, should determine the rules of society.
    (D) The free market is the best way to determine the economic course of a society.

5. Prime Minister George Grenville later challenged Benjamin Franklin's statements that the American colonists should have representation in Parliament by claiming

    (A) the colonists had virtual representation in Parliament, meaning that Parliament represented all subjects of the British king.
    (B) the Stamp Act would be only the first of many internal taxes that the Americans would be expected to pay.
    (C) no subject of the king had the right to challenge Parliament's authority.
    (D) by refusing to pay the taxes imposed by Parliament, the Americans were committing treason.

6. Which of the following actions most closely mirrors the arguments presented in this quotation by Benjamin Franklin?

    (A) Anti-Federalist arguments in favor of adding a Bill of Rights to the U.S. Constitution
    (B) Representatives of the colonies convening the Stamp Act Congress to protest the laws of Parliament
    (C) South Carolina implementing the doctrine of nullification in the 1830s
    (D) The business-friendly policies of Presidents Calvin Coolidge and Herbert Hoover in the 1930s

Questions 7–9 refer to the following passage:

"As a means of effecting this end I suggest for your consideration the propriety of setting apart an ample district west of the Mississippi, and without the limit of any State or Territory now formed, to be guaranteed to the Indian tribes as long as they shall occupy it.... There they may be secured in the enjoyment of governments of their own choice, subject to no other control from the United States than such as may be necessary to preserve peace on the frontier and between the several tribes. There the benevolent may endeavor to teach them the arts of civilization....

"This emigration would be voluntary, for it would be as cruel and unjust to compel the aborigines to abandon the graves of their fathers and seek a home in a distant land. But they should be distinctly informed that if they remain within the limits of the States they must be subject to their laws...."

—President Andrew Jackson, Address to Congress, 1829

7. Which author was most critical of the policy being described here by President Jackson?

   (A) Rachel Carson in *Silent Spring*
   (B) Ralph Ellison in *Invisible Man*
   (C) Helen Hunt Jackson in *A Century of Dishonor*
   (D) William Lloyd Garrison in *The Liberator*

8. The policy described most immediately led to

   (A) peace between Indian tribes and white settlers.
   (B) the forced removal of the Cherokee from their homeland.
   (C) the first Treaty of Fort Laramie, which guaranteed Indian possession of lands west of the Mississippi River.
   (D) a negotiated settlement between the tribes of the Southeast and the U.S. government, by which the tribes were allowed to remain on their lands for ten years.

9. President Jackson's policy was later altered by the

   (A) Homestead Act of 1862.
   (B) Immigration Act of 1921.
   (C) Supreme Court decision in *Plessy v. Ferguson*.
   (D) Dawes Act of 1887.

Questions 10–12 refer to the following passage:

"I am in Birmingham because injustice is here.... Moreover, I am cognizant of the interrelatedness of all communities and states. I cannot sit idly by in Atlanta and not be concerned about what happens in Birmingham. Injustice anywhere is a threat to justice everywhere. We are caught in an inescapable network of mutuality, tied in a single garment of destiny. Whatever affects one directly affects all indirectly. Never again can we afford to live with the narrow, provincial 'outside agitator' idea. Anyone who lives inside the United States can never be considered an outsider anywhere in this country...."

—Martin Luther King Jr., "Letter from a Birmingham Jail," April 16, 1963

10. Based on this quotation, what can you infer about the efforts of Martin Luther King and others in the civil rights movement of the 1950s?

    (A) The civil rights movement was not finding success through nonviolent methods.
    (B) Advocates for civil rights were coordinating their efforts to raise awareness of racial segregation across the country.
    (C) King was focused on ending segregation in Birmingham only.
    (D) King was willing to compromise his principles and would be a violent agitator if necessary.

11. Which of the following Supreme Court decisions was the primary contributor to the system of segregation that Martin Luther King and others were trying to end?

    (A) *Dred Scott v. Sandford* (1857)
    (B) *Brown v. Board of Education of Topeka* (1954)
    (C) *Worcester v. Georgia* (1831)
    (D) *Plessy v. Ferguson* (1896)

12. Martin Luther King was in jail in Birmingham, Alabama, because of his belief in protesting injustice through the use of

    (A) targeted assassinations of segregationist public officials.
    (B) massive letter-writing campaigns denouncing segregated businesses.
    (C) violent self-defense.
    (D) nonviolent direct action.

Questions 13–16 refer to the following passage:

"One-half of the people of this nation today are utterly powerless to blot from the statute books an unjust law, or to write there a new and a just one. The women, dissatisfied as they are with this form of government, that enforces taxation without representation,—that compels them to obey laws to which they have never given their consent,— that imprisons and hangs them without a trial by a jury of their peers, that robs them, in marriage, of the custody of their own persons, wages and children,—are this half of the people left wholly at the mercy of the other half, in direct violation of the spirit and letter of the declarations of the framers of this government, every one of which was based on the immutable principle of equal rights to all."

—Susan B. Anthony, "I Stand Before You Under Indictment," speech (excerpt), 1873

13. On which of these documents is Susan B. Anthony basing her appeal for women's equality?

    (A) Articles of Confederation
    (B) Proclamation of Amnesty and Reconstruction
    (C) Compromise of 1850
    (D) Declaration of Independence

14. Which other nineteenth-century reform movement made similar arguments to those written here by Susan B. Anthony?

    (A) The temperance movement
    (B) Utopian communities
    (C) The abolition movement
    (D) Public school advocates

15. Susan B. Anthony and others in the women's rights movement had a major influence on the ratification of which of the following?

    (A) The Nineteenth Amendment
    (B) The Equal Rights Amendment
    (C) The Fifteenth Amendment
    (D) The Twenty-sixth Amendment

16. The language of this passage by Susan B. Anthony demonstrates which of the following continuities in U.S. history?

    (A) Debates over free speech
    (B) Debates over voting rights
    (C) Debates over federal power and states' rights
    (D) Debates over the procedures of amending the Constitution

Questions 17–20 refer to the following image:

—"Forty-Millionaire Carnegie in his Great Double Role,"
The Saturday Globe, July 9, 1892

17. Which of the following statements best represents the criticism of Andrew Carnegie found in this cartoon?

    (A) Carnegie was able to give away a great deal of money only because he violated his workers' rights.
    (B) Carnegie did not give enough of his considerable fortune to charity.
    (C) Carnegie was dividing his attention and was therefore not as successful in either of his main endeavors.
    (D) Carnegie's ruthless business practices were causing him to lose touch with his working-class origins.

18. Which of the following was another common criticism of Andrew Carnegie?

    (A) As an immigrant, Carnegie had no right to own controlling interests in major American industries.
    (B) Carnegie did nothing to prevent the use of violence against his workers when they asked for better wages and working conditions.
    (C) Carnegie was seen as the epitome of American success, but he was not even the richest man in America.
    (D) Too much of Carnegie's philanthropic efforts were concentrated on his homeland of Scotland, denying Americans the benefits of his charity.

19. Which of the following was NOT designed to empower the government to regulate the increasing wealth and power of the industrialists in the late nineteenth and early twentieth centuries?

    (A) Sherman Anti-Trust Act (1890)
    (B) Interstate Commerce Act (1887)
    (C) Federal Trade Commission Act (1914)
    (D) Newlands Reclamation Act (1902)

20. The actions taken by Andrew Carnegie that were critiqued in the cartoon reflected the thinking of which of the following concepts?

    (A) The Social Gospel
    (B) "Survival of the Fittest"
    (C) The Gospel of Wealth
    (D) "Rugged individualism"

Questions 21–23 refer to the following passage:

"Wherever I go—the street, the shop, the house, or the steamboat—I hear the people talk in such a way as to indicate that they are yet unable to conceive of the Negro as possessing any rights at all. Men who are honorable in their dealings with their white neighbors will cheat a Negro without feeling a single twinge of their honor. To kill a Negro they do not deem murder; to debauch a Negro woman they do not think fornication; to take the property away from a Negro they do not consider robbery…

"The reason of all this is simple and manifest. The whites esteem the blacks their property by natural right, and however much they may admit that the individual relations of masters and slaves have been destroyed by the war and the President's emancipation proclamation, they still have an ingrained feeling that the blacks at large belong to the whites at large, and whenever opportunity serves they treat the colored people just as their profit, caprice or passion may dictate."

—Congressional testimony of Col. Samuel Thomas, Assistant Commissioner, Bureau of Refugees, Freedmen and Abandoned Lands, 1865

21. According to this official from the Freedmen's Bureau, how had southern society reacted to the end of the Civil War?

    (A) Blacks were able to freely travel around the country without fear of reprisal.
    (B) The only way for southern whites to demonstrate their manhood was to mistreat freed slaves.
    (C) Southern whites were willing to accept the freedom of slaves as long as the slaves did not ask for voting rights.
    (D) The freed slaves were experiencing discrimination and limitations on their rights similar to their treatment under slavery.

22. The Fourteenth Amendment attempted to eliminate the societal conditions described in this passage by

    (A) revoking the voting rights of all known members of the Confederate government and soldiers of the Confederate Army.
    (B) granting citizenship and guaranteeing equal protection under the law to former slaves.
    (C) creating a special appeals process that expedited civil rights claims directly to the Supreme Court.
    (D) ensuring that former slaves received the forty acres of land promised to them by General William Sherman and the Freedmen's Bureau Bill of 1866.

23. Which of the following events of the twentieth century reflects a continuation of the attitudes of southern whites as described in this passage?

    (A) The Great Migration
    (B) Jim Crow legislation
    (C) The Civil Rights Act of 1957
    (D) The March on Washington for Jobs and Freedom

Questions 24–26 refer to the following passage:

"SECTION 1.

"Be it enacted by the Senate and the House of Representatives of the United States of America in Congress assembled, That it shall be lawful for the President of the United States at any time during the continuance of this act, to order all such aliens as he shall judge dangerous to the peace and safety of the United States, or shall have reasonable grounds to suspect are concerned in any treasonable or secret machinations against the government thereof, to depart out of the territory of the United States, within such time as shall be expressed in such order, which order shall be served on such alien by delivering him a copy thereof, or leaving the same at his usual abode, and returned to the office of the Secretary of State, by the marshal or other person to whom the same shall be directed."

—An Act Concerning Aliens (excerpt), 1798

24. The legislative act, excerpted above, enjoyed widespread public support, despite opposition from Democratic-Republican leaders, because, in part,

    (A) President John Adams was extremely popular; any opposition to him was seen as treasonous.
    (B) Irish immigration was changing the composition of many American cities; many Americans wondered if the United States could retain its Anglo-Saxon heritage without limiting immigration.
    (C) federal authorities had uncovered and thwarted a plot by disgruntled North Carolina farmers to assassinate President John Adams; desperate times, it seemed, called for desperate measures.
    (D) large numbers of Americans had become intensely critical of the revolutionary French government during the Quasi-War with France; restricting the ability of French immigrants to participate in American politics seemed reasonable.

25. Leaders of the Democratic-Republican Party responded to legislative acts, such as the one excerpted, by

    (A) calling for the impeachment of President John Adams.
    (B) challenging the laws in the Supreme Court.
    (C) putting forth the theory of state nullification of federal legislation.
    (D) boycotting the elections of 1800.

26. The governmental action allowed for in the excerpt is similar to government actions taken

    (A) against Mexican Americans during the Mexican-American War (1846–1848).
    (B) during the "Red Scare" following World War I.
    (C) in the aftermath of the sit-in strikes of the 1930s.
    (D) as part of the COINTELPRO program, initiated by the Federal Bureau of Investigation against protest movements in the 1960s.

Questions 27–29 refer to the following passage:

"Lincoln was strongly antislavery, but he was not an abolitionist or a Radical Republican and never claimed to be one. He made a sharp distinction between his frequently reiterated personal wish that 'all men everywhere could be free' and his official duties as a legislator, congressman, and president in a legal and constitutional system that recognized the South's right to property in slaves. Even after issuing the Emancipation Proclamation he continued to declare his preference for gradual abolition. While his racial views changed during the Civil War, he never became a principled egalitarian in the manner of abolitionists such as Frederick Douglass or Wendell Phillips or Radical Republicans like Charles Sumner."

—Eric Foner, *The Fiery Trial*, 2010

27. Which of the following statements best describes Eric Foner's argument about President Abraham Lincoln's views on slavery?

    (A) President Lincoln was a consistent supporter of the abolitionist cause.
    (B) President Lincoln was reluctant to be ideologically associated with advocates like Frederick Douglass.
    (C) In his ambition to become president, Abraham Lincoln declared his desire to use his constitutional powers to end slavery.
    (D) President Lincoln had continually changing views on slavery and abolition that did not always fit into the prevailing political categories.

28. How did President Lincoln's issuance of the Emancipation Proclamation alter the course of the Civil War?

    (A) The war came to a swift conclusion because the Proclamation made the Confederacy realize the futility of their cause.
    (B) The war grew in scope because the Proclamation caused Great Britain to join the fight on the side of the Union.
    (C) President Jefferson Davis of the Confederacy vowed massive resistance to any Union effort to free the slaves.
    (D) The war aims of the United States were no longer exclusively focused on the preservation of the Union.

29. Which of these statements best describes the Emancipation Proclamation?

    (A) It guaranteed the freedom of all slaves living within the boundaries of the United States at the conclusion of the Civil War.
    (B) It freed only the slaves in states and portions of states in rebellion against the United States at the time it was issued.
    (C) It declared that the freedom of the slaves was conditional upon the agreement of individual southern states to sign a peace treaty with the U.S. government.
    (D) It prohibited the use of slaves in combat in both the Union and Confederate Armies.

Questions 30–31 refer to the following passage:

"The only force which is strong enough to break down social convention is economic necessity.... The economic necessity which has forced women out of the home and into the world of business has completely annihilated the old idea that a woman should eat only in the privacy of her household or in the homes of her friends, has created the absolutely new social phenomenon of women eating in public, unescorted by men, by the tens of thousands, and has given rise to a wholly new phase of the restaurant business."

—*The New York Times*, October 15, 1905

30. Which of the following groups would have most likely supported the scenario described in this passage?

    (A) Ku Klux Klan
    (B) American Temperance Union
    (C) National Woman Suffrage Association
    (D) Southern Christian Leadership Conference

31. The scenario described in the passage above is most directly reflected in the ideas of which of the following?

    (A) Civil Rights Act of 1964
    (B) Equal Rights Amendment
    (C) Pure Food and Drug Act
    (D) Interstate Commerce Act

Questions 32–34 refer to the following passage:

Did [this treaty] not... annex Louisiana, and squander millions in a week? Have we not seen in France, how early and how effectually the conqueror takes care to prevent another rival from playing the same game, by which he himself prevailed against his predecessor? Let any man, who has any understanding, exercise it to see that the American jacobin party, by rousing the popular passions, inevitably augments the powers of government, and contracts within narrower bounds, and on a less sound foundation, the privileges of the people. Facts, yes facts, that speak in terror to the soul, confirm this speculative reasoning. What limits are there to the prerogatives of the present administration? And whose business is it, and in whose power does it lie, to keep them within those limits? Surely not in the senate: the small States are now in vassalage, and they obey the nod of Virginia. Not in the judiciary: that fortress, which the Constitution had made too strong for an assault, can now be reduced by famine. The Constitution, alas! that sleeps with Washington, having no mourners but the virtuous, and no monument but history. Louisiana, in open and avowed defiance of the Constitution, is by treaty to be added to the union; the bread of the children of the union is to be taken and given to the dogs. Judge then, good men and true, judge by the effects, whether the tendency of the intrigues of the party was to extend or contract the measure of popular liberty."

—Fisher Ames, "The Republican. No. II," first printed in *The Boston Gazette*, July 26, 1804

32. Which of the following points is Ames making in regard to the treaty he refers to in this letter?

    (A) The treaty violated the Constitution and will expand the powers of the government.
    (B) The treaty will entangle the United States with the affairs of European countries.
    (C) The treaty will quite likely lead to war with American Indian tribes in the region.
    (D) The treaty will stifle economic growth in the United States.

33. The argument made by Ames is most similar to which of the following arguments from earlier in American history?

    (A) Arguments by Quakers in the 1780s against provisions in the Constitution concerning slavery
    (B) Arguments by the British in the 1760s in favor of preventing the colonists from migrating beyond the Appalachian Mountains
    (C) Arguments by the Democratic-Republicans in the 1790s against the creation of a national bank
    (D) Arguments by the Federalists in the 1790s in favor of free speech limitations during national crises

34. The treaty that is the subject of the Ames's letter would later lead to which of the following conflicts?

    (A) Conflicts between northern and southern states over the expansion of slavery into new territories
    (B) Conflicts between the United States and Great Britain over shipping rights on the high seas
    (C) Conflicts between Federalists and Democratic-Republicans over the proper balance between maintaining security and ensuring basic civil liberties
    (D) Conflicts between nativists and advocates of open borders over immigration policy

Questions 35–38 refer to the following passage:

"The economic ills we suffer have come upon us over several decades. They will not go away in days, weeks, or months, but they will go away. They will go away because we as Americans have the capacity now, as we've had in the past, to do whatever needs to be done to preserve this last and greatest bastion of freedom. In this present crisis, government is not the solution to our problem; government is the problem....

"It is my intention to curb the size and influence of the Federal establishment and to demand recognition of the distinction between the powers granted to the Federal Government and those reserved to the States or to the people. All of us need to be reminded that the Federal Government did not create the States; the States created the Federal Government."

—Ronald Reagan, First Inaugural Address, January 21, 1981

35. The conservative political revival that led to President Ronald Reagan's election in 1980 held the view that

   (A) political leaders in the 1960s and 1970s did not do enough to challenge the racial and economic status quo.
   (B) the United States had relied too heavily on military solutions and needed to pursue a more isolationist foreign policy.
   (C) religious leaders had become too assertive in governmental policy and had blurred the separation of church and state.
   (D) liberal laws and court decisions in the 1960s and a general moral decline were undermining the United States.

36. Which of the following would have most likely agreed with President Reagan's statement that the federal government was created by the states and the federal government's role should be limited?

   (A) The Anti-Federalists
   (B) The Whig Party
   (C) The Mugwumps
   (D) The Progressives

37. Which of the following ongoing debates in U.S. history is expressed in the quotation?

   (A) Debates over the powers of the president
   (B) Debates over participation in elections
   (C) Debates over federal power over the economy
   (D) Debates over federal power over international affairs

38. One way in which President Reagan acted on his rhetoric in the passage was to

   (A) increase the military budget.
   (B) work with Congress to cut taxes and government spending.
   (C) eliminate the Department of Housing and Urban Development.
   (D) prohibit pay increases for government workers.

Questions 39–40 refer to the following passage:

"Our energy plan will also include a number of specific goals, to measure our progress toward a stable energy system. These are the goals we set for 1985:
- Reduce the annual growth rate in our energy demand to less than 2 percent.
- Reduce gasoline consumption by 10 percent below its current level.
- Cut in half the portion of U.S. oil which is imported, from a potential level of sixteen million barrels to six million barrels a day.
- Establish a strategic petroleum reserve of one billion barrels, more than six months' supply.
- Increase our coal production by about two-thirds to more than one billion tons a year.
- Insulate 90 percent of American homes and all new buildings.
- Use solar energy in more than two and one-half million houses."

—President Jimmy Carter, speech (excerpt), April 18, 1977

39. The passage above reflects which of the following continuities of U.S. history?

    (A) Concern for working-class Americans
    (B) The shifting role of the federal government
    (C) Concern for natural resources and their environmental impact
    (D) The role of the United States in world diplomacy

40. President Jimmy Carter's speech, excerpted above, was primarily a reaction to which of the following events?

    (A) The Soviet Union's invasion of Afghanistan
    (B) The Iran hostage crisis
    (C) A series of embargoes enacted by the Middle East–dominated organization known as OPEC
    (D) Terrorist bombings that targeted U.S. military personnel

Questions 41–43 refer to the following image:

—William Carson, "A Bigger Job Than He Thought For," *Sunday Globe* (Utica, NY), 1899

41. The 1899 cartoon shown above makes the point that

    (A) insurgents in Cuba were being manipulated by Spain into resisting the presence of American troops.
    (B) native Hawaiians behaved in a childlike manner when the Hawaiian islands were annexed by the United States.
    (C) the United States misread the reaction of the Filipino people when it acquired the Philippines following the Spanish-American War.
    (D) the task of completing the Panama Canal was more time consuming, and more costly, than the United States had originally anticipated.

42. The cartoon reflects which of the following continuities in U.S. history?

    (A) Debates over extending constitutional rights to peoples in territories acquired by the United States
    (B) Debates over the wisdom of asserting American control over foreign possessions
    (C) Debates over the morality of tactics used by the United States in wars of colonial independence
    (D) Debates over allowing the Central Intelligence Agency to engage in covert operations in foreign countries

43. The event depicted in the cartoon represents which of the following?

    (A) A shift in American foreign policy from "gunboat diplomacy" to "dollar diplomacy"
    (B) The beginning of a period of isolation from world affairs
    (C) A shift from "brinksmanship" to détente
    (D) The beginning of a period of imperialistic activities by the United States

Questions 44–45 refer to the following passage:

"I marvel not a little, right worshipful, that since the first discovery of America (which is now full four score and ten years), after so great conquests and plantings of the Spaniards and Portuguese there, that we of England could never have the grace to set fast footing in such fertile and temperate places as are left as yet unpossessed of them. But...I conceive great hope that the time approacheth and now is that we of England may share and part stakes [divide the prize] (if we will ourselves) both with the Spaniard and the Portuguese in part of America and other regions as yet undiscovered.

"And surely if there were in us that desire to advance the honor of our country which ought to be in every good man, we would not all this while have [neglected] the possessing of these lands which of equity and right appertain unto us, as by the discourses that follow shall appear most plainly."

—Richard Hakluyt, *Divers Voyages Touching the Discovery of America and the Islands Adjacent,* 1582

44. The ideas expressed in the passage above most closely reflect the influence of which of the following?

    (A) The Enlightenment philosophy of natural rights
    (B) The economic policy of mercantilism
    (C) The religious philosophy of predestination
    (D) The social contract theory

45. By following the ideas of Richard Hakluyt, England was eventually able to

    (A) drive the French and Portuguese governments into bankruptcy.
    (B) conquer large parts of Africa in the eighteenth century.
    (C) establish several colonies along the Atlantic coastline of North America.
    (D) destroy the Dutch commercial empire.

Questions 46–49 refer to the following passage:

"The God that holds you over the pit of hell, much as one holds a spider, or some loathsome insect, over the fire, abhors you, and is dreadfully provoked; his wrath towards you burns like fire; he looks upon you as worthy of nothing else, but to be cast into the fire; he is of purer eyes than to bear to have you in his sight; you are ten thousand times so abominable in his eyes as the most hateful venomous serpent is in ours. You have offended him infinitely more than ever a stubborn rebel did his prince: and yet 'tis nothing but his hand that holds you from falling into the fire every moment: 'tis to be ascribed to nothing else, that you did not go to hell the last night; that you was suffered to awake again in this world, after you closed your eyes to sleep: and there is no other reason to be given why you have not dropped into hell since you arose in the morning, but that God's hand has held you up: there is no other reason to be given why you ha[ve]n't gone to hell since you have sat here in the house of God, provoking his pure eyes by your sinful wicked manner of attending his solemn worship: yea, there is nothing else that is to be given as a reason why you don't this very moment drop down into hell."

—Jonathan Edwards, "Sinners in the Hands of an Angry God" (excerpt), 1741.

46. An important point that Jonathan Edwards is making in the sermon is that

    (A) despite the sinful nature of humanity, God has given individuals a chance to rectify their sins.
    (B) human beings are born inherently good, but are corrupted by the evils of society.
    (C) God is merciless, allowing sinners and saints alike to suffer in the fires of hell.
    (D) it is not important what you believe in life, just as long as you live your life in a moral and ethical manner.

47. The sermon by Jonathan Edwards was a central text of

    (A) Transcendentalism.
    (B) Mormonism.
    (C) the Great Awakening.
    (D) the Social Gospel.

48. Which of the following describes the context that Jonathan Edwards was preaching in?

    (A) There had been a marked decline in piety in Puritan New England; Edwards hoped to rekindle the fires of New England church members.
    (B) The government of Massachusetts had disestablished the Congregational Church, forcing preachers like Edwards to travel from town to town in search of adherents.
    (C) New England had experienced a wave of immigrants from all over Europe, including many Catholics, Jews, Protestants from a variety of sects, and non-believers; Edwards hoped to convert them to teachings of the Congregational Church.
    (D) New England was recently devastated by war with American Indians; Edwards sought to reassure the survivors that God did, indeed, exist.

49. Jonathan Edwards was part of a broader religious movement that impacted colonial American society by

    (A) encouraging colonists to question and challenge the legitimacy of British authorities.
    (B) citing the immorality of slavery and stressing the importance of ending the institution.
    (C) asserting the importance of developing amicable relations with American Indians.
    (D) fostering changes in colonists' understandings of God, themselves, and the world around them.

Questions 50–52 refer to the following image:

Ford Motor Company, advertisment, 1926

50. What does the above image reflect about the decade of the 1920s?

   (A) Consumer safety was the primary concern of leading manufacturing companies.
   (B) Automobiles were a rare commodity and therefore extremely expensive.
   (C) New technologies such as automobiles were unproven and unsafe, requiring extensive propaganda in order to make consumers interested in them.
   (D) Consumer products were increasingly affordable and highly desired by the public as a sign of status.

51. Like other consumer products such as radios and home electric appliances, automobiles were often offered to consumers through

   (A) payment plans, which allowed consumers to spread full payment over time.
   (B) self-manufacturing kits, which reduced the costs for the companies selling the products.
   (C) exclusive retail stores, which prevented consumers from buying products at the lowest possible price.
   (D) incentives such as rebates, which consumers could acquire by agreeing to sell products for the manufacturer.

52. The consumer economy of the 1920s most directly shows the influence of which of the following?

   (A) Manifest destiny and territorial expansion
   (B) The Industrial Revolution and a spirit of entrepreneurship
   (C) Reconstruction and the "Redemption" of the South
   (D) World War I and international cooperation

Questions 53–55 refer to the following table:

Wholesale Price Index of Farm Products
(Based on 1910–1914 = 100)

1866	140
1870	112
1876	89
1880	80
1882	99
1886	68
1890	71
1896	56
1900	71

53. Which of the following describes an important reason for the trend reflected in the figures in the table above?

   (A) The number of family farms increased in the 1870s and 1880s, as thousands of "new immigrant" families settled in the rural Midwest.
   (B) Population stagnated as the spread of birth control and the growth of the middle class led to falling birthrates.
   (C) Mechanization of agriculture, improved techniques, and an increase in acres under cultivation created agricultural surpluses.
   (D) American expansion into Latin America resulted in surplus agricultural products from Central and South America flooding American markets.

54. Which of the following was a demand of the Populist Party in the 1880s and 1890s to address the situation reflected in the figures in the table?

   (A) A national sales tax
   (B) Government funding for the purchase of agricultural machinery
   (C) "Internal improvements" in the West, including railroads and canals
   (D) An end to the gold standard and a shift to currency backed by silver as well as gold

55. Which of the following describes developments in the 1870s, 1880s, and 1890s that occurred, in part, as a result of the trend indicated in the chart?

   (A) The federal government established agencies that oversaw agricultural production in the United States, limiting production of certain products.
   (B) The United States lowered import tariffs in order to stimulate international trade and reduce surpluses of agricultural products.
   (C) Farmers created local and regional networks to challenge and resist corporate control of agricultural markets.
   (D) Major agricultural producers invested in the establishment of a transcontinental railroad network to more effectively transport agricultural goods to urban markets.

STOP If there is still time remaining, you may review your answers.

Part B: Short-Answer Questions

> **DIRECTIONS:** Answer Question 1 *and* Question 2. Answer either Question 3 *or* Question 4.
>
> During the AP exam, a Short-Answer Response booklet will be distributed. You must write your response to each question on the lined page designated for that response. Each response is expected to fit within the space provided.
>
> In your responses, be sure to address all parts of the questions you answer. Use complete sentences; an outline or bulleted list alone is not acceptable. You may plan your answers in this exam booklet, but no credit will be given for notes written in this booklet. (40 minutes)

Question 1

"Martin Luther King famously exhorted the nation to 'rise up and live out the true meaning of its creed....' He reinforced a cry for democracy with political sacrifice, and dreams of brotherhood collided in his anguished voice with the cruelties of race.... King balanced an imperative for equal votes with the original prophetic vision of equal souls before God. He grounded one foot in patriotism, one foot in ministry, and both in nonviolence. The movement he led climbed from obscurity to command the center stage of American politics in 1963, when President Johnson declared racial segregation a moral issue "as old as the Scriptures...as clear as the American Constitution.' A year later, after President Lyndon Johnson signed a landmark law to abolish segregation by sex as well as race, King accepted the Nobel Peace Prize...

[In 1965] thousands of ordinary Americans will answer King's overnight call for a nonviolent pilgrimage to Selma. Three of them will be murdered, but the quest to march beyond Pettus Bridge will release waves of political energy from the human nucleus of freedom. The movement will transform national politics to win the vote."
Taylor Branch, historian, At Canaan's Edge: America in the King Years, 1965–1968, 2006

"[T]hese local movements should not be viewed as protest activity designed to persuade and coerce the federal government to act on behalf of black civil rights. There was a constant tension between the national black leaders, who saw mass protest as an instrument for reform, and local leaders and organizers who were often more interested in building enduring local institutions rather than staging marches and rallies for a national audience. Local black leadership sought goals that were quite distinct from the national civil rights agenda. Even in communities where King played a major role, as in Albany, Birmingham, and Selma, he was compelled to work with local leaders who were reluctant, to say the least, to implement strategies developed by outsiders.

"Black communities mobilized not merely to prod the federal government into action but to create new social identities for participants and for all Afro-Americans.... The notion of a black freedom struggle seeking a broad range of goals suggests...that there was much continuity between the period before 1965 and the period after."
Clayborne Carson, historian, "Civil Rights Reform and the Black Freedom Struggle,"
in Charles W. Eagles, ed., The Civil Rights Movement in America, 1986

1. Using the excerpts above, answer (a), (b), and (c).

    (a) Briefly describe ONE major difference between Branch's and Carson's historical interpretations of the American civil rights movement.

    (b) Briefly explain how ONE specific historical event or development that is not explicitly mentioned in the excerpts could be used to support Branch's interpretation.

    (c) Briefly explain how ONE specific historical event or development that is not explicitly mentioned in the excerpts could be used to support Carson's interpretation.

Question 2

—"A Party of Patches," *Judge Magazine*, 1891

2. Using the image above, answer (a), (b), and (c).

   (a) Briefly describe ONE perspective about politics in the 1890s expressed in this image.
   (b) Briefly describe ONE specific historical development that led to the political development depicted in the cartoon.
   (c) Briefly explain ONE effect that the political development depicted in the cartoon had on the United States in the period 1891 to 1920.

> **DIRECTIONS:** Answer either Question 3 or Question 4.

Question 3 or 4

3. Answer (a), (b), and (c). Confine your response to the period.

    (a) Briefly describe ONE specific historical similarity between President George Washington's Farewell Address (1796) and the Monroe Doctrine (1823) in regard to U.S. foreign policy.
    (b) Briefly describe ONE specific historical difference between President George Washington's Farewell Address and the Monroe Doctrine in regard to U.S. foreign policy.
    (c) Briefly explain ONE specific historical reason for a difference between President George Washington's Farewell Address and the Monroe Doctrine in regard to U.S. foreign policy.

4. Answer (a), (b), and (c).

    (a) Briefly describe ONE specific historical similarity between the United States' entrance into World War I and its entrance into World War II.
    (b) Briefly describe ONE specific historical difference between the United States' entrance into World War I and its entrance into World War II.
    (c) Briefly explain ONE specific historical reason for a difference between the United States' entrance into World War I and its entrance into World War II.

Section II

TOTAL TIME—1 HOUR AND 40 MINUTES

Part A: Document-Based Question

SUGGESTED READING AND WRITING TIME: 1 HOUR

It is suggested that you spend 15 minutes reading the documents and 45 minutes writing your response.
Note: You may begin writing your response before the reading period is over.

> **DIRECTIONS:** Question 1 is based on the accompanying documents. The documents have been edited for the purpose of this exercise.
>
> In your response, you should do the following:
>
> - Respond to the prompt with a historically defensible thesis or claim that establishes a line of reasoning.
> - Describe a broader historical context relevant to the prompt.
> - Support an argument in response to the prompt using at least four documents.
> - Use at least one additional piece of specific historical evidence (beyond that found in the documents) relevant to an argument about the prompt.
> - For at least two documents, explain how or why each document's point of view, purpose, historical situation, and/or audience are relevant to an argument.
> - Demonstrate a complex understanding of a historical development related to the prompt through sophisticated argumentation and/or effective use of evidence.

Question 1

1. Evaluate the extent of change in the ways in which Americans addressed and debated immigration policy in two different time periods—in the period 1750–1800 and in the period 1875–1925.

> **DOCUMENT 1**
>
> **Source:** Benjamin Franklin, *Observations Concerning the Increase of Mankind, Peopling of Countries, etc.* (1753).
>
> Why should the [Germans] be suffered to swarm into our Settlements, and by herding together establish their Language and Manners to the Exclusion of ours? Why should *Pennsylvania*, founded by the *English*, become a Colony of *Aliens*, who will shortly be so numerous as to Germanize us instead of our Anglifying them, and will never adopt our Language or Customs, any more than they can acquire our Complexion.

DOCUMENT 2

Source: J. Hector St. John De Crevecoeur, *Letters From An American Farmer*, Letter III (1782).

What then is the American, this new man? He is either an European, or the descendant of an European, hence that strange mixture of blood, which you will find in no other country. I could point out to you a family whose grandfather was an Englishman, whose wife was Dutch, whose son married a French woman, and whose present four sons have now four wives of different nations. *He* is an American, who leaving behind him all his ancient prejudices and manners, receives new ones from the new mode of life he has embraced, the new government he obeys, and the new rank he holds. He becomes an American by being received in the broad lap of our great *Alma Mater*. Here individuals of all nations are melted into a new race of men, whose labours and posterity will one day cause great changes in the world. Americans are the western pilgrims, who are carrying along with them that great mass of arts, sciences, vigour, and industry which began long since in the east; they will finish the great circle. The Americans were once scattered all over Europe; here they are incorporated into one of the finest systems of population which has ever appeared, and which will hereafter become distinct by the power of the different climates they inhabit. The American ought therefore to love this country much better than that wherein either he or his forefathers were born.

DOCUMENT 3

Source: Theodore Sedgwick, from debate in the House of Representatives over Naturalization Bill, 1794.

And shall we alone adopt the rash theory that the subjects of all governments despotic, monarchical, and aristocratical are, as soon as they set foot on American ground, qualified to participate in administering the sovereignty of our country? Shall we hold the benefits of American citizenship so cheap as to invite, nay, almost bribe, the discontented, the ambitious, and the avaricious of every country to accept them? . . .

A war, the most cruel and dreadful which has been known for centuries, was now raging in those in all those countries from which emigrants were to be expected. The most fierce and unrelenting passions were engaged in a conflict, which shock to their foundations all the ancient political structures of Europe. . . . Could any reasonable man believe, that men who, actuated by such passions, had fought on grounds so opposite, almost equally distant from the happy mean we had chosen, would here mingle in social affections with each other, or with us? That their passions and prejudices would subside as soon as they should set foot in America? or that, possessing those passions and prejudices, they were qualified to make or to be made the governors of Americans?

DOCUMENT 4

Source: Joseph McDonnell, *Labor Standard*, June 30, 1878.

The cry that the "Chinese must go" is both narrow and unjust. It represents no broad or universal principle. It is merely a repetition of the cry that was raised years ago by American Indians against the immigration of Irishmen, Englishmen, Germans and others from European nations. It now ill becomes those, or the descendants of those, against whom this cry was raised in past years, to raise a similar tocsin against a class of foreigners who have been degraded by ages of oppression. . . .

The feeling at the bottom of the "Know Nothing" movement IN ITS EARLY DAYS was certainly a general one against low wages, and if it had raised the cry:

No low wages.
No cheap labor!

Instead of sounding the intolerant, silly, and shameful cry against Irishmen, Englishmen, Germans and all other "foreigners," it would have accomplished incalculable good. As it was it fell into the hands of infamous, scheming politicians, who pandered to the worst prejudices of the masses by raising a cry against men of various religious faiths and foreign nationalities. This policy suited them; it raised them to prominence and office and allowed what they IN THEIR HEARTS desired, the onward march of low wages.

DOCUMENT 5

Source: Joseph Keppler, "Welcome to All!" *Puck*, 1880.

WELCOME TO ALL!

Credit: Granger, NYC

DOCUMENT 6

Source: Madison Grant, *The Passing of the Great Race* (1916).

These new immigrants were no longer exclusively members of the Nordic race as were the earlier ones who came of their own impulse to improve their social conditions. The transportation lines advertised America as a land flowing with milk and honey, and the European governments took the opportunity to unload upon careless, wealthy, and hospitable America the sweepings of their jails and asylums. The result was that the new immigration, while it still included many strong elements from the north of Europe, contained a large and increasing number of the weak, the broken, and the mentally crippled of all races drawn from the lowest stratum of the Mediterranean basin and the Balkans, together with hordes of the wretched, submerged populations of the Polish Ghettos.

DOCUMENT 7

Source: Frank Beard, "Columbia's Unwelcome Guests," 1885.

Credit: Granger, NYC

Part B: Long Essay (Question 2, 3, or 4)

SUGGESTED WRITING TIME: 40 MINUTES

DIRECTIONS: Answer Question 2 or Question 3 or Question 4.

In your response, you should do the following:

- Respond to the prompt with a historically defensible thesis or claim that establishes a line of reasoning.
- Describe a broader historical context relevant to the prompt.
- Support an argument in response to the prompt using at least two pieces of specific and relevant evidence.
- Use historical reasoning (e.g., comparison, causation, continuity or change) to frame or structure an argument that addresses the prompt.
- Demonstrate a complex understanding of a historical development related to the prompt through sophisticated argumentation and/or effective use of evidence.

2. Evaluate the relative importance of the causes of the French and Indian War (1754–1763).

3. Evaluate the relative importance of the causes of the Mexican-American War (1846–1848).

4. Evaluate the relative importance of the causes of the Spanish-American War (1898).

Answers and Explanations

Section I

PART A: MULTIPLE-CHOICE QUESTIONS

1. **(B)** The cartoonist Herblock was pointing out that the growing anti-Communist sentiment in the United States following World War II could become a threat to the civil liberties of Americans. The hysterical figure climbing the ladder is about to extinguish the torch of liberty in a rash reaction to someone claiming that fire is a danger.

2. **(D)** In 1798, President John Adams and the Federalist Party in Congress were concerned that Americans supportive of France and French immigrants in America were working to undermine the U.S. government. This led to the passage of the Alien and Sedition Acts, which were criticized as violations of the liberties guaranteed by the Bill of Rights.

3. **(A)** After President Harry S. Truman vetoed the McCarran Internal Act in 1950, Congress overrode his veto. Truman criticized the act, saying it represented "the greatest danger to freedom of speech, press, and assembly since the Alien and Sedition Laws of 1798." The act required groups deemed to be "subversive" to register with the federal government, prohibited some members of these groups from becoming American citizens, created an investigatory agency to find people suspected of engaging in subversive activities, and gave the president the power to detain suspected subversive people in the event of an emergency. Critics of the act echoed the sentiment of the cartoonist—that the act was an overreaction to perceived threats.

4. **(A)** John Locke's contract theory was well known among the American colonial elites such as Franklin and was a foundational principle of American democracy. The concept is integral to both the Declaration of Independence and the Constitution of the United States.

5. **(A)** Grenville's argument that the colonies of the British Empire had virtual representation was criticized in both Parliament and the American colonies as illogical and not at all founded in British law. The backlash against Grenville's policies led to the repeal of the Stamp Act later in 1766.

6. **(B)** Benjamin Franklin was an early proponent of colonial unity, often arguing that the thirteen British colonies in America should work together for the betterment of all. A prime example of this type of advocacy was Franklin's famous "Join or Die" political cartoon from the French and Indian War era. His testimony to British officials in 1766 was directly related to the Stamp Act and colonial actions to protest against the stamp tax, such as the Stamp Act Congress. Franklin and other colonial leaders argued that the colonies should be given representation in Parliament if Parliament was going to tax the colonies.

7. **(C)** Published in 1881, Helen Hunt Jackson's book, *A Century of Dishonor*, was a scathing indictment of U.S. policy toward Indian tribes over the previous century. Jackson sent the book to every member of Congress, but it did not have as strong an impact as she had hoped.

8. **(B)** The Indian Removal Act put Jackson's policy request into law in 1830. It took several years of political and legal maneuvering, but the Indian Removal Act was eventually implemented during the presidency of Jackson's successor, Martin Van Buren. The Cherokee tribe, unlike the other affected tribes, resisted the pressure to sign a treaty that would cede their ancestral lands. The result of their resistance was their forcible removal, leading to the deaths of thousands of Cherokee.

9. **(D)** The Dawes Act established a system of land allotments to Indian tribes, granting 160 acres to the head of a family, and allowed for a method by which Indians could receive U.S. citizenship. The Dawes Act ended the reservation system of community ownership of land for Indian tribes and made the assimilation of Indians into American culture a matter of national policy.

10. **(B)** Martin Luther King Jr. was only one of many civil rights leaders across the country, but he was probably the most prominent by the end of the 1950s. King coordinated his activist effort for civil

rights with many of those civil rights leaders, culminating with the March on Washington for Jobs and Freedom in August 1963, which was organized by King, labor leader A. Phillip Randolph, and various activist groups.

11. **(D)** Racial segregation was given the endorsement of the Supreme Court with the 1896 *Plessy v. Ferguson* decision, which established the "separate but equal" doctrine. Using that allowance, many states continued and expanded the Jim Crow laws that disenfranchised and discriminated against African Americans.

12. **(D)** Martin Luther King Jr. followed the precedent set by Henry David Thoreau and Mohandas Gandhi and practiced nonviolent protest methods. King knew that in order to win the struggle for civil rights, advocates for racial equality must occupy the moral high ground. That meant that he did not support the use of violence as a means to achieve the end of segregation or to acquire voting rights.

13. **(D)** Susan B. Anthony and other advocates for women's rights often appealed to America's founding documents in their arguments for equality. In this quote, she echoes the list of grievances against the king of England found in the Declaration of Independence—taxation without representation, withholding trial by jury, depriving them of property without due process—as a way to connect the women's rights movement to the leaders of the Revolution and their struggle for freedom.

14. **(C)** Abolitionists sought freedom for slaves and felt that the promises outlined in the Declaration of Independence, namely that "all men are created equal," should and did apply to all people. Those promises could not be fulfilled until slaves were granted their freedom.

15. **(A)** The Nineteenth Amendment, ratified in 1920, gave women the right to vote on a nationwide basis. It was the result of at least seventy-two years of effort on the part of women's rights advocates, who had been arguing for equal suffrage since the adoption of the Declaration of Rights and Sentiments at the Seneca Falls Convention in 1848.

16. **(B)** Susan B. Anthony was, along with Elizabeth Cady Stanton, a founder of the National Woman Suffrage Association in 1869. Anthony was arrested for voting in the 1872 presidential election and refused to pay the fine imposed on her by a judge. In addition to women like Susan B. Anthony, other groups that have fought for voting rights include African Americans (Fifteenth Amendment) and people between the age of eighteen and twenty-one years (Twenty-sixth Amendment).

17. **(A)** Andrew Carnegie made sizable philanthropic contributions in both the United States and his homeland of Scotland. The cartoonist draws attention to Carnegie's cash donations and his monetary grants to build libraries while he was simultaneously cutting the wages of the workers in his steel plants. The dichotomous nature of Carnegie's wealth has often been used as a symbol of the "Gilded Age" of the late nineteenth century.

18. **(B)** Workers went on strike at Andrew Carnegie's Homestead Steel plant near Pittsburgh in 1892. Carnegie and his operations manager Henry Clay Frick hired the Pinkerton Detective Agency to defend the plant and the newly hired non-union workers. The strikers and the Pinkertons clashed violently, with the striking workers winning the battle. Pennsylvania state militia later arrived to restore order, allowing Frick to reopen the plant with the non-union workers.

19. **(D)** The Newlands Reclamation Act was part of the environmental legislation of the Progressive era. The law gave the federal government authority over water rights in much of the nation, which paved the way for federal construction of dams and irrigation projects. All of the other choices were federal attempts to regulate or limit the abusive practices of big businesses.

20. **(C)** Andrew Carnegie wrote "Wealth" (also known as "The Gospel of Wealth") in 1889, in which he argued that the newly rich class of industrialists and entrepreneurs had a responsibility to give back to the community. He thought that wealthy people, rather than the government, should administer funds for public-minded projects. He

argued that the wealthy should live modest lifestyles and avoid extravagances.

21. **(D)** Despite the freedom former slaves obtained via the Thirteenth Amendment, this representative of the Freedmen's Bureau said that southern whites were slow to accept the new social conditions brought about by the amendment. Many southern states began to pass restrictive laws in an attempt to continue their dominance.

22. **(B)** In an effort to integrate the freed slaves into American political and social life, and to deny individual states the ability to legally discriminate against Blacks, the Fourteenth Amendment declared, "No state shall make or enforce any law which shall abridge the privileges or immunities of citizens of the United States; nor shall any state deprive any person of life, liberty, or property, without due process of law; nor deny to any person within its jurisdiction the equal protection of the laws."

23. **(B)** Jim Crow legislation was a term used to describe laws passed to disenfranchise Blacks and to systematize racial segregation. Some examples of Jim Crow laws include the poll tax, literacy tests, and separate facilities, including schools, for whites and Blacks. The Jim Crow system was eroded by several Supreme Court decisions in the 1950s, most famously *Brown v. Board of Education* in 1954, and congressional legislation in the 1960s such as the Civil Rights Act of 1964. Additionally, the Twenty-fourth Amendment prohibited the poll tax.

24. **(D)** The Act Concerning Aliens (1798), part of the set of laws known as the Alien and Sedition Acts, enjoyed widespread public support despite opposition from Democratic-Republican leaders because, in part, large numbers of Americans had become intensely critical of the revolutionary French government during the Quasi-War with France. At the time, restricting the ability of French immigrants to participate in American politics seemed reasonable to many Americans. Relations between the United States and France deteriorated in the late 1790s. After an American delegation to Paris was rebuffed (the "XYZ Affair"), Congress allocated money for a maritime conflict with France. Warships were dispatched to the Caribbean and fought French ships in America's first undeclared war, labeled the Quasi-War (1798–1800) by historians. It was in this context that the Alien and Sedition Acts were passed.

25. **(C)** Leaders of the Democratic-Republican Party, notably Thomas Jefferson and James Madison, responded to the Alien and Sedition Acts by putting forth the theory of state nullification of federal legislation. The theory of nullification held that states could declare objectionable laws invalid within their borders. The theory was articulated by Jefferson and Madison in the Virginia and Kentucky resolutions (drafted in 1798 and 1799). The theory was again put forward by John C. Calhoun and other opponents of the Tariff Act of 1828, labeled the "Tariff of Abominations."

26. **(B)** The governmental action allowed for in the excerpt is similar to government actions taken during the "Red Scare" following World War I. The Red Scare was also set in motion by a series of bombs detonated in several cities in 1919 and 1920 by radical groups. In January 1920, Attorney General A. Mitchell Palmer began a broad hunt for suspected radicals. Palmer's Justice Department carried out unwarranted raids, known as "Palmer raids," of suspected radicals' homes. While Palmer did not uncover the makings of an uprising, he did end up deporting over 500 noncitizens. In December 1919, the Russian-born anarchist activist Emma Goldman was deported by the Justice Department. In both cases the government was empowered to deport aliens.

27. **(D)** Historian Eric Foner's 2010 Pulitzer Prize-winning book, *The Fiery Trial*, traces Abraham Lincoln's changing perspectives on slavery and abolition from his youth in Kentucky and Illinois all the way through his assassination in 1865. Foner's book argues that it is difficult to place labels on Lincoln's beliefs on these subjects because Lincoln did not hold a consistent belief throughout his life. Instead, Lincoln's thoughts on slavery changed as he gathered more information on the subject, met new people in his public and private life, and gained power as a politician.

28. **(D)** Until the summer of 1862, when President Abraham Lincoln began contemplating the way he could legally emancipate slaves in the South, he had been repeatedly stating publicly that his primary goal in the war was to save the Union. President Lincoln used the Emancipation Proclamation to marry the freedom of the slaves to the plan of preserving the Union, declaring that the Proclamation was a "military necessity," and allowed for Black men to serve in the U.S. Army.

29. **(B)** The Emancipation Proclamation, despite being a groundbreaking document in U.S. history, was intentionally limited in its scope. President Abraham Lincoln was careful to stay within what he believed to be his constitutional powers in issuing the document. He did so by applying the document only to the emancipation of slaves who were in states that were in rebellion on the date the Proclamation went into effect—January 1, 1863. President Lincoln had been stating, even before he was president, that he did not believe that the federal government had the authority to abolish slavery. But the Civil War was a special circumstance, and President Lincoln believed that his interpretation of the Constitution allowed him special powers in the event of an insurrection. There were also political considerations that President Lincoln needed to take into account, especially the need to keep the slave-holding "Border States" of Delaware, Maryland, Kentucky, and Missouri in the Union. As such, the Emancipation Proclamation exempted those states from its decrees.

30. **(C)** The National Woman Suffrage Association (NWSA) was formed in 1869 and was active in women's rights causes until its merger with the American Woman Suffrage Association in 1890; among its leaders were Elizabeth Cady Stanton and Susan B. Anthony. NWSA advocated an amendment to the U.S. Constitution that would grant women the right to vote on a national basis. In addition to suffrage, NWSA campaigned for a broad-based platform of women's equality including political, social, and cultural issues.

31. **(B)** Women's suffrage activist Alice Paul first wrote the Equal Rights Amendment in 1923, the year it was also first introduced in Congress. The proposed amendment's language guaranteed that the "Equality of rights under the law shall not be denied or abridged by the United States or by any State on account of sex." It was reintroduced in Congress every year until it finally passed in 1970. Congress imposed a time limit for ratification on the Amendment—originally 1979 but later extended until 1982. The Equal Rights Amendment fell short of ratification by eight states (or three, if the rescission of ratification of five states is not counted).

32. **(A)** Ames is arguing that the treaty to purchase the Louisiana Territory was "in open and avowed defiance of the Constitution." The treaty allowed the United States to purchase the Louisiana Territory from France for $15 million. The purchase nearly doubled the territory of the United States and gave the United States control of the Mississippi River and the port city of New Orleans. Ames is voicing a strict constructionist view of the Constitution, asserting that the government has no powers beyond those specified in the Constitution. President Thomas Jefferson also had concerns about the constitutionality of the purchase—the Constitution does not specifically allow for the purchase of additional territory. However, as a matter of expediency, Jefferson set aside his strict constructionist view of the Constitution when the Louisiana Territory became available to the United States. Ames, however, is arguing that the benefits of acquiring the Louisiana Territory are outweighed by the dangerous precedent of expanding the power of the government. He also argues that the United States would be wasting precious financial resources—"the bread of the children of the union is to be taken and given to the dog."

33. **(C)** Ames is arguing that President Thomas Jefferson is pushing the power of the "present administration" beyond what is allowed in the Constitution. This argument is similar to arguments made by the Democratic-Republicans, including Thomas Jefferson himself, in opposition to the plan by Secretary of the Treasury Alexander Hamilton to create a national bank (1790). Jefferson, in the early 1790s, argued that the

Constitution did not permit Congress to create a national bank. It was not among the powers listed in the Constitution. Hamilton countered that the elastic clause of the Constitution, which permits Congress do what it considered "necessary and proper," implicitly allowed for the creation of a national bank.

34. **(A)** The treaty referred to in the question, in which the United States purchased the Louisiana Territory from France, led to intense debates and physical conflict over the future status of slavery in this territory. Northern and southern politicians debated the issue when Missouri applied for statehood in 1819, leading to the 1820 Missouri Compromise. Later, northern and southern politicians debated opening additional areas within the Louisiana Territory up to slavery. The resulting Kansas-Nebraska Act (1854) led to violence in Kansas as proslavery and antislavery men fought for control of the state. Finally, the issue of the expansion of slavery led the nation into the Civil War (1861–1865).

35. **(D)** There were many factors that led to the election of Ronald Reagan as president, but one of the largest factors was the conservative reaction to the growth of government spending on social welfare programs under President Lyndon B. Johnson in the 1960s. President Johnson's "Great Society" agenda included new or expanded government spending to combat poverty, housing shortages, and nutritional needs for millions of Americans. Conservatives like President Reagan believed that issues such as those were not under the purview of the federal government, but rather should be handled by the individual states. In addition, conservatives sought to undo some of the Supreme Court decisions during the period that Earl Warren was the chief justice (1953–1969), especially decisions that hindered law enforcement. Conservatives were also critical of what they perceived to be a moral decline in the United States, as reflected in protest movements, drug use, promiscuity, and rock music.

36. **(A)** During the debate over the ratification of the Constitution of the United States in 1787 and 1788, many people, generally categorized as the Anti-Federalists, argued that the new nation would be best served by a limited national government with a larger role for the individual states, which would allow for the states to respond to the needs of their people on a local level. The Anti-Federalists were satisfied with the structure of the U.S. government under the Articles of Confederation, which had limited the powers of Congress and guaranteed the equality and sovereignty of each state.

37. **(C)** President Ronald Reagan ran on a platform of shrinking the size and spending of the federal government, and his inaugural address takes on that issue directly. President Reagan and the Republican Party had vowed to change the way the federal government interacted with the economic system of the United States, primarily promising to cut taxes, cut spending, and reduce or eliminate regulations on businesses. This was a reversal of policy from much of the twentieth century, where presidents such as Franklin Roosevelt, Dwight Eisenhower, and Lyndon Johnson had used the federal government to shape a changing U.S. economy.

38. **(B)** President Ronald Reagan's economic policies, commonly called supply-side or "trickle-down" economics, were intended to cut taxes and regulations while also cutting government spending in order to reduce the growing national debt. The theory behind much of President Reagan's economic plans was that the wealthy and business owners, with their taxes lowered and restrictions loosened, would be able to invest more money and spur job growth, thereby allowing working-class Americans to have more earning potential.

39. **(C)** President Jimmy Carter's 1977 speech on the energy crisis was part of an ongoing debate in the United States about how best to use natural resources such as petroleum and natural gas. President Carter urged Americans to change their energy consumption habits and advocated for national policies that would protect the environment, help the economy, and promote national defense.

40. **(C)** Starting with the presidential administration of Richard Nixon, the United States had been

subjected to several oil embargoes enacted by the Organization of Petroleum Exporting Countries (OPEC). The embargoes had resulted in gasoline shortages, higher fuel prices, and other economic consequences. President Jimmy Carter was hoping to ease some of the threat of those embargoes by enacting a new national energy policy that would make the United States less reliant on imported petroleum.

41. **(C)** The 1899 cartoon makes the point that the United States misread the situation in the Philippines following the Spanish-American War (1898). Under the provisions of the Treaty of Paris (1898), the United States assumed several of Spain's possessions following the war, including the Philippines, Guam, and Puerto Rico. The United States stated that it would grant the Philippines independence sometime in the future, but for the time being, it held onto the Philippines. Many Filipinos were deeply disappointed in this outcome, hoping to attain independence as Cuba had following the war. A resistance movement developed in the Philippines and a bloody three-year war, known as the Philippine-American War, ensued. Filipino forces were led by Emilio Aguinaldo. The infantilization of the Filipino people in the image can be read on two levels. It serves as a visual pun, comparing Uncle Sam to a parent coming to the realization that a baby is more work than originally thought. Also, it reflects racist attitudes toward the Filipino people.

42. **(B)** The cartoon questions the wisdom of American involvement in the Philippines. The cartoon depicts Uncle Sam trying to discipline an unruly child. It presumes that the child needs disciplining, but it raises the question of whether the time, effort, and resources necessary for such a project are worth it. The cartoon does not allude to the constitutional rights of Filipino people, nor does it refer to the Central Intelligence Agency (D), which did not come into existence until 1947. In addition, the cartoon does not question the morality of the tactics used by the United States in the Philippines (C). A cartoon raising such moral issues might depict the suffering of Filipino people. Rather, the cartoon is weighing the benefits and costs of American control of the Philippines. Similar questions were raised during the war in Vietnam and during other American interventions.

43. **(D)** The cartoon depicts the war in the Philippines, with rebels following the American victory in the Spanish-American War. Many Filipino people expected to gain independence after Spain's defeat. They were deeply disappointed that the United States decided to hold onto the Philippines. This move by the United States marks a turn toward a more imperialistic policy.

44. **(B)** Mercantilism, as practiced by European nations in the sixteenth through the eighteenth centuries, was an economic system by which nations attempted to accumulate wealth by creating a trade surplus, especially by founding colonies on other continents. Mercantilism served to strengthen the power of monarchs and led to intense competition for land and resources between the European nations. Here, the Englishman Richard Hakluyt advocated for English participation in that competition by striving to establish colonies on the Atlantic coast of America.

45. **(C)** Richard Hakluyt wrote extensively on the benefits of establishing colonies in the New World. The arguments he presented in favor of doing so included economic, spiritual, political, and nationalistic benefits for England. England's first permanent colony was established at Jamestown in Virginia in 1607 and, by 1732, there were thirteen colonies along the Atlantic Coast of North America, as well as an English foothold in Canada and island possessions in the Caribbean Sea.

46. **(A)** Edwards is asserting that God gives individuals a chance to rectify their sins because he is merciful. The sermon presents a dark view of humanity, but Edwards offers hope to those who find their way to Jesus. This sermon is one of the central texts of the Great Awakening. The idea that human beings are inherently good but are corrupted by the evils of society (B) is associated with Jean-Jacques Rousseau, one of the philosophers of the French enlightenment. Edwards has a dimmer

view of human nature. In Edwards's view, God is angry, but he is not merciless (C). It is his action, after all, that is preventing us from descending into the fires of hell. Choice (D) describes a more modern view of ethics and morality; Edwards certainly argued that it is important that one believes in the saving grace of Jesus.

47. **(C)** Edwards was a central figure in the Great Awakening. In the face of declining membership in the Congregational Church of New England, preachers such as Edwards attempted to revive flagging piety. By the 1730s, several charismatic ministers attempted to infuse a new passion into religious practice. These ministers, and their followers, were part of a religious resurgence known as the Great Awakening. The movement took a more emotional, and less cerebral, approach to religion. The other choices identify nineteenth-century religious movements.

48. **(A)** By the early 1700s, the white-hot piety of Puritanism had dimmed considerably. The succeeding generations of New England became increasingly interested in commerce and matters of this world rather than spiritual things. They had not endured religious suppression in England, nor had they suffered through the difficulties of settling in the New World. The Great Awakening hoped to revive the intense religious feeling of the previous century. Disestablishment—the severing of links between the church and the state—occurred in many states in the early nineteenth century, not the early eighteenth century (B). New England remained fairly homogeneous throughout the colonial period. It failed to attract immigrants from outside of England (C). There were devastating wars with American Indians in New England, such as King Philip's War, but those wars occurred in the seventeenth century (D).

49. **(D)** Edwards was part of the Great Awakening, and the Great Awakening contributed to changes in colonists' understanding of God, themselves, and the world around them. Specifically, it led to questioning of traditional authorities and encouraged colonists to see themselves as agents for change. It did not specifically encourage a questioning of British policies (A); this did not occur until after the French and Indian War, well after the height of the Great Awakening. Great Awakening ministers did not, for the most part, condemn slavery (B), nor did they encourage better treatment of American Indians (C).

50. **(D)** The Ford Motor Company was known for the policy of its chairman, Henry Ford, to pay his workers well enough to be able to afford the product they were making. American consumers of the 1920s were able to buy more products at affordable prices, but were also subjected to a great deal of advertising that attempted to convince them of the necessity of those purchases in order to increase or maintain their status in society.

51. **(A)** Credit-buying plans offered by companies like the Ford Motor Company allowed consumers to purchase products that they otherwise may not have been able to afford if they had been required to pay the entire purchase price up front. Many consumers were willing to use credit to buy the new products as a way to demonstrate their status in an increasingly status-centered culture. However, the growth of consumer debt was a significant harbinger of the approaching economic calamity of the Great Depression.

52. **(B)** The Industrial Revolution in the United States began in the late 1700s and grew along with the nation throughout the 1800s. American manufacturing had become one of the world's leading exporters of manufactured goods, in no small part because of the contributions of numerous inventors and entrepreneurs like Eli Whitney, Charles Goodyear, John Deere, Cyrus McCormick, and Henry Ford himself.

53. **(C)** The numbers in the table illustrate a major problem for farmers in the post–Civil War period. Commodity prices for agricultural products were falling; in other words, farmers were getting less and less for their produce. It reached a point where it was hardly worth growing crops. The costs of production were almost more than the price they received for their goods. A primary culprit in this situation was mechanization and improved agricultural techniques. These created surpluses that pushed down prices. Another important cause was the tight money supply,

which contributed to deflation. An important demand of the movement was to base currency on silver as well as gold.

54. **(D)** Farmers' organizations, such as the Grange and the Populist Party, wanted more money in circulation so that there would be inflation. Inflation would lead to higher prices for agricultural commodities. The populists demanded an end to the gold standard and a shift to currency backed by silver as well as gold.

55. **(C)** In the last decades of the nineteenth century, farmers organized groups to challenge the corporate-driven policies that were reducing their profitability and potential markets. The Populist Party became a formidable force in the 1890s. The movement challenged the concentration of wealth and power among eastern industrialists and bankers. It supported a national income tax so that those with higher incomes would pay more than the poor would. It also supported free and unlimited coinage of silver. The Populist Party wanted the United States to get off the gold standard and to issue money backed by silver as well. This would increase the amount of money in circulation and would lead to inflation. Farmers supported inflationary policies so that the prices they received for their produce would increase.

PART B: SHORT-ANSWER QUESTIONS

Good responses to question 1

(a) A good response would describe a major difference between Branch's and Carson's historical interpretations of the American civil rights movement, such as:

Branch emphasizes the importance of leadership in shaping and guiding the civil rights movement of the 1950s and 1960s, while Carson puts more emphasis on grassroots organizing. Branch specifically sees the leadership and inspiration of Dr. Martin Luther King Jr. as an essential element of the movement. Carson argues that such national leadership was often at odds with the priorities of local civil rights activists. These local activists were less interested in achieving victories on the national level (such as the Civil Rights Act of 1964 or the Voting Rights Act of 1965) and were more interested in instilling a sense of pride and purpose among African Americans on the local level.

(b) A good response would explain a specific historical event or development that is not explicitly mentioned in the excerpts and that could be used to support Branch's interpretation, such as:

* *The presence of Dr. Martin Luther King Jr. at a particular local campaign brought national attention to the movement. This was evident in the campaign to end segregation in Birmingham, Alabama, in 1963. With heightened attention on the issue of segregation, the movement was better able to pressure the federal government to enact changes.*

* *The 1963 March on Washington, organized by the national leadership of the civil rights movement, was a galvanizing event in the push toward civil rights in the United States. The event, which included King's famous "I Have a Dream" speech, pushed the federal government to pass the Civil Rights Act the following year.*

(c) A good response would explain a specific historical event or development that is not explicitly mentioned in the excerpts and that could be used to support Carson's interpretation, such as:

* *Tensions between local and national leaders can be seen in the civil rights campaign in Albany, Georgia, in late 1961 and 1962. Local activists in the Student Nonviolent Coordinating Committee were somewhat resentful of the presence of Dr. Martin Luther King Jr. in their campaign. The presence of King brought national attention to Albany, but after King and other leaders of the Southern Christian Leadership Conference left town in July 1962, the movement in Albany felt like it had to regroup and refocus the energy of activists. King's presence failed to bring immediate concessions from town leaders in Albany.*

* *The accomplishments of the national civil rights movement—the Civil Rights Act of 1964 and the Voting Rights Act of 1965—were significant, but they took the focus off the struggles of*

activists to achieve economic justice in communities throughout the South. Although the mainstream media presented the civil right struggle as over by 1965, activists in organizations such as the Black Panthers continued the local organizing that had been central to the movement from the 1950s and 1960s, and even earlier.

Good responses to question 2

(a) A good response would explain a perspective about politics in the 1890s expressed in this image, such as:

   * *The cartoon is mocking the efforts of the People's Party (Populist Party) to organize a political campaign. The party, labeled a "Platform of Lunacy," appears to be patched together from other organizations and movements that do not seem to fit well. The entire assemblage of patches appears to be unstable and misguided. The cartoonist is critical of the establishment of the People's Party, which had its founding convention in 1891 in Cincinnati, Ohio, although its formal platform was written the following year in Omaha. The Omaha Platform included a broad range of demands, among them the abolition of national banks, the direct election of senators, an eight-hour working day, a graduated income tax, and government control of railroads, telegraphs, and telephones.*

(b) A good response would explain a specific historical development that led to the political development depicted in the cartoon, such as:

   * *The formation of the People's (Populist) Party in the late 1800s had roots in the discontent of American farmers who felt squeezed by the railroads, banks, and large corporations. Railroads, many farmers argued, overcharged them for shipping their commodities to distant markets.*

   * *The formation of the People's (Populist) Party was the culmination of several efforts by farmers to organize resistance to corporate power and government policies that favored corporations. The Grange (founded in 1867) and the Greenback Party (active 1874 to 1889) were both efforts to address the concerns of farmers.*

   * *The formation of the People's (Populist) Party grew out the concerns of many farmers about the insufficient amount of currency in circulation. Farmers were opposed to the gold standard, which limited the amount of currency to the reserves of gold maintained by the government. The limited amount of currency resulted in deflationary policies, which reduced the price at which farmers were able to sell corn, wheat, and other major crops. Many farmers urged the government to adopt bi-metalism—basing the amount of currency in circulation on stocks of silver as well as gold. The Populist Party took up this demand.*

(c) A good response would explain a specific effect that the change depicted in U.S. foreign policy had on the United States in the period 1891 to 1920, such as:

   * *The United States adopted some of the demands of the People's (Populist) Party. The demand for a graduated income tax was met with ratification of the Sixteenth Amendment. The call for the direct election of senators was met by the ratification of the Seventeenth Amendment. Both amendments were ratified in 1913.*

   * *Many of the demands of the People's (Populist) Party were later taken up by the Progressive movement in the first two decades of the twentieth century. The Populists' call for greater democracy and greater government regulation of big business were echoed in the demands of the progressives. The progressives, however, did not embrace some of the more radical demands of the Populists, such as government ownership of banks.*

Good responses to question 3

(a) Good responses would explain a specific historical similarity between President George Washington's Farewell Address (1796) and the Monroe Doctrine (1823) in regard to U.S. foreign policy, such as:

   * *Both documents assert that the United States should remain at a distance from the affairs of European nations. Washington's Farewell Address urges the United States to avoid permanent alliances with European nations, and the Monroe*

Doctrine urges European nations to refrain from attempting to colonize any independent nations in the Western Hemisphere. Both documents, therefore, sought to avoid conflict with the nations of Europe.

* Both documents were responses to potential foreign policy entanglements for the United States. The context of Washington's Farewell Address was the ongoing conflict between Great Britain and France. Washington hoped to maintain free trade and amicable relations with both nations in the conflict. The context of the Monroe Doctrine was a fear that European powers would try to restore monarchical power in Spain, and that Spain, in turn, would try to reestablish control over the newly independent nations of South America. Further, the United States was concerned about the Russian proclamation of 1821, which asserted its authority over northwestern North America.

(b) Good responses would explain a specific historical difference between Washington's Farewell Address (1796) and the Monroe Doctrine (1823) in regard to U.S. foreign policy, such as:

* The Monroe Doctrine was more assertive than Washington's Farewell Address. Washington merely states that the United States should avoid alliances with European powers. Monroe, on the other hand, warned European nations against attempting interventions in the Americas.

* Washington's Farewell Address touched on many foreign policy points, including the importance of the United States maintaining free trade throughout the world and protecting the rights of merchants. The Monroe Doctrine focused on the importance of political independence rather than on the maintenance of free trade.

(c) Good responses would explain a specific historical reason for a difference between Washington's Farewell Address (1796) and the Monroe Doctrine (1823) in regard to United States foreign policy, such as:

* The most important reason for the difference in the scope and tone of the two documents is the change in the position of the United States on the world stage. At the time of Washington's Farewell Address, the United States was a newly emerging country. Some European powers were expecting the country to fail altogether. As such, the United States was not in a position to make demands on the nations of Europe. Washington merely urged that future presidents avoid permanent alliances with European powers. The Monroe Doctrine was issued after the United States performed well in the War of 1812. Its more assertive tone reflects the changed stature of the United States in the eyes of European nations. Though it was not yet a dominant player in global affairs, the United States had established itself as a stable and growing nation.

Good responses to question 4

(a) Good responses would explain a specific historical similarity between the U.S. entrance into World War I and its entrance into World War II, such as:

* The United States entered both World War I and World War II because of the aggressive actions of belligerent powers—Germany and Japan, respectively. Germany's use of unrestricted submarine warfare that caused the deaths of American citizens and Japan's attack on the U.S. naval base at Pearl Harbor, Hawaii in 1941 were catalysts for American intervention.

* In the lead-up to both interventions, isolationist sentiment was strong among many Americans. In regard to World War I, President Woodrow Wilson ran for reelection in 1916 with the slogan, "He kept us out of war." In the 1930s, many Americans wanted to avoid any future involvement in European affairs and crises after World War I. The America First Committee was a prominent organization opposed to American involvement in World War II.

(b) Good responses would explain a specific historical difference between the U.S. entrance into World War I and its entrance into World War II, such as:

* During World War II, the Japanese attack on Pearl Harbor was seen by Americans as an unjustified attack on U.S. territory. It was clearly

an act of war. The prelude to American involvement in World War I was murkier. The *Lusitania*, for example, was a British ship. Further, German U-boat attacks targeted American ships bringing supplies to belligerents at war.

* Public opinion was more clearly on the side of intervention in World War II. Public opinion was more mixed as the United States intervened in World War I. The United States had to go to great lengths to convince many Americans to support World War I intervention. Those Americans who were still not convinced were subject to the restrictions on free speech imposed by the Espionage and Sedition Acts.

(c) Good responses would explain a specific historical reason for a difference between the U.S. entrance into World War I and its entrance into World War II, such as:

* Public opinion about intervention was different for each of the two world wars because the wars themselves were different. Large numbers of Americans did not see a moral issue in regard to World War I. Although there was much media coverage in the United States about German atrocities against Belgium, many people saw this as biased wartime propaganda. However, once World War II began, most Americans came to see Germany as a genuine threat to democracy and civilization. The goals of Nazism led many Americans to view intervention in World War II as a moral imperative, not simply a strategic decision.

Section II

PART A: DOCUMENT-BASED QUESTION

Question 1

What good responses will include:

A good response would draw on at least four of the documents to present an analysis of each of the elements mentioned in the question: The extent of change in the ways in which Americans addressed immigration to America in two different periods. The first period is decades immediately before and after the United States achieved independence (1750–1800); the second period connects the era of the Gilded Age with the immediate aftermath of World War I (1875–1925).

Thesis (1 point)

The thesis for this question should focus on the historical reasoning process of continuity and change over time. It should note key elements in debates and discussions around immigration in two different time periods and note continuities and/or changes between the two periods. The thesis should make an assertion in regard to the degree of change over time. In regard to continuities, in both periods we see concerns of what it means to be an American, and who is qualified to become one. We see fears and prejudices toward certain groups in both periods. We also see, in both periods, Americans exhibiting a welcoming attitude toward immigration. Broadly speaking, in both periods Americans vigorously debated immigration policy; in both periods, Americans debated legislation to restrict immigration into the United States. In regard to changes, in the earlier period, concerns about immigration centered around identity, while in the later period, concerns included economic fears. The economic concerns of the Gilded Age about low wages and unemployment were not central to the thinking of Americans in the second half of the eighteenth century.

Examples of acceptable thesis statements:

*In both the period 1750 to 1800 and the period 1875 to 1925, Americans fiercely debated immigration policy, with some attempting to preserve a narrow version of national identity and some embracing a more expansive notion of what it means to be American. The anti-immigrant sentiment changed, however, between the two periods. In the latter period, anti-immigrant sentiment, combined with changing attitudes around race, gained a more widespread following. This movement was able to implement more far-reaching restrictions to new immigrants entering the United States in the 1920s. The changes in regard to the debates are more significant than the continuities, especially in regard to tone and impact.

Debates about immigration policy show remarkable continuities between the period 1750 to 1800 and the period 1875 to 1925. In both periods, many Americans were quick to paint immigrants as fundamentally different from white native-born Americans and were ready to enact policies to restrict immigration. While continuities are more prominent, the debates also show changes. In the latter period, anti-immigrant sentiment became more virulent and pointed as concerns about jobs and wages in the industrial economy stoked fear of newcomers.

Contextualization (1 point)

Essays should situate the argument in its historical context by explaining broader historical events, developments, or processes immediately relevant to the question. In this case, students could establish a broader context by discussing the fact that war shaped debates in both periods. During the earlier period, there was war in Europe between France and an alliance of countries headed by Great Britain. This war occurred in the aftermath of the French Revolution. The conflict drew in the United States, which engaged in the "Quasi-War" with France. In the later period, World War I was the backdrop to much of the anti-immigrant sentiment of the late 1910s. In both cases, wartime anxieties led to legislation that restricted immigration. Toward the end of the earlier period, Congress passed the Alien and Sedition Acts; toward the end of the second period, Congress passed the Emergency Quota Act and the National Origins Act, establishing the quota system for immigration. Contextualization could also focus on the political debates in each period—between Federalists and Democratic-Republicans in the first period, and between progressive reformers and isolationist jingoists in the second period.

Evidence (3 points)

Evidence from the Documents (2 points)

In order to receive credit for the first point, the essay should use the content of at least three documents to *address* the topic of the prompt. For the second point the student must use at least four of the documents to *support* an argument in response to the prompt. A good essay should not simply describe the content of the documents one after another. Rather, a good essay should make connections between documents or sections of documents in crafting a convincing argument.

It should be immediately apparent that the first three documents deal with the earlier period (1750–1800), while the last four documents deal with the later period (1875–1925). For the first period, one document (Document 2) expresses a welcoming attitude. J. Hector St. John De Crevecoeur writes positively of the idea that anyone can leave behind their old ways and become an American. He sees great potential for the United States to exist as a multiethnic republic: "Here individuals of all nations are melted into a new race of men." Here, connections can be made between Crevecoeur and the idea of the United States as a "melting pot," popularized in the early twentieth century. Documents 1 and 3 are critical of the influx of immigrants in America. Benjamin Franklin (Document 1) worries that an influx of Germans to Pennsylvania would change that colony's English cultural character. Theodore Sedgwick is concerned about the background of immigrants coming from the warring monarchies of the Old World (Document 3).

For the later period, Documents 4 and 5 are welcoming of new immigrants, while Documents 6 and 7 are harshly anti-immigrant. Document 4 is a sharp rebuttal to the anti-Chinese rhetoric of the 1870s. The cartoon by Joseph Keppler (himself Austrian-born) envisions the United States as Noah's ark—providing a refuge to immigrants from the troubled countries of Europe, which is shrouded in storm clouds (Document 5). Madison Grant, the anthropologist and founder of the American Museum of Natural History, employs racial theories to warn against the influx of non-Nordic peoples (Document 6). The last document, a cartoon by Frank Beard, depicts America being overwhelmed by "unwelcome guests." In the background, the immigrants are depicted as rats scurrying out of the sewers of Italy, Russia, and Germany. The new arrivals are depicted as anarchists, socialists, and the Mafia. The purpose of the cartoon is to persuade readers of the dangers of America's unrestricted immigration policies (Document 7).

Evidence Beyond the Documents (1 point)

Students will earn one point if they use at least one piece of historical evidence (beyond that found in the documents) relevant to an argument about the prompt. The specific evidence students use will depend on the approach of the essay. From the first period (1750–1800), students might cite the Quaker presence in Pennsylvania, the American Revolution, the French Revolution and the violence of the 1790s, the Quasi-War with France, or conflicts between Federalists and Democratic-Republicans. For the latter period (1875–1920), students might cite the Chinese Exclusion Act, the "new immigration," eugenics, World War I, the "Red Scare" of the post–World War I period, or the Emergency Quota Act (1921) and the National Origins Act (1924).

Analysis and Reasoning (2 points)

Sourcing (1 point)

For at least two of the documents, students must explain how or why the document's point of view, purpose, historical situation, and/or audience are relevant to an argument. It is not enough simply to identify an element of sourcing. A discussion of a document's point of view, purpose, historical situation, and/or audience should explain how that aspect of the document influences its meaning and sheds light on its credibility and/or limitations in regard to the argument of the essay. For instance, students could note that the point of view of the cartoonist Joseph Keppler (Document 5) is that of an immigrant—he was born in Austria. This could help explain the document's pro-immigrant sentiment and its concern for the deteriorating state of Europe (as depicted by the distant storm clouds). For Document 7, students could note the historical situation of the cartoon. It was created in 1885. The first half of the decade of the 1880s witnessed two significant trends that the cartoonist, Frank Beard, was responding to—the growth of labor militancy and the surge in immigration from eastern and southern Europe. Recent immigrants—depicted as dangerous radicals and terrorists—helped propel the Knights of Labor to nearly 800,000 members by the middle of the decade.

Historical Complexity (1 point)

Students must develop their argument by expanding upon the thesis. Students can earn one point if they can demonstrate a complex understanding of the historical development that is the focus of the prompt through sophisticated argumentation and/or effective use of evidence. For example, a more complex thesis might acknowledge both continuities *as well as* changes in regard to public sentiment toward immigrants. For instance, anti-immigrant sentiment existed in both periods (a continuity), but the tone of anti-immigrant sentiment changed over time. In the earlier period, the opposition focused on the ability of immigrants to fit into the culture of the United States; in the later period, we see outright racism toward entire groups. Students may also earn the point for historical complexity by explaining relevant and insightful connections within and across time periods. Students could extend their analysis to include time periods not included in the essay, such as debates around Irish and German immigration of the pre–Civil War period or debates around immigration from Central American– and Muslim-majority countries in the late twentieth and early twenty-first centuries. In addition, the complex understanding point can be earned by effectively using **seven** of the documents to support your argument, or by sourcing at least **four** of the documents. Finally, the point can be earned by demonstrating a sophisticated understanding of different perspectives relevant to the prompt. For instance, the essay could discuss reactions to the immigration debate by immigrant groups themselves, as seen through activism and ethnic newspapers.

PART B: LONG ESSAY QUESTIONS

Question 2

What good responses will include:

A good response to long essay question #2 will discuss the causes of the French and Indian War and analyze the relative importance of the different causes of the war.

Thesis (1 point)

Students will earn one point for presenting a historically defensible thesis or claim that establishes a line of reasoning. The thesis, which must consist of one or more sentences and must be located in either the introduction or the conclusion, must be more than a restatement of the prompt. In this case, students must make a convincing claim about the relative importance of different causes of the French and Indian War (1754–1763). In addition, the student should explain why the cause or causes they chose were most significant in understanding the war.

Examples of acceptable thesis statements:

* *The origins of the French and Indian War can be found in both the Old World and the New. The war was caused by ongoing bitter rivalries between France and Great Britain over power and authority around the world. However, the most proximate and prominent cause of the war was competition between France and Great Britain over control of the interior of the North American continent.*

* *On the one hand, the French and Indian War was caused by the competing claims of France, Great Britain, and American Indian groups over control of the Ohio River Valley region. More significantly, however, the war was caused by the competing mercantilist goals of Great Britain and France to control the lucrative North Atlantic trade.*

Contextualization (1 point)

Students will earn one point if they describe a broader historical context relevant to the prompt. Contextualizing the French and Indian War could include a discussion of the long struggle among the different European powers and the different American Indian groups to establish control of North America. Since the seventeenth century, battles occurred as the English, the Dutch, the Spanish, and various American Indian groups sought preeminence over different areas. The Beaver Wars of the 1600s and several other "French and Indian wars" between 1688 and 1748 all led to a redrawing of boundaries but did not conclusively settle the issue of who would control the interior of North America. Alternatively, students could contextualize the French and Indian War of 1754 to 1763 by looking at conflicts between France and Great Britain in Europe and at sea. In some ways, the conflict over control of North America was an extension of European conflicts over political dominance and dynastic claims.

Evidence (2 points)

Students will earn one point for *providing* specific examples of at least two pieces of evidence relevant to the topic of the prompt—the causes of the French and Indian War. They will earn a second point if they use this evidence to *support* their argument. The specific evidence the student chooses will vary depending on the approach of the essay. Students could discuss the growing population of the British colonies in the 1700s and the expansion of British settlements beyond the Appalachian Mountains into lands adjacent to the Ohio River. Virginia authorities dispatched a young George Washington into the Ohio River Valley to establish land claims there. In addition, students could discuss attempts by France to establish a presence in this same area by building a chain of fortifications, including Fort Duquesne. Students could discuss the Iroquois Confederacy and the Covenant Chain seeking to establish control of the Ohio River Valley, as well as resistance by other American Indian groups.

Analysis and Reasoning (2 points)

Students must develop their argument by expanding upon the thesis. Students can earn up to two points in this section. One point will be granted if the student successfully uses historical reasoning (in this case, causation) to frame or structure an argument that addresses the prompt. Students can earn a second point if they can demonstrate a complex understanding of the historical development that is the focus of the prompt through sophisticated argumentation and/or effective use of evidence.

For the first point, an essay could explain and evaluate several different causes of the war—British and French ambitions in North America, the growth of colonial populations, shifting American Indian territorial claims, and the evolution of the fur trade. The essay should be able to explain why certain causes are more important than others. The point for historical complexity could be earned in several ways, including looking at effects as well as causes. Students could discuss tightening of British colonial policies as a result of the war, and how heavy-handed British policies contributed to tensions between Great Britain and its colonists. Or, students could qualify or modify their argument by considering diverse or alternative views or evidence, such as the perspective of American Indians in regard to the ongoing conflicts between Great Britain and France. For this final point, students can also incorporate additional evidence (at least four pieces) that supports a nuanced or complex argument relevant to the prompt.

Question 3

What good responses will include:

A good response to long essay question 3 will discuss the causes of the Mexican-American War and analyze the relative importance of the different causes of the war.

Thesis (1 point)

Students will earn one point for presenting a historically defensible thesis or claim that establishes a line of reasoning. The thesis, which must consist of one or more sentences and must be located in either the introduction or the conclusion, must be more than a restatement of the prompt. In this case, a thesis must make a convincing claim about the relative importance of different causes of the Mexican-American War (1846–1848). In addition, the student should explain why the cause or causes they chose were the most significant in understanding the war.

Examples of acceptable thesis statements:

* *Although the immediate cause of the Mexican-American War was a conflict over the site of the border between the United States and Texas, the more important cause was a shift in the electorate toward expansionism. This was evident in the election of 1844, when the Democratic Party, and its nominee James K. Polk, won the presidency on a platform of westward expansion and Texas annexation.*

* *The Mexican-American War was caused by the confluence of major cultural and economic developments in antebellum America. In regard to cultural causes, many Americans came to believe in the superiority of Protestant, Anglo-American practices and institutions. However, the most important causes of the war were economic. American leaders prioritized the expansion of commerce and trade to the West and to Asia; acquiring northern Mexico (including California) was essential to this mission.*

Contextualization (1 point)

Students will earn one point if they describe a broader historical context relevant to the prompt. Contextualizing the Mexican-American War could include a discussion of the idea of "manifest destiny," which refers to the movement of individuals to the West, as well as to the political extension of U.S. territory. The term captured the fervor of the westward expansion movement, implying that it was God's plan that the United States take over and settle the entire continent. Students could also note that the war with Mexico occurred in the context of growing tensions between the United States and Mexico.

Evidence (2 points)

Students will earn one point for *providing* specific examples of at least two pieces of evidence relevant to the topic of the prompt—causes of the Mexican-American War. They will earn a second point if they use this evidence to *support* their argument. The specific evidence the student chooses will vary depending on the approach of the essay. Students, for instance, might mention the opposition of Abraham Lincoln, then a member of the House of Representatives, to going to war with Mexico. He challenged President Polk's assertion that "American blood has been shed on American soil." He repeatedly challenged the president to show him the spot where American blood had been shed. This specific evidence could be used to substantiate claims of political tensions between Whigs and Democrats on the eve of the war. These tensions played out in the election of 1844, which Polk won, ensuring a more aggressive foreign policy in terms of westward expansion.

Analysis and Reasoning (2 points)
Students must develop their argument by expanding upon the thesis. Students can earn up to two points in this section. One point will be granted if the student successfully uses historical reasoning (in this case, causation) to frame or structure an argument that addresses the prompt. Students can earn a second point if they can demonstrate a complex understanding of the historical development that is the focus of the prompt through sophisticated argumentation and/or effective use of evidence.

For the first point, students could explain and evaluate several causes of the war, such as the border dispute between the United States and Mexico. Texas had recently (1845) been annexed by the United States. Mexico said the border between Texas and Mexico was at the Nueces River. However, the United States insisted it was at the Rio Grande, 150 miles to the south. Students could also mention the election of the expansionist James K. Polk as president in 1844. Polk was determined to extend the borders of the United States to the Pacific Ocean. The ideas of manifest destiny could be discussed as a causal factor, but a specific development cannot be used for more than one point. Therefore, if the ideas of manifest destiny were used to establish contextualization, they cannot also be used as a causal factor.

The point for historical complexity could be earned in several ways, including the use of different themes. The prompt is built around the theme of "America and the World"; students could corroborate their thesis by employing the theme of "Culture and Society." For example, students could discuss cultural factors that paved the way for war, including a belief in Anglo-Saxon superiority. Many Americans felt that it was their duty to bring civilization and democratic principles to the lands controlled by Mexico. Students could also explain relevant and insightful connections within and/or across periods. In this case, the student could draw connections between the lead-up to the Mexican-American War and the lead-up to any other war in American history. Such connections could focus on the significance of economic factors in explaining the push toward war. The student could draw comparisons between the desire for expanded trade with Asia in the lead-up to the Mexican-American War and concerns about American sugar production in Cuba in the lead-up to the Spanish-American War. For this final point, students can also incorporate additional evidence (at least four pieces) that supports a nuanced or complex argument relevant to the prompt.

Question 4

What good responses will include:

A good response to long essay question 4 will discuss the causes of the Spanish-American War and to analyze the relative importance of the different causes of the war.

Thesis (1 point)
Students will earn one point for presenting a historically defensible thesis or claim that establishes a line of reasoning. The thesis, which must consist of one or more sentences and must be located in either the introduction or the conclusion, must be more than a restatement of the prompt. In this case, students must make a convincing claim about the relative importance of different causes of the Spanish-American War (1898). In addition, the student should explain

why the cause or causes they chose were the most significant in understanding the war.

Examples of acceptable thesis statements:

* *The Spanish-American War seemed, on the surface, to be about American concern for the fate of the Cuban people. Media coverage of the Cuban Rebellion aroused American empathy for neighboring people attempting to free themselves from European rule. However, a more important reason for American interest in Cuba was economic; America wanted to secure its extensive investments in Cuban sugar production.*

* *The decision by the United States to declare war against Spain in 1898 was prompted by Spain's actions in Cuba—its treatment of the Cuban people and, many Americans believed, its actions in the sinking of the U.S. battleship Maine. However, the long-term motivation of the war—for the United States to compete with the powers of Europe in terms of imperialist ambitions—is more significant in understanding U.S. actions in 1898.*

Contextualization (1 point)

Students will earn one point if they describe a broader historical context relevant to the prompt. Contextualizing the Spanish-American War could include a discussion of imperialist ventures by the powerful nations of Europe during the late 1800s. Another strategy would be to note that the U.S. economy was rapidly expanding in the years leading up to the war. Many industrial leaders and policymakers argued that the growing American economy necessitated overseas colonies, both for raw materials and for new markets for manufactured goods.

Evidence (2 points)

Students will earn one point for *providing* specific examples of at least two pieces of evidence relevant to the topic of the prompt—short-term and long-term causes of the Spanish-American War. They will earn a second point if they use this evidence to *support* their argument. The specific evidence the student chooses will vary depending on the approach of the essay. Students, for instance, might mention José Martí, the history of the Cuban independence movement, "yellow journalism," William Randolph Hearst, Joseph Pulitzer, Governor Valeriano Weyler, concentration camps, sugar production, the political background of President William McKinley, the American Anti-Imperialist League, Mark Twain, Josiah Strong and racial justifications for imperialism, Alfred Mahan and naval power, or a host of other details.

Analysis and Reasoning (2 points)

Students must develop their argument by expanding upon the thesis. Students can earn up to two points in this section. One point will be granted if the student successfully uses historical reasoning (in this case, causation) to frame or structure an argument that addresses the prompt. Students can earn a second point if they demonstrate a complex understanding of the historical development that is the focus of the prompt through sophisticated argumentation and/or effective use of evidence.

For the first point, students could discuss long-term factors such as the push for imperial expansion. By the late nineteenth century, U.S. political leaders were looking beyond the nation's borders to expand its influence and power. The United States was expanding trade with Asia and Hawaii. Earlier in the 1890s, American businessmen had wrested control of the island of Hawaii from local rulers. Acquiring parts of Spain's empire was on the minds of American political and economic leaders. In terms of short-term causes of the war, students could mention the conflict in Cuba over independence from Spain. Cuban rebels had been struggling with Spain for decades. The conflict in Cuba highlights another cause for U.S. concern. American-owned sugar plantations were suffering damage caused by the fighting in Cuba. Economic interests supplemented humanitarian interests. In 1898, the U.S. battleship *Maine* exploded and sank in the harbor of Havana, Cuba. Many in the United States thought that the destruction of the ship was the work of Spain, especially after American newspapers bluntly accused Spain of the crime, despite the scarcity of evidence. This sensationalistic, irresponsible coverage of events is known as *yellow journalism*. Finally, intercepted correspondence between Spanish officials, the De Lôme letter, revealed their unflattering opinions of President William McKinley.

The second point, for historical complexity, could be earned in a variety of ways, including by considering diverse or alternative views or evidence. For example, students could discuss evidence from the viewpoint of Cuban revolutionaries to challenge the assertion that the United States intervened in Cuba for altruistic reasons. Many Cuban revolutionaries were deeply conflicted about the participation of the United States in their war for independence. The Cuban revolution had been explicitly biracial in its composition and outlook; many leaders wondered if the segregationist United States would honor that perspective (the *Plessy v. Ferguson* decision was made two years before the war, in 1896). Further, they wondered whether the United States would grant Cuba autonomy. Their concerns were justified and challenged the narrative that concern for Cuban independence was a driving factor in the United States declaration of war on Spain. For this final point, students can also incorporate additional evidence (at least four pieces) that supports a nuanced or complex argument relevant to the prompt.

Scoring the Test

The AP United States History test is composed of four parts grouped into two sections. The multiple-choice test is scored with one point given for each correct answer.

- *There is no penalty for guessing,* so you should answer every question on the test.
- The Document-Based Question is given a score from 0 to 7.
- The Long Essay is given a score from 0 to 6.

To attain your final AP score, the following method should be used:

Multiple-Choice Score × 1.31 = _____

\+

Short-Answer Score × 4.0 = _____

\+

DBQ Score × 6.43 = _____

\+

Long Essay Score × 4.5 = _____

Total of all above scores is composite score = _____ **(round it)**

Score Range	AP Score
111–180	5
91–110	4
76–90	3
57–75	2
>56	1

To get a final score for the test, compare your composite score to the chart directly above.

Once you have scored each section of the test, place the score on the appropriate line above. When you are done, do the computations to get your final score. Remember that this test is designed to mimic the AP exam, but the conditions of taking a practice exam are very different from the conditions of taking the actual exam. Further, keep in mind that your scoring of the written sections may differ from the scoring of the professional readers who score the actual exam. This test is only an approximate predictor of success on the actual exam. Do not stop studying just because you got a good score here.

Index

A

Abolitionism, 161, 187–188, 191, 195–196
Abortion, 342, 345, 355, 376
Abraham Accords, 393
Absolute immunity, 370
Abstract expressionism, 328
Abu Ghraib prison, 390
Adams, John, 117–118, 136, 141
Adams, John Quincy, 140, 143, 153
Adams-Onís Treaty (1819), 143, 156
Addams, Jane, 233, 263
Administration of Justice Act, 99
Advertising, 280
Affirmative action, 354
Affluence, 335–336
Affordable Care Act, 369, 375
Afghanistan, 380, 388–389
African Americans, 163–164
   in armed forces, 299, 301–302
   Black Lives Matter movement, 378
   civil rights movement, 328–330
   cultures of, 165–166
   exclusion from political process, 204
   Harlem Renaissance, 283
   in post–Civil Rights era, 378
   Progressive era, 265
   World War II and, 299, 301–302
African Methodist Episcopal (AME) Church, 165
African slave trade, 50–51, 72
Africans, cultural adaptation by, 52–53
Agricultural Adjustment Act, 289
Agriculture, 63–64, 145, 215–216
AI technologies, 383
AIDS, 376–377
Albany Plan, 94
Alger, Horatio, 233
Algonquian peoples, 45, 63, 76
Alien and Sedition Acts (1798), 119–120, 121
Alliances, 93, 117
Allied Powers, 272
al-Qaeda, 388
Amendments
   Eighteenth, 270, 286
   Fifteenth, 114, 198, 264
   First, 66, 114
   Fourteenth, 197–198, 203–204, 223
   overview of, 114
   Second, 114, 379
   Seventeenth, 266
   Thirteenth, 197
   Twelfth, 136
   Twenty-second, 119
America in the World theme, 15
American and Regional Culture theme, 15–16
American Anti-Imperialist League, 257
American Colonization Society, 162
American Federation of Labor (AFL), 229, 291
American identity, 13
American Indian Movement, 343
American Indians
   after American Revolution, 123
   boarding schools for, 221
   British forces and, 116
   in California, 184
   Constitution and, 118
   cultural adaptation by, 52–53
   Europeans and, conflicts between, 77–79
   and Florida, 156
   French diplomacy with, 60
   in Great Depression, 274
   of Great Plains, 45
   in North America, 79
   political alliances, 93
   racial hierarchy and, 78–79
   resistance by, 221–222
   spiritual practices, 159–160
   westward settlers and, 155–156
American Recovery and Reinvestment Act, 374
American Revolution
   causes and nature of, 125–126
   phases of, 105
   role of women in, 100
American System, 137, 139, 155
Anarchism, 236
Anglicanism, 83
Antebellum society, 151, 169
Anthony, Susan B., 198
Anti-Asian sentiment, 218
Anti-Drug Abuse Act, 378
Anti-federalism, 113
Anti-immigrant sentiments, 186–187, 278
Anti-Saloon League, 270
Antislavery movement, 162–163
Antiwar movement, 346–347
AP U.S. History examination
   content of, 18
   document-based questions, 23–29
   long essay questions, 29–31
   multiple-choice questions, 19–21
   overview of, 17–19
   short-answer questions, 21–23
   time periods for, 19
Appalachians, 111
Architecture, 122
Argumentation, 9–11
Arkansas, Little Rock Crisis in, 330
Arms race, 331–332
"Aroostook War," 144
"Arsenal of democracy," 299
Articles of Confederation, 108–111, 126
Artificial intelligence (AI) technologies, 383
Artisans, and American Revolution, 100
Asia, 319
Asian Americans, 344
Asylum, 161
Atomic bomb, 304, 307
Australian ballot, 266
Automobile, 280
Automobile industry, 374

B

Baby boom, 325
Bacon, Nathaniel, 80
Bacon's Rebellion, 79–80, 124
Baehr v. Lewin, 377
Bailout, government, 374
Bakke v. University of California, 354
Banking, 139, 144
Barbados, 70
Barbary Wars, 141
Basic Health Program, 375
Battle of Fallen Timbers, 124
Battle of Gettysburg, 195, 197
Battle of Midway, 302
Battle of the Coral Sea, 302
Battle of the Little Big Horn, 220
Battle of Tippecanoe, 155
Bay of Pigs, 331
Beat literary movement, 328
Beaver Wars, 76
Bellamy, Edward, 236
Berlin Airlift, 319
Berlin Blockade, 319
Berlin Wall, 381
Bessemer process, 224
Bible, 285
Biden, Joe, 168, 196, 369, 370, 389, 390, 391, 392, 393, 394, 395
"Big Stick," 260

Bill of Rights, 113–114
Bin Laden, Osama, 389, 390
Birmingham Campaign, 338
"Black Cabinet," 294
Black Codes, 199–200
Black Death, 46
"Black Legend," 53
Black Lives Matter, 378
Black Panther Party, 339
"Black Power!," 339
"Bleeding Kansas," 189–190
Bonaparte, Napoleon, 107, 138, 141
Boston Massacre (1770), 98
Boston Port Act, 99
Boston Tea Party, 99
Boxer Rebellion, 260
Bracero program, 300
Bradford, William, 65
"Brandeis Brief," 267
Brandenberg v. Ohio, 342
Bretton Woods Conference, 304
British North America
    anglicization of, 83
    colonial patterns, 61–62
    colonist oppression in, 86
    geography and regional development in, 62–71
    regional differences in, 86
    religious toleration in, 83–84
    self-government in, 82–83
Brown, John, 188
Brown v. Board of Education of Topeka, 203, 328, 329, 330
Bryan, William Jennings, 238–239, 269
Buffalo, 220
"Buffalo Bill" Cody's Wild West show, 234
Buren, Martin Van, 156
Bush, George H. W., 365, 381
Bush, George W., 365, 367, 372, 389, 391–392, 394
Bush Doctrine, 392

C

Calhoun, John C., 153–154, 155
California
    American Indians in, 184
    Dust Bowl and, 294–295
    Gold Rush, 179–180
    statehood of, 185–186
California Trail, 179
Calvert, Cecelius, 64
Calvin, John, 47, 65
Calvinism, 65
Camp David Accords, 349
Canals, 146
Capitalism, 74
Capitol attack (2021), 369
Carnegie, Andrew, 225–226, 229, 235
Carolina, 70
Carolina Regulators movement, 124
Caroline incident, 144
Carpetbaggers, 201
Carson, Rachel, 350
Carter, Jimmy, 140, 349–350, 351, 353
Carter Doctrine, 350
Casablanca Conference, 303

Casta system, 51
Catawba, 74
Cato's Letters, 85
Causation, history reasoning process, 12
Central America, 380–381
Central Park, 235
Central Powers, 272
Change, continuity and, 12
Charles II, 61, 68, 70, 75
Chavez, Cesar, 343
Checks and balances, 115
Chesapeake Bay region, 62–63, 64
Chief Little Crow, 183–184
Child labor, 267–268
Childrearing, 325
Children, 227
China, 143, 260, 319–320, 322, 382–383, 394–395
Chinese Exclusion Act, 218
Chinese immigrants, 218
Chinook people, 46
Church and state, separation of, 66, 67, 341, 342–343
CIA, 333
Citizenship, 203–204, 283
Civil liberties, 194, 276
Civil Rights Act (1866), 200
Civil Rights Act (1964), 203, 339, 341
Civil rights movement, 328–330, 356
Civil War, 192–197, 220
    causation, 204–205
Civilian Conservation Corps, 290
Civil-service reform, 240
Class, 149–150. *See also* Middle class; Poverty; Wealthy class
Clay, Henry, 139, 155, 186
Clayton Antitrust Act, 270
Cleveland, Grover, 230
Climate change, 390–391
Clinton, Bill, 366–367, 371, 372, 378, 381
Clinton, Hillary, 368, 372, 393
Coal, 224
Coercive Acts, 99
Cohens v. Virginia, 137
Cold War, 317–322, 355. *See also* "Red Scare"
Colfax, Louisiana, 201–202
Colonial America
    democracy in, 84
    economic growth in, 70, 71
    governance in, 71
    political instability in, 76–79
    religious pluralism in, 81–82
    resistance to British policies, 97–100
    slavery in northern compared with southern, 80
    taxation in, 94–95
Colonialism, 255
Colonization, 58–62
    American Colonization Society, 162
Colorado War, 184
Columbian Exchange, 47–49
Columbus, Christopher, 48
Committee on Public Information (CPI), 274
Committees of correspondence, 97–98

Committees of Safety, 100
Common Sense (Paine), 101, 103
Commonwealth v. Hunt, 149
Communication, 146
Communism, 320, 355, 381
Communist Party, 277, 290, 324
Comparison, history reasoning process, 11
Compromise of 1850, 186
Compromise of 1877, 202
Concord, 104
Confederacy, 194–195
Confiscation Acts, 196
Conformity, 327–328, 356
Congregational Church, 68
Congress of Industrial Organizations, 291
Congress on Racial Equality (CORE), 338
Connecticut, 67
Conquistadores, 49
Consensus history, 306
Conservationism, 271
Conservative movement, 365–366
Constitution. *See also* Amendments
    description of, 112
    framing of, 112
    interpreting, 119
    ratification of, 113
    and slavery, 112
    structure of government under, 115
Constitutions, state, 108–109
Consumerist culture, 83
Containment, 318, 319–322
Contextualization, 8–9
Continuity, and change, 12
"Contract with America," 366
Corporate ethic, 236
Corporations, 145, 224, 226, 236
Corruption, 240, 243
Cotton, 147, 167
Cotton gin, 146, 147
Counter-Reformation, 47
COVID-19 pandemic, 369, 379, 384
Coxey's Army, 236
Crimea, 394
"Cross of Gold" speech, 238
Crowds, 98
Crusades, 46
Cuba, 185, 258, 259, 331, 394
Cuban Missile Crisis, 321–322
Currency, 105, 240, 241
Custer, George, 220
Custer's Last Stand (1876), 220

D

DACA, 388
Dakota War, 183–184
Darwinism
    Reform, 263
    Social, 232–233
Davis, Jefferson, 192
Dawes Severalty Act (1887), 221, 294
Dayton Agreement, 382
D-Day, 303
Debs, Eugene V., 229–230, 269

Debts, 110, 120, 298
Declaration of Independence, 102, 103, 105, 106
Decolonization, 332
Defense of Marriage Act, 377
Deference, 68
Deferred Action for Childhood Arrivals (DACA), 388
Deindustrialization, 384
Deism, 82
Delaware, 69
Democracy, 151–152
Democratic participation, 264
Democratic Party, 191, 200–201, 239–240, 293, 340–341, 371
Democratic-Republicans, 119–120, 135–136
Deng Xiaoping, 382
Denmark Vesey conspiracy, 164
Department of Homeland Security, 390
Desert culture, 45
Desert Land Act (1877), 217
Détente, 322
Dewey, John, 273
Digital Revolution, 383
Direct primaries, 266
Disease, 49
Dix, Dorothea, 161, 163
Dobbs v. Jackson Women's Health Organization, 376
Document-based questions, 23–29
Dodd-Frank Wall Street Reform and Consumer Protection Act, 374–375
"Dollar diplomacy," 261
Domesticity, 151, 163, 236–237
Dominican Republic, 331
Dominion of New England, 75, 84
"Domino theory," 334
Donner Party, 179
"Don't Ask, Don't Tell," 377
"Double V" campaign, 301–302, 329
Douglas, Stephen, 186, 189, 191–192
Douglass, Frederick, 165, 188, 256
Dred Scott v. Sandford, 190
Du Bois, W. E. B., 223, 264
Dust Bowl, 284, 294–295
Dutch colonies, 59, 60–61
Dylan, Bob, 348

E

Economic crisis, 373–374. *See also* Great Depression
Economic inequality, 386
Edict of Nantes, 83
Education, 122, 161
Egalitarianism, 68, 69, 106
Eighteenth Amendment, 270, 286
Eisenhower, Dwight D., 303, 320–321, 322, 333
Election of 1844, 182
Election of 1848, 185
Election of 1856, 191
Election of 1860, 191–192
Election of 1876, 202
Election of 1896, 238–239
Election of 1912, 269

Election of 2000, 367, 396
Election of 2016, 393
Election of 2020, 369
Electoral college, 202
Emancipation Proclamation, 196
Embargo Act (1807), 141
Emergency Quota Act of 1921, 12, 283
Emerson, Ralph Waldo, 159
Encomienda, 49, 50, 53, 59, 79
Energy, 349–350
Energy policy, 390–391
Enforcement Act of 1870, 202
Engel v. Vitale, 342–343
English Bill of Rights, 75
Enlightenment, 82, 85, 101–102, 106, 107
Environmental conservation, 270, 271
Environmental movement, 351–352
Equal Rights Amendment (ERA), 354
"Era of Good Feelings," 136–137, 140, 152, 168
Erie Canal, 146
Escobedo v. Illinois, 341–342
Espionage, 321, 324
Espionage Act, 276
Ethnicity, 232
Europe, 296
    exploration and conquest, 46–47
    migrations from, 148
    World War II in, 302
European Romanticism, 180
Examination, AP U.S. History. *See* AP U.S. History examination
Excise tax, 120–121
Executive branch of government, 115
Executive Order 9835, 323
"Exoduster" movement, 230

F

Factory system, 150
Family structures, 375
Farmers, 215–216, 222, 287
Farming, 219
Federal deficit, 371
Federal Emergency Relief Act, 289
Federal Employee Loyalty and Security Program (1947), 323
Federal Reserve Act, 269–270
Federal Reserve System, 269
Federal Trade Commission, 270
Federalism, 115
Federalist Number 10, 113
Federalist Number 51, 113, 115
Federalists, 113–114, 115, 119–120, 136
Feminist movement, 376
Feudalism, 46
Fifteenth Amendment, 114, 198, 264
Fifth Amendment, 114
"Fifty-four forty or fight," 144
Fillmore, Millard, 181, 186
First Amendment, 66, 114
First Continental Congress, 99–100
Fishing, 73
Five Points neighborhood, 186
Fletcher v. Peck, 145
Florida, 156
Floyd, George, 378

Flushing Remonstrance, 66, 84
Ford, Henry, 280
Foreclosures, 373–374
Foreign policy, 258, 295–298, 353
Foreign trade, 226, 371–372
Fort Sumter, 192
Four Corners region, of Southwest, 44
Fourteen Points, 275
Fourteenth Amendment, 197–198, 203–204, 223
Fourth Amendment, 114
France
    American Indian diplomacy with, 60
    New World colonies of, 59–60
Franklin, Benjamin, 94
"Free labor" ideology, 191, 232
Free public education, 161
Free speech, 342
Free trade, 141
Freedman's Bureau, 200
"Freedom now!," 339
Freedom of press, 85, 342, 346
Freedom Rides, 338
"Free-labor" model, 187
Free-Soil Party, 185, 191
Fremont, John C., 191
French and Indian Wars, 76–77, 93–97
French Revolution, 107, 117
Friedan, Betty, 344
Fugitive Slave Act, 187
Fugitive Slave Law, 186
Fulton, Robert, 146
Fur trade, 72, 76

G

Gabriel's Rebellion, 164
Gadsden Purchase, 182
"Gag rule," 140
Garfield, James A., 240
Garrison, William Lloyd, 161
Gaspee affair, 98, 101
Gay liberation movement, 344–345
Gay rights movement, 376, 377
Gender, 100, 101, 106–107, 151
General Agreement on Trade and Tariffs (GATT), 371–372
Gentility, 151
"Gentleman's Agreement," 261
George, Henry, 236
Georgia, 70–71
German immigrants, 148
Gettysburg Address, 197
Ghost Dance movement, 222
G.I. Bill, 325
Gibbons v. Ogden, 137
Gideon v. Wainwright, 341
Gig economy, 386
Gilded Age, 215, 225, 279, 282
    government and politics in, 237–242
    immigration and migration in, 230–233, 242
    labor in, 226–230
    reform in, 235–237
Glasgow Climate Pact, 391
Glass-Steagall Act, 289, 373, 374
Globalization, 372

Glorious Revolution, 75, 84
Gold Rush, 179–180
Good Neighbor Policy, 296
Gore, Al, 367
Government
    bailouts, 373–374
    promotion of Western expansion, 180–181
    structure under Constitution, 115
Grange, 215, 216
Granger Laws, 216
Grant, Ulysses S., 195, 221, 240
Great Awakening, 82
    second, 158
    third, 285
Great Basin, 44–45
Great Britain, 85
    Jay's Treaty and, 116–117
Great Compromise, 112
Great Depression, 255, 286–288, 293–294, 295, 307
Great Lakes region, 76, 95
Great Migration, 66, 278
Great Plains, 44–45
Great Railroad Strike of 1877, 228
Great Recession, 373–374
Great Society, 335–338
Greece, 318
Greenback Party, 215
Griswold v. Connecticut, 342, 345
Guatemala, 331
Gulf of Tonkin Resolution, 334
Gun control, 379
Gun violence, 379

H
Haight-Ashbury, 348
Haiti, 107–108, 382
Half-Breeds, 240
Halfway Covenant, 68
Hamas, 393
Hamilton, Alexander, 113, 117, 119, 120, 136, 139
Harlem Renaissance, 283
Harper's Ferry, 188
Harrington, Michael, 336
Harris, Kamala, 370
Harrison, William Henry, 155
Hartford Convention, 142
Hat Act (1732), 75
Hawaii, 256
Hay-Bunau-Varilla Treaty (1903), 260
Hayes, Rutherford B., 202
Haymarket Incident, 228–229
Health care, 369, 371
    reform, 372, 375
Henry VIII, King, 47
Hetch Hetchy Valley, 271
"Hippie" movement, 348
Hiroshima, 304
Hispanos, 216
Hiss, Alger, 324
Historical thinking skills, 5–11
    argumentation, 9–11
    claims and evidence in sources, 7–8
    contextualization, 8–9
    developments and processes, 5–6
    making connections, 9
    sourcing and situation, 6–7
History reasoning processes, 11–12
Hitler, Adolf, 296
HIV. *See* AIDS
Ho Chi Minh, 333, 334
Hobbes, Thomas, 85, 102
Hollywood, 324
Holocaust, 300–301
"Holy experiment," 69
Homestead Act (1862), 181, 216, 220
Hoover, Herbert, 287–288, 307
Horizontal integration, 226
House of Burgesses, 71, 84, 124
Housing crisis, 373–374
Hudson River School, 157
Huerta, Delores, 343
Hull House, 233
Huron people, 73
Hutchinson, Anne, 67

I
"I Have a Dream" (King speech), 339
Identity, 13
Immigration, 148, 186, 230–233, 242, 243, 273, 387–388
Immigration and Nationality Act of 1965, 337–338
Immigration Restriction Act, 278
Impeachment, 366–367, 369, 370
Imperialism, 255–257, 261, 305
Income gap, 386
Indentured servants/servitude, 64, 72–73
Indian Intercourse Act of 1834, 156
Indian Peace Commission (1867), 220
Indian Removal Act (1830), 155
Indian Reorganization Act (1934), 221, 294
"Indian Territory," 156, 183
"Indian Wars," 123
Indigo, 72
Industrial capitalism, 266–267
Industrial revolution, 150
Industrialization, 193, 224–226, 256, 258
Inflation, 105, 110, 240
Inflation Reduction Act, 370
Infrastructure Investment and Jobs Act, 370
Initiative, 266
Insular Cases, 259
International trade. *See* Foreign trade
Internet, 384
Interstate Highway Act, 326
Interventionists, 298
Intolerable Acts, 99
Investigative journalism, 263
Iran, 333
Iran Hostage Crisis, 349
Iran Nuclear Deal, 392
Iran-Contra Scandal, 380–381
Iranian Revolution, 349, 350, 391
Iraq, 389, 392
Irish immigrants, 148, 186
Iron Act (1750), 75
Iroquois, 76, 159–160
Iroquois League, 45
"Island hopping," 302
Isolationism, 272, 296–297, 298
Israel, 349, 392–393
Israel-Hamas War, 393
Iwo Jima, 303–304

J
Jackson, Andrew, 153–156, 168
Jackson, Helen Hunt, 221
Jackson State University, 347
James II, 75
Jamestown, 62–63
Japan, 181, 303–304, 307
Japanese Americans, 300
Jay, John, 113, 117
Jay's Treaty, 116–117
Jefferson, Thomas, 119–120, 136, 140, 141
Jim Crow laws, 203, 223, 264
Johnson, Andrew, 199, 200
Johnson, Lyndon B., 331, 336, 340, 341, 371, 378
Joint-stock company, 48
Journalism, 234, 258, 263
Judicial review, 137
Judiciary Act of 1789, 119
Judiciary Act of 1801, 137
Judiciary branch of government, 115
"Juneteenth," 196
Jungle, The, 267

K
Kansas, 189–190
Kansas-Nebraska Act, 189
Kellogg-Briand Pact, 296
Kennedy, John F., 322, 336, 340
Kent State University, 347
Kentucky Resolution, 121
Kerry, John, 392
Keynesian economics, 293
Khrushchev, Nikita, 322
King, Martin Luther, Jr., 329, 339, 340
King George's War, 77
King Philip's War, 78
King William's War, 77
Knights of Labor, 228
Know-Nothing Party, 187, 191
Korean War, 320
Korematsu v. United States, 299, 300
Ku Klux Klan, 202, 204, 230, 264, 279, 285, 342
Kyoto Protocol, 391

L
Labor unions, 149–150, 323, 385
Laborers, and American Revolution, 100
Laissez-faire, 233, 237, 266–267
Land Ordinances (1784 and 1785), 111
Las Casas, Bartolomé de, 50, 53, 59
Latin America, 108, 331, 387
League of Nations, 275–276, 296
Lee, Robert E., 188
Legislative branch of government, 115
Leisure, 234
Levittown, 326

Lewis and Clark expedition, 138
Lexington, 104
Liberalism, 336–337
Liberty Party, 162
Lincoln, Abraham, 191–192, 199
Lindbergh, Charles, 298
Literature, 284, 297
Little Rock Crisis, 330
Locke, John, 83, 85, 107
Long Essay questions, 29–31
"Lost cause" myth, 205
"Lost Generation" literary movement, 284
Louis XVI, King, 117
Louisiana Purchase, 138
Love Canal, 351
Lovejoy, Elijah, 163
Lowell system, 150–151
Luther, Martin, 47, 65

M

MacArthur, Douglas, 320
Macon's Bill No. 2, 142
Madison, James, 113, 141
Mahan, Alfred Thayer, 255
Malcolm X, 339–340
Manifest destiny, 179–181
Mao Zedong, 320
Mapp v. Ohio, 341
Marbury v. Madison, 115, 137
March on Washington (1963), 339
Market economy, 145
Market Revolution, 144–145, 149–150
Marketing, 224–225
Maroons, 50–51
Marshall, John, 341
Marshall Court, 137–138
Marshall Plan, 318–319
Maryland, 64
Mass culture, 281
Mass media, 281
Massachusetts Bay Colony, 66
Massachusetts Government Act, 99
Mayflower Compact, 65–66
McCain, John, 390
McCarran Internal Security Act (1950), 323
McCarthy, Joseph, 323, 324, 325
McCarthyism, 323, 324, 325
McCulloch v. Maryland, 137
Me Too Movement, 376
Meat-packing Industry, 267
Mechanization, of agriculture, 215
Medicaid, 371
Medicare, 371
Mercantilism, 74–75
Metacomet, 78
Mexican Revolution, 262
Mexican-American War, 181–184, 216
Mexican-Americans, 295
Mexico, 181–183, 300
Middle class, 151, 233–235, 325
Middle East, 349–350, 382, 392–393
Migrations, 148–149, 184, 186, 230, 278, 294–295, 300
and settlement, 14

Military, African Americans in, 299, 301–302
"Military-Industrial Complex," 331–332
Mining, 217–218
Minstrel shows, 188–189
Miranda v. Arizona, 342
Missionaries, 256
Missions, 118
Mississippi, 195
Mississippi River, 116
Missouri Compromise, 140, 184, 189, 190
Mobs, 98
Molasses Act, 73, 76
Monroe, James, 143
Monroe Doctrine, 143
Montgomery bus boycott, 329
Moral Majority, 355
Mormonism, 158–159, 180
Morrill Land Grant Act (1862), 181
Morse, Samuel, 146
Motion picture industry, 281
Mott, Lucretia, 163
Muckrakers, 263
Muckraking journalism, 234
Mueller Report, 393
Mugwumps, 240
Muir, John, 271
Muller v. Oregon, 267
Multiple-choice questions, 19–21
Music, 328, 348–349
My Lai Massacre, 335

N

NAFTA, 371
Nagasaki, 304
Nat Turner's Rebellion, 165
National Aeronautics and Space Administration (NASA), 321
National Association for the Advancement of Colored People (NAACP), 264
National culture, 122, 156–158
National identity, 13
National Industrial Recovery Act, 289, 290
National Origins Act, 283
National Park System, 271
National Rifle Association (NRA), 379
Native Americans. see American Indians
Nativism, 187, 232, 278, 282–283
Naturalization, 283
Naval power, 255
Navigation Acts, 74–75
Nazi-Soviet Pact (1939), 298
Negro Plot of 1741, 69
Neutrality Act, 122
New Amsterdam, 61, 69
New Deal, 288–295, 307
New England
American Indian–European conflicts in, 77–79
colonial, economy of, 72–73
colonies, 65–68
dominion of, 75, 84

town meetings in, 71
New Hampshire, 67
New Jersey, 69
New Left, 347–348
"New Look," in foreign policy, 320–321
New Right, 365–366, 395
"New South," 214, 222–223
New World colonies
Dutch, 59, 60–61
economic growth of, 72–73
French, 59–60
New York, 69, 80
New York Times Co. v. United States, 347
New York Times v. Sullivan, 342, 346
Newspapers, 234
Nineteenth Amendment, 114
Ninth Amendment, 114
Nixon, Richard, 321, 322, 354, 356
"No Child Left Behind," 367–368
Non-Intercourse Act of 1809, 141, 147
North America
democracy in, 84
governance in, 71
North Atlantic Treaty Organization (NATO), 319
North Carolina, 64
Northwest Ordinance, 111
Northwest Territory, 111
NSC-68, 319
Nuclear energy, 350
Nuclear policy, 332
Nuclear war, 324
Nullification crisis, 153–154
Nuremberg trials, 296, 305
Nye Committee, 297

O

Obama, Barack, 368, 369, 374, 375, 379, 388, 390, 392, 394, 395
Obergefell v. Hodges, 377
Oil, 224, 225
Oil industry, 349
Okinawa, 303–304
"Old China Trade," 143
Old West, 234, 243
Olive Branch Petition, 102–103
Oñate, Juan de, 52
"One-person, one-vote," 342
Open Door Policy, 260
"Operation Desert Storm," 381
Oregon, 144, 267
Oregon Trail, 179
Organization of Petroleum Exporting Countries (OPEC), 349
Organized labor, 276–277, 290
Ostend Manifesto, 185
Other America: Poverty in the United States, The (Harrington), 336
Overland trails, 179
Overproduction, 287

P

Pacific Northwest, 144
Pacific Railroad Act (1862), 181, 216
Pacific theater, 302
Paine, Thomas, 100, 101, 103
Palestine, 392–393

Palmares, 51
Panama, 260
Panama Canal, 260, 353
Panay incident, 297
Panic of 1819, 144–145
Panic of 1837, 149, 154
Panic of 1893, 241, 256, 286
Panic of 1907, 269, 286–287
Paris Agreement, 391
Parks, Rosa, 329
Partial Test Ban Treaty, 322
Patient Protection and Affordable Care Act, 375
Patriot Act, 389–390
Paxton Boys, 96–97, 124
"Peace policy," 221
"Peaceful coercion," 141
Pearl Harbor, 298
Pendleton Act, 240
Penitentiary movement, 161
Pennsylvania, 68, 109, 120–121, 124
    economic opportunity in, 96
Pentagon Papers, 347
Pequot War, 78
Perry, Matthew C., 181
Persian Gulf War, 381
Personal liberty laws, 187
Philippines, 259
Pinchot, Gifford, 271
Pinckney's Treaty, 116
Platt Amendment, 259
Plessy v. Ferguson, 204, 223, 330
Plymouth, 65–66
"Political correctness," 368
Politics, and power, 14–15
Polk, James, 144
Pontiac's Rebellion, 95–96
Popé's Rebellion, 79
Popular sovereignty, 185
Populist Party and movement, 238–239, 242–243
Portugal, 48–49
Potsdam Conference, 305
Poverty, 227, 335–336
Pragmatism, 263
Prayer, 342–343
"Praying Indians," 78
Predestination, 65
Preservationism, 271
Print culture, 83
PRISM, 390
Proclamation Act (1763), 96
Professional Air Traffic Controllers' Organization (PATCO), 385
Progressive movement, 262–271, 288, 305–306
Progressivism, 262–264
    industrial capitalism and, 266–267
Prohibition, 270, 286
Prostitution, 242
Protestant evangelicalism, 101
Protestant Reformation, 47, 65
Public education, 161
Public health debates, 379
Public opinion, 258
Public parks, 234–235

Pueblo people, 44, 52
Pueblo Revolt, 79
Pullman Strike, 229–230
Puritanism, 65, 67
Putin, Vladimir, 394
"Putting-out system," 150

Q
al-Qaeda, 388–389
Quakerism, 68, 69, 82
Quarantine Speech, 297
Quartering Acts (1765 and 1774), 95, 99
Quebec Act, 99
Queen Anne's War, 77
Questions
    long essay, 29–31
    multiple-choice, 19–21
    short-answer, 21–23
"Quiet revolution," 345
Quota system, 283

R
Race, 180, 279, 283
Racial hierarchy, 78–79, 80
Racial violence, 279
Racism, 86, 162, 188–189, 264
Radio, 281
Railroads, 147, 216, 225
Reagan, Nancy, 378
Reagan, Ronald, 288, 365–366, 371, 378, 395
Reaganomics, 288, 366, 371
Reapportionment, 342
Recall, 266
Reconstruction, 197–204, 205
Reconstruction Acts of 1867, 200
Red Cloud's War, 220
"Red Scare," 277, 322–325
Redemptioners, 72–73
Redlining, 326
Referendum, 266
Reform Darwinism, 263
Reform movements, 160–161, 169
Regionalism, 284
Religious toleration, 83–84
Renaissance, 46–47
Repartimiento, 50, 59
Republican motherhood, 107
Republican Party, 191, 199, 200–201, 239, 240, 341, 366
Republicanism, 103
Reservation system, 183
Rhode Island, 67
Rice, 72
Right to privacy, 342
Right to vote, 114
Riis, Jacob, 231
Roads, 146
Robber barons, 242
Rock 'n' roll music, 328
Rockefeller, John D., 226
Roe v. Wade, 342, 345, 355, 376
Rolfe, John, 63
Romanticism, 157–158, 270
Roosevelt, Eleanor, 294
Roosevelt, Franklin D., 288–293, 297, 299, 300, 307, 340

Roosevelt, Theodore, 234, 260–261, 268–271, 286–287, 288
Roosevelt Recession, 292
Rosenberg, Ethel, 324
Rosenberg, Julius, 324
"Rosie the Riveter," 299
Russia, 394
Russo-Ukrainian War, 394

S
Sacco, Nicola, 277
Salem witch trials, 68
Sales tax, 121
Saloons, 231
"Salutary neglect," 93
Same-sex marriage, 377
Sampson, Deborah, 100
Sand Creek Massacre, 184
Sanders, Bernie, 386
Santa Fe Trail, 179
Savagery, 79
"Save America" rally, 370
Savings and loan associations, 373
Scalawags, 201
Schenck v. United States, 276
School shootings, 347, 379
Scientific management, 265, 280
Scots-Irish, 96
"Scottsboro Boys" case, 294
SEAL Team Six, 390
Second Amendment, 114, 379
Second Bank of the United States, 144, 154
Second Continental Congress, 100, 103, 108
Second Great Awakening, 158
Second New Deal, 292
Second Treaty of Fort Laramie, 220
Sectionalism, 139
Secure Ammunition and Firearms Enforcement (SAFE) Act, 379
Securities and Exchange Commission, 290
Sedition Act, 276
Segregation, 203, 222–223, 264
Selma to Montgomery March, 339
Seminole Wars, 156
Senators, 266
Seneca Falls Convention, 163
"Separate but equal" doctrine, 223
Separation of church and state, 66, 67, 341, 342–343
Sepúlveda, Juan Ginés de, 53
Service sector, 385
Servicemen's Readjustment Act (1944), 325
Settlement house movement, 233
Seventeenth Amendment, 266
Seventh Amendment, 114
Sexual revolution, 345
Sharecropping, 202–203, 222
Shays's Rebellion, 110, 120, 121, 124
Shelby County v. Holder, 341
Sheridan, Philip, 220
Sherman Antitrust Act, 229, 237, 267, 270

Short-answer questions, 21–23
Sierra Club, 271
Silent Spring (Carson), 351
Sit-down strike, 291
Sit-ins, 338
Sixth Amendment, 114
Slater, Samuel, 150
Slater Mill, 150
Slaughterhouse cases, 203–204, 223
Slave trade, 72
Slavery, 64, 169, 204–205
    abolition of, 106, 161, 195–196
    African slave trade, 50–51
    Bible and, 166
    in British New World, 79–81
    Constitution and, 112
    cultural resistance to, 165–166
    defense of, 166, 194
    Dred Scott v. Sandford, 190
    Emancipation Proclamation, 196
    in Haiti, 107–108
    Lincoln speech on, 195
    racism development and, 86
    rebellions, 164–165
    regional attitudes toward, 125
    resistance to, 81
    in southern and northern colonies, compared, 80
    in southern colonies, 72
    southern defense of, 166, 194
    in southern states, 125, 166–167
    transition from servitude to, 80
    in West, 167–168
    in West Indies, 69–70, 72
Smith, Adam, 74, 103
Smith Act, 325
Snowden, Edward, 390
Social Darwinism, 232–233
Social Security Act, 292
Social Security reform, 372
Social structures, 16
Socialism, 236
Somalia, 381–382
South Carolina, 64, 70
Southern colonies, 72, 80
Southern states
    isolation of, 139
    "New South," 214, 222–223
    segregation in, 203, 222–223, 264
    slavery in, 125, 166–167
Soviet Union, 322, 355, 381
Spain
    exploitation by, 50
    exploration by, 48–49
    Mississippi River conflicts, 116
    New World colonies, 59
Spanish America, 51, 59
Spanish missions, 118
Spanish-American War, 257–259
Specie Circular (1836), 154
"Spinning bees," 100, 101
Sports, 235
Sputnik, 321
"Square Deal," 268
St. Louis (ship) episode, 301, 307
Stagflation, 353
Stalwarts, 240

Stamp Act (1765), 95, 97–98
Standing armies, 99
Stanton, Elizabeth Cady, 163, 198
State and church, separation of, 66, 67, 341, 342–343
States. *See also* Southern states
    constitutions of, 108–109
    northern, 187–188
Steamboats, 146
Steel, 224, 225
Stevens, Thaddeus, 200
Stimulus package, 374
Stock market, 287
Stonewall riots, 376
Stono, South Carolina, rebellion, 81
Stowe, Harriet Beecher, 188
Strategic Arms Limitation Talks (SALT), 321, 322
Strike Wave of 1946, 323
Strikes, 291
Students for a Democratic Society (SDS), 347–348
Suburbia, 326
Sugar, 70, 72
Sugar Act (1764), 94–95
Sumner, Charles, 190
Sunbelt, 386–387
Superfund programs, 351
Supreme Court, 137, 145, 203–204, 283, 292, 299, 330, 346, 376, 377
    Warren Court decisions of, 341–343

T

Taft, William Howard, 261, 269
Taft-Hartley Act, 323, 385
Takao Ozawa v. United States, 283
Tammany Hall, 241–242
Tariff Act of 1828, 121
Tariff of Abominations, 153
Tariffs, 120, 121, 139, 241, 295
Taxation, 94–95, 97–100
Taylor, Frederick Winslow, 265, 280
Taylor, Zachary, 182
Tea Act (1773), 99
Tea Party, 368
Technological innovation, 223–224, 383–384
Tehran Conference, 304
Telegraph, 146, 217
Telephone, 217
Television, 327
Temperance movement, 160, 242
Tennessee Valley Authority, 289
Tenth Amendment, 114
Tenure of Office Act, 200
Terrorism, 389–390
Tet Offensive, 335
Texas, 167–168
Texas annexation, 182
Themes in U.S. history, 13–16
    America in the World, 15
    American and Regional Culture, 15–16
    geographic and environmental factors, 14
    identity, 13
    migration and settlement, 14

    politics and power, 14–15
    social structures, 16
    work, exchange, and technology, 14
Third Amendment, 114
Thirteenth Amendment, 197
Thoreau, Henry David, 159
Three Mile Island, 351–352
"Three-Fifths Compromise," 112
Tilden, Samuel J., 202
Timber Culture Act (1873), 217
Tinker v. Des Moines, 342
Title IX of the Educational Amendments, 321, 344
Tobacco, 63–64, 72
Tocqueville, Alexis de, 152
Tokugawa shogunate, 181
Townshend Acts (1767), 98
Trade, 71–76, 140–144, 147. *See also* African slave trade; Foreign trade
"Trail of Tears," 156
Transcendentalism, 159
Transportation, 146–147
Treaty of Fort Harmar (1789), 123
Treaty of Fort Laramie, 183, 220
Treaty of Fort McIntosh (1785), 123
Treaty of Fort Stanwix, 123
Treaty of Ghent (1814), 142–143
Treaty of Greenville, 124
Treaty of Guadalupe Hidalgo, 182
Treaty of Paris (1763), 94, 105
Treaty of Paris (1783), 107, 116, 123, 144, 156
Treaty of Paris (1898), 257, 258–259
Treaty of Tordesillas, 48–49
Treaty of Tripoli, 66
Treaty of Versailles, 276
Treaty of Wanghia (1844), 143
Triangle Factory Fire, 263–264
Triple Alliance, 272
Triple Entente, 272
Truman, Harry S., 329
Truman Doctrine, 318
Trump, Donald, 365, 368–370, 384, 388, 390, 391, 392, 393, 394, 395
Trump Administration, 168
Trustees of Dartmouth College v. Woodward, 145
Tulsa race riot, 279
Turkey, 318
Turner, Nat, 165
Twain, Mark, 225
Twelfth Amendment, 136
Twenty-second Amendment, 119
Twenty-sixth Amendment, 114
Two-party system, 135–136, 190–191, 239

U

U-2 incident, 321
Ukraine, 352, 369, 394
Uncle Tom's Cabin (Stowe), 188
Underconsumption, 287
Unions, 149–150, 323, 385
United Farm Workers, 343
United States, 380. *See also specific topics*
    critical period, 109–110
    Cuba and, 185

debts in, 120, 298
economy of, 120
foreign policy, 332
nuclear policy, 332
in World War I, 271–279, 306
in World War II, 297–304, 307
United States v. Bhagat Singh Thind, 283
United States v. Cruikshank, 202
United States v. Nixon, 354
"Unwritten Constitution," 119
Urban America, 241–242
Urban renewal, 327
Urban rioting, 340
U.S. Capitol attack (2021), 369
U.S. history, themes in. *See* Themes in U.S. history
U.S. Steel, 225, 269, 287
USS *Maine*, 258
USS *Panay*, 297
Utopian communities, 159

V

Vaccines, 379
Vanzetti, Bartolomeo, 277
V-E Day, 303
Vermont, 106
Vertical Integration, 226
Vietnam War, 333–335, 345–346, 356
Virginia, 62–63, 79–80
Virginia Company, 71, 75
Virginia Plan, 112
Virginia Resolution, 121
Voting rights, 114
Voting Rights Act (1965), 203, 341

W

Wabash River, American defeat at, 123–124
Wagner Act, 290, 292
Walker, David, 165
Wallace, George, 341
Walpole, Robert, 75–76
Waltham-Lowell System, 147
War Hawks, 155
War of 1812, 142–143, 148
War of the Regulation, 124
War Powers Act, 335
Warren, Earl, 341
Warsaw Pact, 319
Washington, Booker T., 223, 264
Washington, George, 104, 119, 120, 122, 141
Washington Conference, 303
Washington Disarmament Conference, 304
Watergate scandal, 354
Wealthy class, 235, 242
Webster-Ashburton Treaty, 144
Wells, Ida B., 223, 256
Wesley, John, 165
West Indies, 69–70, 72, 116–117
Westward expansion, 167–168, 169, 179–180
economic development and, 215–218
Mexican-American War and, 181–183
Old West memory and reality in, 234, 243
social and cultural development, 218–222
Wheat, 72–73
Whigs, 153–155, 185, 191
Whip Inflation Now (WIN) campaign, 353
Whiskey Rebellion (1794), 120–121, 124
"White Flight," 326–327
"White Man's Burden, The," 256
White superiority, 52–53
Whitefield, George, 82
Whitney, Eli, 146, 147
Whittaker Chambers, 324
Wilderness, 270–271
Williams, Roger, 67
Wilmot Proviso, 182–183, 184–185
Wilson, Woodrow, 261–262, 264, 269–270, 273–274
Witch trials, 68
"Wokeness," 368
Women
in American Revolution, 100
in antebellum society, 151
domesticity of, 151, 163, 236–237
in Great Depression, 294
in labor force, 227
liberation movement by, 344
in military, 301
opportunities for, 282
in professions, 376
Progressive movement and, 262–263
rights movement by, 163, 198
"Rosie the Riveter," 299
suffrage movement, 265–266
Women's Army Auxiliary Corps (WAAC), 301
Women's March on Washington, 376
Wool Act (1699), 75
World War I, 271–279, 306
World War II, 297–304, 306, 307

Y

Yellow journalism, 234, 258
Yugoslavia, 382

Z

Zelenskyy, Volodymyr, 394